RETIREMENT PLACES r·a·t·e·d

All you need to plan your retirement or select your second home

DAVID SAVAGEAU

PRENTICE
HALL
PRESS

New York • London • Toronto • Sydney • Tokyo • Singapore

Acknowledgements

I'm indebted to competent people at Prentice Hall's Deerfield office: Catherine Fay, Beth Lofchie, and Diane Rote.

I owe the most to Karen Katz, the editor for this edition. Enthusiastic, objective, energetic, understanding, professional, whiz; all these words apply.

Thanks also to the following for their insights, data, or help in completing this edition: Mary Allen, Lisa Clyde, Jerry Davis, Bob Dick, Corina Eckl, Warren Fisher, Norm Gourly, Carol Green, Bill and Joanne Hoffman, Michael Hunt, Claire Jensen, Chuck Longino, Pat McCabe, Dick McDonough, Ian Nielsen, Rogelio Saenz, Mary Jo Schneider, Ed Sherman, and Howard Stambler.

Thanks also to Drs. Thomas F. Bowman, George Giuliani, and M. Ronald Mingé, for permission to adapt their "Prospering Test" to retirement relocation; to Darlene Oldakowski and Tom Potts of Aaron D. Cushman Associates for their survey of housing prices and rental options in each of the retirement places; and to the hundreds of Century 21 Real Estate Corporation brokers who responded.

Finally, special thanks are due Woods & Poole Economics, Inc., of Washington, DC, for their population and income estimates and employment forecasts for each of the retirement places. The use of this information and the conclusions drawn from it are solely the responsibility of the author.

Publisher's Note

 Published by Prentice Hall Press
A division of Simon & Schuster Inc.
15 Columbus Circle
New York, NY 10023

Library of Congress Catalog Card No.: 90-7714
ISBN: 0-13-778929-7

Printed in the United States of America

Third Edition 1990

Contents

Preface

Readers will note the differences in the final rankings for the 117 places profiled in both the 1987 and 1990 editions. There are four reasons for this.

1. The interval effect. With 131 places in the 1987 edition and 151 in this one, the ranks of the 117 places common to both editions will necessarily change. Deming, New Mexico, for example, has nearly the same Personal Safety score as it had in the previous edition, yet its rank in this factor slipped from 87 to 104. Deming isn't getting more dangerous; it's just that 16 other places with better Personal Safety ratings have moved it to a lower ranking.

2. Time series data. Local population figures (for deriving per capita access to public golf courses, for example), prices (for measuring living costs), and personal incomes (for gauging how far Social Security benefits will stretch in a given place) have increased at varying rates since the previous edition was published.

3. New scoring elements and methods. The scoring in three chapters has been refined by new data elements, slight changes in scoring methods, or both.

MONEY MATTERS: For the first time, cost indexes for food, transportation, and miscellaneous goods and services are included when adjusting local household income for living costs.

SERVICES: Figures for public libraries have been included in this chapter for the first time. In addition, the scoring for continuing education has been weighted in favor of public colleges and universities, since these institutions are more likely to offer tuition waivers or reductions to older adults.

HOUSING: Except for dropping median prices and using typical prices from Century 21 Real Estate Corporation's survey for this book, the scoring method is identical to that of the 1987 edition. Rank differences are due to varying rates of housing price inflation among regions.

4. An entirely new chapter. For the first time, *Retirement Places Rated* has a seventh chapter.

WORKING: The subject of employment after retirement has been given a separate chapter for three reasons: (1) nearly one in four people continue to work part-time for a few years immediately after they start receiving Social Security benefits; (2) an additional quarter of their contemporaries indicate they, too, would work part-time if they found a good opportunity; and (3) a successful strategy for weathering future inflation is to build wealth in the early retirement years by working part-time.

As a result of these changes, the rankings better reflect what each retirement place has to offer older adults.

Introduction

"The best place to retire," says Dr. Robert Butler, former head of the National Institute on Aging, "is the neighborhood where you spent your life."

Who's going to argue with that? You have more practical knowledge and influence in the place where you've lived than you may ever have in an unfamiliar location. For all the hype about moving on, the number of older adults who actually settle each year in another state wouldn't crowd the route for the Cotton Bowl parade.

There's more to it than just convenience. The psychic connection that comes with raising children, working at a job, and paying off a mortgage in one town may be missed in a new one. When you move you can take the philodendron, the oak blanket chest, the canoe, and the car, but you can't necessarily pack a deep sense of place.

For you, perhaps, relocation is unthinkable. You've known your neighbors for years, your doctor knows you, you don't need to look up the bank's phone number, ask for directions to a discount hardware store, or scratch your head for the name of the one person in city hall who can get the sewer fixed. What you may ultimately want from retirement is R and R in familiar territory, not an agenda that takes high energy and risk just to sink new roots.

If all this is true, by all means stay where you are. But possibly—just possibly—there is someplace in this country where you might prosper more than where you now live. And possibly, too, it is a lack of objec-tive information that keeps you from taking a look.

RETIREMENT PLACES RATED

Since 1983, this guide has profiled retirement places throughout the country. The public response confirms that people want reliable, practical information about places. This new edition takes the same approach as its predecessors and has been thoroughly updated, revised, and expanded.

Retirement Places Rated is meant for those who are planning for retirement and are weighing the pluses and minuses of moving or staying. It is a guide offering a wealth of facts about 151 carefully chosen places, places that together attract a large number of retired persons who make interstate moves.

It is more than simply a collection of interesting and useful information about places, however. It also rates and ranks these places on the basis of seven factors influencing the quality of retirement life: money matters, climate, jobs, services, housing, leisure, and personal safety.

Retirement Places Rated doesn't treat mid- or later life as a kind of springtime or a second career, turning point, third age, or transformation. The book simply gives you the facts you need to start evaluating other locations in this country where you might live. After using the book, your hunch that you've never had it so good might well be confirmed. On the other hand, you may be in for a surprise.

1

FINDING YOUR WAY IN THE CHAPTERS

Each of *Retirement Places Rated*'s seven main chapters has five parts:

- The **Introduction** gives basic information on the chapter's topic, interspersed with facts and figures to help you evaluate places.
- **Scoring** explains how the places are rated. Here, several places are selected as "scoring examples" to show why one performs better than another.
- **Rankings** orders the 151 places from first to last by their *Retirement Places Rated* score.
- The **Place Profiles** are capsule comparisons, arranged alphabetically by place, covering all the elements used to rate the retirement places. Here you can see differences among the areas at a glance.
- The **Et Cetera** section expands on topics mentioned in the introduction and also contains information on related subjects. These range all the way from state-by-state college tuition breaks for older adults to essays on such subjects as state tax breaks for older adults and tactics for avoiding property crime.

The last chapter, "Putting It All Together," adds up the ranks to identify America's best all-around retirement places and describes the strengths and weaknesses of the top 30.

The Last Move?

Most people move 11 times in their lifetime. The common reasons are job changes or job transfers, shifts out of rental housing into home ownership, and moves up to larger homes. Is retirement yet another reason to move? For most people, not at all.

Each year, fewer than half a million persons over 60 pack up and relocate to another state. Another million and a half simply move out of a big house into smaller housing within the same city. Consider your own options. You might:

- Stay at your present address. Forty-seven out of 50 persons over age 60 do, according to the latest census statistics on geographic mobility.
- Stay close to town but sell or rent your home and move to another address, possibly an apartment, condominium, or smaller home. One in 29 older adults takes this route.
- Move out of town to another part of the state—to occupy a vacation home year-round, perhaps. Just one in every 73 older adults does this.
- Move to another state. For every 94 older adults, only one of them takes this course.

Clearly, hometown turf wins out over the distant happy valley. Even if you aren't thrilled with your present environment, you still have to decide whether moving is the key to a satisfying later life. The rule for successful relocation is that "destination pull" must be much, much stronger than "origin push." The time-consuming and expensive process of moving anywhere you wish shouldn't be plunged into without careful planning and investigation.

WHERE ARE THESE PLACES?

If you were asked, in a kind of geographic word-association test, to name seven states that spring to mind when you hear the word *retirement,* you might well say Arizona, California, Florida, New Mexico, North Carolina, South Carolina, and Texas.

You'd be right, of course.

For 40 years, these states have attracted half of all older adults who packed up and moved to another state. Several of their cities—Phoenix, San Diego, Fort Myers, Albuquerque, Asheville, Charleston, and McAllen—are as synonymous with retirement as any in the country.

But other states outside the Sun Belt also belong in retirement geography. Oregon and Washington are drawing thousands of equity-rich Californians. The 160-mile stretch of New Jersey's sandy Atlantic coastline from Cape May up to Monmouth owes a good part of its economic rebound to older newcomers hailing from New York and Philadelphia. Meanwhile, real estate catalogs mailed out of the Smokey Mountains to retirement-planning Atlantans and Washingtonians are getting fatter and fatter.

It's no secret that places in every part of the country benefit from retirement relocation. If each of these places was to be daubed in red on a blank map of the United States, the nation would look as if it had measles. They are found along rural roads within commuting distance of big cities, on the edges of forested federal lands, along rocky ocean coastlines, in river valleys, around lakes, on mountain slopes, and in desert crossroads with striking distant vistas. To identify likely places from among the hundreds of possibilities, *Retirement Places Rated* uses several criteria.

Each place had to have a 1990 area population greater than 10,000. A smaller population may signal a lower level of human services. Moreover, the place should be growing. Between 1985 and 1990, the U.S. population grew 4.4%; the retirement places profiled here together grew 12%.

In addition, the place should be attractive to older adults. In almost all of the retirement places in this guide, there is a much greater number of persons 60 to 65 years of age today than there were persons 50 to 55 years of age a decade previously. This simple demographic exercise indicates the place is drawing older newcomers.

The place should be relatively safe. The U.S. annual average crime rate, for example, is 5,567 per

RETIREMENT REGIONS

In addition to the 151 retirement places in this book, you'll see references to 17 *regions* where these places are found. Few retirement regions match the political boundaries shown in a road atlas; most embrace parts of more than one state, and some states are apportioned among more than one region. Southport, North Carolina, for example, is grouped with Fairhope–Gulf Shores, Alabama, and other South Atlantic and Gulf Coast spots because it has more in common with them than with New Appalachia places like Asheville or the Mid-South area of Chapel Hill.

Big Ten Country
Ann Arbor, MI
Bloomington–Brown County, IN
Iowa City, IA
Madison, WI
State College, PA

California Coast
Salinas–Seaside–Monterey, CA
San Diego, CA
San Luis Obispo, CA
Santa Rosa–Petaluma, CA
Santa Barbara, CA

Desert Southwest
El Centro–Calexico–Brawley, CA
Lake Havasu City–Kingman, AZ
Las Vegas, NV
Phoenix–Tempe–Scottsdale, AZ
Prescott, AZ
St. George–Zion, UT
Tucson, AZ
Yuma, AZ

Florida
Bradenton, FL
Daytona Beach, FL
Fort Lauderdale–Hollywood–
    Pompano Beach, FL
Fort Myers–Cape Coral–Sanibel
    Island, FL
Fort Walton Beach, FL
Gainesville, FL
Key West–Key Largo–Marathon, FL
Lakeland–Winter Haven, FL
Melbourne–Titusville–Palm Bay, FL
Miami–Hialeah, FL
Naples, FL
New Port Richey, FL
Ocala, FL
Orlando, FL
Panama City, FL
Pensacola, FL
St. Augustine, FL
St. Petersburg–Clearwater–
    Dunedin, FL
Sarasota, FL
Vero Beach, FL
West Palm Beach–Boca Raton–
    Delray Beach, FL

Hawaii
Honolulu, HI
Maui, HI

Mid-Atlantic Metro Belt
Canandaigua, NY
Cape May, NJ
Charlottesville, VA
Columbia County, NY
Easton–Chesapeake Bay, MD
Lancaster County, PA
Martinsburg–Charles Town, WV

Monticello–Liberty, NY
New Paltz–Ulster County, NY
Ocean City–Assateague Island, MD
Ocean County, NJ
Pike County, PA
Rehoboth Bay–Indian River Bay, DE
Virginia Beach–Norfolk, VA

Mid-South
Aiken, SC
Athens, GA
Chapel Hill, NC
Crossville, TN
Lexington–Fayette, KY
Murray–Kentucky Lake, KY
Paris–Big Sandy, TN
Thomasville, GA

New Appalachia
Asheville, NC
Blacksburg, VA
Brevard, NC
Clayton, GA
Hendersonville, NC
Lake Lanier, GA

New England
Amherst–Northampton, MA
Bar Harbor–Frenchman Bay, ME
Bennington, VT
Burlington, VT
Camden–Penobscot Bay, ME
Cape Cod, MA
Hanover, NH
Keene, NH
Laconia–Lake Winnipesaukee, NH
North Conway–White Mountains, NH
Portsmouth–Dover–Durham, NH

North Woods
Charlevoix–Boyne City, MI
Door County, WI
Eagle River, WI
Houghton Lake, MI
Petoskey–Straits of Mackinac, MI
Traverse City–Grand Traverse
    Bay, MI

Ozarks and Ouachitas
Benton County, AR
Branson–Table Rock Lake, MO
Fayetteville, AR
Grand Lake, OK
Harrison, AR
Hot Springs National Park, AR
Mountain Home–Bull Shoals, AR

Pacific Northwest
Bellingham, WA
Bend, OR
Eugene–Springfield, OR
Grants Pass, OR
Medford–Ashland, OR
Newport–Lincoln City, OR

Oak Harbor–Whidbey Island, WA
Olympia, WA
Port Townsend, WA
San Juan Islands, WA
Wenatchee, WA

Rio Grande Country
Alamogordo, NM
Albuquerque, NM
Brownsville–Harlingen, TX
Carlsbad–Artesia, NM
Deming, NM
Las Cruces, NM
Los Alamos, NM
McAllen–Edinburg–Mission, TX
Roswell, NM
Santa Fe, NM

Rocky Mountains
Boise, ID
Coeur d'Alene, ID
Colorado Springs, CO
Fort Collins–Loveland, CO
Grand Junction, CO
Hamilton–Bitterroot Valley, MT
Kalispell, MT

South Atlantic and Gulf Coasts
Biloxi–Gulfport–Pass Christian, MS
Brunswick–Golden Isles, GA
Charleston, SC
Edenton–Albemarle Sound, NC
Fairhope–Gulf Shores, AL
Hilton Head–Beaufort, SC
Myrtle Beach, SC
New Bern, NC
Rockport–Aransas Pass, TX
St. Tammany Parish, LA
Savannah, GA
Southport, NC

Tahoe Basin and the Other California
Amador County, CA
Carson City–Minden, NV
Chico–Paradise, CA
Clear Lake, CA
Grass Valley–Truckee, CA
Red Bluff–Sacramento Valley, CA
Redding, CA
Reno, NV
South Lake Tahoe–Placerville, CA
Twain Harte–Yosemite, CA

Texas Interior
Athens–Cedar Creek Lake, TX
Austin, TX
Burnet–Marble Falls–Llano, TX
Canton–Lake Tawakoni, TX
Fredericksburg, TX
Kerrville, TX
New Braunfels, TX
San Antonio, TX

Population Growth

Fastest-Growing Retirement Places	Population Increase 1985–1990
St. George–Zion, UT	40.5%
Yuma, AZ	28.9
Carson City–Minden, NV	25.7
New Port Richey, FL	25.5
Vero Beach, FL	25.3
St. Tammany Parish, LA	25.2
Lake Havasu City–Kingman, AZ	24.3
Fort Myers–Cape Coral–Sanibel Island, FL	24.1
Clear Lake, CA	24.0
Southport, NC	24.0
West Palm Beach–Boca Raton–Delray Beach, FL	23.4

Source: Woods & Poole Economics, Inc., population forecasts.

Population Size

Largest Retirement Places	1990 Population
San Diego, CA	2,390,682
Phoenix–Tempe–Scottsdale, AZ	2,129,907
Miami–Hialeah, FL	1,886,152
Fort Lauderdale–Hollywood–Pompano Beach, FL	1,271,407
San Antonio, TX	1,262,346
Orlando, FL	1,054,481
Virginia Beach–Norfolk, VA	966,902
West Palm Beach–Boca Raton–Delray Beach, FL	894,121
St. Petersburg–Clearwater–Dunedin, FL	881,049
Honolulu, HI	845,741

Smallest Retirement Places	1990 Population
San Juan Islands, WA	10,406
Clayton, GA	11,572
Edenton–Albemarle Sound, NC	13,668
Fredericksburg, TX	16,309
Rockport–Aransas Pass, TX	17,757
Eagle River, WI	17,956
Deming, NM	18,186
Houghton Lake, MI	20,016
Los Alamos, NM	20,320
Charlevoix–Boyne City, MI	20,633

Source: Woods & Poole Economics, Inc., population forecasts.

100,000 people. In three out of four of the places profiled here, it's much less.

The place should be affordable, too. The money it takes to live in nine out of 10 of the places included in this book is less than U.S. average estimated costs for a two-person, retired household.

The place should have both natural and man-made amenities. Most of the places included here are gifted either with large areas of federal recreation land, state recreation land, lakes, or an ocean coastline. Several have all four. In addition, nearly all offer a high level of human services.

Based on personal visits, the demographic evidence, the advice of experts, and recommendations from hundreds of older adults, *Retirement Places Rated* profiles 151 places. Ninety-two are in the Sun Belt; retirement relocation is largely a march to milder climates, that much is certain. Because there is a growing counter-stream to attractive places outside this region, 59 of these are profiled. In all, 40 states are represented. Although these places do not by any means include every desirable destination, they do include many of the country's best, and they represent the variety of places many persons are choosing for retirement.

A WORD ABOUT THE RETIREMENT PLACE-NAMES

The 151 places profiled here aren't towns or cities. For good reason, they are counties.

Thanks to the car, the space you can cover on a typical day has expanded since the nostalgic era when Main Street truly was the noisy, exciting center of things. Now people likely live in one town, work in another, visit friends in still another, shop at a mall several miles away, and escape to the countryside—all within an easy drive.

It is no different in retirement places. Metropolitan San Diego not only takes in the country's 6th biggest city, it also includes Chula Vista, Oceanside, Escon-

dido, El Cajon, and other suburban places, and the desert east of the Cuyamaca Mountains to boot. Several retirement destinations in this guide include more than one county. Orlando, for instance, encompasses urbanized Orange County plus two suburban counties, Osceola and Seminole.

County names often ring a bell with travelers. Hawaii's Maui, Wisconsin's Door County, and New Jersey's Cape May are three such places. Other counties—Santa Fe in New Mexico, Bennington in Vermont, and San Luis Obispo on the southern California coast—have the same name as their well-known seats of government. In these cases, it's natural to call the retirement place by its county name.

But county names aren't usually tossed about in discourse. Washington County, Arkansas, is one of 31 counties honoring the first president of the United States. The name draws a blank to Texans, Louisianans, Missourians, and Oklahomans (neighboring states which have their *own* Washington County). Fayetteville, home of the University of Arkansas and the seat of Washington County, is better recognized by everyone.

Another case is Barnstable County, Massachusetts, which includes all of Cape Cod from Buzzards Bay out old U.S. 6 on the famous sandy spit of land to Provincetown. Cape Cod elbowed Barnstable County aside in popular New England usage centuries ago.

Sometimes the name given a retirement place is that of the one or two biggest population centers; thus New Mexico's Luna County becomes Deming, and Arizona's Mohave County becomes Lake Havasu City–Kingman. In other instances, the name of a town may be paired with a well-known natural feature;

Edenton–Albemarle Sound identifies Chowan County, North Carolina; likewise, New Hampshire's Carroll County becomes North Conway–White Mountains.

The following chart names the 151 places as they are used throughout *Retirement Places Rated* and shows their component counties. The Retirement Place Finder in the book's Appendix lists towns, cities, and unincorporated areas located within these counties.

151 Retirement Places

Retirement Places and Component Counties	1985 Population	1990 Population	Growth, 1985–1990
Aiken, SC Aiken County	115,600	128,576	11.2%
Alamogordo, NM Otero County	49,900	51,924	4.1
Albuquerque, NM Bernalillo County	464,400	499,620	7.6
Amador County, CA Amador County	23,200	25,774	11.1
Amherst–Northampton, MA Hampshire County	140,900	147,115	4.4
Ann Arbor, MI Washtenaw County	262,000	273,386	4.3
Asheville, NC Buncombe County	168,400	175,269	4.1
Athens, GA Clarke County	77,600	78,517	1.2
Athens–Cedar Creek Lake, TX Henderson County	52,100	58,918	13.1
Austin, TX Hays, Travis, and Williamson counties	697,500	798,105	14.4
Bar Harbor–Frenchman Bay, ME Hancock County	43,600	45,301	3.9
Bellingham, WA Whatcom County	112,700	117,789	4.5
Bend, OR Deschutes County	66,800	74,787	12.0
Bennington, VT Bennington County	35,000	37,078	5.9
Benton County, AR Benton County	86,700	98,093	13.1
Biloxi–Gulfport–Pass Christian, MS Hancock and Harrison counties	201,100	213,942	6.4
Blacksburg, VA Montgomery County	79,100	82,735	4.6
Bloomington–Brown County, IN Brown and Monroe counties	113,100	119,502	5.7
Boise, ID Ada County	192,400	201,683	4.8
Bradenton, FL Manatee County	174,600	197,525	13.1
Branson–Table Rock Lake, MO Stone and Taney counties	41,500	49,048	18.2
Brevard, NC Transylvania County	25,600	26,694	4.3
Brownsville–Harlingen, TX Cameron County	252,000	277,314	10.0
Brunswick–Golden Isles, GA Glynn County	59,100	63,847	8.0
Burlington, VT Chittenden and Grand Isle counties	127,100	141,109	11.0
Burnet–Marble Falls–Llano, TX Burnet and Llano counties	35,100	39,937	13.8
Camden–Penobscot Bay, ME Knox County	34,800	36,467	4.8
Canandaigua, NY Ontario County	91,300	95,410	4.5
Canton–Lake Tawakoni, TX Van Zandt County	37,400	40,963	9.5
Cape Cod, MA Barnstable County	165,400	193,562	17.0
Cape May, NJ Cape May County	90,300	98,930	9.6
Carlsbad–Artesia, NM Eddy County	51,900	53,596	3.3
Carson City–Minden, NV Carson City and Douglas County	58,600	73,653	25.7
Chapel Hill, NC Orange County	82,600	92,313	11.8
Charleston, SC Charleston County	285,800	292,150	2.2
Charlevoix–Boyne City, MI Charlevoix County	19,700	20,633	4.7
Charlottesville, VA Albemarle, Fluvanna, and Greene counties; Charlottesville City	119,700	126,467	5.7
Chico–Paradise, CA Butte County	162,400	181,018	11.5
Clayton, GA Rabun County	10,900	11,572	6.2
Clear Lake, CA Lake County	47,700	59,146	24.0
Coeur d'Alene, ID Kootenai County	66,800	72,174	8.0
Colorado Springs, CO El Paso County	367,200	406,945	10.8
Columbia County, NY Columbia County	60,300	62,283	3.3
Crossville, TN Cumberland County	31,100	34,075	9.6
Daytona Beach, FL Volusia County	310,800	348,600	12.2
Deming, NM Luna County	17,600	18,186	3.3

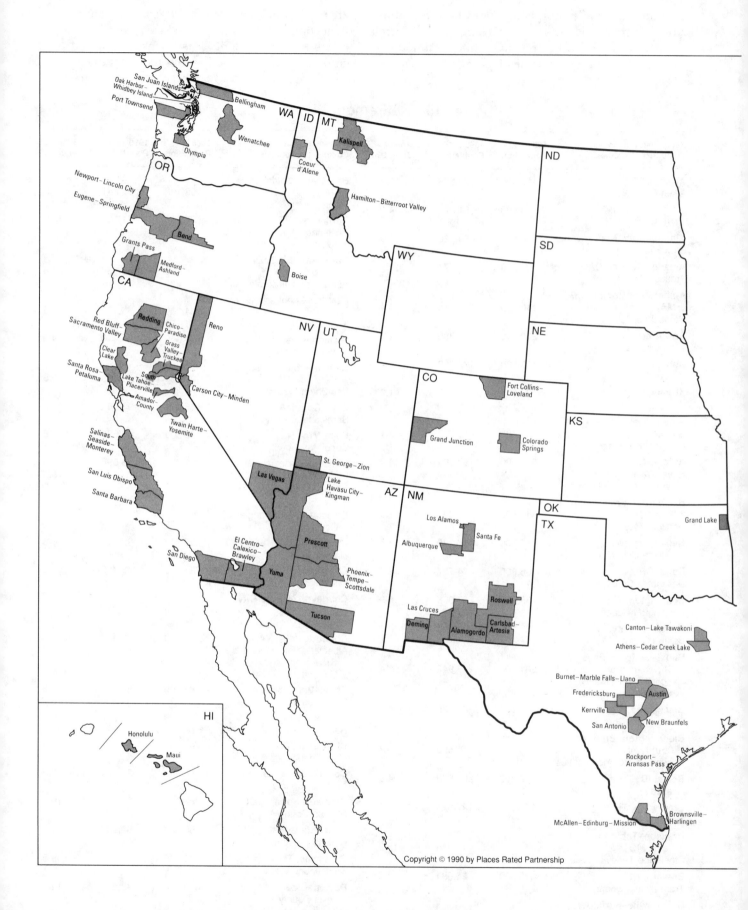

San Juan Islands
Oak Harbor – Whidbey Island
Port Townsend
Bellingham
WA ID MT
Wenatchee
Olympia
Kalispell
Coeur d'Alene
ND
Hamilton – Bitterroot Valley
OR
Newport – Lincoln City
Eugene – Springfield
SD
Grants Pass
Bend
WY
Medford – Ashland
Boise
CA
Red Bluff – Sacramento Valley
Redding
Chico – Paradise
Reno
NV UT
NE
Clear Lake
Grass Valley – Truckee
Santa Rosa – Petaluma
South Lake Tahoe – Placerville
CO
Fort Collins – Loveland
Amador County
Carson City – Minden
Salinas – Seaside – Monterey
Twain Harte – Yosemite
Grand Junction
Colorado Springs
KS
San Luis Obispo
St. George – Zion
Santa Barbara
Las Vegas
Lake Havasu City – Kingman
AZ NM
OK
Los Alamos
Santa Fe
Grand Lake
Albuquerque
TX
San Diego
El Centro – Calexico – Brawley
Prescott
Phoenix – Tempe – Scottsdale
Yuma
Roswell
Las Cruces
Canton – Lake Tawakoni
Tucson
Deming
Alamogordo
Carlsbad – Artesia
Athens – Cedar Creek Lake

Burnet – Marble Falls – Llano
Fredericksburg
Austin
Kerrville
New Braunfels
San Antonio

Rockport – Aransas Pass

HI
Honolulu
Maui

McAllen – Edinburg – Mission
Brownsville – Harlingen

Copyright © 1990 by Places Rated Partnership

Retirement Places

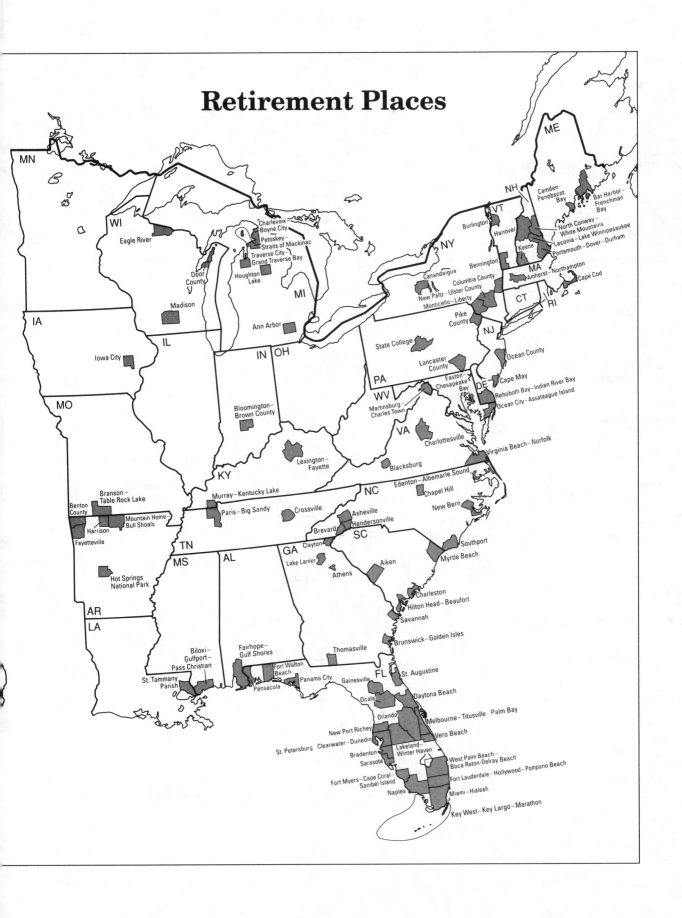

Retirement Places and Component Counties	1985 Population	1990 Population	Growth, 1985–1990
Door County, WI Door County	26,200	28,326	8.1
Eagle River, WI Vilas County	17,400	17,956	3.2
Easton–Chesapeake Bay, MD Talbot County	26,900	27,768	3.2
Edenton–Albemarle Sound, NC Chowan County	13,200	13,668	3.5
El Centro–Calexico– Brawley, CA Imperial County	105,800	107,627	1.7
Eugene–Springfield, OR Lane County	263,900	262,649	–0.5
Fairhope–Gulf Shores, AL Baldwin County	89,900	100,324	11.6
Fayetteville, AR Washington County	105,700	109,452	3.5
Fort Collins–Loveland, CO Larimer County	170,700	186,063	9.0
Fort Lauderdale– Hollywood–Pompano Beach, FL Broward County	1,020,200	1,271,407	13.5
Fort Myers–Cape Coral– Sanibel Island, FL Lee County	266,800	331,175	24.1
Fort Walton Beach, FL Okaloosa County	135,100	161,415	19.5
Fredericksburg, TX Gillespie County	15,500	16,309	5.2
Gainesville, FL Alachua County	173,700	190,723	9.8
Grand Junction, CO Mesa County	90,900	89,661	–1.4
Grand Lake, OK Delaware County	27,900	30,016	7.6
Grants Pass, OR Josephine County	66,600	73,655	10.6
Grass Valley–Truckee, CA Nevada County	67,700	82,300	21.6
Hamilton–Bitterroot Valley, MT Ravalli County	24,700	26,443	7.1
Hanover, NH Grafton County	68,500	75,788	10.6
Harrison, AR Boone County	27,700	29,446	6.3
Hendersonville, NC Henderson County	66,200	73,074	10.4
Hilton Head–Beaufort, SC Beaufort County	80,400	95,735	19.1
Honolulu, HI Honolulu County	811,100	845,741	4.3
Hot Springs National Park, AR Garland County	74,600	77,043	3.3
Houghton Lake, MI Roscommon County	18,600	20,016	7.6
Iowa City, IA Johnson County	85,500	88,028	3.0

Retirement Places and Component Counties	1985 Population	1990 Population	Growth, 1985–1990
Kalispell, MT Flathead County	57,300	61,054	6.6
Keene, NH Cheshire County	65,500	71,187	8.7
Kerrville, TX Kerr County	34,700	40,949	18.0
Key West–Key Largo– Marathon, FL Monroe County	71,100	80,418	13.1
Laconia–Lake Winnipesaukee, NH Belknap County	45,600	51,723	13.4
Lake Havasu City– Kingman, AZ Mohave County	71,600	88,997	24.3
Lake Lanier, GA Hall County	84,400	86,793	2.8
Lakeland–Winter Haven, FL Polk County	368,400	399,718	8.5
Lancaster County, PA Lancaster County	387,300	413,925	6.9
Las Cruces, NM Dona Ana County	118,700	135,879	14.5
Las Vegas, NV Clark County	550,700	651,440	18.3
Lexington–Fayette, KY Bourbon, Clark, Fayette, Jessamine, Scott, and Woodford counties	329,600	338,924	2.8
Los Alamos, NM Los Alamos County	18,000	20,320	12.9
Madison, WI Dane County	341,400	359,302	5.2
Martinsburg–Charles Town, WV Berkeley and Jefferson counties	83,400	88,709	6.4
Maui, HI Maui and Kalawao counties	85,500	102,368	19.7
McAllen–Edinburg– Mission, TX Hidalgo County	355,800	394,041	10.7
Medford–Ashland, OR Jackson County	138,400	145,199	4.9
Melbourne–Titusville– Palm Bay, FL Brevard County	347,600	383,416	10.3
Miami–Hialeah, FL Dade County	1,744,500	1,886,152	8.1
Monticello–Liberty, NY Sullivan County	67,500	68,395	1.3
Mountain Home–Bull Shoals, AR Baxter and Marion counties	42,200	46,606	10.4
Murray–Kentucky Lake, KY Calloway County	28,900	28,944	0.2
Myrtle Beach, SC Horry County	126,500	154,648	22.3
Naples, FL Collier County	117,100	142,139	21.4
New Bern, NC Craven County	79,400	86,206	8.6
New Braunfels, TX Comal County	46,600	56,240	20.7

Retirement Places and Component Counties	1985 Population	1990 Population	Growth, 1985–1990
New Paltz–Ulster County, NY Ulster County	162,800	170,420	4.7
New Port Richey, FL Pasco County	237,200	297,645	25.5
Newport–Lincoln City, OR Lincoln County	36,600	37,095	1.4
North Conway–White Mountains, NH Caroll County	30,600	36,034	17.8
Oak Harbor–Whidbey Island, WA Island County	48,600	53,742	10.6
Ocala, FL Marion County	164,800	198,405	20.4
Ocean City–Assateague Island, MD Worcester County	35,100	39,628	12.9
Ocean County, NJ Ocean County	380,800	433,016	13.7
Olympia, WA Thurston County	141,900	160,114	12.8
Orlando, FL Orange, Osceola, and Seminole counties	862,600	1,054,481	22.2
Panama City, FL Bay County	114,600	134,073	17.0
Paris–Big Sandy, TN Benton and Henry counties	44,100	45,675	3.6
Pensacola, FL Escambia County	262,900	287,789	9.5
Petoskey–Straits of Mackinac, MI Emmet County	23,700	25,327	6.9
Phoenix–Tempe–Scottsdale, AZ Maricopa County	1,816,700	2,129,907	17.2
Pike County, PA Pike County	21,200	24,598	16.0
Port Townsend, WA Jefferson County	17,800	20,711	16.4
Portsmouth–Dover–Durham, NH Rockingham and Strafford counties	304,600	359,315	18.0
Prescott, AZ Yavapai County	83,400	99,501	19.3
Red Bluff–Sacramento Valley, CA Tehama County	44,100	46,574	5.6
Redding, CA Shasta County	130,500	143,614	10.0
Rehoboth Bay–Indian River Bay, DE Sussex County	106,700	117,345	10.0
Reno, NV Washoe County	219,800	242,183	10.2
Rockport–Aransas Pass, TX Aransas County	17,600	17,757	0.9
Roswell, NM Chaves County	56,100	55,610	−0.9
St. Augustine, FL St. Johns County	67,900	82,269	21.2
St. George–Zion, UT Washington County	35,200	49,456	40.5
St. Petersburg–Clearwater–Dunedin, FL Pinellas County	803,800	881,049	9.6
St. Tammany Parish, LA St. Tammany Parish	140,800	176,275	25.2
Salinas–Seaside–Monterey, CA Monterey County	329,400	374,475	13.7
San Antonio, TX Bexar County	1,139,100	1,262,346	10.8
San Diego, CA San Diego County	2,132,600	2,390,682	12.1
San Juan Islands, WA San Juan County	8,900	10,406	16.9
San Luis Obispo, CA San Luis Obispo County	188,100	229,526	22.0
Santa Barbara, CA Santa Barbara County	331,200	370,971	12.0
Santa Fe, NM Santa Fe County	84,200	95,122	13.0
Santa Rosa–Petaluma, CA Sonoma County	334,100	387,731	16.1
Sarasota, FL Sarasota County	243,500	276,124	13.4
Savannah, GA Chatham County	215,700	219,783	1.9
South Lake Tahoe–Placerville, CA El Dorado County	103,900	120,587	16.1
Southport, NC Brunswick County	45,600	56,530	24.0
State College, PA Centre County	114,200	117,115	2.6
Thomasville, GA Thomas County	38,100	38,275	0.5
Traverse City–Grand Traverse Bay, MI Grand Traverse County	58,100	64,831	11.6
Tucson, AZ Pima County	585,000	637,333	8.9
Twain Harte–Yosemite, CA Tuolumne County	40,600	47,208	16.3
Vero Beach, FL Indian River County	77,700	97,350	25.3
Virginia Beach–Norfolk, VA Chesapeake, Norfolk, Portsmouth, Suffolk, and Virginia Beach cities	884,300	966,902	9.3
Wenatchee, WA Chelan County	49,300	52,317	6.1
West Palm Beach–Boca Raton–Delray Beach, FL Palm Beach County	724,300	894,121	23.4
Yuma, AZ Yuma County	84,800	109,283	28.9

Source: Woods & Poole Economics, Inc., population forecasts, 1990.

Making the Chapters Work For You

There are three points of view on rating places. The first says that defining what's good for all people at all times is not only unfair, it's impossible and shouldn't be tried at all. The second says you can but you shouldn't because measuring a touchy thing like "liveability" makes places unwilling competitors of one another and often leads to wrong conclusions. The third says you can, as long as you make clear what your statistical yardsticks are and go on to use them consistently.

Although the first and second positions may be valid, *Retirement Places Rated* sides with the third.

RATING PLACES: AN OLD AMERICAN TRADITION

It may seem the height of effrontery, this business of judging places from best to worst with numbers. After all, how can intangible things like friendliness and optimism be measured with statistics? Yet *numeracy* is almost as strong a national character trait as *literacy*. When it comes to picking a new place to live, we've been digesting numbers for a long, long time.

To sell colonists on settling in Maryland rather than in Virginia, 17th-century boosters assembled figures showing heavier livestock, more plentiful game, and lower mortality from summer diseases and Indian attacks.

California for Health, Wealth, and Residence, just one volume in a library of post-Civil War guides touting the West's superior quality of life, gathered data to show the climate along the southern Pacific coast to be the world's best. Not so, countered the Union Pacific Railroad's land office in 1871; settlers will find the most "genial and healthy seasons" in western Kansas.

In our own century, the statistical nets were flung even wider. "There are plenty of Americans who regard Kansas as almost barbaric," noted H.L. Mencken back in 1931, "just as there are other Americans who shudder whenever they think of Arkansas, Ohio, Indiana, Oklahoma, Texas, or California." Mencken wrote these words in his *American Mercury* magazine to introduce his formula for measuring the progress of civilization in each of the states. He mixed the number of Boy Scouts and *Atlantic Monthly* subscribers with lynchings and pellagra cases, added a dash of *Who's Who* listings along with rates for divorce and murder, threw in figures for rainfall and gasoline consumption, and found that, hands down, Mississippi was the worst American state. Few were surprised by his finding, since Mencken didn't like the South anyway. Massachusetts, a state he admired, came out best.

But the Bay State was demoted in 1978 when Chase Econometrics, a major consulting firm, rated it the worst state for retirement. And the best state according to the Chase forecasters? Utah.

Rating Retirement Places: One Way

Retirement Places Rated is more useful than any system that just looks at states. When it comes to finding your own spot for retirement, you would do well to ignore the shopworn truisms about states and their track records in attracting older adults.

Thinking of Florida as a destination still means having to make a choice from among thousands of cities, towns, and unincorporated places from Escambia County farm country in the panhandle all the way down some 900 miles to Key West. People don't retire to states, they retire to specific places.

Moreover, statewide averages hide local realities. For some persons, there may be a world of difference between Alamogordo and Santa Fe in New Mexico, and these differences may be more important in retirement than the differences between California and Florida.

Certainly this book is more objective than the hearsay that travelers share at an interstate highway rest stop or at an airport gate. Each of the 151 places is rated by seven factors that most persons planning for retirement deem highly important.

- **Money Matters** looks at typical personal incomes and taxes, and it also measures the costs for items such as food and health care.
- **Housing** also looks at costs, including property taxes, utility bills, and average sales prices, and it also notes whether condominiums, mobile homes, and rental apartments are available.
- **Climate** rates mildness; that is, where air temperatures remain closest to a low of 65 degrees Fahrenheit and a high of 80 degrees throughout the year; where, in fact, you can spend most of your days outdoors if you wish.
- **Personal Safety** measures the annual rate of violent and property crimes per 100,000 people in each retirement place.
- **Services** evaluates the relative supply of health care, public transportation, and continuing education amenities in each place.
- The chapter on **Working** compares the local prospects for jobs in three basic industries

most promising to older adults: finance, insurance, and real estate; retail trade; and services.

- **Leisure Living** counts recreational and cultural assets such as public golf courses, good restaurants, symphony orchestras and opera companies, and lakes and national parks.

You may fault *Retirement Places Rated*'s choice of criteria. Admittedly, this book's measurements for health care, public transportation, continuing education, and the performing arts favor big places over small ones. On the other hand, the ratings for personal safety and costs of living favor small places over big ones. The standards for warm, occasionally hot climates and outdoor recreation assets are certainly not everyone's. But they have nothing to do with population size.

Rating Retirement Places: Your Way

At the end of this book, in the chapter entitled "Putting It All Together," money matters, housing, climate, personal safety, community services, working, and leisure living get equal weight to identify retirement places with across-the-board strengths.

You may not agree with this system. You may give more weight to personal safety than to good fishing spots. For you, a place where fixed income goes further might be more important than an abundance of physicians, an ocean coastline, or a busy performing arts calendar. To identify which factors are more important and which factors are less, you might want to take stock of your own preferences.

YOUR PREFERENCE INVENTORY

The following Preference Inventory has 42 pairs of statements. For each pair, decide which statement is more important to you when judging a retirement place. Even if both statements are equally important or neither is important, select one anyway. If you can't decide quickly, pass up the item but return to it after you complete the rest of the inventory.

Don't worry about being consistent. The paired statements aren't repeated. There aren't any right or wrong answers, only those that are best for you. Although the inventory takes about 15 minutes to finish, there is no time limit. You may want to ask your spouse or a friend to use one of the extra preference profiles on the last page of this chapter. Comparing your Preference Inventory with another person's can be an interesting exercise.

Directions

For each numbered item, decide which of the two statements is more important to you when choosing a

place to retire. Mark the box next to that statement. Be sure to make a choice for all items.

1. A. ☐ The local costs of living,
   or
   B. ☐ The median sales price of a house.

2. C. ☐ The duration of the winter,
   or
   D. ☐ The raw odds of being a victim of crime.

3. E. ☐ Opportunities for taking college courses,
   or
   F. ☐ Opportunities for volunteer work.

4. A. ☐ How far Social Security benefits will stretch,
   or
   G. ☐ Access to public golf courses.

5. B. ☐ Local adults-only housing developments,
   or
   C. ☐ How hot is summer and how cold is winter.

6. D. ☐ Local homicides, burglaries, and holdups,
   or
   E. ☐ Physicians and accredited hospitals.

7. F. ☐ Five-year forecast for job growth in an area,
   or
   G. ☐ Nearby national parks and forests.

8. A. ☐ Typical household incomes in an area,
   or
   C. ☐ Elevation, humidity, and temperatures.

9. B. ☐ The number of rental apartments in an area,
   or
   D. ☐ How free an area is from criminal activity.

10. C. ☐ A mild, four-season climate,
    or
    E. ☐ Academic programs at local colleges.

11. D. ☐ The local crime rate,
    or
    F. ☐ Variety of volunteer opportunities.

12. E. ☐ Local library acquisition budgets,
    or
    G. ☐ Ocean coastlines and inland lakes.

13. A. ☐ The bite state and local taxes might take,
    or
    F. ☐ Retired Senior Volunteer programs.

14. B. ☐ Local life-care residences,
    or
    G. ☐ Symphonies, operas, and theatres.

15. C. ☐ Annual temperature extremes,
    or
    F. ☐ Service Corps of Retired Executives programs.

16. A. ☐ Where the living is inexpensive,
    or
    D. ☐ The odds of being burglarized.

17. B. ☐ Mobile-home parks in an area,
    or
    E. ☐ Health care and public transportation.

18. C. ☐ The length of the growing season,
    or
    G. ☐ Camping, fishing, and hiking.

19. D. ☐ The local property crime rate,
    or
    G. ☐ Local theatre, symphony, and opera seasons.

20. A. ☐ Low state and local taxes,
    or
    E. ☐ Opportunities for going to college.

21. B. ☐ New housing developments in an area,
    or
    F. ☐ Self-employment opportunities.

22. A. ☐ Places where fixed incomes go further,
    or
    B. ☐ Typical property taxes in an area.

23. C. ☐ The number of rainy and snowy days,
    or
    D. ☐ Annual violent and property crime rates.

24. E. ☐ Accredited short-term, acute care hospitals,
    or
    F. ☐ Outlook for part-time employment.

25. A. ☐ Tax bites and health care costs in an area,
    or
    G. ☐ Golf, movies, and good restaurants.

26. B. ☐ Local market values of housing,
    or
    C. ☐ The number of clear and cloudy days.

27. D. ☐ Local criminal activity,
    or
    E. ☐ Public transit alternatives to driving a car.

28. F. ☐ Job opportunities in the tourist trade,
    or
    G. ☐ The area's fine arts calendar.

29. A. ☐ The local costs of living index,
    or
    C. ☐ The number of stormy days throughout the year.

30. B. ☐ The number of condominiums in an area,
    or
    D. ☐ Local burglaries, robberies, and assaults.

31. C. ☐ Humidity, elevation, and wind speed,
    or
    E. ☐ Public library branches and collections.

32. D. ☐ How safe the area is from violent crime,
    or
    F. ☐ Forecasted employment growth in retail trade.

33. E. ☐ Access to specialized medical care,
    or
    G. ☐ Local night life.

34. A. ☐ Where physician fees are low,
    or
    F. ☐ Opportunities for work in the service sector.

35. B. ☐ Typical utility bills in an area,
    or
    G. ☐ Boating, fishing, and swimming.

36. C. ☐ Annual amounts of rain and snow,
    or
    F. ☐ Forecasted employment growth.

37. A. ☐ Where a fixed income will stretch further,
    or
    D. ☐ Local criminal activity.

38. B. ☐ Taxes on residential property,
    or
    E. ☐ Continuing education at local colleges.

39. C. ☐ How cold the winters are,
    or
    G. ☐ Access to the great outdoors.

40. D. ☐ Annual burglary and robbery rates,
    or
    G. ☐ The local performing arts calendar.

41. A. ☐ Local household incomes,
    or
    E. ☐ The local supply of public transportation.

42. B. ☐ Structured retirement housing in an area,
    or
    F. ☐ Forecasted job growth.

Source: Adapted from "The Prospering Test," courtesy Thomas F. Bowman, Ph.D.; George Giuliani, Ph.D.; and M. Ronald Minge, Ph.D.

Plotting Your Preference Profile

It is important that you make a choice for each of the 42 items. Have you left any unchecked? If not, you're ready to draw your Preference Profile.

First Step. Count all the marks you've made in the boxes next to the letter A. Then enter the number of "A" statements on the line next to the words "Money Matters" on your Preference Profile. In the same way, count the number of statements for each of the other letters. Enter their totals in their respective places on your Preference Profile.

Second Step. Now plot your totals on the blank chart. Place a dot on the appropriate line for each of the numbers and connect the dots to form a line graph of your results (see the Sample Preference Profile).

Analyzing Your Preference Profile

Each of the seven factors in your Preference Profile—money matters, housing, climate, personal safety, community services, working after retirement, and recreation—is not only a major concern when identifying a likely place to retire; it also has a complete chapter in this book. The purpose of the Preference Inventory is to help you decide the relative importance of each of the chapters to you personally.

If your scores are high for one or two of these factors, you may want to give extra attention to the chapters covering them. Likewise, if your scores are low for any of the seven, you may not need to give as much consideration to them as you would the ones with high scores. Bear in mind that the inventory *orders* your preferences in a hierarchy, that each of the factors has some importance to you, and that none should be entirely ignored.

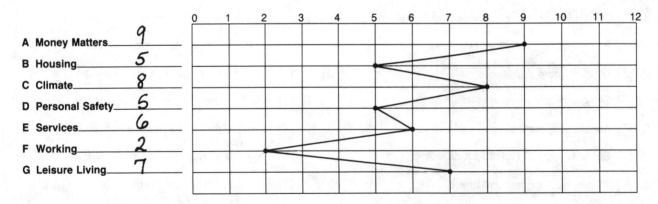

Sample Preference Profile

Your Preference Profiles

	0	1	2	3	4	5	6	7	8	9	10	11	12
A Money Matters													
B Housing													
C Climate													
D Personal Safety													
E Services													
F Working													
G Leisure Living													

	0	1	2	3	4	5	6	7	8	9	10	11	12
A Money Matters													
B Housing													
C Climate													
D Personal Safety													
E Services													
F Working													
G Leisure Living													

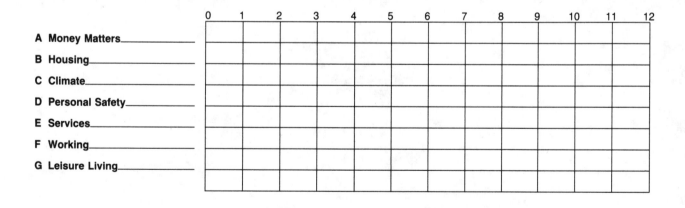

	0	1	2	3	4	5	6	7	8	9	10	11	12
A Money Matters													
B Housing													
C Climate													
D Personal Safety													
E Services													
F Working													
G Leisure Living													

Money Matters

"Let price decide which place is best," say some economists. "It will be the most expensive place because it is the most desirable." Good luck explaining that to people who've fled costly New York for Florida, pricey California for Nevada, or even middle-money Florida for the lower-cost Carolinas.

Because of all the windowed envelopes—interest, dividends, annuities, pensions, and Social Security checks—that come to your forwarding address, you needn't stay anywhere that's unaffordable. The best economic reason you'll ever need for leaving your hometown is the chance to enjoy a lower cost of living somewhere else for the final quarter of your life.

MONEY IN RETIREMENT: GETTING IT

"Money's no problem," any accountant will tell you. "Lack of money . . . now *that's* a problem." Can you afford to retire? More to the point, can you swing retirement where you're living now—or might there be somewhere else where you can do it more easily?

Lack of enough money to retire causes many people to cling to unsatisfactory jobs. For those who do retire, it crimps plans for travel or for year-round living in a warm, sunny, clean-air place where the bass fishing is good. It indefinitely defers the dream of a small part-time business, the book you've been meaning to write, or the boat you want to build. And it works hardships on your family.

A simple approach for deciding whether you can stop working and settle in another part of the country is to look at how your own circumstances stack up against typical retired persons who've retired recently, and weigh your own income and spending habits against typical incomes and living costs in other places.

In retirement, there isn't just one source of income but many. Apart from Social Security, there is a multitude of annuities, Individual Retirement Accounts (IRAs) and Keogh Plans, some 6,000 government-employee plans (federal civil service, military, state, and municipal) and one-half million private pension plans, each of which has different rules for age of eligibility, years of service required, payouts, and how spouses are covered.

For a typical husband and wife just embarking on retirement, the main income sources—in descending dollar amounts—are Social Security benefits, earnings from a job or self-employment, private pensions, and asset income.

Where the Money Comes From

Of every 100 newly retired couples in the United States . . .	receive a median income of . . .	annually from . . .
84	$2,160	Interest, dividends, rents, and royalties
50	$10,056	Social Security, when both spouses are eligible
47	$6,048	Social Security, when just the husband is eligible
46	$5,652	Husband's private pension
17	$5,016	Earnings, when only the husband works
17	$7,992	Earnings, when only the wife works
10	$12,648	Earnings, when both work
7	$9,084	Private pensions for both spouses
3	$2,568	Wife's private pension
1	$3,648	Social Security, when just the wife is eligible

Source: Social Security Bulletin.

Social Security

Social Security is money paid out by the federal government at the end of each month to retired persons who paid into the system during their working years. While determining benefits is complex, in general, annual earnings up to the year of eligibility for retirement are averaged and adjusted for inflation to derive an Average Index of Monthly Earnings (AIME). A benefit formula is then applied to the AIME to determine your Primary Insurance Amount (PIA). The percent of the PIA that you actually get depends on when you retire.

Currently, you are eligible for 100 percent of your PIA when you turn 65, the "normal" retirement age defined by the Social Security program 55 years ago. Reduced benefits equal to 80 percent of your PIA are available at age 62. For every month after age 62 you put off claiming your benefits, the 20 percent *early retirement penalty* is reduced by 0.56 percent (or 6.67 percent a year) so that your full PIA is earned at 65. If you stay on the job after 65, you receive a *delayed retirement credit* of three percent a year. If you work and put off claiming Social Security benefits until you're 68, for instance, you would receive benefits equal to 109 percent of your PIA.

In 1990, the maximum monthly check comes to $975 for a single worker, $1,462 for a couple with one dependent spouse, and $1,950 for a couple when both spouses are eligible. The average amount mailed out each month to a retired couple is $966, or $11,592 a year.

Earnings

Once you start collecting Social Security and private pension checks, there's almost nothing you can do to dramatically increase their amounts. If they aren't enough, the surest way of boosting your income is to get a job. The options run all the way from an eight-hour-a-day, 50-week-a-year new career to part-time or seasonal work.

Average Income for Two

LOWEST

McAllen–Edinburg–Mission, TX	$16,445
Brownsville–South Padre Island, TX	$17,388
Deming, NM	$20,125
Grand Lake, OK	$21,255
Southport, NC	$21,723
St. George–Zion, UT	$21,918
Las Cruces, NM	$22,034
Hamilton–Bitterroot Valley, MT	$23,068
Lake Havasu City–Kingman, AZ	$23,147
Paris–Big Sandy, TN	$23,295

HIGHEST

Los Alamos, NM	$53,346
Ann Arbor, MI	$46,359
Fort Lauderdale–Hollywood–Pompano Beach, FL	$46,091
Cape Cod, MA	$45,453
West Palm Beach–Boca Raton–Delray Beach, FL	$45,095
Sarasota, FL	$44,082
Santa Barbara, CA	$44,100
Carson City–Minden, NV	$44,750
Easton–Chesapeake Bay, MD	$43,719
Santa Rosa–Petaluma, CA	$42,689

Source: Woods & Poole Economics. Inc., personal income estimates.

Though savings, investments, and pension income don't affect the amount of your Social Security check, there is a ceiling on how much you can make on the job and still collect the Social Security benefits coming to you. If you're under 65 and your income exceeds $6,480, your benefits will be reduced by $1 for every $2 you're earning over the ceiling. If you're between 65 and 70 and you're making more than $8,800, your benefits will be cut by $1 for every $3 you're paid over the ceiling. After age 70, these reductions no longer apply.

Private Pensions

Everyone working in government contributes to a pension. Just half of all workers in the private sector are covered by an employer pension plan, however. And only half of these will ever see the money because of vesting requirements. Unlike the Social Security sys-

Preretirement and Postretirement Income Equivalents

A standard rule knocking about in folk wisdom is the one which states: "If your retirement income is 66 to 75 percent of what it was when you were working, you'll never notice a change in your standard of living." Actually, higher-income people need a lower percentage because their preretirement income is dramatically reduced by the federal income tax bite.

To keep your preretirement standard of living,

you'll need roughly . . .	or . . .	of a gross preretirement income of . . .
$14,000	70%	$20,000
$19,800	66%	$30,000
$24,800	62%	$40,000
$29,000	58%	$50,000
$33,000	55%	$60,000
$37,100	53%	$70,000

tem, to which workers contribute no matter how many different jobs they hold, private pensions are the equivalent of a corporate loyalty test—at least for the standard eight or 10 years of service required before an employee is vested and shares in a pension fund. Unlike Social Security, too, most employer pension plans don't have a cost-of-living escalator clause.

The typical amount of income from a public or private pension is $8,000 for a newly retired couple that is eligible for payments. While the amount isn't paltry, it isn't lavish, either. According to a recent study from the Social Security Administration, only seven out of 100 retired people who collect pension checks from their old employer rely on them for at least half their income.

Assets

Dividends from blue-chip stock investments you've made over the years; rents from real estate you own; royalties from your invention, song, computer software, best-selling book, or oil well; and interest from IRAs, Keogh Plans, certificates of deposit, passbook savings accounts, and loans are examples of asset income.

Like private pensions and earnings from a job, income from assets supplements Social Security for a more comfortable retirement. Nearly nine out of every 10 households that are newly retired count on money from these sources.

MONEY IN RETIREMENT: SPENDING IT

If you're thinking of moving, consider how far your income would stretch elsewhere. Average personal incomes in different places provide the first clue. Comparing local living costs completes the picture.

Scraping by on $35,108 a Year

Do personal incomes reflect local living costs? For the most part, yes.

A Bureau of Labor Statistics study showed that two-thirds of the difference in personal incomes between, say, Orlando and Olympia indicates their different costs of living; the rest is due to different employers, worker skills, and prevailing wages.

To reckon income for a typical two-person household, *Retirement Places Rated* doubled per capita income figures from Woods & Poole Economics, Inc., of Washington, DC. Among all the places featured in this book, the average is $35,108, ranging from $53,346 in Los Alamos, New Mexico, to $16,445 in McAllen–Edinburg–Mission, Texas.

So much for two-person household incomes. Are they really helpful in estimating living costs for a retired couple? They are if you consider to what extent Social Security checks can replace the income of a two-person household in retirement places. Please read on.

Local Social Security "Replacement Rates"

You'll never live comfortably on Social Security alone; these payments by themselves were never intended to completely support you in retirement. If you are a $51,300-a-year employee retiring at 65 with maximum earnings in "covered employment" (a job in which wages are deducted for Social Security) each year since 1951, for example, you can expect a monthly check of $975. That's only $11,700 a year. If you have a dependent spouse over 65, this amount is boosted by $488, for a combined benefit of $1,462, or $17,550 a year. Even though Social Security increases with the cost of living, the money comes way short of the dollars you were pulling down at work.

One useful indicator of how far your Social Security benefits will go is the rate at which your benefits would replace average personal incomes around the country. In mid-1990, the average benefits for a retired couple are $11,592. That won't replace much of

Putting It All Together

Lowest Living Costs	Cost-of-Living Index
Fayetteville, AR	81
Harrison, AR	81
Benton County, AR	83
Grand Lake, OK	83
Athens–Cedar Creek Lake, TX	84
Burnet–Marble Falls–Llano, TX	84
Paris–Big Sandy, TN	84
St. Tammany Parish, LA	84
Branson–Table Rock Lake, MO	85
Brownsville–Harlingen, TX	85
Canton–Lake Tawakoni, TX	85
Fredericksburg, TX	85
Kerrville, TX	85
Mountain Home–Bull Shoals, AR	85
Murray–Kentucky Lake, KY	85

Highest Living Costs	Cost-of-Living Index
Santa Barbara, CA	158
San Luis Obispo, CA	156
Salinas–Seaside–Monterey, CA	152
Maui, HI	151
Honolulu, HI	145
Santa Rosa–Petaluma, CA	138
San Diego, CA	135
Carson City–Minden, NV	128
Los Alamos, NM	127
Hanover, NH	126
Portsmouth–Dover–Durham, NH	124
San Juan Islands, WA	124
Key West–Key Largo–Marathon, FL	123
Cape Cod, MA	121
Santa Fe, NM	121

A place's cost-of-living index is derived from unrounded indexes for food, housing, health care, transportation, and all other expenses. The average cost-of-living index for the retirement places is 100.

the income a typical San Franciscan, New Yorker, or Chicagoan is accustomed to.

In certain places in Rio Grande Country, the Ozarks and Ouachitas, and New Appalachia, however, Social Security checks go a lot further in replacing local household incomes. Small wonder that retired persons who've moved over the last 40 years have tended to quit richer areas with high living costs for poorer places with low personal incomes. They were in search of spots where their own Social Security and pension benefits could be stretched; in short, where living costs were lower.

Local Costs of Living

It's a "black hole," the *Wall Street Journal* commented on just what is meant by *cost of living*. So what if the Consumer Price Index has gone up eightfold since the start of World War II; what does all that have to do with the high price of getting by in Santa Barbara as opposed to a small town in the Ozarks?

A few years ago, a special committee appointed by the Department of Labor to look into better ways to measure cost-of-living differences between places threw in the towel. Given the infinite range of consumer tastes and household tactics for saving a dollar, the only way to pin down why life in one place was more

expensive than in another was to focus on the weather's effect on clothing costs and household utility bills. Then look at taxes.

Taxes certainly do make a difference. But clothing and home energy bills? Not that much. According to one retailer, the cost difference between cotton and synthetic wardrobes in the Sun Belt and woolen and down-filled Frost Belt clothing amounts to less than one percent of a household's budget. As for the comparative costs of keeping warm in the North Woods winter and staying cool in Florida, often the only difference is the season during which local residents pay most of their bill.

One firm that counsels transferred employees adopts an 80/20 rule. In its experience, 80 percent of the difference in living costs between where you've come from and where you're going comes down to two things: housing and taxes. The other 20 percent comes from prices for everything from a splint for a broken thumb to frozen orange juice, soap flakes, and a shampoo, trim, and blow-dry at a salon.

To measure what it costs to live in each place, *Retirement Places Rated* looks at cost indexes for food, housing, health care, transportation, and other miscellaneous expenses. To produce an overall cost-of-living index, these items are weighted according to the Bureau of Labor Statistics' latest survey on spending among older households.

Against a national yardstick of 100, these overall cost-of-living indexes range from a high of 158 in Santa Barbara, California, to a low of 81 in Fayetteville, Arkansas.

 ## SCORING: Money Matters

If the money you and your spouse receive from a combination of Social Security, a private pension, plus interest and dividends from investments made over the years amounts to $28,000, will it stretch farther in the Rio Grande Country than on the California Coast? Do costs of living really vary tremendously among different places, or can skillful budgeting keep your head above water anywhere you choose to live?

To help you compare each place's differences, *Retirement Places Rated* looks at three factors: (1) the average income for a two-person household, (2) the combined cost-of-living indexes for food, housing, health care, transportation, and all other expenses, and (3) the extent that average 1990 Social Security benefits for a retired couple ($11,592) can replace income adjusted by those cost-of-living indexes.

Each place starts with a base score of zero. Points are added or subtracted using these indicators:

1. *Local average two-person household income adjusted for living costs.* Income is adjusted upward or downward by the cost-of-living index. For example, Honolulu's typical $37,125 household income is adjusted upward by 144 percent (since its cost-of-living index is 144) for an adjusted income of $53,460. Yuma's $24,853 household income is adjusted downward (multiplied by 95 percent, since its cost-of-living index is 95) to $23,610.

2. *Social Security replacement rate.* Average Social Security benefits for a retired couple ($11,592) replace the income in each place at different rates. The benefits replace only 21.61 percent of the adjusted income in Honolulu, for example, but replace 49.27 percent in Yuma. This local replacement rate is then multiplied by 100 to derive a score. Honolulu's and Yuma's scores, then, are 2,161 and 4,927, respectively.

SCORING EXAMPLES

Look at two places from sections of the country that represent economic opposites: McAllen–Edinburg–Mission on the bank of the Rio Grande in historically poor southernmost Texas, and the affluent Easton–Chesapeake Bay area on Maryland's Eastern Shore, a place attracting people from Baltimore and Washington, DC.

McAllen–Edinburg–Mission, Texas (#1)

Of all places profiled in this book, a winter resort lined with palms, bougainvillea, poinsettias, and citrus trees in the lower Rio Grande valley has the lowest income ($16,445) for a two-person household. McAllen–Edinburg–Mission means poverty to some. To others it means low costs of living.

The Texas tax bite is forgiving. There are no personal income taxes here. Though sales taxes are high, food and medicine are exempt and there are always bargains to be found in tax-free stores across the river in Mexico. In metropolitan McAllen–Edinburg–Mission, health care, housing, food, transportation, and other expenses together form a cost-of-living factor that is 88 percent of the U.S. average.

Adjusting local income downward (multiplying it by 88 percent) produces $14,471. Typical Social Security benefits replace 80.49 percent of that adjusted income, giving this place a score of 8,049.

Easton–Chesapeake Bay, Maryland (#135)

People are financially well-off in Talbot County, Maryland, where Easton is the seat of government. From the water, shorefront Georgian mansions can be spotted; in town are branch offices of Wall Street brokerage houses and many expensive shops. The place ranks near the top in personal income, not just in the Old Line State but in the nation. A retired couple here, however, may not do nearly so well as elsewhere.

Against a national yardstick of 100, food here is no more expensive than average, and health care and other items are a shade less. But high housing, utilities, and property taxes push the cost-of-living index up to 104. Social Security for a typical retired couple replaces only 25.48 percent of the $45,467 income (adjusted upward from $43,719 by living costs) that a two-person household needs to get by. This produces a money matters score of 2,548.

RANKINGS: Money Matters

Retirement Places Rated chooses three criteria to rank 151 places for money matters: (1) the average income for a two-person household, (2) cost-of-living indicators for food, housing, health care, transportation, and all other household expenses, and (3) the extent that average Social Security benefits for a retired couple ($11,592) can replace income adjusted for living costs.

Retirement Places from First to Last

Rank	Score	Rank	Score	Rank	Score
1. McAllen–Edinburg–Mission, TX	8,049	41. Coeur d'Alene, ID	4,522	85. Redding, CA	3,698
2. Brownsville–Harlingen, TX	7,812	41. Panama City, FL	4,522	86. Bradenton, FL	3,656
3. Grand Lake, OK	6,600	43. Lakeland–Winter Haven, FL	4,508	87. Savannah, GA	3,650
4. Deming, NM	6,387	44. Clear Lake, CA	4,490	88. Hendersonville, NC	3,638
5. Southport, NC	6,129	44. St. Tammany Parish, LA	4,490	89. Twain Harte–Yosemite, CA	3,615
				90. Hilton Head–Beaufort, SC	3,601
6. Paris–Big Sandy, TN	5,955	46. Gainesville, FL	4,449		
7. St. George–Zion, UT	5,872	47. Blacksburg, VA	4,448	91. Boise, ID	3,582
8. Hamilton–Bitterroot Valley, MT	5,643	48. San Antonio, TX	4,419	92. Grass Valley–Truckee, CA	3,563
9. Crossville, TN	5,481	49. Grand Junction, CO	4,416	93. Tucson, AZ	3,509
10. Athens–Cedar Creek Lake, TX	5,459	50. Thomasville, GA	4,410	94. Virginia Beach–Norfolk, VA	3,504
				95. Petoskey–Straits of Mackinac, MI	3,496
11. Las Cruces, NM	5,394	51. Prescott, AZ	4,399		
12. Houghton Lake, MI	5,348	52. Bloomington–Brown County, IN	4,360	96. Eugene–Springfield, OR	3,474
13. Clayton, GA	5,283	53. Kalispell, MT	4,357	97. Oak Harbor–Whidbey Island, WA	3,440
14. Lake Havasu City–Kingman, AZ	5,156	54. New Port Richey, FL	4,333	98. Medford–Ashland, OR	3,438
15. Biloxi–Gulfport–Pass Christian, MS	5,144	55. Aiken, SC	4,237	99. Bar Harbor–Frenchman Bay, ME	3,414
		55. Athens, GA	4,237	100. Bend, OR	3,405
16. Alamogordo, NM	5,022	57. Charlevoix–Boyne City, MI	4,173		
17. Harrison, AR	4,968	58. Benton County, AR	4,150	101. Austin, TX	3,391
18. Canton–Lake Tawakoni, TX	4,964	59. Asheville, NC	4,054	102. Lexington–Fayette, KY	3,366
19. Eagle River, WI	4,951	60. Brunswick–Golden Isles, GA	4,043	103. Orlando, FL	3,363
20. Fayetteville, AR	4,940			104. Phoenix–Tempe–Scottsdale, AZ	3,223
		60. Daytona Beach, FL	4,043	105. Amador County, CA	3,221
21. Yuma, AZ	4,927	62. Fort Collins–Loveland, CO	4,039		
22. Martinsburg–Charles Town, WV	4,894	63. Fredericksburg, TX	4,023	106. Albuquerque, NM	3,204
23. Ocala, FL	4,862	64. Pike County, PA	4,016	107. Door County, WI	3,168
24. Edenton–Albemarle Sound, NC	4,848	65. New Braunfels, TX	4,015	108. Charlottesville, VA	3,148
25. Brevard, NC	4,841			108. Columbia County, NY	3,148
		66. Charleston, SC	3,996	110. Chapel Hill, NC	3,107
26. Rockport–Aransas Pass, TX	4,832	67. St. Augustine, FL	3,992		
27. Mountain Home–Bull Shoals, AR	4,814	68. Ocean City–Assateague Island, MD	3,960	111. Monticello–Liberty, NY	3,075
28. Branson–Table Rock Lake, MO	4,813	69. Port Townsend, WA	3,955	112. Ocean County, NJ	3,074
29. El Centro–Calexico–Brawley, CA	4,795	70. Bellingham, WA	3,896	113. Traverse City–Grand Traverse Bay, MI	3,068
30. Pensacola, FL	4,775			114. New Paltz–Ulster County, NY	3,059
		71. Newport–Lincoln City, OR	3,887	115. South Lake Tahoe–Placerville, CA	3,023
31. Carlsbad–Artesia, NM	4,765	72. Burnet–Marble Falls–Llano, TX	3,842		
31. Myrtle Beach, SC	4,765	73. Fort Meyers–Cape Coral–Sanibel Island, FL	3,797	116. Lancaster County, PA	2,994
33. Red Bluff–Sacramento Valley, CA	4,725	74. Melbourne–Titusville–Palm Bay, FL	3,787	117. Bennington, VT	2,989
34. Fairhope–Gulf Shores, AL	4,640	75. Camden–Penobscot Bay, ME	3,783	118. Amherst–Northampton, MA	2,982
35. Grants Pass, OR	4,630			119. Canandaigua, NY	2,968
		76. Kerrville, TX	3,771	120. Iowa City, IA	2,933
36. Roswell, NM	4,613	77. Wenatchee, WA	3,749		
37. Murray–Kentucky Lake, KY	4,611	78. Colorado Springs, CO	3,747	121. Laconia–Lake Winnipesaukee, NH	2,907
38. New Bern, NC	4,595	79. State College, PA	3,745	122. Key West–Key Largo–Marathon, FL	2,900
39. Fort Walton Beach, FL	4,584	80. Vero Beach, FL	3,723	123. Keene, NH	2,889
40. Hot Springs National Park, AR	4,577	81. Lake Lanier, GA	3,719	124. Miami–Hialeah, FL	2,868
		82. Chico–Paradise, CA	3,708	125. Naples, FL	2,865
		83. Rehoboth Bay–Indian River Bay, DE	3,704		
		84. Olympia, WA	3,701		

Rank	Score
126. Santa Fe, NM	2,860
127. St. Petersburg–Clearwater– Dunedin, FL	2,846
128. Las Vegas, NV	2,842
129. Madison, WI	2,840
130. Sarasota, FL	2,737
131. North Conway–White Mountains, NH	2,666
132. Burlington, VT	2,640
133. Cape May, NJ	2,581
134. West Palm Beach–	

Rank	Score
Boca Raton–Delray Beach, FL	2,572
135. Easton–Chesapeake Bay, MD	2,548
136. Fort Lauderdale–Hollywood– Pompano Beach, FL	2,525
137. Portsmouth–Dover– Durham, NH	2,404
138. San Juan Islands, WA	2,380
139. San Luis Obispo, CA	2,342
140. Hanover, NH	2,340
141. Reno, NV	2,326
142. Maui, HI	2,272

Rank	Score
143. Ann Arbor, MI	2,237
144. San Diego, CA	2,232
145. Salinas–Seaside– Monterey, CA	2,170
146. Honolulu, HI	2,161
147. Cape Cod, MA	2,110
148. Carson City–Minden, NV	2,026
149. Santa Rosa–Petaluma, CA	1,975
150. Los Alamos, NM	1,707
151. Santa Barbara, CA	1,658

 PLACE PROFILES: Money Matters

The pages that follow highlight certain cost-of-living features in the retirement places. These include the factors used to rank the places—estimated average income for a two-person household and the cost of food, housing, health care, transportation, and all other expenses against an average of 100.

The information comes from these sources: Advisory Commission on Intergovernmental Relations, *Significant Features of Fiscal Federalism*, 1990; American Chamber of Commerce Researchers Association, "Inter-City Cost of Living Index," 4th quarter, 1989, and 1st quarter, 1990; Commerce Clearing House, *State Tax Guide*, 1990; Equicor Group Marketing, *1989 Hospital Daily Service Charges*, 1990; Minnesota Revenue Department, *Comparison of 1988 Individual Income Tax Burdens by State*, 1989; U.S. Department of Health and Human Services, Health Care Financing Administration, unpublished data, 1990; Woods & Poole Economics, Inc., unpublished county income estimates, 1990.

A star (★) preceding a place's name indicates it is one of the top 20 places for money matters.

Aiken, SC
Typical Household Income: $29,477
State and Local Taxes: $1,594
Cost-of-Living Indexes
Food: 94
Housing: 78
Health Care: 97
Transportation: 101
All Other: 103
Score: 4,237   **Rank: 55**

★ Alamogordo, NM
Typical Household Income: $25,152
State and Local Taxes: $1,138
Cost-of-Living Indexes
Food: 107
Housing: 72
Health Care: 98
Transportation: 100
All Other: 99
Score: 5,022   **Rank: 16**

Albuquerque, NM
Typical Household Income: $34,714
State and Local Taxes: $1,570
Cost-of-Living Indexes
Food: 98
Housing: 115
Health Care: 104
Transportation: 101
All Other: 98
Score: 3,204   **Rank: 106**

Amador County, CA
Typical Household Income: $31,427
State and Local Taxes: $1,321
Cost-of-Living Indexes
Food: 103
Housing: 141
Health Care: 105
Transportation: 102
All Other: 101
Score: 3,221   **Rank: 105**

Amherst–Northampton, MA
Typical Household Income: $34,449
State and Local Taxes: $1,654
Cost-of-Living Indexes
Food: 108
Housing: 129
Health Care: 113
Transportation: 106
All Other: 102
Score: 2,982   **Rank: 118**

Ann Arbor, MI
Typical Household Income: $46,359
State and Local Taxes: $2,151
Cost-of-Living Indexes
Food: 102
Housing: 131
Health Care: 108
Transportation: 103
All Other: 102
Score: 2,237   **Rank: 143**

Asheville, NC
Typical Household Income: $30,388
State and Local Taxes: $1,724
Cost-of-Living Indexes
  Food: 99
  Housing: 84
  Health Care: 95
  Transportation: 98
  All Other: 100
Score: 4,054   **Rank: 59**

Athens, GA
Typical Household Income: $29,548
State and Local Taxes: $1,462
Cost-of-Living Indexes
  Food: 98
  Housing: 82
  Health Care: 85
  Transportation: 97
  All Other: 100
Score: 4,237   **Rank: 55**

★ Athens–Cedar Creek Lake, TX
Typical Household Income: $25,255
State and Local Taxes: $213
Cost-of-Living Indexes
  Food: 92
  Housing: 59
  Health Care: 94
  Transportation: 98
  All Other: 97
Score: 5,459   **Rank: 10**

Austin, TX
Typical Household Income: $36,912
State and Local Taxes: $213
Cost-of-Living Indexes
  Food: 100
  Housing: 76
  Health Care: 100
  Transportation: 100
  All Other: 101
Score: 3,391   **Rank: 101**

Bar Harbor–Frenchman Bay, ME
Typical Household Income: $32,847
State and Local Taxes: $1,874
Cost-of-Living Indexes
  Food: 101
  Housing: 109
  Health Care: 97
  Transportation: 101
  All Other: 101
Score: 3,414   **Rank: 99**

Bellingham, WA
Typical Household Income: $31,191
State and Local Taxes: $250
Cost-of-Living Indexes
  Food: 100
  Housing: 83
  Health Care: 135
  Transportation: 95
  All Other: 100
Score: 3,896   **Rank: 70**

Bend, OR
Typical Household Income: $30,781
State and Local Taxes: $2,055
Cost-of-Living Indexes
  Food: 101
  Housing: 132
  Health Care: 106
  Transportation: 98
  All Other: 101
Score: 3,405   **Rank: 100**

Bennington, VT
Typical Household Income: $35,115
State and Local Taxes: $1,170
Cost-of-Living Indexes
  Food: 102
  Housing: 127
  Health Care: 107
  Transportation: 103
  All Other: 102
Score: 2,989   **Rank: 117**

Benton County, AR
Typical Household Income: $33,805
State and Local Taxes: $1,611
Cost-of-Living Indexes
  Food: 90
  Housing: 59
  Health Care: 89
  Transportation: 84
  All Other: 103
Score: 4,150   **Rank: 58**

★ Biloxi–Gulfport–Pass Christian, MS
Typical Household Income: $25,771
State and Local Taxes: $980
Cost-of-Living Indexes
  Food: 93
  Housing: 70
  Health Care: 82
  Transportation: 98
  All Other: 98
Score: 5,144   **Rank: 15**

Blacksburg, VA
Typical Household Income: $26,663
State and Local Taxes: $1,266
Cost-of-Living Indexes
  Food: 97
  Housing: 97
  Health Care: 93
  Transportation: 104
  All Other: 96
Score: 4,448   **Rank: 47**

Bloomington–Brown County, IN
Typical Household Income: $28,753
State and Local Taxes: $1,063
Cost-of-Living Indexes
  Food: 100
  Housing: 82
  Health Care: 98
  Transportation: 93
  All Other: 99
Score: 4,360   **Rank: 52**

Boise, ID
Typical Household Income: $36,017
State and Local Taxes: $2,199
Cost-of-Living Indexes
  Food: 91
  Housing: 74
  Health Care: 86
  Transportation: 100
  All Other: 101
Score: 3,582   **Rank: 91**

Bradenton, FL
Typical Household Income: $34,497
State and Local Taxes: $164
Cost-of-Living Indexes
  Food: 99
  Housing: 76
  Health Care: 99
  Transportation: 99
  All Other: 100
Score: 3,656   **Rank: 86**

Branson–Table Rock Lake, MO
Typical Household Income: $28,258
State and Local Taxes: $1,197
Cost-of-Living Indexes
　Food: 99
　Housing: 67
　Health Care: 82
　Transportation: 81
　All Other: 102
Score: 4,813　　　　　　　　　　　Rank: 28

Brevard, NC
Typical Household Income: $26,673
State and Local Taxes: $1,513
Cost-of-Living Indexes
　Food: 99
　Housing: 72
　Health Care: 93
　Transportation: 96
　All Other: 100
Score: 4,841　　　　　　　　　　　Rank: 25

★ **Brownsville–Harlingen, TX**
Typical Household Income: $17,388
State and Local Taxes: $213
Cost-of-Living Indexes
　Food: 101
　Housing: 65
　Health Care: 89
　Transportation: 97
　All Other: 91
Score: 7,812　　　　　　　　　　　Rank: 2

Brunswick–Golden Isles, GA
Typical Household Income: $32,233
State and Local Taxes: $1,595
Cost-of-Living Indexes
　Food: 99
　Housing: 70
　Health Care: 95
　Transportation: 96
　All Other: 99
Score: 4,043　　　　　　　　　　　Rank: 60

Burlington, VT
Typical Household Income: $37,716
State and Local Taxes: $1,256
Cost-of-Living Indexes
　Food: 103
　Housing: 145
　Health Care: 104
　Transportation: 104
　All Other: 102
Score: 2,640　　　　　　　　　　　Rank: 132

Burnet–Marble Falls–Llano, TX
Typical Household Income: $35,856
State and Local Taxes: $213
Cost-of-Living Indexes
　Food: 100
　Housing: 56
　Health Care: 89
　Transportation: 95
　All Other: 99
Score: 3,842　　　　　　　　　　　Rank: 72

Camden–Penobscot Bay, ME
Typical Household Income: $30,548
State and Local Taxes: $1,742
Cost-of-Living Indexes
　Food: 104
　Housing: 98
　Health Care: 97
　Transportation: 101
　All Other: 101
Score: 3,783　　　　　　　　　　　Rank: 75

Canandaigua, NY
Typical Household Income: $36,265
State and Local Taxes: $2,182
Cost-of-Living Indexes
　Food: 105
　Housing: 110
　Health Care: 94
　Transportation: 111
　All Other: 107
Score: 2,968　　　　　　　　　　　Rank: 119

★ **Canton–Lake Tawakoni, TX**
Typical Household Income: $27,537
State and Local Taxes: $213
Cost-of-Living Indexes
　Food: 93
　Housing: 61
　Health Care: 88
　Transportation: 98
　All Other: 98
Score: 4,964　　　　　　　　　　　Rank: 18

Cape Cod, MA
Typical Household Income: $45,453
State and Local Taxes: $2,182
Cost-of-Living Indexes
　Food: 104
　Housing: 157
　Health Care: 104
　Transportation: 105
　All Other: 103
Score: 2,110　　　　　　　　　　　Rank: 147

Cape May, NJ
Typical Household Income: $39,947
State and Local Taxes: $1,051
Cost-of-Living Indexes
　Food: 102
　Housing: 137
　Health Care: 100
　Transportation: 100
　All Other: 101
Score: 2,581　　　　　　　　　　　Rank: 133

Carlsbad–Artesia, NM
Typical Household Income: $26,308
State and Local Taxes: $1,190
Cost-of-Living Indexes
　Food: 110
　Housing: 71
　Health Care: 109
　Transportation: 106
　All Other: 95
Score: 4,765　　　　　　　　　　　Rank: 31

Carson City–Minden, NV
Typical Household Income: $44,750
State and Local Taxes: $231
Cost-of-Living Indexes
　Food: 97
　Housing: 182
　Health Care: 125
　Transportation: 105
　All Other: 100
Score: 2,026　　　　　　　　　　　Rank: 148

Chapel Hill, NC
Typical Household Income: $34,773
State and Local Taxes: $1,973
Cost-of-Living Indexes
　Food: 99
　Housing: 122
　Health Care: 103
　Transportation: 100
　All Other: 101
Score: 3,107　　　　　　　　　　　Rank: 110

Charleston, SC
Typical Household Income: $30,320
State and Local Taxes: $1,639
Cost-of-Living Indexes
  Food: 100
  Housing: 90
  Health Care: 89
  Transportation: 97
  All Other: 100
Score: 3,996   Rank: 66

Charlevoix–Boyne City, MI
Typical Household Income: $27,626
State and Local Taxes: $1,282
Cost-of-Living Indexes
  Food: 104
  Housing: 84
  Health Care: 105
  Transportation: 112
  All Other: 109
Score: 4,173   Rank: 57

Charlottesville, VA
Typical Household Income: $35,140
State and Local Taxes: $1,669
Cost-of-Living Indexes
  Food: 97
  Housing: 119
  Health Care: 93
  Transportation: 104
  All Other: 96
Score: 3,148   Rank: 108

Chico–Paradise, CA
Typical Household Income: $29,003
State and Local Taxes: $1,219
Cost-of-Living Indexes
  Food: 102
  Housing: 119
  Health Care: 120
  Transportation: 102
  All Other: 100
Score: 3,708   Rank: 82

★Clayton, GA
Typical Household Income: $24,542
State and Local Taxes: $1,214
Cost-of-Living Indexes
  Food: 102
  Housing: 67
  Health Care: 93
  Transportation: 100
  All Other: 100
Score: 5,283   Rank: 13

Clear Lake, CA
Typical Household Income: $26,860
State and Local Taxes: $1,129
Cost-of-Living Indexes
  Food: 101
  Housing: 86
  Health Care: 120
  Transportation: 100
  All Other: 98
Score: 4,490   Rank: 44

Coeur d'Alene, ID
Typical Household Income: $27,822
State and Local Taxes: $1,699
Cost-of-Living Indexes
  Food: 102
  Housing: 78
  Health Care: 96
  Transportation: 98
  All Other: 98
Score: 4,522   Rank: 41

Colorado Springs, CO
Typical Household Income: $34,034
State and Local Taxes: $1,329
Cost-of-Living Indexes
  Food: 93
  Housing: 76
  Health Care: 102
  Transportation: 104
  All Other: 96
Score: 3,747   Rank: 78

Columbia County, NY
Typical Household Income: $35,451
State and Local Taxes: $2,133
Cost-of-Living Indexes
  Food: 108
  Housing: 112
  Health Care: 106
  Transportation: 90
  All Other: 101
Score: 3,148   Rank: 108

★Crossville, TN
Typical Household Income: $24,652
State and Local Taxes: $252
Cost-of-Living Indexes
  Food: 98
  Housing: 66
  Health Care: 84
  Transportation: 93
  All Other: 97
Score: 5,481   Rank: 9

Daytona Beach, FL
Typical Household Income: $31,067
State and Local Taxes: $164
Cost-of-Living Indexes
  Food: 102
  Housing: 74
  Health Care: 100
  Transportation: 100
  All Other: 101
Score: 4,043   Rank: 60

★Deming, NM
Typical Household Income: $20,125
State and Local Taxes: $910
Cost-of-Living Indexes
  Food: 105
  Housing: 61
  Health Care: 105
  Transportation: 107
  All Other: 101
Score: 6,387   Rank: 4

Door County, WI
Typical Household Income: $37,210
State and Local Taxes: $2,187
Cost-of-Living Indexes
  Food: 104
  Housing: 98
  Health Care: 92
  Transportation: 98
  All Other: 97
Score: 3,168   Rank: 107

★Eagle River, WI
Typical Household Income: $26,175
State and Local Taxes: $1,539
Cost-of-Living Indexes
  Food: 99
  Housing: 71
  Health Care: 115
  Transportation: 96
  All Other: 96
Score: 4,951   Rank: 19

Easton–Chesapeake Bay, MD
Typical Household Income: $43,719
State and Local Taxes: $2,696
Cost-of-Living Indexes
  Food: 100
  Housing: 114
  Health Care: 99
  Transportation: 101
  All Other: 98
Score: 2,548   **Rank: 135**

Edenton–Albemarle Sound, NC
Typical Household Income: $24,876
State and Local Taxes: $1,411
Cost-of-Living Indexes
  Food: 102
  Housing: 91
  Health Care: 98
  Transportation: 101
  All Other: 95
Score: 4,848   **Rank: 24**

El Centro–Calexico–Brawley, CA
Typical Household Income: $26,833
State and Local Taxes: $1,128
Cost-of-Living Indexes
  Food: 99
  Housing: 76
  Health Care: 100
  Transportation: 98
  All Other: 94
Score: 4,795   **Rank: 29**

Eugene–Springfield, OR
Typical Household Income: $31,967
State and Local Taxes: $2,135
Cost-of-Living Indexes
  Food: 97
  Housing: 116
  Health Care: 104
  Transportation: 99
  All Other: 99
Score: 3,474   **Rank: 96**

Fairhope–Gulf Shores, AL
Typical Household Income: $26,713
State and Local Taxes: $1,106
Cost-of-Living Indexes
  Food: 100
  Housing: 82
  Health Care: 92
  Transportation: 101
  All Other: 98
Score: 4,640   **Rank: 34**

★Fayetteville, AR
Typical Household Income: $29,090
State and Local Taxes: $1,387
Cost-of-Living Indexes
  Food: 91
  Housing: 61
  Health Care: 74
  Transportation: 89
  All Other: 93
Score: 4,940   **Rank: 20**

Fort Collins–Loveland, CO
Typical Household Income: $32,623
State and Local Taxes: $1,274
Cost-of-Living Indexes
  Food: 94
  Housing: 70
  Health Care: 107
  Transportation: 93
  All Other: 98
Score: 4,039   **Rank: 62**

Fort Lauderdale–Hollywood–Pompano Beach, FL
Typical Household Income: $46,091
State and Local Taxes: $164
Cost-of-Living Indexes
  Food: 101
  Housing: 90
  Health Care: 119
  Transportation: 103
  All Other: 104
Score: 2,525   **Rank: 136**

Fort Myers–Cape Coral–Sanibel Island, FL
Typical Household Income: $33,855
State and Local Taxes: $164
Cost-of-Living Indexes
  Food: 101
  Housing: 67
  Health Care: 102
  Transportation: 101
  All Other: 101
Score: 3,797   **Rank: 73**

Fort Walton Beach, FL
Typical Household Income: $26,739
State and Local Taxes: $164
Cost-of-Living Indexes
  Food: 102
  Housing: 85
  Health Care: 100
  Transportation: 98
  All Other: 98
Score: 4,584   **Rank: 39**

Fredericksburg, TX
Typical Household Income: $33,969
State and Local Taxes: $213
Cost-of-Living Indexes
  Food: 96
  Housing: 61
  Health Care: 89
  Transportation: 98
  All Other: 96
Score: 4,023   **Rank: 63**

Gainesville, FL
Typical Household Income: $28,659
State and Local Taxes: $164
Cost-of-Living Indexes
  Food: 99
  Housing: 76
  Health Care: 94
  Transportation: 95
  All Other: 100
Score: 4,449   **Rank: 46**

Grand Junction, CO
Typical Household Income: $29,288
State and Local Taxes: $1,143
Cost-of-Living Indexes
  Food: 103
  Housing: 70
  Health Care: 98
  Transportation: 101
  All Other: 95
Score: 4,416   **Rank: 49**

★Grand Lake, OK
Typical Household Income: $21,255
State and Local Taxes: $1,076
Cost-of-Living Indexes
  Food: 90
  Housing: 59
  Health Care: 89
  Transportation: 84
  All Other: 103
Score: 6,600   **Rank: 3**

Grants Pass, OR
Typical Household Income: $23,325
State and Local Taxes: $1,557
Cost-of-Living Indexes
   Food: 98
   Housing: 126
   Health Care: 104
   Transportation: 97
   All Other: 99
Score: 4,630   **Rank: 35**

Grass Valley–Truckee, CA
Typical Household Income: $29,866
State and Local Taxes: $1,255
Cost-of-Living Indexes
   Food: 102
   Housing: 127
   Health Care: 103
   Transportation: 102
   All Other: 98
Score: 3,563   **Rank: 92**

★Hamilton–Bitterroot Valley, MT
Typical Household Income: $23,068
State and Local Taxes: $1,126
Cost-of-Living Indexes
   Food: 100
   Housing: 69
   Health Care: 98
   Transportation: 101
   All Other: 96
Score: 5,643   **Rank: 8**

Hanover, NH
Typical Household Income: $39,215
State and Local Taxes: $132
Cost-of-Living Indexes
   Food: 103
   Housing: 175
   Health Care: 96
   Transportation: 105
   All Other: 104
Score: 2,340   **Rank: 140**

★Harrison, AR
Typical Household Income: $28,798
State and Local Taxes: $1,373
Cost-of-Living Indexes
   Food: 90
   Housing: 54
   Health Care: 89
   Transportation: 84
   All Other: 103
Score: 4,968   **Rank: 17**

Hendersonville, NC
Typical Household Income: $31,283
State and Local Taxes: $1,775
Cost-of-Living Indexes
   Food: 98
   Housing: 107
   Health Care: 97
   Transportation: 99
   All Other: 101
Score: 3,638   **Rank: 88**

Hilton Head–Beaufort, SC
Typical Household Income: $32,172
State and Local Taxes: $1,740
Cost-of-Living Indexes
   Food: 100
   Housing: 103
   Health Care: 97
   Transportation: 96
   All Other: 100
Score: 3,601   **Rank: 90**

Honolulu, HI
Typical Household Income: $37,125
State and Local Taxes: $2,702
Cost-of-Living Indexes
   Food: 110
   Housing: 224
   Health Care: 110
   Transportation: 110
   All Other: 103
Score: 2,161   **Rank: 146**

Hot Springs National Park, AR
Typical Household Income: $29,360
State and Local Taxes: $1,399
Cost-of-Living Indexes
   Food: 96
   Housing: 67
   Health Care: 87
   Transportation: 93
   All Other: 98
Score: 4,577   **Rank: 40**

★Houghton Lake, MI
Typical Household Income: $24,081
State and Local Taxes: $1,118
Cost-of-Living Indexes
   Food: 101
   Housing: 66
   Health Care: 94
   Transportation: 101
   All Other: 103
Score: 5,348   **Rank: 12**

Iowa City, IA
Typical Household Income: $37,352
State and Local Taxes: $1,657
Cost-of-Living Indexes
   Food: 100
   Housing: 122
   Health Care: 98
   Transportation: 100
   All Other: 96
Score: 2,933   **Rank: 120**

Kalispell, MT
Typical Household Income: $28,565
State and Local Taxes: $1,394
Cost-of-Living Indexes
   Food: 102
   Housing: 79
   Health Care: 98
   Transportation: 101
   All Other: 98
Score: 4,357   **Rank: 53**

Keene, NH
Typical Household Income: $35,315
State and Local Taxes: $132
Cost-of-Living Indexes
   Food: 102
   Housing: 141
   Health Care: 96
   Transportation: 102
   All Other: 100
Score: 2,889   **Rank: 123**

Kerrville, TX
Typical Household Income: $36,240
State and Local Taxes: $213
Cost-of-Living Indexes
   Food: 101
   Housing: 56
   Health Care: 83
   Transportation: 101
   All Other: 98
Score: 3,771   **Rank: 76**

Key West–Key Largo–Marathon, FL
Typical Household Income: $32,580
State and Local Taxes: $164
Cost-of-Living Indexes
  Food: 103
  Housing: 163
  Health Care: 107
  Transportation: 106
  All Other: 102
Score: 2,900   **Rank: 122**

Laconia–Lake Winnipesaukee, NH
Typical Household Income: $38,436
State and Local Taxes: $132
Cost-of-Living Indexes
  Food: 102
  Housing: 109
  Health Care: 94
  Transportation: 103
  All Other: 101
Score: 2,907   **Rank: 121**

★ Lake Havasu City–Kingman, AZ
Typical Household Income: $23,147
State and Local Taxes: $906
Cost-of-Living Indexes
  Food: 103
  Housing: 94
  Health Care: 110
  Transportation: 93
  All Other: 98
Score: 5,156   **Rank: 14**

Lake Lanier, GA
Typical Household Income: $32,445
State and Local Taxes: $1,605
Cost-of-Living Indexes
  Food: 98
  Housing: 91
  Health Care: 89
  Transportation: 99
  All Other: 100
Score: 3,719   **Rank: 81**

Lakeland–Winter Haven, FL
Typical Household Income: $27,619
State and Local Taxes: $164
Cost-of-Living Indexes
  Food: 98
  Housing: 69
  Health Care: 103
  Transportation: 99
  All Other: 112
Score: 4,508   **Rank: 43**

Lancaster County, PA
Typical Household Income: $35,712
State and Local Taxes: $862
Cost-of-Living Indexes
  Food: 102
  Housing: 119
  Health Care: 88
  Transportation: 103
  All Other: 107
Score: 2,994   **Rank: 116**

★ Las Cruces, NM
Typical Household Income: $22,034
State and Local Taxes: $997
Cost-of-Living Indexes
  Food: 105
  Housing: 84
  Health Care: 105
  Transportation: 107
  All Other: 101
Score: 5,394   **Rank: 11**

Las Vegas, NV
Typical Household Income: $36,448
State and Local Taxes: $231
Cost-of-Living Indexes
  Food: 95
  Housing: 134
  Health Care: 117
  Transportation: 105
  All Other: 100
Score: 2,842   **Rank: 128**

Lexington–Fayette, KY
Typical Household Income: $35,672
State and Local Taxes: $1,442
Cost-of-Living Indexes
  Food: 99
  Housing: 89
  Health Care: 103
  Transportation: 95
  All Other: 104
Score: 3,366   **Rank: 102**

Los Alamos, NM
Typical Household Income: $53,346
State and Local Taxes: $2,413
Cost-of-Living Indexes
  Food: 105
  Housing: 177
  Health Care: 105
  Transportation: 107
  All Other: 101
Score: 1,707   **Rank: 150**

Madison, WI
Typical Household Income: $39,682
State and Local Taxes: $2,333
Cost-of-Living Indexes
  Food: 103
  Housing: 106
  Health Care: 86
  Transportation: 108
  All Other: 99
Score: 2,840   **Rank: 129**

Martinsburg–Charles Town, WV
Typical Household Income: $24,913
State and Local Taxes: $1,122
Cost-of-Living Indexes
  Food: 97
  Housing: 86
  Health Care: 103
  Transportation: 98
  All Other: 101
Score: 4,894   **Rank: 22**

Maui, HI
Typical Household Income: $33,702
State and Local Taxes: $2,453
Cost-of-Living Indexes
  Food: 113
  Housing: 237
  Health Care: 115
  Transportation: 113
  All Other: 108
Score: 2,272   **Rank: 142**

★ McAllen–Edinburg–Mission, TX
Typical Household Income: $16,445
State and Local Taxes: $213
Cost-of-Living Indexes
  Food: 101
  Housing: 72
  Health Care: 89
  Transportation: 97
  All Other: 91
Score: 8,049   **Rank: 1**

Medford–Ashland, OR
Typical Household Income: $29,904
State and Local Taxes: $1,997
Cost-of-Living Indexes
  Food: 99
  Housing: 141
  Health Care: 109
  Transportation: 98
  All Other: 99
Score: 3,438   Rank: 98

Melbourne–Titusville–Palm Bay, FL
Typical Household Income: $32,883
State and Local Taxes: $164
Cost-of-Living Indexes
  Food: 101
  Housing: 77
  Health Care: 100
  Transportation: 100
  All Other: 101
Score: 3,787   Rank: 74

Miami–Hialeah, FL
Typical Household Income: $36,516
State and Local Taxes: $164
Cost of Living Indexes
  Food: 101
  Housing: 118
  Health Care: 131
  Transportation: 108
  All Other: 106
Score: 2,868   Rank: 124

Monticello–Liberty, NY
Typical Household Income: $36,435
State and Local Taxes: $2,192
Cost of Living Indexes
  Food: 105
  Housing: 123
  Health Care: 85
  Transportation: 88
  All Other: 94
Score: 3,075   Rank: 111

Mountain Home–Bull Shoals, AR
Typical Household Income: $28,365
State and Local Taxes: $1,352
Cost-of-Living Indexes
  Food: 90
  Housing: 66
  Health Care: 90
  Transportation: 84
  All Other: 103
Score: 4,814   Rank: 27

Murray–Kentucky Lake, KY
Typical Household Income: $29,574
State and Local Taxes: $1,195
Cost-of-Living Indexes
  Food: 102
  Housing: 66
  Health Care: 91
  Transportation: 85
  All Other: 96
Score: 4,611   Rank: 37

Myrtle Beach, SC
Typical Household Income: $26,486
State and Local Taxes: $1,432
Cost-of-Living Indexes
  Food: 95
  Housing: 87
  Health Care: 88
  Transportation: 94
  All Other: 95
Score: 4,765   Rank: 31

Naples, FL
Typical Household Income: $40,369
State and Local Taxes: $164
Cost-of-Living Indexes
  Food: 101
  Housing: 92
  Health Care: 117
  Transportation: 105
  All Other: 103
Score: 2,865   Rank: 125

New Bern, NC
Typical Household Income: $26,773
State and Local Taxes: $1,519
Cost of Living Indexes
  Food: 99
  Housing: 86
  Health Care: 98
  Transportation: 99
  All Other: 97
Score: 4,595   Rank: 38

New Braunfels, TX
Typical Household Income: $33,428
State and Local Taxes: $213
Cost-of-Living Indexes
  Food: 97
  Housing: 67
  Health Care: 99
  Transportation: 91
  All Other: 97
Score: 4,015   Rank: 65

New Paltz–Ulster County, NY
Typical Household Income: $36,592
State and Local Taxes: $2,202
Cost-of-Living Indexes
  Food: 108
  Housing: 111
  Health Care: 107
  Transportation: 90
  All Other: 101
Score: 3,059   Rank: 114

New Port Richey, FL
Typical Household Income: $29,283
State and Local Taxes: $164
Cost-of-Living Indexes
  Food: 100
  Housing: 73
  Health Care: 100
  Transportation: 100
  All Other: 100
Score: 4,333   Rank: 54

Newport–Lincoln City, OR
Typical Household Income: $30,139
State and Local Taxes: $2,012
Cost-of-Living Indexes
  Food: 96
  Housing: 99
  Health Care: 110
  Transportation: 98
  All Other: 99
Score: 3,887   Rank: 71

North Conway–White Mountains, NH
Typical Household Income: $41,072
State and Local Taxes: $132
Cost-of-Living Indexes
  Food: 103
  Housing: 115
  Health Care: 95
  Transportation: 103
  All Other: 101
Score: 2,666   Rank: 131

Oak Harbor–Whidbey Island, WA
Typical Household Income: $30,405
State and Local Taxes: $250
Cost-of-Living Indexes
  Food: 107
  Housing: 103
  Health Care: 143
  Transportation: 122
  All Other: 109
Score: 3,440   Rank: 97

Ocala, FL
Typical Household Income: $26,179
State and Local Taxes: $164
Cost-of-Living Indexes
  Food: 103
  Housing: 78
  Health Care: 79
  Transportation: 94
  All Other: 99
Score: 4,862   Rank: 23

Ocean City–Assateague Island, MD
Typical Household Income: $31,241
State and Local Taxes: $1,927
Cost-of-Living Indexes
  Food: 101
  Housing: 81
  Health Care: 98
  Transportation: 100
  All Other: 99
Score: 3,960   Rank: 68

Ocean County, NJ
Typical Household Income: $40,211
State and Local Taxes: $1,058
Cost-of-Living Indexes
  Food: 105
  Housing: 76
  Health Care: 102
  Transportation: 100
  All Other: 102
Score: 3,074   Rank: 112

Olympia, WA
Typical Household Income: $32,964
State and Local Taxes: $250
Cost-of-Living Indexes
  Food: 96
  Housing: 84
  Health Care: 134
  Transportation: 95
  All Other: 100
Score: 3,701   Rank: 84

Orlando, FL
Typical Household Income: $36,511
State and Local Taxes: $164
Cost-of-Living Indexes
  Food: 104
  Housing: 81
  Health Care: 102
  Transportation: 97
  All Other: 101
Score: 3,363   Rank: 103

Panama City, FL
Typical Household Income: $27,716
State and Local Taxes: $164
Cost-of-Living Indexes
  Food: 102
  Housing: 77
  Health Care: 100
  Transportation: 99
  All Other: 99
Score: 4,522   Rank: 41

★Paris–Big Sandy, TN
Typical Household Income: $23,295
State and Local Taxes: $238
Cost-of-Living Indexes
  Food: 101
  Housing: 62
  Health Care: 91
  Transportation: 85
  All Other: 96
Score: 5,955   Rank: 6

Pensacola, FL
Typical Household Income: $27,138
State and Local Taxes: $164
Cost-of-Living Indexes
  Food: 101
  Housing: 73
  Health Care: 100
  Transportation: 95
  All Other: 96
Score: 4,775   Rank: 30

Petoskey–Straits of Mackinac, MI
Typical Household Income: $33,087
State and Local Taxes: $1,535
Cost-of-Living Indexes
  Food: 104
  Housing: 83
  Health Care: 105
  Transportation: 112
  All Other: 109
Score: 3,496   Rank: 95

Phoenix–Tempe–Scottsdale, AZ
Typical Household Income: $37,565
State and Local Taxes: $1,470
Cost-of-Living Indexes
  Food: 99
  Housing: 80
  Health Care: 117
  Transportation: 102
  All Other: 104
Score: 3,223   Rank: 104

Pike County, PA
Typical Household Income: $29,352
State and Local Taxes: $708
Cost-of-Living Indexes
  Food: 105
  Housing: 107
  Health Care: 85
  Transportation: 88
  All Other: 94
Score: 4,016   Rank: 64

Port Townsend, WA
Typical Household Income: $29,839
State and Local Taxes: $250
Cost-of-Living Indexes
  Food: 96
  Housing: 94
  Health Care: 134
  Transportation: 95
  All Other: 100
Score: 3,955   Rank: 69

Portsmouth–Dover–Durham, NH
Typical Household Income: $38,969
State and Local Taxes: $132
Cost-of-Living Indexes
  Food: 103
  Housing: 156
  Health Care: 116
  Transportation: 114
  All Other: 107
Score: 2,404   Rank: 137

Prescott, AZ
Typical Household Income: $27,618
State and Local Taxes: $1,081
Cost-of-Living Indexes
  Food: 97
  Housing: 91
  Health Care: 103
  Transportation: 94
  All Other: 99
Score: 4,399   Rank: 51

Red Bluff–Sacramento Valley, CA
Typical Household Income: $26,023
State and Local Taxes: $1,094
Cost-of-Living Indexes
  Food: 101
  Housing: 83
  Health Care: 108
  Transportation: 100
  All Other: 97
Score: 4,725   Rank: 33

Redding, CA
Typical Household Income: $30,164
State and Local Taxes: $1,268
Cost-of-Living Indexes
  Food: 102
  Housing: 110
  Health Care: 110
  Transportation: 101
  All Other: 99
Score: 3,698   Rank: 85

Rehoboth Bay–Indian River Bay, DE
Typical Household Income: $29,963
State and Local Taxes: $1,357
Cost-of-Living Indexes
  Food: 106
  Housing: 110
  Health Care: 99
  Transportation: 103
  All Other: 99
Score: 3,704   Rank: 83

Reno, NV
Typical Household Income: $42,274
State and Local Taxes: $231
Cost-of-Living Indexes
  Food: 96
  Housing: 154
  Health Care: 111
  Transportation: 99
  All Other: 103
Score: 2,326   Rank: 141

Rockport–Aransas Pass, TX
Typical Household Income: $26,919
State and Local Taxes: $213
Cost-of-Living Indexes
  Food: 104
  Housing: 63
  Health Care: 99
  Transportation: 104
  All Other: 99
Score: 4,832   Rank: 26

Roswell, NM
Typical Household Income: $28,053
State and Local Taxes: $1,269
Cost-of-Living Indexes
  Food: 106
  Housing: 70
  Health Care: 91
  Transportation: 98
  All Other: 97
Score: 4,613   Rank: 36

Salinas–Seaside–Monterey, CA
Typical Household Income: $35,078
State and Local Taxes: $1,474
Cost-of-Living Indexes
  Food: 103
  Housing: 257
  Health Care: 117
  Transportation: 101
  All Other: 102
Score: 2,170   Rank: 145

San Antonio, TX
Typical Household Income: $30,597
State and Local Taxes: $213
Cost-of-Living Indexes
  Food: 97
  Housing: 65
  Health Care: 99
  Transportation: 91
  All Other: 97
Score: 4,419   Rank: 48

San Diego, CA
Typical Household Income: $38,545
State and Local Taxes: $1,620
Cost-of-Living Indexes
  Food: 103
  Housing: 184
  Health Care: 129
  Transportation: 119
  All Other: 108
Score: 2,232   Rank: 144

San Juan Islands, WA
Typical Household Income: $39,388
State and Local Taxes: $250
Cost-of-Living Indexes
  Food: 113
  Housing: 140
  Health Care: 143
  Transportation: 122
  All Other: 109
Score: 2,380   Rank: 138

San Luis Obispo, CA
Typical Household Income: $31,744
State and Local Taxes: $1,334
Cost-of-Living Indexes
  Food: 102
  Housing: 259
  Health Care: 117
  Transportation: 119
  All Other: 101
Score: 2,342   Rank: 139

Santa Barbara, CA
Typical Household Income: $44,100
State and Local Taxes: $1,853
Cost-of-Living Indexes
  Food: 102
  Housing: 266
  Health Care: 112
  Transportation: 119
  All Other: 103
Score: 1,658   Rank: 151

Santa Fe, NM
Typical Household Income: $33,494
State and Local Taxes: $1,515
Cost-of-Living Indexes
  Food: 109
  Housing: 145
  Health Care: 112
  Transportation: 115
  All Other: 106
Score: 2,860   Rank: 126

Santa Rosa–Petaluma, CA
Typical Household Income: $42,689
State and Local Taxes: $1,794
Cost of Living Indexes
  Food: 102
  Housing: 209
  Health Care: 114
  Transportation: 104
  All Other: 103
Score: 1,975   Rank: 149

Sarasota, FL
Typical Household Income: $44,082
State and Local Taxes: $164
Cost-of-Living Indexes
  Food: 100
  Housing: 86
  Health Care: 100
  Transportation: 100
  All Other: 102
Score: 2,737   Rank: 130

Savannah, GA
Typical Household Income: $33,770
State and Local Taxes: $1,671
Cost-of-Living Indexes
  Food: 98
  Housing: 81
  Health Care: 106
  Transportation: 98
  All Other: 102
Score: 3,650   Rank: 87

South Lake Tahoe–Placerville, CA
Typical Household Income: $32,392
State and Local Taxes: $1,361
Cost-of-Living Indexes
  Food: 102
  Housing: 151
  Health Care: 110
  Transportation: 105
  All Other: 101
Score: 3,023   Rank: 115

★Southport, NC
Typical Household Income: $21,723
State and Local Taxes: $1,232
Cost-of-Living Indexes
  Food: 96
  Housing: 68
  Health Care: 89
  Transportation: 98
  All Other: 96
Score: 6,129   Rank: 5

St. Augustine, FL
Typical Household Income: $31,020
State and Local Taxes: $164
Cost-of-Living Indexes
  Food: 97
  Housing: 85
  Health Care: 98
  Transportation: 102
  All Other: 95
Score: 3,992   Rank: 67

★St. George–Zion, UT
Typical Household Income: $21,918
State and Local Taxes: $1,328
Cost-of-Living Indexes
  Food: 96
  Housing: 67
  Health Care: 99
  Transportation: 103
  All Other: 103
Score: 5,872   Rank: 7

St. Petersburg–Clearwater–Dunedin, FL
Typical Household Income: $41,936
State and Local Taxes: $164
Cost-of-Living Indexes
  Food: 100
  Housing: 91
  Health Care: 100
  Transportation: 100
  All Other: 100
Score: 2,846   Rank: 127

St. Tammany Parish, LA
Typical Household Income: $30,804
State and Local Taxes: $948
Cost-of-Living Indexes
  Food: 99
  Housing: 61
  Health Care: 84
  Transportation: 96
  All Other: 93
Score: 4,490   Rank: 44

State College, PA
Typical Household Income: $29,971
State and Local Taxes: $723
Cost-of-Living Indexes
  Food: 101
  Housing: 101
  Health Care: 104
  Transportation: 115
  All Other: 99
Score: 3,745   Rank: 79

Thomasville, GA
Typical Household Income: $30,202
State and Local Taxes: $1,494
Cost-of-Living Indexes
  Food: 97
  Housing: 66
  Health Care: 96
  Transportation: 97
  All Other: 97
Score: 4,410   Rank: 50

Traverse City–Grand Traverse Bay, MI
Typical Household Income: $36,526
State and Local Taxes: $1,695
Cost-of-Living Indexes
  Food: 104
  Housing: 93
  Health Care: 105
  Transportation: 112
  All Other: 109
Score: 3,068   Rank: 113

Tucson, AZ
Typical Household Income: $34,277
State and Local Taxes: $1,341
Cost-of-Living Indexes
  Food: 97
  Housing: 88
  Health Care: 117
  Transportation: 92
  All Other: 105
Score: 3,509   Rank: 93

Twain Harte–Yosemite, CA
Typical Household Income: $28,597
State and Local Taxes: $1,202
Cost-of-Living Indexes
  Food: 101
  Housing: 136
  Health Care: 105
  Transportation: 101
  All Other: 100
Score: 3,615   Rank: 89

Vero Beach, FL
Typical Household Income: $34,268
State and Local Taxes: $164
Cost-of-Living Indexes
  Food: 98
  Housing: 76
  Health Care: 98
  Transportation: 99
  All Other: 97
Score: 3,723   Rank: 80

Virginia Beach–Norfolk, VA
Typical Household Income: $34,043
State and Local Taxes: $1,616
Cost-of-Living Indexes
  Food: 101
  Housing: 86
  Health Care: 93
  Transportation: 108
  All Other: 101
Score: 3,504   Rank: 94

Wenatchee, WA
Typical Household Income: $33,526
State and Local Taxes: $250
Cost-of-Living Indexes
  Food: 99

  Housing: 72
  Health Care: 125
  Transportation: 102
  All Other: 99
Score: 3,749   Rank: 77

West Palm Beach–Boca Raton–Delray Beach, FL
Typical Household Income: $45,095
State and Local Taxes: $164
Cost-of-Living Indexes
  Food: 101
  Housing: 95
  Health Care: 109
  Transportation: 102
  All Other: 102
Score: 2,572   Rank: 134

Yuma, AZ
Typical Household Income: $24,853
State and Local Taxes: $973
Cost-of-Living Indexes
  Food: 95
  Housing: 86
  Health Care: 99
  Transportation: 100
  All Other: 100
Score: 4,927   Rank: 21

 ET CETERA: Money Matters

Question: Where in America can you find rock-bottom property taxes, no personal income tax on any of your retirement income, no sales tax on the basics you'll need like food and medicine, no inheritance taxes for your heirs to pay, and a minimum of nickel-and-dime fees for licensing a car or for taking out a fishing license?

Answer: Dream on. The ideal tax haven would have to have the low property taxes of Louisiana, Alaska's forgiveness of taxes on personal income, and the absence of sales taxes as in Oregon. Unfortunately, you just can't find all these tax breaks together in any one state.

When you retire, federal taxes will take the same bite whether you live in Hanover, Honolulu, or Hot Springs. But state taxes differ dramatically. Sales taxes, excise taxes, license taxes, income taxes, intangibles taxes, property taxes, estate taxes, and inheritance taxes are just some of the forms state taxes take. Depending on where you live, you may encounter all of them or only several.

Property Taxes. Taxes on land and the buildings on it—whether they are homes, farms, industrial plants, or commercial buildings—are the biggest sources of cash for local governments. Property taxes are imposed not by states but by more than 20,000 cities, townships, counties, school districts, sanitary districts, hospital districts, and other special districts in the nation. All the states do is specify the maximum rate on the market value of the property, or a percentage of it, as the legal standard for local assessors to fol-

low. The local assessor determines the value to be taxed. If you think the valuation is too high, you have a limited right of appeal.

You can't escape property taxes in any state except Alaska (there you must be over 65 to take advantage of that break), but you can find dramatically low rates in certain parts of the country. Nationally, the average bills on homes amount to 1.15 percent of their market value, while the average bills in Alabama, Hawaii, Louisiana, and Wyoming are less than half that rate. In addition, several states allow specific exemptions, without income qualifications, on property valuation for older homeowners.

Sales Taxes. Sometimes called "retail taxes" or consumption taxes, sales taxes are collected on the purchase of goods at the store level. After property taxes, sales taxes account for the largest source of revenue for state and local governments. Unlike property taxes, however, they will not be deductible from your federal tax return after 1991. Nationally, the median sales tax is five percent of retail sales. If you're living in Connecticut, you're paying the nation's highest state rate, eight percent. But the highest combined state and local rate is the 10 percent levied on goods at New Orleans International Airport. Alaska, Delaware, Montana, New Hampshire, and Oregon collect no sales taxes at all. To a retired couple, this could mean saving $300 to $600 a year. But you can avoid much of that cost in states where such basics as food, medicine, and clothing are exempt from sales taxes.

Personal Income Taxes. When federal income taxes

<table>
<tr><td colspan="4">

Taxing the Necessities

You'll pay sales tax on groceries in . . .

Alabama	Mississippi	Tennessee
Arkansas	Missouri	Utah
Georgia	New Mexico	Virginia
Hawaii	North Carolina	West Virginia
Idaho	Oklahoma	Wyoming
Kansas	South Carolina	
Louisiana	South Dakota	

And sales tax on medicine in . . .

Louisiana	New Mexico

But no sales tax on clothing in . . .

Connecticut	New Jersey
Massachusetts	Pennsylvania
Minnesota	Rhode Island

And NO sales tax, period, in . . .

Alaska	New Hampshire
Delaware	Oregon
Montana	

Source: Commerce Clearing House, *State Tax Guide*, 1990.

Taxes are paid by all taxpayers, not just those of retirement age.

</td></tr>
</table>

were enacted in 1914, two states—Mississippi and Wisconsin—were already collecting income taxes on their own. It was only during the 1920s and 1930s that the majority of states began to raise cash by tapping personal incomes. Today 40 states impose the tax; two —New Hampshire and Tennessee—apply it only to income from interest and dividends; one—Connecticut —applies it only to income from capital gains and dividends; and seven—Alaska, Florida, Nevada, South Dakota, Texas, Washington, and Wyoming—don't tax income at all.

STATE DEATH TAXES

Most persons need never worry about federal estate taxes. The law lets you leave as much as you wish to your spouse and up to an additional $600,000 to other heirs tax-free. In some states, however, inheritances valued at $100 can be hit by death taxes. Depending on where you live, there are three kinds: a "pickup" tax, an inheritance tax, or an estate tax.

The pickup tax doesn't cost you or your heirs anything. It picks up for the state some of the money that the estate would otherwise pay to the federal government. It is the only death tax in 25 states. If you live in any of them, you won't have to worry about the pickup tax unless your estate is subject to the federal tax.

The inheritance tax, applicable in 18 states, may amount to a good deal of money depending on who the heirs are and how much they get. Property left to a spouse, however, is tax-free in 11 of these states.

The estate tax is used in seven states. The amount they collect is determined solely by the size of the

State Treatment of Death Taxes

State	Pickup Only	Pickup and Estate	Pickup and Inheritance
Alabama	•		
Alaska	•		
Arizona	•		
Arkansas	•		
California	•		
Colorado	•		
Connecticut			•
Delaware			•
Florida	•		
Georgia	•		
Hawaii	•		
Idaho	•		
Illinois	•		
Indiana			•
Iowa			•
Kansas			•
Kentucky			•
Louisiana			•
Maine	•		
Maryland			•
Massachusetts		•	
Michigan			•
Minnesota	•		
Mississippi		•	
Missouri	•		
Montana			•
Nebraska			•
Nevada	•		
New Hampshire			•
New Jersey			•
New Mexico	•		
New York		•	
North Carolina			•
North Dakota	•		
Ohio		•	
Oklahoma		•	
Oregon	•		
Pennsylvania			•
Rhode Island		•	
South Carolina		•	
South Dakota			•
Tennessee			•
Texas	•		
Utah	•		
Vermont	•		
Virginia	•		
Washington	•		
West Virginia	•		
Wisconsin			•
Wyoming	•		

Source: American Association of Retired Persons, Tax Aid Program, 1990.

Note: Three states will become pickup-only states by phasing out their estate or inheritance taxes, as follows: Rhode Island by the last day of 1990; South Carolina by June 30, 1991; Wisconsin by the last day of 1991. Transfers to spouse are exempt in Connecticut, Indiana, Kansas, Kentucky, Montana, Nebraska, New Hampshire, New Jersey, North Carolina, Oklahoma, South Dakota, and Wisconsin.

estate. Mississippi allows a $600,000 exemption; the exemption in Massachusetts is only $200,000. The relationship of the heirs to the person who left the estate has no bearing unless the heir is a surviving spouse.

State Tax Treatment of Retirement Income

State	Pension Income Exclusions			Social Security Benefits Fully Exempted	Additional Personal Exemptions	Additional Credit
	State	Federal	Private			
Alabama	pending	pending		•		
Arizona	partial	partial		•	•	
Arkansas	partial	partial	partial	•		•
California				•		•
Colorado	partial	partial	partial		•	
Delaware	partial	partial	partial	•	•	
Georgia	partial	partial	partial	•	•	
Hawaii	•		•	•	•	
Idaho	partial	partial		•		•
Illinois	•	•		•		
Indiana		partial		•	•	
Iowa	partial	partial				•
Kansas	•	•			•	
Kentucky	•	•		•		•
Lousiana	•	•	partial	•	•	
Maine				•		•
Maryland	partial	partial		•	•	
Massachusetts	•			•	•	
Michigan	pending	pending	pending	•	•	
Minnesota	partial	partial	partial		•	
Mississippi	partial	partial	partial	•		•
Missouri	partial	partial	partial*		•	
Montana	•	•	partial		•	
Nebraska						
New Jersey	partial	partial	partial	•	•	
New Mexico	partial	partial	partial	•	•	
New York	•	•	partial	•		
North Carolina	partial	partial	partial	•	•	
North Dakota		partial			•	
Ohio				•		•
Oklahoma	partial	partial		•	•	
Oregon	partial	partial		•	•	
Pennsylvania	•	•	•	•		
Rhode Island						
South Carolina	partial	partial	partial	•	•	
Utah	partial	partial	partial		•	
Vermont						
Virginia	partial	partial	partial	•	•	
West Virginia	partial	partial	partial			
Wisconsin						•

Source: National Conference of State Legislatures.

*Missouri's partial exclusion of private pensions begins in tax year 1991.

Alaska, Florida, Nevada, South Dakota, Tennessee, Texas, Washington, and Wyoming do not tax personal incomes from any source. Connecticut taxes only capital gains and dividends; New Hampshire and Tennessee tax only income from dividends and interest. Rhode Island and Vermont calculate personal income taxes as a percentage of federal income tax; therefore, provisions in the federal tax code are implicitly recognized.

STATE RETIREMENT INCOME TAX PROFILES

From 1977 to 1987, state tax collections increased 144%, outrunning the 121% rise in federal taxes and the 88% rise in inflation. Today, some state and local taxes can total almost half the size of the federal tax bite.

Of the 43 states with some kind of income tax, 35 base the taxes on federal returns, typically taking a portion of what you pay the IRS, or using your federal adjusted gross income or taxable income as the starting point for their own computation. However, these states take differing views on income from Social Security, government pensions, and private em-ployer pensions.

The following brief descriptions of how states treat retirement income come from the National Conference of State Legislatures' May 1990 survey. The best way to learn what your income taxes will be in a new state is to write for its *resident* income tax form and instructions, fill it out, and compare the bottom line with that of your current state.

ALABAMA fully exempts Social Security benefits and federal civil service and military pensions. The state also fully exempts state or local government pensions, but limits the exemption to $8,000 for public safety employees. Except for defined-benefit plans, private employer pensions are taxed.

Information and tax forms: Alabama Department of Revenue, 64 N. Union Street, Montgomery 36130; (205) 261-3362.

ALASKA repealed its personal income tax in 1979.

Information: Alaska Department of Revenue, P.O. Box SA, Juneau 99811; (907)465-2320.

ARIZONA fully exempts Social Security benefits, excludes $2,500 from state or local, federal civil service, and military employee pensions, and allows additional personal exemptions. Private employer pensions are taxed.

Information and tax forms: Arizona Department of Revenue, 1600 W. Monroe, Phoenix 85007; (602)255-3572.

ARKANSAS fully exempts Social Security benefits, excludes $6,000 from all employer pensions—government and private—and allows additional personal tax credits.

Information and tax forms: Arkansas Department of Finance and Administration, P.O. Box 1272, Little Rock 72203; (501)682-7000.

CALIFORNIA tax code fully exempts Social Security benefits. Pensions from all government and private employers are taxable.

Information and tax forms: California Franchise Tax Board, P.O. Box 115, Rancho Cordova 95741; (916)369-4543.

COLORADO excludes $20,000 from all private and government employer pensions and allows a double standard deduction for taxpayers over 65. Half of Social Security benefits are taxable for single taxpayers with income over $25,000 and married taxpayers with income over $32,000.

Information and tax forms: Colorado Department of Revenue, 1375 Sherman Street, Denver 80216; (303)866-3091.

CONNECTICUT taxes only income from dividends and interest.

Information and tax forms: Connecticut Department of Revenue, 92 Farmington Avenue, Hartford 06105; (203)566-7120.

DELAWARE fully exempts Social Security benefits, excludes $3,000 from all government and private employer pensions, and allows an additional standard deduction to older taxpayers.

Information and tax forms: Delaware Division of Revenue, 820 N. French Street, Wilmington 19801; (302)571-3315.

FLORIDA doesn't tax personal income.

Information: Florida Department of Revenue, Carlton Building, Tallahassee 32399; (904)488-5050.

GEORGIA fully exempts Social Security benefits, excludes $10,000 from all government and private employer pensions, and allows an additional standard deduction to older taxpayers.

Information and tax forms: Georgia Department of Revenue, 270 Washington Street, SW, Atlanta 30334; (404)656-4015.

HAWAII fully exempts Social Security benefits, all government and private employer pensions, and allows additional personal exemptions for older taxpayers.

Information and tax forms: Hawaii Department of Taxation, P.O. Box 259, Honolulu 96809; (808)548-7650.

IDAHO fully exempts Social Security benefits, excludes $10,788 from government employer pensions, and allows additional credits for older taxpayers. Income from private employer pensions is taxable.

Information and tax forms: Idaho Department of Revenue and Taxation, 700 W. State Street, Boise 83722; (208)334-7660.

ILLINOIS fully exempts Social Security benefits, excludes all government employer pension income, and allows additional personal exemptions for older taxpayers. Income from private employer pension plans is taxable.

Information and tax forms: Illinois Department of Revenue, 101 W. Jefferson, Springfield 62708; (217)785-2602.

INDIANA fully exempts Social Security benefits, excludes $2,000 from federal civil service and military pensions, and allows additional personal exemptions for older taxpayers. State or local government and private employer pensions currently are taxable.

Information and tax forms: Indiana Department of Revenue, 202 State Office Building, Indianapolis 46204; (317)232-2101.

IOWA, for tax year 1990, excludes $2,500 from state or local, federal civil service, and military pensions and allows an additional credit to older taxpayers. Half of Social Security benefits are taxable for single taxpayers with income over $25,000 and married taxpayers with income over $32,000. Private employer pension income is fully taxable.

Information and tax forms: Iowa Department of Revenue Administration, Hoover State Office Building, Des Moines 50319; (515)281-3204.

KANSAS excludes income from state or local government and federal civil service pensions and allows older taxpayers a double standard deduction. Half of Social Security benefits are taxable for single taxpayers with income over $25,000 and married taxpayers with income over $32,000. Private pensions are fully taxable.

Information and tax forms: Kansas Department of Revenue, 915 Harrison, Topeka 66625; (913)296-3909.

KENTUCKY fully exempts Social Security benefits, excludes all government employer pensions, and allows additional credits to older taxpayers. Private employer pensions are fully taxable.

Information and tax forms: Kentucky Department of Revenue, Revenue Cabinet, Frankfort 40620; (502)565-3226.

LOUISIANA fully exempts Social Security benefits and all government employer pensions, exempts $6,000 from private employer pensions, and allows additional personal exemptions for older taxpayers.

Information and tax forms: Louisiana Department of Revenue and Taxation, P.O. Box 201, Baton Rouge 70821; (504)925-7680.

MAINE fully exempts Social Security benefits and allows additional personal exemptions to older taxpayers. Income from all government and private employer pensions is taxable.

Information and tax forms: Maine Bureau of Taxation, 24 State Office Building, Augusta 04333; (207)289-2076.

MARYLAND fully exempts Social Security benefits, excludes $2,500 from military pensions, excludes an amount equal to the difference between maximum Social Security benefits and what the taxpayer actually receives for all other government pensions, and

allows an additional standard deduction to older taxpayers. Private employer pensions are taxable.

Information and tax forms: Maryland Department of Revenue, P.O. Box 466, Annapolis 21404; (301)974-3801.

MASSACHUSETTS excludes income from government employer pensions, fully exempts Social Security benefits, and allows additional personal exemptions for older taxpayers. Private employer pension income is fully taxable.

Information and tax forms: Massachusetts Department of Revenue, 100 Cambridge Street, Boston 02204; (617)727-4201.

MICHIGAN fully exempts Social Security benefits, fully excludes military pensions and $7,500 from all other employer pensions, and allows older adults an additional personal exemption.

Information and tax forms: Michigan Department of Revenue, Treasury Building, Lansing 48922; (517)373-3227.

MINNESOTA excludes $8,000 of income from any source less any nontaxable retirement or disability income, and allows a double standard deduction for persons over 65.

Information and tax forms: Minnesota Department of Revenue, 658 Cedar Street, St. Paul 55145; (612)296-3401.

MISSISSIPPI fully exempts Social Security benefits, excludes $6,000 from government pensions and $5,000 from private pensions, and allows older taxpayers an additional personal exemption.

Information and tax forms: Mississippi State Tax Commission, 202 Woolfolk Building, Jackson 39201; (601)359-1100.

MISSOURI excludes $6,000 from government and (for tax year 1991 and after) private pensions and allows a double standard deduction for older adults. Half of Social Security benefits are taxable for single taxpayers with income over $25,000 and married taxpayers with income over $32,000.

Information and tax forms: Missouri Department of Revenue, P.O. Box 311, Jefferson City 65105; (314)751-4450.

MONTANA fully excludes state or local, federal civil service, and military pensions, $3,600 of private employer pensions, and allows older taxpayers an additional personal exemption. Half of Social Security benefits are taxable for single taxpayers with income over $25,000 and married taxpayers with income over $32,000.

Information and tax forms: Montana Department of Revenue, Mitchell Building, Helena 59620; (406)444-2460.

NEBRASKA taxes half of Social Security benefits for

single taxpayers with income over $25,000 and married taxpayers with income over $32,000. Government and private employer pensions are fully taxable.

Information and tax forms: Nebraska Department of Revenue, 301 Centennial Mall South, Lincoln 68509; (402)471-2971.

NEVADA doesn't tax personal income.

Information: Nevada Department of Taxation, 1340 S. Curry Street, Carson City 89710; (702)885-4892.

NEW HAMPSHIRE taxes only income from dividends and interest.

Information and tax forms: New Hampshire Department of Revenue Administration, P.O. Box 457, Concord 03302; (603)271-2191.

NEW JERSEY fully exempts Social Security benefits, excludes $7,500 from all government and private pensions, and allows an additional personal exemption to older taxpayers.

Information and tax forms: New Jersey Department of the Treasury, CN-240, Trenton 08646; (609)292-5185.

NEW MEXICO fully exempts Social Security benefits and excludes up to $8,000 income from any source for persons over 65, depending on income level.

Information and tax forms: New Mexico Taxation and Revenue Department, P.O. Box 630, Santa Fe 87509; (505)988-2290.

NEW YORK fully exempts Social Security benefits, government employer pensions, and $20,000 of private pensions.

Information and tax forms: New York Department of Taxation and Finance, State Campus, Building 9, Albany 12227; (518)457-2244.

NORTH CAROLINA fully exempts Social Security benefits, $4,000 from government pensions, $2,000 from private employer pensions, and allows an additional personal exemption to older taxpayers. For taxpayers receiving more than one pension, the maximum exclusion is $4,000.

Information and tax forms: North Carolina Department of Revenue, P.O. Box 25000, Raleigh 27640; (919)733-7211.

NORTH DAKOTA excludes an amount equal to $5,000, less Social Security benefits, from public safety employee, federal civil service, and military pensions, and allows a double standard deduction for taxpayers over 65. Half of Social Security benefits are taxable for single taxpayers with income over $25,000 and married taxpayers with income over $32,000. Private employer pensions are fully taxable.

Information and tax forms: North Dakota State Tax Department, State Capitol Building, Bismarck 58505; (701)224-2770.

OHIO fully exempts Social Security benefits and allows additional tax credits for taxpayers over 65. All government and private pensions are fully taxable.

Information and tax forms: Ohio Department of Taxation, 30 E. Broad Street, Columbus 43216; (614)466-2166.

OKLAHOMA fully exempts Social Security benefits, excludes $5,500 of state and local, federal civil service, and military pensions, and allows an additional personal exemption to older taxpayers. Private pensions are fully taxable.

Information and tax forms: Oklahoma Tax Commission, 2501 Lincoln Boulevard, Oklahoma City 73194; (405)521-3115.

OREGON fully exempts Social Security benefits and state or local government pensions, excludes $5,000 from federal civil service and military pensions, and allows an additional personal exemption for older adults. The $5,000 exclusion is reduced as income rises over $30,000. Legislation to reduce the state or local pension exclusion to $5,000 has been enacted but awaits referendum in November 1990.

Information and tax forms: Oregon Department of Revenue, 955 Center Street NE, Salem 97310; (502)378-3363.

PENNSYLVANIA fully exempts income from Social Security and all government and private pensions.

Information and tax forms: Pennsylvania Department of Revenue, Strawberry Square, Harrisburg 17120; (717)783-3680.

RHODE ISLAND claims a flat 22.96 percent of taxpayer's federal income tax liability but allows an additional personal exemption to older taxpayers.

Information and tax forms: Rhode Island Division of Taxation, 289 Promenade Street, Providence 02908; (401)277-3050.

SOUTH CAROLINA fully exempts Social Security benefits, excludes $3,000 from all government and private employer pensions, and allows a double standard deduction for persons over 65.

Information and tax forms: South Carolina Tax Commission, P.O. Box 125, Columbia 29201; (803)734-1830.

SOUTH DAKOTA doesn't tax personal income.

Information: South Dakota Department of Revenue, 700 Governors Drive, Pierre 57501; (605)773-3311.

TENNESSEE taxes only income from dividends and interest on bonds, notes, and mortgages.

Information and tax forms: Tennessee Department of Revenue, 500 Deaderick Street, Nashville, 37242; (615)741-2461.

TEXAS doesn't tax personal income.

Information: Texas Department of Revenue, 111 E. 17th Street, Austin 78774; (512)463-1000.

UTAH tax code excludes up to $7,500 from any source, depending on income level. Half of Social Security benefits are taxable for single taxpayers with income over $25,000 and married taxpayers with income over $32,000.

Information and tax forms: Utah Tax Commission, 160 E. 300 South, Salt Lake City 84134; (801)530-6088.

VERMONT claims a flat 25 percent of taxpayer's federal income tax liability, and allows additional personal exemptions for persons over 65.

Information and tax forms: Vermont Department of Taxes, 109 State Street, Montpelier 05602; (802)828-2523.

VIRGINIA fully exempts Social Security benefits, excludes $6,000 of income from any source for persons 62 to 64, and $12,000 of income from any source for persons 65 and over. These exclusions are reduced by the amount of Social Security or Railroad Retirement benefits the taxpayer receives.

Information and tax forms: Virginia Department of Taxation, P.O. Box 6-L, Richmond 23282; (804)367-8005.

WASHINGTON doesn't tax personal income.

Information: Washington Department of Revenue, General Administration Building, Olympia 98504; (206)753-5574.

WEST VIRGINIA excludes $2,000 from all government employer pensions. Each taxpayer aged 65 and over may exclude $8,000 of income from any source. Pension exclusions (which may not exceed a total of $6,000) count toward the $8,000 ceiling.

Information and tax forms: West Virginia Tax Department, State Capitol, Charleston 25305; (304)348-2501.

WISCONSIN excludes federal civil service and military pensions, certain benefits from municipal pensions for persons covered as of the end of 1963, and allows additional personal tax credits to older adults. Half of Social Security benefits are taxable for single taxpayers with income over $25,000 and married taxpayers with income over $32,000. Private pension income is fully taxable.

Information and tax forms: Wisconsin Department of Revenue, P.O. Box 8933, Madison 53708; (608)266-6466.

WYOMING doesn't tax personal income.

Information: Wyoming Department of Revenue and Taxation, 122 W. 25th Street, Cheyenne 82002; (307)777-7961.

Personal Income Taxes on Municipal Bonds

State	State's Own Bonds	Other States' Bonds
Alabama		•
Arizona		•
Arkansas		•
California		•
Colorado		•
Connecticut		•
Delaware		•
Georgia		•
Hawaii		•
Idaho		•
Illinois	•	•
Indiana		
Iowa	•	•
Kansas	•	•
Kentucky		•
Louisiana		•
Maine		•
Maryland		•
Massachusetts		•
Michigan		•
Minnesota		•
Mississippi		•
Missouri		•
Montana		•
Nebraska		
New Hampshire		•
New Jersey		•
New Mexico		
New York		•
North Carolina		•
North Dakota		•
Ohio		•
Oklahoma	•	•
Oregon		•
Pennsylvania		•
Rhode Island		•
South Carolina		•
Tennessee		•
Utah		
Vermont		
Virginia		•
West Virginia		•
Wisconsin	•	•

Source: Commerce Clearing House, *State Tax Guide*, 1990.

A • indicates municipal bonds are taxable.

MUNICIPAL BONDS AREN'T TAX EXEMPT EVERYWHERE

Even though income from state and local government obligations, collectively called "municipal bonds," is exempt from federal income tax, it isn't necessarily exempt from state personal income taxes. Thirty-eight states tax income from out-of-state municipal bonds as well. Only five states—Indiana, Nebraska, New Mexico, Utah, and Vermont—don't tax the income at all. Alaska, Florida, Nevada, South Dakota, Texas, Washington, and Wyoming do not tax personal income from any source.

FEDERAL TAXES AREN'T
DEDUCTIBLE EVERYWHERE

Of the 40 states with broad-based income taxes, 12 allow taxpayers to deduct federal income taxes. Is this an advantage? It is if you're deciding between two states with similar tax rates, but only one of them allows you to deduct. In the latter case, your effective tax rate would be less. The following states allow deductions of federal income taxes:

Alabama	Missouri
Arizona	Montana
Iowa	North Dakota
Kansas	Oklahoma
Kentucky	Oregon
Louisiana	Utah

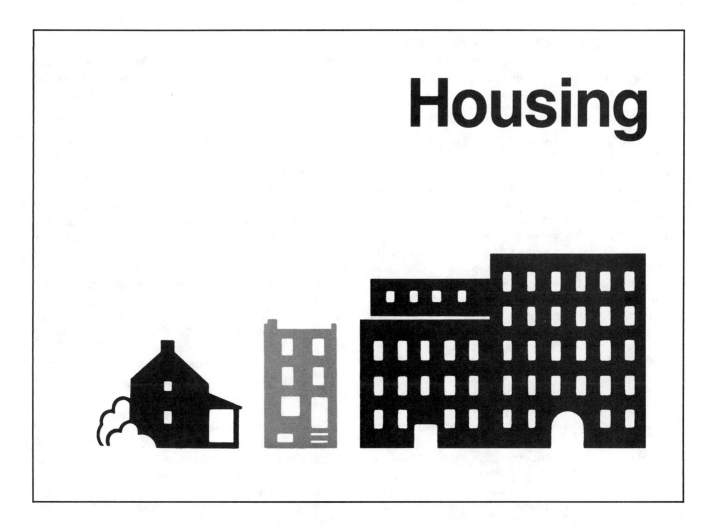

Housing

"You can't get too much housing," real estate sales-people and homebuilders tell their customers when they want to push the tax and investment advantages of owning a home on your own piece of ground.

But when you retire, you may find you've finally got too much housing indeed. The phenomenon is called "overhousing," and it crops up when your children grow up, leave home, and scatter like tumbleweeds in the wind.

There's no mistaking the signs. Bedrooms are full of furniture but closed off, the creaking and settling you once heard at night when everything was still are now heard all the time, and those bills for property taxes, insurance, and upkeep on the family's sentimental shrine are as high as they ever were, and they still have to be paid.

Overhousing isn't just an empty-nester symptom. If you plan to see the country after you retire, your empty home and its yard running to weeds will worry you when you're supposed to be enjoying yourself. What's more, your home is your biggest asset; seven of every 10 retired persons in this country own their homes, and 85 percent of these people have paid off their mortgages. Might your home's market value, which has appreciated over the years, be turned into cash and put to better use?

Certainly developers, investors, and marketers think so. "Move over, baby boomers," *Builder*, a construction trade magazine, announces. "Make way for your elders, who will constitute housing's hottest market for the rest of the century." If you're 55 to 65, you're now part of the "go-go" market for adults-only housing developments. If you're 65 to 75, you're a "go slow" customer for newfangled congregate housing. And if you're over 75, stop worrying; "no go" continuing-care facilities are springing up everywhere.

While these types of housing are attracting many residents, the seven alternatives for more independent living are the same and as plentiful as they ever were for retired people: *buying* a smaller house, condominium, or mobile home; or *renting* an apartment, smaller home, condominium, or mobile home.

TYPICAL HOUSING CHOICES . . .

If the burdens of overhousing lead you to put the old ark up for sale, heed the advice of other retired persons and scale down your housing needs when you scout for another address. *Buying down* to smaller, less expensive shelter can not only give you more income—it can boost your leisure time, too.

If you're thinking of buying down in a distant

retirement place, it helps to know in advance what kinds of typical housing choices are there, what the average rent would be for an apartment, and since most relocating retired people end up buying a single-family house, how much that would cost.

Single Houses

Older adults are no different from everyone else in the kind of roof they prefer overhead. Surveys by the National Association of Home Builders as well as the U.S. League of Savings Institutions show a common detached house is the overwhelming favorite.

If you open the front door of this typical American home, you'll find yourself in a structure that has a single-level, 1,600-square-foot floor plan enclosing six rooms (three bedrooms, one bath, a living room, and a complete kitchen); an insulated attic and storm windows to conserve the heat from the gas-fired, warm-air furnace; and no basement. This house is kept cool during hot spells by a central air-conditioning unit. It is also connected to city water and sewerage lines.

So much for the national composite. Among the 68 million single houses in the United States, a buyer can choose from many building styles—Cape Cods, Cape Annes and Queen Annes, mountain A-frames, American and Dutch colonials, desert adobes, cabins of peeled pine log, Greek revivals, Puget Sounds, cat-slides, saltboxes, exotic glass solaria, futuristic earth berms, Victorians, plantation cottages, ubiquitous split-levels, and California bungalows.

But in retirement places, the number of single homes you'll actually find among the other options—apartments, condominiums, and mobile homes—varies considerably.

Condominiums

Condominium was nothing more than an obscure Latin word before a new legal form of housing tenure was imported from Puerto Rico to the U.S. mainland in 1960. Under the arrangement, you could own outright an apartment, townhouse, or single house in a multiple-unit development. As an owner, you were subject to property taxes and could sell, lease, bequeath, and furnish that legally described cube of air space independently of other unit owners.

What's more, you owned the elevators, heating plant, streets, parking spaces, garden landscaping, tennis courts, swimming pool, lights, and walkways in common with the rest of the development's residents.

Throughout the 1970s, condominiums were marketed to young people making their way out of the rental market and older adults who wanted to unload large houses for smaller ones. While the construction boom has subsided in many sections of the country, the fact that the number of condos grew from nothing in 1960 to more than 4 million today certainly vouches for their appeal.

Condo housing ranges all the way from units in high-rise buildings and low-rise garden apartments to row townhouse developments and even mobile-home parks. In several Florida metropolitan areas, in San Diego, and in resorts like Hilton Head–Beaufort and Maui, condos outnumber single homes in the "for sale" market. In more rural retirement places, condos are a negligible part of the housing mix.

Mobile Homes

The big plus of mobile homes is that they are the cheapest kind of housing you can buy. That they are affordable doesn't mean mobile homes resemble the drafty, 300-square-foot trailers that housed many defense workers during World War II or the somewhat larger tin cans built during the 1950s that were parked in enclaves beyond the railroad tracks.

Mobile homes now average 14 feet by 70 feet, offering nearly 1,000 square feet of living space. A 70-foot-long Double Wide can enclose three bedrooms, two ceramic-tiled baths, a living room, a dining room, and a full kitchen. These mobile homes are typically marketed complete: appliances, furniture, draperies, and carpeting are included in the price, as are the built-in plumbing, heating, air-conditioning, and electrical systems.

Outside, owners landscape with grass, trees, and shrubberies. When carports, porches, sheds, patios, and pitched shake roofs are added to the basic structures, sharp-eyed tax assessors sometimes mistake them for conventional houses.

The only time the mobile home is mobile is when it leaves the factory and is trucked in one or more sections to a concrete foundation on the owner's property or at one of 24,000 trailer parks in the country. When it gets there, the wheels, axle, and towing tongue are taken off. After that, the only element that hints of its origins as a trailer is the welded I-beam chassis, which becomes hidden structural reinforcement once the unit is winched onto the concrete pad and plumbed. When it's in place, the mobile home becomes more or less permanent; no more than three percent of them will ever be jacked up and rolled off to a new site.

Mobile homes are a big part of the Sun Belt housing mix. Last year, half of all newly built mobile homes were trucked to just eight states: California, Florida, Georgia, Louisiana, North Carolina, Oklahoma, South Carolina, and Texas. You'll search long and hard for a mobile-home park in Hawaii, the less rural parts of New England, and larger cities where the high cost of land offsets any savings from buying a mobile home.

Renting an Apartment

It can happen. One day you're out with a real estate broker scouting for a condo or small home and you spot an immaculate, stately old building near downtown with flowers in front and no sign but one: Apart-

The Lot Factor

Any real estate broker touting a suburban ranch or condo can tick off the basic factors that figure into the sales price. Aside from seller's greed, the factors are quality of original construction, turnover rate in the neighborhood, current condition, and location. But these are of secondary importance to local supply and demand.

Cut off a slice of a tract development in suburban San Antonio and drop it in the middle of California's San Diego County and you can see supply and demand at work. The transplanted homes will more than double in value, not because they are roomier and built with better materials but because of the more intense competition for housing in much of Southern California. You can still find well-cared-for three-bedroom ranches in San Antonio for less than $100,000 and nearly identical homes in San Diego for $200,000. The location of the site, more than any other factor, is the best single determinant of a home's sales price.

Based on Federal Housing Administration data, the value of the lot on which a typical house is built represents 19 percent of the home's sales price. However, the percentage varies considerably depending on where this typical house is found. In Hawaii, the cost of the site is half the price of the home; in California, it's 32 percent. In Kansas, it's only 13 percent.

Land Costs as Percentage of House Prices

HIGHEST		LOWEST	
Hawaii	50%	Kansas	13%
California	32	Indiana	14
Connecticut	26	Georgia	15
Oregon	26	Iowa	15
Washington	26	Michigan	15
Nevada	25	Missouri	15

ment for Rent. The next day you're a tenant. Unlike younger newcomers who usually rent after relocating, most retired persons buy. But renting may be smart for the short term; it allows you to remain flexible, since you need not stay in an apartment beyond the term of the lease if you decide to buy or to relocate to a different retirement place.

Renting is also cheaper. Rents haven't gone up as fast as the costs of owning. Other pluses: you don't need to come up with a large down payment; taxes, insurance, repairs, and sometimes utilities are the landlord's headaches. What's more, vacancy rates are predicted to climb as more and more renters buy. In some overbuilt Sun Belt retirement places—San Antonio and Phoenix, for example—landlords are offering month-to-month arrangements or leases with six months free rent.

Retirement Places Rated defines an apartment as simply a rental unit in a structure with two or more rental units; this definition includes rental duplexes, triplexes, and fourplexes. Don't be put off by the image of

impersonal blocks of large, high-rise tower complexes near a place's central business district. Only one out of 50 apartments is in a building of 13 stories or more, and only one out of 10 is in a building higher than three stories. Make note: apartments make up a large chunk of housing, not only in bigger retirement places, but in smaller places dominated by state universities.

. . . AND TYPICAL HOUSING PRICES

If you sell your home, you'll likely realize enough cash to buy another home, perhaps a smaller one. Or you might buy a mobile home or condo. You might even rent, investing the money from the sale of your old home to provide retirement income.

Of course, if you decide to buy, what you buy and where you buy it greatly influence the price you pay. At the national level, prices are lowest for mobile homes, rise for resale condominiums, move higher for resale detached homes, higher still for new condominiums, and then peak for new homes.

The price difference between a mobile home and a site-built house is almost entirely due to labor costs. It takes a small builder's crew 60 to 90 days to erect a typical three-bedroom tract house. A mobile home takes 80 to 100 hours at the factory. In 1990, when the average square-foot cost of building a conventional home was $55, exclusive of land, the cost of manufacturing a mobile home was $25 per square foot.

If you want to strike a compromise between small-scale living and the satisfaction of owning your own address, consider the condominium form of ownership. In a new condominium, you'll have less interior space to look after (1,250 square feet, on average, versus 1,700 square feet for a new single home). Moreover, the tax advantages of ownership are yours at a lower cost (on average, new condos cost 10 to 15 percent less than new single homes).

SHOPPING FOR PROPERTY TAXES

Being overhoused doesn't only mean finding yourself with a surplus of living space. You can be *financially* overhoused, too, especially when you pay property taxes on a home that has increased in value at a time when income has abruptly become fixed.

Just because you're getting older doesn't mean the tax assessor will take notice and graciously lower your home's tax bill. Property tax relief, in the states that offer it to older adults, usually comes after specific income tests. The only place in this country where persons over 65 can completely forget their property taxes is Alaska (a state, incidentally, with the lowest proportion of people over 65). Why not shop for favorable property taxes the way corporations do when they plan moves?

In recent years, homeowners who organized to fight confiscatory property taxes likened them to a

Property Tax Bills in the Retirement Places

LOWEST

Alamogordo, NM
Benton County, AR
Brevard, NC
Deming, NM
Fairhope–Gulf Shores, AL
Fayetteville, AR
Harrison, AR
Mountain Home–Bull Shoals, AR
Rehoboth Bay–Indian River Bay, DE
St. Tammany Parish, LA

Among 151 places, the average tax on *Retirement Places Rated*'s model home is $1,170. In the places listed above, taxes are less than $500; in the places listed below, they are more than $2,500.

HIGHEST

Ann Arbor, MI
Bend, OR
Bennington, VT
Burlington, VT
Eugene–Springfield, OR
Grants Pass, OR
Hanover, NH
Medford–Ashland, OR
Salinas–Seaside–Monterey, CA
San Luis Obispo, CA
Santa Barbara, CA

Source: Century 21 Real Estate Corporation survey for Places Rated Partnership, May 1990.

In Some Places, Older Isn't Always Cheaper

Most of us live in homes built years ago that were bought, lived in, and sold by a succession of owners. We all confirm the "filtering theory" of housing, which states that houses filter down from their high-income original owners to middle-income buyers and finally to lower-income owners. To put it another way, high-income households tend to live in newer homes, and lower-income households occupy older homes.

Sounds obvious, doesn't it?

However, when the real estate sections of *Yankee* magazine, the *Boston Globe,* the *Hartford Courant, Down East Magazine,* the *New York Times Magazine,* and the *Washington Post* list antique Cape Cod-style homes and Georgian country mansions built in the last century for hundreds of thousands of dollars, you're looking at a big exception to this theory. Nowhere is this more apparent than in the Amherst–Northampton area in western Massachusetts, Maryland's Eastern Shore, and Charlottesville, Virginia.

Nevertheless, the theory holds true for most of the country and for most of the retirement places, too. The older the housing, the lower the price.

ransom they were forced to pay to save their homes from the tax assessor's auction block. Using this analogy, Oregonians buy their homes back every 44 years, since Oregon's average residential property tax rate is 2.26 percent of a home's market value. In Louisiana, the "ransom" period is 454 years because of an extremely low average rate of .22 percent. The difference in these figures illustrates the wide variation in property taxes around the country.

Property taxes can vary locally, too, and be madly confusing to property owners. In California, two homes on the same street with identical sales prices and physical characteristics can have substantially different, yet legally impeccable, tax bills if one of them was sold before the approval of Proposition 13 and the other after. In Texas, a home's value can be assessed at different levels at different times of the year by different assessors.

WHAT DIFFERENCE DOES AGE MAKE?

Scuff over the sawdust and around the empty nail kegs, the stacked sheetrock, and the crated fiberglass shower stall in a newly framed ranch in a suburban housing development, and you might wonder why the builder is asking a bundle for something he's putting up so quickly.

They don't build them the way they used to. Wraparound porches are rarely found. A porch is now merely a recessed space at the home's entrance. The 10-foot interior ceiling common before World War II has been replaced by the 8-foot standard. The kind of formal stairway with well-turned balusters and waxed rails that Andy Hardy used to slide down are no longer necessary—most new homes are erected on a single level. Milled red oak fascias and moldings have become too expensive for common use; walls are envelopes of three-eighths gypsum board fastened to studs rather than the old "mud jobs" of plaster on lath; and solid six-panel interior doors have lost out to hollow-core flush doors of hemlock veneer.

On the other hand, the seasonal threat of damp and flooded cellars arises less often, simply because there aren't many cellars being excavated. Polyvinyl chloride and copper have replaced galvanized iron for water pipes; cast-iron radiators no longer interfere with furniture arrangement; knob-and-tube wiring has surrendered to safer electrical circuitry; and pressure-treated wood has eliminated termite and dry-rot risks along the sills. Indeed, 20 percent of a new home's breathtaking price is due to builders' using superior materials for some types of jobs, according to a recent Prudential Insurance Company study.

HOME ENERGY REQUIREMENTS

If you don't count the loan initiation fees and closing costs that new homeowners pay to float their mortgages, then fuel and electricity for the home were among the fastest-rising items on the Consumer Price Index since 1967. What was once a minor and predictable expense, amounting to less than one percent of a

Air-Conditioning Needs: The Top Hot-Weather Retirement Places	
Retirement Place	Annual Hours Over 80° F
El Centro–Calexico–Brawley, CA	3,185
Yuma, AZ	3,185
Phoenix–Tempe–Scottsdale, AZ	2,815
Key West–Key Largo–Marathon, FL	2,720
Rockport–Aransas Pass, TX	2,531
McAllen–Edinburg–Mission, TX	2,527
Miami–Hialeah, FL	2,408
Lake Havasu City–Kingman, AZ	2,360
Las Vegas, NV	2,360
Fort Lauderdale–Hollywood–Pompano, FL	2,342

Source: Department of Defense, *Engineering Weather Data*, 1978.

Heating Needs: The Top 10 Cold-Weather Retirement Places	
Retirement Place	Heating-Degree Days
Eagle River, WI	9,339
Kalispell, MT	8,554
Houghton Lake, MI	8,347
Burlington, VT	7,876
Door County, WI	7,876
Madison, WI	7,730
Traverse City–Grand Traverse Bay, MI	7,698
Bennington, VT	7,681
Hanover, NH	7,680
Petoskey–Straits of Mackinac, MI	7,669

Source: National Oceanic and Atmosphere Administration, *Climatography of the United States, Series 81*, no date.

household's budget 25 years ago, may now amount to more than the cost of medical care or clothing, in spite of the recent drop in oil prices.

Three factors account for the $1,286 difference between the annual average residential utility bills in Wenatchee, Washington, and Yuma, Arizona: local climate, the form of energy used to keep interiors comfortable, and the energy's source.

Counting Hours

Texans say that their Gulf Coast is one long stretch where air conditioning, like food and water, is a basic necessity without which all humanity would go mad and die. Here, a meteorologist measuring humidity with a psychrometer whenever the temperature climbs over 80 degrees Fahrenheit will count nearly 2,500 hours every year when the instrument's bulb stays wet from moist air. New Delhi records similar numbers, and so does Kinshasa, capital of Zaire. These 2,500-odd hours are the equivalent of more than 200 days per year having uncomfortable, sweaty, 12-hour periods of high humidity.

In desert retirement locations such as Las Vegas, Phoenix, and Tucson, the days are much drier, but the number of hours there when the temperature is more than 80 degrees Fahrenheit is even greater than the number found on the Texas Gulf Coast. These hours were first counted by Defense Department building engineers in the late 1940s and updated in 1978 for a worldwide inventory of military installations. Not only are these hours useful for gauging how hot a given place is over time, but they also signal how often your home's air conditioner may be humming.

Counting Days

In 1915, Eugene P. Milener, an engineer with the Gas Company of Baltimore, made a discovery for which he received little recognition outside his industry. The amount of natural gas needed to keep houses warm can be accurately predicted for every degree that the outdoor temperature falls below 32 degrees. Natural gas utilities still use this measurement, called a "heating-degree day," to estimate consumption patterns among their customers.

Heating-degree days are the number of degrees the daily average temperature drops below 65. Heating your home isn't usually necessary when the temperature outdoors is more than 65, but furnaces are fired up when the outdoors gets colder. Thus, a heating-degree day indicates the number of degrees of heating required to keep a house at 65. If, for example, the temperature on a winter day is 35, that day has 30 heating-degree days, meaning that 30 degrees of heating are called for.

The average for annual heating-degree days (total heating-degree days over the year) in the United States is 4,643, ranging from none in the Hawaiian Islands at sea level to nearly 20,000 in the Brooks Range of Alaska. The number of annual heating-degree days in a given year tells you how cold it gets and also how often you'll need to run a home's heating system to keep the indoors comfortable.

Household Energy Geography

Can you recall the Korean War years when the rumbling of coal trucks along their delivery routes was a familiar urban street sound? Three-dollar-a-ton black anthracite was the dominant home heating fuel everywhere east of the Mississippi except for Florida and New England. The blue flame of piped-in natural gas, the dominant heating fuel today, was just starting to burn in new refrigerators, stoves, clothes dryers, and in new home furnaces. The electric utilities were just beginning to offer rate incentives to buyers of total-electric homes.

Coal today is largely gone from the home-energy scene. In spite of heavy marketing of airtight coal stoves as an auxiliary means of heating houses, the number of homes burning this fuel declined by more than one million over the past decade. The major options in urban retirement places, from most expensive to least in cost per million British thermal units (Btu), are electricity, piped-in natural gas, and fuel oil or kerosene. In the rural parts of some retirement places,

Atomic Retirement Places

Retirement Place	Nuclear Power Plants
Charlevoix–Boyne City, MI	1
Miami–Hialeah, FL	2
Phoenix–Tempe–Scottsdale, AZ	3
Portsmouth–Dover–Durham, NH	1
San Diego, CA	3
San Luis Obispo, CA	2
Southport, NC	2

Source: United States Council for Energy Awareness, 1990.

A large part of the residential electric power in the places above comes (or will soon come) from local nuclear power plants.

there's bottled gas and wood.

Electricity. In 1950, the only place where most of the homes were total-electric was the small desert town of Las Vegas, seat of Nevada's Clark County. The power there was the cheapest in the country because it was generated by falling water at the new Boulder Canyon hydroelectric project some 25 miles southeast. Power is still cheap in Las Vegas, relative to nuclear-generated or fossil-fuel-generated power that residential customers pay for elsewhere in the country. So is the power that heats and lights homes in the Puget Sound area, the Oregon Cascades, and the Kentucky and Tennessee lakes region, places that also get their power from major hydroelectric projects.

Although most American homes are heated with natural gas, electricity is the dominant choice in new homes. Since 1970, the number of total-electric homes tripled. The reason: it costs much less to wire a new house for electric resistance heat than to install a gas or oil furnace with piping and sheet-metal hot-air conduits. Total-electric homes predominate in 57 retirement places.

- Typical consumption: 17,956 kilowatt-hours per year
- Typical bill: $1,217 per year
- Cost per million Btu: $19.58

Bottled Gas. Bottled, or liquified petroleum (LP), gas is derived from oil and sold in compressed or liquid form. Like residual fuel oil, it requires on-site storage tanks. Unlike piped-in natural gas and electricity, it offers the advantage of an on-hand supply in case of interrupted service. In rural retirement spots, particularly in the Ozarks, it is the fuel of choice for heat and even for running air conditioners and refrigerators.

Most mobile homes from New England to the Desert Southwest are also heated by bottled gas. While this fuel is more expensive than piped-in natural gas, in the future it may be cheaper—given the dramatic drop in the price of crude oil from which LP is derived.

- Typical consumption: 1,145 gallons per year
- Typical bill: $993

- Cost per million Btu: $9.46

Natural Gas. In 63 retirement places, the major source for heating a house is a by-product of oil drilling that for many years flamed at the wellhead for lack of a market. Natural gas, a fossil fuel, has meant inexpensive heat for most householders, mainly because the federal government has regulated its interstate price. Even after deregulation, its price continues to drop.

Natural gas hasn't ever been cheap to residential customers at the ends of the continental transmission lines that start in Louisiana and Texas gas fields, however. Transportation costs explain why natural gas isn't preferred in New England or Mid-Atlantic Metro Belt retirement places, where oil is the least expensive of fuels, or in the Pacific Northwest, where hydro-generated electricity costs the least. The American Gas Association provides the following figures:

- Typical consumption: 10,200 cubic feet per year
- Typical bill: $606
- Cost per million Btu: $5.94

Oil and Kerosene. Though their prices have tumbled recently because of worldwide overproduction, #2 heating oil and kerosene were the only items on the Consumer Price Index to sextuple in cost between 1967 and 1980. High cost is one reason that the number of homes heated with fuel oil or kerosene declined by more than two million during the 1970s. You won't find the price varying greatly by location, but you will find those distillates of imported crude to be the most common heating fuel in 26 retirement places, mainly in New England, the Mid-Atlantic Metro Belt, and in western North Carolina.

- Typical consumption: 1,043 gallons per year
- Typical bill: $490 per year
- Cost per million Btu: $6.96

Wood. Anyone who feeds a wood stove has heard the homely proverb about this fuel: it warms you twice, first when you cut and stack it, and second when you watch it burn. From Rocky Mountain piñon to hickory and ash from Ozark forests, it is burned in three million homes. Among retirement places, many of the homes in Hamilton–Bitterroot Valley, Montana, and Twain Harte–Yosemite, California, are heated with wood because it is cheap and available right outside a householder's door.

Nationally, the cost of a cord of good, seasoned hardwood varies a great deal. You can buy half a cord for $300 in Manhattan, or, with a little sweat and permission, you can gather fallen timber in local state forests gratis. The U.S. Forest Service determines energy content for various kinds of wood; consumption and price figures come from the U.S. Department of Energy:

- Typical consumption: 2.8 cords per year
- Typical bill: $350
- Cost per million Btu: $5.34 (mixed hardwood)

Keeping It Running

Utility bills for home heating and cooling, lighting, and running appliances cost $1,259 up in New Paltz–Ulster County, New York, but only $928 in Coeur d'Alene, Idaho. Why such a great difference?

The high number of annual heating-degree days in both places is a sign of long winters, certainly. But in New Paltz–Ulster County, the cost of natural gas plus the electricity bills mailed to Consolidated Edison's residential customers are among the country's highest. As for Coeur d'Alene, homes there are total-electric and get their bills from the Washington Water Power Company, the distributor of cheaper hydro-generated power.

If your only retirement concern is dodging both winter heating and summer air-conditioning bills, head for Hawaii. Unfortunately, you'll still be writing big monthly checks to the local electric power company. There are few heated homes here, and air conditioning isn't necessary. But the cost of electricity to keep your water hot, food cool, lamps lit, and appliances running is about as high as it gets anywhere. Why? Because power is generated by imported fuel oil.

 **SCORING:** Housing

---

Is housing less expensive in the North Woods than in New Appalachia or New England? When it comes to paying property taxes, would you be better off choosing the Ozark corner of Arkansas over Florida? Might a move to Yuma, Arizona, in February haunt you in August when you realize how much air conditioning costs?

To help answer these questions, *Retirement Places Rated* tallies the three biggest dollar expenses of homeownership: utility bills, property taxes, and mortgage payments. The total of these three equals the amount you can expect to pay each year for the basics of homeowning. It also represents each retirement place's score.

Each place starts with a base score of zero. Points are added according to the following indicators:

1. *Utility bills.* Annual utility bills are estimated for a home that uses natural gas for space heating, water heating, and cooking because this fuel is available everywhere and is the most frequent chosen in most of the retirement places. Also included in the utility bills are the costs of electricity for lighting, running appliances, and air conditioning based on local bills for 500 kilowatt-hours of monthly consumption as reported by the Department of Energy. In retirement places where total-electric homes predominate, utility bills reflect the annual cost of using 18,000 kilowatt-hours of electricity per year.
2. *Property taxes.* Property taxes are estimates for a typical 1,600-square-foot, single-family, detached home with two or three bedrooms, one and a half baths, and a garage.
3. *Mortgage payments.* Annual mortgage payments are based on a 10 percent, 25-year mortgage on the sales price of a typical home, after making a one-fifth down payment.

SCORING EXAMPLES

A large city in the Texas Interior, a small place in Rio Grande Country, and a Hawaiian paradise illustrate the scoring method for housing.

San Antonio, Texas (#15)

"The bank owns this one" isn't an uncommon phrase in San Antonio real estate advertising. Texas is coming out of hard times brought on by the mid-1980s slump in the oil patch, but rebounding from the Savings and Loan scandals will take a few more years. The consequences reach even this city dominated by defense employment.

Browse through a book of multiple listings and you're struck by one thing: condominiums aren't a major form of housing in San Antonio as they are elsewhere. The photographs show brick or Texas-rock suburban ranches set back from the street on large lawns. Prices differ widely from the hundreds of thousands in Elm Creek to the low fifties in some neighborhoods near Randolph Air Force Base and Fort Sam Houston. For a typical 1,600-square-foot, two- or three-bedroom home here, the sales price is $61,100, a five percent appreciation over the previous 12 months. Utility bills are $795, property taxes $1,200, and mortgage payments $5,327, totaling $7,322, the lowest homeowning costs among retirement places with more than half a million people.

Roswell, New Mexico (#32)

With a typical sales price of $72,200, housing in Chaves County, New Mexico, is more affordable than in most places. Indeed, the most expensive house here is a $200,000 golf-course contemporary with splendid mountain views.

They say here that buffalo grass doesn't put up much resistance to developers. House lots are quite inexpensive in the open plains outside of Roswell, the county seat and historic cattle town.

This place is more old than new. Just one home in 20 has been built since 1980, whereas one in eight predates World War II. Most are single homes occupied by their owners. There are no condos to speak of, but the local supply of rental apartments and mobile homes means there are reasonable alternatives to buying a home. Utility bills in Roswell are $902, property taxes $635, and mortgage payments $6,295, totaling $7,832, among the lowest homeowning costs of all the retirement places.

Maui, Hawaii (#148)

Thousands of miles to the west of Roswell, the Pacific islands that make up Maui, Hawaii, have some of the highest homeowner costs in the United States. The typical sales price of a Maui home is $290,000. Moreover, prices here have increased 40 percent. This home is likely to be a high-rise condominium, and is likely to have been built within the last 10 years. Maui has a greater percentage of year-round housing units that are condos than any other retirement place. Owing to the distance from stateside manufacturers and the astronomical cost of land, there aren't any mobile homes here. Also, unlike the freehold tenure common to most of the United States mainland, many homes here are built on ground leased for 99 years.

Even though most homes in Maui aren't air conditioned or heated, the bills from Maui Electric, Ltd., for using 500 kilowatt-hours of electricity just to cook, run appliances, and light your home in the evening come to $63 each month, or $755 a year. With Hawaii's exceptionally low effective rate, however, the property tax bill on this $290,000 dwelling comes to only $600 a year. But mortgage payments amount to $25,283. Add them all together and you get homeowner costs of $26,638 a year.

 RANKINGS: Housing

Three criteria are used to rank places for basic costs of owning a house over one year: (1) typical utility bills, (2) property taxes, and (3) mortgage payments. The sum of these items is the score for each place.

Places receiving tie scores get the same rank and are listed alphabetically.

Retirement Places from First to Last

Rank	Score	Rank	Score	Rank	Score
1. Harrison, AR	6,103	20. Murray–Kentucky Lake, KY	7,453	36. Eagle River, WI	8,019
2. Burnet–Marble Falls–Llano, TX	6,271	21. New Braunfels, TX	7,483	37. McAllen–Edinburg–Mission, TX	8,040
3. Kerrville, TX	6,279	22. Branson–Table Rock Lake, MO	7,499	38. Alamogordo, NM	8,052
4. Benton County, AR	6,605	23. Hot Springs National Park, AR	7,540	39. Brevard, NC	8,065
5. Athens–Cedar Creek Lake, TX	6,607	24. Fort Myers–Cape Coral–Sanibel Island, FL	7,542	40. Wenatchee, WA	8,112
6. Grand Lake, OK	6,680	25. Clayton, GA	7,553	41. Pensacola, FL	8,209
7. St. Tammany Parish, LA	6,856			42. New Port Richey, FL	8,245
8. Fayetteville, AR	6,858	26. St. George–Zion, UT	7,558	43. Boise, ID	8,268
9. Fredericksburg, TX	6,868	27. Southport, NC	7,681	44. Daytona Beach, FL	8,305
10. Canton–Lake Tawakoni, TX	6,881	28. Lakeland–Winter Haven, FL	7,706	45. El Centro–Calexico–Brawley, CA	8,498
11. Deming, NM	6,889	29. Hamilton–Bitterroot Valley, MT	7,801		
12. Paris–Big Sandy, TN	6,911	30. Fort Collins–Loveland, CO	7,816	46. Ocean County, NJ	8,527
13. Rockport–Aransas Pass, TX	7,078			46. Vero Beach, FL	8,527
14. Brownsville–Harlingen, TX	7,279	31. Biloxi–Gulfport–Pass Christian, MS	7,823	48. Colorado Springs, CO	8,531
15. San Antonio, TX	7,322	32. Roswell, NM	7,832	49. Gainesville, FL	8,546
16. Crossville, TN	7,362	33. Brunswick–Golden Isles, GA	7,835	50. Bradenton, FL	8,565
17. Thomasville, GA	7,376	34. Grand Junction, CO	7,909	51. Austin, TX	8,579
18. Houghton Lake, MI	7,390	35. Carlsbad–Artesia, NM	7,928	52. Melbourne–Titusville–Palm Bay, FL	8,625
19. Mountain Home–Bull Shoals, AR	7,422			53. Panama City, FL	8,631
				54. Aiken, SC	8,720

Rank	Score		Rank	Score		Rank	Score
55. Coeur d'Alene, ID	8,724		87. Prescott, AZ	10,224		117. Lancaster County, PA	13,323
			88. Lake Lanier, GA	10,252		118. Charlottesville, VA	13,330
56. Ocala, FL	8,803		89. Naples, FL	10,339		119. Iowa City, IA	13,676
57. Kalispell, MT	8,880		90. Traverse City–Grand Traverse			120. Chapel Hill, NC	13,727
58. Phoenix–Tempe–Scottsdale,			Bay, MI	10,474			
AZ	9,001						
59. Ocean City–			91. Lake Havasu City–Kingman,			121. Monticello–Liberty, NY	13,782
Assateague Island, MD	9,061		AZ	10,502		122. Grants Pass, OR	14,139
60. Savannah, GA	9,135		92. Port Townsend, WA	10,567		123. Bennington, VT	14,267
			93. West Palm Beach–Boca			124. Grass Valley–Truckee, CA	14,317
61. Orlando, FL	9,152		Raton–Delray Beach, FL	10,705		125. Amherst–Northampton, MA	14,471
62. Bloomington––Brown County,			94. Blacksburg, VA	10,870			
IN	9,228		95. Camden–Penobscot Bay, ME	10,967		126. Ann Arbor, MI	14,677
63. Athens, GA	9,257					127. Bend, OR	14,776
64. Fairhope–Gulf Shores, AL	9,263		96. Door County, WI	10,971		128. Las Vegas, NV	15,100
65. Petoskey–Straits of Mackinac,			97. Newport–Lincoln City, OR	11,131		129. Twain Harte–Yosemite, CA	15,265
MI	9,337		98. State College, PA	11,375		130. Cape May, NJ	15,414
			99. Oak Harbor–Whidbey Island,				
66. Red Bluff–Sacramento Valley,			WA	11,558		131. San Juan Islands, WA	15,738
CA	9,356		100. Hilton Head–Beaufort, SC	11,593		132. Medford–Ashland, OR	15,786
67. Bellingham, WA	9,369					133. Amador County, CA	15,792
68. Olympia, WA	9,408		101. Madison, WI	11,878		134. Keene, NH	15,848
69. Las Cruces, NM	9,433		102. Pike County, PA	12,008		135. Santa Fe, NM	16,250
70. Asheville, NC	9,441		103. Hendersonville, NC	12,038			
			104. Bar Harbor–Frenchman Bay,			136. Burlington, VT	16,323
70. Charlevoix––Boyne City, MI	9,441		ME	12,237		137. South Lake Tahoe–	
72. Fort Walton Beach, FL	9,527		105. Laconia–Lake Winnipesaukee,			Placerville, CA	16,978
72. St. Augustine, FL	9,527		NH	12,254		138. Reno, NV	17,276
74. New Bern, NC	9,618					139. Portsmouth–Dover–Durham,	
75. Martinsburg–Charles Town,			106. Canandaigua, NY	12,334		NH	17,483
WV	9,621		107. Redding, CA	12,350		140. Cape Cod, MA	17,584
			108. Rehoboth Bay–Indian River				
76. Sarasota, FL	9,625		Bay, DE	12,386		141. Key West–Key Largo–	
77. Yuma, AZ	9,664		109. New Paltz–			Marathon, FL	18,354
78. Virginia Beach–Norfolk, VA	9,673		Ulster County, NY	12,425		142. Hanover, NH	19,658
79. Clear Lake, CA	9,677		110. Columbia County, NY	12,603		143. Los Alamos, NM	19,882
80. Myrtle Beach, SC	9,775					144. Carson City–Minden, NV	20,446
			111. Miami–Hialeah, FL	12,798		145. San Diego, CA	20,706
81. Tucson, AZ	9,906		112. Easton–Chesapeake Bay,				
82. Lexington–Fayette, KY	9,956		MD	12,806		146. Santa Rosa–Petaluma, CA	23,461
83. Fort Lauderdale–Hollywood–			113. Albuquerque, NM	12,872		147. Honolulu, HI	25,165
Pompano Beach, FL	10,067		114. North Conway–White			148. Maui, HI	26,638
84. Charleston, SC	10,088		Mountains, NH	12,952		149. Salinas–Seaside–Monterey,	
85. St. Petersburg–Clearwater–			115. Eugene–Springfield, OR	13,044		CA	28,856
Dunedin, FL	10,190					150. San Luis Obispo, CA	29,110
			116. Chico–Paradise, CA	13,322			
86. Edenton–Albemarle Sound,						151. Santa Barbara, CA	29,901
NC	10,193						

PLACE PROFILES: Housing

On the following pages are capsule descriptions of housing costs in each retirement place. Data under the first category, **Model Home**, show the typical sales price for a 1,600-square-foot, site-built, single-level, two- or three-bedroom home with one and a half bathrooms and a garage. Property taxes on this home are given in estimated annual dollar amounts. Recent appreciation is the percent increase or decrease in the home's price between May 1989 and May 1990.

The heating season, under **Energy Requirements**, is the number of heating-degree days per year (see p. 47 for explanation). The typical source is the prevailing local mode—natural gas, oil, total electric, or bottled gas—for home heating. The number of hours for air conditioning represents the normal number of hours per year when the outside temperature climbs over 80 degrees Fahrenheit. Utilities costs for space and water heating, cooling, lighting, and appliances are estimated annual dollar amounts.

Data under the last heading, **Alternative Housing**, indicate whether condominiums, mobile homes, and rental homes and apartments are also available. Rent figures are estimated monthly dollar amounts.

Information comes from these sources: Advisory Commission on Intergovernmental Relations, *Significant Features of Fiscal Federalism* (property taxes), 1990; American Gas Association, *Gas Facts* (residential gas bills), 1990; Century 21 Corporation, survey for Places Rated Partnership (property taxes, sales price, price appreciation, and rental market), May 1990; U.S. Department of Commerce, Bureau of the Census, *Housing Permits and Construction Contracts* (new home construction), annually, 1980–1989, and National Oceanic and Atmospheric Administration, *Climatography of the United States, Series 81* (heating-degree days), no date; U.S. Department of Defense, *Engineering Weather Data* (air conditioning hours), no date; U.S. Department of Energy, *Typical Electric Bills* (residential electric bills), 1990; U.S. Department Labor, Bureau of Labor Statistics, *Consumer Price Index* (mortgage costs, rent, and residential oil bills), monthly, 1987–1990.

A star (★) preceding a place's name highlights it as one of the 20 best places for homeowning costs.

Aiken, SC
Model Home
Sales price: $81,900
Property taxes: $590
Recent appreciation: 6%
Energy Requirements
Heating season: 2,547 degree days
Typical source: natural gas
Air conditioning: 1,431 hours
Utilities cost: $989
Alternative Housing
Condos, mobile homes
Rental homes ($500)
Score: 8,720   **Rank: 54**

Alamogordo, NM
Model Home
Sales price: $76,200
Property taxes: $250
Recent appreciation: none
Energy Requirements
Heating season: 3,172 degree days
Typical source: natural gas
Air conditioning: 1,790 hours
Utilities cost: $1,159
Alternative Housing
Mobile homes
Rental homes ($525)
Score: 8,052   **Rank: 38**

Albuquerque, NM
Model Home
Sales price: $123,500
Property taxes: $1,087
Recent appreciation: −5%
Energy Requirements
Heating season: 4,292 degree days
Typical source: natural gas
Air conditioning: 1,130 hours
Utilities cost: $1,018
Alternative Housing
Condos, mobile homes
Apartments ($575)
Rental homes ($690)
Score: 12,872   **Rank: 113**

Amador County, CA
Model Home
Sales price: $149,300
Property taxes: $1,568
Recent appreciation: 12%
Energy Requirements
Heating season: 5,800 degree days
Typical source: bottled gas
Air conditioning: 621 hours
Utilities cost: $1,208
Alternative Housing
Condos, mobile homes
Rental homes ($950)
Score: 15,792   **Rank: 133**

Amherst–Northampton, MA
Model Home
Sales price: $139,700
Property taxes: $1,173
Recent appreciation: −10%
Energy Requirements
Heating season: 6,576 degree days
Typical source: oil
Air conditioning: 500 hours
Utilities cost: $1,118
Alternative Housing
Condos, mobile homes
Apartments ($700)
Rental homes ($975)
Score: 14,471   **Rank: 125**

Ann Arbor, MI
Model Home
Sales price: $123,500
Property taxes: $2,594
Recent appreciation: 10%
Energy Requirements
Heating season: 6,306 degree days
Typical source: natural gas
Air conditioning: 511 hours
Utilities cost: $1,317
Alternative Housing
Condos
Apartments ($630)
Rental homes ($790)
Score: 14,677   **Rank: 126**

Asheville, NC
Model Home
Sales price: $86,500
Property taxes: $874
Recent appreciation: 5%
Energy Requirements
Heating season: 4,237 degree days
Typical source: oil
Air conditioning: 610 hours
Utilities cost: $1,026
Alternative Housing
Condos, mobile homes
Apartments ($440)
Rental homes ($550)
Score: 9,441   **Rank: 70**

Athens, GA
Model Home
Sales price: $85,200
Property taxes: $878
Recent appreciation: 3%
Energy Requirements
Heating season: 2,822 degree days
Typical source: natural gas
Air conditioning: 1,122 hours
Utilities cost: $952
Alternative Housing
Condos, mobile homes
Apartments ($440)
Rental homes ($550)
Score: 9,257   **Rank: 63**

★ Athens–Cedar Creek Lake, TX
Model Home
  Sales price: $58,900
  Property taxes: $1,100
  Recent appreciation: –2%
Energy Requirements
  Heating season: 2,272 degree days
  Typical source: natural gas
  Air conditioning: 1,855 hours
  Utilities cost: $372
Alternative Housing
  Condos, mobile homes
  Rental homes ($500)
Score: 6,607   **Rank: 5**

Austin, TX
Model Home
  Sales price: $79,000
  Property Taxes: $1,114
  Recent appreciation: –8%
Energy Requirements
  Heating season: 1,737 degree days
  Typical source: natural gas
  Air conditioning: 2,243 hours
  Utilities cost: $577
Alternative Housing
  Condos, mobile homes
  Apartments ($460)
  Rental homes ($575)
Score: 8,579   **Rank: 51**

Bar Harbor–Frenchman Bay, ME
Model Home
  Sales price: $111,100
  Property taxes: $1,355
  Recent appreciation: none
Energy Requirements
  Heating season: 7,240 degree hours
  Typical source: oil
  Air conditioning: 137 hours
  Utilities cost: $1,195
Alternative Housing
  Condos, mobile homes
  Apartments ($560)
  Rental homes ($700)
Score: 12,237   **Rank: 104**

Bellingham, WA
Model Home
  Sales price: $85,300
  Property taxes: $938
  Recent appreciation: 15%
Energy Requirements
  Heating season: 5,738 degree days
  Typical source: total electric
  Air conditioning: 40 hours
  Utilities cost: $994
Alternative Housing
  Condos, mobile homes
  Apartments ($440)
  Rental homes ($550)
Score: 9,369   **Rank: 67**

Bend, OR
Model Home
  Sales price: $125,400
  Property taxes: $2,834
  Recent appreciation: 35%
Energy Requirements
  Heating season: 7,117 degree days
  Typical source: total electric
  Air conditioning: 375 hours
  Utilities cost: $1,009

Alternative Housing
  Condos, mobile homes
  Apartments ($640)
  Rental homes ($800)
Score: 14,776   **Rank: 127**

Bennington, VT
Model Home
  Sales price: $114,500
  Property taxes: $2,897
  Recent appreciation: 5%
Energy Requirements
  Heating season: 7,681 degree days
  Typical source: oil
  Air conditioning: 335 hours
  Utilities cost: $1,388
Alternative Housing
  Condos, mobile homes
  Apartments ($600)
  Rental homes ($750)
Score: 14,267   **Rank: 123**

★ Benton County, AR
Model Home
  Sales price: $61,100
  Property taxes: $391
  Recent appreciation: 3%
Energy Requirements
  Heating season: 3,976 degree days
  Typical source: natural gas
  Air conditioning: 1,013 hours
  Utilities cost: $887
Alternative Housing
  Condos, mobile homes
  Apartments ($360)
  Rental homes ($450)
Score: 6,605   **Rank: 4**

Biloxi–Gulfport–Pass Christian, MS
Model Home
  Sales price: $73,300
  Property taxes: $557
  Recent appreciation: none
Energy Requirements
  Heating season: 1,496 degree days
  Typical source: natural gas
  Air conditioning: 2,052 hours
  Utilities cost: $875
Alternative Housing
  Condos, mobile homes
  Apartments ($380)
  Rental homes ($475)
Score: 7,823   **Rank: 31**

Blacksburg, VA
Model Home
  Sales price: $101,700
  Property taxes: $997
  Recent appreciation: 6%
Energy Requirements
  Heating season: 4,307 degree days
  Typical source: natural gas
  Air conditioning: 799 hours
  Utilities cost: $1,007
Alternative Housing
  Condos, mobile homes
  Apartments ($520)
  Rental homes ($650)
Score: 10,870   **Rank: 94**

Bloomington–Brown County, IN
Model Home
  Sales price: $79,900
  Property taxes: $999
  Recent appreciation: 6%

Energy Requirements
Heating season: 4,905 degree days
Typical source: natural gas
Air conditioning: 848 hours
Utilities cost: $1,263
Alternative Housing
Condos, mobile homes
Apartments ($400)
Rental homes ($500)
Score: 9,228   **Rank: 62**

Boise, ID
Model Home
Sales price: $76,000
Property taxes: $825
Recent appreciation: 6%
Energy Requirements
Heating season: 5,833 degree days
Typical source: total electric
Air conditioning: 706 hours
Utilities cost: $817
Alternative Housing
Condos, mobile homes
Apartments ($375)
Rental homes ($480)
Score: 8,268   **Rank: 43**

Bradenton, FL
Model Home
Sales price: $72,800
Property taxes: $670
Recent appreciation: 2%
Energy Requirements
Heating season: 597 degree days
Typical source: total electric
Air conditioning: 2,154 hours
Utilities cost: $1,549
Alternative Housing
Condos, mobile homes
Apartments ($480)
Rental homes ($600)
Score: 8,565   **Rank: 50**

Branson–Table Rock Lake, MO
Model Home
Sales price: $67,500
Property taxes: $560
Recent appreciation: 6%
Energy Requirements
Heating season: 4,406 degree days
Typical source: bottled gas
Air conditioning: 1,058 hours
Utilities cost: $1,054
Alternative Housing
Condos, mobile homes
Rental homes ($450)
Score: 7,499   **Rank: 22**

Brevard, NC
Model Home
Sales price: $75,600
Property taxes: $410
Recent appreciation: 8%
Energy Requirements
Heating season: 4,072 degree days
Typical source: oil
Air conditioning: 610 hours
Utilities cost: $1,064
Alternative Housing
Condos, mobile homes
Rental homes ($480)
Score: 8,065   **Rank: 39**

★ Brownsville–Harlingen, TX
Model Home
Sales price: $60,600
Property taxes: $1,200
Recent appreciation: 5%
Energy Requirements
Heating season: 650 degree days
Typical source: natural gas
Air conditioning: 2,295 hours
Utilities cost: $795
Alternative Housing
Condos, mobile homes
Apartments ($400)
Rental homes ($500)
Score: 7,279   **Rank: 14**

Brunswick–Golden Isles, GA
Model Home
Sales price: $69,700
Property taxes: $718
Recent appreciation: 4%
Energy Requirements
Heating season: 1,331 degree days
Typical source: total electric
Air conditioning: 1,365 hours
Utilities cost: $1,040
Alternative Housing
Condos, mobile homes
Apartments ($380)
Rental homes ($475)
Score: 7,835   **Rank: 33**

Burlington, VT
Model Home
Sales price: $135,400
Property taxes: $3,426
Recent appreciation: 3%
Energy Requirements
Heating season: 7,876 degree days
Typical source: oil
Air conditioning: 263 hours
Utilities cost: $1,092
Alternative Housing
Condos, mobile homes
Apartments ($700)
Rental homes ($860)
Score: 16,323   **Rank: 136**

★ Burnet–Marble Falls–Llano, TX
Model Home
Sales price: $51,800
Property taxes: $730
Recent appreciation: none
Energy Requirements
Heating season: 2,163 degree days
Typical source: total electric
Air conditioning: 1,715 hours
Utilities cost: $1,025
Alternative Housing
Mobile homes
Rental homes ($1,000)
Score: 6,271   **Rank: 2**

Camden–Penobscot Bay, ME
Model Home
Sales price: $99,100
Property taxes: $1,209
Recent appreciation: none
Energy Requirements
Heating season: 7,353 degree days
Typical source: oil
Air conditioning: 236 hours
Utilities cost: $1,118

Alternative Housing
  Condos
  Apartments ($520)
  Rental homes ($650)
Score: 10,967   **Rank: 95**

Canandaigua, NY
Model Home
  Sales price: $103,100
  Property taxes: $2,134
  Recent appreciation: 5%
Energy Requirements
  Heating season: 6,656 degree days
  Typical source: natural gas
  Air conditioning: 419 hours
  Utilities cost: $1,211
Alternative Housing
  Condos, mobile homes
  Rental homes ($660)
Score: 12,334   **Rank: 106**

★ Canton–Lake Tawakoni, TX
Model Home
  Sales price: $59,200
  Property taxes: $835
  Recent appreciation: 2%
Energy Requirements
  Heating season: 2,272 degree days
  Typical source: natural gas
  Air conditioning: 1,855 hours
  Utilities cost: $885
Alternative Housing
  Condos, mobile homes
  Rental homes ($550)
Score: 6,881   **Rank: 10**

Cape Cod, MA
Model Home
  Sales price: $172,700
  Property taxes: $1,451
  Recent appreciation: –9%
Energy Requirements
  Heating season: 5,395 degree days
  Typical source: oil
  Air conditioning: 164 hours
  Utilities cost: $1,077
Alternative Housing
  Condos
  Apartments ($880)
  Rental homes ($1,100)
Score: 17,584   **Rank: 140**

Cape May, NJ
Model Home
  Sales price: $137,300
  Property taxes: $2,200
  Recent appreciation: 2%
Energy Requirements
  Heating season: 4,946 degree days
  Typical source: oil
  Air conditioning: 508 hours
  Utilities cost: $1,244
Alternative Housing
  Condos
  Apartments ($440)
  Rental homes ($550)
Score: 15,414   **Rank: 130**

Carlsbad–Artesia, NM
Model Home
  Sales price: $73,200
  Property taxes: $644
  Recent appreciation: none

Energy Requirements
  Heating season: 3,202 degree days
  Typical source: natural gas
  Air conditioning: 1,813 hours
  Utilities cost: $902
Alternative Housing
  Condos, mobile homes
  Rental homes ($450)
Score: 7,928   **Rank: 35**

Carson City–Minden, NV
Model Home
  Sales price: $206,500
  Property taxes: $1,425
  Recent appreciation: 12%
Energy Requirements
  Heating season: 5,753 degree days
  Typical source: natural gas
  Air conditioning: 574 hours
  Utilities cost: $1,018
Alternative Housing
  Condos, mobile homes
  Apartments ($1,050)
  Rental homes ($1,300)
Score: 20,446   **Rank: 144**

Chapel Hill, NC
Model Home
  Sales price: $127,800
  Property taxes: $1,291
  Recent appreciation: 3%
Energy Requirements
  Heating season: 3,454 degree days
  Typical source: total electric
  Air conditioning: 977 hours
  Utilities cost: $1,294
Alternative Housing
  Condos
  Apartments ($640)
  Rental homes ($800)
Score: 13,727   **Rank: 120**

Charleston, SC
Model Home
  Sales price: $96,400
  Property taxes: $694
  Recent appreciation: none
Energy Requirements
  Heating season: 1,904 degree days
  Typical source: natural gas
  Air conditioning: 1,252 hours
  Utilities cost: $989
Alternative Housing
  Condos, mobile homes
  Apartments ($480)
  Rental homes ($600)
Score: 10,088   **Rank: 84**

Charlevoix–Boyne City, MI
Model Home
  Sales price: $77,000
  Property taxes: $1,617
  Recent appreciation: 6%
Energy Requirements
  Heating season: 7,669 degree days
  Typical source: natural gas
  Air conditioning: 301 hours
  Utilities cost: $1,111
Alternative Housing
  Condos
  Rental homes ($450)
Score: 9,441   **Rank: 70**

Charlottesville, VA
Model Home
Sales price: $126,400
Property taxes: $1,239
Recent appreciation: 8%
Energy Requirements
Heating season: 4,162 degree days
Typical source: natural gas
Air conditioning: 826 hours
Utilities cost: $1,071
Alternative Housing
Condos
Apartments ($640)
Rental homes ($800)
Score: 13,330   **Rank: 118**

Chico–Paradise, CA
Model Home
Sales price: $127,800
Property taxes: $1,342
Recent appreciation: 25%
Energy Requirements
Heating season: 2,865 degree days
Typical source: natural gas
Air conditioning: 1,410 hours
Utilities cost: $838
Alternative Housing
Condos, mobile homes
Apartments ($650)
Rental homes ($820)
Score: 13,322   **Rank: 116**

Clayton, GA
Model Home
Sales price: $66,800
Property taxes: $688
Recent appreciation: none
Energy Requirements
Heating season: 3,672 degree days
Typical source: bottled gas
Air conditioning: 1,011 hours
Utilities cost: $1,041
Alternative Housing
Condos, mobile homes
Rental homes ($430)
Score: 7,553   **Rank: 25**

Clear Lake, CA
Model Home
Sales price: $82,500
Property taxes: $866
Recent appreciation: 10%
Energy Requirements
Heating season: 2,460 degree days
Typical source: total electric
Air conditioning: 1,200 hours
Utilities cost: $1,618
Alternative Housing
Mobile homes
Apartments ($425)
Rental homes ($530)
Score: 9,677   **Rank: 79**

Coeur d'Alene, ID
Model Home
Sales price: $76,800
Property taxes: $1,050
Recent appreciation: none
Energy Requirements
Heating season: 6,564 degree days
Typical source: total electric
Air conditioning: 363 hours
Utilities cost: $978

Alternative Housing
Condos, mobile homes
Apartments ($480)
Rental homes ($600)
Score: 8,724   **Rank: 55**

Colorado Springs, CO
Model Home
Sales price: $79,700
Property taxes: $800
Recent appreciation: −2%
Energy Requirements
Heating season: 6,473 degree days
Typical source: natural gas
Air conditioning: 644 hours
Utilities cost: $782
Alternative Housing
Condos, mobile homes
Apartments ($480)
Rental homes ($600)
Score: 8,531   **Rank: 48**

Columbia County, NY
Model Home
Sales price: $106,700
Property taxes: $2,209
Recent appreciation: 8%
Energy Requirements
Heating season: 6,888 degree days
Typical source: oil
Air conditioning: 420 hours
Utilities cost: $1,092
Alternative Housing
Mobile homes
Apartments ($550)
Rental homes ($680)
Score: 12,603   **Rank: 110**

★Crossville, TN
Model Home
Sales price: $65,800
Property taxes: $586
Recent appreciation: 3%
Energy Requirements
Heating season: 4,744 degree days
Typical source: total electric
Air conditioning: 1,150 hours
Utilities cost: $1,040
Alternative Housing
Mobile homes
Rental homes ($425)
Score: 7,362   **Rank: 16**

Daytona Beach, FL
Model Home
Sales price: $70,100
Property taxes: $645
Recent appreciation: 3%
Energy Requirements
Heating season: 897 degree days
Typical source: total electric
Air conditioning: 1,675 hours
Utilities cost: $1,549
Alternative Housing
Condos, mobile homes
Apartments ($480)
Rental homes ($600)
Score: 8,305   **Rank: 44**

★Deming, NM
Model Home
Sales price: $63,900
Property taxes: $300
Recent appreciation: none

Energy Requirements
  Heating season: 3,294 degree days
  Typical source: natural gas
  Air conditioning: 1,848 hours
  Utilities cost: $1,018
Alternative Housing
  Mobile homes
  Apartments ($320)
  Rental homes ($400)
Score: 6,889   **Rank: 11**

Door County, WI
Model Home
  Sales price: $93,100
  Property taxes: $1,890
  Recent appreciation: 5%
Energy Requirements
  Heating season: 7,876 degree days
  Typical source: oil
  Air conditioning: 264 hours
  Utilities cost: $964
Alternative Housing
  Condos
  Apartments ($360)
  Rental homes ($450)
Score: 10,971   **Rank: 96**

Eagle River, WI
Model Home
  Sales price: $64,800
  Property taxes: $1,315
  Recent appreciation: 3%
Energy Requirements
  Heating season: 9,339 degree days
  Typical source: bottled gas
  Air conditioning: 436 hours
  Utilities cost: $1,054
Alternative Housing
  Mobile homes
  Rental homes ($415)
Score: 8,019   **Rank: 36**

Easton–Chesapeake Bay, MD
Model Home
  Sales price: $129,200
  Property taxes: $555
  Recent appreciation: 15%
Energy Requirements
  Heating season: 4,299 degree days
  Typical source: oil
  Air conditioning: 635 hours
  Utilities cost: $987
Alternative Housing
  Condos
  Apartments ($640)
  Rental homes ($800)
Score: 12,806   **Rank: 112**

Edenton–Albemarle Sound, NC
Model Home
  Sales price: $90,600
  Property taxes: $915
  Recent appreciation: 5%
Energy Requirements
  Heating season: 2,956 degree days
  Typical source: total electric
  Air conditioning: 980 hours
  Utilities cost: $1,379
Alternative Housing
  Condos
  Rental homes ($400)
Score: 10,193   **Rank: 86**

El Centro–Calexico–Brawley, CA
Model Home
  Sales price: $74,300
  Property taxes: $780
  Recent appreciation: 6%
Energy Requirements
  Heating season: 1,005 degree days
  Typical source: total electric
  Air conditioning: 3,185 hours
  Utilities cost: $1,240
Alternative Housing
  Mobile homes
  Rental homes ($475)
Score: 8,498   **Rank: 45**

Eugene–Springfield, OR
Model Home
  Sales price: $113,900
  Property taxes: $2,574
  Recent appreciation: 8%
Energy Requirements
  Heating season: 4,739 degree days
  Typical source: total electric
  Air conditioning: 441 hours
  Utilities cost: $539
Alternative Housing
  Condos, mobile homes
  Apartments ($590)
  Rental homes ($730)
Score: 13,044   **Rank: 115**

Fairhope–Gulf Shores, AL
Model Home
  Sales price: $92,100
  Property taxes: $359
  Recent appreciation: 8%
Energy Requirements
  Heating season: 1,529 degree days
  Typical source: natural gas
  Air conditioning: 1,844 hours
  Utilities cost: $874
Alternative Housing
  Condos, mobile homes
  Apartments ($475)
  Rental homes ($590)
Score: 9,263   **Rank: 64**

★**Fayetteville, AR**
Model Home
  Sales price: $63,800
  Property taxes: $408
  Recent appreciation: 2%
Energy Requirements
  Heating season: 3,938 days
  Typical source: natural gas
  Air conditioning: 966 hours
  Utilities cost: $887
Alternative Housing
  Mobile homes
  Apartments ($400)
  Rental homes ($500)
Score: 6,858   **Rank: 8**

Fort Collins–Loveland, CO
Model Home
  Sales price: $71,200
  Property taxes: $762
  Recent appreciation: 2%
Energy Requirements
  Heating season: 6,599 degree days
  Typical source: natural gas
  Air conditioning: 647 hours
  Utilities cost: $846
Alternative Housing
  Condos, mobile homes
  Apartments ($440)
  Rental homes ($550)
Score: 7,816   **Rank: 30**

Fort Lauderdale–Hollywood–Pompano Beach, FL
Model Home
Sales price: $88,300
Property taxes: $812
Recent appreciation: 5%
Energy Requirements
Heating season: 244 degree days
Typical source: total electric
Air conditioning: 2,342 hours
Utilities cost: $1,556
Alternative Housing
Condos
Apartments ($640)
Rental homes ($800)
Score: 10,067   **Rank: 83**

Fort Myers–Cape Coral–Sanibel Island, FL
Model Home
Sales price: $63,700
Property taxes: $586
Recent appreciation: 10%
Energy Requirements
Heating season: 457 degree days
Typical source: total electric
Air conditioning: 1,863 hours
Utilities cost: $1,402
Alternative Housing
Condos, mobile homes
Apartments ($480)
Rental homes ($600)
Score: 7,542   **Rank: 24**

Fort Walton Beach, FL
Model Home
Sales price: $86,300
Property taxes: $794
Recent appreciation: 2%
Energy Requirements
Heating season: 1,361 degree days
Typical source: total electric
Air conditioning: 1,788 hours
Utilities cost: $1,210
Alternative Housing
Condos
Apartments ($440)
Rental homes ($550)
Score: 9,527   **Rank: 72**

★ Fredericksburg, TX
Model Home
Sales price: $59,700
Property taxes: $842
Recent appreciation: –10%
Energy Requirements
Heating season: 2,107 degree days
Typical source: natural gas
Air conditioning: 1,715 hours
Utilities cost: $821
Alternative Housing
Mobile homes
Rental homes ($375)
Score: 6,868   **Rank: 9**

Gainesville, FL
Model Home
Sales price: $76,200
Property taxes: $701
Recent appreciation: 3%
Energy Requirements
Heating season: 1,081 degree days
Typical source: total electric
Air conditioning: 1,724 hours
Utilities cost: $1,202

Alternative Housing
Condos, mobile homes
Apartments ($400)
Rental homes ($500)
Score: 8,546   **Rank: 49**

Grand Junction, CO
Model Home
Sales price: $72,100
Property taxes: $700
Recent appreciation: 5%
Energy Requirements
Heating season: 5,605 degree days
Typical source: natural gas
Air conditioning: 988 hours
Utilities cost: $923
Alternative Housing
Condos, mobile homes
Apartments ($360)
Rental homes ($450)
Score: 7,909   **Rank: 34**

★ Grand Lake, OK
Model Home
Sales price: $60,500
Property taxes: $460
Recent appreciation: 3%
Energy Requirements
Heating season: 3,587 degree days
Typical source: natural gas
Air conditioning: 1,399 hours
Utilities cost: $945
Alternative Housing
Mobile homes
Rental homes ($375)
Score: 6,680   **Rank: 6**

Grants Pass, OR
Model Home
Sales price: $119,600
Property taxes: $2,703
Recent appreciation: 10%
Energy Requirements
Heating season: 4,912 degree days
Typical source: total electric
Air conditioning: 590 hours
Utilities cost: $1,009
Alternative Housing
Mobile homes
Apartments ($600)
Rental homes ($750)
Score: 14,139   **Rank: 122**

Grass Valley–Truckee, CA
Model Home
Sales price: $130,000
Property taxes: $1,365
Recent appreciation: 15%
Energy Requirements
Heating season: 4,900 degree days
Typical source: total electric
Air conditioning: 647 hours
Utilities cost: $1,618
Alternative Housing
Condos, mobile homes
Apartments ($640)
Rental homes ($800)
Score: 14,317   **Rank: 124**

Hamilton–Bitterroot Valley, MT
Model Home
Sales price: $70,100
Property taxes: $939
Recent appreciation: 3%

Energy Requirements
  Heating season: 7,187 degree days
  Typical source: natural gas
  Air conditioning: 303 hours
  Utilities cost: $750
Alternative Housing
  Condos, mobile homes
  Rental homes ($450)
Score: 7,801   **Rank: 29**

Hanover, NH
Model Home
  Sales price: $180,300
  Property taxes: $2,795
  Recent appreciation: 5%
Energy Requirements
  Heating season: 7,680 degree days
  Typical source: oil
  Air conditioning: 312 hours
  Utilities cost: $1,144
Alternative Housing
  Condos
  Apartments ($880)
  Rental homes ($1,100)
Score: 19,658   **Rank: 142**

★**Harrison, AR**
Model Home
  Sales price: $51,300
  Property taxes: $328
  Recent appreciation: 2%
Energy Requirements
  Heating season: 3,537 degree days
  Typical source: total electric
  Air conditioning: 1,207 hours
  Utilities cost: $1,302
Alternative Housing
  Mobile homes
  Apartments ($280)
  Rental homes ($350)
Score: 6,103   **Rank: 1**

Hendersonville, NC
Model Home
  Sales price: $112,800
  Property taxes: $1,139
  Recent appreciation: 4%
Energy Requirements
  Heating season: 4,266 degree days
  Typical source: oil
  Air conditioning: 610 hours
  Utilities cost: $1,064
Alternative Housing
  Condos, mobile homes
  Apartments ($380)
  Rental homes ($475)
Score: 12,038   **Rank: 103**

Hilton Head–Beaufort, SC
Model Home
  Sales price: $109,200
  Property taxes: $786
  Recent appreciation: 5%
Energy Requirements
  Heating season: 1,941 degree days
  Typical source: total electric
  Air conditioning: 1,393 hours
  Utilities cost: $1,287
Alternative Housing
  Condos, mobile homes
  Apartments ($560)
  Rental homes ($700)
Score: 11,593   **Rank: 100**

Honolulu, HI
Model Home
  Sales price: $258,000
  Property taxes: $1,316
  Recent appreciation: 5%
Energy Requirements
  Heating season: 0 degree days
  Typical source: total electric
  Air conditioning: 1,342 hours
  Utilities cost: $1,356
Alternative Housing
  Condos
  Apartments ($1,280)
  Rental homes ($1,600)
Score: 25,165   **Rank: 147**

Hot Springs National Park, AR
Model Home
  Sales price: $68,900
  Property taxes: $441
  Recent appreciation: 1%
Energy Requirements
  Heating season: 2,729 degree days
  Typical source: natural gas
  Air conditioning: 1,643 hours
  Utilities cost: $1,092
Alternative Housing
  Condos, mobile homes
  Apartments ($350)
  Rental homes ($440)
Score: 7,540   **Rank: 23**

★**Houghton Lake, MI**
Model Home
  Sales price: $57,800
  Property taxes: $1,214
  Recent appreciation: 4%
Energy Requirements
  Heating season: 8,347 degree days
  Typical source: natural gas
  Air conditioning: 218 hours
  Utilities cost: $1,137
Alternative Housing
  Mobile homes
  Rental homes ($400)
Score: 7,390   **Rank: 18**

Iowa City, IA
Model Home
  Sales price: $117,200
  Property taxes: $2,297
  Recent appreciation: none
Energy Requirements
  Heating season: 6,404 degree days
  Typical source: natural gas
  Air conditioning: 615 hours
  Utilities cost: $1,161
Alternative Housing
  Condos, mobile homes
  Apartments ($440)
  Rental homes ($550)
Score: 13,676   **Rank: 119**

Kalispell, MT
Model Home
  Sales price: $80,700
  Property taxes: $1,081
  Recent appreciation: 7%
Energy Requirements
  Heating season: 8,554 degree days
  Typical source: natural gas
  Air conditioning: 26 hours
  Utilities cost: $763

Alternative Housing
Condos, mobile homes
Apartments ($400)
Rental homes ($500)
Score: 8,880   **Rank: 57**

Keene, NH
Model Home
Sales price: $141,700
Property taxes: $2,196
Recent appreciation: none
Energy Requirements
Heating season: 6,969 degree days
Typical source: oil
Air conditioning: 335 hours
Utilities cost: $1,298
Alternative Housing
Condos, mobile homes
Apartments ($560)
Rental homes ($700)
Score: 15,848   **Rank: 134**

★ Kerrville, TX
Model Home
Sales price: $54,900
Property taxes: $774
Recent appreciation: 2%
Energy Requirements
Heating season: 2,399 degree days
Typical source: natural gas
Air conditioning: 1,715 hours
Utilities cost: $718
Alternative Housing
Condos, mobile homes
Apartments ($400)
Rental homes ($500)
Score: 6,279   **Rank: 3**

Key West–Key Largo–Marathon, FL
Model Home
Sales price: $175,000
Property taxes: $1,610
Recent appreciation: 10%
Energy Requirements
Heating season: 26 degree days
Typical source: total electric
Air conditioning: 2,720 hours
Utilities cost: $1,487
Alternative Housing
Condos
Apartments ($880)
Rental homes ($1,000)
Score: 18,354   **Rank: 141**

Laconia–Lake Winnipesaukee, NH
Model Home
Sales price: $106,700
Property taxes: $1,654
Recent appreciation: none
Energy Requirements
Heating season: 7,315 degree days
Typical source: oil
Air conditioning: 398 hours
Utilities cost: $1,298
Alternative Housing
Condos, mobile homes
Apartments ($475)
Rental homes ($595)
Score: 12,254   **Rank: 105**

Lake Havasu City–Kingman, AZ
Model Home
Sales price: $91,800
Property taxes: $850
Recent appreciation: 4%

Energy Requirements
Heating season: 2,425 degree days
Typical source: total electric
Air conditioning: 2,360 hours
Utilities cost: $1,649
Alternative Housing
Condos, mobile homes
Apartments ($475)
Rental homes ($580)
Score: 10,502   **Rank: 91**

Lake Lanier, GA
Model Home
Sales price: $94,500
Property taxes: $973
Recent appreciation: 5%
Energy Requirements
Heating season: 3,267 degree days
Typical source: total electric
Air conditioning: 1,077 hours
Utilities cost: $1,040
Alternative Housing
Apartments ($480)
Rental homes ($600)
Score: 10,252   **Rank: 88**

Lakeland–Winter Haven, FL
Model Home
Sales price: $66,200
Property taxes: $609
Recent appreciation: 3%
Energy Requirements
Heating season: 678 degree days
Typical source: total electric
Air conditioning: 1,759 hours
Utilities cost: $1,325
Alternative Housing
Condos, mobile homes
Apartments ($340)
Rental homes ($425)
Score: 7,706   **Rank: 28**

Lancaster County, PA
Model Home
Sales price: $120,900
Property taxes: $1,693
Recent appreciation: 12%
Energy Requirements
Heating season: 5,283 degree days
Typical source: oil
Air conditioning: 654 hours
Utilities cost: $1,090
Alternative Housing
Condos, mobile homes
Apartments ($400)
Rental homes ($500)
Score: 13,323   **Rank: 117**

Las Cruces, NM
Model Home
Sales price: $86,600
Property taxes: $762
Recent appreciation: none
Energy Requirements
Heating season: 3,194 degree days
Typical source: natural gas
Air conditioning: 1,848 hours
Utilities cost: $1,120
Alternative Housing
Condos, mobile homes
Apartments ($440)
Rental homes ($550)
Score: 9,433   **Rank: 69**

Las Vegas, NV
Model Home
Sales price: $149,600
Property taxes: $1,032
Recent appreciation: 15%
Energy Requirements
Heating season: 2,601 degree days
Typical source: total electric
Air conditioning: 2,360 hours
Utilities cost: $1,025
Alternative Housing
Condos, mobile homes
Apartments ($760)
Rental homes ($950)
Score: 15,100   **Rank: 128**

Lexington–Fayette, KY
Model Home
Sales price: $93,200
Property taxes: $811
Recent appreciation: 2%
Energy Requirements
Heating season: 4,729 degree days
Typical source: natural gas
Air conditioning: 954 hours
Utilities cost: $1,019
Alternative Housing
Condos, mobile homes
Apartments ($480)
Rental homes ($600)
Score: 9,956   **Rank: 82**

Los Alamos, NM
Model Home
Sales price: $197,200
Property taxes: $1,735
Recent appreciation: none
Energy Requirements
Heating season: 6,007 degree days
Typical source: natural gas
Air conditioning: 686 hours
Utilities cost: $954
Alternative Housing
Condos
Rental homes ($1,200)
Score: 19,882   **Rank: 143**

Madison, WI
Model Home
Sales price: $99,800
Property taxes: $2,026
Recent appreciation: 7%
Energy Requirements
Heating season: 7,730 degree days
Typical source: natural gas
Air conditioning: 485 hours
Utilities cost: $1,151
Alternative Housing
Condos, mobile homes
Apartments ($800)
Rental homes ($1,000)
Score: 11,878   **Rank: 101**

Martinsburg–Charles Town, WV
Model Home
Sales price: $90,300
Property taxes: $623
Recent appreciation: 8%
Energy Requirements
Heating season: 5,152 degree days
Typical source: natural gas
Air conditioning: 702 hours
Utilities cost: $1,125

Alternative Housing
Mobile homes
Apartments ($520)
Rental homes ($650)
Score: 9,621   **Rank: 75**

Maui, HI
Model Home
Sales price: $290,000
Property taxes: $600
Recent appreciation: 40%
Energy Requirements
Heating season: 0 degree days
Typical source: total electric
Air conditioning: 1,414 hours
Utilities cost: $755
Alternative Housing
Condos
Apartments ($960)
Rental homes ($1,200)
Score: 26,638   **Rank: 148**

McAllen–Edinburg–Mission, TX
Model Home
Sales price: $71,400
Property taxes: $1,007
Recent appreciation: 2%
Energy Requirements
Heating season: 696 degree days
Typical source: natural gas
Air conditioning: 2,527 hours
Utilities cost: $808
Alternative Housing
Condos, mobile homes
Apartments ($400)
Rental homes ($500)
Score: 8,040   **Rank: 37**

Medford–Ashland, OR
Model Home
Sales price: $134,600
Property taxes: $3,042
Recent appreciation: 10%
Energy Requirements
Heating season: 4,930 degree days
Typical source: total electric
Air conditioning: 630 hours
Utilities cost: $1,009
Alternative Housing
Condos, mobile homes
Apartments ($720)
Rental homes ($900)
Score: 15,786   **Rank: 132**

Melbourne–Titusville–Palm Bay, FL
Model Home
Sales price: $73,100
Property taxes: $673
Recent appreciation: none
Energy Requirements
Heating season: 611 degree days
Typical source: total electric
Air conditioning: 2,088 hours
Utilities cost: $1,579
Alternative Housing
Condos
Apartments ($440)
Rental homes ($550)
Score: 8,625   **Rank: 52**

Miami–Hialeah, FL
Model Home
Sales price: $116,800
Property taxes: $1,075
Recent appreciation: 5%

Energy Requirements
Heating season: 206 degree days
Typical source: total electric
Air conditioning: 2,408 hours
Utilities cost: $1,541
Alternative Housing
Condos
Apartments ($640)
Rental homes ($800)
Score: 12,798   **Rank: 111**

Monticello–Liberty, NY
Model Home
Sales price: $115,600
Property taxes: $2,393
Recent appreciation: none
Energy Requirements
Heating season: 6,556 degree days
Typical source: oil
Air conditioning: 623 hours
Utilities cost: $1,311
Alternative Housing
Rental homes ($750)
Score: 13,782   **Rank: 121**

★Mountain Home–Bull Shoals, AR
Model Home
Sales price: $65,400
Property taxes: $419
Recent appreciation: 2%
Energy Requirements
Heating season: 3,852 degree days
Typical source: total electric
Air conditioning: 966 hours
Utilities cost: $1,302
Alternative Housing
Condos, mobile homes
Rental homes ($420)
Score: 7,422   **Rank: 19**

★Murray–Kentucky Lake, KY
Model Home
Sales price: $67,200
Property taxes: $585
Recent appreciation: 6%
Energy Requirements
Heating season: 3,893 degree days
Typical source: total electric
Air conditioning: 1,160 hours
Utilities cost: $1,009
Alternative Housing
Mobile homes
Apartments ($350)
Rental homes ($430)
Score: 7,453   **Rank: 20**

Myrtle Beach, SC
Model Home
Sales price: $92,300
Property taxes: $665
Recent appreciation: none
Energy Requirements
Heating season: 2,023 degree days
Typical source: total electric
Air conditioning: 1,204 hours
Utilities cost: $1,063
Alternative Housing
Condos, mobile homes
Apartments ($600)
Rental homes ($750)
Score: 9,775   **Rank: 80**

Naples, FL
Model Home
Sales price: $91,200
Property taxes: $839
Recent appreciation: 23%
Energy Requirements
Heating season: 345 degree days
Typical source: total electric
Air conditioning: 1,890 hours
Utilities cost: $1,549
Alternative Housing
Condos, mobile homes
Apartments ($600)
Rental homes ($750)
Score: 10,339   **Rank: 89**

New Bern, NC
Model Home
Sales price: $83,900
Property taxes: $847
Recent appreciation: 8%
Energy Requirements
Heating season: 2,786 degree days
Typical source: total electric
Air conditioning: 1,160 hours
Utilities cost: $1,456
Alternative Housing
Condos, mobile homes
Apartments ($440)
Rental homes ($550)
Score: 9,618   **Rank: 74**

New Braunfels, TX
Model Home
Sales price: $67,300
Property taxes: $949
Recent appreciation: none
Energy Requirements
Heating season: 1,570 degree days
Typical source: natural gas
Air conditioning: 2,004 hours
Utilities cost: $667
Alternative Housing
Condos, mobile homes
Apartments ($400)
Rental homes ($500)
Score: 7,483   **Rank: 21**

New Paltz–Ulster County, NY
Model Home
Sales price: $103,500
Property taxes: $2,142
Recent appreciation: –5%
Energy Requirements
Heating season: 7,447 degree days
Typical source: oil
Air conditioning: 460 hours
Utilities cost: $1,259
Alternative Housing
Apartments ($520)
Rental homes ($650)
Score: 12,425   **Rank: 109**

New Port Richey, FL
Model Home
Sales price: $71,800
Property taxes: $661
Recent appreciation: 3%
Energy Requirements
Heating season: 717 degree days
Typical source: total electric
Air conditioning: 2,154 hours
Utilities cost: $1,325

Alternative Housing
  Condos, mobile homes
  Apartments ($530)
  Rental homes ($660)
Score: 8,245   **Rank: 42**

Newport–Lincoln City, OR
Model Home
  Sales price: $92,200
  Property taxes: $2,084
  Recent appreciation: 15%
Energy Requirements
  Heating season: 5,235 degree days
  Typical source: total electric
  Air conditioning: 296 hours
  Utilities cost: $1,009
Alternative Housing
  Rental homes ($625)
Score: 11,131   **Rank: 97**

North Conway–White Mountains, NH
Model Home
  Sales price: $113,500
  Property taxes: $1,759
  Recent appreciation: 8%
Energy Requirements
  Heating season: 7,612 degree days
  Typical source: oil
  Air conditioning: 398 hours
  Utilities cost: $1,298
Alternative Housing
  Condos, mobile homes
  Apartments ($575)
  Rental homes ($720)
Score: 12,952   **Rank: 114**

Oak Harbor–Whidbey Island, WA
Model Home
  Sales price: $107,600
  Property taxes: $1,184
  Recent appreciation: 12%
Energy Requirements
  Heating season: 5,380 degree days
  Typical source: total electric
  Air conditioning: 53 hours
  Utilities cost: $994
Alternative Housing
  Condos, mobile homes
  Apartments ($550)
  Rental homes ($690)
Score: 11,558   **Rank: 99**

Ocala, FL
Model Home
  Sales price: $77,100
  Property taxes: $709
  Recent appreciation: 3%
Energy Requirements
  Heating season: 700 degree days
  Typical source: total electric
  Air conditioning: 1,824 hours
  Utilities cost: $1,371
Alternative Housing
  Condos, mobile homes
  Apartments ($400)
  Rental homes ($500)
Score: 8,803   **Rank: 56**

Ocean City–Assateague Island, MD
Model Home
  Sales price: $84,400
  Property taxes: $600
  Recent appreciation: none

Energy Requirements
  Heating season: 4,303 degree days
  Typical source: oil
  Air conditioning: 461 hours
  Utilities cost: $1,103
Alternative Housing
  Condos
  Apartments ($440)
  Rental homes ($550)
Score: 9,061   **Rank: 59**

Ocean County, NJ
Model Home
  Sales price: $70,800
  Property taxes: $1,200
  Recent appreciation: none
Energy Requirements
  Heating season: 5,128 degree days
  Typical source: oil
  Air conditioning: 586 hours
  Utilities cost: $1,154
Alternative Housing
  Condos
  Apartments ($680)
  Rental homes ($850)
Score: 8,527   **Rank: 46**

Olympia, WA
Model Home
  Sales price: $81,600
  Property taxes: $1,300
  Recent appreciation: 15%
Energy Requirements
  Heating season: 5,530 degree days
  Typical source: total electric
  Air conditioning: 117 hours
  Utilities cost: $994
Alternative Housing
  Condos, mobile homes
  Apartments ($480)
  Rental homes ($600)
Score: 9,408   **Rank: 68**

Orlando, FL
Model Home
  Sales price: $83,200
  Property taxes: $765
  Recent appreciation: 5%
Energy Requirements
  Heating season: 704 degree days
  Typical source: total electric
  Air conditioning: 1,675 hours
  Utilities cost: $1,132
Alternative Housing
  Condos, mobile homes
  Apartments ($520)
  Rental homes ($650)
Score: 9,152   **Rank: 61**

Panama City, FL
Model Home
  Sales price: $77,000
  Property taxes: $708
  Recent appreciation: 3%
Energy Requirements
  Heating season: 1,388 degree days
  Typical source: total electric
  Air conditioning: 1,908 hours
  Utilities cost: $1,210
Alternative Housing
  Condos, mobile homes
  Apartments ($480)
  Rental homes ($600)
Score: 8,631   **Rank: 53**

★ Paris–Big Sandy, TN
Model Home
Sales price: $61,500
Property taxes: $547
Recent appreciation: 5%
Energy Requirements
Heating season: 3,882 degree days
Typical source: total electric
Air conditioning: 1,160 hours
Utilities cost: $1,002
Alternative Housing
Mobile homes
Rental homes ($350)
Score: 6,911   **Rank: 12**

Pensacola, FL
Model Home
Sales price: $72,300
Property taxes: $665
Recent appreciation: 3%
Energy Requirements
Heating season: 1,578 degree days
Typical source: total electric
Air conditioning: 1,884 hours
Utilities cost: $1,240
Alternative Housing
Condos
Apartments ($450)
Rental homes ($560)
Score: 8,209   **Rank: 41**

Petoskey–Straits of Mackinac, MI
Model Home
Sales price: $75,800
Property taxes: $1,592
Recent appreciation: 6%
Energy Requirements
Heating season: 7,669 degree days
Typical source: natural gas
Air conditioning: 301 hours
Utilities cost: $1,137
Alternative Housing
Condos, mobile homes
Apartments ($400)
Rental homes ($500)
Score: 9,337   **Rank: 65**

Phoenix–Tempe–Scottsdale, AZ
Model Home
Sales price: $82,200
Property taxes: $850
Recent appreciation: none
Energy Requirements
Heating season: 1,552 degree days
Typical source: natural gas
Air conditioning: 2,815 hours
Utilities cost: $985
Alternative Housing
Condos, mobile homes
Apartments ($480)
Rental homes ($600)
Score: 9,001   **Rank: 58**

Pike County, PA
Model Home
Sales price: $116,600
Property taxes: $700
Recent appreciation: 10%
Energy Requirements
Heating season: 5,415 degree days
Typical source: oil
Air conditioning: 460 hours
Utilities cost: $1,142
Alternative Housing
Condos, mobile homes
Rental homes ($500)
Score: 12,008   **Rank: 102**

Port Townsend, WA
Model Home
Sales price: $97,500
Property taxes: $1,073
Recent appreciation: 16%
Energy Requirements
Heating season: 5,842 degree days
Typical source: total electric
Air conditioning: 0 hours
Utilities cost: $994
Alternative Housing
Mobile homes
Apartments ($500)
Rental homes ($625)
Score: 10,567   **Rank: 92**

Portsmouth–Dover–Durham, NH
Model Home
Sales price: $157,500
Property taxes: $2,441
Recent appreciation: –10%
Energy Requirements
Heating season: 7,089 degree days
Typical source: oil
Air conditioning: 220 hours
Utilities cost: $1,311
Alternative Housing
Condos
Apartments ($560)
Rental homes ($700)
Score: 17,483   **Rank: 139**

Prescott, AZ
Model Home
Sales price: $96,800
Property taxes: $800
Recent appreciation: 3%
Energy Requirements
Heating season: 4,956 degree days
Typical source: natural gas
Air conditioning: 925 hours
Utilities cost: $985
Alternative Housing
Condos, mobile homes
Apartments ($500)
Rental homes ($620)
Score: 10,224   **Rank: 87**

Red Bluff–Sacramento Valley, CA
Model Home
Sales price: $87,200
Property taxes: $916
Recent appreciation: 5%
Energy Requirements
Heating season: 2,688 degree days
Typical source: natural gas
Air conditioning: 1,515 hours
Utilities cost: $838
Alternative Housing
Condos, mobile homes
Apartments ($450)
Rental homes ($560)
Score: 9,356   **Rank: 66**

Redding, CA
Model Home
Sales price: $119,300
Property taxes: $1,253
Recent appreciation: 20%
Energy Requirements
Heating season: 2,610 degree days
Typical source: natural gas
Air conditioning: 1,515 hours
Utilities cost: $696

Alternative Housing
  Condos, mobile homes
  Apartments ($480)
  Rental homes ($600)
Score: 12,350   **Rank: 107**

Rehoboth Bay–Indian River Bay, DE
Model Home
  Sales price: $125,900
  Property taxes: $332
  Recent appreciation: 6%
Energy Requirements
  Heating season: 4,303 degree days
  Typical source: oil
  Air conditioning: 456 hours
  Utilities cost: $1,077
Alternative Housing
  Condos, mobile homes
  Rental homes ($550)
Score: 12,386   **Rank: 108**

Reno, NV
Model Home
  Sales price: $172,800
  Property taxes: $1,192
  Recent appreciation: 3%
Energy Requirements
  Heating season: 6,022 degree days
  Typical source: natural gas
  Air conditioning: 647 hours
  Utilities cost: $1,018
Alternative Housing
  Condos, mobile homes
  Apartments ($880)
  Rental homes ($1,100)
Score: 17,276   **Rank: 138**

★Rockport–Aransas Pass, TX
Model Home
  Sales price: $61,900
  Property taxes: $873
  Recent appreciation: none
Energy Requirements
  Heating season: 1,011 degree days
  Typical source: natural gas
  Air conditioning: 2,531 hours
  Utilities cost: $808
Alternative Housing
  Condos
  Apartments ($480)
  Rental homes ($600)
Score: 7,078   **Rank: 13**

Roswell, NM
Model Home
  Sales price: $72,200
  Property taxes: $635
  Recent appreciation: none
Energy Requirements
  Heating season: 3,697 degree days
  Typical source: natural gas
  Air conditioning: 1,617 hours
  Utilities cost: $902
Alternative Housing
  Mobile homes
  Apartments ($375)
  Rental homes ($460)
Score: 7,832   **Rank: 32**

St. Augustine, FL
Model Home
  Sales price: $82,300
  Property taxes: $757
  Recent appreciation: 4%

Energy Requirements
  Heating season: 1,327 degree days
  Typical source: total electric
  Air conditioning: 1,725 hours
  Utilities cost: $1,595
Alternative Housing
  Condos, mobile homes
  Apartments ($480)
  Rental homes ($600)
Score: 9,527   **Rank: 72**

St. George–Zion, UT
Model Home
  Sales price: $70,700
  Property taxes: $686
  Recent appreciation: none
Energy Requirements
  Heating season: 3,425 degree days
  Typical source: total electric
  Air conditioning: 789 hours
  Utilities cost: $709
Alternative Housing
  Condos, mobile homes
  Apartments ($360)
  Rental homes ($450)
Score: 7,558   **Rank: 26**

St. Petersburg–Clearwater–Dunedin, FL
Model Home
  Sales price: $91,900
  Property taxes: $845
  Recent appreciation: 3%
Energy Requirements
  Heating season: 551 degree days
  Typical source: total electric
  Air conditioning: 1,881 hours
  Utilities cost: $1,333
Alternative Housing
  Condos, mobile homes
  Apartments ($520)
  Rental homes ($650)
Score: 10,190   **Rank: 85**

★St. Tammany Parish, LA
Model Home
  Sales price: $66,700
  Property taxes: $200
  Recent appreciation: none
Energy Requirements
  Heating season: 1,465 degree days
  Typical source: natural gas
  Air conditioning: 1,733 hours
  Utilities cost: $841
Alternative Housing
  Condos, mobile homes
  Apartments ($580)
  Rental homes ($725)
Score: 6,856   **Rank: 7**

Salinas–Seaside–Monterey, CA
Model Home
  Sales price: $286,300
  Property taxes: $3,006
  Recent appreciation: 15%
Energy Requirements
  Heating season: 2,959 degree days
  Typical source: natural gas
  Air conditioning: 14 hours
  Utilities cost: $889
Alternative Housing
  Condos, mobile homes
  Apartments ($680)
  Rental homes ($850)
Score: 28,856   **Rank: 149**

★ San Antonio, TX
Model Home
Sales price: $61,100
Property taxes: $1,200
Recent appreciation: 5%
Energy Requirements
Heating season: 1,570 degree days
Typical source: natural gas
Air conditioning: 2,004 hours
Utilities cost: $795
Alternative Housing
Condos, mobile homes
Apartments ($400)
Rental homes ($500)
Score: 7,322　　　　　　　**Rank: 15**

San Diego, CA
Model Home
Sales price: $200,500
Property taxes: $2,105
Recent appreciation: 18%
Energy Requirements
Heating season: 1,507 degree days
Typical source: natural gas
Air conditioning: 130 hours
Utilities cost: $1,120
Alternative Housing
Condos, mobile homes
Apartments ($720)
Rental homes ($900)
Score: 20,706　　　　　　　**Rank: 145**

San Juan Islands, WA
Model Home
Sales price: $149,700
Property taxes: $1,647
Recent appreciation: 25%
Energy Requirements
Heating season: 5,609 degree days
Typical source: total electric
Air conditioning: 53 hours
Utilities cost: $1,040
Alternative Housing
Condos, mobile homes
Rental homes ($950)
Score: 15,738　　　　　　　**Rank: 131**

San Luis Obispo, CA
Model Home
Sales price: $288,900
Property taxes: $3,033
Recent appreciation: 8%
Energy Requirements
Heating season: 2,472 degree days
Typical source: natural gas
Air conditioning: 329 hours
Utilities cost: $889
Alternative Housing
Condos
Apartments ($960)
Rental homes ($1,200)
Score: 29,110　　　　　　　**Rank: 150**

Santa Barbara, CA
Model Home
Sales price: $297,000
Property taxes: $3,119
Recent appreciation: 12%
Energy Requirements
Heating season: 1,980 degree days
Typical source: natural gas
Air conditioning: 44 hours
Utilities cost: $889

Alternative Housing
Condos
Apartments ($960)
Rental homes ($1,200)
Score: 29,901　　　　　　　**Rank: 151**

Santa Fe, NM
Model Home
Sales price: $158,700
Property taxes: $1,397
Recent appreciation: 6%
Energy Requirements
Heating season: 6,007 degree days
Typical source: natural gas
Air conditioning: 686 hours
Utilities cost: $1,018
Alternative Housing
Condos
Apartments ($800)
Rental homes ($1,000)
Score: 16,250　　　　　　　**Rank: 135**

Santa Rosa–Petaluma, CA
Model Home
Sales price: $231,600
Property taxes: $2,432
Recent appreciation: 15%
Energy Requirements
Heating season: 3,065 degree days
Typical source: natural gas
Air conditioning: 770 hours
Utilities cost: $838
Alternative Housing
Condos
Apartments ($760)
Rental homes ($950)
Score: 23,461　　　　　　　**Rank: 146**

Sarasota, FL
Model Home
Sales price: $83,800
Property taxes: $771
Recent appreciation: 2%
Energy Requirements
Heating season: 527 degree days
Typical source: total electric
Air conditioning: 2,154 hours
Utilities cost: $1,549
Alternative Housing
Condos, mobile homes
Apartments ($620)
Rental homes ($775)
Score: 9,625　　　　　　　**Rank: 76**

Savannah, GA
Model Home
Sales price: $82,500
Property taxes: $850
Recent appreciation: 3%
Energy Requirements
Heating season: 1,952 degree days
Typical source: natural gas
Air conditioning: 1,515 hours
Utilities cost: $1,093
Alternative Housing
Condos, mobile homes
Apartments ($440)
Rental homes ($550)
Score: 9,135　　　　　　　**Rank: 60**

South Lake Tahoe–Placerville, CA
Model Home
Sales price: $165,100
Property taxes: $1,734
Recent appreciation: 26%

Energy Requirements
Heating season: 6,543 degree days
Typical source: natural gas
Air conditioning: 585 hours
Utilities cost: $850
Alternative Housing
Condos
Apartments ($560)
Rental homes ($700)
Score: 16,978   **Rank: 137**

Southport, NC
Model Home
Sales price: $64,700
Property taxes: $653
Recent appreciation: 5%
Energy Requirements
Heating season: 2,423 degree days
Typical source: total electric
Air conditioning: 683 hours
Utilities cost: $1,387
Alternative Housing
Condos, mobile homes
Apartments ($360)
Rental homes ($450)
Score: 7,681   **Rank: 27**

State College, PA
Model Home
Sales price: $108,500
Property taxes: $900
Recent appreciation: 6%
Energy Requirements
Heating season: 6,132 degree days
Typical source: oil
Air conditioning: 351 hours
Utilities cost: $1,015
Alternative Housing
Condos
Apartments ($560)
Rental homes ($700)
Score: 11,375   **Rank: 98**

★ Thomasville, GA
Model Home
Sales price: $66,300
Property taxes: $683
Recent appreciation: none
Energy Requirements
Heating season: 1,872 degree days
Typical source: natural gas
Air conditioning: 780 hours
Utilities cost: $913
Alternative Housing
Mobile homes
Rental homes ($425)
Score: 7,376   **Rank: 17**

Traverse City–Grand Traverse Bay, MI
Model Home
Sales price: $85,600
Property taxes: $1,798
Recent appreciation: 6%
Energy Requirements
Heating season: 7,698 degree days
Typical source: natural gas
Air conditioning: 308 hours
Utilities cost: $1,214
Alternative Housing
Condos
Apartments ($440)
Rental homes ($600)
Score: 10,474   **Rank: 90**

Tucson, AZ
Model Home
Sales price: $92,900
Property taxes: $950
Recent appreciation: 2%
Energy Requirements
Heating season: 1,707 degree days
Typical source: natural gas
Air conditioning: 2,243 hours
Utilities cost: $856
Alternative Housing
Condos, mobile homes
Apartments ($520)
Rental homes ($650)
Score: 9,906   **Rank: 81**

Twain Harte–Yosemite, CA
Model Home
Sales price: $143,900
Property taxes: $1,511
Recent appreciation: 15%
Energy Requirements
Heating season: 4,800 degree days
Typical source: bottled gas
Air conditioning: 647 hours
Utilities cost: $1,208
Alternative Housing
Condos, mobile homes
Apartments ($720)
Rental homes ($900)
Score: 15,265   **Rank: 129**

Vero Beach, FL
Model Home
Sales price: $75,600
Property taxes: $696
Recent appreciation: none
Energy Requirements
Heating season: 503 degree days
Typical source: total electric
Air conditioning: 2,276 hours
Utilities cost: $1,240
Alternative Housing
Condos
Apartments ($475)
Rental homes ($580)
Score: 8,527   **Rank: 46**

Virginia Beach–Norfolk, VA
Model Home
Sales price: $88,700
Property taxes: $869
Recent appreciation: none
Energy Requirements
Heating season: 3,488 degree days
Typical source: natural gas
Air conditioning: 990 hours
Utilities cost: $1,071
Alternative Housing
Condos, mobile homes
Apartments ($500)
Rental homes ($400)
Score: 9,673   **Rank: 78**

Wenatchee, WA
Model Home
Sales price: $79,400
Property taxes: $873
Recent appreciation: 6%
Energy Requirements
Heating season: 6,805 degree days
Typical source: total electric
Air conditioning: 351 hours
Utilities cost: $316

Alternative Housing
Condos, mobile homes
Apartments ($400)
Rental homes ($500)
Score: 8,112   **Rank: 40**

West Palm Beach–Boca Raton–
Delray Beach, FL
Model Home
Sales price: $95,000
Property taxes: $874
Recent appreciation: –5%
Energy Requirements
Heating season: 299 degree days
Typical source: total electric
Air conditioning: 2,276 hours
Utilities cost: $1,549
Alternative Housing
Condos

Apartments ($720)
Rental homes ($900)
Score: 10,705   **Rank: 93**

Yuma, AZ
Model Home
Sales price: $83,000
Property taxes: $825
Recent appreciation: 4%
Energy Requirements
Heating season: 1,005 degree days
Typical source: total electric
Air conditioning: 3,185 hours
Utilities cost: $1,602
Alternative Housing
Condos, mobile homes
Apartments ($520)
Rental homes ($650)
Score: 9,664   **Rank: 77**

 ET CETERA: Housing

YOUR $125,000 DECISION

Prior to 1987, capital gains were taxed up to a maximum of 20 percent. Tax reform now treats capital gains as ordinary income. Your house is a capital asset, and if you sell it at a profit, your capital gains are taxable in the year you sell. A loss on the sale, however, isn't deductible.

There are two important exceptions to this rule that can help you put off the payment of taxes or eliminate them altogether: the "rollover" available to sellers of any age and the one-time exclusion, which can be taken advantage of only by sellers 55 and over.

The Rollover. If you sell your house at a profit, the tax on the profit may be postponed if, within two years from the date you sell, you buy another house and pay as much or more than the sale price of your old house. This time limit works forward and backward: you can buy the new house as long as 24 months before or 24 months after you sell your old house. If you anticipate retiring, this rule allows you to buy a vacation home up to two years before you sell your principal residence and claim the rollover when you move into the vacation home for full-time living.

If the price of your new home is less than the sale price of your old one, part of the profit will be taxable during the year. The profit will also be taxable during the year in which you sold in the event that you don't buy a new principal residence but instead rent an apartment or house.

The rollover can be used over and over again until the day you sell your home and don't buy another. When that happens, the taxes are due on all the accumulated profits realized in all your principal residences sold over prior years. That is an ideal time to claim the one-time exclusion.

The Exclusion. If either you or your spouse are 55 by the day you sell your home at a profit, and you've owned and used the home as your principal residence for at least three of the five years ending on the day the property is sold, you can elect to exclude up to $125,000 of profit from tax altogether ($62,500 for married persons filing separately).

The exclusion can be claimed only once, so don't use it to shelter a paltry gain if you anticipate an even larger gain later on. Also, if you sell your house and buy another, you can postpone all or part of your gain anyway. If you take the exemption and later wish you hadn't, you can revoke your decision within three years after filing your return for the year the sale occurred or within two years of the time the tax for that year was paid, whichever is later.

Remember, too, that once the exclusion is claimed by a married couple, it cannot be claimed again by either spouse. Divorced or widowed persons who jointly used the exemption with their previous spouses are branded for life in the eyes of the IRS.

HOME-EQUITY CONVERSION: LIVING "ON THE HOUSE"

If you're over 65 and own a home, you're likely to possess an asset that has appreciated dramatically over the years. Economists put the total value of homes owned by people over 65 in the United States at more than $1 trillion.

Home-equity conversion, or reverse-equity plans, are designed to help older house-rich and cash-poor homeowners unlock the value of their home and convert it into additional retirement income without being forced to move. Unlike common home-equity loans available to most homeowners, you don't have to show sufficient monthly income for a commercial bank's approval. Some plans involve actual transfer of title to the property; others do not. Some provide income for only a specified period; others provide income for life.

Deciding which plan is best takes careful thought; interested homeowners should seek the advice of an attorney for help in weighing the benefits and liabilities of specific plans. The following are three major variations:

A **Reverse Appreciation Mortgage** (RAM) is a loan paid out in monthly installments to the homeowner by a lender, thereby creating a debt (hence the word *mortgage*) that increases each month. The house must be free of mortgage or lien, since the amount of the loan is determined by the price the home would fetch if the property were put up for sale. The loan comes due at the end of the term or when the owner dies or decides to sell the property. The RAM is repaid out of money from the sale of the house or from other resources.

A **sale-leaseback** lets you stay in your home for the rest of your life as long as you're physically able. You sell your house to an investor who leases the property back to you at a fixed rent for as long as you can or want to live in the house. You receive a down payment and a monthly mortgage payment from the investor, who is responsible for taxes, maintenance, and insurance on the property. The investor takes full possession of the property when you choose to move out of the house or in the event of your death.

Deferred payment loans are home-improvement loans offered most often by city governments or neighborhood housing service agencies. They are generally open to all ages and charge low or no interest. The loan comes due when the owner dies or sells the property. In either case, the deferred loan is then paid out of cash from the sale of the house or at the estate settlement.

PROPERTY TAXES

Although the dollar amount of your home's recent property tax bills may seem to ratchet upward with each reassessment, there is some slight comfort in knowing that the rate at which your home is being taxed is actually going down.

Over the past 10 years, while the prices of existing homes were rising, the average effective property tax rates dropped from 2 percent of these values to less than 1.15 percent nationwide. Economists expect the downward trend to continue.

Nowhere in the United States can you own a home and entirely escape property taxes (except in Alaska, but you have to be 65). But homeowners in certain states (like Louisiana, where the statewide average property tax rate is .22 percent) shoulder less of a burden than do homeowners in other states (such as Oregon, which has an average tax rate of 2.26, or nearly 10 times that of Louisiana).

Exemptions

When you shop for low property taxes around the country, adopt a circumspect attitude when you hear of places that give retired people additional property tax relief. Are any of these benefits, by themselves, worth a move? Read on.

Homestead exemptions are specific dollar amounts deducted by local assessors when they compute your bill. In Hawaii, for example, homeowners over 60 get an exemption of $40,000; when they turn 70, the exemption increases to $50,000. All homeowners in Florida receive a $25,000 exemption if they are permanent residents. According to the Washington, D.C.-based Advisory Commission on Intergovernmental Relations, 19 states grant exemptions to *all* homeowners:

Alabama	Massachusetts
California	(local option)
Florida	Minnesota
Georgia	Mississippi
Hawaii	New Jersey
Idaho	New Mexico
Illinois	Oklahoma
Indiana	Texas
Iowa	Wisconsin
Louisiana	Wyoming

Nine states allow special exemptions or credits to *older homeowners* without any income qualifications: Alaska, Hawaii, Illinois, Kentucky, Mississippi, New Jersey, South Carolina, Texas, and West Virginia.

Do the exemptions in these states translate into much hard cash? Except in Alaska—where you can forget property taxes once you turn 65—not really. Based on statewide average property tax rates, you'll save $204 in Hawaii ($255 if you're over 70), $54 in Illinois, $160 in Kentucky, $144 in South Carolina, and $138 in West Virginia.

The bottom line? Property tax exemptions can be an extra benefit in retirement, but if you're planning a move, you'd do well to put other considerations, such as energy cost and house prices, first.

Deferrals

Seventeen states allow older persons to legally postpone payment of all or part of their property taxes. In property tax deferral programs, the state pays the tax for the retired homeowner and puts a lien on the property, secured by its sale value. Generally, below-market interest is charged each year on the amount postponed. The tax-deferral loan comes due when the home is sold, given away, or when the owner dies, in which case the heirs or estate must pay what's due.

California	North Dakota
Colorado	Oregon
Florida	Tennessee
Georgia	Texas
Illinois	Utah
Iowa	Virginia
Massachusetts	Washington
Michigan	Wisconsin
New Hampshire	

A SINGLE-HOUSE MISCELLANY

Each year, the Federal Housing Authority reports on the characteristics of existing single-family homes whose mortgages it insures. Here's a geography of nine of these features.

Lot Size. Imagine a house lot with 85 feet of frontage and 100 feet of depth. The 8,500 square feet it encloses is the average lot size for a resale house in the United States. Resale houses sitting on lots over half an acre (21,780 square feet) are more frequently found in Connecticut, Georgia, Maine, New Hampshire, and North Carolina than in the other states.

Construction and Exterior. In frame construction, the wood frame supports the floors and roof; in masonry construction, the exterior masonry wall serves as the support. Except in the Texas Interior, masonry construction using local stone has virtually disappeared in new houses. Concrete-block masonry construction, however, is a common technique in Arizona and Florida, where either spray-paint or stucco is used on the exterior. Everywhere else, the majority of new houses are of frame construction.

Aluminum siding is the preferred exterior in Maryland and Ohio; wood is the choice in Georgia, Maine, Massachusetts, New Hampshire, and Washington. Exteriors of brick or stucco are preferred in California, Louisiana, Nevada, Oklahoma, South Carolina, and Texas.

Stories. The word *story* originally referred to tiers of stained-glass or painted windows that described a special event. The common definition today is "the space between the floor and the ceiling, roof, or the floor above, in the case of a multistory home." It has nothing to do with the height of a house; a house that appears from the outside to be two stories may actually be a single story with a cathedral ceiling. Two-thirds of existing houses in this country have only one story. However, in Arizona, California, Florida, Louisiana, Mississippi, New Mexico, Oklahoma, and Texas single-story houses constitute more than 90 percent of resale homes. Multistory resale homes, on the other hand, predominate in the District of Columbia, Maine, Maryland, Massachusetts, New Jersey, New York, and Pennsylvania.

Basements. The basement is an area of full-story height below the first floor that is not meant for year-round living. Only 15 percent of new houses have basements; they've become too expensive to excavate.

In seven states, however, two out of three resale houses have a full basement, reflecting a pattern of locating the furnace below grade and a preference for extra living space. These states are Connecticut, Iowa, Maine, Massachusetts, Minnesota, New Hampshire, and Wisconsin.

Most resale houses have no basements at all. More than two-thirds of the houses in Arizona, Florida, Louisiana, Mississippi, New Mexico, and Texas simply rest on a concrete slab poured on the ground. In Alabama, Arkansas, North Carolina, Oregon, South Carolina, and Tennessee, a majority of existing houses have a crawl space (an unfinished accessible space below the first floor that is usually less than full-story height).

Bathrooms. Bathrooms are either full (a tub or shower stall, a sink, and a toilet) or half (just a sink and toilet). Just one of five resale homes have both a full bathroom and a half bathroom. In Hawaii, Mississippi, New Hampshire, New Mexico, North Carolina, and South Carolina, however, more than one-third of resale homes have both full and half bathrooms.

Garages and Carports. Garages, as everyone knows, are completely enclosed shelters for automobiles; carports are roofed shelters that aren't completely enclosed. Six out of 10 houses, new and old, have garages; one in 10 has only a carport. Only in Arizona, Hawaii, Louisiana, and Mississippi is this pattern reversed.

Fireplaces. Flueless, imitation fireplaces, like dinettes and rumpus rooms, are memories of the 1950s. Nearly half of new American homes now have a working fireplace and chimney. Resale homes with a fireplace can be found most frequently in the northern timber states of Idaho, Minnesota, Montana, Oregon, and Washington, and also in North Carolina and Pennsylvania.

Swimming Pools. You won't find new houses built on speculation with in-ground swimming pools anywhere. Builders have learned that few buyers shop for shelter *and* a swimming pool at the same time. Among resale homes, less than two percent have them. You're most likely to find them in Arizona, California, Nevada, and surprisingly, Maine and New York.

Enclosed Porches. A porch is a covered addition or recessed space at the entrance of a home. These Main Street lookouts have disappeared from new home markets. You'll find enclosed porches on eight percent of resale homes in this country. In Connecticut, Iowa, Maine, Massachusetts, New Jersey, and New York, more than 20 percent of these homes have them.

Resale Houses and New Houses

If a single, detached house is your preference, consider the pluses and minuses of resale houses versus new houses.

In most markets, resale homes are less expensive than equivalent new homes and are available in broader price ranges, with more architectural styles and loca-

Annual Home Price Appreciation

Prices have dropped in . . .	By . . .
Amherst–Northampton, MA	–10%
Fredericksburg, TX	–10
Portsmouth–Dover–Durham, NH	–10
Cape Cod, MA	–9
Austin, TX	–8
Albuquerque, NM	–5
New Paltz–Ulster County, NY	–5
West Palm Beach–Boca Raton–Delray Beach, FL	–5
Colorado Springs, CO	–2
Athens–Cedar Creek Lake, TX	–2

Prices have increased in . . .	By . . .
Bellingham, WA	15%
Easton–Chesapeake Bay, MD	15
Grass Valley–Truckee, CA	15
Las Vegas, NV	15
Newport–Lincoln City, OR	15
Olympia, WA	15
Salinas–Seaside–Monterey, CA	15
Santa Rosa–Petaluma, CA	15
Twain Harte–Yosemite, CA	15
Port Townsend, WA	16
San Diego, CA	18
Redding, CA	20
Naples, FL	23
Chico–Paradise, CA	25
San Juan Islands, WA	25
South Lake Tahoe–Placerville, CA	26
Bend, OR	35
Maui, HI	40

Source: Century 21 Real Estate Corporation survey for Places Rated Partnership, May 1990.

tions in town. Resale homes usually have had their minor defects, often unforseen when the home was new, corrected by the seller. But the age of the structure may signal problems. Repairs to the roof, floor coverings, appliances, and mechanical systems, which have depreciated over the years, may be necessary during the first two years you own the house. More importantly, as a neighborhood matures, some homes are maintained better than others and price disparities develop, which can affect your own home's value.

New houses in new, homogeneous neighborhoods portend more rapid appreciation in value over equivalent resale houses. You can have a new house covered by an extended homeowner warranty to protect you from major structural defects. If timing permits, you also can "customize" the house with options and extras and have the opportunity to select colors, appliance brands, and technological features such as heating and air-conditioning systems. But the drawback to new homes in many communities is their 10 to 20 percent price premium over equivalent resale homes.

Buying a new home is more complicated, too, since many more decisions have to be made about finish details and landscaping, all of which may mean frequent site visits to confer with the builder.

Duplexes

If you're a first-time investor considering a home for rental income, a duplex (a house divided into apart-ments for two households) often is a better buy than a single house because of a better relation between price and income. A duplex might be bought for eight to 10 times its annual rental income, where a single house might cost 13 to 15 times what it could bring in rent.

You might consider buying a duplex, renting one of the apartments, and occupying the other yourself. This is particularly attractive in college towns. From Ann Arbor, Michigan, to State College, Pennsylvania, college towns have more rental properties and renters than other retirement places. Aside from the income and depreciation you would have from the rental unit, if you live alone, congenial tenants—perhaps a graduate student and family—can watch the house should you want to do some traveling. You can also trade lower rent for maintenance help.

A MOBILE-HOME MISCELLANY

According to Foremost Insurance Company surveys, the average age of a mobile-home owner is climbing past middle age, and persons over 60 now comprise 35 percent of the market. Mobile homes made up one-third of all new housing purchased in the United States last year. Living in one makes sense if you are on a limited budget. It also presents two major problems: (1) this type of housing doesn't appreciate in value everywhere, and (2) owners are subject to sometimes arbitrary eviction from mobile-home parks.

Are Mobile Homes Investments?

Whether real estate salespeople tout houses, condos, townhouses, or mobile homes, they've all learned the five factors that influence price tags: quality of original construction, the neighborhood's turnover rate, supply and demand for housing, current upkeep, and location.

With these factors at work in the housing market, mobile homes, like automobiles, tend to go down in value as they get older. According to the American Institute of Real Estate Appraisers, the typical mobile home in a typical park depreciates 10 percent the first year and between five and six percent each year thereafter.

This isn't the case in all parts of the country. In seven states, all but two of them in the West, mobile homes appreciated at a modest annual rate, according to a survey from the Foremost Insurance Company. These states are Alaska, Arizona, California, Florida, New Jersey, Oregon, and Washington. In the central states, values kept pace with new home costs. In the eastern third of the country, however, mobile homes declined in value from the moment they were first winched onto a permanent pad.

Do mobile homes make good investments?

Yes, if you want to live in Florida, New Jersey, Arizona, or the Pacific Coast states but can't afford to buy a house or a condominium in the competitive real estate markets there. While the appreciation in mobile homes lags behind that of conventional houses, you still have a good chance to make money when you sell.

Perhaps, if you have your sights set on a destination in the Rocky Mountain states, the Ozarks, northern Michigan, or Texas but can't afford conventional housing. Search carefully for a well-managed park near popular resorts or natural outdoor endowments.

No, if you're headed for the southeastern states, Pennsylvania, New York, or New England and have enough money to buy conventional housing. Mobile homes here have a history of depreciating when prices for existing site-built homes have gone up.

Tenant Rights for Mobile-Home Owners

Except in New Mexico, the Uniform Residential Landlord and Tenant Act doesn't protect mobile-home owners who rent space in a mobile-home park. In most states, a park owner can evict you for any reason. The park owner rarely gives leases and can demand sharp rent increases and a variety of costly fees once you've spent money moving your mobile home to the park. You may be forced to sell at a loss if the park owner tells you to get out and no other park has space for your home.

Twelve states have passed "just cause" laws to protect mobile-home owners from being arbitrarily evicted from mobile-home parks, according to a survey by the American Mobilehome Association. Just causes for eviction include nonpayment of rent, being tried and convicted of a crime, violation of reasonable park rules, or conversion of park land to other uses. The states are:

Arizona	Oregon
California	New Jersey
Colorado	New Mexico
Florida	New York
Illinois	Utah
Nevada	Washington

A CONDO MISCELLANY

Condominiums are pushed to people making their way out of the rental market and older persons drawn to maintenance-free living at a lower cost, often in adults-only developments. While the construction boom has faded in certain parts of the country, the fact that condominiums account for 15 percent of all new housing units since 1970 certainly vouches for their appeal.

Ten Negatives

The complaints reported by the Urban Land Institute 20 years ago in an extensive survey of condominium residents are still being raised today. Among them are:

* noisy children and undesirable neighbors
* pets
* parking problems
* poor association management
* ticky-tacky construction
* dishonest salespeople
* renters in other units
* thin party walls
* long rows of identically designed houses
* unneeded and overpromoted recreation facilities

If you are thinking of condominium living in your retirement, these complaints are a guide to judging condominium developments. Ask questions of the association and the broker. What are the restrictions on pets? Children? How are they enforced? Does each unit have an assigned parking space? Are there rules in the association's bylaws limiting the number of rental units? What is the average tenure of the unit owners? Of the renters? Are any units set aside for time shares? Is their number restricted?

As a retired person, you are one of the two major targets of condominium marketing. The other is the young person or family buying their first home. Both groups want lower costs, freedom from house and yard maintenance in a ready-made environment, social life, and recreation facilities, all with the tax advantages of ownership. There isn't any reason the two groups can't live together harmoniously in the same development. In well-managed condominiums they do. But in other developments, the mix can prove unhappy.

Legal Protection for Condo Buyers

Many state legislatures recognize that consumers have little protection at the point of purchasing a condominium. Eleven states have enacted comprehensive statutes to deal with condominium ownership based on the Uniform Condominium Act (1980) drawn up by the National Conference of Commissioners on Uniform State Laws. The states are:

Maine	North Carolina
Minnesota	Pennsylvania
Missouri	Rhode Island
Nebraska	Virginia
New Hampshire	Washington
New Mexico	

The act covers owners' associations, developers' activities, eminent domain, separate titles and taxation, and safeguards for condominium buyers. Among its provisions are:

* The developer must provide you with a Public Offering Statement, accurately and fully disclosing a schedule for completion of all construction, the total number of condominium units, the bylaws of the owners' association, copies of any contracts or leases that you must sign, a current balance sheet and projected one-year budget for the owners' as-

sociation, and a statement of the monthly common assessments you'll have to pay.

- After signing a purchase agreement, you still have 15 days to cool off, after which you can either cancel the agreement without penalty or accept conveyance of the property.
- If you buy a condominium without first being given the Public Offering Statement, you are entitled to receive from the developer an amount equal to 10 percent of the sales price of the unit you bought.
- The developer and real estate agent must guarantee that the unit you are buying is free from defective materials, is built according to sound engineering and construction standards, and conforms to local codes.

CAVEAT EMPTOR: SUBDIVISION LOTS

Every year real estate developers ring up billions of dollars in interstate land sales. During the 1970s, one of the results of this lucrative business was to leave one million Americans with real estate they didn't want and couldn't sell. Many of these buyers who found themselves holding title to swampland or desert were retired persons looking for a spot to put up a vacation home or permanent residence.

Buying out-of-state land is always risky, especially if the buyer doesn't visit the property. Even if you do see the homesite before buying, it may be very difficult to be sure the developer will actually follow through on promised amenities. The slick promotional brochure will describe golf courses, landscaped parks, swimming pools, clubhouses, and marinas, but any promise not clearly outlined in the sales contract isn't enforceable. What you consider to be a sound retirement investment may turn out to be no more of a sure thing than your prospects at the $2 window at the track.

"You can always resell your lot if you change your mind," the salesperson will tell you. "In fact, the developer will buy it back from you." What is not revealed is that the price you are paying for the lot has already inflated to nearly twice its real value to cover the advertising and other initial sales costs. Where do you suppose the money comes from for the fancy literature, the gourmet dinners fed to prospective buyers, the free trips often proffered to hot prospects who want to see what they're buying? Right out of that earnest money you're about to write a check for, that's where! So even if you do successfully resell your lot, you may take a heavy loss on the transaction.

A Land Buyer's Rights

Federal legislation amended in 1984 to protect the land buyer applies to brokers and developers who subdivide land into 100 or more lots and sell or advertise them in more than one state. Some of the provisions arc:

- The buyer has seven calendar days to back out of any sales agreement. A legal or legitimate reason isn't necessary for cancellation.
- A buyer who fails to receive a property report before signing a purchase agreement may cancel the agreement up to two years from the time of signing.
- A buyer who doesn't receive a warranty deed within 180 days of signing a purchase agreement may, in most cases, cancel the agreement.
- Buyers who legally revoke their contracts are entitled to a refund.
- For a period up to three years after signing the purchase contract, the buyer may sue the seller if he:

  Sells property without giving the property report to the buyer before he signs the contract.

  Sells any property when the property report contains any false facts or omits a material fact.

  Provides or distributes promotional material that is inconsistent with material in the property report.

AN APARTMENT MISCELLANY

The kind of apartment building you choose to live in definitely makes a difference in your monthly costs. In larger cities where apartments are a significant part of the housing mix, rents for a typical four-room, 850-square-foot unit are higher in high-rise elevator buildings (U.S. median $541) than in walk-ups or elevator buildings of three stories or fewer (U.S. median $480), according to the latest Institute of Real Estate Management survey. The least expensive kind of building is the garden apartment, defined as a group of low-rise apartment buildings on a large landscaped lot under one manager. The national monthly rental for this kind of building is $400.

You'll find the annual turnover rate, defined as newly occupied apartments as a percentage of all the apartments in the building in a year's time, also varies by the kind of building. Around the country, high-rise elevator buildings have the lowest turnover rate (U.S. median 31 percent), whereas the turnover rate in walk-ups and elevator buildings of three or fewer stories is half again that rate (U.S. median 46 percent). The kind of apartment building with the most transient population is the garden apartment, in which 74 percent of the tenants moved in within the previous 12 months.

The Rule of 156

One useful way of determining the rent for a house is to divide its market value by 156. Using this rule plus

Apartment Rent in the Retirement Places

LOWEST	Typical Rent
Harrison, AR	$280
Paris–Big Sandy, TN	$280
Fredericksburg, TX	$300
Grand Lake, OK	$300
Deming, NM	$320
Edenton–Albemarle Sound, NC	$320
Houghton Lake, MI	$320
Eagle River, WI	$330
Crossville, TN	$340
Lakeland–Winter Haven, FL	$340
Thomasville, GA	$340

HIGHEST	Typical Rent
Honolulu, HI	$1,280
Carson City–Minden, NV	$1,040
Maui, HI	$960
San Luis Obispo, CA	$960
Santa Barbara, CA	$960
Cape Cod, MA	$880
Hanover, NH	$880
Key West–Key Largo–Marathon, FL	$880
Burnet–Marble Falls–Llano, TX	$800
Madison, WI	$800
Reno, NV	$800
Santa Fe, NM	$800

Source: Century 21 Real Estate Corporation survey for Places Rated Partnership, May 1990.

the prices of houses given in the Place Profiles, it isn't difficult to figure roughly what it would cost you to rent a house in a given retirement area, assuming that the landlord has realistic expectations for the rate of return on property.

In Honolulu, the rent would be about $1,200; in Cape Cod, $1,100; in Roswell, New Mexico, $460. The rule of 156 may seem unfair to landlords, since there is only an eight percent return from which maintenance and taxes must be paid. Bear in mind, however, that landlords rarely buy houses for the rental income they may bring; rather, they buy them for their market appreciation and rent them during the interim merely to cover expenses.

Renters' Legal Rights

Nineteen states have enacted landlord–tenant laws based on the Uniform Residential Landlord and Tenant Act (1972), a piece of model legislation drawn up by the National Conference of Commissioners on Uniform State Laws. These states are:

Alaska	Nebraska
Arizona	New Mexico
Connecticut	Oklahoma
Florida	Oregon
Hawaii	Rhode Island
Iowa	South Carolina
Kansas	Tennessee
Kentucky	Virginia
Michigan	Washington
Montana	

The landlord–tenant act defines rights and obligations of both parties to a lease on an apartment or house, and it also specifies the way disputes can be resolved. Among its provisions are the following:

- If your dispute with a landlord leads you to complain to the local housing board, join a tenants' group, or bring suit against the landlord, your landlord may not retaliate by cutting services, raising your rent, or evicting you.
- If the landlord doesn't make needed repairs, and the cost of the repairs isn't more than $100 or half the rent, whichever is greater, you may make repairs and deduct the expense from your monthly rent.
- After you vacate the apartment or house, any money you've deposited as security must be returned. If there are any deductions from the deposit for damages or other reasons, these deductions must be itemized.
- If the landlord doesn't live up to the terms of the lease, you may recover damages in small-claims court.

Climate

"The fortunate people of the planet," John Kenneth Galbraith wrote years ago in *Harper's*, "are those who live by the seasons. There is far more difference between a Vermont farm in the summer and that farm in the winter than there is between San Diego and São Paulo. This means that people who live where the seasons are good and strong have no need to travel; they can stay at home and let change come to them. This simple truth will one day be recognized and then we will see a great reverse migration from Florida to Maine and on into Quebec."

Galbraith's forecast might cause many a white-shoed Sun Belt real estate promoter to sit up and say "Huh?" They can relax, however. The migration to the sun will continue, demographers predict, until well into the 21st century. So, what else is new? Americans say they prefer mild, sunny climates, and when asked where in the country these climates are, they point to the fast-growing lower half of the Pacific Coast, Florida, and anywhere along the South Atlantic and Gulf coasts. Certainly this area, between 25 and 35 degrees latitude, has been drawing older adults for decades.

But other places north of the Mason–Dixon line and hundreds of miles from ocean beaches benefit from retirement growth, and many of these enjoy

mild climates, too. Some of these places might surprise you.

What has always been surprising is the enormous variety of global climates found right here at home. Northern maritime, extremely mild Mediterranean, southerly mountain, lowland desert, tropical "paradise," desert highland, rugged northern continental, windward slope, leeward slope, and humid subtropical climates—you name it, you'll meet up with it somewhere in the United States.

Climate is a part of your circumstances that can't be bought, built, remodeled, or relocated. A place's climate is there for keeps, and the weather events that make up a place's climate—rain, snow, heat, cold, drought, wind—will have a profound effect on the rest of your life.

FIVE FACTORS TO KEEP IN MIND

If you can live anywhere you wish and are open to all the variety this country offers, know that a combination of water, latitude, elevation, prevailing winds, and mountains lies behind any area's climate.

Water, particularly an ocean, takes the edge off temperature. It warms up slowly, holds much more heat than land, and cools more slowly. Places on the water tend to be cooler in summer and warmer in winter than others away from water. The hottest it gets in July on the Santa Monica Pier in Los Angeles is 75 degrees Fahrenheit; meanwhile, 15 miles north in the San Fernando Valley, it's 95. Golfers in the suburbs west of Boston store their clubs from Thanksgiving till the onset of Spring; golfers 45 miles southeast on Cape Cod, with water on three sides, can play almost all year round.

Places located in the country's heartland see wide swings of temperature. These continental climates tend to be even more rigorous in the higher *latitudes*. The closer to the poles you get, the more exaggerated are the seasonal shifts because polar and very northerly locations undergo the greatest seasonal variation in the amount and intensity of sunlight. In Fairbanks, Alaska, for example, the average day in December is only 4 hours long. In late June, the day has lengthened to 18 hours and the sun's heat is intense. Places in the North and Far North, then, experience Siberian winters and sun-baked summers.

Though some medical studies show reduced odds of heart disease and cancer the higher one lives above sea level, higher *elevations* can have the same negative effect on comfort as higher latitudes. Each 1,000 feet above sea level lowers a thermometer reading by 3.3 degrees Fahrenheit. In New Mexico, for example, there are just 3 degrees difference in annual average temperature between two weather stations at similar elevations, one in the extreme northeast and the other in the extreme southwest. However, at two weather stations just 15 miles apart, but differing in elevation by 4,700 feet, the average annual temperatures differ by 16 degrees.

In the United States, places that combine high altitudes with southerly latitudes get the best of both worlds, enjoying the mild, short winters of the South and the cooler nights and crisp falls of the North. Asheville, Brevard, and Hendersonville in the southern Appalachian Mountains, and Los Alamos and Santa Fe in the mountains of the Southwest have long been known for their mild, four-season climates.

To understand how *prevailing winds* influence climate, consider a pair of places 3,200 miles apart: Port Townsend, Washington, and Bar Harbor–Frenchman Bay, Maine. Both are at similar northern latitudes. Both, in their respective ocean settings, peek through some of the foggiest mornings in the United States.

You'd naturally suppose the two have similar climates. But Port Townsend is milder because of the winds that blow from west to east across the continent. The West Coast is a landfall for air that has moved thousands of miles over water; cities even far inland still feel some of the beneficial effects of the Pacific winds. Interior cities in the East feel few consequences of the Atlantic save on those rare occasions when the prevailing wind direction turns. Sad to say, this reversal of wind direction often means a storm.

Mountain ranges act as giant barriers, deflecting and channeling winds, rain, and snow. Mountain people aren't relating folk tales when they tell visitors that the weather on one side of a mountain range is often radically different from that on the other. In winter, for example, the Great Divide shields Colorado Springs from much of the bitter cold air that moves down the continent from the Arctic. Because of this, mountain ranges are natural dividing points between climate zones.

AMERICA'S MAJOR CLIMATE REGIONS

Mountains indeed mark the seven major climate regions of the continental United States. The Pacific Coast is quite mild, and the northern portion of the Great Interior quite rigorous. The Intermountain Plateau lying between the Cascade–Sierra Nevada range to the west and the Rocky Mountains to the east is noted for its dryness. Some of the best climates for variety and mildness are found in the southern portion of this area. The southern half of the Appalachian Mountains region also offers climates both mild and variable.

Most Americans live in the large climatic zone that includes the Great Interior, Southern Plains, and Lowlands regions. Ironically, this zone also happens to be the least desirable for human comfort. Those who live in its northern part are plagued by severe winters and hot, humid summers with springs and autumns that are all too short. In the southern portion, winters are mild and springs and autumns are longer, but the steam-bath summers are uncomfortable. The climate of the East Coast is similar to that of the Great Interior, but milder and somewhat damper. Right on the coast, winters are milder and summers noticeably cooler. Several retirement places with excellent climates are here, notably New Jersey's Cape May and Ocean counties, Ocean City–Assateague Island in Maryland, and Rehoboth Bay–Indian River Bay in southern Delaware.

The high country that includes the Rockies, the Cascades, the Sierra Nevadas, and the northern half of the Appalachians is home to resort areas owing to the cool, crisp, sunny summers with cold nights and winters that provide plenty of snow for outdoor sports. Several places in the valleys of these mountains are popular with older adults who prefer a stimulating yet not too mild climate.

The Alaskan climate varies from bitterly cold in the northern tundra area—one-fifth of the state lies north of the Arctic Circle—to relatively mild (for Alaska) temperatures on the southern coast, which sees abundant rainfall.

Hawaii is the only state situated in the tropical zone, officially defined as any area where temperatures don't drop below 64 degrees. These islands experience small temperature changes, with summer

Climate Regions of the United States

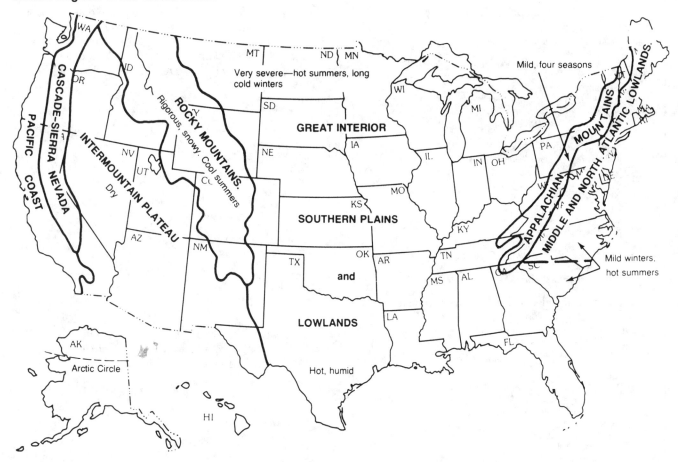

averaging only 4 to 8 degrees higher than winter. Moisture-bearing trade winds from over the Pacific provide a system of natural ventilation for the heat associated with these tropical climates.

SO, WHAT'S COMFORTABLE?

Mop the sweat from pulling a balky lawnmower's starter cord a dozen times on a July afternoon, hack away at the ice on the car's windshield one morning in January, or look out the window on any wet and gray day and you're forgiven for fantasizing about a place where it's never hot or cold and always bright.

It is a fantasy, indeed. Not only would you likely get bored with an endless sequence of identically dry, sunny days with tepid temperatures, you'd also find that none of the places profiled here have climates that match this mythical pattern 365 days a year. Because the thermometer is the most useful instrument for telling how comfortable you might be outdoors, however, *Retirement Places Rated* considers air temperature in rating climate.

Temperature

Beware of chamber of commerce blandishments about a place's annual average temperature. San Francisco's is 57 degrees. So is St. Louis's. But San Francisco enjoys both a diurnal (24 hour) temperature range of 12 degrees and an annual range (the difference between January's and July's average temperatures) of 12 degrees. St. Louis has a diurnal range of 17 degrees and an annual range of 47. The temperature swings in these two cities highlight the difference between a marine climate and a continental climate. San Francisco's climate is somewhat cool and remarkably stable year-round. St. Louis's is neither.

Among retirement regions, the greatest annual temperature ranges (up to 77 degrees) are found in the North Woods, the Rocky Mountains, and northern parts of New England. The greatest diurnal temperature swings (up to 37 degrees) are in high desert parts of the Rio Grande and Desert Southwest regions. The smallest diurnal *and* annual temperature swings are in Hawaii and along the Pacific Coast.

More than any other climate variables, temperature—and temperature changes—influence comfort and daily activities. Many older adults readily adapt to wide temperature swings. Others, even if they are in excellent health, need a much longer time. "In rapid weather changes," noted the late bioclimatologist H. E. Landsberg, the human body sometimes "lags behind the events in its attempts to keep all factors in equilibrium. Thus, a person may always be a bit out

The Mildest Winters

Bradenton, FL
Brownsville–Harlingen, TX
Daytona Beach, FL
Fort Lauderdale–Hollywood–Pompano Beach, FL
Fort Myers–Cape Coral–Sanibel Island, FL
Gainesville, FL
Honolulu, HI
Key West–Key Largo–Marathon, FL
Lakeland–Winter Haven, FL
Maui, HI
McAllen–Edinburg–Mission, TX
Melbourne–Titusville–Palm Bay, FL
Miami–Hialeah, FL
Naples, FL
New Port Richey, FL
Ocala, FL
Orlando, FL
San Diego, CA
Sarasota, FL
St. Petersburg–Clearwater–Dunedin, FL
Vero Beach, FL
West Palm Beach–Boca Raton–Delray Beach, FL

These places experience fewer than 90 monthly degrees of variation from a high of 80 degrees Fahrenheit and low of 65 during December, January, and February.

The Mildest Summers

Ann Arbor, MI
Asheville, NC
Blacksburg, VA
Bloomington–Brown County, IN
Cape May, NJ
Charlottesville, VA
Crossville, TN
Hendersonville, NC
Iowa City, IA
Lake Lanier, GA
Lexington–Fayette, KY
Ocean City–Assateague Island, MD
Rehoboth Bay–Indian River Bay, DE
San Diego, CA
State College, PA

These retirement places experience fewer than 25 monthly degrees of variation from a high of 80 degrees Fahrenheit and low of 65 during June, July, and August.

The National Oceanic and Atmospheric Administration (NOAA) measures cloudiness during daylight hours. A day is *clear* if clouds form 0% to 30% of the sky cover, *partly cloudly* if clouds are 40% to 70% of the sky cover, and *cloudy* if clouds are 80% to 100% of the sky cover.

Clearest Places

	Clear Days
Yuma, AZ	246
Chico–Paradise, CA	219
Las Vegas, NV	216
Phoenix, AZ	214
Tucson, AZ	198
Las Cruces, NM	194
Red Bluff–Sacramento Valley, CA	176
Roswell, NM	176
Santa Rosa–Petaluma, CA	176
Grass Valley–Truckee, CA	175
Albuquerque, NM	172
Santa Fe, NM	172
Reno, NV	165
St. George–Zion, UT	153
San Diego, CA	150

Listed above are retirement places described in the Place Profiles with 150 or more days of clear, sunny skies in a normal year.

Cloudy Places

	Cloudy Days
Port Townsend, WA	246
Bellingham, WA	229
Oak Harbor–Whidbey Island, WA	229
San Juan Islands, WA	229
Olympia, WA	228
Hamilton–Bitterroot Valley, MT	213
Kalispell, MT	213
Newport–Lincoln City, OR	210
Charlevoix–Boyne City, MI	209
Petoskey–Straits of Mackinac, MI	209
Traverse City–Grand Traverse Bay, MI	209
Eugene–Springfield, OR	207
Bennington, VT	206
Burlington, VT	204

Listed above are places described in the Place Profiles with 200 or more cloudy days in a normal year.

of balance and not feel well even though he has no specific disease."

Bioclimatologists—scientists who study the connection between weather and health—generally agree that temperatures that don't fall far below 65 degrees Fahrenheit are ideal for outdoor work and play. Under that point, the body's metabolism is pressed to maintain its normal warm core temperature. Eventually, you either put on extra clothing or you go indoors. *Retirement Places Rated* fixes 65 degrees as a standard for mildness at the low end of the thermometer.

At the thermometer's upper end, 80 degrees marks an optimum. Under experimental conditions, a person lying nude in a dark room neither gains nor loses body heat if the dry air temperature is 86 degrees. At most locations in this country, however, an 80-degree air temperature indicates the point above which hu-

midity starts to increase felt heat up to and beyond normal 86-degree skin temperature. Just as the body works harder to maintain a warmer core temperature when the thermometer falls below 65 degrees, so also is it pressed to maintain a cooler core temperature when the thermometer rises above 80.

This 15-degree swing between a low of 65 and a high of 80 is a sufficiently stimulating daily temperature variation for many older adults. It means a cool point at night below which home heating may be necessary and a warm point during the day above which the human body starts to gain heat.

None of the 151 retirement places *exactly* matches this cool night–warm day cycle 365 days a year. However, if you count each degree of monthly mean temperature variation (from a low of 65 and a high of 80) during June, July, and August, the retirement places with the mildest summers may surprise you. San Diego and the Hawaiian Islands aside, these places are on the Atlantic Coast above Chesapeake Bay and in the country's interior.

What surprises no one are the places that experience mild winters. They make up a nearly all-Florida list. Certainly, places in the Sunshine State enjoy mild weather for most of the year. In the summer months, however, their weather turns hellish with high temperatures and humidity.

Humidity

After air temperature, humidity—the amount of moisture in the air—is the major factor in climatic comfort. As anyone who has suffered a hot, humid summer knows, humidity intensifies heat. A hot day that is humid is uncomfortable because the body's natural cooling process of evaporation is retarded.

But there is another reason damp air increases felt heat in the summertime. Just as warm air holds more moisture, so damp air holds heat better and longer. In hot, humid climates, heat is retained in the damp air even after the sunset, resulting in nights that are almost as hot as the days.

Again You Wonder, "What's Comfortable?"

Is all this statistical searching for the ideal year-round retirement climate merely an illusion, much like the quest for perfect health, an honest man, or the Holy Grail?

Perhaps it is. Thousands of retired persons living in Florida vacate during the Sunshine State's summers for a cottage on the Jersey Shore, the New England Coast, or a cabin in the southern Appalachians. Thousands of others shun the broiling Desert Southwest summers for Sierra or Rocky Mountain foothills. Still others, absolutely bored by the unvaryingly paradise-like climate in the Virgin Islands or Hawaii, head back to the mainland in search of four-season weather.

This migration isn't exclusively American. Older adults from northern Europe who live in Spain, southern Italy, Greece, or North Africa routinely pack up and return to their native country for a summer climate that's milder than the one on the Mediterranean coast.

Having acknowledged this, it is still possible to rate places that approach a climatic ideal by pointing to conditions that detract from maximum comfort. Please read on.

 SCORING: Climate

Mild won't always mean a winterless, perpetually Mediterranean climate; it is simply the absence of great variations or extremes of temperature. Older adults tend to be better off in comfortable, stable weather conditions than they are in climates that make large physiological demands and where radical weather changes come on quickly.

Retirement Places Rated defines milder climates as those whose monthly low temperatures remain closest to 65 degrees Fahrenheit coupled with monthly high temperatures of 80 degrees. Deviations from this comfort zone are negatives. Each place, then, starts with a base score of 1,000 from which points are subtracted according to the following indicators:

1. *Variation from a high of 80.* For each month of the year, one point is subtracted for each degree the average daily high temperature varies from 80 degrees. Miami–Hialeah, Florida, for example, loses points for summer months where the average daily high exceeds 80 degrees. Burlington, Vermont, loses 364 points for an 11-month stretch when the daily high is *under* 80.

2. *Variation from a low of 65.* The day's low temperature usually occurs in the early morn-

ing hours. For each month of the year, one point is subtracted for each degree the average daily low temperature varies from 65 degrees. Reno, Nevada, for example, loses 398 points; not only will you need blankets there most nights, you'll need to heat the bedroom, too.

SCORING EXAMPLES

Metropolitan Phoenix and all of Florida experience two climate types favored by many footloose older adults: desert and subtropical.

Phoenix–Tempe–Scottsdale, AZ (#53)

If Phoenix's summertime temperatures of 40 years ago were to have persisted today, the Arizona capital would be rated much higher by *Retirement Places Rated*'s standards for climate mildness.

According to climatologists at Arizona State University, afternoon high temperatures during June, July, and August have remained constant over the years, but low temperatures during those months are now eight degrees hotter than they were in 1948. These eight degrees make the difference between formerly bearable warm nights and currently oppressive hot ones. The change is due to a twelvefold increase in population since the end of World War II.

Long-time residents who recall the old desert-cowtown days blame the heat on humidity caused by evaporating surface water in backyard swimming pools, municipal fountains, man-made lakes, and winter vegetable irrigation in the Salt River Valley. Actually, atmospheric moisture hasn't changed much since the late 1940s.

According to ASU scientists, modern Phoenix, with a metropolitan population of 2.1 million persons, has all the characteristics of a classic *urban heat island:* (1) the ability of concrete and asphalt to absorb and store more radiant energy than natural vegetation and soil, (2) low winds, (3) man-made sources of heat, particularly the automobile, and (4) a persistent high-pressure cell that traps air pollution, creating a blanket effect.

Certainly, temperatures in the Valley of the Sun are mild most of the year. Catch a televised Phoenix Cardinals football game in November and you may wish you were there. The biggest comfort liability here, however, is an intense period from mid-May through September when temperatures rarely drop to 65 degrees at night and usually top 100 degrees during the day. The total monthly degrees of variation from a low of 65 and high of 80, almost all of it during the summer months, results in a loss of 336 points.

Florida (21 Retirement Places)

Climate is Florida's greatest natural resource. It permits winter vegetables, tropical fruits, and even gladioli and chrysanthemums to be grown almost all year, and it annually brings in billions of dollars from visitors fleeing a long, northern winter.

And it is the biggest factor behind the Sunshine State's explosive population growth. Summers here are long, warm, and humid enough to leave a heavy dew on cars each morning and patches of mold in unventilated closets. Winters, though subject to periodic invasions of cool to occasionally cold air from the north, are mild because of the southern latitude and also because no point in the state is more than 70 miles from an ocean beach.

Daily sea breezes temper the summer heat along the coast and as far inland as 30 miles. Afternoon thunderstorms occur about half of the days in summer everywhere but are frequently accompanied by a rapid 10 degree to 20 degree drop in temperature, resulting in comfortable weather for the rest of the day.

Though there may seem to be little climatic difference among places here, there is a geographic pattern to their climate ratings: stations on the lower coasts are warmer in winter and cooler in summer than coastal stations at a higher latitude and stations in the interior. Miami–Hialeah, Fort Lauderdale–Hollywood–Pompano Beach, and West Palm Beach–Boca Raton–Delray Beach—the three top-rated places in Florida—are on the lower East Coast where onshore winds passing over the Gulf Stream exert a warming influence in winter and a cooling influence in summer.

 **RANKINGS:** Climate

A retirement place's score for climate is based on two criteria for each month of the year: (1) its average daily high variation from 80 degrees Fahrenheit and (2) its average daily low variation from 65 degrees Fahrenheit. Because the principal source, the National Oceanic and Atmospheric Administration's (NOAA) *Local Climatological Data,* does not provide information for all of the 151 retirement places, the scores for some are calculated from NOAA's *Series 20* publications.

Places that receive tie scores get the same rank and are listed alphabetically. The retirement places described in detail in the Place Profiles are shown in boldface type.

Retirement Places from First to Last

Rank	Score	Rank	Score	Rank	Score
1. **Maui, HI**	925	Marathon, FL	838	19. Ocala, FL	796
2. **Honolulu, HI**	902	10. Melbourne–Titusville–		20. McAllen–Edinburg–Mission,	
3. **Miami–Hialeah, FL**	867	Palm Bay, FL	832	TX	793
4. Fort Lauderdale–Hollywood–		11. **Lakeland–Winter Haven, FL**	828	21. **St. Augustine, FL**	786
Pompano Beach, FL	861	12. **Orlando, FL**	825	22. Gainesville, FL	782
5. **West Palm Beach–**		13. New Port Richey, FL	817	23. **Rockport–Aransas Pass, TX**	780
Boca Raton–Delray Beach,		14. Bradenton, FL	816	24. **San Diego, CA**	773
FL	859	14. **St. Petersburg–Clearwater–**		25. **Fairhope–Gulf Shores, AL**	749
6. Naples, FL	846	**Dunedin, FL**	816		
6. Vero Beach, FL	846			26. **Brunswick–Golden Isles, GA**	747
8. **Fort Myers–Cape Coral–**		14. Sarasota, FL	816	27. **Biloxi–Gulfport–Pass**	
Sanibel Island, FL	838	17. **Daytona Beach, FL**	814	**Christian, MS**	742
8. **Key West–Key Largo–**		18. **Brownsville–Harlingen, TX**	810	28. **St. Tammany Parish, LA**	738

Rank	Score		Rank	Score		Rank	Score
29. Thomasville, GA	736		68. Salinas–Seaside–Monterey, CA	617		111. **Cape Cod, MA**	459
30. Pensacola, FL	734		70. Brevard, NC	615		112. Los Alamos, NM	457
31. Panama City, FL	730					113. Oak Harbor–Whidbey Island, WA	452
31. **San Antonio, TX**	730		70. **Hendersonville, NC**	615		114. Bellingham, WA	449
33. **Hilton Head–Beaufort, SC**	729		72. Harrison, AR	606		115. **Santa Fe, NM**	447
34. **Savannah, GA**	726		73. **Clayton, GA**	605			
35. **Austin, TX**	724		74. **Las Cruces, NM**	597		116. **Boise, ID**	446
			75. Grand Lake, OK	593		117. **Port Townsend, WA**	444
35. Fort Walton Beach, FL	724					118. Ann Arbor, MI	439
37. New Braunfels, TX	722		76. **Mountain Home–Bull Shoals, AR**	592		119. **State College, PA**	438
38. Fredericksburg, TX	721		76. **Murray–Kentucky Lake, KY**	592		120. San Juan Islands, WA	437
39. **Athens–Cedar Creek Lake, TX**	709		78. **Charlottesville, VA**	587			
40. **Charleston, SC**	708		79. Ocean City–Assateague Island, MD	584		121. Iowa City, IA	431
			80. Paris–Big Sandy, TN	581		122. Pike County, PA	430
41. **Southport, NC**	697					123. Carson City–Minden, NV	429
42. El Centro–Calexico–Brawley, CA	696		81. **St. George–Zion, UT**	580		124. New Paltz–Ulster County, NY	424
42. **Myrtle Beach, SC**	696		82. Fayetteville, AR	578		125. **Colorado Springs, CO**	410
44. **Kerrville, TX**	692		83. Benton County, AR	575			
44. **Tucson, AZ**	692		84. **Asheville, NC**	574		126. Amherst–Northampton, MA	406
			85. **Roswell, NM**	568		127. **Fort Collins–Loveland, CO**	405
44. **Yuma, AZ**	692					128. Canandaigua, NY	404
47. Burnet–Marble Falls–Llano, TX	685		86. Branson–Table Rock Lake, MO	566		129. Columbia County, NY	400
48. New Bern, NC	683		86. Rehoboth Bay–Indian River Bay, DE	566		129. **Reno, NV**	400
49. **Aiken, SC**	679		88. **Cape May, NJ**	563			
50. Canton–Lake Tawakoni, TX	676		89. Easton–Chesapeake Bay, MD	561		131. **Coeur d'Alene, ID**	397
			90. Deming, NM	560		132. **Bennington, VT**	371
51. San Luis Obispo, CA	672					133. **Bend, OR**	354
52. Edenton–Albemarle Sound, NC	665		91. Blacksburg, VA	555		134. Bar Harbor–Frenchman Bay, ME	346
53. **Phoenix–Tempe–Scottsdale, AZ**	664		92. **Lexington–Fayette, KY**	554			
54. Redding, CA	661		93. **Albuquerque, NM**	553		134. **Camden–Penobscot Bay, ME**	346
55. **Red Bluff–Sacramento Valley, CA**	655		94. **Clear Lake, CA**	543			
			94. Twain Harte–Yosemite, CA	543		136. Hamilton–Bitterroot Valley, MT	343
56. **Hot Springs National Park, AR**	652		96. Crossville, TN	534		137. Monticello–Liberty, NY	340
57. **Lake Lanier, GA**	644		97. Amador County, CA	533		138. **Madison, WI**	337
58. South Lake Tahoe–Placerville, CA	643		98. Grants Pass, OR	525		139. Hanover, NH	333
59. **Athens, GA**	642		99. Ocean County, NJ	518		139. Portsmouth–Dover–Durham, NH	333
60. Carlsbad–Artesia, NM	638		100. **Eugene–Springfield, OR**	515			
						141. **Burlington, VT**	324
61. **Virginia Beach–Norfolk, VA**	634		101. Martinsburg–Charles Town, WV	506		142. Door County, WI	321
62. **Chico–Paradise, CA**	629		102. **Lancaster County, PA**	497		143. Charlevoix–Boyne City, MI	316
63. **Las Vegas, NV**	628		103. Bloomington–Brown County, IN	493		143. **Petoskey–Straits of Mackinac, MI**	316
64. **Chapel Hill, NC**	626		104. **Medford–Ashland, OR**	492			
65. **Santa Rosa–Petaluma, CA**	625		104. Prescott, AZ	492		143. Traverse City–Grand Traverse Bay, MI	316
			106. **Newport–Lincoln City, OR**	487			
66. **Santa Barbara, CA**	623		107. **Grand Junction, CO**	469		146. **Keene, NH**	315
67. Lake Havasu City–Kingman, AZ	621		108. **Grass Valley–Truckee, CA**	465		147. Laconia–Lake Winnipesaukee, NH	314
68. Alamogordo, NM	617		109. Wenatchee, WA	464		148. **North Conway–White Mountains, NH**	307
			110. **Olympia, WA**	460		149. Houghton Lake, MI	285
						150. **Kalispell, MT**	263
						151. **Eagle River, WI**	261

 PLACE PROFILES: Climate

The following pages describe climate at weather stations in 81 retirement places. These places were chosen because they represent distinct parts of the country with distinct climate types, or because they embrace large numbers of retired persons, or both.

The data come from the National Oceanic and Atmospheric Administration (NOAA) series, *Local Climatological Data.* (Scores for most of the retirement places not included in the following profiles are calculated from NOAA's *Series 20* publications.)

The climate data presented in *Retirement Places Rated* are NOAA's "30-Year Normals" or averages collected over 3 decades. Every 10 years, the data for the new decade are added into the normal, and the data for the earliest 10 years are dropped to flatten out anomalies and weather extremes. Atypical events such as a freak blizzard in San Antonio or a heat wave that might occur once every 50 years in Coeur d'Alene have little effect on each place's 30-year normal.

These summaries describe each place's distinctive climate and terrain features. When terrain is described, it is usually how it influences a place's climate. Few people would deny that terrain is an important element on its own; for many, it is as important as climate. Some prefer mountains or seacoasts, others rolling hills or flatwoods forests, while still others favor stark desert vistas. Rather than rating terrain, *Retirement Places Rated* simply describes it briefly and lets you decide.

The table of average temperatures on the right-hand side of each profile gives you a clear idea of the monthly temperature ranges for each place. If you want to know how hot it gets in Albuquerque in July, for example, look at the table in Albuquerque's profile. In July the daily high temperatures (which usually occur in mid-afternoon) average 92 degrees Fahrenheit. That sounds hot, and it is. But look at the average daily low temperature (a point reached in the early morning) for the same month. It is 65 degrees. July in Albuquerque means hot days and cool nights. This fits New Mexico's largest city's dry, desert location and 5,314 foot elevation.

Rounding out each place's climate picture are data for relative humidity, wind speed, snowfalls and rainfalls, clear and cloudy days, storm days, very hot and very cold days, and precipitation days (days on which there is at least .01 inch of precipitation).

A unique graphic in each profile is the circular picture showing the length of the seasons. Seasonal change is best defined by weather conditions, human activities, and growth or dormancy of plant life rather than by the calendar. In *Retirement Places Rated* the seasons are defined as follows: Summer begins when the mean monthly temperature rises above 60 degrees Fahrenheit; summer ends when it falls below 60. Winter begins when the average daily low falls below 32 degrees and ends when it rises above that mark. The remaining portions of the year constitute fall and spring. In the seasonal graph, winter is the black segment, spring and fall appear as gray, and summer is white.

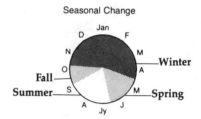

If you look at several of these seasonal graphs you'll see that the length of the seasons vary. Winter is a tiny sliver in Hot Springs and a full half circle in Colorado Springs. Some places have no four-season climates. Places along the Atlantic and Gulf coasts usually have only two—spring and summer. Some, like Miami–Hialeah, have only one—perpetual summer.

A star (★) preceding a place's name highlights it as one of the top 20 places for climate mildness.

Aiken, SC

Terrain: Aiken, county seat of South Carolina's Aiken County, lies across the Savannah River from Augusta, Georgia. The dividing line between the Piedmont Plateau and the Coastal Plain, known as the fall line, passes through the Savannah River basin in a northeast–southwest direction near here. The terrain is mainly flat, with low rise hills to the west.

Climate: Warm and mild, with occasional hot spells. In the winter, measureable snow is a rarity and remains on the ground only a short time. In 100 years of weather records, a temperature of zero or colder has never been reached. The growing season approaches 250 days, from mid-March to mid-November, although frosts have been reported as late as April 21 and as early as October 17.

Pluses: Very brief winters.   **Minuses:** Hot.

Elevation: 136 feet

Relative Humidity: 72%
Wind Speed: 6.6 mph

Seasonal Change

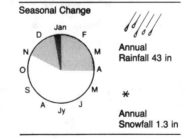

Annual Rainfall 43 in

*

Annual Snowfall 1.3 in

Clear 110 days   Partly Cloudy 107 days   Cloudy 148 days

Precipitation Days: 107 Storm Days: 55

Average Temperatures		
	Daily High	Daily Low
January	57	34
February	61	36
March	67	42
April	77	51
May	84	59
June	90	67
July	91	70
August	90	69
September	85	63
October	77	51
November	67	40
December	59	34

Zero-Degree Days: 0
Freezing Days: 59
90-Degree Days: 63

Score: 679   **Rank: 49**

Albuquerque, NM

Terrain: Rests in the Rio Grande Valley 55 miles southwest of Santa Fe, and is surrounded by mountains, most of them to the east. These mountainous areas receive more precipitation than does the city proper. With an annual rainfall of 8 inches, only the most hardy desert flora can grow. However, successful farming—primarily fruit and produce—is carried out in the valley by irrigation.

Climate: Arid continental. No muggy days. Half the moisture falls between July and September in the form of brief but severe thunderstorms. Long drizzles are unknown. These storms do not greatly interfere with outdoor activities and they have a moderating effect on the heat. The hottest month is July, with temperatures reaching 90° F almost constantly. However, the low humidity and cool nights make the heat much less felt.

Pluses: Sunny and dry, with mild winters.

Minuses: Dust storms.

Score: 553 **Rank: 93**

Elevation: 5,314 feet

Relative Humidity: 37%
Wind Speed: 9 mph

Seasonal Change

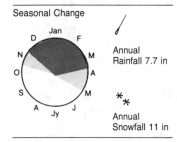

Annual Rainfall 7.7 in

Annual Snowfall 11 in

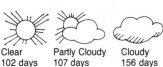

Clear 172 days   Partly Cloudy 111 days   Cloudy 82 days

Precipitation Days: 59   Storm Days: 43

Average Temperatures		
	Daily High	Daily Low
January	47	24
February	53	27
March	59	32
April	70	41
May	80	51
June	90	60
July	92	65
August	90	63
September	83	57
October	72	45
November	57	32
December	48	25

Zero-Degree Days: 1
Freezing Days: 123
90-Degree Days: 61

Asheville, NC

Terrain: Located on both banks of the French Broad River, near the center of the basin of the same name. Two miles upstream from Asheville, the Swannanoa River joins the French Broad River from the east. The entire valley is called the Asheville Plateau and is flanked on the east and west by mountain ranges. Thirty miles south, the Blue Ridge Mountains form an escarpment, with an average elevation of 2,700 feet. Tallest peaks near Asheville are Mount Mitchell (6,684 feet), 20 miles northeast, and Big Pisgah (5,721 feet), 16 miles southwest.

Climate: Temperate but invigorating. Considerable variation in temperature occurs from day to day throughout the year. The valley has a pronounced effect on wind direction, which is mostly from the northwest. Destructive weather events are rare. However, the French Broad Valley is subject to flooding, with especially high flooding occurring in 12-year cycles.

Pluses: Long spring, beginning early.

Minuses: Drizzly, flood-prone.

Score: 574 **Rank: 84**

Elevation: 2,207 feet

Relative Humidity: 59%
Wind Speed: 7.7 mph

Seasonal Change

Annual Rainfall 45 in

Annual Snowfall 18 in

Clear 102 days   Partly Cloudy 107 days   Cloudy 156 days

Precipitation Days: 128   Storm Days: 49

Average Temperatures		
	Daily High	Daily Low
January	48	27
February	51	28
March	58	34
April	69	42
May	77	51
June	83	59
July	84	63
August	84	62
September	78	55
October	69	45
November	58	34
December	49	28

Zero-Degree Days: 1
Freezing Days: 106
90-Degree Days: 5

Athens, GA

Terrain: Located in the Piedmont Plateau section of northeast Georgia. The land is rolling to hilly, with elevations ranging between 600 and 800 feet. The Atlantic Ocean 200 miles to the southeast, the Gulf of Mexico 275 miles to the south, and the southern Appalachian Mountains to the north and northwest, all exert some influence on the city's climate, resulting in moderate summer and winter weather.

Climate: Summers are warm and somewhat humid, but there is a noticeable absence of prolonged periods of extreme heat. The mountains to the north serve as a partial barrier to extremely cold airflows; as a result, the city's winters aren't severe. Cold spells are short-lived, interspersed with periods of warm southerly airflow, making normal outside activities possible throughout most of the year. Precipitation is evenly distributed during the year. Measurable amounts of snow occur infrequently.

Pluses: Mild winters.

Minuses: Humid summers, frequent serious dry spells.

Score: 642 **Rank: 59**

Elevation: 802 feet

Relative Humidity: 56%
Wind Speed: 7.4 mph

Seasonal Change

Annual Rainfall 50 in

Annual Snowfall 2 in

Clear 113 days   Partly Cloudy 105 days   Cloudy 147 days

Precipitation Days: 111   Storm Days: 52

Average Temperatures		
	Daily High	Daily Low
January	53	33
February	56	35
March	63	40
April	74	50
May	82	58
June	88	66
July	90	69
August	88	68
September	83	82
October	74	51
November	63	40
December	54	34

Zero-Degree Days: 0
Freezing Days: 54
90-Degree Days: 48

Athens–Cedar Creek Lake, TX

Terrain: Athens, seat of Henderson County, is located in the pine and post oak area of East Texas, about 70 air miles southeast of Dallas. The surrounding rolling to hilly terrain drains to the Neches River on the east and the Trinity River on the west. Cedar Creek Reservoir, 5 miles northwest, is one of the most popular recreation areas in the state. Nestled among the post oaks and pines, the lakes offer innumerable campsites, excellent fishing, swimming, and boating.
Climate: Humid subtropical, with hot summers. Rainfall is about 39 inches annually, evenly distributed. July and August, though, are somewhat dry. Winters are mild, with temperatures almost always rising above freezing in the daytime. No zero temperatures on record. Spring and fall are the best seasons, and are long. There are sufficient changes to make the weather interesting. The growing season is long (260 days); flowers bloom as late as December, as early as March.

Pluses: Mild winters, lovely springs and falls.

Minuses: Hot, humid summers.

Score: 709　　　　　　　　**Rank: 39**

Elevation: 490 feet

Relative Humidity: 68%
Wind Speed: 10.8 mph

Seasonal Change

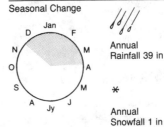

Annual Rainfall 39 in

Annual Snowfall 1 in

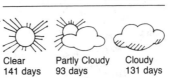

Clear 141 days　　Partly Cloudy 93 days　　Cloudy 131 days

Precipitation Days: 55　　Storm Days: 52

Average Temperatures		
	Daily High	Daily Low
January	58	36
February	63	41
March	69	46
April	79	56
May	85	63
June	91	69
July	96	72
August	96	71
September	90	66
October	81	56
November	70	47
December	62	40

Zero-Degree Days: 0
Freezing Days: 33
90-Degree Days: 95

Austin, TX

Terrain: Located on the Colorado River where it crosses the Balcones escarpment, which separates the Texas hill country from the blackland prairies of East Texas. Elevations within the city limits vary from 400 feet to 900 feet above sea level. Native trees include cedar, oak, walnut, mesquite, and pecan.
Climate: Subtropical. Although summers are hot, the nights are a bit cooler, with temperatures usually dropping into the 70s. Winters are mild, with below-freezing temperatures on fewer than 25 days; strong northers may bring cold spells, but these rarely last more than a few days. Precipitation is well distributed, but heaviest in late spring, with a secondary rainfall peak in September. With summer come heavy thunderstorms; in winter, the rain tends to be slow and steady. Snowfall (1 inch per year) is inconsequential. Prevailing winds are southerly. Destructive weather infrequent. Freeze-free season: 270 days. Average date of last freeze: March 3. First freeze: November 28.

Pluses: Mild winters.

Minuses: Hot.

Score: 724　　　　　　　　**Rank: 35**

Elevation: 570 feet

Relative Humidity: 56%
Wind Speed: 9.3 mph

Seasonal Change

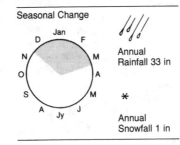

Annual Rainfall 33 in

Annual Snowfall 1 in

Clear 115 days　　Partly Cloudy 116 days　　Cloudy 134 days

Precipitation Days: 82　　Storm Days: 41

Average Temperatures		
	Daily High	Daily Low
January	60	39
February	64	43
March	71	48
April	79	58
May	85	65
June	92	71
July	95	74
August	96	74
September	89	68
October	81	59
November	70	48
December	63	42

Zero-Degree Days: 0
Freezing Days: 23
90-Degree Days: 101

Bend, OR

Terrain: Located along the western border of the Great Basin, near the center of the state. The Cascade foothills rise immediately west of the city and terrace upwards to crests of 10,000 feet about 10 miles away. The rolling plateau extends south and east from Bend into California, Nevada, and Idaho. To the north, the plateau is cut by canyons and drainage streams that feed into the Columbia River.
Climate: Bend has primarily the continental climate of the Great Basin. The mountains moderate the more extreme temperatures of summer. Precipitation is generally light (12 inches of rain annually as opposed to 60 inches to 100 inches on the coast!) because the high Cascades block the moisture-laden Pacific winds. Moderate days and cool nights characterize the climate here. Even in July the temperature may drop to freezing one night. There is, on the average, only one day per year with rainfall of an inch or more.

Pluses: Scenic terrain. Dry and mild, with cool nights.

Minuses: Large temperature shifts. Too dry for some.

Score: 354　　　　　　　　**Rank: 133**

Elevation: 3,599 feet

Relative Humidity: 45%
Wind Speed: 7 mph

Seasonal Change

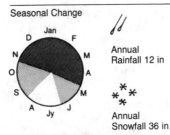

Annual Rainfall 12 in

Annual Snowfall 36 in

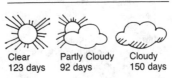

Clear 123 days　　Partly Cloudy 92 days　　Cloudy 150 days

Precipitation Days: 33　　Storm Days: 8

Average Temperatures		
	Daily High	Daily Low
January	41	21
February	46	24
March	50	24
April	57	28
May	65	34
June	73	40
July	82	44
August	80	43
September	74	37
October	63	31
November	49	26
December	43	23

Zero-Degree Days: 3
Freezing Days: 190
90-Degree Days: 11

Bennington, VT

Terrain: This historic city is nestled in the valley of the Walloomsac River, which is a part of the Hudson River drainage system. At 700 feet, it is surrounded by mountains. Mount Anthony (2,300 feet) is nearby to the southwest. A ridge of the Green Mountains, at a similar altitude, lies a few miles to the east. The terrain is more open to the west, though many hills rise to 1,000 feet between Bennington and the Hudson.

Climate: The surrounding mountains tend to modify the local climate, especially those to the east, which block some effects of the coastal storms, called "northeasters," which pass along the Atlantic Coast (125 miles distant). There are large differences of temperature, both daily and annually. Winters are cold and snowy, which accounts for the region's many fine ski resorts. Summers are very comfortable, with daytime temperatures in the 70s and low 80s and nighttime temperatures in the 50s.

Pluses: Beautiful summers. Scenic terrain. Great winter skiing.

Minuses: Long and fairly rigorous winters.

Score: 371 **Rank: 132**

Elevation: 670 feet

Relative Humidity: 55%
Wind Speed: 8.8 mph

Seasonal Change

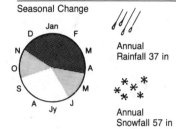

Annual Rainfall 37 in

Annual Snowfall 57 in

Clear 57 days
Partly Cloudy 102 days
Cloudy 206 days

Precipitation Days: 88   Storm Days: 25

Average Temperatures		
	Daily High	Daily Low
January	31	11
February	35	14
March	43	23
April	58	34
May	70	43
June	78	52
July	82	56
August	80	54
September	73	47
October	62	38
November	49	30
December	35	17

Zero-Degree Days: 17
Freezing Days: 166
90-Degree Days: 8

Biloxi–Gulfport–Pass Christian, MS

Terrain: In speaking of the Mississippi Gulf Coast, one usually thinks of the thickly settled area stretching from St. Louis Bay at Pass Christian to Biloxi Bay and Ocean Springs. This area is climatologically homogeneous, and a summary of any town (in this case, Biloxi–Gulfport) is applicable to the others. The terrain is flat, consisting of low-lying delta floodplains sloping down to sand beaches and rather shallow harbors and bays.

Climate: The Gulf waters have a modifying effect on the local climate that is not felt farther inland. Temperatures of 90° F or higher occur only half as often here as they do in Hattiesburg, 60 miles north. However, there is no such reverse effect on cold air moving down from the north in winter. Rainfall is plentiful and is heaviest in July, with totals in March and September following close behind. Damage from hurricanes and tropical storms can occur six to seven times a year.

Pluses: Warm, mild beach climate.

Minuses: Relatively chilly winters; hurricane-prone.

Score: 742 **Rank: 27**

Elevation: 15 feet

Relative Humidity: 65%
Wind Speed: 9.1 mph

Seasonal Change

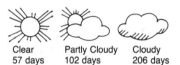

Annual Rainfall 59 in

Annual Snowfall 0 in

Clear 100 days
Partly Cloudy 119 days
Cloudy 146 days

Precipitation Days: 75   Storm Days: 94

Average Temperatures		
	Daily High	Daily Low
January	61	42
February	64	44
March	70	51
April	77	59
May	84	71
June	90	71
July	91	73
August	91	73
September	88	69
October	80	58
November	70	49
December	64	44

Zero-Degree Days: 0
Freezing Days: 11
90-Degree Days: 52

Boise, ID

Terrain: Cradled in the valley of the Boise River about 8 miles below the mouth of a mountain canyon, where this valley widens. The Boise Mountains rise to a height of 5,000 feet to 6,000 feet within 8 miles. Their slopes are partially mantled with sagebrush and chaparral, changing to stands of fir, spruce, and pine trees higher up.

Climate: Almost a typical upland continental climate in summer but one tempered by periods of cloudy or stormy and mild weather during almost every winter. The cause of this modification in the winter months is the flow of warm, moist Pacific air, called Chinook winds. While this air is considerably moderated by the time it reaches Boise, its effect is nonetheless felt. Summer hot spells rarely last longer than a few days, but temperatures may reach 100° F each year. However, due to the low humidity, the average 5:00 PM July temperature of 62° F is comfortable. In general, the climate is dry and temperate, with enough variation to be stimulating.

Pluses: Mild; low humidity.

Minuses: Stormy winters.

Score: 446 **Rank: 116**

Elevation: 2,868 feet

Relative Humidity: 52%
Wind Speed: 9 mph

Seasonal Change

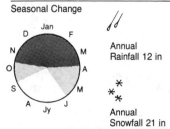

Annual Rainfall 12 in

Annual Snowfall 21 in

Clear 124 days
Partly Cloudy 90 days
Cloudy 151 days

Precipitation Days: 91   Storm Days: 15

Average Temperatures		
	Daily High	Daily Low
January	37	21
February	44	27
March	52	31
April	61	37
May	71	44
June	78	51
July	91	59
August	88	57
September	78	49
October	65	39
November	49	31
December	39	25

Zero-Degree Days: 2
Freezing Days: 124
90-Degree Days: 43

★ Brownsville–Harlingen, TX

Terrain: Situated at the extreme southern tip of Texas, on the Mexican border, and on the alluvial soils of the Rio Grande. The only more southerly city in America is Key West, Florida. The Gulf of Mexico is 18 miles to the east, and more than half the land toward the coast consists of tidal marshlands, which have the net effect of "moving" the coast 10 miles nearer to the city.

Climate: Humid subtropical. It's always summer here, accounting for the area's agricultural importance in growing citrus fruits, cotton, and warm-weather vegetables. Part of the climate is man-made: irrigation, used for all the crops, adds considerably to the humidity. Summer temperatures follow a predictable pattern of lower 90s in the day and middle 70s at night. Gulf breezes help temper the summer heat. This is a popular tourist spot in the winter months. The normal daily January minimum temperature is 51° F.

Pluses: Long growing season.   **Minuses:** Hot.

Score: 810   **Rank: 18**

Elevation: 20 feet

Relative Humidity: 61%
Wind Speed: 11.7 mph

Seasonal Change

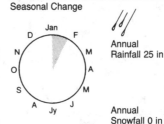

Annual
Rainfall 25 in

Annual
Snowfall 0 in

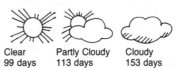

Clear   Partly Cloudy   Cloudy
96 days   138 days   131 days

Precipitation Days: 73   Storm Days: 24

Average Temperatures		
	Daily High	Daily Low
January	70	51
February	73	54
March	77	59
April	83	67
May	87	71
June	91	75
July	93	76
August	93	76
September	90	73
October	85	66
November	78	59
December	72	53

Zero-Degree Days: 0
Freezing Days: 2
90-Degree Days: 102

Brunswick–Golden Isles, GA

Terrain: The city of Brunswick, and neighboring St. Simons Island, which lies across the Intracoastal Waterway, are located on Georgia's southeast coast. Land surface is flat, and elevation averages from 10 feet to 15 feet. Much of the surrounding area is marshland. Fine beaches are plentiful. The low terrain and low latitude East Coast location of the area make it vulnerable to occasional tropical storms, though their full force is felt only infrequently.

Climate: The area enjoys mild and relatively short winters due to the moderating effect of coastal waters. There are only 11 days below freezing in the average winter, and no zero days. Summers are warm and humid, but very high temperatures are rare. Heat waves are usually interrupted by thundershowers, and even in the summer the nights are usually pleasant. Most of the annual 53 inches of rain falls in the summer and early autumn.

Pluses: Warm, mild climate with little temperature change.   **Minuses:** Can be hot and humid, with frequent rain.

Score: 747   **Rank: 26**

Elevation: 13 feet

Relative Humidity: 60%
Wind Speed: 8 mph

Seasonal Change

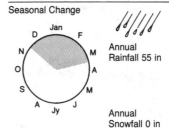

Annual
Rainfall 55 in

Annual
Snowfall 0 in

Clear   Partly Cloudy   Cloudy
99 days   113 days   153 days

Precipitation Days: 74   Storm Days: 72

Average Temperatures		
	Daily High	Daily Low
January	61	42
February	62	44
March	69	50
April	76	58
May	82	66
June	87	72
July	90	74
August	89	74
September	85	71
October	77	61
November	69	51
December	63	44

Zero-Degree Days: 0
Freezing Days: 11
90-Degree Days: 75

Burlington, VT

Terrain: Located on the eastern shore of Lake Champlain at the widest part of that lake. About 35 miles to the west lie the highest peaks of the Adirondacks; the foothills of the Green Mountains begin 10 miles to the east and southeast.

Climate: Burlington's northerly latitude assures the variety and vigor of a true New England climate. Lake Champlain, however, has a tempering effect; during the winter months, temperatures along the lakeshore often run from 5 degrees to 10 degrees warmer than those at the airport 3.5 miles away. The summer, while not long compared with most, is quite pleasant, with only four 90-degree days per year on the average. Fall is cool, extending through October. Winters are cold, with intense cold snaps (usually not lasting long) formed by high-pressure systems moving down from central Canada and Hudson Bay. Because of its location in the path of the St. Lawrence Valley storm track and the effects of the lake, Burlington is one of the cloudiest cities in the United States.

Pluses: Cool summers.   **Minuses:** Long, cold winters.

Score: 324   **Rank: 141**

Elevation: 340 feet

Relative Humidity: 60%
Wind Speed: 8.8 mph

Seasonal Change

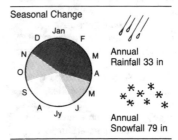

Annual
Rainfall 33 in

Annual
Snowfall 79 in

Clear   Partly Cloudy   Cloudy
58 days   103 days   204 days

Precipitation Days: 153   Storm Days: 25

Average Temperatures		
	Daily High	Daily Low
January	26	8
February	28	9
March	38	20
April	53	33
May	66	44
June	77	54
July	81	59
August	78	56
September	70	49
October	59	39
November	44	30
December	30	15

Zero-Degree Days: 28
Freezing Days: 163
90-Degree Days: 5

Camden–Penobscot Bay, ME

Terrain: Penobscot Bay lies at the mouth of the Penobscot River in the middle of Maine's seacoast. Although low-lying, the coastal terrain is very rugged and rocky in most places, allowing for hundreds of bays, islands, peninsulas, and harbors. Just to the northeast of Penobscot Bay lies the smaller Frenchman Bay, containing Mount Desert Island and Acadia National Park. Vegetation consists of evergreen coniferous trees, maple, birch, and scrub oak, and many marshes and ponds with cranberry bogs. Fruit orchards, truck farming, and fishing are the predominant coastal industries.

Climate: The Atlantic Ocean has a considerable modifying effect on the local climate, resulting in cool summers and winters that are very mild for so northerly a location. Though fall is generally mild, spring comes late and the weather isn't really warm until July.

Pluses: Cool summers. Winters relatively mild.

Minuses: Long winters. Cold, damp springs.

Score: 346　　　　　　　　**Rank: 134**

Elevation: 49 feet

Relative Humidity: 60%
Wind Speed: 8.7 mph

Seasonal Change

Annual Rainfall 47 in

Annual Snowfall 60 in

Clear 106 days　Partly Cloudy 98 days　Cloudy 161 days

Precipitation Days: 85　Storm Days: 21

Average Temperatures		
	Daily High	Daily Low
January	32	14
February	34	14
March	41	24
April	52	33
May	63	42
June	72	50
July	78	56
August	77	55
September	69	48
October	60	39
November	48	31
December	36	18

Zero-Degree Days: 11
Freezing Days: 152
90-Degree Days: 4

Cape Cod, MA

Terrain: Cape Cod is a crooked spit of land that juts out into the Atlantic Ocean from the southeastern corner of Massachusetts, stretching roughly 80 miles from the Cape Cod Canal (at Buzzards Bay) to its tip at Provincetown. The western end of the cape is higher and hillier than the eastern, or "outer cape," which is almost flat and treeless. The sandy soil, arranged in rolling hills and dunes, supports scrub oak and pine trees, while dune grasses and low trees grow on the outer cape.

Climate: Mild, cool, and maritime, with cool summers and cold, wet winters that are seldom severe. Summer temperatures are usually ideal for outdoor recreation. Both zero and 90° F days are very rare.

Pluses: Mild four-season climate, with long and pleasant falls.

Minuses: Winters wet and sleety. Summers can be damp and foggy.

Score: 459　　　　　　　　**Rank: 111**

Elevation: 35 feet

Relative Humidity: 60%
Wind Speed: 13 mph

Seasonal Change

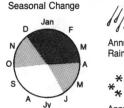

Annual Rainfall 43 in

Annual Snowfall 24 in

Clear 97 days　Partly Cloudy 114 days　Cloudy 154 days

Precipitation Days: 79　Storm Days: 14

Average Temperatures		
	Daily High	Daily Low
January	38	23
February	39	23
March	44	29
April	53	37
May	64	46
June	73	56
July	79	62
August	78	61
September	72	55
October	63	46
November	53	37
December	42	26

Zero-Degree Days: 1
Freezing Days: 115
90-Degree Days: 2

Cape May, NJ

Terrain: Located at New Jersey's southernmost point on a peninsula between the mouth of Delaware Bay and the Atlantic Ocean. The surrounding flat terrain is composed of tidal marshes and beach sand.

Climate: Continental, but the moderating influence of the Atlantic Ocean is apparent throughout the year. Summers are relatively cooler, winters warmer than those of other places at the same latitude. During the warm season, sea breezes in the late morning and afternoon prevent excessive heat. On occasion, sea breezes may lower the temperature between 15 degrees and 20 degrees within a half hour. Temperatures of 90° F or higher are recorded only about three times a year here. Fall is long, lasting until almost mid-November. On the other hand, warming is somewhat delayed in the spring. Ocean temperatures range from an average near 37° F in winter to 72° F in August. Precipitation is moderate and well distributed throughout the year, but great variation is seen from year to year in precipitation during the late summer and early fall (August, September, and October).

Pluses: Moderate temperatures.

Minuses: Late springs.

Score: 563　　　　　　　　**Rank: 88**

Elevation: 10 feet

Relative Humidity: 60%
Wind Speed: 11.4 mph

Seasonal Change

Annual Rainfall 46 in

Annual Snowfall 16 in

Clear 96 days　Partly Cloudy 108 days　Cloudy 161 days

Precipitation Days: 112　Storm Days: 25

Average Temperatures		
	Daily High	Daily Low
January	41	28
February	42	28
March	50	35
April	60	44
May	69	53
June	78	62
July	83	67
August	83	67
September	77	62
October	67	51
November	56	42
December	46	32

Zero-Degree Days: 1
Freezing Days: 15
90-Degree Days: 16

Chapel Hill, NC

Terrain: Situated in the transition zone between the Coastal Plain and the Piedmont Plateau of North Carolina. The surrounding topography is rolling, with elevations from 200 feet to 500 feet within a 10-mile radius.

Climate: Because it is located between mountains to the west and the Atlantic Coast to the east and south, the metro area enjoys a favorable climate. The mountains form a partial barrier to cold air masses moving eastward from the nation's interior, so that there are very few days in the heart of the winter when the temperature falls below 20° F. Tropical air is present over the eastern and central sections of North Carolina during much of the summer, bringing warm temperatures and high humidity. In midsummer, afternoon temperatures reach 90° F or higher on an average of every fourth day. Rainfall is well distributed throughout the year. July has, on the average, the greatest amount of rainfall, and November the least.

Pluses: Mild four-season climate.

Minuses: Long, humid summers.

Score: 626 **Rank: 64**

Elevation: 441 feet

Relative Humidity: 54%
Wind Speed: 7.9 mph

Seasonal Change

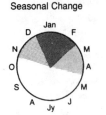

Annual
Rainfall 43 in

Annual
Snowfall 7 in

Clear
113 days

Partly Cloudy
107 days

Cloudy
145 days

Precipitation Days: 112 Storm Days: 46

Average Temperatures		
	Daily High	Daily Low
January	51	30
February	53	31
March	61	37
April	72	47
May	79	55
June	86	63
July	88	67
August	87	66
September	82	60
October	72	48
November	62	38
December	52	31

Zero-Degree Days: 0
Freezing Days: 82
90-Degree Days: 25

Charleston, SC

Terrain: Before the expansion began in 1960, Charleston was limited to the peninsula bounded on the west and south by the Ashley River, on the east by the Cooper River, and on the southeast by a spacious harbor that contains historic Fort Sumter. The terrain is generally level and the soil sandy to sandy loam. Because of the low elevation, a portion of the city and nearby coastal islands are vulnerable to tidal flooding.

Climate: Generally temperate, modified considerably by the ocean. Summer is warm and humid, but temperatures over 100° F are infrequent. Most rain—41% of the annual total—occurs then. The fall passes from an Indian summer to the prewinter cold spells that begin in November. From late September to early November, the weather is very pleasant, being cool and sunny. Winters are mild; temperatures of 20° F or less are very unusual. Spring is warm, windy, and changeable. Most storms occur then.

Pluses: Pleasant falls, mild winters.

Minuses: Hot, humid, stormy.

Score: 708 **Rank: 40**

Elevation: 48 feet

Relative Humidity: 56%
Wind Speed: 8.8 mph

Seasonal Change

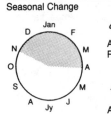

Annual
Rainfall 52 in

Annual
Snowfall .5 in

Clear
101 days

Partly Cloudy
113 days

Cloudy
151 days

Precipitation Days: 115 Storm Days: 56

Average Temperatures		
	Daily High	Daily Low
January	60	37
February	62	39
March	68	45
April	76	53
May	83	61
June	88	68
July	89	71
August	89	71
September	85	66
October	77	55
November	68	44
December	61	32

Zero-Degree Days: 0
Freezing Days: 36
90-Degree Days: 47

Charlottesville, VA

Terrain: Located in the center of Albemarle County, which is on the Central Piedmont Plateau. The Blue Ridge Mountains are on the western edge of the county. These and several smaller ranges make the topography vary from rolling to quite steep. Elevations range from 300 feet to 800 feet, with some points in the Blue Ridge as high as 3,200 feet.

Climate: Modified continental, with mild winters and warm, humid summers. The mountains produce various steering and blocking effects on storms and air masses. Chesapeake Bay to the east further modifies the climate, making it warmer in winter, cooler in summer. Precipitation is well distributed throughout the year, with the maximum in July, the minimum in January. Tornadoes and violent storms are rare, but severe thunderstorms occur each year.

Pluses: Scenic mountain terrain. Mild four-season climate.

Minuses: Summers can be hot and rainy.

Score: 587 **Rank: 78**

Elevation: 870 feet

Relative Humidity: 55%
Wind Speed: 8.3 mph

Seasonal Change

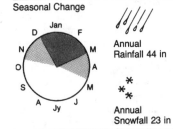

Annual
Rainfall 44 in

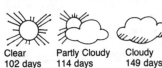

Annual
Snowfall 23 in

Clear
102 days

Partly Cloudy
114 days

Cloudy
149 days

Precipitation Days: 116 Storm Days: 45

Average Temperatures		
	Daily High	Daily Low
January	44	26
February	46	28
March	56	36
April	68	46
May	76	55
June	83	62
July	87	67
August	86	66
September	80	60
October	69	49
November	59	39
December	47	30

Zero-Degree Days: 0
Freezing Days: 87
90-Degree Days: 35

Chico–Paradise, CA

Terrain: Lies in the northern third of the Sacramento River valley in the foothills of the Sierra Nevada. Chico is about 6 miles east of the Sacramento River. The lower slopes of the nearby Sierra foothills are cut by well-defined canyons draining from northeast to southwest. To the west the Coast Ranges rise up to 7,000 feet; to the east, the peaks of the Sierra Nevada reach as high as 9,000 feet. Thus, the towns of the upper valley are sheltered from ocean breezes and the extreme dryness of the Great Basin.

Climate: As a result of its inland location, the Chico–Paradise region experiences a considerable range of temperature. However, even in winter the average low temperature is not below freezing, which enhances the region's agricultural productivity, particularly in fruit- and nut-growing. The Chico–Paradise area receives 26 inches of rain per year, most of it in the cooler winter months.

Pluses: Mild, sunny, variable.   **Minuses:** Hot summer days.

Score: 629   **Rank: 62**

Elevation: 230 feet

Relative Humidity: 35%
Wind Speed: 8 mph

Seasonal Change

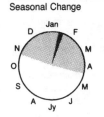

Annual
Rainfall 26 in

Annual
Snowfall .6 in

Clear
219 days

Partly Cloudy
57 days

Cloudy
89 days

Precipitation Days: 62   Storm Days: 7

Average Temperatures	Daily High	Daily Low
January	54	36
February	60	39
March	65	41
April	72	44
May	81	51
June	89	57
July	95	61
August	94	59
September	89	55
October	79	48
November	64	41
December	54	37

Zero-Degree Days: 0
Freezing Days: 36
90-Degree Days: 92

Clayton, GA

Terrain: Located in Habersham and Rabun counties is the Mountain and Intermountain Plateau Province of northeast Georgia. The terrain is hilly to mountainous, with elevations averaging 1,500 feet. To the north, some of the mountains rise above 3,000 feet.

Climate: Nearby mountains, and higher mountains farther north, have a marked influence. Summer heat is tempered by the higher elevations. The contrast of valley and hill exposures results in wide variations in winter low temperatures. Generally, places halfway up the mountain slopes remain warmer during winter nights than do places on the valley floor. Summers are quite pleasant, with warm days and cool nights. Winters are cold but not severe. Spring is changeable and sometimes stormy. Fall is clear and sunny, with chilly nights.

Pluses: Ideal mountain climate, with cool nights year round.

Minuses: Large daily temperature shifts. Stormy springs.

Score: 605   **Rank: 73**

Elevation: 1,470 feet

Relative Humidity: 60%
Wind Speed: 6.8 mph

Seasonal Change

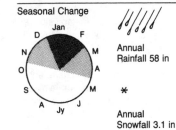

Annual
Rainfall 58 in

Annual
Snowfall 3.1 in

Clear
122 days

Partly Cloudy
100 days

Cloudy
143 days

Precipitation Days: 86   Storm Days: 70

Average Temperatures	Daily High	Daily Low
January	51	28
February	54	29
March	62	36
April	72	43
May	77	51
June	83	58
July	85	62
August	85	62
September	80	56
October	72	44
November	62	35
December	54	30

Zero-Degree Days: 0
Freezing Days: 73
90-Degree Days: 26

Clear Lake, CA

Terrain: Clear Lake is located at an elevation of 1,347 feet in one of California's major recreational and agricultural areas. The rounded mountains of the Coast Range surround the lake on all sides, reaching heights of 3,000 feet to 4,000 feet. A broad valley extends from the lake southward, and the smaller Scott's Valley is directly northwest. Clear Lake is about 40 miles due east of the coast and Point Arena.

Climate: Winters here are cool and wet, and summers are warm and dry. The Pacific remains the dominant climatic influence, but it is modified by the lake's high, mountainous location. There are marked seasonal differences here, and greater temperature extremes than at coastal locations. About 60% of the 29 inches of rain annually falls in the winter months. Summers can be hot, but nights are cool.

Pluses: Scenic setting. Mild, warm climate with seasonal variations.

Minuses: A bit hot and dry.

Score: 543   **Rank: 94**

Elevation: 1,347 feet

Relative Humidity: 55%
Wind Speed: 7.4 mph

Seasonal Change

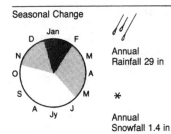

Annual
Rainfall 29 in

Annual
Snowfall 1.4 in

Clear
148 days

Partly Cloudy
112 days

Cloudy
105 days

Precipitation Days: 50   Storm Days: 9

Average Temperatures	Daily High	Daily Low
January	52	32
February	57	34
March	62	35
April	69	39
May	77	43
June	84	48
July	94	52
August	92	50
September	88	48
October	76	42
November	62	36
December	54	33

Zero-Degree Days: 0
Freezing Days: 74
90-Degree Days: 74

Coeur d'Alene, ID

Terrain: The city lies north of Coeur d'Alene Lake, which is about 30 miles long and 2 miles wide. To the east and southwest the city is sheltered by forested hills or low mountains. To the north and northwest lies Rathdrum Prairie. The Coeur d'Alene, St. Joe, and St. Maries rivers drain the heavily forested mountains between the lake and the Bitterroot Mountains, which form the boundary between Idaho and Montana. Within a 10-mile radius of the city, quite a few mountain peaks rise over 4,000 feet.

Climate: Can be generally described as temperate, with dry summers and rainy winters. Though seasonal variation is large, it is less so than most other locations this far north. Rain is heaviest from autumn to early spring. Sunshine records haven't been kept here, but for nearby (and similar) Spokane, they reveal sun 20% of the time in January, 81% in July.

Pluses: Dry, warm summers.   **Minuses:** Long, rainy winters.

Score: 397   **Rank: 131**

Elevation: 2,158 feet

Relative Humidity: 35%
Wind Speed: 8 mph

Seasonal Change

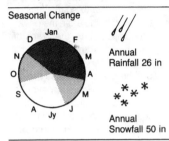

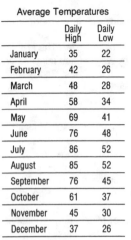

Annual Rainfall 26 in

Annual Snowfall 50 in

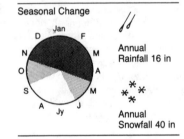

Clear 85 days   Partly Cloudy 89 days   Cloudy 191 days

Precipitation Days: 73   Storm Days: 14

Average Temperatures		
	Daily High	Daily Low
January	35	22
February	42	26
March	48	28
April	58	34
May	69	41
June	76	48
July	86	52
August	85	52
September	76	45
October	61	37
November	45	30
December	37	26

Zero-Degree Days: 4
Freezing Days: 141
90-Degree Days: 29

Colorado Springs, CO

Terrain: At an elevation of more than 6,000 feet, Colorado Springs is located in relatively flat semiarid country on the eastern slope of the Rocky Mountains. Immediately to the west, the mountains rise abruptly to heights ranging from 10,000 feet to 14,000 feet. To the east lies the gently undulating prairie land of eastern Colorado. The land slopes upward to the north, reaching an average height of 8,000 feet within 20 miles, at the top of Palmer Lake Divide.

Climate: The terrain of the area, particularly its wide range of elevations, helps to give Colorado Springs the pleasant plains-and-mountain mixture of climate that has established it as a desirable place to live. Precipitation is generally light, with 80% of it falling between April 1 and September 30. Heavy downpours accompany summer thunderstorms. Temperatures are on the mild side for a city in this latitude and at this elevation.

Pluses: Dry, sunny, variable.   **Minuses:** Long winters.

Score: 410   **Rank: 125**

Elevation: 6,170 feet

Relative Humidity: 38%
Wind Speed: 10.4 mph

Seasonal Change

Annual Rainfall 16 in

Annual Snowfall 40 in

Clear 130 days   Partly Cloudy 119 days   Cloudy 116 days

Precipitation Days: 87   Storm Days: 59

Average Temperatures		
	Daily High	Daily Low
January	41	16
February	44	19
March	48	23
April	59	33
May	68	43
June	78	51
July	84	57
August	82	56
September	75	47
October	64	37
November	50	25
December	43	19

Zero-Degree Days: 7
Freezing Days: 162
90-Degree Days: 15

★ Daytona Beach, FL

Terrain: Located on the Atlantic Ocean, with the Halifax River, part of the Intracoastal Waterway, running through the city. The land is flat, with no elevations above 35 feet. Soil is mainly sandy.

Climate: Nearness to the ocean results in a climate tempered by land and sea breezes. In the summer, the number of hours of 90° F or more is relatively small due to the beginning of the sea breeze at midday and the occurrence of local afternoon thundershowers which lower the temperature to the more comfortable 80s. Winters, although subject to cold airflows from the north, are relatively mild because of the city's ocean setting and southerly latitude.

Pluses: Mild winters.   **Minuses:** Hot, stormy summers.

Score: 814   **Rank: 17**

Elevation: 41 feet

Relative Humidity: 61%
Wind Speed: 9 mph

Seasonal Change

Annual Rainfall 48 in

Annual Snowfall 0 in

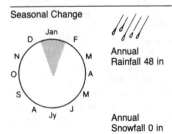

Clear 92 days   Partly Cloudy 137 days   Cloudy 136 days

Precipitation Days: 115   Storm Days: 78

Average Temperatures		
	Daily High	Daily Low
January	69	48
February	70	49
March	75	53
April	80	59
May	85	65
June	88	71
July	90	73
August	89	73
September	87	72
October	81	65
November	75	56
December	70	49

Zero-Degree Days: 0
Freezing Days: 6
90-Degree Days: 54

Eagle River, WI

Terrain: Wisconsin's Vilas County, of which Eagle River is the seat, borders on the western end of the Upper Peninsula of Michigan. The entire area was once part of a great, dense white pine forest, but is now covered with second growth. Within a 20-mile radius of the town are more than 200 lakes, some with identical names. The area is known for its walleye and muskie fishing, and for its winter sports.
Climate: Continental, and largely determined by the movement and interaction of large air masses. Winters are long and cold, while summers are warm and pleasant, with cool nights. Weather changes can be expected every few days in winter and spring. Spring and fall are short, with rapid transition from winter to summer and vice versa. The average number of thunderstorms per year is 30. With an average of 39 days when the temperature drops below zero, this should be considered a rigorous climate.

Pluses: Warm, pleasant summers.

Minuses: Long, cold winters.

Score: 261　　　　　　　　　　　　　　　　**Rank: 151**

Elevation: 1,647 feet

Relative Humity: 55%
Wind Speed: 8.5 mph

Seasonal Change

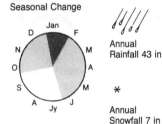

Annual Rainfall 31 in

Annual Snowfall 56 in

Clear 89 days　Partly Cloudy 102 days　Cloudy 174 days

Precipitation Days: 66　Storm Days: 30

Average Temperatures		
	Daily High	Daily Low
January	23	3
February	26	4
March	36	15
April	53	30
May	67	42
June	75	52
July	80	57
August	78	54
September	68	46
October	57	37
November	38	24
December	26	10

Zero-Degree Days: 39
Freezing Days: 182
90-Degree Days: 6

Eugene–Springfield, OR

Terrain: Situated at the southern end of the fertile Willamette Valley. This valley is bounded on both sides by mountain ranges: the Cascades to the east and the Coast Ranges to the west. To the north, the valley widens and levels out. Hills of the rolling, wooded Coast Ranges begin about 5 miles west of the airport and rise to between 1,500 feet and 2,000 feet midway between the city and the Pacific, 50 miles to the west. The Cascades, 75 miles east, reach heights of 10,000 feet. These sheltering ranges and the proximity of the ocean contribute heavily to Eugene's extremely mild climate. This is one of the nation's most important agricultural and lumbering areas.
Climate: Very mild maritime climate. Temperature minima below 20° F occur only five times a year. The temperature rarely reaches the mid-90s. Seasonal change is gradual, with intermediate seasons being as long as summer and winter.

Pluses: Mild; gradual change of seasons.

Minuses: Cloudy, damp.

Score: 515　　　　　　　　　　　　　　　　**Rank: 100**

Elevation: 373 feet

Relative Humity: 73%
Wind Speed: 7.6 mph

Seasonal Change

Annual Rainfall 43 in

Annual Snowfall 7 in

Clear 77 days　Partly Cloudy 81 days　Cloudy 207 days

Precipitation Days: 137　Storm Days: 5

Average Temperatures		
	Daily High	Daily Low
January	46	33
February	52	35
March	55	37
April	61	39
May	68	44
June	74	49
July	83	51
August	81	51
September	77	47
October	64	42
November	53	38
December	47	36

Zero-Degree Days: 0
Freezing Days: 54
90-Degree Days: 15

Fairhope–Gulf Shores, AL

Terrain: Located on the Gulf of Mexico near the entrance to Mobile Bay. Ecologies here range from sea level sandy beaches and saltmarshes to typically southern mixed forests. Elevations vary from sea level to no more than 250 feet inland.
Climate: Subtropical. Although destructive hurricanes are extremely infrequent, this seems due more to chance than to location. The area is subject to hurricanes from the West Indies and the Gulf of Mexico. The normal annual rainfall amount here is one of the highest in the continental United States. It is evenly distributed throughout the year, with a slight maximum at the height of the summer thunderstorm season (there are thunderstorms every other day during July and August). Most of these storms are showers; long periods of continuous rain are rare. The growing season averages 274 days, enough for citrus fruits to be grown in the area.

Pluses: Mild winters, ample and even precipitation.

Minuses: Hot and muggy summers with frequent thunderstorms; area prone to hurricanes.

Score: 749　　　　　　　　　　　　　　　　**Rank: 25**

Elevation: 45 feet

Relative Humity: 73%
Wind Speed: 9.2 mph

Seasonal Change

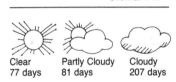

Annual Rainfall 67 in

Annual Snowfall .4 in

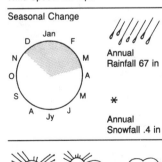

Clear 100 days　Partly Cloudy 117 days　Cloudy 148 days

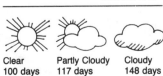

Precipitation Days: 124　Storm Days: 80

Average Temperatures		
	Daily High	Daily Low
January	62	42
February	65	43
March	71	50
April	78	57
May	85	64
June	90	70
July	91	72
August	90	72
September	87	68
October	79	57
November	70	49
December	64	43

Zero-Degree Days: 0
Freezing Days: 19
90-Degree Days: 81

Fort Collins–Loveland, CO

Terrain: Located on the eastern slope of the Rocky Mountains between Denver and Cheyenne, Wyoming, the Fort Collins-Loveland area lies in some of the most spectacular mountain terrain in the country. Steep cliffs (some nearly vertical), high waterfalls, and forested mountain slopes cut by swift rivers are all found to the west. Within 30 miles to the east, the landscape settles into grassland prairies of the Great Plains.

Climate: Near the center of the continent, Fort Collins and Loveland are removed from any major source of airborne moisture and are further shielded from rainfall by the high Rockies to the west. In wintertime, cold air masses from Canada may bring temperatures well below zero at night. In summer, hot, dry air from the desert to the southwest brings with it daytime temperatures of 90° F. However, felt heat is low because of dryness.

Pluses: Semirigorous four-season climate. Spectacular terrain.

Minuses: Cold winters. Hot, dry summers.

Score: 405   **Rank: 127**

Elevation: 5,004 feet

Relative Humidity: 35%
Wind Speed: 9 mph

Seasonal Change

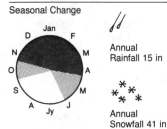

Annual Rainfall 15 in

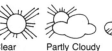

Annual Snowfall 41 in

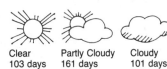

Clear 118 days   Partly Cloudy 128 days   Cloudy 119 days

Precipitation Days: 37   Storm Days: 50

Average Temperatures		
	Daily High	Daily Low
January	41	13
February	45	19
March	50	23
April	60	33
May	70	43
June	80	51
July	86	57
August	83	55
September	75	45
October	65	35
November	50	23
December	44	17

Zero-Degree Days: 15
Freezing Days: 175
90-Degree Days: 17

★ Fort Myers–Cape Coral–Sanibel Island, FL

Terrain: Located on the Caloosahatchee River, about 15 miles from the Gulf of Mexico, Fort Myers and Cape Coral sit on land that is level and low, with lush greenery.

Climate: Subtropical, with temperature extremes of both summer and winter checked by the influence of the Gulf. The average annual mean temperature is a warm 74° F, with averages ranging from the low 60s in January to the low 80s in the summer months. Winters are mild, with many bright, warm days and moderately cool nights. Maximum temperatures average in the low 90s from June through the first part of September, with daily highs of 90° F or greater on 80% of the days. Rainfall averages more than 50 inches annually, with two-thirds of this total coming between June and September. Most rain falls as late afternoon or early evening thunderstorms, which in the summer bring welcome relief from the heat and occur almost every day.

Pluses: Mild, sunny winters.

Minuses: Hot, humid, stormy.

Score: 838   **Rank: 8**

Elevation: 15 feet

Relative Humidity: 56%
Wind Speed: 8.2 mph

Seasonal Change

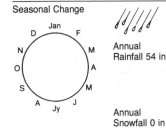

Annual Rainfall 54 in

Annual Snowfall 0 in

Clear 103 days   Partly Cloudy 161 days   Cloudy 101 days

Precipitation Days: 112   Storm Days: 93

Average Temperatures		
	Daily High	Daily Low
January	75	52
February	76	53
March	80	57
April	85	62
May	89	66
June	91	72
July	91	72
August	92	74
September	90	73
October	85	66
November	80	59
December	76	54

Zero-Degree Days: 0
Freezing Days: 1
90-Degree Days: 106

Grand Junction, CO

Terrain: Situated in a large mountain valley at the junction of the Colorado and Gunnison rivers, Grand Junction lies on the western slope of the Rocky Mountains. The city's climate is marked by wide seasonal temperature changes, but thanks to the protection of the surrounding mountains, sudden and severe weather changes are infrequent. Elevations on the valley floor average about 4,600 feet above sea level, with mountains on all sides reaching as high as 12,000 feet.

Climate: The interior location, coupled with the ring of high mountains, results in low rainfall, and agriculture depends heavily on irrigation, derived from mountain streams and runoff. Winter snows are frequent but light, and do not remain long. In the summer, relative humidity is very low, making the region as dry as parts of Arizona. Sunny days predominate in all seasons.

Pluses: Four-season climate milder than others in comparable latitudes.

Minuses: Low rainfall. Some hot weather.

Score: 469   **Rank: 107**

Elevation: 4,843 feet

Relative Humidity: 40%
Wind Speed: 8.1 mph

Seasonal Change

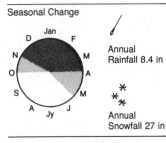

Annual Rainfall 8.4 in

Annual Snowfall 27 in

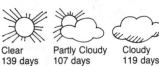

Clear 139 days   Partly Cloudy 107 days   Cloudy 119 days

Precipitation Days: 70   Storm Days: 33

Average Temperatures		
	Daily High	Daily Low
January	37	17
February	44	23
March	53	30
April	65	39
May	76	49
June	86	57
July	93	64
August	89	62
September	81	53
October	68	42
November	51	29
December	39	20

Zero-Degree Days: 7
Freezing Days: 137
90-Degree Days: 66

Grass Valley–Truckee, CA

Terrain: Located on the western slope of the Sierra Nevada. The climate is primarily that of a mountainous region, in this instance modified by the proximity of the Sacramento Valley to the west. The temperature and snowfall can vary greatly from one town to the next in Nevada County, due to the high peaks and ridges of the Sierra Nevada, which serve to block air masses from the coast and the Great Basin, and to channel warm, moist air to high elevations where the moisture is extracted in the form of rain or snow.

Climate: The average annual temperature for the area is about 50° F, with the mean wintertime low being around 29° F and the mean high temperature in the summertime about 76° F. The temperature range during the year is great, with occasional lows at zero and highs in the low 90s. Though the climate is generally mild during most of the year, blizzard conditions and very deep snows (245 inches at Blue Canyon) may prevail during the winter.

Pluses: Spectacular scenery. Pleasant summers and falls.

Minuses: High elevations have blizzard conditions in winter.

Score: 465 **Rank: 108**

Elevation: 5,280 feet

Relative Humidity: 35%
Wind Speed: 8 mph

Seasonal Change

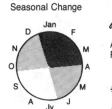

Annual Rainfall 67.6 in

Annual Snowfall 240 in

Clear	Partly Cloudy	Cloudy
175 days	64 days	126 days

Precipitation Days: 89   Storm Days: 12

Average Temperatures		
	Daily High	Daily Low
January	43	30
February	44	31
March	45	31
April	52	36
May	60	43
June	68	50
July	78	59
August	76	57
September	73	53
October	63	45
November	52	37
December	46	33

Zero-Degree Days: 0
Freezing Days: 100
90-Degree Days: 1

Hendersonville, NC

Terrain: Hendersonville and Brevard are located in the mountainous southwestern part of the state, just above the South Carolina border. The relief is mostly broken, mountainous, and rugged, with some very steep slopes and high waterfalls. There is a large intermountain valley, with rolling to strongly rolling mountain meadows. The cool climate favors the growth of pasture grasses, potatoes, apples and tree fruits, cabbage, and late truck crops.

Climate: Mildly continental, with considerable differences in temperature between winter and summer. It is mild and pleasant from late spring to late fall, and summer nights are always cool, even following hot afternoons. Hendersonville, Brevard and the cities surrounding them have long been famous as recreational and health resorts.

Pluses: Ideal mild four-season climate.

Minuses: Pronounced temperature shifts possible.

Score: 615 **Rank: 70**

Elevation: 2,153 feet

Relative Humidity: 60%
Wind Speed: 7 mph

Seasonal Change

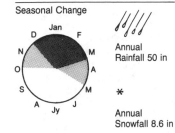

Annual Rainfall 50 in

Annual Snowfall 8.6 in

Clear	Partly Cloudy	Cloudy
110 days	103 days	152 days

Precipitation Days: 132 Storm Days: 47

Average Temperatures		
	Daily High	Daily Low
January	48	28
February	52	30
March	60	37
April	70	47
May	78	55
June	84	63
July	87	67
August	86	66
September	80	60
October	70	47
November	60	38
December	51	31

Zero-Degree Days: 0
Freezing Days: 80
90-Degree days: 8

Hilton Head–Beaufort, SC

Terrain: This area comprises a group of islands in the southern tip of the state. The land is low and flat with elevations mostly under 25 feet. There are dozens of islands of various shapes and sizes, and on them are fresh and saltwater streams, inlets, rivers, and sounds. Most of the islands (except Hilton Head and Port Royal) contain much swampy area. The best beaches are found on Hilton Head, Fripps, and Hunting islands.

Climate: The island group is just on the edge of the balmy subtropical climate enjoyed by Florida and the Caribbean islands. The surrounding water produces a maritime climate, with mild winters, hot summers, and temperatures that shift slowly. The inland Appalachian Mountains block much cold air from the northern interior, and the Gulf Stream moderates the climate considerably.

Pluses: Mild, yet with more seasonal change than places to the south.

Minuses: Summers can be uncomfortably hot and humid.

Score: 729 **Rank: 33**

Elevation: 25 feet

Relative Humidity: 65%
Wind Speed: 7.2 mph

Seasonal Change

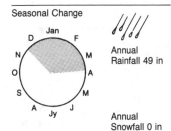

Annual Rainfall 49 in

Annual Snowfall 0 in

Clear	Partly Cloudy	Cloudy
102 days	112 days	151 days

Precipitation Days: 115 Storm Days: 77

Average Temperatures		
	Daily High	Daily Low
January	59	38
February	61	42
March	67	46
April	76	55
May	82	62
June	86	68
July	89	71
August	89	71
September	84	67
October	77	57
November	69	47
December	61	39

Zero-Degree Days: 0
Freezing Days: 31
90-Degree Days: 39

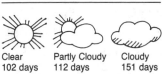

★ Honolulu, HI

Terrain: Oahu, the island on which Honolulu is located, is the third largest of the Hawaiian Islands. The Koolau Range, at an average height of 2,000 feet, parallels the northeast coast. The Waianae Mountains, somewhat higher in elevation, parallel the west coast. Much of the city lies along the coastal plain, leeward (relative to the trade winds) of the Koolaus.

Climate: Mild marine tropical. Honolulu shows the least seasonal temperature change of any American city: The difference between the mean January minimum temperature and the August maximum mean temperature is only about 22 degrees. Honolulu's location just south of the Tropic of Cancer in the Pacific Ocean assures this mildness. It has no snow, fog, or freezing weather, and an average of only nine 90-degree days and seven thunderstorms a year. There are no heating-degree days here. Although it can be uncomfortably warm occasionally, the persistent trade winds give relief.

Pluses: Extremely mild.   **Minuses:** A bit monotonous.

Score: 902   **Rank: 2**

Elevation: 15 feet

Relative Humidity: 67%
Wind Speed: 11.8 mph

Seasonal Change

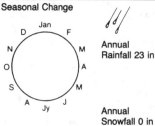

Annual
Rainfall 23 in

Annual
Snowfall 0 in

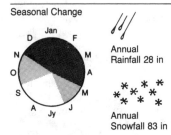

Clear   Partly Cloudy   Cloudy
90 days   174 days   101 days

Precipitation Days: 102   Storm Days: 7

Average Temperatures		
	Daily High	Daily Low
January	79	65
February	79	65
March	80	66
April	81	68
May	84	70
June	86	72
July	87	73
August	87	74
September	87	73
October	86	72
November	83	70
December	80	67

Zero-Degree Days: 0
Freezing Days: 0
90-Degree Days: 9

Hot Springs National Park, AR

Terrain: This region, famous for its fishing and thermal springs, is located in Garland County in south-central Arkansas. The city of Hot Springs is adjacent to Hot Springs National Park and is in the eastern part of the Ouachita Mountain system. It is near the boundary between the highland (Ozark) and delta regions of the state.

Climate: The irregular topography, with elevations varying from 400 feet to 1,000 feet, has considerable effect on the microclimate of the area, particularly with regard to temperature extremes, ground fog, and precipitation. The climate is generally mild, and favors outdoor activities almost year round. However, the area is subject to storms, flash floods, and extreme heat and cold. Winter temperatures fall below freezing only half the time. Summers are warm and long, springs changeable. The freeze-free growing period is long: 225 days.

Pluses: Long, warm summers.   **Minuses:** Hot, muggy spells in
         Mild winters.   summer.

Score: 652   **Rank: 56**

Elevation: 630 feet

Relative Humidity: 55%
Wind Speed: 8.1 mph

Seasonal Change

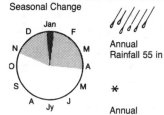

Annual
Rainfall 55 in

Annual
Snowfall 3 in

Clear   Partly Cloudy   Cloudy
119 days   101 days   145 days

Precipitation Days: 72   Storm Days: 79

Average Temperatures		
	Daily High	Daily Low
January	52	31
February	57	34
March	65	41
April	75	52
May	82	59
June	89	67
July	93	71
August	93	70
September	87	63
October	77	53
November	63	42
December	55	35

Zero-Degree Days: 0
Freezing Days: 47
90-Degree Days: 90

Houghton Lake, MI

Terrain: This resort area is located in north-central Lower Michigan. Houghton Lake, the largest inland lake in the state, lies within Michigan's central plateau, which is 1,000 feet above sea level. The land around the lake is level to rolling, gradually dropping off toward the east and, more rapidly, to the south; to the north are hills and ridges 100 feet to 300 feet higher. However, the region's thick woods and abundant streams and lakes make it a natural tourist and recreation area.

Climate: The daily and seasonal temperature range is greater here than along Michigan's shorelines, where the modifying effects of the various Great Lakes can be felt. Rainfall is heaviest in the summer, with 60% of it falling between April and September. Winters here are cold and snowy, though not as snowy as those in locations to the north and west. Cloudiness is greatest in late fall and winter. The growing season is only 90 days.

Pluses: Excellent fishing, hunt-   **Minuses:** Long, cold winters.
         ing, water sports.   Cloudy.

Score: 285   **Rank: 149**

Elevation: 1,149 feet

Relative Humidity: 64%
Wind Speed: 8.9 mph

Seasonal Change

Annual
Rainfall 28 in

Annual
Snowfall 83 in

Clear   Partly Cloudy   Cloudy
70 days   98 days   197 days

Precipitation Days: 144   Storm Days: 36

Average Temperatures		
	Daily High	Daily Low
January	26	9
February	28	8
March	37	16
April	53	31
May	65	40
June	75	50
July	79	54
August	77	53
September	68	46
October	58	37
November	42	27
December	30	16

Zero-Degree Days: 25
Freezing Days: 175
90-Degree Days: 2

Kalispell, MT

Terrain: Kalispell, the seat of Flathead County, is located 8 miles northwest of the north end of Flathead Lake, in the valley of the same name. The climate of Flathead Valley differs from that found east of the Continental Divide (40 miles east of Kalispell), largely because of the high mountains to the east, which block cold air from Alberta in the wintertime. These rise 4,500 feet above the valley floor, and assure frequent and beneficial rains by cooling the moist ocean air arriving from the west. In addition to Flathead, the valley contains four smaller lakes and numerous streams and sloughs.

Climate: There is more precipitation on the eastern side of the valley than the western. In winter, the eastern portion receives 68 inches of snow, the western only 49 inches. Kalispell is windy, with intense winds often reaching 30 mph to 40 mph. Winter is cold; summers are pleasant and dry.

Pluses: Beautiful, rugged northern mountain country.

Minuses: Can be cold, cloudy, windy.

Score: 263   **Rank: 150**

Elevation: 2,965 feet

Relative Humidity: 51%
Wind Speed: 6.8 mph

Seasonal Change

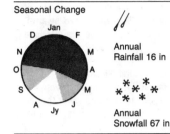

Annual Rainfall 16 in

Annual Snowfall 67 in

Clear 71 days   Partly Cloudy 81 days   Cloudy 213 days

Precipitation Days: 131   Storm Days: 23

Average Temperatures		
	Daily High	Daily Low
January	27	11
February	34	16
March	41	20
April	54	30
May	64	38
June	70	44
July	81	48
August	79	46
September	68	39
October	54	31
November	39	23
December	31	17

Zero-Degree Days: 17
Freezing Days: 191
90-Degree Days: 15

Keene, NH

Terrain: Located in southwestern New Hampshire, in the relatively flat Ashuelot River Valley, which is about 2 miles wide near the city. The valley is about 500 feet above sea level and is surrounded by hills. Peaks of 1,300 feet to 1,500 feet are within 5 miles of Keene. High peaks of the White Mountains lie 80 miles north northwest, while the main ridge of the Green Mountains lies 40 miles west.

Climate: Semirigorous continental, characterized by changeable weather, large annual and daily temperature ranges, and great differences between the same seasons in different years. In common with most of New England, there is no "rainy" or "dry" season, but rather, abundant rainfall year round. Summers are delightful but short, winters moderately cold and fairly long, and springs and falls pleasant, changeable, and brief.

Pluses: Fine four-season climate, a bit on the rugged side.

Minuses: Brief summers.

Score: 315   **Rank: 146**

Elevation: 490 feet

Relative Humidity: 60%
Wind Speed: 10.4 mph

Seasonal Change

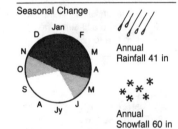

Annual Rainfall 41 in

Annual Snowfall 60 in

Clear 90 days   Partly Cloudy 109 days   Cloudy 166 days

Precipitation Days: 83   Storm Days: 24

Average Temperatures		
	Daily High	Daily Low
January	29	6
February	32	8
March	41	20
April	55	31
May	68	41
June	77	51
July	81	56
August	79	54
September	70	46
October	59	36
November	45	27
December	32	13

Zero-Degree Days: 16
Freezing Days: 167
90-Degree Days: 11

Kerrville, TX

Terrain: Kerr County lies across the hills, valleys, and uplands of the rolling Hill Country of southwest Texas, at the edge of the Edwards Plateau. The western part of the county is on a rolling plain covered with cedars and live oak trees. The eastern part breaks into the deep valleys of the Guadalupe River and its tributaries. Kerr County is an outstanding tourist resort area for hunting deer, turkey, and other game.

Climate: Mainly continental in character, especially in the winter, with wide swings of temperature both daily and seasonally. Rainfall tapers off from east to west rather sharply, from annual totals of 32 inches in the east to only 24 inches in the west. Winter precipitation is mostly slow, steady, light rain. Summer months are dry and hot. Falls are pleasant but can be stormy due to "northers" and Gulf storms moving north.

Pluses: Minimal winter. Warm.

Minuses: Summers can be hot.

Score: 692   **Rank: 44**

Elevation: 1,650 feet

Relative Humidity: 50%
Wind Speed: 9.3 mph

Seasonal Change

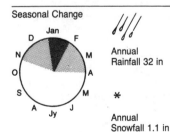

Annual Rainfall 32 in

Annual Snowfall 1.1 in

Clear 116 days   Partly Cloudy 114 days   Cloudy 135 days

Precipitation Days: 50   Storm Days: 51

Average Temperatures		
	Daily High	Daily Low
January	61	33
February	64	37
March	71	42
April	78	51
May	84	59
June	90	66
July	94	68
August	95	67
September	89	62
October	80	52
November	68	40
December	63	34

Zero-Degree Days: 0
Freezing Days: 60
90-Degree days: 101

★ Key West–Key Largo–Marathon, FL

Terrain: Laced together by the 53-mile Overseas Highway, the Florida Keys are an island chain swinging in a southwesterly arc from the tip of the Florida peninsula. The average elevation here is just 8 feet. The soil is a thin layer of sand, or marfill, overlying a stratum of Oolitic limestone. Much of the shoreline is filled mangrove swamp. The waters surrounding these islands are shallow, and there is little wave action because outlying reefs break any established wave pattern.

Climate: Because of the nearness of the Gulf Stream, the Florida Keys have a notably mild, tropical-maritime climate in which the average winter temperatures are only about 14 degrees lower than in summer. There is no known record of frost, ice, sleet, or snow here. Prevailing easterly tradewinds and sea breezes suppress the usual summertime heat.

Pluses: Single-season, subtropical marine climate.

Minuses: Hurricanes. Frequent summer thunderstorms. Humid year-round.

Score: 838

Rank: 8

Elevation: 8 feet

Relative Humidity: 67%
Wind Speed: 11.2 mph

Seasonal Change

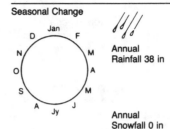

Annual Rainfall 38 in

Annual Snowfall 0 in

Clear	Partly Cloudy	Cloudy
100 days	163 days	102 days

Precipitation Days: 111   Storm Days: 63

Average Temperatures	Daily High	Daily Low
January	76	66
February	77	67
March	79	70
April	83	74
May	85	76
June	88	79
July	89	80
August	90	80
September	88	78
October	84	75
November	80	71
December	76	67

Zero-Degree Days: 0
Freezing Days: 0
90-Degree Days: 43

Lake Lanier, GA

Terrain: Lake Lanier, the most popular lake in the Army Corps of Engineers system, is a huge reservoir noted for its fishing, recreational facilities, and beauty. It is located in central Hall County, a short distance beyond Atlanta's northeast suburbs, in an area where the Piedmont Plateau joins the Blue Ridge foothills. The soil surrounding the lake is sandy clay loam and the terrain is rolling to hilly. Elevation in Gainesville, the Hall County seat, is around 1,200 feet but varies considerably over the county.

Climate: Due to its elevation and proximity to the higher elevation of the mountains to the north and northwest, Gainesville has a comparatively mild summer climate. Some hot days can be expected, but fewer than half the days in summer reach 90°F, and summer nights are almost always comfortable. Winters are not severe, though cold weather can be expected. There is usually snow every year, but accumulations are rare.

Pluses: Mild yet variable, with seasonal changes.

Minuses: Rainy. Tornado danger. Can be hot.

Score: 644

Rank: 57

Elevation: 1,170 feet

Relative Humidity: 60%
Wind Speed: 9.1 mph

Seasonal Change

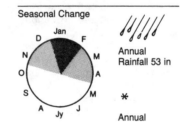

Annual Rainfall 53 in

Annual Snowfall 3 in

Clear	Partly Cloudy	Cloudy
112 days	105 days	148 days

Precipitation Days: 84   Storm Days: 70

Average Temperatures	Daily High	Daily Low
January	50	31
February	54.	32
March	63	39
April	73	48
May	79	56
June	84	63
July	87	67
August	87	66
September	81	61
October	71	49
November	61	40
December	53	33

Zero-Degree Days: 0
Freezing Days: 63
90-Degree Days: 48

★ Lakeland–Winter Haven, FL

Terrain: Located slightly west of the center of the Florida peninsula in the rolling lake-ridge section, 50 miles from the Gulf of Mexico and 70 miles from the Atlantic Ocean. Lakeland's elevation of 236 feet above sea level is the highest of any town or city in the Florida peninsula.

Climate: Classified as subtropical because of its low latitude and the proximity of the Gulf of Mexico and the Atlantic Ocean. Winters are pleasant, characterized by bright warm days, cool nights, and moderately light rainfall. Occasionally, major cold waves overspread the area, bringing temperatures down to the low 30s and mid-20s. Summers are long with high temperatures moderated in the afternoon by thundershowers.

Pluses: Mild, pleasant winters.

Minuses: Hot summers; frequent thundershowers.

Score: 828

Rank: 11

Elevation: 236 feet

Relative Humidity: 60%
Wind Speed: 6.9 mph

Seasonal Change

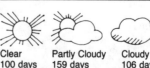

Annual Rainfall 49 in

Annual Snowfall 0 in

Clear	Partly Cloudy	Cloudy
100 days	159 days	106 days

Precipitation Days: 120   Storm Days: 100

Average Temperatures	Daily High	Daily Low
January	71	51
February	72	52
March	76	56
April	82	62
May	87	67
June	90	71
July	90	73
August	90	73
September	88	72
October	82	66
November	76	58
December	72	53

Zero-Degree Days: 0
Freezing Days: 2
90-Degree Days: 83

Lancaster County, PA

Terrain: Situated in the heart of Pennsylvania Dutch country in the southeastern part of the state, Lancaster lies about 100 miles northwest of the Atlantic and 30 miles southeast of the Blue Ridge Mountains. All around the city, the rich farmland—flat to gently rolling—is extensively cultivated.

Climate: Because of its proximity to the ocean and the protection afforded by the mountains of central Pennsylvania, Lancaster enjoys a comparatively moderate climate. Conditions range from relatively mild in winter to warm and humid in summer, with weather changes every few days throughout the year. Cold air outbreaks in winter can result in zero or near zero temperatures, but these are rare. Hot spells occur each summer, during which afternoons are uncomfortable. However, nights are generally cooler—in the 70s—and the heat spells don't last more than a few days.

Pluses: Mild four-season climate.

Minuses: Humid, can be muggy.

Score: 497　　　　　　　　**Rank: 102**

Elevation: 255 feet

Relative Humidity: 55%
Wind Speed: 7.7 mph

Seasonal Change

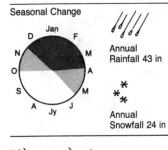

Annual Rainfall 43 in

Annual Snowfall 24 in

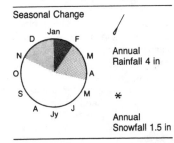

Clear 86 days　　Partly Cloudy 107 days　　Cloudy 172 days

Precipitation Days: 77　　Storm Days: 46

Average Temperatures		
	Daily High	Daily Low
January	41	23
February	43	22
March	52	29
April	65	38
May	76	49
June	83	58
July	87	62
August	84	61
September	78	53
October	67	42
November	54	32
December	42	24

Zero-Degree Days: 2
Freezing Days: 135
90-Degree Days: 27

Las Cruces, NM

Terrain: The seat of Dona Ana County, Las Cruces is located in the Rio Grande River Valley, about 25 miles north of the Texas border. The wide, level valley runs northwest to southeast through this area, with rolling desert bordering it to the southwest and west. About 12 miles to the east the Organ Mountains, with peaks above 8,500 feet, form a rugged backdrop for the city. The northwest portion of the valley narrows, and is bordered by low hills and buttes.

Climate: Arid continental, characterized by low rainfall, moderately warm summers, and mild, pleasant winters. The rainfall, at 8 inches per year, is light. But since almost all of it falls during the summer growing months, considerable forage is available on nearby grazing lands. The rain falls in brief showers; drizzles are unknown. Summers are hot, but the nights are cool. Winters tend to be mild and sunny.

Pluses: Warm and sunny, even in winter.

Minuses: Summer afternoons can be hot and dusty.

Score: 597　　　　　　　　**Rank: 74**

Elevation: 3,881 feet

Relative Humidity: 40%
Wind Speed: 9.5 mph

Seasonal Change

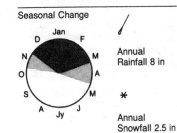

Annual Rainfall 8 in

Annual Snowfall 2.5 in

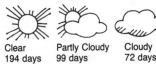

Clear 194 days　　Partly Cloudy 99 days　　Cloudy 72 days

Precipitation Days: 21　　Storm Days: 58

Average Temperatures		
	Daily High	Daily Low
January	56	25
February	62	28
March	72	34
April	77	41
May	85	49
June	94	59
July	94	65
August	92	64
September	87	56
October	78	44
November	65	30
December	58	26

Zero-Degree Days: 0
Freezing Days: 111
90-Degree Days: 101

Las Vegas, NV

Terrain: Situated near the center of a broad desert valley surrounded by mountains ranging from 2,000 feet to 10,000 feet higher than the valley's floor. These mountains act as effective barriers to moisture-laden storms moving eastward from the Pacific Ocean, so that Las Vegas sees very few overcast or rainy days.

Climate: Summers are typical of a desert climate—low humidity with maximum temperatures in the 100-degree levels. Nearby mountains contribute to relatively cool nights, with minimums between 70° F and 75° F. Springs and falls are ideal: Outdoor activities are rarely interrupted by adverse weather conditions. Winters, too, are mild, with daytime averages of 60° F, clear skies, and warm sunshine.

Pluses: Mild year-round climate with especially pleasant springs and falls.

Minuses: High winds, though infrequent, bring dust and sand.

Score: 628　　　　　　　　**Rank: 63**

Elevation: 2,180 feet

Relative Humidity: 20%
Wind Speed: 9 mph

Seasonal Change

Annual Rainfall 4 in

Annual Snowfall 1.5 in

Clear 216 days　　Partly Cloudy 84 days　　Cloudy 65 days

Precipitation Days: 24　　Storm Days: 15

Average Temperatures		
	Daily High	Daily Low
January	56	33
February	61	37
March	68	42
April	78	50
May	88	59
June	97	67
July	104	75
August	102	73
September	95	65
October	81	53
November	66	41
December	57	34

Zero-Degree Days: 0
Freezing Days: 41
90-Degree Days: 131

Lexington–Fayette, KY

Terrain: Located in the heart of the Kentucky Bluegrass region on a gently rolling plateau with varying elevations of 900 feet to 1,050 feet. The surrounding country is noted for its beauty, fertile soil, excellent grass, stock farms, and burley tobacco. There are no bodies of water nearby that are large enough to have an effect on climate.

Climate: Decidedly continental, temperate, yet subject to sudden large but brief changes in temperature. Precipitation is evenly distributed throughout the winter, spring, and summer, with an average of 12 inches falling in each of these seasons. Snowfall is variable, but the ground does not retain snow for more than a few days at a time. The months of September and October are the most pleasant of the year; they have the least precipitation, the most clear days, and generally comfortable temperatures.

Pluses: Temperate four-season climate with pleasant falls.

Minuses: Large diurnal temperature range.

Score: 554　　　　　　　　　　**Rank: 92**

Elevation: 989 feet

Relative Humidity: 60%
Wind Speed: 9.6 mph

Seasonal Change

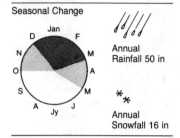

Annual Rainfall 50 in

Annual Snowfall 16 in

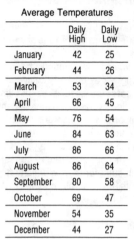

Clear 95 days　Partly Cloudy 102 days　Cloudy 168 days

Precipitation Days: 130　Storm Days: 47

Average Temperatures		
	Daily High	Daily Low
January	42	25
February	44	26
March	53	34
April	66	45
May	76	54
June	84	63
July	86	66
August	86	64
September	80	58
October	69	47
November	54	35
December	44	27

Zero-Degree Days: 2
Freezing Days: 97
90-Degree Days: 16

Madison, WI

Terrain: Madison sits on a narrow isthmus of land between Lakes Mendota (15 square miles) and Monona (5 square miles). Normally these lakes are frozen from December 17 to April 5. Most farming is dairying, with field crops mainly of corn, oats, and alfalfa. The majority of fruits grown are apples, strawberries, and raspberries.

Climate: Continental, typical of interior North America, with a large annual temperature range and frequent short periods of temperature changes. Winter temperatures average 20° F and summer ones 68° F. The most common air masses are of polar origin, with occasional outbreaks of arctic air during the winter. Much of the precipitation falls between May and September. Lighter winter precipitation falls over a longer period of time.

Pluses: Pleasant summers with moderate growing season; even precipitation.

Minuses: Long, severe winters.

Score: 337　　　　　　　　　　**Rank: 138**

Elevation: 866 feet

Relative Humidity: 61%
Wind Speed: 9.9 mph

Seasonal Change

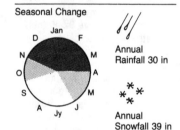

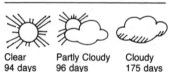
Annual Rainfall 30 in

Annual Snowfall 39 in

Clear 94 days　Partly Cloudy 96 days　Cloudy 175 days

Precipitation Days: 117　Storm Days: 40

Average Temperatures		
	Daily High	Daily Low
January	25	8
February	30	11
March	39	21
April	56	35
May	67	45
June	77	55
July	81	59
August	80	57
September	71	49
October	61	39
November	43	26
December	30	14

Zero-Degree Days: 25
Freezing Days: 164
90-Degree Days: 12

★ Maui, HI

Terrain: The most centrally located of Hawaii's major islands, Maui lies between Oahu and the Big Island of Hawaii. The island is mountainous, with the peaks of west Maui rising to almost 6,000 feet, and those to the southeast rising to over 10,000 feet.

Climate: The outstanding features of Maui's climate are the equable temperatures from day to day and season to season; the marked variation in rainfall on the island from season to season and place to place; the persistence of winds from the northeast quadrant; and the rarity of severe storms. For a visitor from the mainland, the steady, mild temperature is probably the biggest surprise. The normal temperature range between the warmest month (August) and the coldest (February) is only eight degrees! At Kahului, where these data were recorded, the average mean humidity is fairly high (72%) and the rainfall is low, averaging under 30 inches.

Pluses: Very mild maritime climate.

Minuses: Monotonous.

Score: 925　　　　　　　　　　**Rank: 1**

Elevation: 103 feet

Relative Humidity: 58%
Wind Speed: 12.9 mph

Seasonal Change

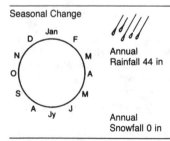
Annual Rainfall 44 in

Annual Snowfall 0 in

Clear 124 days　Partly Cloudy 149 days　Cloudy 92 days

Precipitation Days: 202　Storm Days: 8

Average Temperatures		
	Daily High	Daily Low
January	80	64
February	79	64
March	80	64
April	82	66
May	84	67
June	85	69
July	86	70
August	87	71
September	87	70
October	86	69
November	83	68
December	80	66

Zero-Degree Days: 0
Freezing Days: 0
90-Degree Days: 0

Medford–Ashland, OR

Terrain: Located in a mountain valley formed by the famous Rogue River and one of its tributaries, Bear Creek. Most of the valley ranges in elevation from 1,300 feet to 1,400 feet above sea level. The valley's outlet to the ocean 80 miles west is the narrow canyon of the Rogue.
Climate: Moderate, with marked seasonal characteristics. Late fall, winter, and early spring are cloudy, damp, and cool. The remainder of the year is warm, dry, and sunny. The rain shadow afforded by the Siskiyous and the Coast Range results in relatively light rainfall, most of which falls in the wintertime. Snowfalls are very light and seldom remain on the ground more than 24 hours. Winters are mild, with the temperatures just dipping below freezing during December and January. Summer days can reach 90° F, but nights are cool. The climate is ideal for truck and fruit farming, and the area is dotted with orchards.

Pluses: Very mild four-season climate. Sunny summers.

Minuses: Half the year is damp and cloudy.

Score: 492　　　　　　　　**Rank: 104**

Elevation: 1,298 feet

Relative Humidity: 67%
Wind Speed: 4.8 mph

Seasonal Change

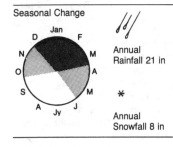

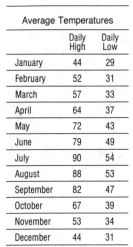

Annual Rainfall 21 in

Annual Snowfall 8 in

Clear 117 days　Partly Cloudy 79 days　Cloudy 169 days

Precipitation Days: 101　Storm Days: 9

Average Temperatures		
	Daily High	Daily Low
January	44	29
February	52	31
March	57	33
April	64	37
May	72	43
June	79	49
July	90	54
August	88	53
September	82	47
October	67	39
November	53	34
December	44	31

Zero-Degree Days: 0
Freezing Days: 90
90-Degree Days: 54

★ Miami–Hialeah, FL

Terrain: Located on the lower east coast of Florida. To the east lies Biscayne Bay, and east of it Miami Beach. The surrounding countryside is level and sparsely wooded.
Climate: Essentially subtropical marine, characterized by a long, warm summer with abundant rainfall and a mild, dry winter. The Atlantic Ocean greatly influences the city's small range of daily temperature and aids the rapid warming of colder air masses that pass to the east of the state. During the early morning hours, more rainfall occurs at Miami Beach than at the airport (9 miles inland), while during the afternoon the reverse is true. Even more striking is the difference in the annual number of days over 90° F: at Miami Beach, 15 days; at the airport, 60. Freezing temperatures occur occasionally in surrounding farming districts but almost never near the ocean. In 1977, for the first time in Miami's history, traces of snow were reported. Tropical hurricanes affect the area and are the most frequent in early fall.

Pluses: Single-season, subtropical marine climate.

Minuses: Hurricanes. Frequent thunderstorms.

Score: 867　　　　　　　　**Rank: 3**

Elevation: 12 feet

Relative Humidity: 62%
Wind Speed: 9.2 mph

Seasonal Change

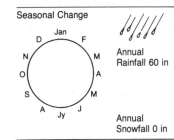

Annual Rainfall 60 in

Annual Snowfall 0 in

Clear 76 days　Partly Cloudy 172 days　Cloudy 117 days

Precipitation Days: 129　Storm Days: 75

Average Temperatures		
	Daily High	Daily Low
January	76	59
February	77	59
March	80	63
April	83	68
May	85	71
June	88	74
July	89	76
August	90	76
September	88	75
October	85	71
November	80	65
December	77	60

Zero-Degree Days: 0
Freezing Days: 0
90-Degree Days: 30

Mountain Home–Bull Shoals, AR

Terrain: Bull Shoals Dam and the White River lakes (Beaver, Table Rock, Bull Shoals, and Norfork) are located in the Arkansas–Missouri Ozark Mountain country. These lakes are really reservoirs, with a water surface area of 290 square miles. Elevations in the area vary from 500 feet to 1,400 feet. The most rugged terrain is near Beaver Dam. Gently rolling hills surround Lake Norfork. The country is rugged and wooded, with farms small and scattered. This area is one of the most famous fishing spots in the country. In addition, the woods are full of game such as deer, turkey, duck, and quail.
Climate: Primarily modified continental, with warm summers and mild winters. Each year it can vary from warm and humid maritime to cold and dry continental, but it is relatively free from climatic extremes.

Pluses: Scenic. Great recreational opportunities. Mild winters.

Minuses: Some winter cold snaps and summer heat waves. Subject to ice and sleet.

Score: 592　　　　　　　　**Rank: 76**

Elevation: 900 feet

Relative Humidity: 55%
Wind Speed: 11 mph

Seasonal Change

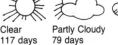

Annual Rainfall 42 in

Annual Snowfall 7.6 in

Clear 119 days　Partly Cloudy 96 days　Cloudy 150 days

Precipitation Days: 68　Storm Days: 81

Average Temperatures		
	Daily High	Daily Low
January	46	24
February	51	28
March	60	36
April	72	47
May	79	55
June	86	63
July	91	67
August	90	66
September	84	59
October	74	47
November	60	36
December	50	29

Zero-Degree Days: 0
Freezing Days: 88
90-Degree Days: 69

Murray–Kentucky Lake, KY

Terrain: The Two Rivers Breaks area covers several hundred square miles in western Kentucky. Elevations vary from 350 feet to 600 feet. Lakes Barkley and Kentucky were formed by damming the Tennessee and Cumberland rivers. The thin finger of land between them is called Land Between the Lakes recreation area. The entire area, both in Kentucky and Tennessee, is famous for fishing.

Climate: Temperate, with moderately cold winters and warm, humid summers. Precipitation is ample and well-distributed throughout the year. Most days, even those in winter, are suitable for outdoor activity, with temperatures in winter reaching 50° F or more 11 to 16 days per month. Spring and fall are the most comfortable seasons, with fall being remarkably free from storms or cold. There are about 52 thunderstorms per year. The sunniest months are September and October; the cloudiest is January.

Pluses: Milder than many locations farther north. Scenic.

Minuses: Fairly damp. Summers can be uncomfortable.

Score: 592 **Rank: 76**

Elevation: 450 feet

Relative Humidity: 60%
Wind Speed: 8 mph

Seasonal Change

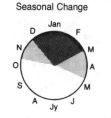

Annual Rainfall 49 in

*

Annual Snowfall 8 in

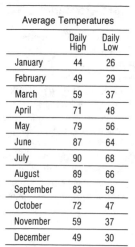

Clear 102 days   Partly Cloudy 108 days   Cloudy 155 days

Precipitation Days: 76   Storm Days: 53

Average Temperatures		
	Daily High	Daily Low
January	44	26
February	49	29
March	59	37
April	71	48
May	79	56
June	87	64
July	90	68
August	89	66
September	83	59
October	72	47
November	59	37
December	49	30

Zero-Degree Days: 1
Freezing Days: 87
90-Degree Days: 67

Myrtle Beach, SC

Terrain: Located in the center of the long coastal area known as the Grand Strand, which extends for 43 miles and has a populated area only a few blocks wide. The land is low and swampy inland, and the entire area is quite flat, with no elevations greater than 50 feet above sea level. There are many more trees and wooded areas than are usually found in a beach area. The beaches themselves are of white sand, and the water is quite clean, as there are no harbors, shipping, or major industries nearby. Also, no rivers or streams empty into the sea for a distance of almost 30 miles.

Climate: Mild winters and warm summers are the rule. The ocean has a pronounced modifying effect on temperatures, and the Blue Ridge Mountains inland block much cold air from the interior. Some tropical storms reach the area every few years.

Pluses: Warm, mild, steady.

Minuses: Can be hot and muggy. Tropical storms.

Score: 696 **Rank: 42**

Elevation: 25 feet

Relative Humidity: 65%
Wind Speed: 8.8 mph

Seasonal Change

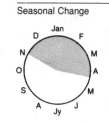

Annual Rainfall 48 in

Annual Snowfall 0 in

Clear 102 days   Partly Cloudy 110 days   Cloudy 153 days

Precipitation Days: 112   Storm Days: 76

Average Temperatures		
	Daily High	Daily Low
January	57	35
February	59	36
March	64	42
April	73	52
May	80	61
June	84	67
July	88	70
August	89	70
September	83	65
October	75	53
November	68	44
December	58	35

Zero-Degree Days: 0
Freezing Days: 54
90-Degree Days: 28

Newport–Lincoln City, OR

Terrain: These places lie directly on the Pacific Coast, with marine climates typical of Oregon's coastal area. Although this climate summary describes Newport, it is applicable to Lincoln City, 25 miles north. Just to the east of Newport's city limits, the foothills of the Coast Range begin their fairly steep ascent to ridges which are 2,000 feet to 3,000 feet high 12 miles east of the city. Though part of the city sits at the water's edge, a considerable portion of it is built on level bench land about 150 feet above sea level.

Climate: Newport receives warm, moist air from the Pacific. Accordingly, summers are mild and pleasant. In the winter, the air releases its moisture over the cold landmass, resulting in frequent clouds and rain from November through March. Some 70% of the annual rainfall occurs during these winter months. Very high and very low temperatures are almost nonexistent.

Pluses: Very mild maritime climate, with cool summers, mild winters.

Minuses: Cloudy, wet winters with little sun or snow.

Score: 487 **Rank: 106**

Elevation: 136 ft

Relative Humidity: 60%
Wind Speed: 7.6 mph

Seasonal Change

Annual Rainfall 63 in

*

Annual Snowfall 1.2 in

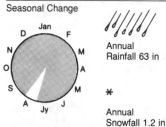

Clear 75 days   Partly Cloudy 80 days   Cloudy 210 days

Precipitation Days: 122   Storm Days: 3

Average Temperatures		
	Daily High	Daily Low
January	50	39
February	51	39
March	53	40
April	56	42
May	59	46
June	62	49
July	64	51
August	65	51
September	65	49
October	61	46
November	56	42
December	51	40

Zero-Degree Days: 0
Freezing Days: 17
90-Degree Days: 0

North Conway–White Mountains, NH

Terrain: North Conway, long famous as a recreation and resort area for both winter and summer sports and summer recreation, lies nestled in the White Mountains. About 20 miles south is Lake Winnipesaukee, the state's largest, noted for year-round recreation and fine fishing. From the lake to the ski resorts around North Conway, the terrain rises dramatically from elevations of about 2,000 feet to more than 6,000 feet in the Presidential Range. The area is generally rugged, scenic, and heavily forested. Interspersed between ranges and peaks are broad valleys suitable for dairy and truck farming.

Climate: Semirigorous continental, with delightful summers that aren't too hot. Summer nights are cool, and the days usually sunny. Falls are pleasant, and famous throughout the region for the bright colors of the foliage. Winters are long, snowy, and sometimes very cold for periods of several days to a week. Springs changeable.

Pluses: Scenic. Pleasant summers.

Minuses: Winters are long and snowy.

Score: 307 **Rank: 148**

Elevation: 720 feet

Relative Humidity: 60%
Wind Speed: 6.8 mph

Seasonal Change

Annual Rainfall 45 in

Annual Snowfall 98 in

Clear 93 days | Partly Cloudy 111 days | Cloudy 161 days

Precipitation Days: 90   Storm Days: 46

Average Temperatures	Daily High	Daily Low
January	30	8
February	33	10
March	41	19
April	54	30
May	66	40
June	76	49
July	81	53
August	78	52
September	71	45
October	61	35
November	45	27
December	32	13

Zero-Degree Days: 25
Freezing Days: 187
90-Degree Days: 7

Olympia, WA

Terrain: The capital of the state of Washington, Olympia lies at the southernmost end of Puget Sound, some 60 miles south-southwest of Seattle. The Olympic Peninsula, with its fine remnants of the Pacific Northwest rain forests, active glaciers, and alpine meadows, lies to the northwest. The city and vicinity are quite well protected by the Coast Range from the strong south and southwest winds accompanying many Pacific storms during the fall and winter.

Climate: Characterized by warm, generally dry summers and wet, mild winters. Fall rains begin in October and continue with few interruptions until spring. During the rainy season there is little variation in temperature, with days in the 40s and 50s and nights in the 30s, and constant cloud cover. The summer highs are between 60° F and 80° F, with up to 20 days without rain. The summer is marked by clear skies at night and frequent morning fog.

Pluses: Mild winters, dry summers.

Minuses: Cloudy, damp, rainy.

Score: 460 **Rank: 110**

Elevation: 195 feet

Relative Humidity: 70%
Wind Speed: 6.7 mph

Seasonal Change

Annual Rainfall 51 in

Annual Snowfall 19 in

Clear 49 days | Partly Cloudy 88 days | Cloudy 228 days

Precipitation Days: 163   Storm Days: 5

Average Temperatures	Daily High	Daily Low
January	44	30
February	49	32
March	54	33
April	60	37
May	67	41
June	72	46
July	78	49
August	77	48
September	72	45
October	61	40
November	51	35
December	46	33

Zero-Degree Days: 0
Freezing Days: 89
90-Degree Days: 6

★ Orlando, FL

Terrain: Located in the central section of the Florida peninsula, almost surrounded by lakes. The countryside is flat, with no natural barriers to exterior weather systems.

Climate: Because of the surrounding water, relative humidity remains high year-round, hovering near 90% at night and dipping to 50% in the afternoon. The rainy season extends from June through September; afternoon thundershowers occur daily. Rain is light during the winter, and snow and sleet are rare. Winter temperatures may drop to freezing at night, but days are usually pleasant, with brilliant sunshine.

Pluses: Mild.

Minuses: Humid year-round; hot summers with daily thundershowers.

Score: 825 **Rank: 12**

Elevation: 106 feet

Relative Humidity: 60%
Wind Speed: 8.7 mph

Seasonal Change

Annual Rainfall 51 in

Annual Snowfall 0 in

Clear 94 days | Partly Cloudy 148 days | Cloudy 123 days

Precipitation Days: 116   Storm Days: 81

Average Temperatures	Daily High	Daily Low
January	71	50
February	72	52
March	76	56
April	82	61
May	86	66
June	89	71
July	90	73
August	90	74
September	88	72
October	83	66
November	76	57
December	72	52

Zero-Degree Days: 0
Freezing Days: 2
90-Degree Days: 104

Petoskey–Straits of Mackinac, MI

Terrain: The Straits of Mackinac are located in the northernmost part of Lower Michigan, where the waters of Lake Michigan meet those of Lake Huron. The land north of the straits forms Michigan's Upper Peninsula. The town of Petoskey is located some 30 miles south of the straits, on the south shore of Little Traverse Bay on the Lake Michigan shore. The terrain is generally level or gently undulating, with sandy and gravelly soils. The region abounds with lakes ideal for fishing and summer recreation.

Climate: Though rigorous because of its interior and northerly location, the climate is modified by the presence of the lakes on either side. Consequently, summertime temperatures average at least 5 degrees cooler than locations in the southern part of the state. However, winters are quite severe, with cold spells that may last for a week and snowfall that averages almost 75 inches.

Pluses: Pleasant summers with cool nights. Crisp falls.

Minuses: Long, cold, snowy winters.

Score: 316   **Rank: 143**

Elevation: 586 feet

Relative Humidity: 60%
Wind Speed: 8 mph

Seasonal Change

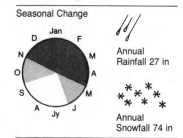

Annual Rainfall 27 in

Annual Snowfall 74 in

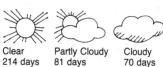

Clear 68 days   Partly Cloudy 88 days   Cloudy 209 days

Precipitation Days: 67   Storm Days: 33

Average Temperatures		
	Daily High	Daily Low
January	28	13
February	30	11
March	37	18
April	51	30
May	64	40
June	74	50
July	80	57
August	78	56
September	69	49
October	58	40
November	43	29
December	32	19

Zero-Degree Days: 14
Freezing Days: 147
90-Degree Days: 9

Phoenix–Tempe–Scottsdale, AZ

Terrain: Located in the center of the Salt River Valley, on a broad, oval, nearly flat plain. To the south, west, and north are nearby mountain ranges, and 35 miles to the east are the famous Superstition Mountains, which rise to an elevation of 5,000 feet.

Climate: Typical desert, with low annual rainfall and low humidity. Daytime temperatures are high throughout the summer. Winters are mild, but nighttime temperatures frequently drop below freezing during December, January, and February. The valley floor is generally free of wind except during the thunderstorm season in July and August, when local gusts flow from the east. The majority of days are clear and sunny, except for July and August; then, considerable afternoon cloudiness builds up over nearby mountains.

Pluses: Dry, two-season desert climate.

Minuses: Hot summers.

Score: 664   **Rank: 53**

Elevation: 1,107 feet

Relative Humidity: 32%
Wind Speed: 6.3 mph

Seasonal Change

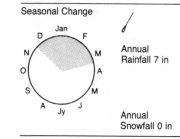

Annual Rainfall 7 in

Annual Snowfall 0 in

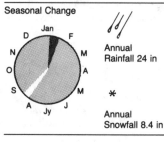

Clear 214 days   Partly Cloudy 81 days   Cloudy 70 days

Precipitation Days: 34   Storm Days: 23

Average Temperatures		
	Daily High	Daily Low
January	65	38
February	69	41
March	75	45
April	84	52
May	93	60
June	102	68
July	105	78
August	102	76
September	98	69
October	88	57
November	75	45
December	66	39

Zero-Degree Days: 0
Freezing Days: 32
90-Degree Days: 164

Port Townsend, WA

Terrain: Located at the eastern end of the Strait of Juan de Fuca, on the Quimper Peninsula. Here Admiralty Inlet leads into Puget Sound.

Climate: Predominantly marine, with cool summers, mild winters, moist air, and small daily temperature variation. Summers are cool and rather dry. The average summertime temperature is 65° F to 70° F during the day and about 55° F at night. The air temperature seldom tops 75° F. In winter, the daily temperatures are in the 40s in the daytime, dropping to the 30s at night. Like most other places in this region, the area is often foggy and cloudy.

Pluses: Cool, mild, maritime climate.

Minuses: Beach and sunbathing weather very scarce.

Score: 444   **Rank: 117**

Elevation: 32 feet

Relative Humidity: 70%
Wind Speed: 8.6 mph

Seasonal Change

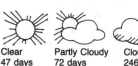

Annual Rainfall 24 in

Annual Snowfall 8.4 in

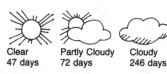

Clear 47 days   Partly Cloudy 72 days   Cloudy 246 days

Precipitation Days: 64   Storm Days: 8

Average Temperatures		
	Daily High	Daily Low
January	45	33
February	48	36
March	50	36
April	55	39
May	61	44
June	65	48
July	69	51
August	68	51
September	66	49
October	58	43
November	50	38
December	46	35

Zero-Degree Days: 0
Freezing Days: 40
90-Degree Days: 0

Red Bluff–Sacramento Valley, CA

Terrain: Located at the northern end of the Sacramento Valley, which is the northern half of the great Central Valley of California. Mountains surround the city on three sides, forming a huge horseshoe: The Coast Range is located 30 miles west, the Sierra Nevada system 40 miles east, and the Cascade Range about 50 miles north-northeast. The western part of the valley floor is mostly rolling hills with scrub oak trees. The Sacramento River flows in a north-south direction through the eastern portion of the valley, through fertile orchards and grain lands.
Climate: Precipitation is confined mostly to rain during the winter and spring months. Snowfall is infrequent and light. In the hot months (June through September), temperatures often exceed 100° F, but nighttime temperatures are almost always comfortable. The summer and fall are nearly cloudless, and the resulting warm days are ideal for fruit drying.

Pluses: Warm, dry, sunny.　　**Minuses:** Hot summer days.

Score: 655　　　　**Rank: 55**

Elevation: 342 feet

Relative Humidity: 49%
Wind Speed: 8.7 mph

Seasonal Change

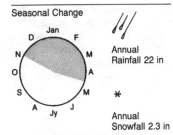

Annual Rainfall 22 in

Annual Snowfall 2.3 in

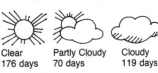

Clear 176 days　Partly Cloudy 70 days　Cloudy 119 days

Precipitation Days: 70　Storm Days: 10

Average Temperatures		
	Daily High	Daily Low
January	54	37
February	60	40
March	64	43
April	72	47
May	81	54
June	89	62
July	98	67
August	96	64
September	91	60
October	78	52
November	64	43
December	55	38

Zero-Degree Days: 0
Freezing Days: 21
90-Degree Days: 99

Reno, NV

Terrain: Located at the west edge of Truckee Meadows in a semiarid plateau lying in the lee of the Sierra Nevada. To the west, this range rises to elevations of 9,000 feet to 10,000 feet, and hills to the east reach 6,000 feet to 7,000 feet. The Truckee River, flowing from the Sierra Nevada eastward through Reno, drains into Pyramid Lake to the northeast.
Climate: Sunshine is abundant throughout the year. Temperatures are mild, but the daily range may exceed 45 degrees. Even when afternoons reach the upper 90s, a light jacket is needed shortly after sunset. Nights with a minimum temperature over 60° F are rare. Afternoon temperatures are moderate, and only about ten days a year fail to reach a level above freezing. Humidity is very low during the summer months and moderately low during winter.

Pluses: Mild, sunny climate in alpine setting.　　**Minuses:** Considerable daily temperature variation. Little precipitation.

Score: 400　　　　**Rank: 129**

Elevation: 4,400 feet

Relative Humidity: 44%
Wind Speed: 6.4 mph

Seasonal Change

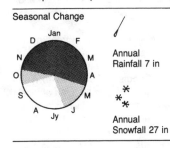

Annual Rainfall 7 in

Annual Snowfall 27 in

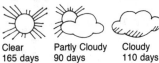

Clear 165 days　Partly Cloudy 90 days　Cloudy 110 days

Precipitation Days: 49　Storm Days: 13

Average Temperatures		
	Daily High	Daily Low
January	45	18
February	51	23
March	56	25
April	64	30
May	72	37
June	80	43
July	91	47
August	89	45
September	82	39
October	70	31
November	56	24
December	46	20

Zero-Degree Days: 3
Freezing Days: 189
90-Degree Days: 52

Rockport–Aransas Pass, TX

Terrain: Aransas County is a flat coastal plain, with many bays and inlets. Elevations range from sea level to 50 feet. The sandy loam and coastal clay soils are dotted with mesquite and live oak. About 90% of the agricultural income is derived from livestock, chiefly beef cattle. For recreation, many fishing, hunting, and camping facilities are available, including Goose Island State Park.
Climate: Humid subtropical, with warm summers. Also, the prevailing southeasterly winds off the Gulf provide a climate that is predominantly maritime. Winters are pleasantly mild, with freezing temperatures occurring at night, and only about 10 times per year. Summers are warm and humid, but the heat is moderated somewhat by Gulf breezes. Spring and fall are the most pleasant months, with moderate temperatures and changeable weather.

Pluses: Mild, warm, maritime climate, with little daily change.　　**Minuses:** Hot and muggy in summer. Monotonous.

Score: 780　　　　**Rank: 23**

Elevation: 15 feet

Relative Humidity: 80%
Wind Speed: 12 mph

Seasonal Change

Annual Rainfall 37 in

Annual Snowfall 0 in

Clear 103 days　Partly Cloudy 120 days　Cloudy 142 days

Precipitation Days: 49　Storm Days: 37

Average Temperatures		
	Daily High	Daily Low
January	65	45
February	68	49
March	73	55
April	79	63
May	84	69
June	89	75
July	92	76
August	92	75
September	89	72
October	83	64
November	74	55
December	68	48

Zero-Degree Days: 0
Freezing Days: 10
90-Degree Days: 77

Roswell, NM

Terrain: Located in a valley in southern New Mexico amid higher land masses that modify air masses, especially the cold outbreaks in winter.

Climate: Conforms to the basic trend of four seasons. Summers are warm and dry. Half of the annual precipitation falls then. In the fall, frosty nights alternate with warm days of extremely low humidity. Winter is the season of least precipitation and is characterized by subfreezing temperatures at night followed by considerable warming in the day. The wind speed is in excess of 25 mph on some 60 days a year, usually between February and May.

Pluses: Low humidity year round. Long summers. Abundance of clear days.

Minuses: Cold nights. High winds.

Score: 568   **Rank: 85**

Elevation: 3,669 feet

Relative Humidity: 42%
Wind Speed: 8.9 mph

Seasonal Change

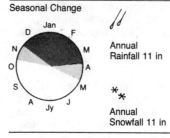

Annual Rainfall 11 in

Annual Snowfall 11 in

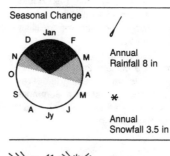

Clear 176 days   Partly Cloudy 111 days   Cloudy 78 days

Precipitation Days: 47   Storm Days: 31

Average Temperatures		
	Daily High	Daily Low
January	55	21
February	61	25
March	68	31
April	78	41
May	86	51
June	94	60
July	95	64
August	93	62
September	87	54
October	77	42
November	65	29
December	57	22

Zero-Degree Days: 0
Freezing Days: 94
90-Degree Days: 75

St. Augustine, FL

Terrain: Located in northwest Florida on a peninsula with the Matanzas and North rivers on the east and south and the San Sebastian on the west. These rivers and saltwater lagoons lie between the city and Anastasia Island and the Atlantic Ocean beyond. The surrounding terrain is level.

Climate: Humid, subtropical. The atmosphere is moist, with an average relative humidity of about 75%, ranging from a high of 90% in early morning to about 55% in late afternoon. The average daily sunshine ranges from five and one-half hours in December to nine hours in May. The greatest amount of rain, mostly in the form of local thundershowers, falls during the last summer months, when a measurable amount can be expected every other day.

Pluses: Pleasant winters.

Minuses: Hot, stormy summers.

Score: 786   **Rank: 21**

Elevation: 6 feet

Relative Humidity: 75%
Wind Speed: 8.5 mph

Seasonal Change

Annual Rainfall 54 in

Annual Snowfall 0 in

Clear 98 days   Partly Cloudy 128 days   Cloudy 139 days

Precipitation Days: 116   Storm Days: 64

Average Temperatures		
	Daily High	Daily Low
January	64	45
February	66	46
March	72	52
April	77	59
May	83	66
June	87	71
July	89	73
August	88	73
September	86	72
October	79	64
November	72	54
December	66	48

Zero-Degree Days: 0
Freezing Days: 11
90-Degree Days: 85

St. George–Zion, UT

Terrain: St. George, at an elevation of 2,700 feet, is located 2 miles north of the junction of the Virgin and Santa Clara rivers in the fairly broad Virgin River Valley of southwestern Utah. Fifteen miles north the Pine Valley Mountains rise to over 10,000 feet. The same distance west are the Beaver Dam Mountains, rising to 7,000 feet. To the east and south is principally high plateau land. Nearby Zion National Park is noted for its spectacular canyons and rock formations.

Climate: Semiarid (steppe) type, with the most striking features being bright sunshine, small annual precipitation, dryness and purity of air, and large daily variations in temperature. Summers are characterized by hot, dry weather, with temperatures over 100° F occurring frequently during July and August. However, the low humidity makes these high temperatures somewhat bearable. Winters are short and mild, with the Rocky Mountains blocking cold air masses from the north and east.

Pluses: Very sunny, dry, and warm.

Minuses: Can be very hot and dry in summer.

Score: 580   **Rank: 81**

Elevation: 2,880 feet

Relative Humidity: 25%
Wind Speed: 8.7 mph

Seasonal Change

Annual Rainfall 8 in

Annual Snowfall 3.5 in

Clear 153 days   Partly Cloudy 103 days   Cloudy 109 days

Precipitation Days: 24   Storm Days: 48

Average Temperatures		
	Daily High	Daily Low
January	53	26
February	61	32
March	67	37
April	76	44
May	86	52
June	96	61
July	102	68
August	99	66
September	94	57
October	81	45
November	65	34
December	55	27

Zero-Degree Days: 0
Freezing Days: 95
90-Degree Days: 117

★ St. Petersburg–Clearwater–Dunedin, FL

Terrain: Located in flat topography on the Gulf coast of Florida.
Climate: An outstanding feature is the summer thunderstorm season. On the average, there are 88 days of thundershowers per year, occurring mostly in the afternoons in July, August, and September. The resulting temperature drop from 90° F to 70° F produces an agreeable physiologic reaction. Temperature throughout the year is modified by the waters of the Gulf of Mexico and surrounding bays. Snowfall is negligible, and freezing temperatures are rare; during the cooling season, however, night ground fogs occur frequently because of the flat terrain.

Pluses: Mild Gulf climate.

Minuses: Gulf hurricanes, regular summer thundershowers.

Score: 816   **Rank: 14**

Elevation: 11 feet

Relative Humidity: 57%
Wind Speed: 8.7 mph

Seasonal Change

Annual Rainfall 49 in

Annual Snowfall 0 in

Clear 98 days   Partly Cloudy 140 days   Cloudy 127 days

Precipitation Days: 107 Storm Days: 88

Average Temperatures		
	Daily High	Daily Low
January	71	50
February	72	52
March	76	56
April	82	62
May	88	67
June	90	72
July	90	74
August	90	74
September	89	73
October	84	66
November	77	56
December	72	51
Zero-Degree Days: 0		
Freezing Days: 4		
90-Degree Days: 81		

St. Tammany Parish, LA

Terrain: Located in an area of level pinewoods along the north shore of Lake Pontchartrain (610 square miles) and the west bank of the Pearl River, which divides Louisiana from Mississippi. A 24 mile causeway across the lake connects the parish with New Orleans.
Climate: Best described as humid, with Lake Pontchartrain and the nearby Gulf of Mexico modifying the temperature and decreasing the range of temperatures. Heavy and frequent rains are typical, and there are daily afternoon thunderstorms from mid-June through September. From December to March, precipitation is likely to be steady rain of two or three days duration, instead of showers. During the winter and spring, cold rain forms fogs.

Pluses: Tropical climate moderated by water.

Minuses: Hot and humid; heavy rains and fogs; flood-prone.

Score: 738   **Rank: 28**

Elevation: 9 feet

Relative Humidity: 77%
Wind Speed: 8.4 mph

Seasonal Change

Annual Rainfall 57 in

✳
Annual Snowfall .2 in

Clear 109 days   Partly Cloudy 120 days   Cloudy 136 days

Precipitation Days: 113 Storm Days: 68

Average Temperatures		
	Daily High	Daily Low
January	63	40
February	66	41
March	72	48
April	79	55
May	86	62
June	91	68
July	92	71
August	92	70
September	88	67
October	81	55
November	71	46
December	65	41
Zero-Degree Days: 0		
Freezing Days: 13		
90-Degree Days: 67		

San Antonio, TX

Terrain: Located between the Edwards Plateau and the Gulf Coastal Plain of south-central Texas. Terrain is rolling. Vegetation consists of grasses and live oak trees, along with mesquite and cacti. Soils are blackland clay and silty loam.
Climate: Two-season, with mild weather during normal winter months and a long, hot summer. Though 140 miles from the Gulf of Mexico, the city feels the influence of its hot moist air. Thunderstorms and rains have occurred in every month of the year, but they are most common during the summer, with most rain falling in May and September. The winds during the winter are from the north, and from the south in the summer. Skies are clear more than 30% of the time, and cloudy about 30%.

Pluses: No winter; attractive terrain.

Minuses: Hot, muggy summers.

Score: 730   **Rank: 31**

Elevation: 794 feet

Relative Humidity: 55%
Wind Speed: 9.3 mph

Seasonal Change

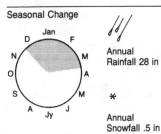

Annual Rainfall 28 in

✳
Annual Snowfall .5 in

Clear 110 days   Partly Cloudy 117 days   Cloudy 138 days

Precipitation Days: 81 Storm Days: 36

Average Temperatures		
	Daily High	Daily Low
January	62	40
February	66	43
March	73	49
April	80	59
May	86	66
June	92	72
July	96	74
August	96	73
September	90	69
October	82	59
November	71	48
December	64	42
Zero-Degree Days: 0		
Freezing Days: 22		
90-Degree Days: 111		

San Diego, CA

Terrain: Located on San Diego Bay in the southwest corner of California near the Mexican border. Its coastal location is backed by coastal foothills and mountains to the east.

Climate: One of the mildest in North America: typically marine, sometimes called Mediterranean. There are no freezing days and an average of only three 90-degree days each year. San Diego has abundant sunshine and mild sea breezes. Only two seasons occur here: a dry, mild summer and a spring that is cooler, with some rain. Storms are practically unknown, though there is considerable fog along the coast, and many low clouds in early morning and evening during the summer.

Pluses: One of the best climates for sun and mildness.

Minuses: Paradise climate lacking variety and seasonal contrasts.

Score: 773   **Rank: 24**

Elevation: 28 feet

Relative Humidity: 61%
Wind Speed: 6.7 mph

Seasonal Change

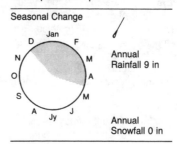

Annual Rainfall 9 in

Annual Snowfall 0 in

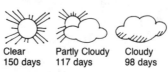

| Clear | Partly Cloudy | Cloudy |
| 150 days | 117 days | 98 days |

Precipitation Days: 41   Storm Days: 3

Average Temperatures		
	Daily High	Daily Low
January	65	46
February	66	48
March	66	50
April	68	54
May	69	57
June	71	60
July	75	64
August	75	65
September	77	63
October	74	58
November	70	52
December	66	54

Zero-Degree Days: 0
Freezing Days: 0
90-Degree Days: 3

Santa Barbara, CA

Terrain: Located in the Santa Maria Valley 150 miles north of Los Angeles and 250 miles south of San Francisco. The valley is flat and fertile, opening onto the Pacific Ocean at its widest point and tapering inland at a distance of 30 miles from the coast. It is bounded by the foothills of the San Rafael Mountains, the Solomon Hills, and the Casmalia Hills.

Climate: Rainfall season, typical of the California coast, is winter. During the rest of the year, particularly from June to October, there is little or no precipitation. Clear, sunshiny afternoons prevail on most days. At night and in the morning, however, the California stratus and fog appear.

Pluses: Year-round mildness moving through gradual transitions.

Minuses: No distinct seasonal changes, night and morning fogs.

Score: 623   **Rank: 66**

Elevation: 238 feet

Relative Humidity: 74%
Wind Speed: 7 mph

Seasonal Change

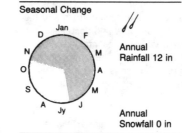

Annual Rainfall 12 in

Annual Snowfall 0 in

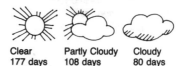

| Clear | Partly Cloudy | Cloudy |
| 177 days | 108 days | 80 days |

Precipitation Days: 45   Storm Days: 2

Average Temperatures		
	Daily High	Daily Low
January	63	38
February	64	40
March	64	41
April	66	44
May	67	47
June	70	50
July	72	52
August	72	53
September	74	51
October	73	48
November	69	42
December	64	39

Zero-Degree Days: 0
Freezing Days: 24
90-Degree Days: 6

Santa Fe, NM

Terrain: This historic city, the capital of New Mexico and seat of Santa Fe County, sits in the Rio Grande Valley in the north-central section of the state. It is situated amid the rolling foothills of the Sangre de Cristo Mountains, which rise to peaks of 10,000 feet. Westward the terrain slopes downward to the Rio Grande River, some 20 miles away. The high mountains to the east protect the city from much of the cold air of winter. The city's historic legacy, cultural facilities, and fine climate have long attracted tourists and retired people.

Climate: Semiarid continental, with cool and pleasant summers. Days are in the 80s, but nights in the 50s. Long cloudy periods are unknown. Winters are crisp, clear, and sunny, with considerable daytime warming.

Pluses: Beautiful scenery. Mild, sunny, four-season climate.

Minuses: Wide temperature range and high altitude may present health problems for some persons.

Score: 447   **Rank: 115**

Elevation: 7,200 feet

Relative Humidity: 30%
Wind Speed: 9 mph

Seasonal Change

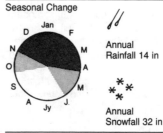

Annual Rainfall 14 in

Annual Snowfall 32 in

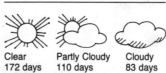

| Clear | Partly Cloudy | Cloudy |
| 172 days | 110 days | 83 days |

Precipitation Days: 37   Storm Days: 54

Average Temperatures		
	Daily High	Daily Low
January	41	19
February	45	23
March	52	27
April	62	35
May	71	43
June	81	52
July	84	57
August	82	55
September	77	49
October	65	38
November	52	27
December	43	21

Zero-Degree Days: 1
Freezing Days: 152
90-Degree Days: 7

Santa Rosa–Petaluma, CA

Terrain: Located in the east-central portion of the Petaluma–Santa Rosa–Russian River valley, which extends northwestward from San Pablo Bay, about 45 miles from the Golden Gate Bridge. This valley runs parallel to the Pacific Coast, with only low hills (300 feet to 500 feet) between it and the ocean 25 miles southwest. Higher hills rise to the east of the metro area, with greater elevations about 10 miles farther east, in the foothills of the Coast Ranges.

Climate: The nearness of the ocean and the surrounding topography join with the prevailing westerly circulation to produce a predominantly southerly air flow year-round. However, the area is sufficiently far inland to assure it a more varied climate than San Francisco's. Summers are warmer, winters cooler, and there is more daily temperature shift, as well as less fog and drizzle.

Pluses: Mild, yet sunnier and warmer than coastal locations.

Minuses: Some hot weather.

Score: 625   **Rank: 65**

Elevation: 167 feet

Relative Humidity: 55%
Wind Speed: 7 mph

Seasonal Change

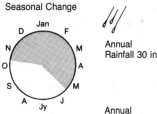

Annual Rainfall 30 in

Annual Snowfall 0 in

Clear 176 days	Partly Cloudy 109 days	Cloudy 80 days

Precipitation Days: 47   Storm Days: 4

Average Temperatures		
	Daily High	Daily Low
January	57	36
February	63	39
March	66	39
April	70	41
May	75	45
June	81	49
July	84	51
August	84	51
September	84	50
October	78	45
November	66	40
December	60	37
Zero-Degree Days: 0		
Freezing Days: 43		
90-Degree Days: 33		

Savannah, GA

Terrain: Surrounded by flat land, low and marshy to the north and east, rising to several feet above sea level to the west and south. About half the land to the west and south is clear of trees; the other half is woods, much of which lie in swamp.

Climate: Temperate with a seasonal mean temperature of 51° F in winter, 64° F in spring, 80° F in summer, and 66° F in autumn. Summer temperatures are moderated by thundershowers almost every afternoon. Sunshine is adequate in all seasons; seldom are there more than two or three days in succession without it. The long growing season is accompanied by abundant rain.

Pluses: Mild winters, pleasant autumns.

Minuses: Low, marshy terrain; humid summers.

Score: 726   **Rank: 34**

Elevation: 51 feet

Relative Humidity: 74%
Wind Speed: 8.1 mph

Seasonal Change

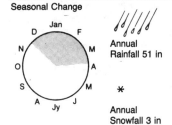

Annual Rainfall 51 in

Annual Snowfall 3 in

Clear 104 days	Partly Cloudy 113 days	Cloudy 148 days

Precipitation Days: 112   Storm Days: 64

Average Temperatures		
	Daily High	Daily Low
January	61	39
February	64	41
March	70	46
April	78	54
May	85	62
June	89	69
July	91	71
August	90	71
September	85	67
October	78	56
November	69	45
December	62	39
Zero-Degree Days: 0		
Freezing Days: 35		
90-Degree Days: 54		

Southport, NC

Terrain: Located on the Atlantic Ocean in the Tidewater section of North Carolina at the extreme southeastern corner of the state. The surrounding terrain, typical of the state's Coastal Plain, is low-lying (the average elevation is less than 40 feet) and level. There are many rivers, creeks, and lakes nearby, most with considerable swampy growth surrounding them. Large tracts of southern mixed forest alternate with cultivated fields.

Climate: The climate here shows a strong maritime influence. Summers are warm and humid, but excessive heat is rare. During the colder part of the year, polar air masses reach the coastal areas, causing sharp temperature drops. However, much of the coldness of these air masses has diminished by the time they reach this area. Rainfall is ample and well distributed, with most occurring in summer in the form of thundershowers. In winter, rain may fall steadily for several days. Snowfall is very slight. Some tropical storms reach the Cape Fear area every few years.

Pluses: Warm, moist, mild and steady.

Minuses: Hot and muggy summers; prone to tropical storms.

Score: 697   **Rank: 41**

Elevation: 20 feet

Relative Humidity: 75%
Wind Speed: 8.9 mph

Seasonal Change

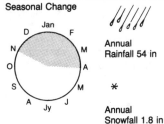

Annual Rainfall 54 in

Annual Snowfall 1.8 in

Clear 113 days	Partly Cloudy 106 days	Cloudy 146 days

Precipitation Days: 117   Storm Days: 46

Average Temperatures		
	Daily High	Daily Low
January	57	36
February	59	38
March	65	44
April	74	52
May	81	61
June	87	68
July	89	72
August	88	71
September	84	66
October	75	55
November	67	44
December	58	38
Zero-Degree Days: 0		
Freezing Days: 49		
90-Degree Days: 28		

State College, PA

Terrain: Located in Centre County, the geographic center of Pennsylvania. The orientation of the ridges and valleys of the Appalachian Mountains is northeast to southwest. Elevations within Centre County vary from 977 feet to 2,400 feet. The largest valley in the area is Nittany Valley, much of which is under cultivation. The surrounding higher elevations are covered with second-growth forests.

Climate: A composite of the relatively dry midwestern continental climate and the more humid climate characteristic of the eastern seaboard. Prevailing westerly winds carry weather disturbances from the interior of the country into the area. Coastal storms occasionally affect the local weather as they move toward the northeast, but generally, the Atlantic is too distant to have a noticeable effect on the climate. Winters are cold and relatively dry, with thick cloud cover. Summer and fall are the most pleasant seasons of the year.

Pluses: Nice falls, summers.

Minuses: Humid, lots of cloudy days.

Score: 438   **Rank: 119**

Elevation: 1,200 feet

Relative Humidity: 55%
Wind Speed: 7.8 mph

Seasonal Change

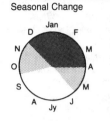

Annual Rainfall 37 in

Annual Snowfall 48 in

Clear 66 days   Partly Cloudy 114 days   Cloudy 185 days

Precipitation Days: 122   Storm Days: 35

Average Temperatures		
	Daily High	Daily Low
January	33	18
February	36	19
March	45	27
April	59	38
May	70	48
June	79	57
July	82	61
August	81	60
September	74	52
October	62	41
November	49	33
December	37	23

Zero-Degree Days: 4
Freezing Days: 132
90-Degree Days: 8

Tucson, AZ

Terrain: Lies at the foot of the Catalina Mountains in a flat to gently rolling valley floor in southern Arizona.

Climate: Desert, characterized by a long, hot season beginning in April and ending in October. Temperature maxima above 90° F are the rule during this period; on 41 days each year, on the average, the temperature reaches 100° F. These high temperatures are modified by low humidity, reducing discomfort. Tucson lies in the zone receiving more sunshine than any other in the United States. Clear skies or very thin, high clouds permit intense surface heating during the day and active radiational cooling at night, a process enhanced by the characteristic atmospheric dryness.

Pluses: Clear, warm, dry.

Minuses: Intense summer heat.

Score: 692   **Rank: 44**

Elevation: 2,555 feet

Relative Humidity: 30%
Wind Speed: 8.2 mph

Seasonal Change

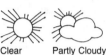

Annual Rainfall 11 in

Annual Snowfall 2 in

Clear 198 days   Partly Cloudy 89 days   Cloudy 78 days

Precipitation Days: 50   Storm Days: 40

Average Temperatures		
	Daily High	Daily Low
January	64	38
February	67	40
March	72	44
April	81	50
May	90	58
June	98	66
July	98	74
August	95	72
September	93	67
October	84	56
November	72	45
December	65	39

Zero-Degree Days: 0
Freezing Days: 21
90-Degree Days: 139

Virginia Beach–Norfolk, VA

Terrain: Located on low level land, with Chesapeake Bay immediately to the north, Hampton Roads to the west, and the Atlantic Ocean to the east.

Climate: The metro area is in a favorable geographic position, being north of the track of hurricanes and tropical storms and south of high-latitude storm systems. Winters are mild. Springs and falls are especially pleasant. Summers, though, are warm, humid, and long. A temperature of zero has never been recorded here, although there is occasional snow.

Pluses: Four-season climate suited for year-round outdoor activities.

Minuses: Long, humid summers.

Score: 634   **Rank: 61**

Elevation: 30 feet

Relative Humidity: 58%
Wind Speed: 10.6 mph

Seasonal Change

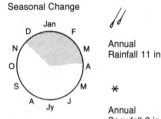

Annual Rainfall 45 in

Annual Snowfall 7 in

Clear 110 days   Partly Cloudy 102 days   Cloudy 153 days

Precipitation Days: 115   Storm Days: 37

Average Temperatures		
	Daily High	Daily Low
January	49	32
February	50	33
March	57	39
April	68	48
May	76	57
June	84	66
July	87	70
August	85	69
September	80	64
October	70	53
November	61	43
December	51	34

Zero-Degree Days: 0
Freezing Days: 54
90-Degree Days: 30

★ West Palm Beach–Boca Raton–Delray Beach, FL

Terrain: Located on the coastal sand ridge of southeastern Florida. The entire coastal ridge is only about 5 miles wide and in early times the Everglades reached to its western edge. Now most of the swampland has been drained for development. The Atlantic Ocean forms the eastern edge, and the Gulf Stream flows northward 2 miles offshore, its nearest approach to the Florida coast.

Climate: Because of its southerly location near the ocean, the area has an equable climate. Winters are pleasantly warm. Summer daytime temperatures are high but are tempered by the ocean breeze, and by the frequent formation of cumulus clouds which shade the land without completely obscuring the sun. Rarely does the thermometer climb beyond 95° F. The moist, unstable air in this area results in frequent showers, usually of short duration.

Pluses: Single season, sub-tropical climate.

Minuses: Hurricanes, frequent summer thunder-storms.

Score: 859

Rank: 5

Elevation: 21 feet

Relative Humidity: 60%
Wind Speed: 9.4 mph

Seasonal Change

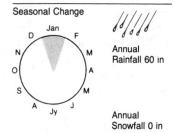

Annual Rainfall 60 in

Annual Snowfall 0 in

Clear 73 days

Partly Cloudy 155 days

Cloudy 137 days

Precipitation Days: 132 Storm Days: 79

Average Temperatures		
	Daily High	Daily Low
January	75	56
February	76	56
March	79	60
April	83	65
May	86	69
June	88	73
July	90	74
August	90	74
September	88	75
October	84	70
November	80	63˙
December	76	57

Zero-Degree Days: 0
Freezing Days: 1
90-Degree Days: 55

Yuma, AZ

Terrain: Yuma is located in the extreme southwest corner of Arizona, near the California and Mexican borders. The land is typical desert-steppe, with dry, sandy, and dusty soil, scant vegetation, and craggy buttes and mountains that take their characteristic texture from wind erosion rather than water erosion. The various mountain ranges that surround Yuma are perhaps the dominant geologic features. They include the Trigo, Chocolate, Castle Dome, Mohawk, and Gila ranges.

Climate: Yuma's climate is definitely a desert product. Home heating is necessary from late October to mid-April. However, outdoor activities can be conducted comfortably during this period from 10:00 AM to 5:00 PM. It is very dry, with many places in the world receiving more rain in a year than has fallen in Yuma in the past 90 years. Yuma is officially the sunniest place in America.

Pluses: America's sunniest spot.

Minuses: Hot, dry, dusty.

Score: 692

Rank: 44

Elevation: 194 feet

Relative Humidity: 32%
Wind Speed: 7.8 mph

Seasonal Change

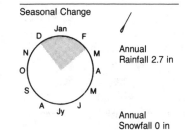

Annual Rainfall 2.7 in

Annual Snowfall 0 in

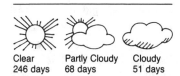

Clear 246 days

Partly Cloudy 68 days

Cloudy 51 days

Precipitation Days: 16   Storm Days: 7

Average Temperatures		
	Daily High	Daily Low
January	67	43
February	73	46
March	78	50
April	86	57
May	93	64
June	101	71
July	106	81
August	104	81
September	100	74
October	90	62
November	77	50
December	68	44

Zero-Degree Days: 0
Freezing Days: 2
90-Degree Days: 168

 ET CETERA: Climate

CLIMATE AND HEALTH

Relative humidity, barometric pressure, and altitude are just a few factors related to climate or terrain that can influence your physical well-being. There is no proven link between longevity and climate, although the three places on the globe whose populations have the highest percentage of centenarians—the Caucasus Mountains of the Soviet Union, the mountains of Bolivia, and northwestern India—are all in southerly latitudes at high elevations. But in America, where careful records have been kept for generations, a sim-

ilar situation does not exist. In fact, most of the longest average life spans have been recorded in states with severe climates—Minnesota, North Dakota, and Iowa, for example.

It has been shown, however, that people with certain chronic diseases or disorders are far more comfortable in some climates than others. Asthmatics generally do best in warm, dry places that have a minimum of airborne allergens and no molds. People with rheumatism or arthritis find comfort in warm, moist southerly climates where the weather is constant and the atmospheric pressure undergoes the least daily change. Those who suffer from tuberculosis or emphysema seem to do best in the lower elevations of mountainous locales with lots of clear air and sunshine.

A brief classic in the field of bioclimatology is H. E. Landsberg's *Weather and Health* (1969). Landsberg details some of the relationships that have been observed between climate and the aggravation of (or relief from) various physical afflictions. Drawing on this and other sources, *Retirement Places Rated* describes some basic weather phenomena and suggests how they can affect the way you feel.

Weather Stages: Beware of 3 and 4

The weather changes that cause the human body to react have been carefully studied by meteorologists and classified into six basic stages, which make up the clear–stormy–clear cycle that is constantly repeated all over the planet. The stages in the cycle have been linked to some of the joys and tragedies of human existence.

Stage 1. Cool, high-pressure air, with few clouds and moderate winds, followed by . . .

Stage 2. Perfectly clear, dry air, high pressure, and little wind, leading to . . .

Stage 3. Considerable warming, steady or slightly falling pressure, and some high clouds, until . . .

Stage 4. The warm, moist air gets into the lower layers; pressure falls, clouds thicken, precipitation is common, and the wind picks up speed; then . . .

Stage 5. An abrupt change takes place; showery precipitation is accompanied by cold, gusty winds, rapidly rising pressure, and falling humidity as the moisture in the air is released.

Stage 6. Gradually, the pressure rises still farther and the clouds diminish; temperatures reach low levels and the humidity continues to drop, leading back to . . .

Stage 1. Cool, high-pressure air . . .

Of course, these phases aren't equally long, either in any given sequence or in the course of a year. During winter, all six stages may follow one another within three days, while in the summer two weeks may pass before the cycle is completed.

Obviously, the "beautiful weather" stages 1 and 2 stimulate the body very little. They make few demands that cannot be met by adequate clothing and housing. In contrast, weather stages 4 and 5 are often violent; they stir us up, both mentally and physically.

That weather phases affect the human body is beyond question; the records of hospital births and deaths prove it. For example, in the case of human pregnancy, in far more cases than statistical accident would permit, labor begins on days that are in weather

stage 3. Coronary thrombosis—"heart attack"—shows a strong peak of frequency in weather stages 3 and 4, and a definite low in stages 1 and 6. Bleeding ulcers and migraine attacks peak in stage 4, too.

Weather events affect moods and behavior. There is a strong correlation between weather stage 3 and suicide, behavior problems in schoolchildren, and street riots. A study in Poland over a five-year period (1966–70) showed that accident rates in factory workers doubled during cyclonic weather conditions (stages 3 and 4: periods of falling pressure, rising temperatures and humidity, which signal the onset of stormy weather) and returned to normal low levels in fair weather. Animals as well as humans are affected. Dogcatchers are invariably busiest during stages 3, 4, and 5 because dogs become restless, stray from their homes, and wander through the streets.

The Three Determinants of Human Comfort

As the six weather stages suggest, everyday human comfort is influenced by three basic climatic factors: humidity, temperature, and barometric pressure.

Humidity. Humidity, or the amount of moisture in the air, is closely related to air temperature in determining the comfort level of the atmosphere. Much of the discomfort and nervous tension experienced at the approach of stormy weather (weather stage 4), for example, is the result of rising temperatures and humidity. These atmospheric conditions are also related, at least in part, to the behavioral problems and medical emergencies described previously.

Extremely high levels of atmospheric moisture, such as those experienced most of the time in the Pacific Northwest and around the Gulf of Mexico and southern Atlantic Coast, aren't usually the cause of direct discomfort except in persons suffering from certain types of arthritis or rheumatism. But even in these cases, the mild temperatures found in these maritime locations usually do much to offset discomfort. In fact, the stability of the barometric pressure (which means small or gradual shifts in the air pressure) in these areas makes them ideal for people with muscle and joint pain.

But damp air coupled with low temperatures can be uncomfortable. Most people who've experienced damp winters, especially in places with high winds, complain that the cold, wet wind seems to go right through them. And the harmful effect of cold, damp air on pulmonary diseases, particularly tuberculosis, has long been known. With this in mind, it's wise to consider carefully before moving to the northerly coastal locations on the Eastern Seaboard—Cape Cod and the coast of Maine, for example—where these conditions are common during the winter.

Perhaps the most noticeable drawback to very moist air is the wide variety of organisms it supports. Bacteria, and the spores of fungi and molds, thrive in moist air but are almost absent in dry air. If the air is moist

Temperature, Humidity, and Apparent Temperature

Apparent Temperature

Air Temperature (°F)	0	5	10	15	20	25	30	35	40	45	50	55	60	65	70	75	80	85	90	95	100
110	99	102	105	108	112	117	123	130	137	143	150										
105	95	97	100	102	105	109	113	118	123	129	135	142	149								
100	91	93	95	97	99	101	104	107	110	115	120	126	132	138	144						
95	87	88	90	91	93	94	96	98	101	104	107	110	114	119	124	130	136				
90	83	84	85	86	87	88	90	91	93	95	96	98	100	102	106	109	113	117	122		
85	78	79	80	81	82	83	84	85	86	87	88	89	90	91	93	95	97	99	102	105	108
80	73	74	75	76	77	77	78	79	79	80	81	81	82	83	85	86	86	87	88	89	91
75	69	69	70	71	72	72	73	73	74	74	75	75	76	76	77	77	78	78	79	79	80
70	64	64	65	65	66	66	67	67	68	68	69	69	70	70	70	70	71	71	71	71	72

Relative Humidity (%)

Locate the air temperature at the left and the relative humidity along the bottom. The intersection of the horizontal row of figures opposite the temperature with the vertical row of figures above the relative humidity is the apparent temperature. For example, an air temperature of 85 degrees feels like 89 degrees at 55 percent relative humidity; but when the humidity is 90 percent, 85 degrees feels like 102.

and also warm, the problem is multiplied. Therefore, people prone to bacterial skin infections, fungal infections such as athlete's foot, or mold allergies should carefully check out places with high humidities before moving there.

On the other end of the spectrum, very dry air produces effects that are perceptible almost immediately and can cause discomfort within a day. When the relative humidity falls below 50 percent, most persons experience dry nasal passages and perhaps a dry, tickling throat. In the dry areas of the Southwest, where the humidity can drop to 20 percent or less, many people experience nosebleeds, flaking skin, and constant sore throats.

Temperature. Many bioclimatologists maintain that the human body is most comfortable and productive at "65–65," meaning an air temperature of 65 degrees with 65 percent humidity. High relative humidity intensifies the felt effect of high temperatures (see the table "Temperature, Humidity, and Apparent Temperature") because it impairs the evaporative cooling effect of sweating. At apparent temperatures as low as 80 to 90 degrees Fahrenheit, a person may begin to suffer symptoms of heat stress. The degree of heat stress experienced will vary depending on age, health, and body characteristics; generally speaking, infants, young children, and older adults are most likely to be affected by high temperature/humidity combinations. In the summer of 1980, record heat waves accompanied by high humidity swept the Southwest, leaving hundreds dead.

The map "Apparent Temperatures (July)" shows how felt temperatures vary across the country. The places in America where the highest temperatures are constantly recorded are mainly in the desert areas of the Great Basin (the southern half of the plateau between the Sierra Nevada to the west and the Rocky Mountains to the east), the Great Interior Valley of California, and parts of the High Plains regions of New Mexico, Oklahoma, and Texas. However, these areas are generally dry, so the effects of the high

temperatures on the body are not particularly noticeable or damaging. This is especially true of locations west of eastern New Mexico.

America's southeastern quadrant (which includes those states that border the Gulf of Mexico and the southern half of the Atlantic Coast) has temperatures that are less spectacularly high but humidity that can be oppressive. Most people would find a 90-degree day in Biloxi–Gulfport or Orlando far more uncomfortable than they would a day of the same temperature in Las Vegas or Yuma, Arizona.

What about cold temperatures? Throughout the 1960s and 1970s, most older adults shunned cold weather in favor of the hot and sunny beach climates of the Sun Belt. Now, many are discovering the benefits of seasonal change and some cold weather, particularly around the holiday season. *Retirement Places Rated* includes many retirement places that have cold weather. Some of these—most notably in Michigan, Wisconsin, and Montana—have winters that can be rigorous and are not for the faint of heart.

Cold weather can have an adverse effect on persons with heart or circulatory ailments. According to H. E. Landsberg, these diseases follow a seasonal pattern, with a peak of deaths occurring in January and February. The cooling of the extremities can place greater stress on the heart as it tries to maintain a safe body temperature; breathing very cold air can tax the heart–lung system, and some persons who have hardening of the coronary arteries may get chest pains when outdoors in a cold wind. Cold weather can also increase blood pressure, with adverse consequences for those with circulatory problems. Although extremely cold (polar) weather inhibits the survival of respiratory germs, these microbes thrive in a damp, cloudy, cool climate and contribute to a high incidence of influenza, bronchitis, and colds.

As the body gets older, its circulatory system loses effectiveness. Add to this another natural consequence of aging—the decreased rate of metabolism that keeps the body warm—and you have partially explained

Apparent Temperatures (July)

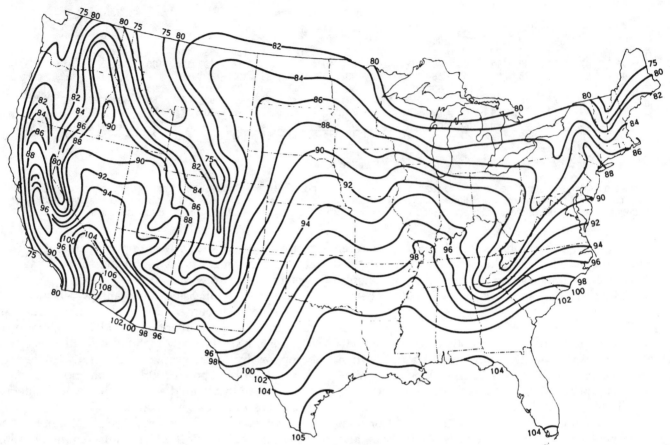

Source: National Oceanic and Atmospheric Administration, National Climatic Center, Asheville, North Carolina.

older adults' needs for higher household temperatures. Therefore, the expense of heating costs in a cool climate may offset the appeal of seasonal changes and winter weather.

But despite the dangers of extremes of heat or cold, sudden wide shifts of temperature in either direction constitute the gravest threat to human health. When the weather (and especially the temperature) changes suddenly and dramatically, the rates of cardiac arrest, respiratory distress, stroke, and other medical emergencies skyrocket.

Sudden atmospheric cooling can bring on attacks of asthma, bronchitis, and stroke. Heart attacks and other associated symptoms are also more frequent following these periods of rapid cooling. Often these are produced by changing air masses during autumn, particularly by the passage of a cold frontal system following a quickly falling barometer.

A sudden rise in the temperature may precipitate its own assortment of medical emergencies, among them heat stroke, heart attack, and stroke. During a heat wave, the nighttime maximum air temperature is far more significant than the daytime maximum. This is because the body recuperates during the night. A hot night prevents the body from reestablishing its thermal equilibrium and tends to lessen the amount of sleep a person gets, thus increasing fatigue. Hospital employees call these sudden temperature shifts, which cause so much discomfort and harm, especially to older adults, "ambulance weather." It's a term that proves to be accurate, if unseemly. A study of the New York City heat wave of July 1966 revealed that the death rate more than doubled during the period of record temperature. The number of deaths from flu and pneumonia rose 315 percent, from strokes more than 176 percent, from heart attacks 161 percent, and from cancer 128 percent.

Barometric pressure. Even though most people may be unaware of the source of their discomfort, barometric pressure and its wide and rapid fluctuations are extremely powerful influences on human performance, comfort, and health. Pressure changes are felt even more keenly by older adults, whose bodies are generally more sensitive to change. As previously stated, the rapid fall of pressure that signals the arrival of storms and advancing cold fronts can trigger episodes of asthma, heart disease, stroke, and pain in the joints. People with rheumatism or arthritis may suffer unduly if they live in places where pressure changes are continual and rapid. The map "Pressure Changes from Day to Day (February)" shows the regions with greatest and least pressure changes during

Pressure Changes from Day to Day (February)

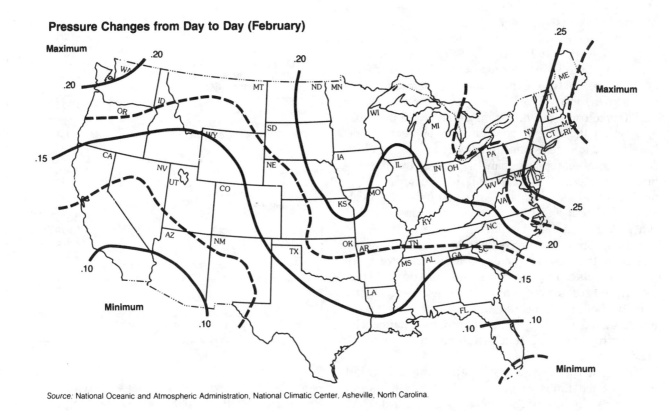

Source: National Oceanic and Atmospheric Administration, National Climatic Center, Asheville, North Carolina.

an average day in February, when joint pain and other discomforts reach their peak.

As the map shows, the northern and eastern sections of the country experience the greatest variance, averaging a barometric change of .20 inch to .25 inch from one day to the next. (In summer, when pressure changes are relatively small, the average change in these regions is approximately .10 inch.) States in the southern latitudes, particularly Florida and southern California, show the least change, only about .10 inch in February (and less than .05 inch in summer). Of course, these figures are averages, and along the Gulf and Atlantic coasts, large and rapid pressure changes are caused on occasion by hurricanes.

The pressure changes map, and the phenomenon it depicts, explain perhaps more than any other single reason why so many older adults have chosen to move to Florida and the Gulf Coast. Additionally, due to the stabilizing and modifying effects that large bodies of water have on temperature and pressure, weather conditions by seacoasts are steadier than those of most inland, desert, or mountain locations.

Although the climates found in Florida and the other Gulf states are not as pleasant year-round as they are advertised to be, there is no denying that the semitropical climate—hot, humid, monotonous, and even depressing as it might be to some—is just about perfect for people with severe rheumatoid joint pain or those who cannot tolerate sudden changes in the weather.

Questing for Relief

People with heart conditions should definitely avoid extreme heat and cold, rapid temperature variations, and extreme and sudden pressure changes. This can rule out most interior regions as well as northerly ones, even those on coastal locations. Recommended are places that have warm, mild, and steady weather. Mountains and high altitudes should be avoided on two counts: less oxygen and strain caused by steep grades. Best bets are southerly coastal locations where sea-level, oxygen-rich air and stable pressures and temperatures predominate most of the year. Look along the coast of the Mid-Atlantic Metro Belt southward all the way around the Florida peninsula and westward along the Gulf. Also look along the southern third of the Pacific coastline.

Emphysema brings a completely different set of problems and solutions. In general, excessive dampness, coupled with cool or cold weather, is harmful. This eliminates all northerly locations, particularly the Pacific Northwest, New England, and the North Woods. Southerly coastal locations are better, but the air is perhaps still too damp. Seek out warm, sunny, dry climates such as those found in Arizona, New Mexico, Utah, Nevada, and the interior valleys of California. Remember to avoid high elevations.

Asthma is a complex disorder that is not yet completely understood. While it is believed to be an autoimmune disorder similar to allergies, it may be precipitated or worsened by different things in different individuals. Your wisest course is to consult medical specialists first to determine the specific cause of your attacks. Asthmatics seem to do best in the pollen-free, dry, warm air found in greatest abundance in the Desert Southwest. Because the air on the desert floor can be dusty, seeking a moderate altitude there may be beneficial.

Tuberculosis, recently considered a waning disease, is on the rise. It generally strikes people who have weakened resistance to infection, making older adults more susceptible than the rest of the population. Treatment is multifaceted, but an area that is mild, dry, sunny, and has clear air helps a great deal. Mountain locations have always been popular and can provide relief if the altitude isn't excessive. Because dampness isn't recommended, the dry, sunny places in the southern mountains of the West are preferable to locations in the southern Appalachians. Ocean breezes are thought to be beneficial, too, and may be better for people who cannot tolerate the more rugged climate of the interior mountains. Hawaii or the coast of southern California would be ideal.

For people with rheumatic pains, and discomfort in amputated limbs or in old scar tissue, the warm and steady climates of the subtropics are perfect. Here the surrounding water keeps temperatures and pressures from shifting quickly, and the prevailing warmth is soothing. It would be hard to miss with any seafront location from Myrtle Beach, South Carolina, south to the Florida Keys, around and up the west coast of the Florida peninsula, westward along the Gulf and down all the way to the mouth of the Rio Grande. Southern California and Hawaii, of course, shouldn't be overlooked.

Life at the Top

Many mountain resort areas got their start as 19th-century health retreats. Back then, "night air" and "bad air" were seen as causes for chronic respiratory diseases. The antidote demanded by well-to-do patients (and prescribed by their doctors) was "pine air" and a high altitude.

While most mountain air is clear and relatively free from pollutants, it also contains less oxygen. A rapid change to a high altitude is risky for people with heart diseases and arteriosclerosis. If you suffer from asthma, emphysema, or anemia, you should consult local physicians before moving to any place more than 2,000 feet above sea level. Even if all indications point to a positive reaction on your part, it would be wise to take up residence for at least several months before making a permanent move.

For those who can tolerate the high country, the advantages of such locations are well known. Because atmospheric temperature decreases with increasing elevation (about 3.3 degrees Fahrenheit per 1,000 feet), places at high elevations in southerly locales (such as

High Retirement Places	
	Elevation Above Sea Level
Santa Fe, NM	7,200 feet
South Lake Tahoe–Placerville, CA	6,260
Colorado Springs, CO	6,170
Prescott, AZ	5,366
Albuquerque, NM	5,314
Grass Valley–Truckee, CA	5,280
Fort Collins–Loveland, CO	5,004
Grand Junction, CO	4,843
Carson City–Minden, NV	4,687
Reno, NV	4,400
Deming, NM	4,336
Las Cruces, NM	3,881
Roswell, NM	3,669
Bend, OR	3,599
Hamilton–Bitterroot Valley, MT	3,572
Kalispell, MT	2,965
St. George–Zion, UT	2,880
Boise, ID	2,868
Twain Harte–Yosemite, CA	2,577
Tucson, AZ	2,555

Source: National Oceanic and Atmospheric Administration, Local Climatological Data and Climatography of the United States.

Santa Fe, New Mexico, or Asheville and Hendersonville–Brevard in North Carolina) enjoy the long summers and mild winters typical of the South, and also the cool summers, crisp autumns, and absence of mugginess usually associated with more northerly areas.

Since altitude puts a certain amount of stress on the body's circulatory system and lungs, becoming acclimated to high places leads to good health. A higher altitude accelerates respiration and increases the lung capacity, strengthens the heart, increases the metabolic rate, and boosts the number and proportion of red blood cells.

In the United States, the highest town with a post office is Climax, Colorado. At 11,350 feet, Climax is beyond the comfort range of many older adults. Up here, a 3-minute egg takes 7 minutes to boil, corn on the cob needs to be on the fire 45 minutes, and home-brewed beer matures in half the expected time. Yet many of the 4,000 residents love it. The incidence of infection is amazingly low, and insects are practically unknown. In the East, the highest town of any size is Highlands, North Carolina, in the Great Smoky Mountains. Though less than half as high as Climax, Highlands and the neighboring towns offer the cool, clear air and invigorating climate that have long drawn people to the mountains.

NATURAL HAZARDS

We're all familiar—even if only through television or newspapers—with the awesome destruction that nature can unleash. Perhaps no sight in recent memory was more dramatic than the 1980 eruption of Mount St. Helens, with an initial blast equivalent to that of

10 million tons of TNT, that blew off the topmost 1,300 feet of the mountain. Volcanic eruptions can wipe out lives and property in an instant. Fortunately, however, volcanoes usually give warning of impending activity, as did Mount St. Helens. Even more fortunately, the places where volcanic activity is a potential hazard are very few. A number of violent natural events are much more common and widespread, and although they may be less cataclysmic than a full-blown volcanic eruption, they can cause great damage and present life-threatening conditions. Many of these natural hazards follow definite geographic patterns within the United States, and some retirement places are at much greater risk than others.

The Sun Belt Is Also a Storm Belt

Most severe storms occur in the southern half of the nation. For this reason, one might say the Sun Belt is also a storm belt.

Thunderstorms and Lightning. Thunderstorms are common and don't usually cause death. But lightning kills 200 Americans a year. It remains the most common and frequent natural danger. At any given moment there are about 2,000 thunderstorms in progress around the globe; in the time it takes you to read this paragraph, lightning will have struck the earth 700 times.

Florida, the Sunshine State, is actually the country's stormiest state, with three times as much thunder and lightning as any other. California, Oregon, and Washington are the three most storm-free states. In a typical year, coastal California towns average between 2 and 5 thunderstorm episodes. Most American towns average between 35 and 50. Fort Myers, Florida, averages 128. (A thunderstorm episode represents the presence of a single storm cell; a place like Fort Myers can register 4 or 5 episodes in a single day.)

The Place Profiles earlier in this chapter tell how many thunderstorm days each place can expect in an average year. The southeastern quadrant of our country generally receives more rain and thunderstorms than the rest, although the thunderstorms of the Great Plains are awesome spectacles.

Tornadoes. While they are not nearly as large or long-lived as hurricanes and release much less total force, tornadoes have more killing power concentrated in a small area than any other storm known. For absolute ferocity and wind speed, a tornado has no rival.

The hallmark of this vicious inland storm is the huge, snakelike funnel cloud that sweeps and bounces along the ground, destroying buildings, sweeping up cars, trains, livestock, and trees, and sucking them up hundreds of feet into the whirling vortex. Wind speeds close to 300 miles per hour have been recorded.

Although no one can tell for certain just where particular tornadoes might touch down, their season, origin, and direction of travel are fairly predictable. Tornado season reaches its peak in late spring and early summer, and most storms originate in the central and southern Great Plains, in the states of Oklahoma, Texas, Arkansas, Kansas, and Missouri. After forming in the intense heat and rising air of the plains, these storms proceed toward the northeast at speeds averaging 25–40 miles per hour. Most tornadoes do not last long or travel far. Half of all tornadoes reported travel less than 5 miles on the ground; a rare few have been tracked for more than 200 miles.

Of all the 151 retirement places, the lake locations in Oklahoma, any location in Texas or Arkansas, and even the locations in Kentucky and Tennessee, have a high potential for tornado damage and danger (see map "Tornado and Hurricane Risk Areas"). Nearly one-third of all tornadoes ever reported in the United States have occurred within the boundaries of Kansas, Oklahoma, and Texas.

Hurricanes. Giant tropical cyclonic storms that originate at sea, hurricanes are unmatched for sheer power over a very large area. Hurricanes last for days, measure hundreds of miles across, and release tremendous energy in the form of high winds, torrential rains, lightning, and tidal surges. They occur in late summer and fall, and strike the Gulf states and southern segments of the Atlantic Coast primarily, though they will also strike locations farther north (see map "Tornado and Hurricane Risk Areas"). Like thunderstorms, hurricanes are much less frequent, and less severe, on the Pacific Coast.

Hurricanes usually originate in the tropical waters of the Atlantic Ocean. They occur toward summer's end because it takes that long for the water temperature and evaporation rate to rise sufficiently to begin the cyclonic, counterclockwise rotation of a wind system around a low-pressure system. When the wind velocities are less than 39 miles per hour, this cyclone is called a "tropical depression"; when wind velocities are between 39 and 74 miles per hour, the cyclone is called a "tropical storm." And when the winds reach 74 miles per hour, the storm becomes a hurricane.

Often the greatest danger and destruction from hurricanes aren't due to the winds but to the tidal surges that sweep ashore with seas 15 feet or more higher than normal high tides. Although Florida and the southern coasts are most vulnerable to hurricanes, locations as far north as Cape Cod and the coast of Maine are by no means untouched.

Earthquake Hazard

California and the Pacific Northwest may be relatively free of the thunderstorms, tornadoes, and hurricanes that buffet other parts of the country. But these states are in the area of the country most prone to earthquake damage. A glance at the map "Earthquake Hazard Zones," which predicts not only the probability of

Tornado and Hurricane Risk Areas

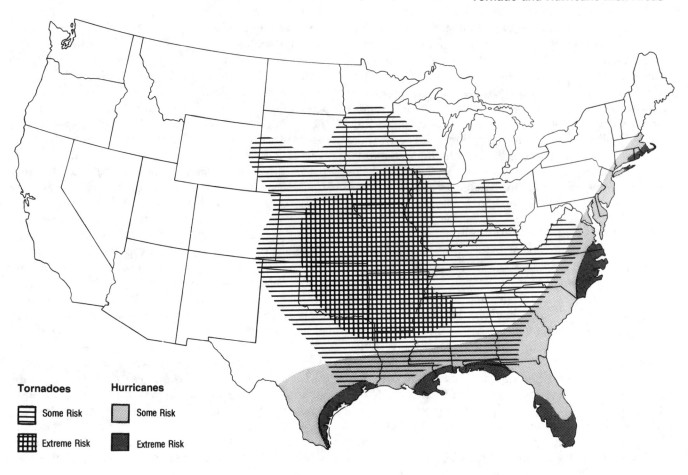

Tornadoes

Some Risk

Extreme Risk

Hurricanes

Some Risk

Extreme Risk

Earthquake Hazard Zones

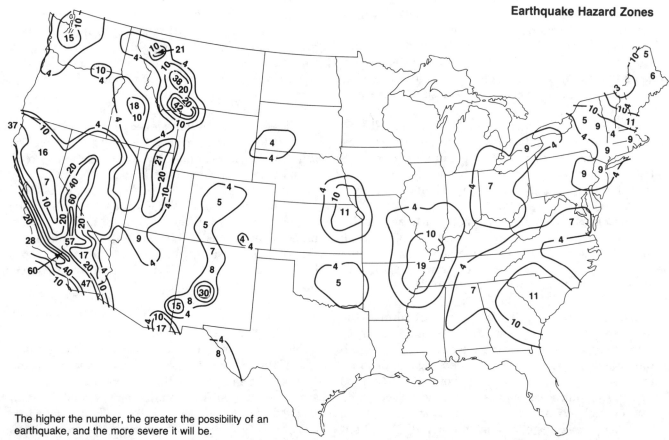

The higher the number, the greater the possibility of an earthquake, and the more severe it will be.

Source: U.S. Geological Survey Open-File Report 76-416, 1976.

earthquakes but also their severity, confirms this.

All retirement places in California, Nevada, and Utah have the potential for substantial earthquake damage. Some locations in Oregon (such as Bend, Medford–Ashland, and Newport–Lincoln City) are relatively safe, but the Puget Sound area of Washington has experienced two major shocks in the past 35 years, both causing considerable damage. Portions of Montana and Idaho also are very vulnerable to earthquakes.

Other pockets of earthquake risk might surprise you. Albuquerque is situated in a danger area, and so is Deming, New Mexico. The resorts of the South Carolina and Georgia coasts sit in the middle of a quake-sensitive zone that was the site of the strongest quake ever measured east of the Mississippi (it happened in Charleston, South Carolina, in 1886). The entire New England region shares a danger roughly comparable to this area; Boston has suffered a severe quake and remains earthquake-prone today. A series of quakes occurred in southeastern Missouri in 1811–12, changing the course of the Mississippi River and creating a major lake. There is still some risk in this area, which includes the retirement places in western Kentucky and Tennessee and part of the Ozarks.

When It Comes to Natural Hazards, Can Anyone Win?

After studying the maps for a while, you may come to the dismal conclusion that you cannot win: where one natural disaster area stops, another begins. Some areas, like the coasts of South Carolina and Georgia, appear to possess a triple-whammy combination of earthquake, tornado, and hurricane hazards.

Studying the map more closely, you might begin to detect retirement areas that seem safer than others. One such area is the Pacific Northwest, with the exception of the significant earthquake risk around Puget Sound. Parts of Arizona, Utah, and New Mexico, too, are relatively free from disaster risk. The southern Appalachians, despite a moderate earthquake risk, do not experience many storms, due to the protection of the mountains. But some parts of the region are flood-prone. And moderate earthquake risk seems almost unavoidable anywhere but the frigid North Central Plains or the steamy, tornado-ridden flatlands of Texas and the Gulf states.

So, as with most things in life, when it comes to avoiding natural disasters, you can only pay your money and take your chances.

HAY FEVER SUFFERERS, TAKE NOTE

It doesn't come from hay, and it doesn't cause a fever, but that's not much consolation to the 18 million Americans afflicted with hay fever.

Hay fever is an allergic reaction of the eyes, nose, or throat to certain airborne particles. These particles may be any of pollen from seed-bearing trees, grasses, and weeds, or spores from certain molds. The term originated in Britain 150 years ago, when people assumed its feverlike symptoms had something to do with the fall haying. Most individuals might think that once they're into adulthood, they already know whether they have hay fever. But if you were to relocate, would you suddenly and mysteriously develop a continual runny nose and minor sore throat? Allergy problems aren't always alleviated by relocation, and sometimes a new allergen—absent where you used to live—can turn up to cause you problems with hay fever.

The incidence of hay fever varies around the world. In the Arctic, for example, it doesn't exist. Because of low temperatures and poor soil, arctic plants are small and primitive. In the tropics and subtropics, there is very little hay fever because the plants are generally flowered and produce pollen that is so heavy it cannot become airborne.

It is in the temperate regions that one finds the greatest amounts of irritating pollen. The worst places in America for hay fever are the middle regions, where grasses and trees without flowers predominate. Because farming continually disrupts the soil and therefore encourages the growth of weeds (especially the most troublesome of them all, ragweed), America's heartland is the most hay fever-ridden area. It extends from the Rockies to the Appalachian chain, and from the Canadian border down to the Mid-South.

Yet no areas of the country, except Alaska and the southern half of Florida, are free from hay fever—it's simply a question of degree.

Some retirement places that were once havens for asthmatics and hay fever sufferers are now less free of allergens. Examples are many of the fast-growing areas of the Desert Southwest. In the 1950s, Tucson was virtually free of ragweed pollen. Its desert location precluded the growth of weeds, grasses, and trees that cause hay fever. But as more and more people moved into the area, more trees were planted and lawns seeded. The result? A pollen index that's still good but not nearly as good as it used to be.

Personal Safety

In a coffee shop high up in Wisconsin's Door County peninsula, the talk one winter morning was of a condo break-in. Missing were a shopping bag of Pampers and a baby's crib. Left behind were a state-of-the-art stereo system, Waterford crystal, the silver, and a closet full of high-fashion ski-wear. Maybe people should all start locking their doors, the locals in the coffee shop agreed.

In Barnstable District Court on Cape Cod one spring day, two dozen persons were arraigned for a variety of offenses that wouldn't open the eyes of a police reporter for the Miami *Herald* or the San Antonio *Light*: possession of marijuana and conspiracy to violate controlled substance laws, operating under the influence and speeding, breaking and entering with intent to commit a felony, giving a false name to a police officer, and assault and battery.

In reality, Door County has no crime problem and Cape Cod hasn't much of one until the summer tourists come. Indeed, the odds of your being a crime victim in three out of four of the 151 places profiled in *Retirement Places Rated* are below the national average. Some are so safe you could hardly pay someone to assault you. Others, by comparison, seem just plain dangerous.

If you decide on retirement in Door County, the odds of your meeting up with violent crime in a year's residence are 1 in 3,147. Should you settle on Miami, the chances are 1 in 57. One could say that retirement on the southeast Florida coast is 55 times more dangerous than it is on the Lake Michigan shore in northern Wisconsin.

But raw odds distort the local crime picture. In spite of the popular idea that older persons are the preferred targets of crooks, you are more likely to have your pocket picked or your purse snatched than you are of being victimized by all other crimes. So why the need for a chapter on personal safety if your retirement years are statistically safer than all the years preceding?

The simple answer is that you are a different kind of crime victim whenever you have to trim back shrubbery along your home's foundation to limit a thief's potential hiding places, or have to get rid of the mailbox and install a mail slot in your front door, or have to check your car's door locks when driving down a darkened avenue, or have to keep feeling for your wallet at street festivals, or have to use only empty elevators, or have to stay indoors evenings more than you really care to. In some places such tactics are advised, in others they are merely prudent, and in still others they may not be necessary at all.

CRIME RISK: EIGHT CONNECTIONS

Why some places are safer than others is a topic guaranteed to get politicians, police, and citizens into arguments. For all the disagreement, criminologists have pinned down several factors.

Transience affects crime. Stable neighborhoods where people know each other and look out for one another's safety and property regardless of how many police cruise the area are a big deterrent. Strangers living next to each other in high turnover areas usually mean a high crime rate. Moreover, resorts that draw strangers—Myrtle Beach, South Carolina, and Ocean City, Maryland, for example—have serious crime problems. When visitors are added to year-round residents, the higher population improves the chances that victim and crook will eventually meet.

Population size is tied to crime rates. The safer retirement places—Fredericksburg, Texas, and Mountain Home, Arkansas, for instance—are rural. The more dangerous places—Miami is the extreme example—are urban. The rule doesn't always hold, certainly. Honolulu's crime rate looks like that of Kalispell, Montana. Key West's crime rate resembles San Antonio's.

Climate has a striking connection with breaking the law. Cops and crooks are busier in warmer parts of the country than in colder ones. Moreover, in the Sun Belt and in the Frost Belt, these adversaries are especially active during July and August when all crimes except robbery are more likely to occur. Since people spend more time outdoors during these months, they are more vulnerable. Homes are more unprotected during this season, too, because they are more frequently left with open windows and unlocked doors. Robbery, the cold weather exception, is highest in December because pedestrians carrying packages and shops doing brisk holiday business make attractive targets.

Even the local *traffic* is a factor. The ease with which a criminal can drive off down the street, escape onto an arterial road, and later be lost on the Interstate is an encouragement. One reason behind Los Alamos' low crime rate is that few crooks are dumb enough to commit a robbery when the only way out of town is down a winding, mountain road.

Time of day is still another factor. After sundown most cars are stolen, most retail businesses are held up, most persons are assaulted, and most thefts are committed. Burglaries, purse-snatchings, and pocket-pickings, on the other hand, happen more often during daylight hours.

Age and sex figure into the equation, too. Some 40 million persons in this country have arrest records for offenses other than traffic tickets. Most are male. In fact, half the people picked up by the police are under 20 years of age and four-fifths are male. None of this should be taken to mean that persons knock off gas stations, boost cars, or get involved in bar fights *because*

Crime Trends

Are the crime scores improving for some places and getting worse for others? The answer to both parts of the question is yes.

FALLING CRIME RATES

Charlevoix–Boyne City, MI
Coeur d'Alene, ID
Fairhope–Gulf Shores, AL
Fort Walton Beach, FL
Hamilton–Bitterroot Valley, MT
Kalispell, MT
Las Cruces, NM
Panama City, FL
Paris–Big Sandy, TN
San Juan Islands, WA
Santa Fe, NM
Vero Beach, FL

Crime scores for the places listed above have improved by more than 15%.

RISING CRIME RATES

Athens–Cedar Creek Lake, TX
Branson–Table Rock Lake, MO
Brevard, NC
Clayton, GA
Edenton–Albemarle Sound, NC
Kerrville, TX
New Braunfels, TX
Port Townsend, WA
Red Bluff–Sacramento Valley, CA
Redding, CA
St. George–Zion, UT
Thomasville, GA

Crime scores for the places listed above have worsened by more than 30%.

Source: Retirement Places Rated average annual score for the period 1985 through 1989 for each place compared with their 1985 scores.

they are young men, but these characteristics are associated with other factors in crime.

Economics play a role. Every time the nation's unemployment rate goes up 10 percent, police make a half million more arrests, according to a Johns Hopkins University study on unemployment's hidden costs. But joblessness and loss of income won't automatically make a place dangerous. Many of the safer places in America are poorer than average and suffer job losses during business slumps. Some more affluent communities, given similar sets of circumstances, aren't as safe as they appear: rich offenders tend to be arrested less frequently than poor ones, especially on suspicion. Once arrested, they are convicted less frequently. This is particularly true in juvenile cases involving thefts and break-ins.

Police strength, too, is related to crime rates. Manhattan has 1,300 sworn uniformed police officers per square mile. It's natural to think that safety rises or falls in direct proportion to the size of the local constabulary, but it just isn't so. Police definitely fight crime, but most of what they do is after the fact. They respond to complaints; they follow up on tips; they catch criminals; and they appear at trial. A large num-

Safer vs. More Dangerous Retirement Places

If you look at the crime rates for places detailed in the Place Profiles later in this chapter, one thing stands out. Whether you're talking of crimes of violence (which account for just 10 percent of all lawbreaking) or property crime, larger Sun Belt resorts suffer more from criminal activity than smaller, more rural places.

Violent Crime in the Retirement Places

SAFEST RETIREMENT PLACES	Violent Crime Rate
Door County, WI	31
Oak Harbor–Whidbey Island, WA	52
Mountain Home–Bull Shoals, AR	59
Los Alamos, NM	69
Bar Harbor–Frenchman Bay, ME	71

DANGEROUS RETIREMENT PLACES	Violent Crime Rate
Miami–Hialeah, FL	1,383
Brunswick–Golden Isles, GA	1,069
Albuquerque, NM	967
Charleston, SC	958
Key West–Key Largo–Marathon, FL	867

Source: FBI, unpublished "Crime by County" reports, 1985, 1986, 1987, 1988, and 1989.

The violent crime rate is the sum of rates for murder, forcible rape, robbery, and aggravated assault. The U.S. average is 613.

Property Crime in the Retirement Places

SAFEST RETIREMENT PLACES	Property Crime Rate
Mountain Home–Bull Shoals, AR	988
Paris–Big Sandy, TN	988
Los Alamos, NM	1,247
Brevard, NC	1,269
Southport, NC	1,512

DANGEROUS RETIREMENT PLACES	Property Crime Rate
El Centro–Calexico–Brawley, CA	9,220
Myrtle Beach, SC	8,312
Ocean City–Assateague Island, MD	8,150
Yuma, AZ	8,097
San Antonio, TX	8,023

Source: FBI, unpublished "Crime by County" reports, 1985, 1986, 1987, 1988, and 1989.

The property crime rate is the sum of rates for burglary, larceny-theft, and motor-vehicle theft. The U.S. average is 4,954.

---

ber of police per capita usually means a high-crime area rather than an area where crime is being prevented.

TRACKING CRIME

Every year some 16,000 police departments send figures of the number of crimes reported in their cities and towns to the FBI in Washington. Because of their seriousness, frequency, and likelihood of being reported, eight crimes make up the FBI's Crime Index. Four are classified as violent; four are property crimes:

Violent Crimes	Property Crimes
murder	burglary
forcible rape	larceny-theft
robbery	motor-vehicle theft
aggravated assault	arson

Because victims sometimes think it futile to file complaints, crimes aren't always reported and this affects the accuracy of the FBI's Crime Index. Even if a complaint is filed, the investigating officer's definition of the crime may affect the numbers. Purse-snatching is either a robbery or a larceny depending on the jurisdiction. Likewise, a slap in the face is either an aggravated or simple assault depending on motive.

Moreover, in the past, some cops either padded the figures to oust a judge considered soft on crime or to persuade the city council to increase the department's budget, or they fudged the number of crimes to create an image of effective law enforcement.

It's important to distinguish between the *incidence* of crime and the crime *rate*. Incidence is simply how many crimes are reported in a given place. In Lancaster, Pennsylvania, police investigate an average of 400 aggravated assaults a year. Far to the southwest, Las Cruces, New Mexico, police handle 300 similar cases. From these figures you might think that Lancaster is more dangerous than Las Cruces. But 413,000 people live in Lancaster while only 136,000 live in Las Cruces.

A truer measure of safety is the crime rate—the number of crimes per 100,000 people. Lancaster's assault rate is 94.2. Las Cruces' rate is 270.4, or more than twice that of Lancaster. But neither of these retirement places experiences assault rates near the national average—352.4.

SCORING: Personal Safety

The single crime the police file the most reports on is theft, whether it's a stolen garden hose or a shoplifted fur coat. Yet the FBI counts these heists as heavily as first-degree murder when it determines a place's crime rate.

Maui, for instance, has a total crime rate of 7,243, roughly on par with Las Vegas. But the two places aren't equally dangerous. Las Vegas' violent crime rate is more than twice as high as Maui's (796 versus 319). Although the Hawaiian island has a high property crime rate, it's safer than Las Vegas.

The realistic way to rate places for personal safety is simple: for each place, *Retirement Places Rated* averages the rates for violent and property crimes for the latest five-year period for which FBI data are available, but since property crimes are much less serious than crimes against people, they get one-tenth the weight of violent crimes. (Although arson has been a property crime since 1979, arson figures aren't included in the scoring because they are unavailable for many of the retirement places.) Each place starts with a base score of zero, and points are added according to these indicators:

1. *Violent crime rate.* The rates for all violent crimes—murder, rape, robbery, and aggravated assault—are totaled.
2. *Property crime rate.* The rates for burglary, larceny-theft, and motor-vehicle theft are added together, and the result is divided by 10.

The sum of a place's violent crime rate and one-tenth its property crime rate, rounded off, represents the score (the higher the score, the more dangerous the place).

SCORING EXAMPLES

A spa in the Arkansas Ouachitas, a Sun Belt capital, a New England college town, and a popular Florida resort show the scoring method for personal safety.

Hot Springs National Park, Arkansas (#98)

If resorts are saddled with sensational crime rates, this one is an exception. Adding its violent crime rate (472) to one-tenth its property crime rate (475) results in a total score of 947, a middlingly safe record.

It wasn't always this way. Up until 1967, when Governor Winthrop Rockefeller ordered state troopers to break up the craps tables, bulldoze the slot machines into a gravel pit, and close down the brothels, Hot Springs had a hundred-year, wide-open tradition for lawlessness.

Today, the locals will tell you that one-third of the annual crime occurs during the spring racing season at Oaklawn Park, and that the only other thing that distinguishes this retirement place in the eyes of the law is the phenomenal number of speeding tickets handed out on I-30 and on US 270 by the Arkansas Highway Patrol's Troop K.

Miami–Hialeah, Florida (#151)

In contrast to Hot Springs, metropolitan Miami has a crime score of 2,150, the sum of its violent crime rate (1,383) and one-tenth its property crime rate (767). The idea that this area is the national crime capital isn't taken from made-for-TV movies, it's based on fact.

Beset by rapid population growth and caught in the crosscurrents of the drug trade, criminal activity is so startlingly high in Dade County that the American Society of Criminology decided against holding its convention there this year because of the city's dubious reputation.

In Miami's favor, the crime rate is edging downward. Even so, in a typical year some 200,000 violent and property crimes are reported to the Metro-Dade police and their fellow officers in Hialeah, Miami, Miami Beach, and Opa-locka. Most of the 100,000 arrests are for larceny, drunk driving, possession and sale of drugs, prostitution and commercial vice, and disorderly conduct.

Amherst–Northampton, Massachusetts (#19)

If higher crime rates go along with young populations, Amherst–Northampton is an exception to the rule. One of every four people here is a student at the Five Colleges—Amherst, Hampshire, Mount Holyoke, Smith, and the University of Massachusetts. Yet Amherst–Northampton and surrounding Hampshire County experience crime rates far below the national average. Moreover, these rates have been dropping throughout the 1980s.

Theft is the most common complaint among the 3,200 crimes reported to the police in a typical year. Adding Amherst–Northampton's violent crime rate (157) to one-tenth its property crime rate (227) produces a total score of 384.

Fort Lauderdale–Hollywood–Pompano Beach, Florida (#125)

If there are a million visitors in Florida on a typical day, a hundred thousand of them are probably having fun on a Broward County beach. Given New England's weather, undergraduates from Amherst–Northampton's Five Colleges no doubt join the student migration here each spring break.

That's just the problem, according to Florida's Division of Tourism. Resorts here see too much carousing by young outsiders, *plus* scams by professional crooks from the Frost Belt and not a little violence carried out by persons just passing through. Because statistics don't take into account the number of visitors when per capita crime rates are figured, resorts seem more dangerous places to live in than they actually are.

Certainly Fort Lauderdale–Hollywood–Pompano Beach has less crime than neighboring Miami–Hialeah to the south and West Palm Beach–Boca Raton–Delray Beach immediately north. Lumping year-round residents and seasonal visitors together when calculating the crime rate might brighten the picture. Even so, the violent crime rate (662) and one-tenth the property crime rate (561) here are far above the national average, producing a crime score of 1,223.

RANKINGS: Personal Safety

In ranking 151 retirement places for personal safety, *Retirement Places Rated* uses two criteria: (1) the violent crime rate, and (2) the property crime rate divided by 10. The sum of these rates is the retirement place's score. The higher the score, the more dangerous the place.

Places receiving tie scores get the same rank and are listed in alphabetical order.

Retirement Places from First to Last

Rank	Score	Rank	Score	Rank	Score
1. Mountain Home–Bull Shoals, AR	158	43. New Paltz–Ulster County, NY	609	88. Burlington, VT	866
2. Los Alamos, NM	194	44. Bennington, VT	610	89. Panama City, FL	875
3. Paris–Big Sandy, TN	201	45. Columbia County, NY	612	90. Santa Barbara, CA	883
4. Southport, NC	239				
5. Brevard, NC	243	46. Fayetteville, AR	615	91. Lexington–Fayette, KY	886
		47. Grass Valley–Truckee, CA	623	92. Iowa City, IA	890
6. Oak Harbor–Whidbey Island, WA	247	48. Fort Myers–Cape Coral–Sanibel Island, FL	628	93. Eugene–Springfield, OR	891
7. Door County, WI	253	49. Ocean County, NJ	630	94. Twain Harte–Yosemite, CA	893
8. Fredericksburg, TX	263	50. New Bern, NC	631	95. Sarasota, FL	905
9. Harrison, AR	310				
10. Branson–Table Rock Lake, MO	318	51. Petoskey–Straits of Mackinac, MI	638	96. McAllen–Edinburg–Mission, TX	908
		52. Kerrville, TX	646	97. New Braunfels, TX	927
11. Bar Harbor–Frenchman Bay, ME	325	53. Prescott, AZ	651	98. Hot Springs National Park, AR	947
12. Clayton, GA	326	54. Bend, OR	667	99. Chico–Paradise, CA	951
13. Keene, NH	338	55. Laconia–Lake Winnipesaukee, NH	675	99. Wenatchee, WA	951
14. Grand Lake, OK	351				
15. Hamilton–Bitterroot Valley, MT	367	56. Olympia, WA	676	101. Biloxi–Gulfport–Pass Christian, MS	963
		57. Grand Junction, CO	677	102. Melbourne–Titusville–Palm Bay, FL	971
16. Crossville, TN	369	58. San Luis Obispo, CA	679	103. Houghton Lake, MI	977
17. Hanover, NH	373	59. Asheville, NC	681	104. Deming, NM	979
18. Camden–Penobscot Bay, ME	374	60. New Port Richey, FL	682	105. Red Bluff–Sacramento Valley, CA	1,001
19. Amherst–Northampton, MA	384				
20. Benton County, AR	386	61. Athens–Cedar Creek Lake, TX	688	106. Rockport–Aransas Pass, TX	1,008
		62. Charlottesville, VA	704	107. Maui, HI	1,011
21. Edenton–Albemarle Sound, NC	398	63. Lake Lanier, GA	715	108. Las Cruces, NM	1,036
22. Lancaster County, PA	399	64. Grants Pass, OR	718	109. Ocala, FL	1,042
23. San Juan Islands, WA	406	65. Coeur d'Alene, ID	721	110. St. Petersburg–Clearwater–Dunedin, FL	1,061
24. Charlevoix–Boyne City, MI	422				
25. State College, PA	436	66. Easton–Chesapeake Bay, MD	723	111. Cape Cod, MA	1,068
		66. Traverse City–Grand Traverse Bay, MI	723	111. Colorado Springs, CO	1,068
26. Hendersonville, NC	441	68. Madison, WI	741	113. Aiken, SC	1,070
27. Canandaigua, NY	445	69. Santa Fe, NM	743	114. Daytona Beach, FL	1,072
28. Pike County, PA	464	70. Bellingham, WA	759	115. Cape May, NJ	1,081
29. Canton–Lake Tawakoni, TX	468				
30. Eagle River, WI	480	71. Monticello–Liberty, NY	763	115. Virginia Beach–Norfolk, VA	1,081
		72. Medford–Ashland, OR	772	117. Alamogordo, NM	1,083
31. Burnet–Marble Falls–Llano, TX	481	73. Newport–Lincoln City, OR	773	118. Redding, CA	1,121
32. North Conway–White Mountains, NH	482	74. Carlsbad–Artesia, NM	780	119. Austin, TX	1,126
33. Murray–Kentucky Lake, KY	494	75. Kalispell, MT	783	120. Athens, GA	1,142
34. Fort Walton Beach, FL	495				
35. Portsmouth–Dover–Durham, NH	497	76. Honolulu, HI	785	121. Salinas–Seaside–Monterey, CA	1,143
		77. Carson City–Minden, NV	789	122. Roswell, NM	1,162
36. Martinsburg–Charles Town, WV	512	77. Chapel Hill, NC	789	123. St. Augustine, FL	1,189
37. Amador County, CA	553	79. South Lake Tahoe–Placerville, CA	791	124. San Diego, CA	1,215
38. Blacksburg, VA	564	80. Boise, ID	798	125. Fort Lauderdale–Hollywood–Pompano Beach, FL	1,223
39. St. George–Zion, UT	570				
40. Fairhope–Gulf Shores, AL	594	81. Vero Beach, FL	799	126. Lakeland–Winter Haven, FL	1,225
		82. St. Tammany Parish, LA	814	127. Pensacola, FL	1,238
41. Port Townsend, WA	596	83. Thomasville, GA	816	128. Reno, NV	1,265
42. Bloomington–Brown County, IN	606	84. Fort Collins–Loveland, CO	844	129. Brownsville–Harlingen, TX	1,267
		85. Naples, FL	845	129. Clear Lake, CA	1,267
		86. Santa Rosa–Petaluma, CA	846		
		87. Rehoboth Bay–Indian River Bay, DE	855		

Rank	Score	Rank	Score	Rank	Score
131. Lake Havasu City–Kingman, AZ	1,273	137. Hilton Head–Beaufort, SC	1,409	145. West Palm Beach–Boca Raton–Delray Beach, FL	1,507
132. Savannah, GA	1,307	138. El Centro–Calexico–Brawley, CA	1,429		
133. Phoenix–Tempe–Scottsdale, AZ	1,330	138. Gainesville, FL	1,429	146. Charleston, SC	1,532
134. Ann Arbor, MI	1,352	140. Las Vegas, NV	1,438	147. Key West–Key Largo–Marathon, FL	1,572
135. Bradenton, FL	1,369			148. Yuma, AZ	1,596
		141. Tucson, AZ	1,463	149. Albuquerque, NM	1,720
136. Ocean City–Assateague Island, MD	1,402	142. Orlando, FL	1,471	150. Brunswick–Golden Isles, GA	1,779
		143. San Antonio, TX	1,483	151. Miami–Hialeah, FL	2,150
		144. Myrtle Beach, SC	1,505		

 PLACE PROFILES: Personal Safety

The Place Profiles show each retirement place's average annual rates for seven crimes: murder, rape, robbery, aggravated assault, burglary, larceny-theft, and motor-vehicle theft for the latest five years for which data are available. These rates are divided into violent and property categories and a total rate for each of these categories is given. A star (★) preceding a place's name highlights it as one of the top 20 places for personal safety.

The next-to-last column indicates the crime trend over five years: 39 retirement places have an arrow

pointing downward, meaning their *Retirement Places Rated* crime rates during this period have dropped more than 5 percent; 59 places have an arrow pointing upward, meaning their rates have risen more than 5 percent; a dash for the remaining 53 places means the rates have neither risen nor dropped more than 5 percent.

All figures are from the FBI's unpublished "Crime by County" annual reports for 1985, 1986, 1987, 1988, and 1989.

	Violent Crime Rates					Property Crime Rates						
	Murder	Rape	Robbery	Assault	Total	Burglary	Larceny-Theft	Motor-Vehicle Theft	Total	SCORE	TREND	RANK
United States	8.3	35.7	217.0	352.4	613.4	1,332	3,088	534	4,954	1,109	–	
Aiken, SC	7.8	42.9	90.6	566.0	707	1,363	2,018	243	3,624	1,070	▼	113
Alamogordo, NM	1.9	8.9	34.6	484.3	530	1,559	3,711	260	5,530	1,083	–	117
Albuquerque, NM	11.4	56.2	259.9	639.4	967	2,457	4,575	501	7,533	1,720	▲	149
Amador County, CA	8.9	5.0	8.7	240.6	263	1,017	1,747	136	2,900	553	▼	37
★ Amherst–Northampton, MA	1.5	12.4	19.7	123.4	157	633	1,442	197	2,272	384	▼	19
Ann Arbor, MI	6.0	74.5	162.2	449.4	692	1,382	4,739	479	6,600	1,352	▲	134
Asheville, NC	5.8	23.7	71.5	189.8	291	1,147	2,519	237	3,903	681	▲	59
Athens, GA	5.3	55.8	116.1	343.6	521	1,597	4,330	286	6,212	1,142	▲	120
Athens–Cedar Creek Lake, TX	13.7	12.2	27.3	252.3	306	1,659	2,008	157	3,824	688	▲	61
Austin, TX	10.3	65.7	158.2	235.9	404	2,066	4,781	377	7,224	1,126	–	119
★ Bar Harbor–Frenchman Bay, ME	2.3	10.0	5.0	53.6	71	690	1,727	125	2,541	325	–	11
Bellingham, WA	3.1	41.5	33.4	144.1	222	1,337	3,763	271	5,371	759	–	70
Bend, OR	6.6	43.8	27.2	79.1	157	1,158	3,690	260	5,107	667	–	54
Bennington, VT	2.9	5.6	15.2	115.6	139	1,121	3,371	217	4,710	610	▲	44
★ Benton County, AR	3.1	9.0	11.1	116.1	139	753	1,577	141	2,471	386	▼	20
Biloxi–Gulfport–Pass Christian, MS	8.9	55.9	123.7	221.8	410	2,157	3,019	352	5,528	963		101
Blacksburg, VA	2.4	18.9	15.3	133.5	170	688	3,104	145	3,937	564	▲	38
Bloomington–Brown County, IN	2.8	15.1	16.1	219.4	253	792	2,532	206	3,530	606	–	42
Boise, ID	3.1	32.1	42.0	245.1	322	1,311	3,226	219	4,755	798	▲	80

	Violent Crime Rates					Property Crime Rates						
	Murder	Rape	Robbery	Assault	Total	Burglary	Larceny-Theft	Motor-Vehicle Theft	Total	SCORE	TREND	RANK
United States	**8.3**	**35.7**	**217.0**	**352.4**	**613.4**	**1,332**	**3,088**	**534**	**4,954**	**1,109**	–	
Bradenton, FL	6.8	47.5	164.4	564.4	783	1,869	3,597	388	5,855	1,369	▼	135
★ Branson–Table Rock Lake, MO	2.4	7.1	9.2	134.5	153	308	1,276	61	1,645	318	▲	10
★ Brevard, NC	3.1	7.7	7.8	97.2	116	363	830	75	1,269	243	▲	5
Brownsville–Harlingen, TX	7.6	25.7	90.7	533.6	658	1,935	3,559	601	6,095	1,267	▲	129
Brunswick–Golden Isles, GA	9.9	75.9	220.2	762.8	1069	2,172	4,536	391	7,100	1,779	–	150
Burlington, VT	1.4	28.8	51.6	90.0	143	1,590	5,368	269	7,227	866		88
Burnet–Marble Falls–Llano, TX	3.9	19.1	8.7	195.2	227	755	1,669	115	2,539	481	▲	31
★ Camden–Penobscot Bay, ME	1.7	20.7	8.6	57.2	88	534	2,196	128	2,858	374	–	18
Canandaigua, NY	2.0	18.4	20.7	137.8	179	663	1,923	74	2,660	445	–	27
Canton–Lake Tawakoni, TX	3.7	12.2	25.7	143.7	185	1,091	1,524	214	2,829	468	▲	29
Cape Cod, MA	2.8	23.6	36.5	470.8	534	1,837	3,171	338	5.345	1,068	–	111
Cape May, NJ	2.8	56.2	90.3	205.1	354	1,999	5,018	254	7,271	1,081	–	115
Carlsbad–Artesia, NM	6.2	21.2	40.4	236.4	304	1,149	3,461	150	4,760	780	–	74
Carson City–Minden, NV	0.0	29.9	82.1	281.1	393	878	2,839	241	3,958	789	–	77
Chapel Hill, NC	8.1	27.7	51.3	171.7	259	1,594	3,461	246	5,301	789	–	77
Charleston, SC	9.9	64.2	217.4	666.5	958	1,549	3,787	400	5,736	1,532	–	146
Charlevoix–Boyne City, MI	1.0	51.3	18.1	99.6	170	669	1,749	101	2,519	422	▼	24
Charlottesville, VA	7.3	29.2	67.4	186.3	261	797	3,437	198	4,432	704	–	62
Chico–Paradise, CA	4.3	40.3	58.6	317.4	421	1,665	3,290	346	5,301	951	▲	99
★ Clayton, GA	5.4	1.8	3.6	128.7	140	927	791	143	1,861	326	▲	12
Clear Lake, CA	9.7	34.0	41.6	721.1	806	1,741	2,615	247	4,603	1,267	▼	129
Coeur d'Alene, ID	2.1	26.3	27.0	252.0	307	1,149	2,821	167	4,138	721	▼	65
Colorado Springs, CO	5.4	61.1	130.7	226.2	423	1,812	4,236	401	6,448	1,068	▲	111
Columbia County, NY	3.5	8.0	22.7	328.6	363	724	1,679	92	2,495	612	–	45
★ Crossville, TN	3.3	11.8	31.5	99.7	146	799	1,154	275	2,227	369	▲	16
Daytona Beach, FL	7.4	41.7	153.7	345.9	549	1,760	3,204	266	5,230	1,072	▼	114
Deming, NM	4.6	24.2	41.2	350.6	421	1,583	3,719	286	5,588	979	–	104
★ Door County, WI	2.3	11.4	3.1	13.8	31	453	1,692	78	2,222	253	▼	7
Eagle River, WI	3.4	22.8	11.5	101.5	139	1,294	1,889	226	3,409	480	▲	30
Easton–Chesapeake Bay, MD	4.3	26.9	53.7	336.7	422	770	2,115	133	3,017	723	▲	66
Edenton–Albemarle Sound, NC	10.4	13.4	26.7	156.0	207	672	1,208	39	1,919	398	▲	21
El Centro–Calexico–Brawley, CA	8.6	31.9	157.7	428.1	626	2,417	5,022	584	8,023	1,429	–	138
Eugene–Springfield, OR	4.1	41.4	86.2	161.0	293	1,685	3,990	307	5,982	891	–	93
Fairhope–Gulf Shores, AL	7.7	18.7	37.0	233.4	297	981	1,851	136	2,969	594	▼	40
Fayetteville, AR	4.3	25.0	27.8	144.7	202	1,125	2,772	236	4,133	615	▲	46
Fort Collins–Loveland, CO	3.7	29.6	29.6	275.5	338	1,051	3,800	201	5,052	844	–	84
Fort Lauderdale–Hollywood–Pompano Beach, FL	8.9	36.3	298.2	318.5	662	1,621	3,469	523	5,612	1,223	▼	125
Fort Myers–Cape Coral–Sanibel Island, FL	6.7	26.6	118.8	137.7	290	1,070	2,057	257	3,384	628	▼	48
Fort Walton Beach, FL	4.1	25.1	46.2	140.6	216	782	1,846	164	2,792	495	▼	34
★ Fredericksburg, TX	5.1	2.5	3.9	68.7	80	573	1,179	76	1,828	263	▼	8
Gainesville, FL	7.0	56.0	175.5	585.4	824	1,962	3,822	271	6,055	1,429	–	138

	Violent Crime Rates					Property Crime Rates						
	Murder	Rape	Robbery	Assault	Total	Burglary	Larceny-Theft	Motor-Vehicle Theft	Total	SCORE	TREND	RANK
United States	8.3	35.7	217.0	352.4	613.4	1,332	3,088	534	4,954	1,109	–	
Grand Junction, CO	3.6	18.7	35.4	161.9	220	1,068	3,316	186	4,570	677	▲	57
★ Grand Lake, OK	5.0	13.7	7.2	90.6	117	888	1,271	181	2,340	351	▲	14
Grants Pass, OR	8.0	36.1	41.9	105.3	191	1,530	3,443	290	5,263	718	–	64
Grass Valley–Truckee, CA	7.2	15.3	22.7	281.9	327	857	1,906	192	2,955	623	▲	47
★ Hamilton–Bitterroot Valley, MT	3.2	3.3	4.9	134.3	146	335	1,755	122	2,212	367	▼	15
★ Hanover, NH	2.3	15.7	10.0	77.5	106	512	2,059	99	2,670	373	▲	17
★ Harrison, AR	1.4	5.1	5.7	74.2	86	560	1,577	102	2,239	310	▼	9
Hendersonville, NC	7.7	13.7	25.2	148.9	196	780	1,500	177	2,456	441	▲	26
Hilton Head–Beaufort, SC	8.5	47.6	68.1	713.3	838	1,729	3,735	256	5,720	1,409	–	137
Honolulu, HI	4.1	32.7	120.3	91.9	249	1,163	3,839	362	5,364	785	–	76
Hot Springs National Park, AR	9.3	43.1	113.1	306.3	472	1,368	3,058	328	4,755	947	▲	98
Houghton Lake, MI	0.0	64.9	32.1	221.0	318	2,464	3,754	372	6,590	977	▼	103
Iowa City, IA	1.7	43.1	27.5	302.1	374	997	3,969	193	5,160	890	▲	92
Kalispell, MT	4.7	28.9	13.0	236.1	283	938	3,768	295	5,001	783	▼	75
★ Keene, NH	1.8	27.7	10.6	95.5	136	422	1,506	92	2,020	338	▲	13
Kerrville, TX	7.1	12.8	35.0	258.9	314	1,162	2,027	128	3,317	646	▲	52
Key West–Key Largo–Marathon, FL	12.5	53.2	153.7	647.1	867	2,283	4,304	469	7,055	1,572	▼	147
Laconia–Lake Winnipesaukee, NH	2.9	54.2	16.9	146.0	220	1,230	3,084	233	4,547	675	–	55
Lake Havasu City–Kingman, AZ	9.8	23.9	65.1	590.3	689	1,846	3,575	422	5,844	1,273	▲	131
Lake Lanier, GA	5.2	24.5	63.1	219.6	312	1,063	2,639	325	4,027	715	▲	63
Lakeland–Winter Haven, FL	9.3	31.4	168.6	463.2	673	1,657	3,583	290	5,530	1,225	▼	126
Lancaster County, PA	2.0	14.8	49.6	94.2	161	591	1,664	130	2,386	399	–	22
Las Cruces, NM	7.0	42.0	75.9	270.4	395	1,762	4,284	360	6,406	1,036	▼	108
Las Vegas, NV	12.5	68.7	366.8	348.1	796	1,981	3,783	651	6,415	1,438	–	140
Lexington–Fayette, KY	5.7	35.7	115.7	270.1	392	1,217	3,446	272	4,935	886	–	91
★ Los Alamos, NM	1.1	3.0	2.1	63.2	69	218	1,006	24	1,247	194	▲	2
Madison, WI	1.9	25.1	73.2	125.1	225	999	3,911	248	5,158	741	–	68
Martinsburg–Charles Town, WV	5.6	18.0	53.7	103.5	181	1,054	2,041	219	3,314	512	▲	36
Maui, HI	2.6	31.8	45.5	238.6	319	1,837	4,750	337	6,924	1,011	▲	107
McAllen–Edinburg–Mission, TX	7.1	17.9	43.3	300.7	369	1,733	3,274	388	5,394	908	▲	96
Medford–Ashland, OR	4.1	39.4	49.4	200.6	294	1,165	3,367	257	4,789	772	▲	72
Melbourne–Titusville–Palm Bay, FL	5.5	30.0	124.5	358.0	518	1,305	2,992	233	4,529	971	▼	102
Miami–Hialeah, FL	17.4	40.6	608.8	715.9	1,383	2,112	4,450	1,114	7,676	2,150	▼	151
Monticello–Liberty, NY	6.5	27.6	62.8	335.1	432	1,424	1,700	1,189	3,313	763	▼	71
★ Mountain Home–Bull Shoals, AR	3.3	4.7	4.7	46.0	59	217	714	57	988	158	▲	1
Murray–Kentucky Lake, KY	2.0	8.1	18.2	225.1	253	793	1,495	120	2,408	494	–	33
Myrtle Beach, SC	11.8	40.0	132.6	511.2	696	2,332	5,254	511	8,097	1,505	–	144
Naples, FL	12.3	35.9	106.3	251.6	406	1,367	2,770	247	4,385	845	▼	85
New Bern, NC	5.4	21.8	52.2	249.2	329	967	1,891	167	3,025	631	–	50
New Braunfels, TX	8.5	11.5	68.0	359.5	448	1,560	3,002	229	4,790	927	▲	97

	Violent Crime Rates					Property Crime Rates						
	Murder	Rape	Robbery	Assault	Total	Burglary	Larceny-Theft	Motor-Vehicle Theft	Total	SCORE	TREND	RANK
United States	8.3	35.7	217.0	352.4	613.4	1,332	3,088	534	4,954	1,109	–	
New Paltz–Ulster County, NY	3.3	20.6	41.0	276.2	341	816	1,726	138	2,680	609	–	43
New Port Richey, FL	4.6	29.3	40.7	252.3	327	1,007	2,378	171	3,556	682	–	60
Newport–Lincoln City, OR	3.8	31.3	48.1	211.4	295	1,468	3,094	217	4,780	773	▲	73
North Conway–White Mountains, NH	4.4	12.9	4.4	110.7	132	894	2,466	132	3,493	482	–	32
★ Oak Harbor–Whidbey Island, WA	2.0	8.2	7.0	34.6	52	542	1,350	62	1,953	247	▼	6
Ocala, FL	7.5	46.0	119.1	409.9	583	1,716	2,676	208	4,599	1,042	▼	109
Ocean City–Assateague Island, MD	8.1	52.2	70.6	455.7	587	1,996	5,864	290	8,150	1,402	–	136
Ocean County, NJ	1.5	22.9	50.1	149.1	224	935	2,877	254	4,066	630	–	49
Olympia, WA	3.0	41.8	32.6	128.4	206	1,241	3,253	211	4,705	676	▲	56
Orlando, FL	7.7	51.1	252.2	585.1	845	1,961	3,909	392	6,262	1,471	–	142
Panama City, FL	6.5	57.9	74.1	277.3	416	1,104	3,243	247	4,593	875	▼	89
★ Paris–Big Sandy, TN	3.1	4.9	2.7	91.8	103	331	631	27	988	201	▼	3
Pensacola, FL	6.2	55.2	145.5	592.3	799	1,288	2,885	220	4,393	1,238	▼	127
Petoskey–Straits of Mackinac, MI	0.8	50.6	20.3	125.3	197	924	3,359	132	4,415	638	▼	51
Phoenix–Tempe–Scottsdale, AZ	8.6	44.6	174.6	408.7	637	1,892	4,570	472	6,934	1,330	▲	133
Pike County, PA	4.0	16.3	18.6	99.2	138	1,926	1,168	165	3,258	464	–	28
Port Townsend, WA	2.1	11.1	13.4	138.2	165	1,068	3,054	190	4,312	596	▲	41
Portsmouth–Dover–Durham, NH	1.3	20.4	19.8	112.1	133	796	2,656	191	3,643	497	–	35
Prescott, AZ	6.0	14.8	27.5	229.1	277	1,020	2,512	207	3,739	651	▲	53
Red Bluff–Sacramento Valley, CA	7.2	26.7	47.7	434.4	516	1,325	3,283	241	4,848	1,001	▲	105
Redding, CA	8.4	47.6	69.2	506.2	631	1,629	2,970	301	4,900	1,121	▲	118
Rehoboth Bay–Indian River Bay, DE	6.9	71.7	49.7	325.3	454	1,207	2,668	139	4,014	855	–	87
Reno, NV	8.3	80.9	241.6	322.4	653	1,717	3,948	455	6,120	1,265	–	128
Rockport–Aransas Pass, TX	11.3	46.7	36.2	360.5	455	1,883	3,357	289	5,529	1,008	▲	106
Roswell, NM	12.0	39.3	74.3	374.9	501	1,737	4,635	243	6,615	1,162	▲	122
St. Augustine, FL	6.8	38.1	110.7	592.6	748	1,278	2,908	226	4,412	1,189	▼	123
St. George–Zion, UT	3.5	13.9	19.0	124.4	161	606	3,232	250	4,089	570	▲	39
St. Petersburg–Clearwater–Dunedin, FL	4.6	34.1	177.5	369.2	585	1,455	3,092	209	4,756	1,061	▼	110
St. Tammany Parish, LA	8.5	31.7	45.5	342.6	428	1,317	2,291	245	3,853	814	–	82
Salinas–Seaside–Monterey, CA	6.0	40.2	143.3	471.4	661	1,316	3,251	251	4,818	1,143	▲	121
San Antonio, TX	15.9	74.6	270.3	200.4	561	2,721	5,547	952	9,220	1,483	▲	143
San Diego, CA	8.5	33.7	229.0	365.8	637	1,510	3,188	1,085	5,782	1,215	▲	124
San Juan Islands, WA	11.1	4.6	2.1	80.2	98	733	2,194	151	3,078	406	▼	23
San Luis Obispo, CA	4.3	30.9	46.4	218.3	300	1,019	2,559	217	3,795	679	–	58
Santa Barbara, CA	4.9	35.5	85.6	288.7	415	1,107	3,296	286	4,688	883	▲	90
Santa Fe, NM	6.8	18.4	42.0	366.0	433	1,133	1,778	191	3,102	743	▼	69
Santa Rosa–Petaluma, CA	5.4	35.4	77.5	261.3	380	1,445	2,932	285	4,661	846	–	86
Sarasota, FL	5.1	39.9	110.7	279.1	435	1,360	3,145	195	4,699	905	▼	95

	Violent Crime Rates					Property Crime Rates						
	Murder	Rape	Robbery	Assault	Total	Burglary	Larceny-Theft	Motor-Vehicle Theft	Total	SCORE	TREND	RANK
United States	8.3	35.7	217.0	352.4	613.4	1,332	3,088	534	4,954	1,109	–	
Savannah, GA	17.5	57.4	299.4	261.0	635	1,985	4,424	311	6,720	1,307	–	132
South Lake Tahoe–Placerville, CA	7.4	29.4	65.3	255.6	358	1,766	2,316	249	4,330	791	▲	79
★ Southport, NC	8.7	6.0	11.6	61.3	88	668	744	101	1,512	239	▲	4
State College, PA	1.6	20.2	14.3	54.1	90	640	2,731	87	3,458	436	–	25
Thomasville, GA	10.8	27.8	113.5	255.8	408	1,250	2,645	188	4,084	816	▲	83
Traverse City–Grand Traverse Bay, MI	0.0	94.8	20.8	128.4	244	1,061	3,568	163	4,791	723	▲	66
Tucson, AZ	8.0	58.0	171.4	455.0	692	1,968	5,305	432	7,705	1,463	▲	141
Twain Harte–Yosemite, CA	2.9	21.4	17.9	508.3	551	1,194	2,077	157	3,427	893	–	94
Vero Beach, FL	6.2	39.1	98.1	296.9	440	1,193	2,194	198	3,585	799	▼	81
Virginia Beach–Norfolk, VA	12.3	43.1	229.3	214.0	499	1,291	4,075	457	5,823	1,081	–	115
Wenatchee, WA	7.7	50.2	57.4	183.9	299	1,483	4,762	275	6,520	951	–	99
West Palm Beach–Boca Raton–Delray Beach, FL	8.3	47.7	270.5	509.8	836	2,221	3,907	575	6,703	1,507	▼	145
Yuma, AZ	10.6	51.1	138.2	564.5	764	1,887	5,948	476	8,312	1,596	▲	148

 ET CETERA: Personal Safety

RETIREMENT HOUSING DEVELOPMENTS: FOUR FACTORS FOR SECURITY

If you are considering life in a retirement development —whether a high-rise apartment or condominium, trailer park, townhouse complex, housing tract, or enclosed dwelling with adjoining courtyards and interior patios—check for these basic security factors.

Opportunity for Surveillance. The ease with which both residents and police patrols can watch what is going on is determined by the design of the building complex. The ability to survey, supervise, and question strangers depends on how each residence is designed and on its relationship to neighboring dwellings. The proximity of elevator doors to apartment entrances, the number of apartments opening onto each landing, the location and nearness of parking lots and open spaces, the layout of streets and walkways, the evenness and intensity of both exterior and interior lighting —all of these factors affect ease of surveillance.

All entryways and walkways should be clearly visible to residents and police at any time of day or night. This means that the landscaping surrounding them should be low and free from obstacles and heavy foliage. Walkways should be evenly illuminated at night with lamps that are not so bright as to cause light "tunnels."

Clustered housing units where residents know their neighbors are conducive to watchfulness. In large buildings, if only a few apartments open onto a common landing or hallway, the same sort of neighborly concern is promoted.

Differentiation of Space and Territory. The most dangerous places within large buildings are interior public areas with no definite territorial boundaries. Areas seemingly belonging to no one are, in effect, open to everyone. When places are definitely marked off, an intruder will be more obvious, and owners and neighbors will be alerted to potential danger more quickly.

Access Control. Obviously, the quality of locks, doors, door frames, and windows affects the ease with which your residence can be entered. Yet many builders give little attention to these details. Still less attention may be given to entrances, a surprising fact when you consider that the design and layout of entrances are crucial elements in security, since they define territory and boundaries to residents, visitors, and intruders.

Entrances and exits to a complex should be limited in number, and entrance routes should pass near activity areas so that those who come and go can be observed by many people. An increasingly popular type of retirement community designed for metropolitan areas high in crime (like many found in Florida, for example) consists of an enclosed complex of either condominium townhouses or cluster homes surrounded

Crime Compared with Other Events in Life

The rates for some violent crimes are higher than those of other harmful life events. For example, the risk of being a victim of violent crime is higher than the risk of being affected by divorce, death from cancer, or injury or death from a fire. Anyone over 15 years old runs a greater risk of being a violent crime victim, with or without injury, than being hurt in a traffic accident. Still, a person is much more likely to die from natural causes than from being a victim of crime.

Event	Annual Rate per 1,000 Adults
Accidental injury, all circumstances	290.000
Accidental injury at home	105.000
Personal Theft	**82.000**
Accidental injury at work	68.000
Acidental injury in an automobile	23.000
Divorce	23.000
Death, all causes	11.000
Aggravated Assault	**9.000**
Death of a spouse	9.000
Robbery	**7.000**
Heart disease death	4.000
Cancer death	2.000
Accidental death, all circumstances	0.500
Penumonia/influenza death	0.300
Automobile accidental death	0.200
Suicide	0.200
Injury from fire	0.100
Murder	**0.100**
Death from fire	0.003

Source: Bureau of Justice Statistics, *Report to the Nation on Crime and Justice,* 1988.

by a wall or secure fence and connected by courtyards and terraces. The entrance in these developments is usually a single gate guarded by a watchman who probably has closed-circuit television and elaborate communications systems.

Siting and Clustering. The placement of buildings on the grounds and their relationship to one another affect the ease of access. In complexes where the design allows anyone to wander at will between dwellings or through courtyards, the opportunity for crime increases. When residences are clustered so that entrances face each other and access is limited, strangers are less likely to wander through and are more apt to be questioned if they do. The practice of clustering units together, then, limits access naturally and unobtrusively, while at the same time providing a setting for the casual social contacts between neighbors that promote security.

Despite the obvious feeling of security that walls, fences, guard posts, and television scanners provide for retired persons in a community setting, too heavy a concentration of these precautions should be a warning flag to the potential resident. Security measures piled on top of one another, like excessive numbers of police with attack dogs, are an indicator of unacceptably high crime in the area. If, upon inspecting your model community, you sense an inordinate preoccu-

pation with security, it's wise to make local inquiries about crime or simply eliminate the community from consideration altogether.

JUST HOW VULNERABLE ARE YOU?

Most older adults' dread of violent crime is out of proportion to the odds of their being victimized. But the consequences of burglary, robbery, and fraud are certainly real enough. It is difficult enough for anyone to return to a ransacked home or bounce back after being robbed on the street, or defrauded of savings. Why shouldn't older adults living on fixed incomes be more fearful when the impact of these crimes is deeper and longer lasting?

Besides common sense defenses that include staying away from dark streets, locking your doors and windows, not talking to strangers, and being alert, aware, and accompanied when going out, here are a few more defenses drawn from various sources, including the Dade County (Miami) Department of Public Safety and the U.S. Department of Justice.

Burglary Defenses

For most households, minimum security (defined by police as preventing entry into a home through any door or window *except* by destructive force) is enough to frustrate intruders. It's usually *after* they've been burglarized, experts note, that people learn additional ways to make their homes secure.

If your home is going to be hit, the chances are greater that it will happen during the day while you are out (even if you're gardening in the backyard) than at night when you're asleep, and that the burglar will be an unemployed young person who lives in or knows the neighborhood, and that the job will be done on the spur of the moment because the home looks empty and easy to enter.

From the viewpoint of the crook, the job's quick rewards also entail the risk of doing time in jail. He may turn back at any of three points:

1. Casing the house. If doors and windows are in plain sight and the sounds are unmistakable that someone is inside, most intruders will turn down the risk and search instead for an easier target.

TACTICS FOR DEFENSE:
- Trim or remove shrubbery near doors and windows to limit an intruder's potential hiding places.
- Leave your air conditioner's fan on when you are away; most burglaries occur in August, and a silent air conditioner is the crook's tip to an empty house.
- If you leave the house during the day, walk out to the sidewalk and turn and wave at the front door.
- Turn on a radio or a television, porch light

CRIME CLOCK

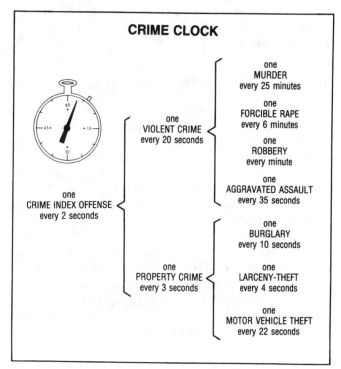

one
CRIME INDEX OFFENSE
every 2 seconds

one
VIOLENT CRIME
every 20 seconds

one
MURDER
every 25 minutes

one
FORCIBLE RAPE
every 6 minutes

one
ROBBERY
every minute

one
AGGRAVATED ASSAULT
every 35 seconds

one
PROPERTY CRIME
every 3 seconds

one
BURGLARY
every 10 seconds

one
LARCENY-THEFT
every 4 seconds

one
MOTOR VEHICLE THEFT
every 22 seconds

Source: FBI, *Crime in the United States,* 1989.
Figures are for 1988.

and yard light, and one or two interior lights (the bathroom is one of the best rooms in which to leave a light on) if you are going out for the evening.

2. Entering the house. Even if the front door is unlocked, an intruder commits a crime once he is inside the house—whether or not anything is stolen. If doors and windows are locked and it looks as if it will take time and energy to break in, he will often go elsewhere.

3. Prowling the house. A burglar inside a target house is a very dangerous person to confront; however, he might still be discouraged if he could not quickly find loot or if he thought the police were on their way.

TACTICS FOR DEFENSE:

- Maintain a secure closet (not a safe) with an outward-opening door for storing furs, cameras, guns, silverware, and jewelry; on the door, install a one-inch deadbolt lock. Place an annunciator alarm on the inside. If the door is paneled or of hollow-core construction, strengthen it with ¾-inch plywood or galvanized sheet steel backing.
- Install a telephone extension in your bedroom and add a rim lock with a 1-inch deadbolt to the interior side of the bedroom door (ideally, a "thumb turn" with *no* exterior key); then if you hear an intruder, you can retreat to the bedroom, lock the door, and call the police.

In addition, you should avoid:

- Displaying guns on interior walls that can be seen from the street. Guns are big drawing cards for burglars.
- Hiding door keys in the mailbox, under the doormat, atop the door casing, in a flowerpot, or any secret place seasoned burglars search first.
- Keeping a safe in your house. If an intruder finds a safe, he will assume you have something of great value and may come back later and force you to open it.
- Leaving window fans and air conditioners in unlocked windows when you are away from home.
- Entering your home or calling out if you find a window or door forced when you return home. Go to a neighbor and call the police. Wait there until the police come.
- Attaching tags on your key ring that identify you, your car, or your address.

Personal Larceny Defenses

Personal larceny with contact, a police blotter term for purse-snatching and pocket-picking, is the only crime that strikes older adults more frequently than the rest of the population. It is a common way a street crook gets cash in a hurry. The target is the person who looks the easiest to attack, has the most money or valuables to lose, and appears the least likely to give chase.

Purses. If you can do without a purse, do without it. Instead, tuck money and credit cards in an inside pocket. If you must carry a purse, carry it under your arm with its opening facing down; if you're attacked, let the purse's contents fall to the ground, then sit down on the sidewalk before you are knocked down.

Wallets. Never carry a wallet in your back pocket; even an amateur can lift it and escape before you realize what's happening. Carry it in the front pocket of your trousers; pin this pocket closed above the wallet with a safety pin, or wrap a large rubber band around the wallet so that it can't be withdrawn smoothly and can't fall through if your pocket is cut by a razor blade.

In addition, you should avoid:

- Letting strangers stop you for conversation.
- Approaching cars parked on the street with motors running
- Flashing your jewelry or cash. This is a signal to street thugs, especially if you seem neither strong nor quick. They may follow you to a more convenient spot for a holdup.
- Walking close to building entrances or shrubbery.
- Getting separated from your purse or wallet in a crowded rest room or other public place, or leaving your purse or wallet unattended in

Neighborhood Crime Watches

It is not uncommon to see a crime in progress without recognizing it as such. Here are some situations that might be observed in any neighborhood. These are situations a trained police officer would investigate if he or she were making the observation.

Situations Involving Vehicles

Situations	Possible Significance
Moving vehicles, especially if moving slowly without lights, following an aimless or repetitive course	Casing for a place to rob or burglarize; drug pusher, sex offender, or vandal
Parked, occupied vehicle, especially at an unusual hour	Lookout for burglary in progress (sometimes two people masquerading as lovers)
Vehicle parked in neighbor's drive being loaded with valuables, even if the vehicle looks legitimate, i.e., moving van or commercial van	Burglary or larceny in progress
Abandoned vehicle with or without license plate	Stolen or abandoned after being used in a crime
Persons loitering around parked cars	Burglary of vehicle contents, theft of accessories, vandalism
Persons detaching accessories and mechanical parts	Theft or vandalism
Apparent business transactions from a vehicle near school, park, or quiet residential neighborhood	Drug sales
Persons being forced into vehicle	Kidnapping, rape, robbery
Objects thrown from a moving vehicle	Disposal of contraband

Situations Involving Property

Situations	Possible Significance
Property in homes, garages, or storage areas, especially if several items of the same kind such as TVs and bicycles	Storage of stolen property

Situations Involving Property

Situations	Possible Significance
Property in vehicles, especially meaningful at night or if property is household goods, appliances, unmounted tape decks, stereo equipment	Stolen property, burglary in progress
Property being removed from a house or building; meaningful if residents are at work, on vacation, or are known to be absent	Burglary or larceny in progress
Open doors, broken doors or windows, or other signs of a forced entry	Burglary in progress or the scene of a recent burglary

Situations Involving Persons

Situations	Possible Significance
Door-to-door solicitors—especially significant if one goes to the back of the house and one stays in front. Can be men or women, clean-cut and well dressed	Casing for burglary, burglary in progress, soliciting violation
Waiting in front of a house	Lookout for burglary in progress
Forced entry or entry through window	Burglary, vandalism, theft
Persons short-cutting through yards	Fleeing the scene of a crime
Persons running, especially if carrying items of value	Fleeing the scene of a crime
Person carrying property, especially if property isn't boxed or wrapped	Offender leaving the scene of a burglary, robbery, or larceny
High volume of human traffic in and out of residence	Drug sales, vice activities, "fence" operation

a shopping cart, or on a counter.
- Mingling with adolescents leaving school or groups of adolescents anywhere.
- Using shortcuts, alleys, or dark ways, and walking through sparsely traveled areas or near thick trees and shrubs.

TYPICAL FRAUDS

P. T. Barnum is credited with the wise but cynical comment that there is "a sucker born every minute and two [con men] to take advantage of him." He spoke from bitter experience; twice in his lifetime he was the victim of swindlers.

Why do people continue to fall for con games? The answer is that the proposals sound too good to pass up and are presented with urgency by persons who

appear to be sincere and honest. The favorite targets of these crooks are older adults who are likely to have liquid assets in their savings accounts.

It's hard to believe that people can still be taken in by the "pigeon drop," a thousand-year-old scam in which the "mark" is expected to ante up some of his or her own money in order to be cut in on an imaginary find of a small fortune. A similar game involves persuading a victim to help bank examiners and the FBI catch an embezzler by withdrawing some of his or her funds and turning them over to the supposed law enforcement officer.

Both of these scams have been exposed time after time, yet victims continue to be bilked out of millions of dollars every year. Consumer and business frauds, too, net billions for their perpetrators. Here are some common examples.

Building Inspector and Contractor Scams

Code violation frauds are perpetrated by crooks working in tandem. One poses as a building inspector who "discovers" serious violations and the need for immediate repairs, for example, to a homeowner's furnace. Shortly afterward the accomplice arrives, pretending to be a repairman who can perform the needed work at low cost. Typically, little or nothing is done to the furnace, but the victim gets a bill for several hundred dollars.

Home improvement swindles are played by con men who usually show up late in the day offering to perform some service such as installing insulation at half price. They claim they have just finished a job in the neighborhood and have material left over, which accounts for the good deal they can pass on to you. You have to make up your mind on the spot and shell out the money immediately. The job probably never gets finished, and the materials used are worth even less than the bargain price you paid.

Work-at-Home Schemes

> **IDEAS, INVENTIONS,** new products needed by innovative manufacturers. Marketing assistance available to individuals, tinkerers, universities, companies. Call free: 1-800-528-6050. Arizona residents: 1-800-352-0458, extension 831.

> **EARN $200** weekly, part-time taking short phone messages at home. Call 1-615-779-3235 extension 267.

> Assemble electronic devices in your home spare time. $300.00—$600.00/week possible. Experience, knowledge, not necessary. No investment. Write for free information. Electronic Development Lab, Drawer 1560-L, Pinellas Park, FL 33565.

Work-at-home schemes are almost exclusively targeted toward older adults who respond to newspaper and magazine advertisements such as the above examples noted in a recent U.S. House of Representatives hearing on mail fraud. The ads promise extra income each month, all yours for addressing envelopes, making wreaths or plaques in your living room, knitting baby bootees, assembling fishing tackle in your basement, growing earthworms, watching television, or raising house plants at home. U.S. Postal Service investigators, who have been looking into these scams for years, say that they haven't encountered one legitimate work-at-home offer that requires payment from the person who responds to the advertisement.

That's the key to work-at-home scams. A fee is required in order for the person to get in on the opportunity. The promotor claims that the money is for a start-up kit or for other expenses. The promise is that the promoter will buy back the finished product or that he will arrange for it to be purchased by others in the marketplace. Unfortunately, the promoter seldom if ever buys back the products, and the consumer is not only robbed of his or her initial cash

---

It's Better If the Check *Isn't* in the Mail

There's one big disadvantage to receiving your Social Security benefits in the mail, according to the Treasury Department. Because of checks being lost, stolen, or otherwise uncashable, you are seven times more likely to encounter a "nonreceipt" problem than persons who have their money directly deposited in a bank.

Direct deposit gives you quicker access to funds and faster posting to interest-bearing accounts. It certainly saves time, especially if you don't drive. It also saves money; some banks offer older adults who sign up for direct deposit free 5.25 percent NOW accounts that otherwise would mean a $5 monthly service charge and require a minimum balance of $1,500.

To sign up for direct deposit, all you have to do is fill out a form from the Treasury Department's Financial Management Service and take it to your bank. Better yet, your bank has copies of the form; ask them to send you one.

---

outlay but is also stuck with a large quantity of products for which there is no market.

Commodities Sales

Commodities swindles have become one of the biggest consumer frauds in years. Government investigators estimate these schemes are defrauding the public of as much as $1 billion a year.

The term *commodities* refers to a wide range of investments, from metals and gems to wholesale food products and foreign currencies. Although most investment firms are reputable, there is a growing number of illegitimate firms which illegally sell off-exchange investments to the unwary. Because commodities issues are complex, even highly educated persons are taken in. Indeed, convicted swindlers have testified in recent congressional hearings that the preferred customer is a retired physician, engineer, college professor, or military officer. Moreover, according to these crooks, the best parts of the country to "mine" are the Midwest and Far West because, they allege, people there are less cynical.

Commodities investments are perfect vehicles for swindlers, since the payment of profits to investors can often be deferred for six months to a year, leaving plenty of time for the operators to skip town before the investors suspect a scam. Moreover, since commodities are by nature very complicated and risky investments, many investors are never sure whether they've been had or not.

There are two basic ways to invest in commodities. The first is to pay the full price and take immediate possession of the items. The second is to buy on margin, which involves putting up a percentage of the total purchase price with the balance being due on a future date.

A commodities scheme typically involves a boiler room full of telephones in which 10 to 100 salespeople make calls to persons who responded to newspaper advertising. The salespersons are paid by commission, and high-pressure sales are the name of the game. In many cases, a sale is consummated on the telephone. If the person called doesn't agree to purchase anything in the initial call, he or she will be inundated with literature and harassed until a sale is made. The salesperson usually requires the deposit to be wired from the investor's bank, leaving no time for second thoughts.

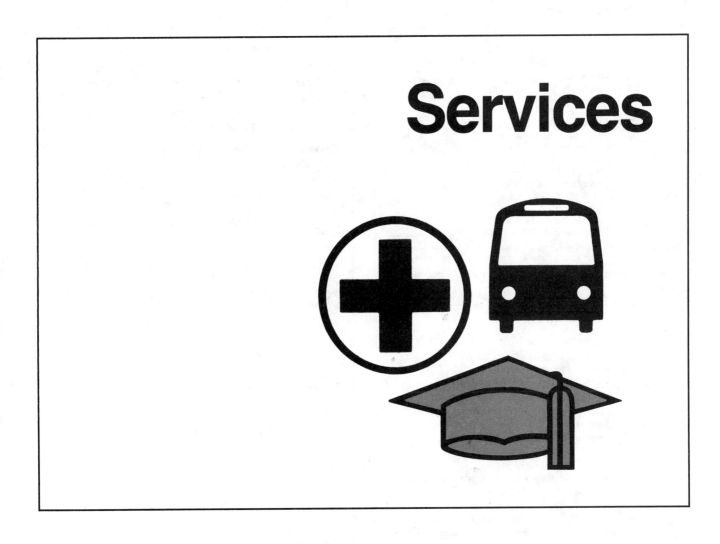

Services

"Here comes the Grey Peril," local planners in many an attractive rural spot whispered to one another in the early 1980s. "They will bid up real estate, string out the visiting nurses, slow down traffic, tap into Meals on Wheels, and vote down school bond issues, all without contributing a nickel to the economy."

Today, places are courting older newcomers as ardently as they chase light industry and fickle tourists. Local economies get better when they float on a cushion of Social Security, pensions, and asset income. Talk to any banker in these places and he or she will bend your ear about how they wouldn't be in business if not for the millions of dollars in CDs they oversee for older depositors.

But the myth persists that greying newcomers want services without paying for them. Let's look at four: health care, public transportation, public libraries, and continuing education.

HEALTH CARE

For many older adults, health care tips the balance in decisions about whether to stay in familiar territory or move to a distant place. In later life, visits to the doctor come more frequently; short hospital stays are a likelihood; and with each passing year, the bills for physican fees and prescriptions get bigger and bigger.

Retirement Places Rated doesn't judge the quality of health care. From Aiken to Yuma, this book simply looks at the place's supply. True enough, larger places have an edge. This doesn't mean that quality health care in a small Ozark clinic is a contradiction. Nor does it necessarily mean that you're better off in a university medical center in San Antonio or Honolulu. The quality of medical care most people get depends on many things, including their ability to pay for it, the luck of the draw, professional incompetence, and human error.

Physicians and Their Specialties

Not every M.D. is listed in the Yellow Pages. Some are hospital administrators, medical school professors, journalists, lawyers, or researchers for pharmaceutical companies. Others work for the federal government's Public Health Service, Veteran's Administration, or Department of Defense service branches. Many are in residency training or are full-time members of hospital staffs. When it comes to the number of physicians per capita, what really counts is the number of doctors who have offices and see patients.

135

**Medical Specialists:
The Top 14 Retirement Places**

Ann Arbor, MI
Burlington, VT
Chapel Hill, NC
Charleston, SC
Charlottesville, VA
Easton–Chesapeake Bay, MD
Gainesville, FL
Hanover, NH
Iowa City, IA
Lexington–Fayette, KY
Los Alamos, NM
Madison, WI
Miami–Hialeah, FL
Petoskey–Straits of Mackinac, MI

Source: Derived from the American Medical Association's *Physician Characteristics and Distribution*, and Woods & Poole Economics, Inc., population estimates.

The number of potential patients per medical specialist in these places is fewer than 1,500.

NORTH CAROLINA: EXPANDING GROUP RECRUITING TWO EXPERIENCED Emergency Physicians. Double coverage and flexible schedule. Excellent total compensation package includes paid vacation. CME time and occurrence malpractice. 22,000 census. Waterfront community. Community hospital closest to Outer Banks and ocean. Send C.V. to Box 1945, c/o JAMA.

CARDIOLOGIST—BC/BE WANTED TO JOIN A WELL-ESTABLISHED solo, Board Certified, non-invasive Cardiologist in a nice Oregon coastal community. Facility available for Echo-Doppler, Holter, Stress test, Cardiac Nuclear Studies, Temporary and Permanent Pacemaker, Swan Ganz, HIS bundle. Excellent salary and benefits. Early partnership. Send C.V. to Box 6199, c/o JAMA.

Where doctors end up practicing is partly determined by sentiment, their perceptions of local quality of life, or both. But mainly it's a matter of economics. The beginning physician has invested three to seven years in graduate medical education and frequently has to start out with a monstrous loan to repay. Some begin work on a hospital staff, develop a practice, get loose from the hospital, and open an office. Others are recruited into partnerships or group practices through advertisements such as the ones above from the *Journal of the American Medical Association.* By whatever means they launch themselves professionally, the major concern of new M.D.s who wish to specialize is a place's covered (i.e., insured) census (i.e., population size).

Depending on how they spend their professional hours, the American Medical Association (AMA) classifies office-based physicians into four groups. Unless they specialize in pediatrics, obstetrics, or child psychiatry, experts predict their typical patients will be in their 60s by the year 2000.

General/family practitioners use all accepted methods

AMA Physician Categories

The American Medical Association (AMA) classifies a physican as a family practitioner, general practitioner, medical specialist, surgeon, or other specialist by 35 specialties in which the physician reports spending the largest number of his or her professional hours.

General/Family Practitioners
General Practice
Family Practice

Medical Specialists
Allergy
Cardiovascular Diseases
Dermatology
Gastroenterology
Internal Medicine
Pediatrics
Pediatric Allergy
Pediatric Cardiology
Pulmonary Diseases

Surgical Specialists
General Surgery
Neurological Surgery
Obstetrics and Gynecology
Ophthalmology
Orthopedic Surgery
Otolaryngology
Plastic Surgery
Colon and Rectal Surgery
Thoracic Surgery
Urology

Other Specialists
Aerospace Medicine
Anesthesiology
Child Psychiatry
Diagnostic Radiology
Forensic Pathology
Neurology
Occupational Medicine
Psychiatry
Pathology
Physical Medicine and Rehabilitation
General Preventive Medicine
Public Health
Radiology
Therapeutic Radiology

of medical care. They treat diseases and injuries, provide preventive care, do routine checkups, prescribe drugs, and do some surgery. They also refer patients to medical specialists.

Medical specialists focus on specific medical disciplines such as cardiology, allergy, gastroenterology, or dermatology. They are the largest of the AMA groups because, frankly, specializing is where the money is. They are likely to give attention to surgical and nonsurgical approaches to treatment. If it is decided that surgery is the method of treatment, they refer patients to surgeons.

Surgical specialists, the best-paid of the AMA's groups, operate on a regular basis several times a week. The letters F.A.C.S. (Fellow of the American College of Surgeons) after a surgeon's name indicate that he or she has passed an evaluation of surgical

Veterans Administration (VA) Hospitals

In addition to hospitals that are both Joint Commission on Accreditation of Hospitals (JCAH) accredited and Medicare-certified, 24 retirement places also have a VA hospital.

Albuquerque, NM
Amherst–Northampton, MA
Ann Arbor, MI
Asheville, NC
Biloxi–Gulfport–Pass Christian, MS
Boise, ID
Canandaigua, NY
Charleston, SC
Fayetteville, AR
Gainesville, FL
Grand Junction, CO
Iowa City, IA
Kerrville, TX
Lexington–Fayette, KY
Madison, WI
Martinsburg–Charles Town, WV
Miami–Hialeah, FL
Phoenix–Tempe–Scottsdale, AZ
Prescott, AZ
Reno, NV
St. Petersburg–Clearwater–Dunedin, FL
San Antonio, TX
San Diego, CA
Tucson, AZ

Medical Schools: A Major Health Care Asset

Medical schools are associated with local teaching hospitals where state-of-the-art techniques, equipment, and therapy are used, and where one can receive care supervised by medical school faculty. Of 127 medical schools in this country, 17 are in places profiled in this book.

Albuquerque, NM—University of New Mexico School of Medicine
Ann Arbor, MI—University of Michigan Medical School
Burlington, VT—University of Vermont College of Medicine
Chapel Hill, NC—University of North Carolina School of Medicine
Charleston, SC—Medical University of South Carolina
Charlottesville, VA—University of Virginia School of Medicine
Gainesville, FL—University of Florida College of Medicine
Hanover, NH—Dartmouth Medical School
Honolulu, HI—University of Hawaii School of Medicine
Iowa City, IA—University of Iowa College of Medicine
Lexington, KY—University of Kentucky College of Medicine
Madison, WI—University of Wisconsin Medical School
Miami–Hialeah, FL—University of Miami School of Medicine
Reno, NV—University of Nevada School of Medicine
San Antonio, TX—University of Texas Health Science Center
San Diego, CA—University of California School of Medicine
Tucson, AZ—University of Arizona College of Medicine

Source: Association of American Medical Colleges, 1990.

training and skills as well as ethical fitness.

Other specialists concentrate on disciplines as familiar as psychiatry and neurology, or as exotic as diagnostic radiology, aerospace medicine, and forensic pathology.

Short-Term General Hospitals

The word *health* can also mean its opposite, *illness*. A hospital is not really a health care institution; its business is to take care of sick people. The truly healthy need little health care except for an occasional shot or checkup; the unhealthy need a lot more.

Just as not all M.D.s see patients, not all hospitals handle typical illnesses and emergencies. Many of the 6,780 U.S. hospitals exclusively treat chronic diseases or alcohol and drug addiction, or they may be burn centers, psychiatric hospitals, or rehabilitation hospitals. *Retirement Places Rated* counts only general hospitals where most patients stay less than 30 days. Nearly all are certified for Medicare participation and most are accredited for acute care by the Joint Commission on Accreditation of Hospitals.

The number of these hospitals and their inpatient beds varies among retirement places. Although the amount of hospital beds isn't as valuable an indicator as it once was before advances in medicine and pharmacology shortened a hospital stay, it is still valid for

gauging relative health care supply. Places with large numbers of beds per capita, for example, are regional medical centers; other places have just one general hospital.

If an area appeals to you, but it hasn't a hospital, don't be discouraged. There are usually good facilities a short drive away. Residents of Ocean City–Assateague Island on Maryland's Eastern Shore may have to drive to Baltimore for specialized care, but Dorchester General Hospital up the shore in Cambridge or Peninsula General Hospital in Salisbury are more than adequate for routine care.

PUBLIC TRANSPORTATION

If it's a toss-up between Cape Cod and Cape May in your mind, in which place can you do without a car? Probably neither one, unless you find a leisure-living development with its own vans or a neighborhood with a nearby bus stop.

Public transportation is a municipal budget-buster. In spite of rising fares, this service operates at a loss

---

Using the Library: 15 Top Places

On average, each person in these locations checks out more
than seven books a year from the local library.

Bar Harbor–Frenchman Bay, ME
Bellingham, WA
Canandaigua, NY
Cape Cod, MA
Deming, NM
Door County, WI
Grand Junction, CO
Hanover, NH
Iowa City, IA
Los Alamos, NM
Madison, WI
Martinsburg–Charles Town, WV
Port Townsend, WA
St. George–Zion, UT
San Juan Islands, WA

Source: Places Rated Partnership survey of state library associations, 1989–90,
and Woods & Poole Economics, Inc., population estimates.

---

nearly everywhere. Transit routes are mapped so that a limited number of buses can serve the greatest number of persons who don't own an automobile and need a reliable, cheap way to get to work or into town for shopping. However, in places where the tab for parking in a downtown garage costs $10, where rush-hour traffic approaches grid-lock, where distances are long and time always seems short, the options for public transportation in retirement places really count.

Fixed route systems pick up passengers at regular stops on a published schedule and provide rides in town or commuter rides from outside of town. Except for San Diego's and Miami's new rapid rail systems, fixed route public transit and "the bus" are synonymous in 87 retirement places.

Demand–response systems are like taxicab services in low-density markets not served by buses. Unlike a Yellow or a Checker cab, however, demand–response vans are operated by local government and the waiting times may be so excessive you may wish you'd called a taxi instead.

PUBLIC LIBRARIES

Until its door is padlocked after a municipal budget cut—as recently happened in Redding, California—one service taken for granted is the local public library.

There are more than 8,500 of them in this country, and 5,000 of these are branches of a city, county, or regional system. From all this, you might expect libraries to be the most plentiful of public services. They aren't. One in nine *Retirement Places Rated* places has just one library; though you'll find current fiction and nonfiction here, you won't locate issues of *Value Line* or the University of California's invaluable *Wellness Letter*.

Libraries and library resources are concentrated in larger places. Sarasota's 318,064 books are shelved in

the main building on the Boulevard of the Arts and in four neighborhood branches; San Diego's 37 libraries house 3.25 million books. But the size of the collection tells only half the story. Measured by the number of books per person, the supply is greater in smaller places, especially college towns and towns in New England where the public library is well into its second century of operation.

CONTINUING EDUCATION

When people look back over their lives, the autobiographies they originally set out to write are different from the ones that finally get written. There is one thread imbedded in the stories: the quick passage through school in youth to a long period of raising a family and working throughout the middle years, ending up in retirement that's all too short. "Is that all there is?," sang Peggy Lee.

Education–work–leisure, called by some the "linear life," doesn't fit people's lengthening life spans. Retirement, frankly, is a period of boredom and anxiety for some who miss the world of work. For others, it would be an empty time indeed if there weren't opportunities for learning new things.

Read the smarmy feature articles frequently run in newspapers 10 years ago about the grandmother who started her masters in social work or the retired banker who got an A in his Modern European History course and you'd think older students were interlopers in the classroom. Today, higher education has cut the tuition fees or waived them entirely for older adults who want to earn a college degree, finish one, or just study for no other reason than fulfillment.

Of the 151 retirement places featured in this book, 118 have at least one college. *Two-year* colleges include junior colleges, community colleges, and technical institutes that offer at least one year of college-level courses leading to an associate degree or are creditable toward a bachelors degree. *Four-year* colleges offer undergraduate courses leading to a bachelor of arts or bachelor of science degree. They typically offer diverse graduate courses, too.

SCORING: Services

Services are in greater supply in bigger places than they are in smaller ones. That's simple common sense. This doesn't mean that your need for a medical specialist, a good public library, a public transit alternative to driving a car, and a schedule of college courses can be met only in places the scale of Miami, Phoenix, or San Diego.

Ranking places by their services will never be done to everyone's satisfaction. "Services" fills a laundry list of everything from trash pickup and street repair, to emergency medical teams and fire protection, to gypsy moth spraying and sewage treatment. If you agree that health care, public transit, libraries, and the chance to take a college course or finish a degree is as good a set of services as any other, then you won't always be disappointed by smaller places, particularly college towns with a medical school.

In spotlighting these services, *Retirement Places Rated* doesn't criticize the quality of local hospitals, the credentials of local physicians, the breadth of local college course offerings, or the local bus fleet's current state of repair. This guide simply indicates the presence or absence of certain services that most persons agree enhance retirement living.

Each place starts with a base score of zero; points are added according to the following criteria.

Health Care

Points are awarded for the number of physicians and hospitals within each place. Access is rated AA, A, B, or C (AA indicating the greatest access and C the least). The place gets points accordingly: 400 points for an AA rating, 300 points for A, 200 points for B, and 100 points for C.

1. *General/family practitioners.*

A retirement place gets a rating of:	if there is one practitioner for every:
AA	3,200 or fewer people
A	4,200 to 3,201 people
B	5,500 to 4,201 people
C	5,501 or more people

2. *Medical specialists.*

A retirement place gets a rating of:	if there is one medical specialist for every:
AA	2,200 or fewer people
A	3,000 to 2,201 people
B	4,750 to 3,001 people
C	4,751 or more people

3. *Surgical specialists.*

A retirement place gets a rating of:	if there is one surgeon for every:
AA	2,000 or fewer people
A	2,750 to 2,001 people
B	3,750 to 2,751 people
C	3,751 or more people

4. *Other specialists.*

A retirement place gets a rating of:	if there is one specialist for every:
AA	2,500 or fewer people
A	3,500 to 2,501 people
B	5,500 to 3,501 people
C	5,501 or more people

5. *Short-term general hospital beds.*

A retirement place gets a rating of:	if, for every 100,000 persons, there are:
AA	500 or more beds
A	350 to 501 beds
B	250 to 351 beds
C	249 or fewer beds in local short-term general hospitals.

Public Transportation

Based on federal Urban Mass Transportation Administration averages for the annual distance a typical bus travels over a fixed route (41,000 miles), a minibus travels in demand–response service (28,500 miles), and a rapid rail car travels over its track (92,000 miles), the total annual fleet mileage in each retirement place is divided by the population and then multiplied by 100.

For example, the Pioneer Valley Transportation Authority's 16 buses in Amherst–Northampton log a total of 656,000 miles in scheduled service annually. This works out to 4.46 miles for each person, good for 446 points.

Public Libraries

The number of public library books per capita in a place is multiplied by 100. Santa Fe's libraries house 204,299 books. This works out to 2.15 books for each resident, good for 215 points.

Continuing Education

All nonprofit colleges and universities with undergraduate programs contribute points. A place's score is 1/100th of its public institution enrollment, 1/200th of its private institution enrollment, plus the percent of the place's population enrolled in all of these institutions times 10.

SCORING EXAMPLES

A Big Ten college town and a small place in the Texas Interior illustrate the scoring method for services.

Iowa City, Iowa (#2)

On the eastern Iowa prairie, there is a center of medical care in every sense of the term. The University of Iowa's College of Medicine, its hospitals and clinics, two other short-term general hospitals, and nearly 300 office-based M.D.s earn Iowa City the maximum 2,000 points in health care.

Iowa City also has a public transit system operating every half hour over 16 different routes, plus demand–response vans in town and buses in suburban Coralville. Riding the university's CAMBUS system between downtown and the hospital, the Oakdale campus, and Hancher Auditorium and the Arena, is free and available to everyone. By *Retirement Places Rated*'s measurement for supply, public transit here is good for 1,772 points.

And finally, with a student population of 30,670, Iowa City is a preeminent college area. The total score of Iowa City is 4,709, which places it comfortably in second place, just 102 points behind the front-runner, San Diego.

Canton–Lake Tawakoni, Texas (#150)

People who opt for small-town living in East Texas are drawn by extremely low costs of living and low crime, not an extensive menu of services. Canton–Lake Tawakoni, for instance, has a small community hospital, but no public transportation, and no local colleges. Physicians who practice here include six GPs and one specialist. The two public libraries house a modest number of books. This marks the extent of services for which Canton–Lake Tawakoni can receive points.

This doesn't mean that Canton and surrounding Van Zandt County aren't good places to live. You can't do without a car and you'll have to look outside the area for specialized medical care and college courses. Fortunately, this retirement place is within commuting distance of Dallas on the west and Tyler on the east via I-20.

 RANKINGS: Services

Five criteria make up the score for a retirement place's supply of selected services: (1) office-based physicians, (2) short-term general hospitals certified for Medicare participation, (3) public transportation, (4) public libraries, and (5) continuing education opportunities at local colleges and universities. Places that receive tie scores get the same rank and are listed alphabetically.

Retirement Places from First to Last

Rank	Score	Rank	Score	Rank	Score
1. San Diego, CA	4,811	18. Bellingham, WA	3,113	36. Santa Rosa–Petaluma, CA	2,467
2. Iowa City, IA	4,709	18. Tucson, AZ	3,113	37. Charlevoix–Boyne City, MI	2,465
3. Miami–Hialeah, FL	4,213	20. Madison, WI	3,097	37. Medford–Ashland, OR	2,465
4. Chapel Hill, NC	4,054			39. Santa Barbara, CA	2,456
5. Honolulu, HI	3,931	21. Chico–Paradise, CA	3,020	40. Olympia, WA	2,435
		22. Reno, NV	2,999		
6. Hanover, NH	3,872	23. New Braunfels, TX	2,996	41. Cape Cod, MA	2,425
7. Los Alamos, NM	3,853	24. Amherst–Northampton, MA	2,953	42. Cape May, NJ	2,420
8. Austin, TX	3,699	25. Burlington, VT	2,951	43. Fort Collins–Loveland, CO	2,416
9. Ann Arbor, MI	3,556			44. Bar Harbor–Frenchman Bay, ME	2,415
10. San Antonio, TX	3,442	26. Lexington–Fayette, KY	2,945		
		27. Eugene–Springfield, OR	2,903	45. Hot Springs National Park, AR	2,403
11. Wenatchee, WA	3,439	28. Albuquerque, NM	2,888		
12. Charlottesville, VA	3,417	29. Savannah, GA	2,816	46. Easton–Chesapeake Bay, MD	2,365
13. Traverse City–Grand Traverse Bay, MI	3,404	30. Charleston, SC	2,802	47. Fort Lauderdale–Hollywood–Pompano Beach, FL	2,309
14. Gainesville, FL	3,392	31. Asheville, NC	2,642	48. Bloomington–Brown County, IN	2,277
15. Phoenix–Tempe–Scottsdale, AZ	3,270	32. St. Petersburg–Clearwater–Dunedin, FL	2,586	49. Houghton Lake, MI	2,271
16. Blacksburg, VA	3,257	33. State College, PA	2,572	50. Murray–Kentucky Lake, KY	2,267
17. Athens, GA	3,243	34. Amador County, CA	2,568		
		35. Santa Fe, NM	2,493		

Rank	Score		Rank	Score		Rank	Score
51. San Luis Obispo, CA	2,223		86. Lakeland–Winter Haven, FL	1,649		118. Eagle River, WI	1,353
52. Boise, ID	2,183		87. Door County, WI	1,632		119. Crossville, TN	1,344
53. Camden–Penobscot Bay, ME	2,176		88. Myrtle Beach, SC	1,624		120. Fredericksburg, TX	1,341
54. West Palm Beach–Boca Raton–Delray Beach, FL	2,158		89. St. Augustine, FL	1,602			
55. Sarasota, FL	2,144		90. Grass Valley–Truckee, CA	1,601		121. Ocean County, NJ	1,237
						122. Clayton, GA	1,229
56. Fayetteville, AR	2,123		91. Hilton Head–Beaufort, SC	1,596		123. Monticello–Liberty, NY	1,213
57. Virginia Beach–Norfolk, VA	2,116		92. Fort Myers–Cape Coral–Sanibel Island, FL	1,592		124. Panama City, FL	1,210
58. Redding, CA	2,094		93. New Paltz–Ulster County, NY	1,587		125. Fairhope–Gulf Shores, AL	1,208
59. Orlando, FL	2,085		94. Edenton–Albemarle Sound, NC	1,583			
60. Bradenton, FL	2,050		95. Mountain Home–Bull Shoals, AR	1,581		126. Brevard, NC	1,184
						127. Yuma, AZ	1,183
61. Pensacola, FL	2,029					128. Grants Pass, OR	1,182
62. Bend, OR	2,018		96. Lancaster County, PA	1,572		129. New Port Richey, FL	1,146
63. Lake Lanier, GA	2,016		97. Prescott, AZ	1,559		130. Benton County, AR	1,073
64. New Bern, NC	1,994		98. Portsmouth–Dover–Durham, NH	1,550			
65. Thomasville, GA	1,992		99. Maui, HI	1,522		131. Clear Lake, CA	1,070
			100. South Lake Tahoe–Placerville, CA	1,517		132. Fort Walton Beach, FL	1,033
66. Grand Junction, CO	1,990					133. McAllen–Edinburg–Mission, TX	1,019
67. Coeur d'Alene, ID	1,977					134. St. Tammany Parish, LA	991
68. Salinas–Seaside–Monterey, CA	1,976		101. Hendersonville, NC	1,506		135. Ocala, FL	946
69. Bennington, VT	1,974		102. Naples, FL	1,504			
70. Petoskey–Straits of Mackinac, MI	1,968		103. Las Cruces, NM	1,492		136. Burnet–Marble Falls–Llano, TX	942
			104. Harrison, AR	1,473		137. Paris–Big Sandy, TN	894
			105. Las Vegas, NV	1,468		138. El Centro–Calexico–Brawley, CA	893
71. Laconia–Lake Winnipesaukee, NH	1,943						
72. Port Townsend, WA	1,926		106. Carlsbad–Artesia, NM	1,460		138. Red Bluff–Sacramento Valley, CA	893
73. Brunswick–Golden Isles, GA	1,924		107. Brownsville–Harlingen, TX	1,444			
74. Daytona Beach, FL	1,920		108. Martinsburg–Charles Town, WV	1,437		140. Lake Havasu City–Kingman, AZ	862
75. Twain Harte–Yosemite, CA	1,907		109. Roswell, NM	1,433			
			110. Columbia County, NY	1,424		141. Oak Harbor–Whidbey Island, WA	849
76. Colorado Springs, CO	1,891					142. Athens–Cedar Creek Lake, TX	819
77. Kalispell, MT	1,875					143. Alamogordo, NM	789
78. Melbourne–Titusville–Palm Bay, FL	1,809		111. Ocean City–Assateague Island, MD	1,408		144. Hamilton–Bitterroot Valley, MT	783
79. Keene, NH	1,795		112. Key West–Key Largo–Marathon, FL	1,401		145. Aiken, SC	765
80. North Conway–White Mountains, NH	1,771		113. Deming, NM	1,397			
			114. Newport–Lincoln City, OR	1,392		146. Southport, NC	722
81. Vero Beach, FL	1,770		115. San Juan Islands, WA	1,388		147. Branson–Table Rock Lake, MO	694
82. Biloxi–Gulfport–Pass Christian, MS	1,748					148. Grand Lake, OK	667
83. Canandaigua, NY	1,680		116. St. George–Zion, UT	1,375		149. Pike County, PA	489
84. Carson City–Minden, NV	1,668		117. Rehoboth Bay–Indian River Bay, DE	1,373		150. Canton–Lake Tawakoni, TX	409
85. Kerrville, TX	1,657					151. Rockport–Aransas Pass, TX	385

PLACE PROFILES: Services

The pages that follow profile the supply of health care, public transportation, public library, and college-level continuing education assets in each of the 151 retirement places.

Health Care, the first heading in each profile, details how many office-based physicians practice in the retirement place according to the American Medical Association's (AMA) basic classifications of general/family practice, surgery, medical specialties, and other specialties. The number of local hospitals accredited by the Joint Commission on Accreditation of Hospitals (JCAH) and certified for Medicare participation by the U.S. Department of Human Services is also included, as is their total number of inpatient beds.

Each item's access rating is shown in the right-hand column (AA indicates the greatest access and C the least). Hospitals with AMA-approved residency programs, VA hospitals, and military hospitals are named. Because VA hospitals aren't part of the Medicare system, and because only military veterans may be patients, they aren't counted when determining a place's access rating.

Public Transportation names the transit agency that regularly operates over a fixed route or has buses or vans in demand–response service. The number of vehicles in the agency's fleet is also given.

Under **Public Libraries** is the total number of public libraries within the retirement place, including central city, suburban, and rural branches, with figures on the size of their book holdings and circulation during their latest fiscal year.

Continuing Education, the last category, shows the types and enrollment sizes of local private and public colleges and universities.

The sources for the information are the American Hospital Association, *Guide to the Health Care Field*, 1989; American Library Association, *American Library Directory, 1989–1990*, 1989; American Medical Association, unpublished data, 1990; Community Transporta-

tion Association of America, *Directory of UMTA-Funded Rural and Specialized Transit Systems*, forthcoming, 1990; Places Rated Partnership survey of state library association annual reports, 1989–1990; Veterans Administration, *Annual Report*, 1989; U.S. Department of Education, *Directory of Postsecondary Institutions*, 1989; and U.S. Department of Transportation, Urban Mass Transportation Administration, *Section 15 Report*, 1989.

A star (★) preceding a retirement place's name highlights it as one of the top 20 place for services.

	Rating
Aiken, SC	
Health Care (600 points)	
Office-Based Physicians	
General/Family Practitioners: 17	C
Medical Specialists: 19	C
Surgical Specialists: 25	C
Other Specialists: 24	B
Short-Term General Hospital: 1 (190 beds)	C
Public Libraries (96 points)	
4 branches, 123,944 books, 311,182 circulation	
Continuing Education (69 points)	
Two-year	
Aiken Technical College (public, 1,350)	
Four-year	
University of South Carolina (public, 2,532)	
Score: 765	**Rank: 145**

	Rating
Alamogordo, NM	
Health Care (600 points)	
Office-Based Physicians	
General/Family Practitioners: 10	B
Medical Specialists: 7	C
Surgical Specialists: 13	C
Other Specialists: 6	C
Short-Term General Hospitals: 3 (104 beds)	C
Public Libraries (144 points)	
1 branch, 74,848 books, 138,734 circulation	
Continuing Education (45 points)	
Two-year	
New Mexico State University (public, 1,541)	
Score: 789	**Rank: 143**

	Rating
Albuquerque, NM	
Health Care (1,600 points)	
Office-Based Physicians	
General/Family Practitioners: 109	B
Medical Specialists: 296	AA
Surgical Specialists: 245	A
Other Specialists: 255	AA
Short-Term General Hospitals: 12 (2,212 beds)	A
Lovelace Medical Center	
Presbyterian Hospital	
University of New Mexico Medical Center	
VA Medical Center	
Public Transportation (734 points)	
Fixed route	
Sun-Tran, 84 buses	
Demand–response	
Sun-Tran, 8 vans	
Public Libraries (107 points)	
12 branches, 535,830 books, 2,285,030 circulation	
Continuing Education (447 points)	
Two-year	
Albuquerque Technical–Vocational Institute (public, 13,117)	
Four-year	
University of New Mexico (public, 24,124)	
Score: 2,888	**Rank: 28**

	Rating
Amador County, CA	
Health Care (1,000 points)	
Office-Based Physicians	
General/Family Practitioners: 12	AA
Medical Specialists: 5	C
Surgical Specialists: 4	C
Other Specialists: 7	B
Short-Term General Hospital: 1 (87 beds)	B
Public Transportation (1,273 points)	
Fixed route	
Amador RTS, 8 buses	
Public Libraries (295 points)	
6 branches, 76,148 books, 114,025 circulation	
Score: 2,568	**Rank: 34**

	Rating
Amherst–Northampton, MA	
Health Care (1,400 points)	
Office-Based Physicians	
General/Family Practitioners: 45	A
Medical Specialists: 73	AA
Surgical Specialists: 42	B
Other Specialists: 77	AA
Short-Term General Hospitals: 2 (264 beds)	C
VA Medical Center	
Public Transportation (446 points)	
Fixed route	
Pioneer Valley TA, 16 buses	
Public Libraries (552 points)	
20 branches, 812,292 books, 905,669 circulation	
Continuing Education (555 points)	
Four-year	
Amherst College (private, 1,570)	
Hampshire College (private, 1,075)	
Mount Holyoke College (private, 1,954)	
Smith College (private, 2,884)	
University of Massachusetts (public, 27,801)	
Score: 2,953	**Rank: 24**

	Rating
★ **Ann Arbor, MI**	
Health Care (1,800 points)	
Office-Based Physicians	
General/Family Practitioners: 63	B
Medical Specialists: 269	AA
Surgical Specialists: 183	AA
Other Specialists: 310	AA
Short-Term General Hospitals: 6 (2,085 beds)	AA
Chelsea Hospital	
McAuley Health Center	
University of Michigan Hospitals	
VA Medical Center	
Public Transportation (600 points)	
Fixed route	
Ann Arbor TA, 40 buses	
Public Libraries (249 points)	
11 branches, 681,100 books, 1,473,898 circulation	
Continuing Education (907 points)	
Two-year	
Washtenaw Community College (public, 9,121)	

Rating

Four-year
Cleary College (private, 1,071)
Concordia College (private, 424)
Eastern Michigan University (public, 21,349)
University of Michigan, Ann Arbor (public, 34,974)
Score: 3,556   **Rank: 9**

Asheville, NC
Health Care (2,000 points)
Office-Based Physicians
General/Family Practitioners: 60	AA
Medical Specialists: 102	AA
Surgical Specialists: 94	AA
Other Specialists: 81	AA
Short-Term General Hospitals: 3 (1,169 beds)	AA
Memorial Mission Hospital
VA Medical Center
Public Transportation (398 points)
Fixed route
Asheville TA, 17 buses
Public Libraries (137 points)
9 branches, 239,704 books, 755,532 circulation
Continuing Education (108 points)
Two-year
Asheville Buncombe Technical College (public, 3,051)
Four-year
Montreat-Anderson College (private, 367)
University of North Carolina (public, 3,200)
Warren Wilson College (private, 523)
Score: 2,642   **Rank: 31**

★ Athens, GA
Health Care (1,800 points)
Office-Based Physicians
General/Family Practitioners: 15	B
Medical Specialists: 37	AA
Surgical Specialists: 59	AA
Other Specialists: 39	AA
Short-Term General Hospitals: 2 (509 beds)	AA
Public Transportation (522 points)
Fixed route
Athens TS, 10 buses
Public Libraries (303 points)
5 branches, 237,851 books, 486,217 circulation
Continuing Education (618 points)
Four-year
University of Georgia (public, 27,176)
Score: 3,243   **Rank: 17**

Athens–Cedar Creek Lake, TX
Health Care (600 points)
Office-Based Physicians
General/Family Practitioners: 12	B
Medical Specialist: 1	C
Surgical Specialists: 5	C
Other Specialists: 2	C
Short-Term General Hospital: 1 (103 beds)	C
Public Libraries (114 points)
2 branches, 67,237 books, 108,750 circulation
Continuing Education (105 points)
Two-year
Trinity Valley Community College (public, 3,893)
Score: 819   **Rank: 142**

★ Austin, TX
Health Care (1,200 points)
Office-Based Physicians
General/Family Practitioners: 179	B
Medical Specialists: 287	A
Surgical Specialists: 303	A
Other Specialists: 251	A
Short-Term General Hospitals: 10 (1,744 beds)	C
Public Transportation (1,307 points)
Fixed route
Capital Area RTS, 66 buses

Rating

Capital MTA, 172 buses
Demand–response
Capital MTA, 24 vans
Public Libraries (140 points)
31 branches, 1,115,710 books, 2,775,156 circulation
Continuing Education (1,052 points)
Two-year
Austin Community College (public, 21,328)
Four-year
Concordia Lutheran College (private, 455)
Huston-Tillotson College (private, 520)
Saint Edward's University (private, 2,536)
Southwest Texas State University (public, 19,375)
Southwestern University (private, 1,119)
University of Texas (public, 50,107)
Score: 3,699   **Rank: 8**

Bar Harbor–Frenchman Bay, ME
Health Care (1,400 points)
Office-Based Physicians
General/Family Practitioners: 16	AA
Medical Specialists: 17	A
Surgical Specialists: 16	B
Other Specialists: 13	A
Short-Term General Hospitals: 3 (139 beds)	B
Public Transportation (453 points)
Fixed route
Downeast Transportation, 5 buses
Public Libraries (542 points)
17 branches, 245,450 books, 331,612 circulation
Continuing Education (20 points)
Four-year
College of the Atlantic (private, 188)
Maine Maritime Academy (public, 479)
Score: 2,415   **Rank: 44**

★ Bellingham, WA
Health Care (1,400 points)
Office-Based Physicians
General/Family Practitioners: 38	AA
Medical Specialists: 41	A
Surgical Specialists: 45	A
Other Specialists: 45	A
Short-Term General Hospitals: 2 (270 beds)	C
Public Transportation (1,173 points)
Fixed route
Whatcom TA, 18 buses
Demand–response
Whatcom County COA, 23 vans
Public Libraries (323 points)
14 branches, 380,351 books, 1,267,038 circulation
Continuing Education (217 points)
Two-year
Whatcom Community College (public, 2,343)
Four-year
Western Washington University (public, 9,398)
Score: 3,113   **Rank: 18**

Bend, OR
Health Care (1,600 points)
Office-Based Physicians
General/Family Practitioners: 23	A
Medical Specialists: 25	A
Surgical Specialists: 42	AA
Other Specialists: 32	AA
Short-Term General Hospitals: 2 (231 beds)	B
Public Transportation (219 points)
Fixed route
City of Bend Transit, 4 buses
Public Libraries (138 points)
3 branches, 103,254 books, 426,709 circulation
Continuing Education (61 points)
Two-year
Central Oregon Community College (public, 2,604)
Score: 2,018   **Rank: 62**

Rating

Bennington, VT
Health Care (1,700 points)
Office-Based Physicians
   General/Family Practitioners: 16   **AA**
   Medical Specialists: 18   **AA**
   Surgical Specialists: 17   **A**
   Other Specialists: 11   **A**
Short-Term General Hospital: 1 (160 beds)   **A**
Public Libraries (236 points)
15 branches, 87,463 books, 138,160 circulation
Continuing Education (39 points)
Four-year
   Bennington College (private, 572)
   Southern Vermont College (private, 635)
Score: 1,974   **Rank: 69**

Benton County, AR
Health Care (1,000 points)
Office-Based Physicians
   General/Family Practitioners: 42   **AA**
   Medical Specialists: 18   **C**
   Surgical Specialists: 15   **C**
   Other Specialists: 15   **C**
Short-Term General Hospitals: 4 (356 beds)   **A**
Public Libraries (60 points)
3 branches, 58,714 books, 139,361 circulation
Continuing Education (13 points)
Four-year
   John Brown University (private, 874)
Score: 1,073   **Rank: 130**

Biloxi–Gulfport–Pass Christian, MS
Health Care (1,200 points)
Office-Based Physicians
   General/Family Practitioners: 35   **C**
   Medical Specialists: 57   **B**
   Surgical Specialists: 81   **A**
   Other Specialists: 50   **B**
Short-Term General Hospitals: 7 (1,740 beds)   **AA**
   VA Medical Center
   U.S. Air Force Hospital, McKeesler
Public Transportation (346 points)
Fixed route
   Mississippi Coast TA, 16 buses
Demand–response
   Mississippi Coast TA, 3 vans
Public Libraries (151 points)
11 branches, 323,569 books, 528,552 circulation
Continuing Education (51 points)
Two-year
   Mississippi Gulf Coast College (public, 3,450)
Score: 1,748   **Rank: 82**

★Blacksburg, VA
Health Care (1,300 points)
Office-Based Physicians
   General/Family Practitioners: 26   **AA**
   Medical Specialists: 24   **B**
   Surgical Specialists: 30   **B**
   Other Specialists: 28   **A**
Short-Term General Hospitals: 2 (290 beds)   **B**
Public Transportation (1,288 points)
Fixed route
   Blacksburg Transit, 26 buses
Public Libraries (124 points)
3 branches, 102,573 books, 443,119 circulation
Continuing Education (544 points)
Four-year
   Virginia Polytechnic Institute (public, 24,637)
Score: 3,257   **Rank: 16**

Bloomington–Brown County, IN
Health Care (1,200 points)
Office-Based Physicians
   General/Family Practitioners: 32   **A**

Rating

   Medical Specialists: 33   **B**
   Surgical Specialists: 35   **B**
   Other Specialists: 42   **A**
Short-Term General Hospital: 1 (347 beds)   **B**
Public Transportation (377 points)
Fixed route
   Bloomington Transit, 11 buses
Public Libraries (104 points)
3 branches, 124,669 books, 806,637 circulation
Continuing Education (595 points)
Four-year
   Indiana University (public, 32,417)
Score: 2,277   **Rank: 48**

Boise, ID
Health Care (1,400 points)
Office-Based Physicians
   General/Family Practitioners: 40   **B**
   Medical Specialists: 71   **A**
   Surgical Specialists: 97   **A**
   Other Specialists: 63   **A**
Short-Term General Hospitals: 3 (726 beds)   **A**
   St. Alphonsus Regional Medical Center
   St. Luke's Regional Medical Center
   VA Medical Center
Public Transportation (428 points)
Fixed route
   Boise Urban Stages, 19 buses
Demand–response
   Boise Urban Stages, 3 vans
Public Libraries (191 points)
9 branches, 386,016 books, 952,457 circulation
Continuing Education (164 points)
Four-year
   Boise State University (public, 10,933)
Score: 2,183   **Rank: 52**

Bradenton, FL
Health Care (1,400 points)
Office-Based Physicians
   General/Family Practitioners: 54   **A**
   Medical Specialists: 70   **A**
   Surgical Specialists: 77   **A**
   Other Specialists: 55   **B**
Short-Term General Hospitals: 2 (895 beds)   **A**
Public Transportation (413 points)
Fixed route
   Bradenton–Manatee County TA, 11 buses
Demand–response
   Manatee County TA, 13 vans
Public Libraries (129 points)
5 branches, 255,143 books, 884,456 circulation
Continuing Education (108 points)
Two-year
   Manatee Community College (public, 7,163)
Score: 2,050   **Rank: 60**

Branson–Table Rock Lake, MO
Health Care (600 points)
Office-Based Physicians
   General/Family Practitioners: 9   **B**
   Medical Specialists: 2   **C**
   Surgical Specialists: 5   **C**
   Other Specialists: 4   **C**
Short-Term General Hospital: 1 (95 beds)   **C**
Public Libraries (61 points)
2 branches, 30,000 books, 45,158 circulation
Continuing Education (33 points)
Four-year
   School of the Ozarks (private, 1,310)
Score: 694   **Rank: 147**

Rating

Brevard, NC
Health Care (1,000 points)
Office-Based Physicians
General/Family Practitioners: 7 — A
Medical Specialists: 6 — B
Surgical Specialists: 8 — B
Other Specialists: 4 — C
Short-Term General Hospital: 1 (88 beds) — B
Public Libraries (156 points)
1 branch, 41,542 books, 131,622 circulation
Continuing Education (29 points)
Two-year
Brevard College (private, 680)
Score: 1,184   Rank: 126

Brownsville–Harlingen, TX
Health Care (600 points)
Office-Based Physicians
General/Family Practitioners: 36 — C
Medical Specialists: 75 — B
Surgical Specialists: 68 — C
Other Specialists: 40 — C
Short-Term General Hospitals: 4 (674 beds) — C
Public Transportation (626 points)
Fixed route
City of Brownsville TS, 17 buses
Town of South Padre Island, 4 buses
Valley Transit, 20 buses
Demand–response
City of Brownsville TS, 2 vans
Public Libraries (92 points)
8 branches, 254,119 books, 335,475 circulation
Continuing Education (126 points)
Two-year
Texas State Technical Institute (public, 2,571)
Texas Southmost Union Junior College (public, 5,522)
Four-year
Pan American University (public, 1,182)
Score: 1,444   Rank: 107

Brunswick–Golden Isles, GA
Health Care (1,700 points)
Office-Based Physicians
General/Family Practitioners: 12 — B
Medical Specialists: 22 — A
Surgical Specialists: 35 — AA
Other Specialists: 30 — AA
Short-Term General Hospital: 1 (340 beds) — AA
Public Libraries (190 points)
1 branch, 121,117 books, 178,366 circulation
Continuing Education (34 points)
Two-year
Brunswick College (public, 1,338)
Score: 1,924   Rank: 73

Burlington, VT
Health Care (1,800 points)
Office-Based Physicians
General/Family Practitioners: 38 — A
Medical Specialists: 108 — AA
Surgical Specialists: 89 — AA
Other Specialists: 98 — AA
Short-Term General Hospitals: 3 (668 beds) — A
Fanny Allen Hospital
Medical Center Hospital of Vermont
Public Transportation (697 points)
Fixed route
Chittenden County TA, 24 buses
Public Libraries (202 points)
20 branches, 284,781 books, 527,925 circulation
Continuing Education (252 points)
Two-year
Champlain College (private, 1,697)
Four-year

Rating

Burlington College (private, 183)
Saint Michael's College (private, 2,287)
Trinity College (private, 999)
University of Vermont (public, 11,096)
Score: 2,951   Rank: 25

Burnet–Marble Falls–Llano, TX
Health Care (700 points)
Office-Based Physicians
General/Family Practitioners: 11 — A
Medical Specialists: 6 — C
Surgical Specialists: 4 — C
Other Specialist: 1 — C
Short-Term General Hospitals: 2 (82 beds) — C
Public Libraries (242 points)
2 branches, 96,667 books, 180,843 circulation
Score: 942   Rank: 136

Camden–Penobscot Bay, ME
Health Care (1,700 points)
Office-Based Physicians
General/Family Practitioners: 9 — A
Medical Specialists: 16 — A
Surgical Specialists: 19 — AA
Other Specialists: 18 — AA
Short-Term General Hospital: 1 (150 beds) — A
Public Libraries (476 points)
12 branches, 173,465 books, 251,607 circulation
Score: 2,176   Rank: 53

Canandaigua, NY
Health Care (1,200 points)
Office-Based Physicians
General/Family Practitioners: 13 — C
Medical Specialists: 40 — A
Surgical Specialists: 40 — A
Other Specialists: 23 — B
Short-Term General Hospitals: 3 (457 beds) — A
VA Medical Center
Public Transportation (172 points)
Fixed route
Onondaga Coach, 4 buses
Public Libraries (209 points)
11 branches, 198,980 books, 695,615 circulation
Continuing Education (99 points)
Two-year
Community College of the Finger Lakes (public, 3,355)
Four-year
Hobart/William Smith Colleges (private, 1,973)
Score: 1,680   Rank: 83

Canton–Lake Tawakoni, TX
Health Care (300 points)
Office-Based Physicians
General/Family Practitioners: 6 — C
Medical Specialist: 1 — C
Short-Term General Hospital: 1 (40 beds) — C
Public Libraries (109 points)
2 branches, 44,662 books, 61,905 circulation
Score: 409   Rank: 150

Cape Cod, MA
Health Care (1,300 points)
Office-Based Physicians
General/Family Practitioners: 38 — B
Medical Specialists: 91 — AA
Surgical Specialists: 74 — A
Other Specialists: 70 — A
Short-Term General Hospitals: 2 (358 beds) — C
Public Transportation (699 points)
Fixed route
Cape Cod RTA, 33 buses
Public Libraries (382 points)
15 branches, 738,988 books, 1,525,928 circulation

Rating

Continuing Education (44 points)
Two-year
    Cape Cod Community College (public, 2,303)
Four-year
    Massachusetts Maritime Academy (public, 600)
Score: 2,425   **Rank: 41**

Cape May, NJ
Health Care (700 points)
Office-Based Physicians
    General/Family Practitioners: 21   B
    Medical Specialists: 23   B
    Surgical Specialists: 22   C
    Other Specialists: 15   C
    Short-Term General Hospital: 1 (239 beds) C
Public Transportation (1,243 points)
Fixed route
    Cape May County TA, 30 buses
Public Libraries (476 points)
4 branches, 471,175 books, 690,351 circulation
Score: 2,420   **Rank: 42**

Carlsbad–Artesia, NM
Health Care (1,100 points)
Office-Based Physicians
    General/Family Practitioners: 13   A
    Medical Specialists: 12   B
    Surgical Specialists: 20   A
    Other Specialists: 4   C
    Short-Term General Hospitals: 2 (181 beds) B
Public Transportation (157 points)
Demand–response
    City of Carlsbad, 3 vans
Public Libraries (177 points)
2 branches, 95,028 books, 260,009 circulation
Continuing Education (26 points)
Two-year
    New Mexico State University, Carlsbad (public, 899)
Score: 1,460   **Rank: 106**

Carson City–Minden, NV
Health Care (900 points)
Office-Based Physicians
    General/Family Practitioners: 22   A
    Medical Specialists: 12   C
    Surgical Specialists: 20   B
    Other Specialists: 20   B
    Short-Term General Hospital: 1 (108 beds) C
Public Transportation (445 points)
Fixed route
    Tahoe TD, 8 buses
Public Libraries (211 points)
2 branches, 155,253 books, 494,500 circulation
Continuing Education (112 points)
Two-year
    Western Nevada Community College (public, 4,736)
Score: 1,668   **Rank: 84**

★**Chapel Hill, NC**
Health Care (2,000 points)
Office-Based Physicians
    General/Family Practitioners: 38   AA
    Medical Specialists: 90   AA
    Surgical Specialists: 74   AA
    Other Specialists: 136   AA
    Short-Term General Hospital: 1 (575 beds) AA
    North Carolina Memorial Hospital
Public Transportation (1,468 points)
Fixed route
    Chapel Hill Transit, 31 buses
Demand–response
    Chapel Hill Transit, 3 vans
Public Libraries (95 points)
2 branches, 87,690 books, 487,887 circulation

Rating

Continuing Education (491 points)
Four-year
    University of North Carolina (public, 23,579)
Score: 4,054   **Rank: 4**

Charleston, SC
Health Care (1,900 points)
Office-Based Physicians
    General/Family Practitioners: 77   A
    Medical Specialists: 221   AA
    Surgical Specialists: 212   AA
    Other Specialists: 174   AA
    Short-Term General Hospitals: 9 (2,247 beds) AA
    Charleston Memorial Hospital
    Medical University Medical Center
    Roper Hospital
    U.S. Naval Hospital
    VA Medical Center
Public Transportation (519 points)
Fixed route
    South Carolina E&G Co., 37 buses
Public Libraries (143 points)
10 branches, 418,211 books, 832,429 circulation
Continuing Education (240 points)
Two-year
    Johnson and Wales University (private, 480)
    Trident Technical College (public, 5,402)
Four-year
    Baptist College at Charleston (private, 1,922)
    Citadel Military College of South Carolina
        (public, 3,339)
    College of Charleston (public, 5,531)
    Medical University of South Carolina (public, 2,066)
Score: 2,802   **Rank: 30**

Charlevoix–Boyne City, MI
Health Care (900 points)
Office-Based Physicians
    General/Family Practitioners: 7   AA
    Medical Specialists: 5   B
    Surgical Specialists: 3   C
    Other Specialists: 2   C
    Short-Term General Hospital: 1 (44 beds) C
Public Transportation (1,357 points)
Demand–response
    Charlevoix County Transit, 10 vans
Public Libraries (208 points)
3 branches, 43,000 books, 62,491 circulation
Score: 2,465   **Rank: 37**

★**Charlottesville, VA**
Health Care (1,900 points)
Office-Based Physicians
    General/Family Practitioners: 33   A
    Medical Specialists: 157   AA
    Surgical Specialists: 102   AA
    Other Specialists: 127   AA
    Short-Term General Hospitals: 2 (910 beds) AA
    University of Virginia Hospitals
Public Transportation (856 points)
Fixed route
    Charlottesville Transit, 10 buses
Demand–response
    Charlottesville JAUNT, 24 vans
Public Libraries (200 points)
6 branches, 253,531 books, 812,913 circulation
Continuing Education (461 points)
Two-year
    Piedmont Virginia Community College (public, 4,104)
Four-year
    University of Virginia (public, 21,615)
Score: 3,417   **Rank: 12**

Rating

Chico–Paradise, CA
Health Care (1,600 points)
Office-Based Physicians
General/Family Practitioners: 62	AA
Medical Specialists: 66	A
Surgical Specialists: 95	AA
Other Specialists: 67	A
Short-Term General Hospitals: 5 (625 beds)	B

Public Transportation (881 points)
Fixed route
Butte County Transit, 10 buses
Chico Area Transit, 5 buses
Demand–response
Butte County Transit, 25 vans
Chico Area Transit, 10 vans
Public Libraries (135 points)
7 branches, 243,619 books, 528,265 circulation
Continuing Education (404 points)
Two-year
Butte College (public, 9,993)
Four-year
California State University (public, 16,031)
Score: 3,020   **Rank: 21**

Clayton, GA
Health Care (1,000 points)
Office-Based Physicians
General/Family Practitioners: 5	AA
Other Specialists: 3	B
Short-Term General Hospitals: 2 (71 beds)	AA

Public Libraries (229 points)
1 branch, 26,520 books, 41,946 circulation
Score: 1,229   **Rank: 122**

Clear Lake, CA
Health Care (800 points)
Office-Based Physicians
General/Family Practitioners: 21	AA
Medical Specialists: 8	C
Surgical Specialists: 7	C
Other Specialists: 7	C
Short-Term General Hospitals: 2 (103 beds)	C

Public Transportation (142 points)
Demand–response
City of Clearlake, 1 van
City of Lakeport, 2 vans
Public Libraries (128 points)
4 branches, 75,786 books, 221,996 circulation
Score: 1,070   **Rank: 131**

Coeur d'Alene, ID
Health Care (1,000 points)
Office-Based Physicians
General/Family Practitioners: 27	AA
Medical Specialists: 12	C
Surgical Specialists: 27	A
Other Specialists: 12	C
Short-Term General Hospital: 1 (171 beds)	C

Public Transportation (702 points)
Fixed route
Panhandle Area Transit, 11 buses
Demand–response
Panhandle Area Transit, 2 vans
Public Libraries (213 points)
8 branches, 153,665 books, 375,142 circulation
Continuing Education (61 points)
Two-year
North Idaho College (public, 2,565)
Score: 1,977   **Rank: 67**

Rating

Colorado Springs, CO
Health Care (1,200 points)
Office-Based Physicians
General/Family Practitioners: 54	C
Medical Specialists: 136	A
Surgical Specialists: 140	B
Other Specialists: 118	A
Short-Term General Hospitals: 7 (1,524 beds)	A

Penrose Hospitals
U.S. Army Community Hospital, Fort Carson
Public Transportation (383 points)
Fixed route
Colorado Springs Transit, 38 buses
Public Libraries (173 points)
9 branches, 705,798 books, 1,001,448 circulation
Continuing Education (135 points)
Two-year
Nazarene Bible College (private, 407)
Pikes Peak Community College (public, 5,014)
Four-year
Colorado College (private, 1,988)
University of Colorado, Colorado Springs
(public, 4,402)
Score: 1,891   **Rank: 76**

Columbia County, NY
Health Care (800 points)
Office-Based Physicians
General/Family Practitioners: 11	C
Medical Specialists: 18	B
Surgical Specialists: 15	C
Other Specialists: 15	B
Short-Term General Hospital: 1 (160 beds)	B

Public Transportation (329 points)
Fixed route
Hudson Bus System, 5 buses
Public Libraries (253 points)
11 branches, 157,373 books, 172,430 circulation
Continuing Education (42 points)
Two-year
Columbia–Greene Community College (public, 1,616)
Score: 1,424   **Rank: 110**

Crossville, TN
Health Care (1,300 points)
Office-Based Physicians
General/Family Practitioners: 13	AA
Medical Specialists: 6	C
Surgical Specialists: 13	A
Other Specialists: 5	C
Short-Term General Hospital: 1 (177 beds)	AA

Public Libraries (44 points)
1 branch, 15,000 books, 90,000 circulation
Score: 1,344   **Rank: 119**

Daytona Beach, FL
Health Care (1,200 points)
Office-Based Physicians
General/Family Practitioners: 70	B
Medical Specialists: 93	B
Surgical Specialists: 116	B
Other Specialists: 107	A
Short-Term General Hospitals: 8 (1,468 beds)	A

Halifax Hospital Medical Center
Public Transportation (369 points)
Fixed route
Volusia TA, 28 buses
Smyrna TS, 2 buses
Demand–response
Volusia TA, 2 vans
Public Libraries (159 points)
15 branches, 554,798 books, 2,195,186 circulation

Rating

Continuing Education (192 points)
Two-year
  Daytona Beach Community College (public, 8,703)
Four-year
  Bethune Cookman College (private, 1,860)
  Embry-Riddle Aeronautical University (private, 5,317)
  Stetson University (private, 2,975)
Score: 1,920   **Rank: 74**

Deming, NM
Health Care (800 points)
Office-Based Physicians
  General/Family Practitioners: 8   AA
Short-Term General Hospital: 1 (118 beds)   AA
Public Transportation (308 points)
Demand–response
  DART, 2 vans
Public Libraries (289 points)
1 branch, 52,591 books, 144,280 circulation
Score: 1,397   **Rank: 113**

Door County, WI
Health Care (1,100 points)
Office-Based Physicians
  General/Family Practitioners: 10   AA
  Medical Specialists: 6   B
  Surgical Specialists: 9   B
  Other Specialists: 4   C
Short-Term General Hospital: 1 (93 beds)   B
Public Libraries (532 points)
8 branches, 150,665 books, 246,862 circulation
Score: 1,632   **Rank: 87**

Eagle River, WI
Health Care (1,000 points)
Office-Based Physicians
  General/Family Practitioners: 5   A
  Medical Specialists: 2   C
  Surgical Specialist: 1   C
  Other Specialists: 2   C
Short-Term General Hospitals: 2 (140 beds)   AA
Public Libraries (353 points)
9 branches, 63,355 books, 118,554 circulation
Score: 1,353   **Rank: 118**

Easton–Chesapeake Bay, MD
Health Care (1,900 points)
Office-Based Physicians
  General/Family Practitioners: 8   A
  Medical Specialists: 25   AA
  Surgical Specialists: 33   AA
  Other Specialists: 13   AA
Short-Term General Hospital: 1 (208 beds)   AA
Public Libraries (361 points)
1 branch, 100,274 books, 184,075 circulation
Continuing Education (103 points)
Two-year
  Chesapeake College (public, 2,247)
Score: 2,365   **Rank: 46**

Edenton–Albemarle Sound, NC
Health Care (1,400 points)
Office-Based Physicians
  General/Family Practitioners: 6   AA
  Medical Specialists: 3   B
  Surgical Specialists: 5   A
  Other Specialists: 2   C
Short-Term General Hospital: 1 (126 beds)   AA
Public Libraries (183 points)
1 branch, 25,080 books, 40,547 circulation
Score: 1,583   **Rank: 94**

El Centro–Calexico–Brawley, CA
Health Care (500 points)
Office-Based Physicians
  General/Family Practitioners: 10   C
  Medical Specialists: 19   C
  Surgical Specialists: 26   C
  Other Specialists: 17   C
Short-Term General Hospitals: 4 (233 beds)   C
Public Transportation (114 points)
Fixed route
  Imperial County DPW, 3 buses
Public Libraries (200 points)
14 branches, 215,694 books, 378,153 circulation
Continuing Education (78 points)
Two-year
  Imperial Valley College (public, 4,039)
Score: 893   **Rank: 138**

Eugene–Springfield, OR
Health Care (1,400 points)
Office-Based Physicians
  General/Family Practitioners: 92   AA
  Medical Specialists: 110   A
  Surgical Specialists: 109   A
  Other Specialists: 94   A
Short-Term General Hospitals: 5 (654 beds)   C
Public Transportation (952 points)
Fixed route
  Lane County MTD, 61 buses
Public Libraries (186 points)
9 branches, 488,924 books, 1,715,465 circulation
Continuing Education (365 points)
Two-year
  Lane Community College (public, 7,623)
Four-year
  Eugene Bible College (private, 153)
  Northwest Christian College (private, 257)
  University of Oregon (public, 18,530)
Score: 2,903   **Rank: 27**

Fairhope–Gulf Shores, AL
Health Care (800 points)
Office-Based Physicians
  General/Family Practitioners: 23   B
  Medical Specialists: 15   C
  Surgical Specialists: 22   C
  Other Specialists: 22   B
Short-Term General Hospitals: 3 (254 beds)   B
Public Transportation (195 points)
Demand–response
  Baldwin County Commission, 7 vans
Public Libraries (166 points)
9 branches, 166,114 books, 394,585 circulation
Continuing Education (47 points)
Two-year
  Faulkner State Junior College (public, 2,348)
Score: 1,208   **Rank: 125**

Fayetteville, AR
Health Care (1,500 points)
Office-Based Physicians
  General/Family Practitioners: 29   A
  Medical Specialists: 33   B
  Surgical Specialists: 51   A
  Other Specialists: 43   A
Short-Term General Hospitals: 4 (704 beds)   AA
  VA Medical Center
  Washington Regional Medical Center
Public Transportation (150 points)
Fixed route
  Ozark Transit, 4 buses

Rating

Public Libraries (197 points)
9 branches, 215,635 books, 511,000 circulation
Continuing Education (277 points)
Four-year
University of Arkansas (public, 14,452)
Score: 2,123   **Rank: 56**

Fort Collins–Loveland, CO
Health Care (1,200 points)
Office-Based Physicians
General/Family Practitioners: 69   AA
Medical Specialists: 46   B
Surgical Specialists: 68   A
Other Specialists: 46   B
Short-Term General Hospitals: 3 (371 beds)   C
Poudre Valley Hospital
Public Transportation (715 points)
Fixed route
Fort Collins Transport, 14 buses
Demand–response
CARE-A-VAN, 27 vans
Public Libraries (195 points)
5 branches, 363,544 books, 1,090,362 circulation
Continuing Education (306 points)
Four-year
Colorado State University (public, 19,885)
Score: 2,416   **Rank: 43**

Fort Lauderdale–Hollywood–Pompano Beach, FL
Health Care (1,400 points)
Office-Based Physicians
General/Family Practitioners: 225   C
Medical Specialists: 719   AA
Surgical Specialists: 578   A
Other Specialists: 411   A
Short-Term General Hospitals: 21 (5,650 beds)   A
Broward General Medical Center
Hollywood Memorial Hospital
Public Transportation (497 points)
Fixed route
Broward County MTA, 154 buses
Public Libraries (136 points)
29 branches, 1,732,253 books, 5,238,849 circulation
Continuing Education (276 points)
Two-year
Broward Community College (public, 21,370)
Four-year
Nova University (private, 7,800)
Score: 2,309   **Rank: 47**

Fort Myers–Cape Coral–Sanibel Island, FL
Health Care (1,100 points)
Office-Based Physicians
General/Family Practitioners: 60   C
Medical Specialists: 116   A
Surgical Specialists: 125   A
Other Specialists: 93   B
Short-Term General Hospitals: 4 (1,163 beds)   B
Public Transportation (297 points)
Fixed route
Lee County Transit, 24 buses
Public Libraries (94 points)
10 branches, 311,027 books, 1,069,169 circulation
Continuing Education (101 points)
Two-year
Edison Community College (public, 7,732)
Score: 1,592   **Rank: 92**

Fort Walton Beach, FL
Health Care (900 points)
Office-Based Physicians
General/Family Practitioners: 21   C
Medical Specialists: 40   B
Surgical Specialists: 44   B
Other Specialists: 27   C

Rating

Short-Term General Hospitals: 5 (626 beds)   A
U.S. Air Force Regional Hospital
Public Libraries (52 points)
5 branches, 84,475 books, 253,170 circulation
Continuing Education (81 points)
Two-year
Okaloosa-Walton Junior College (public, 4,973)
Score: 1,033   **Rank: 132**

Fredericksburg, TX
Health Care (1,100 points)
Office-Based Physicians
General/Family Practitioners: 10   AA
Medical Specialists: 3   C
Surgical Specialists: 5   B
Other Specialists: 2   C
Short-Term General Hospital: 1 (61 beds)   A
Public Libraries (241 points)
1 branch, 39,368 books, 86,966 circulation
Score: 1,341   **Rank: 120**

★**Gainesville, FL**
Health Care (1,800 points)
Office-Based Physicians
General/Family Practitioners: 43   B
Medical Specialists: 120   AA
Surgical Specialists: 123   AA
Other Specialists: 130   AA
Short-Term General Hospitals: 4 (1,689 beds)   AA
Alachua General Hospital
University of Florida, Shands Hospital
VA Medical Center
Public Transportation (762 points)
Fixed route
Gainesville RTS, 30 buses
Demand–response
Gainesville RTS, 8 vans
Public Libraries (142 points)
6 branches, 270,633 books, 862,987 circulation
Continuing Education (687 points)
Two-year
Santa Fe Community College (public, 9,918)
Four-year
University of Florida (public, 35,172)
Score: 3,392   **Rank: 14**

Grand Junction, CO
Health Care (1,500 points)
Office-Based Physicians
General/Family Practitioners: 31   AA
Medical Specialists: 36   A
Surgical Specialists: 34   A
Other Specialists: 23   B
Short-Term General Hospitals: 3 (379 beds)   A
St. Mary's Hospital and Medical Center
VA Medical Center
Public Transportation (62 points)
Demand–response
Mesa County Transportation, 2 vans
Public Libraries (343 points)
6 branches, 307,700 books, 923,100 circulation
Continuing Education (85 points)
Four-year
Mesa College (public, 3,996)
Score: 1,990   **Rank: 66**

Grand Lake, OK
Health Care (600 points)
Office-Based Physicians
General/Family Practitioners: 6   B
Medical Specialists: 3   C
Surgical Specialists: 2   C
Other Specialists: 2   C
Short-Term General Hospital: 1 (59 beds)   C
Public Libraries (67 points)
2 branches, 20,000 books, 57,000 circulation
Score: 667   **Rank: 148**

Rating   Rating

Grants Pass, OR
Health Care (900 points)
Office-Based Physicians
General/Family Practitioners: 14   B
Medical Specialists: 17   B
Surgical Specialists: 22   B
Other Specialists: 14   B
Short-Term General Hospitals: 2 (144 beds)   C
Public Libraries (206 points)
4 branches, 151,684 books, 248,250 circulation
Continuing Education (76 points)
Two-year
Rogue Community College (public, 3,214)
Score: 1,182   **Rank: 128**

Grass Valley–Truckee, CA
Health Care (1,100 points)
Office-Based Physicians
General/Family Practitioners: 34   AA
Medical Specialists: 23   B
Surgical Specialists: 28   B
Other Specialists: 22   B
Short-Term General Hospitals: 2 (183 beds)   C
Public Transportation (399 points)
Fixed route
Nevada County TA, 8 buses
Public Libraries (103 points)
3 branches, 84,727 books, 264,264 circulation
Score: 1,601   **Rank: 90**

Hamilton–Bitterroot Valley, MT
Health Care (700 points)
Office-Based Physicians
General/Family Practitioners: 8   A
Medical Specialists: 3   C
Surgical Specialists: 4   C
Other Specialists: 2   C
Short-Term General Hospital: 1 (48 beds)   C
Public Libraries (83 points)
1 branch, 22,000 books, 50,000 circulation
Score: 783   **Rank: 144**

★Hanover, NH
Health Care (2,000 points)
Office-Based Physicians
General/Family Practitioners: 32   AA
Medical Specialists: 72   AA
Surgical Specialists: 54   AA
Other Specialists: 63   AA
Short-Term General Hospitals: 5 (600 beds)   AA
Mary Hitchcock Hospital
Public Transportation (1,190 points)
Fixed route
Advance Transit, 22 buses
Public Libraries (498 points)
40 branches, 377,237 books, 591,881 circulation
Continuing Education (184 points)
Four-year
Dartmouth College (private, 5,400)
Plymouth State College (public, 3,691)
Score: 3,872   **Rank: 6**

Harrison, AR
Health Care (1,300 points)
Office-Based Physicians
General/Family Practitioners: 16   AA
Medical Specialists: 5   C
Surgical Specialists: 13   A
Other Specialists: 5   C
Short-Term General Hospital: 1 (174 beds)   AA
Public Libraries (125 points)
2 branches, 36,891 books, 125,124 circulation
Continuing Education (47 points)
Two-year
North Arkansas Community College (public, 1,077)
Score: 1,473   **Rank: 104**

Hendersonville, NC
Health Care (1,300 points)
Office-Based Physicians
General/Family Practitioners: 21   A
Medical Specialists: 24   B
Surgical Specialists: 31   A
Other Specialists: 16   B
Short-Term General Hospitals: 2 (336 beds)   A
Public Libraries (177 points)
3 branches, 129,031 books, 386,974 circulation
Continuing Education (29 points)
Two-year
Blue Ridge Technical College (public, 1,223)
Score: 1,506   **Rank: 101**

Hilton Head–Beaufort, SC
Health Care (900 points)
Office-Based Physicians
General/Family Practitioners: 15   C
Medical Specialists: 27   B
Surgical Specialists: 40   A
Other Specialists: 18   B
Short-Term General Hospitals: 3 (212 beds)   C
Public Transportation (557 points)
Fixed route
Lowcountry RTA, 13 buses
Public Libraries (102 points)
2 branches, 97,674 books, 191,101 circulation
Continuing Education (37 points)
Two-year
Beaufort Technical College (public, 979)
University of South Carolina (public, 850)
Score: 1,596   **Rank: 91**

★Honolulu, HI
Health Care (1,300 points)
Office-Based Physicians
General/Family Practitioners: 139   C
Medical Specialists: 518   AA
Surgical Specialists: 395   A
Other Specialists: 337   A
Short-Term General Hospitals: 9 (2,121 beds)   B
Kaiser Permanente Medical Center
Kapiolani Medical Center
Kuakini Medical Center
Queen's Medical Center
St. Francis Medical Center
Tripler Army Medical Center
Public Transportation (1,997 points)
Fixed route
Honolulu DOT, 412 buses
Public Libraries (167 points)
22 branches, 1,408,743 books, 4,571,940 circulation
Continuing Education (467 points)
Two-year
Honolulu Community College (public, 4,270)
Kapiolani Community College (public, 5,465)
Leeward Community College (public, 5,693)
Windward Community College (public, 1,555)
Four-year
Brigham Young University, Hawaii Campus (private, 2,142)
Chaminade University (private, 2,556)
Hawaii Loa College (private, 500)
Hawaii Pacific College (private, 4,560)
University of Hawaii (public, 18,918)
West Oahu College (public, 480)
Score: 3,931   **Rank: 5**

Hot Springs National Park, AR
Health Care (1,600 points)
Office-Based Physicians
General/Family Practitioners: 18   B
Medical Specialists: 34   A

Rating

Surgical Specialists: 39 **AA**
Other Specialists: 23 **A**
Short-Term General Hospitals: 2 (417 beds) **AA**
Public Transportation (639 points)
Fixed route
Hot Springs Transit, 12 buses
Public Libraries (124 points)
1 branch, 95,816 books, 234,642 circulation
Continuing Education (40 points)
Two-year
Garland County Community College (public, 1,729)
Score: 2,403 **Rank: 45**

Houghton Lake, MI
Health Care (600 points)
Office-Based Physicians
General/Family Practitioners: 5 **A**
Medical Specialist: 1 **C**
Surgical Specialist: 1 **C**
Other Specialist: 1 **C**
Public Transportation (1,399 points)
Demand–response
Roscommon Minibus System, 10 vans
Public Libraries (183 points)
2 branches, 36,600 books, 25,000 circulation
Continuing Education (90 points)
Two-year
Kirtland Community College (public, 1,495)
Score: 2,271 **Rank: 49**

★**Iowa City, IA**
Health Care (2,000 points)
Office-Based Physicians
General/Family Practitioners: 29 **AA**
Medical Specialists: 74 **AA**
Surgical Specialists: 78 **AA**
Other Specialists: 102 **AA**
Short-Term General Hospitals: 3 (1,408 beds) **AA**
Mercy Hospital
University of Iowa Hospitals and Clinics
VA Medical Center
Public Transportation (1,772 points)
Fixed route
Coralville Transit, 7 buses
Iowa City Transit, 18 buses
University of Iowa CAMBUS, 11 buses
Demand–response
University of Iowa CAMBUS, 3 vans
Public Libraries (281 points)
5 branches, 247,578 books, 794,500 circulation
Continuing Education (655 points)
Four-year
University of Iowa (public, 30,670)
Score: 4,709 **Rank: 2**

Kalispell, MT
Health Care (1,400 points)
Office-Based Physicians
General/Family Practitioners: 30 **AA**
Medical Specialists: 19 **B**
Surgical Specialists: 25 **A**
Other Specialists: 23 **A**
Short-Term General Hospitals: 2 (209 beds) **B**
Public Transportation (275 points)
Demand–response
Eagle Transit, 6 vans
Public Libraries (148 points)
4 branches, 90,663 books, 299,978 circulation
Continuing Education (52 points)
Two-year
Flathead Valley Community College (public, 1,958)
Score: 1,875 **Rank: 77**

Rating

Keene, NH
Health Care (1,200 points)
Office-Based Physicians
General/Family Practitioners: 19 **A**
Medical Specialists: 24 **A**
Surgical Specialists: 19 **B**
Other Specialists: 21 **A**
Short-Term General Hospital: 1 (173 beds) **C**
Public Libraries (503 points)
23 branches, 358,104 books, 450,636 circulation
Continuing Education (92 points)
Four-year
Franklin Pierce College (private, 1,183)
Keene State College (public, 2,893)
Score: 1,795 **Rank: 79**

Kerrville, TX
Health Care (1,500 points)
Office-Based Physicians
General/Family Practitioners: 9 **B**
Medical Specialists: 18 **A**
Surgical Specialists: 16 **A**
Other Specialists: 14 **A**
Short-Term General Hospitals: 3 (529 beds) **AA**
VA Medical Center
Public Libraries (142 points)
1 branch, 58,328 books, 145,522 circulation
Continuing Education (15 points)
Four-year
Schreiner College (private, 508)
Score: 1,657 **Rank: 85**

Key West–Key Largo–Marathon, FL
Health Care (800 points)
Office-Based Physicians
General/Family Practitioners: 14 **C**
Medical Specialists: 25 **B**
Surgical Specialists: 29 **B**
Other Specialists: 13 **C**
Short-Term General Hospitals: 4 (254 beds) **B**
Public Transportation (408 points)
Fixed route
Key West TA, 8 buses
Public Libraries (179 points)
4 branches, 143,868 books, 326,637 circulation
Continuing Education (14 points)
Two-year
Florida Keys Community College (public, 643)
Score: 1,401 **Rank: 112**

Laconia–Lake Winnipesaukee, NH
Health Care (1,500 points)
Office-Based Physicians
General/Family Practitioners: 16 **A**
Medical Specialists: 24 **AA**
Surgical Specialists: 24 **A**
Other Specialists: 18 **A**
Short-Term General Hospital: 1 (157 beds) **B**
Public Libraries (436 points)
11 branches, 225,730 books, 302,669 circulation
Continuing Education (6 points)
Two-year
New Hampshire Vocational Technical College (public, 213)
Score: 1,943 **Rank: 71**

Lake Havasu City–Kingman, AZ
Health Care (600 points)
Office-Based Physicians
General/Family Practitioners: 17 **B**
Medical Specialists: 15 **C**
Surgical Specialists: 22 **C**
Other Specialists: 16 **C**
Short-Term General Hospitals: 3 (203 beds) **C**

Rating

Public Transportation (92 points)
Fixed route
Colorado River Transit, 2 buses
Public Libraries (87 points)
4 branches, 77,394 books, 228,390 circulation
Continuing Education (83 points)
Two-year
Mohave Community College (public, 3,890)
Score: 862   **Rank: 140**

Lake Lanier, GA
Health Care (1,500 points)
Office-Based Physicians
General/Family Practitioners: 9   C
Medical Specialists: 38   A
Surgical Specialists: 55   AA
Other Specialists: 32   A
Short-Term General Hospitals: 2 (462 beds)   AA
Public Transportation (290 points)
Demand–response
Hall County Dial-A-Ride, 9 vans
Public Libraries (119 points)
3 branches, 103,492 books, 269,226 circulation
Continuing Education (107 points)
Two-year
Gainesville College (public, 2,160)
Lanier Technical Institute (public, 2,438)
Four-year
Brenau College (private, 472)
Score: 2,016   **Rank: 63**

Lakeland–Winter Haven, FL
Health Care (1,200 points)
Office-Based Physicians
General/Family Practitioners: 69   C
Medical Specialists: 138   A
Surgical Specialists: 144   B
Other Specialists: 118   A
Short-Term General Hospitals: 7 (1,502 beds) A
Public Transportation (257 points)
Fixed route
Lakeland Area MTD, 12 buses
Demand–response
Lakeland Area MTD, 3 vans
Public Libraries (94 points)
10 branches, 376,625 books, 646,762 circulation
Continuing Education (98 points)
Two-year
Polk Community College (public, 5,600)
Four-year
Florida Southern College (private, 1,955)
Southeastern College of the Assemblies of God
(private, 1,155)
Warner Southern College (private, 364)
Webber College (private, 302)
Score: 1,649   **Rank: 86**

Lancaster County, PA
Health Care (1,000 points)
Office-Based Physicians
General/Family Practitioners: 137   AA
Medical Specialists: 83   C
Surgical Specialists: 94   C
Other Specialists: 90   B
Short-Term General Hospitals: 5 (1,307 beds) B
Lancaster General Hospital
Public Transportation (317 points)
Fixed route
Red Rose TA, 32 buses
Public Libraries (124 points)
14 branches, 512,582 books, 940,843 circulation
Continuing Education (132 points)
Two-year
Thaddeus Stevens State School of Technology
(public, 425)

Rating

Four-year
Elizabethtown College (private, 1,679)
Franklin and Marshall College (private, 2,684)
Lancaster Bible College (private, 377)
Millersville University of Pennsylvania (public, 7,202)
Score: 1,572   **Rank: 96**

Las Cruces, NM
Health Care (900 points)
Office-Based Physicians
General/Family Practitioners: 31   B
Medical Specialists: 32   B
Surgical Specialists: 39   B
Other Specialists: 30   B
Short-Term General Hospital: 1 (242 beds)   C
Public Transportation (232 points)
Fixed route
Las Cruces Transit, 7 buses
Demand–response
Las Cruces Transit, 1 van
Public Libraries (111 points)
2 branches, 151,173 books, 313,282 circulation
Continuing Education (249 points)
Two-year
New Mexico State University (public, 625)
Four-year
New Mexico State University (public, 13,718)
Score: 1,492   **Rank: 103**

Las Vegas, NV
Health Care (900 points)
Office-Based Physicians
General/Family Practitioners: 110   C
Medical Specialists: 207   B
Surgical Specialists: 203   B
Other Specialists: 179   B
Short-Term General Hospitals: 8 (1,934 beds) B
University Medical Center of Southern Nevada
Public Transportation (157 points)
Fixed route
Las Vegas TS, 25 buses
Public Libraries (110 points)
23 branches, 717,527 books, 2,458,188 circulation
Continuing Education (301 points)
Two-year
Clark County Community College (public, 11,069)
Four-year
University of Nevada (public, 15,000)
Score: 1,468   **Rank: 105**

Lexington–Fayette, KY
Health Care (1,900 points)
Office-Based Physicians
General/Family Practitioners: 101   A
Medical Specialists: 240   AA
Surgical Specialists: 219   AA
Other Specialists: 225   AA
Short-Term General Hospitals: 11 (3,129 beds) AA
Central Baptist Hospital
St. Joseph Hospital
University Hospital
VA Medical Center
Public Transportation (520 points)
Fixed route
LEXTRAN, 43 buses
Public Libraries (157 points)
11 branches, 530,789 books, 1,546,778 circulation
Continuing Education (368 points)
Two-year
Lexington Community College (public, 3,399)
Midway College (private, 340)
Four-year
Asbury College (private, 942)
Asbury Theological Seminary (private, 722)

	Rating
Georgetown College (private, 1,360)	
Transylvania University (private, 970)	
University of Kentucky (public, 22,336)	
Score: 2,945	**Rank: 26**

★ Los Alamos, NM

Health Care (1,600 points)
Office-Based Physicians

	Rating
General/Family Practitioners: 4	B
Medical Specialists: 15	AA
Surgical Specialists: 11	AA
Other Specialists: 8	A
Short-Term General Hospital: 1 (80 beds)	A

Public Transportation (1,614 points)
Fixed route
Los Alamos Bus System, 8 buses
Public Libraries (584 points)
2 branches, 118,621 books, 285,613 circulation
Continuing Education (55 points)
Two-year
University of New Mexico (public, 923)

Score: 3,853	**Rank: 7**

★ Madison, WI

Health Care (1,900 points)
Office-Based Physicians

	Rating
General/Family Practitioners: 105	A
Medical Specialists: 243	AA
Surgical Specialists: 187	AA
Other Specialists: 230	AA
Short-Term General Hospitals: 5 (1,805 beds)	AA

Meriter Hospital
Middleton Memorial Veterans Hospital
St. Mary's Hospital Medical Center
University of Wisconsin Hospitals and Clinics
VA Medical Center
Public Transportation (212 points)
Fixed route
Madison METRO, 144 buses
Demand–response
Madison METRO, 6 vans
Public Libraries (275 points)
24 branches, 987,509 books, 3,147,189 circulation
Continuing Education (710 points)
Two-year
Madison Area Technical College (public, 10,300)
Four-year
Edgewood College (private, 1,110)
University of Wisconsin (public, 44,584)

Score: 3,097	**Rank: 20**

Martinsburg–Charles Town, WV

Health Care (800 points)
Office-Based Physicians

	Rating
General/Family Practitioners: 13	C
Medical Specialists: 19	B
Surgical Specialists: 26	B
Other Specialists: 16	C
Short-Term General Hospitals: 2 (289 beds)	B

VA Medical Center
Public Transportation (324 points)
Fixed route
Eastern Panhandle TA, 7 buses
Public Libraries (232 points)
6 branches, 205,561 books, 706,820 circulation
Continuing Education (82 points)
Four-year
Shepherd College (public, 3,853)

Score: 1,437	**Rank: 108**

Maui, HI

Health Care (1,300 points)
Office-Based Physicians

	Rating
General/Family Practitioners: 32	AA
Medical Specialists: 35	A
Surgical Specialists: 46	A
Other Specialists: 28	B
Short-Term General Hospitals: 3 (189 beds)	C

Public Libraries (183 points)
5 branches, 187,463 books, 430,221 circulation
Continuing Education (39 points)
Two-year
Maui Community College (public, 1,963)

Score: 1,522	**Rank: 99**

McAllen–Edinburg–Mission, TX

Health Care (600 points)
Office-Based Physicians

	Rating
General/Family Practitioners: 74	B
Medical Specialists: 49	C
Surgical Specialists: 67	C
Other Specialists: 44	C
Short-Term General Hospitals: 5 (829 beds)	C

Public Transportation (208 points)
Fixed route
Valley Transit, 20 buses
Public Libraries (100 points)
10 branches, 393,926 books, 940,611 circulation
Continuing Education (111 points)
Four-year
Pan American University (public, 8,887)

Score: 1,019	**Rank: 133**

Medford–Ashland, OR

Health Care (1,500 points)
Office-Based Physicians

	Rating
General/Family Practitioners: 38	A
Medical Specialists: 58	A
Surgical Specialists: 66	A
Other Specialists: 49	A
Short-Term General Hospitals: 3 (531 beds)	A

Public Transportation (678 points)
Fixed route
Rogue Valley TD, 24 buses
Public Libraries (205 points)
15 branches, 298,184 books, 879,693 circulation
Continuing Education (82 points)
Four-year
Southern Oregon State College (public, 4,853)

Score: 2,465	**Rank: 37**

Melbourne–Titusville–Palm Bay, FL

Health Care (1,100 points)
Office-Based Physicians

	Rating
General/Family Practitioners: 71	B
Medical Specialists: 121	B
Surgical Specialists: 124	B
Other Specialists: 125	A
Short-Term General Hospitals: 5 (1,151 beds)	B

Public Transportation (360 points)
Fixed route
Space Coast Area Transit, 20 buses
Demand–response
Space Coast Area Transit, 20 vans
Public Libraries (162 points)
13 branches, 621,264 books, 1,627,080 circulation
Continuing Education (187 points)
Two-year
Brevard Community College (public, 12,377)
Four-year
Florida Institute of Technology (private, 4,117)

Score: 1,809	**Rank: 78**

Rating

★ Miami–Hialeah, FL
Health Care (2,000 points)
Office-Based Physicians
General/Family Practitioners: 711 — AA
Medical Specialists: 1,312 — AA
Surgical Specialists: 1,082 — AA
Other Specialists: 955 — AA
Short-Term General Hospitals: 31 (9,449 beds) — AA
Jackson Memorial Hospital
University of Miami Hospital and Clinics
VA Medical Center
Public Transportation (1,266 points)
Fixed route
Dade County TA, 415 buses
Dade County TA, 74 rapid rail
Public Libraries (143 points)
35 branches, 2,698,205 books, 4,581,194 circulation
Continuing Education (804 points)
Two-year
Miami–Dade Community College (public, 46,035)
Four-year
Barry University (private, 5,238)
Florida International University (public, 17,482)
Miami Christian College (private, 166)
Saint Thomas University (private, 2,500)
University of Miami (private, 11,387)
Score: 4,213   **Rank: 3**

Monticello–Liberty, NY
Health Care (1,000 points)
Office-Based Physicians
General/Family Practitioners: 17 — A
Medical Specialists: 20 — B
Surgical Specialists: 13 — C
Other Specialists: 12 — C
Short-Term General Hospital: 1 (290 beds) — A
Public Libraries (169 points)
9 branches, 115,778 books, 172,221 circulation
Continuing Education (44 points)
Two-year
Sullivan County Community College (public, 1,779)
Score: 1,213   **Rank: 123**

Mountain Home–Bull Shoals, AR
Health Care (1,200 points)
Office-Based Physicians
General/Family Practitioners: 15 — AA
Medical Specialists: 11 — B
Surgical Specialists: 12 — C
Other Specialists: 12 — B
Short-Term General Hospitals: 3 (218 beds) — A
Public Transportation (264 points)
Fixed route
NATS, 3 buses
Public Libraries (117 points)
3 branches, 54,757 books, 185,969 circulation
Score: 1,581   **Rank: 95**

Murray–Kentucky Lake, KY
Health Care (1,300 points)
Office-Based Physicians
General/Family Practitioners: 7 — A
Medical Specialists: 6 — C
Surgical Specialists: 15 — AA
Other Specialists: 4 — C
Short-Term General Hospital: 1 (218 beds) — AA
Public Transportation (425 points)
Fixed route
Murray-Calloway TS, 3 buses
Public Libraries (228 points)
1 branch, 66,061 books, 133,785 circulation
Continuing Education (314 points)
Four-year
Murray State University (public, 7,043)
Score: 2,267   **Rank: 50**

Rating

Myrtle Beach, SC
Health Care (1,000 points)
Office-Based Physicians
General/Family Practitioners: 37 — A
Medical Specialists: 26 — C
Surgical Specialists: 47 — B
Other Specialists: 30 — B
Short-Term General Hospitals: 4 (449 beds) — B
Public Transportation (451 points)
Fixed route
Coastal RTA, 17 buses
Public Libraries (93 points)
4 branches, 144,389 books, 250,588 circulation
Continuing Education (80 points)
Two-year
Horry-Georgetown Technical College (public, 1,658)
Four-year
University of South Carolina (public, 3,176)
Score: 1,624   **Rank: 88**

Naples, FL
Health Care (1,400 points)
Office-Based Physicians
General/Family Practitioners: 39 — A
Medical Specialists: 58 — A
Surgical Specialists: 54 — A
Other Specialists: 41 — A
Short-Term General Hospital: 1 (380 beds) — B
Public Libraries (104 points)
6 branches, 147,748 books, 765,676 circulation
Score: 1,504   **Rank: 102**

New Bern, NC
Health Care (1,100 points)
Office-Based Physicians
General/Family Practitioners: 15 — C
Medical Specialists: 26 — B
Surgical Specialists: 38 — A
Other Specialists: 23 — B
Short-Term General Hospitals: 2 (319 beds) — A
Public Transportation (713 points)
Fixed route
Craven County TS, 15 buses
Public Libraries (128 points)
4 branches, 110,462 books, 261,671 circulation
Continuing Education (52 points)
Two-year
Craven Community College (public, 2,154)
Four-year
East Carolina University, Cherry Point (public, 271)
Score: 1,994   **Rank: 64**

New Braunfels, TX
Health Care (800 points)
Office-Based Physicians
General/Family Practitioners: 20 — AA
Medical Specialists: 7 — C
Surgical Specialists: 14 — C
Other Specialists: 10 — C
Short-Term General Hospital: 1 (105 beds) — C
Public Transportation (2,091 points)
Demand–response
Alamo Area COG, 42 vans
Public Libraries (105 points)
2 branches, 59,154 books, 146,131 circulation
Score: 2,996   **Rank: 23**

New Paltz–Ulster County, NY
Health Care (900 points)
Office-Based Physicians
General/Family Practitioners: 52 — A
Medical Specialists: 56 — B
Surgical Specialists: 45 — C
Other Specialists: 41 — B

Rating

Short-Term General Hospitals: 3 (425 beds)   C
    Benedictine Hospital
Public Transportation (313 points)
    Fixed route
        Kingston Citibus, 4 buses
        Ulster County RTA, 9 buses
Public Libraries (204 points)
    17 branches, 347,217 books, 496,146 circulation
Continuing Education (171 points)
    Two-year
        Ulster County Community College (public, 3,150)
    Four-year
        State University of New York (public, 7,608)
Score: 1,587   **Rank: 93**

New Port Richey, FL
Health Care (700 points)
    Office-Based Physicians
        General/Family Practitioners: 48   C
        Medical Specialists: 80   B
        Surgical Specialists: 66   C
        Other Specialists: 40   C
    Short-Term General Hospitals: 5 (919 beds)   B
Public Transportation (344 points)
    Fixed route
        Pasco Area DHS, 25 buses
Public Libraries (52 points)
    6 branches, 154,336 books, 542,624 circulation
Continuing Education (49 points)
    Two-year
        Pasco-Hernando Community College (public, 2,997)
    Four-year
        Saint Leo College (private, 1,120)
Score: 1,146   **Rank: 129**

Newport–Lincoln City, OR
Health Care (1,000 points)
    Office-Based Physicians
        General/Family Practitioners: 9   A
        Medical Specialists: 14   A
        Surgical Specialists: 9   C
        Other Specialists: 4   C
    Short-Term General Hospitals: 2 (98 beds)   B
Public Transportation (221 points)
    Fixed route
        Newport Area Transit, 2 buses
Public Libraries (171 points)
    2 branches, 63,309 books, 179,974 circulation
Score: 1,392   **Rank: 114**

North Conway–White Mountains, NH
Health Care (1,100 points)
    Office-Based Physicians
        General/Family Practitioners: 10   A
        Medical Specialists: 6   C
        Surgical Specialists: 12   B
        Other Specialists: 10   B
    Short-Term General Hospitals: 2 (138 beds)   A
Public Libraries (671 points)
    18 branches, 241,801 books, 167,783 circulation
Score: 1,771   **Rank: 80**

Oak Harbor–Whidbey Island, WA
Health Care (700 points)
    Office-Based Physicians
        General/Family Practitioners: 15   A
        Medical Specialists: 4   C
        Surgical Specialists: 10   C
        Other Specialists: 6   C
    Short-Term General Hospitals: 2 (71 beds)   C
Public Libraries (149 points)
    1 branch, 80,000 books, 247,779 circulation
Score: 849   **Rank: 141**

Rating

Ocala, FL
Health Care (800 points)
    Office-Based Physicians
        General/Family Practitioners: 30   C
        Medical Specialists: 47   B
        Surgical Specialists: 53   B
        Other Specialists: 48   B
    Short-Term General Hospitals: 2 (434 beds)   C
Public Libraries (86 points)
    7 branches, 170,000 books, 419,000 circulation
Continuing Education (60 points)
    Two-year
        Central Florida Community College (public, 4,000)
Score: 946   **Rank: 135**

Ocean City–Assateague Island, MD
Health Care (400 points)
    Office-Based Physicians
        General/Family Practitioners: 8   B
        Medical Specialists: 3   C
        Other Specialists: 6   C
Public Transportation (724 points)
    Fixed route
        Ocean City Bus System, 7 buses
Public Libraries (283 points)
    3 branches, 112,268 books, 255,053 circulation
Score: 1,408   **Rank: 111**

Ocean County, NJ
Health Care (900 points)
    Office-Based Physicians
        General/Family Practitioners: 36   C
        Medical Specialists: 154   A
        Surgical Specialists: 138   B
        Other Specialists: 53   C
    Short-Term General Hospitals: 4 (1,269 beds)   B
Public Transportation (85 points)
    Fixed route
        Ocean County Area Transit, 9 buses
Public Libraries (160 points)
    3 branches, 693,016 books, 1,602,069 circulation
Continuing Education (92 points)
    Two-year
        Ocean County College (public, 6,214)
    Four-year
        Georgian Court College (private, 2,054)
Score: 1,237   **Rank: 121**

Olympia, WA
Health Care (1,300 points)
    Office-Based Physicians
        General/Family Practitioners: 50   A
        Medical Specialists: 56   A
        Surgical Specialists: 51   B
        Other Specialists: 52   A
    Short-Term General Hospitals: 2 (450 beds)   B
Public Transportation (819 points)
    Fixed route
        Intercity Transit, 32 buses
Public Libraries (199 points)
    5 branches, 318,081 books, 861,200 circulation
Continuing Education (117 points)
    Two-year
        South Puget Sound Community College (public, 3,601)
    Four-year
        Evergreen State College (public, 2,965)
        Saint Martin's College (private, 881)
Score: 2,435   **Rank: 40**

Orlando, FL
Health Care (1,200 points)
    Office-Based Physicians
        General/Family Practitioners: 194   B
        Medical Specialists: 387   A
        Surgical Specialists: 423   A

Rating

Other Specialists: 283 B
Short-Term General Hospitals: 13 (3,537 beds) B
  Florida Hospital Medical Center
  Orlando Regional Medical Center
Public Transportation (272 points)
Fixed route
  Tri-County Transit, 70 buses
Public Libraries (157 points)
16 branches, 1,657,594 books, 4,162,430 circulation
Continuing Education (456 points)
Two-year
  Seminole Community College (public, 6,181)
  Valencia Community College (public, 14,852)
Four-year
  Orlando College (private, 846)
  Rollins College (private, 3,767)
  University of Central Florida (public, 18,094)
Score: 2,085 **Rank: 59**

Panama City, FL
Health Care (1,000 points)
Office-Based Physicians
  General/Family Practitioners: 17 C
  Medical Specialists: 40 B
  Surgical Specialists: 45 B
  Other Specialists: 30 B
Short-Term General Hospitals: 3 (496 beds) A
Public Libraries (123 points)
6 branches, 164,858 books, 310,767 circulation
Continuing Education (87 points)
Two-year
  Gulf Coast Community College (public, 4,975)
Score: 1,210 **Rank: 124**

Paris–Big Sandy, TN
Health Care (800 points)
Office-Based Physicians
  General/Family Practitioners: 7 C
  Medical Specialists: 8 C
  Surgical Specialists: 11 C
  Other Specialists: 6 C
Short-Term General Hospitals: 2 (235 beds) AA
Public Libraries (94 points)
2 branches, 43,000 books, 84,678 circulation
Score: 894 **Rank: 137**

Pensacola, FL
Health Care (1,400 points)
Office-Based Physicians
  General/Family Practitioners: 46 C
  Medical Specialists: 113 A
  Surgical Specialists: 127 A
  Other Specialists: 97 A
Short-Term General Hospitals: 5 (1,696 beds) AA
  Baptist Hospital
  Sacred Heart Hospital
  U.S. Naval Hospital
Public Transportation (271 points)
Fixed route
  Escambia County TS, 19 buses
Public Libraries (120 points)
5 branches, 344,846 books, 1,022,310 circulation
Continuing Education (239 points)
Two-year
  Pensacola Junior College (public, 10,537)
Four-year
  University of West Florida (public, 7,170)
Score: 2,029 **Rank: 61**

Petoskey–Straits of Mackinac, MI
Health Care (1,700 points)
Office-Based Physicians
  General/Family Practitioners: 2 C
  Medical Specialists: 30 AA
  Surgical Specialists: 31 AA

Rating

Other Specialists: 26 AA
Short-Term General Hospital: 1 (260 beds) AA
Public Libraries (187 points)
2 branches, 47,248 books, 83,169 circulation
Continuing Education (82 points)
Two-year
  North Central Michigan College (public, 1,650)
Score: 1,968 **Rank: 70**

★ Phoenix–Tempe–Scottsdale, AZ
Health Care (1,300 points)
Office-Based Physicians
  General/Family Practitioners: 474 B
  Medical Specialists: 858 A
  Surgical Specialists: 878 A
  Other Specialists: 774 A
Short-Term General Hospitals: 29 (6,936 beds) B
  Good Samaritan Medical Center
  Hayden VA Medical Center
  Lincoln Hospital and Medical Center
  Maricopa Medical Center
  Maryvale Samaritan Hospital
  Phoenix Baptist Hospital and Medical Center
  St. Joseph's Hospital and Medical Center
Public Transportation (549 points)
Fixed route
  Phoenix Transit System, 275 buses
Demand–response
  Glendale Dial-A-Ride, 11 vans
  Sun Cities Area Transit, 4 vans
Public Libraries (143 points)
41 branches, 3,056,003 books, 11,921,516 circulation
Continuing Education (1,278 points)
Two-year
  Gateway Community College (public, 5,432)
  Glendale Community College (public, 14,948)
  Mesa Community College (public, 19,577)
  Phoenix College (public, 13,146)
  Rio Salado Community College (public, 14,000)
  Scottsdale Community College (public, 8,000)
  South Mountain Community College (public, 2,874)
Four-year
  Arizona State University (public, 42,500)
  Grand Canyon College (private, 1,813)
  Western International University (private, 1,146)
Score: 3,270 **Rank: 15**

Pike County, PA
Health Care (400 points)
Office-Based Physicians
  General/Family Practitioners: 3 C
  Medical Specialists: 3 C
  Surgical Specialist: 1 C
  Other Specialist: 1 C
Public Libraries (89 points)
1 branch, 21,945 books, 60,653 circulation
Score: 489 **Rank: 149**

Port Townsend, WA
Health Care (900 points)
Office-Based Physicians
  General/Family Practitioners: 7 AA
  Medical Specialist: 1 C
  Surgical Specialists: 6 B
  Other Specialists: 3 C
Short-Term General Hospital: 1 (43 beds) C
Public Transportation (792 points)
Fixed route
  Jefferson TA, 4 buses
Public Libraries (234 points)
2 branches, 48,497 books, 194,370 circulation
Score: 1,926 **Rank: 72**

Rating

Portsmouth–Dover–Durham, NH
Health Care (900 points)
Office-Based Physicians
General/Family Practitioners: 66   B
Medical Specialists: 104   B
Surgical Specialists: 104   B
Other Specialists: 95   B
Short-Term General Hospitals: 6 (606 beds)   C
Public Transportation (217 points)
Fixed route
COAST, 19 buses
Public Libraries (245 points)
46 branches, 880,301 books, 1,572,246 circulation
Continuing Education (188 points)
Two-year
Castle Junior College (private, 166)
New Hampshire Vocational Technical College
(public, 378)
Four-year
School for Lifelong Learning (public, 1,723)
University of New Hampshire (public, 12,483)
Score: 1,550   **Rank: 98**

Prescott, AZ
Health Care (1,200 points)
Office-Based Physicians
General/Family Practitioners: 21   B
Medical Specialists: 22   B
Surgical Specialists: 36   B
Other Specialists: 21   B
Short-Term General Hospitals: 3 (611 beds)   AA
VA Medical Center
Public Libraries (193 points)
14 branches, 191,644 books, 534,330 circulation
Continuing Education (167 points)
Two-year
Yavapai College (public, 6,872)
Four-year
Prescott College (private, 320)
Embry-Riddle Aeronautical University (private, 1,609)
Score: 1,559   **Rank: 97**

Red Bluff–Sacramento Valley, CA
Health Care (700 points)
Office-Based Physicians
General/Family Practitioners: 13   A
Medical Specialists: 8   C
Surgical Specialists: 9   C
Other Specialists: 4   C
Short-Term General Hospital: 1 (76 beds)   C
Public Libraries (193 points)
3 branches, 89,821 books, 176,889 circulation
Score: 893   **Rank: 138**

Redding, CA
Health Care (1,500 points)
Office-Based Physicians
General/Family Practitioners: 46   AA
Medical Specialists: 39   B
Surgical Specialists: 60   A
Other Specialists: 60   AA
Short-Term General Hospitals: 3 (403 beds)   B
Mercy Medical Center
Public Transportation (228 points)
Fixed route
NorCal Transit, 8 buses
Public Libraries (169 points)
10 branches, 242,295 books, 430,412 circulation
Continuing Education (197 points)
Two-year
Shasta College (public, 11,587)
Score: 2,094   **Rank: 58**

Rating

Rehoboth Bay–Indian River Bay, DE
Health Care (1,100 points)
Office-Based Physicians
General/Family Practitioners: 23   B
Medical Specialists: 38   B
Surgical Specialists: 37   B
Other Specialists: 36   A
Short-Term General Hospitals: 3 (382 beds)   B
Public Libraries (227 points)
15 branches, 266,509 books, 473,809 circulation
Continuing Education (46 points)
Two-year
Delaware Technical and Community College
(public, 2,479)
Score: 1,373   **Rank: 117**

Reno, NV
Health Care (1,900 points)
Office-Based Physicians
General/Family Practitioners: 58   A
Medical Specialists: 123   AA
Surgical Specialists: 154   AA
Other Specialists: 121   AA
Short-Term General Hospitals: 5 (1,242 beds)   AA
VA Medical Center
Washoe Medical Center
Public Transportation (694 points)
Fixed route
RTC of Washoe, 41 buses
Public Libraries (158 points)
5 branches, 383,458 books, 799,451 circulation
Continuing Education (247 points)
Two-year
Truckee Meadows Community College (public, 7,688)
Four-year
University of Nevada (public, 9,772)
Score: 2,999   **Rank: 22**

Rockport–Aransas Pass, TX
Health Care (200 points)
Office-Based Physicians
General/Family Practitioners: 3   C
Other Specialists: 3   C
Public Libraries (185 points)
1 branch, 32,798 books, 49,513 circulation
Score: 385   **Rank: 151**

Roswell, NM
Health Care (1,100 points)
Office-Based Physicians
General/Family Practitioners: 9   C
Medical Specialists: 18   B
Surgical Specialists: 20   B
Other Specialists: 14   B
Short-Term General Hospitals: 2 (334 beds)   AA
Public Transportation (151 points)
Demand–response
RSVP Handi-Van, 3 vans
Public Libraries (124 points)
1 branch, 69,142 books, 221,502 circulation
Continuing Education (58 points)
Two-year
Eastern New Mexico University, Roswell (public, 1,632)
New Mexico Military Institute (public, 426)
Score: 1,433   **Rank: 109**

St. Augustine, FL
Health Care (1,000 points)
Office-Based Physicians
General/Family Practitioners: 13   C
Medical Specialists: 24   B
Surgical Specialists: 24   B
Other Specialists: 24   A
Short-Term General Hospitals: 2 (230 beds)   B

Rating

Public Transportation (511 points)
Demand–response
St. John County COA, 15 vans
Public Libraries (65 points)
5 branches, 53,730 books, 168,412 circulation
Continuing Education (26 points)
Four-year
Flagler College (private, 1,166)
Score: 1,602   **Rank: 89**

St. George–Zion, UT
Health Care (800 points)
Office-Based Physicians
General/Family Practitioners: 12   A
Medical Specialists: 5   C
Surgical Specialists: 13   C
Other Specialists: 11   B
Short-Term General Hospital: 1 (116 beds) C
Public Transportation (340 points)
Demand–response
Washington County Minibus, 6 vans
Public Libraries (166 points)
5 branches, 82,236 books, 453,983 circulation
Continuing Education (70 points)
Two-year
Dixie College (public, 2,300)
Score: 1,375   **Rank: 116**

St. Petersburg–Clearwater–Dunedin, FL
Health Care (1,600 points)
Office-Based Physicians
General/Family Practitioners: 189   B
Medical Specialists: 402   AA
Surgical Specialists: 372   A
Other Specialists: 321   A
Short-Term General Hospitals: 19 (5,228 beds) AA
Bayfront Medical Center
VA Medical Center
Public Transportation (649 points)
Fixed route
Suncoast TA, 123 buses
Demand–response
Suncoast TA, 24 vans
Public Libraries (150 points)
20 branches, 1,323,290 books, 3,383,264 circulation
Continuing Education (188 points)
Two-year
Saint Petersburg Junior College (public, 16,116)
Four-year
Eckerd College (private, 1,325)
Score: 2,586   **Rank: 32**

St. Tammany Parish, LA
Health Care (900 points)
Office-Based Physicians
General/Family Practitioners: 24   C
Medical Specialists: 51   B
Surgical Specialists: 60   B
Other Specialists: 44   B
Short-Term General Hospitals: 4 (522 beds) B
Public Libraries (91 points)
10 branches, 160,401 books, 517,067 circulation
Score: 991   **Rank: 134**

Salinas–Seaside–Monterey, CA
Health Care (900 points)
Office-Based Physicians
General/Family Practitioners: 77   B
Medical Specialists: 109   B
Surgical Specialists: 120   B
Other Specialists: 75   B
Short-Term General Hospitals: 6 (819 beds) C
Natividad Medical Center
U.S. Army Community Hospital
Public Transportation (581 points)

Rating

Fixed route
Monterey–Salinas Transit, 38 buses
Demand–response
City of Greenfield, 1 van
City of Soledad, 1 van
King City Transit, 1 van
Monterey–Salinas Transit, 19 vans
Public Libraries (295 points)
23 branches, 1,104,664 books, 2,299,544 circulation
Continuing Education (201 points)
Two-year
Hartnell College (public, 7,014)
Monterey Peninsula College (public, 8,500)
Four-year
Monterey International Studies (private, 533)
Score: 1,976   **Rank: 68**

★**San Antonio, TX**
Health Care (1,400 points)
Office-Based Physicians
General/Family Practitioners: 237   B
Medical Specialists: 503   A
Surgical Specialists: 490   A
Other Specialists: 420   A
Short-Term General Hospitals: 16 (6,271 beds) A
Baptist Medical Center
Bexar County Hospital
Brooke Army Medical Center
Murphy Memorial VA Medical Center
Santa Rosa Medical Center
Public Transportation (1,334 points)
Fixed route
VIA Metro Transit, 399 buses
Demand–response
VIA Metro Transit, 17 vans
Public Libraries (131 points)
19 branches, 1,648,380 books, 2,073,259 circulation
Continuing Education (578 points)
Two-year
Palo Alto College (public, 3,711)
Saint Philip's College (public, 6,027)
San Antonio College (public, 23,344)
Four-year
Incarnate Word College (private, 1,575)
Our Lady of the Lake University (private, 1,780)
Saint Mary's University (private, 3,560)
Trinity University (private, 2,674)
University of Texas (public, 13,134)
University of Texas Health Sciences (public, 2,174)
Score: 3,442   **Rank: 10**

★**San Diego, CA**
Health Care (1,600 points)
Office-Based Physicians
General/Family Practitioners: 616   A
Medical Specialists: 1,099   AA
Surgical Specialists: 1,055   A
Other Specialists: 1,085   AA
Short-Term General Hospitals: 27 (7,085 beds) B
Kaiser Foundation Hospital
Mercy Hospital and Medical Center
U.S. Naval Hospital
University of California Medical Center
VA Medical Center
Public Transportation (1,238 points)
Fixed route
North San Diego TD, 93 buses
San Diego TS, 220 buses
San Diego Trolley, 24 rapid rail
Public Libraries (136 points)
74 branches, 3,252,671 books, 10,409,747 circulation
Continuing Education (1,837 points)
Two-year
Cuyamaca College (public, 3,727)
Grossmont College (public, 15,595)

Rating

Mira Costa College (public, 9,723)
Palomar College (public, 17,557)
San Diego City College (public, 15,728)
San Diego Mesa College (public, 27,000)
San Diego Miramar College (public, 6,982)
Southwestern College (public, 14,066)
Four-year
Christian Heritage College (private, 365)
Coleman College (private, 926)
National University (private, 12,873)
Point Loma Nazarene College (private, 2,165)
San Diego State University (public, 35,821)
United States International University (private, 2,582)
University of California, San Diego (public, 17,227)
University of San Diego (private, 5,858)
Score: 4,811   **Rank: 1**

San Juan Islands, WA
Health Care (1,100 points)
Office-Based Physicians
General/Family Practitioners: 5   AA
Medical Specialist:1   C
Surgical Specialists: 3   B
Other Specialists: 7   AA
Public Libraries (288 points)
2 branches, 29,996 books, 78,940 circulation
Score: 1,388   **Rank: 115**

San Luis Obispo, CA
Health Care (1,300 points)
Office-Based Physicians
General/Family Practitioners: 58   A
Medical Specialists: 81   A
Surgical Specialists: 87   A
Other Specialists: 90   A
Short-Term General Hospitals: 5 (536 beds)   C
Public Transportation (457 points)
Fixed route
City of San Luis Obispo, 7 buses
San Luis Obispo County TA, 6 buses
South County Area Transit, 3 buses
Demand–response
Central Coast RTA, 5 vans
City of Atascadero, 5 vans
City of Morro Bay, 3 vans
City of Paso Robles, 1 van
Public Libraries (114 points)
15 branches, 262,054 books, 1,042,296 circulation
Continuing Education (353 points)
Two-year
Cuesta Community College (public, 8,000)
Four-year
California Polytechnic State University (public, 16,553)
Score: 2,223   **Rank: 51**

Santa Barbara, CA
Health Care (1,700 points)
Office-Based Physicians
General/Family Practitioners: 95   A
Medical Specialists: 210   AA
Surgical Specialists: 199   AA
Other Specialists: 185   AA
Short-Term General Hospitals: 8 (1,009 beds)   B
Santa Barbara Cottage Hospital
Public Transportation (131 points)
Fixed route
Santa Barbara MTD, 50 buses
Demand–response
City of Carpenteria, 1 van
City of Guadalupe, 2 vans
City of Lompoc, 7 vans
Public Libraries (138 points)
17 branches, 513,245 books, 1,630,370 circulation
Continuing Education (487 points)
Two-year

Rating

Allan Hancock College (public, 8,331)
Santa Barbara City College (public, 11,298)
Four-year
University of California (public, 18,003)
Westmont College (private, 1,244)
Score: 2,456   **Rank: 39**

Santa Fe, NM
Health Care (1,700 points)
Office-Based Physicians
General/Family Practitioners: 31   AA
Medical Specialists: 38   A
Surgical Specialists: 48   AA
Other Specialists: 56   AA
Short-Term General Hospitals: 2 (263 beds)   B
Public Transportation (500 points)
Demand–response
Santa Fe Senior Citizens Transit, 17 vans
Public Libraries (215 points)
3 branches, 204,299 books, 359,988 circulation
Continuing Education (78 points)
Two-year
Institute of American Indian Arts (public, 156)
Santa Fe Community College (public, 2,122)
Four-year
College of Santa Fe (private, 1,602)
Saint Johns College (private, 424)
Score: 2,493   **Rank: 35**

Santa Rosa–Petaluma, CA
Health Care (1,400 points)
Office-Based Physicians
General/Family Practitioners: 144   AA
Medical Specialists: 150   A
Surgical Specialists: 160   A
Other Specialists: 140   A
Short-Term General Hospitals: 7 (751 beds)   C
Community Hospital
Public Transportation (508 points)
Fixed route
City of Santa Rosa TA, 13 buses
Sonoma County TA, 35 buses
Public Libraries (163 points)
13 branches, 631,612 books, 2,056,084 circulation
Continuing Education (397 points)
Two-year
Santa Rosa Junior College (public, 24,841)
Four-year
Sonoma State University (public, 6,697)
Score: 2,467   **Rank: 36**

Sarasota, FL
Health Care (1,800 points)
Office-Based Physicians
General/Family Practitioners: 72   A
Medical Specialists: 166   AA
Surgical Specialists: 161   AA
Other Specialists: 124   AA
Short-Term General Hospitals: 3 (1,100 beds)   A
Public Transportation (223 points)
Fixed route
Sarasota County Area Transit, 15 buses
Public Libraries (115 points)
5 branches, 318,064 books, 1,536,786 circulation
Continuing Education (7 points)
Four-year
Ringling School of Art and Design (private, 480)
Score: 2,144   **Rank: 55**

Savannah, GA
Health Care (1,700 points)
Office-Based Physicians
General/Family Practitioners: 40   B
Medical Specialists: 96   A
Surgical Specialists: 123   AA

	Rating
Other Specialists: 92	AA
Short-Term General Hospitals: 3 (1,115 beds)	AA
Memorial Medical Center	

Public Transportation (821 points)
Fixed route
  Savannah TA, 44 buses
Public Libraries (207 points)
  17 branches, 454,316 books, 920,636 circulation
Continuing Education (88 points)
Four-year
  Armstrong State College (public, 3,232)
  Savannah College of Art and Design (private, 1,397)
  Savannah State College (public, 1,932)
Score: 2,816   **Rank: 29**

South Lake Tahoe–Placerville, CA
Health Care (900 points)
Office-Based Physicians

	Rating
General/Family Practitioners: 36	A
Medical Specialists: 19	C
Surgical Specialists: 36	B
Other Specialists: 29	B
Short-Term General Hospitals: 2 (171 beds)	C

Public Transportation (458 points)
Fixed route
  El Dorado TA, 8 buses
Demand–response
  El Dorado TA, 8 vans
Public Libraries (133 points)
  5 branches, 159,798 books, 420,260 circulation
Continuing Education (27 points)
Two-year
  Lake Tahoe Community College (public, 1,467)
Score: 1,517   **Rank: 100**

Southport, NC
Health Care (600 points)
Office-Based Physicians

	Rating
General/Family Practitioners: 11	B
Medical Specialists: 4	C
Surgical Specialists: 8	C
Other Specialists: 5	C
Short-Term General Hospitals: 2 (100 beds)	C

Public Libraries (103 points)
  3 branches, 58,000 books, 200,000 circulation
Continuing Education (20 points)
Two-year
  Brunswick Technical College (public, 713)
Score: 722   **Rank: 146**

State College, PA
Health Care (1,100 points)
Office-Based Physicians

	Rating
General/Family Practitioners: 34	A
Medical Specialists: 35	B
Surgical Specialists: 32	B
Other Specialists: 25	B
Short-Term General Hospitals: 2 (330 beds)	B

Public Transportation (665 points)
Fixed route
  Centre Area TA, 19 buses
Public Libraries (153 points)
  2 branches, 179,739 books, 485,813 circulation
Continuing Education (654 points)
Four-year
  Pennsylvania State University (public, 35,261)
Score: 2,572   **Rank: 33**

Thomasville, GA
Health Care (1,700 points)
Office-Based Physicians

	Rating
General/Family Practitioners: 8	B
Medical Specialists: 15	A
Surgical Specialists: 27	AA
Other Specialists: 19	AA

	Rating
Short-Term General Hospital: 1 (246 beds)	AA

Public Libraries (282 points)
  3 branches, 107,766 books, 257,566 circulation
Continuing Education (11 points)
Two-year
  Thomas College (private, 338)
Score: 1,992   **Rank: 65**

★ Traverse City–Grand Traverse Bay, MI
Health Care (1,800 points)
Office-Based Physicians

	Rating
General/Family Practitioners: 12	B
Medical Specialists: 37	AA
Surgical Specialists: 44	AA
Other Specialists: 35	AA
Short-Term General Hospitals: 2 (370 beds)	AA

Public Transportation (1,391 points)
Fixed route
  Bay Area TA, 22 buses
Public Libraries (133 points)
  4 branches, 85,908 books, 383,789 circulation
Continuing Education (80 points)
Two-year
  Northwestern Michigan College (public, 3,153)
Score: 3,404   **Rank: 13**

★ Tucson, AZ
Health Care (1,500 points)
Office-Based Physicians

	Rating
General/Family Practitioners: 112	C
Medical Specialists: 340	AA
Surgical Specialists: 302	A
Other Specialists: 319	AA
Short-Term General Hospitals: 11 (2,413 beds)	A
Kino Community Hospital	
Palo Verde Hospital	
St. Joseph Hospital and Medical Center	
Tucson Medical Center	
University Medical Center	
VA Medical Center	

Public Transportation (772 points)
Fixed route
  City of Tucson MTS, 120 buses
Public Libraries (129 points)
  19 branches, 820,067 books, 4,217,775 circulation
Continuing Education (712 points)
Two-year
  Pima Community College (public, 26,810)
Four-year
  University of Arizona (public, 34,725)
Score: 3,113   **Rank: 18**

Twain Harte–Yosemite, CA
Health Care (1,500 points)
Office-Based Physicians

	Rating
General/Family Practitioners: 17	AA
Medical Specialists: 14	B
Surgical Specialists: 19	A
Other Specialists: 15	A
Short-Term General Hospitals: 2 (204 beds)	A

Public Transportation (174 points)
Fixed route
  Tuolumne County TA, 2 buses
Public Libraries (169 points)
  13 branches, 80,000 books, 223,828 circulation
Continuing Education (64 points)
Two-year
  Columbia College (public, 2,055)
Score: 1,907   **Rank: 75**

Vero Beach, FL
Health Care (1,500 points)
Office-Based Physicians

	Rating
General/Family Practitioners: 15	C
Medical Specialists: 48	AA

	Rating
Surgical Specialists: 53	AA
Other Specialists: 38	A
Short-Term General Hospitals: 2 (426 beds)	A

Public Transportation (173 points)
Demand–response
Indian River COA, 6 vans
Public Libraries (98 points)
3 branches, 95,250 books, 265,601 circulation
Score: 1,770   **Rank: 81**

Virginia Beach–Norfolk, VA
Health Care (1,300 points)
Office-Based Physicians

	Rating
General/Family Practitioners: 188	B
Medical Specialists: 381	A
Surgical Specialists: 398	A
Other Specialists: 338	A
Short-Term General Hospitals: 11 (3,259 beds)	B

DePaul Hospital
Maryview Medical Center
Portsmouth General Hospital
Sentara Leigh Hospital
Sentara Norfolk General Hospital
U.S. Naval Hospital
Virginia Beach General Hospital
Public Transportation (214 points)
Fixed route
Tidewater TDC, 127 buses
Demand–response
Tidewater TDC, 55 vans
Public Libraries (177 points)
28 branches, 1,710,829 books, 3,987,130 circulation
Continuing Education (425 points)
Two-year
Tidewater Community College (public, 14,976)
Four-year
Norfolk State University (public, 7,458)
Old Dominion University (public, 15,463)
Virginia Wesleyan College (private, 1,116)
Score: 2,116   **Rank: 57**

★**Wenatchee, WA**
Health Care (1,900 points)
Office-Based Physicians

	Rating
General/Family Practitioners: 25	AA
Medical Specialists: 28	AA
Surgical Specialists: 38	AA
Other Specialists: 27	AA
Short-Term General Hospitals: 3 (236 beds)	A

Public Transportation (1,231 points)
Demand–response
Chelan-Douglas COA, 23 vans
Public Libraries (217 points)
4 branches, 113,683 books, 364,698 circulation
Continuing Education (90 points)
Two-year
Wenatchee Valley College (public, 3,100)
Score: 3,439   **Rank: 11**

West Palm Beach–Boca Raton–
Delray Beach, FL
Health Care (1,500 points)
Office-Based Physicians

	Rating
General/Family Practitioners: 173	B
Medical Specialists: 500	AA
Surgical Specialists: 452	AA
Other Specialists: 282	A
Short-Term General Hospitals: 13 (2,944 beds)	B

Public Transportation (316 points)
Fixed route
Palm Beach County TA, 45 buses
Demand–response
Palm Beach County TA, 35 vans
Public Libraries (87 points)
19 branches, 774,428 books, 3,470,229 circulation
Continuing Education (256 points)
Two-year
Palm Beach Junior College (public, 13,364)
Four-year
College of Boca Raton (private, 1,150)
Florida Atlantic University (public, 8,387)
Palm Beach Atlantic College (private, 1,133)
Score: 2,158   **Rank: 54**

Yuma, AZ
Health Care (900 points)
Office-Based Physicians

	Rating
General/Family Practitioners: 19	C
Medical Specialists: 28	B
Surgical Specialists: 30	B
Other Specialists: 20	B
Short-Term General Hospitals: 3 (308 beds)	B

Public Libraries (184 points)
4 branches, 200,784 books, 440,463 circulation
Continuing Education (100 points)
Two-year
Arizona Western College (public, 5,200)
Score: 1,183   **Rank: 127**

ET CETERA: Services

DRIVER LICENSING

When you settle in a new state, you have to surrender your out-of-state driver's license and get a new one. The time permitted to do this ranges from "immediately" in 12 states, up to 30 days in 14 states, up to 90 days in 9 other states, and 120 days in Wyoming. New Hampshire and Vermont allow you as much time as your former state gives newcomers. Hawaii lets you keep your license until it expires.

Required Tests

For a new resident with a valid driver's license from a former state, the requirement for getting a license from the new state varies considerably. In Connecticut, Massachusetts, New Hampshire, and Virginia, a vision test is required but all other tests may be waived. West Virginia requires only a test of the state's rules of the road. Florida, Hawaii, Montana, and Washington require you to get behind the wheel with a license examiner for a road test; in 25 other states, a road test may be waived or required at the discretion of the examiner.

"Problem" Drivers

If your license has been suspended or revoked, you

Getting a Driver's License After Relocating:
A Guide for Persons with a Current License from Their Former State

State	Time Limit	Rules of the Road	Signs and Signals	Vision	Road Test	National Driver License Compact
Alabama	30 days	•	•	•		•
Alaska	90 days	•	•	•		
Arizona	immediately	•	•	•	X	•
Arkansas	immediately	•	•	•		•
California	10 days	•	•	•		•
Colorado	30 days	•	•	•	X	
Connecticut	60 days	X	X	•	X	
Delaware	60 days	•	•	•	X	•
Florida	30 days	•	•	•	•	•
Georgia	30 days	•	•	•		
Hawaii	*	•	•	•	•	•
Idaho	90 days	•	•	•		•
Illinois	90 days	•	•	•		•
Indiana	60 days	•	•	•		•
Iowa	immediately	•	•	•		•
Kansas	90 days	•	•	•		•
Kentucky	immediately	•	•	•		
Louisiana	90 days	•	•	•	X	•
Maine	30 days	•	X	•	X	•
Maryland	30 days	•	•	•	X	•
Massachusetts	immediately	X	X	•		
Michigan	immediately	•	•	•		
Minnesota	60 days	•	•	•	X	
Mississippi	60 days	•	•	•		•
Missouri	immediately	•	•	•	X	•
Montana	90 days	•	•	•	•	•
Nebraska	30 days	•	•	•	X	•
Nevada	45 days	•	•	•	X	
New Hampshire	reciprocal	X	X	•		•
New Jersey	60 days	•	X	•	X	•
New Mexico	30 days	•	X	•		•
New York	30 days	•	•	•		•
North Carolina	30 days	•	•	•	X	
North Dakota	60 days	•	•	•	X	•
Ohio	30 days	•	•	•	X	
Oklahoma	immediately	•	•	•	X	•
Oregon	immediately	•	•	•	X	•
Pennsylvania	60 days	•	•	•	X	
Rhode Island	30 days	•	•	•		•
South Carolina	90 days	•	•	•	X	•
South Dakota	90 days	•	•	•	X	•
Tennessee	90 days	•	•	•	X	•
Texas	30 days	•	•	•	X	
Utah	60 days	•	•	•		•
Vermont	reciprocal	•	•	•	X	
Virginia	30 days	X	X	•		•
Washington	immediately	•	•	•	•	•
West Virginia	immediately	•				•
Wisconsin	immediately	•	•	•	X	•
Wyoming	120 days	•	•	•	X	•

Source: Federal Highway Administration, *Driver's License Administration Requirements and Fees,* 1990.

*In Hawaii, a drivers license from any state is valid until its expiration if the driver is over 18.

• Required.

X May be required or waived at the discretion of the examiner.

won't get a new one simply by moving to another state. Every license application is checked with the National Driver Register, a federal data file of persons whose license to drive has been denied or withdrawn. Moreover, 39 states belong to the National Driver License Compact, an agreement among states to share information on drivers who accumulate tickets in one jurisdiction and try to escape control in another.

Driver Age Discrimination?

Once you start feeling your age, will insurance companies and state highway safety committees consider you dangerous when you get behind the wheel of your automobile?

On the face of it, older drivers have a better accident record than younger drivers; people over 60 represent one in eight persons in this country yet are involved in only one in 15 of the automobile accidents. But the National Safety Council notes that people over 60 drive much less than younger people and actually have a poorer accident record in terms of the miles they drive.

Fifteen years ago, the American Medical Association and the American Association of Motor Vehicle Administrators recommended that no one's license should be placed in jeopardy just because the driver is older, but they also recommended that states reexamine older drivers more frequently than younger drivers. Thirteen states and Washington, D.C., now require special examinations based solely on age.

COLORADO	Reexamination waived for "clean record" drivers under 70.
HAWAII	License renewal every two years for drivers over 65.
ILLINOIS	Complete reexamination every four years for drivers over 69.
INDIANA	Complete reexamination every three years for drivers over 75.
IOWA	License renewal every two years for drivers over 70.
LOUISIANA	Physical examination every four years for drivers over 60.
MAINE	Vision reexamination at age 40, age 52, and 65 and over.
NEW HAMPSHIRE	Complete reexamination for drivers over 75.
NEW MEXICO	License renewal every year for drivers over 75.
OREGON	Vision reexamination at age 50 and over.
PENNSYLVANIA	Physical examination on a random basis for drivers over 45.
RHODE ISLAND	License renewal every two years for drivers over 70.
UTAH	Reexamination waived for "clean record" drivers under 70.
WASHINGTON, D.C.	Vision and reaction examination for drivers over 70; complete reexamination at age 75 and over.

DRIVING DANGER SIGNALS

Researching the records of insurance companies and state police agencies, Dr. Leon Pastalan of the University of Michigan found that older drivers receive a high number of tickets for the following five different traffic violations:

- Rear-end collisions
- Dangerously slow driving
- Failure to yield the right-of-way
- Driving the wrong way on one-way streets
- Illegal turns

Even though people age at different rates, normal changes that affect eyesight, muscle reflexes, and hearing are the reasons older adults are ticketed for these moving violations more often than the rest of the population. Simply recognizing your limitations will help you become a better driver.

Eyesight. Ninety percent of all sensory input needed to drive a car comes through the eyes. As vision loses it sharpness, the typical rectangular black-and-white road signs become hard to read. Night driving is especially risky, because the older we get, the more illumination we need. For example, an 80-year-old needs three times the light that a 20-year-old needs to read. Other problems include loss of depth perception (a major cause of rear-end collisions) and limited peripheral vision (dangerous when making turns at intersections).

You can adjust to these dangers by not driving at night, having regular eye checkups, wearing gray or green-tinted sunglasses on days with high sun glare, and replacing your car's standard rearview mirror with a wide-angle one to aid peripheral vision.

Muscle Reflexes. Many people slow down as they get older. Strength may dwindle, neck and shoulder joints may stiffen, and you may tire sooner. Most important to driving, your reflex reactions may slow. All of these symptoms can affect how safely you enter a busy freeway, change lanes to pass a plodding 18-wheel truck, or avoid a rear-end fender bender.

Ask your physician if any of the medication you're taking might decrease your alertness and ability to drive defensively. On long road trips, take along a companion to share the driving and break the day's distance into short stretches to reduce fatigue. Don't get caught on freeways and major arterial streets during morning and evening rush hours.

Hearing. One in every five persons over 55 and one of every three persons over 65 has impaired hearing. It is a gradual condition and can go unnoticed for a long time. When you can't hear an ambulance siren, a ticket for failing to yield the right-of-way to an emergency vehicle is the likely consequence.

You can compensate for hearing loss by having periodic checkups. When you drive, open a window, turn off the radio, keep the air conditioner fan on low speed, and cut unnecessary conversation.

College Tuition Breaks: Waivers for Older Adults

State	Law	Policy	Minimum Age	All State-Supported Institutions
Alabama		•	60	
Arkansas	•		60	•
California		•	60	
Connecticut	•		62	•
Delaware	•		60	•
Florida	•		62	•
Georgia	•		62	•
Hawaii	•		60	•
Idaho		•	60	•
Illinois	•		65	•
Kansas		•	60	•
Kentucky	•		65	•
Louisiana	•		65	•
Maine		•	65	•
Maryland	•		60	•
Massachusetts	•		65	•
Minnesota	•		62	•
Nevada		•	62	•
New Hampshire		•	65	•
New Jersey	•		65	•
New Mexico	•		65	•
New York	•		60	•
North Carolina	•		65	•
North Dakota		•	65	•
Ohio	•		60	•
Oklahoma		•	65	•
Oregon		•	65	•
Rhode Island	•		65	•
South Carolina	•		60	•
South Dakota		•	65	•
Tennessee	•		60, 65	•
Texas	•		65	•
Utah	•		62	•
Virginia	•		60	•
Washington	•		60	•
Wisconsin		•	62	•

Source: Places Rated Partnership survey, 1990.

COLLEGE TUITION BREAKS FOR OLDER ADULTS

Thirty-six states waive or reduce tuition in their public colleges for persons who've reached a specific age. It's the law in 24 of these states; in the other 12, it's a policy adopted by the state's Board of Regents or its Board of Higher Education.

The limitations on this benefit vary among the states. All of them grant it on a *space-available basis,* which simply means that older students who want to take advantage of the tuition break are admitted to courses only after tuition-paying students have enrolled. Eight states grant the benefit only for *auditing* courses, that is, enrolling for no credit. Four states— Illinois, Maryland, South Carolina, and Virginia—look at the applicant's income to determine eligibility.

College Tuition Breaks: Waiver Limitations

ALABAMA
Tuition and general student fees are waived for courses in all state-supported 2-year colleges.

ARKANSAS
Tuition and general student fees are waived only for credit courses on a space-available basis.

CALIFORNIA
Tuition and general student fees waived only at participating campuses of the California State University system for credit courses on a space-available basis.

CONNECTICUT
Unless the student has been accepted into a degree-granting program, tuition fees are waived for courses only on a space-available basis.

DELAWARE
Tuition and general student fees are waived for auditing courses, or for taking courses for credit, on a space-available basis; students must be formal degree candidates.

FLORIDA
Tuition fees are waived for courses on a space-available basis.

GEORGIA
Tuition fees are waived only for credit courses on a space-available basis; dental, medical, veterinary, and law school courses are excluded. Regular admission procedures are required.

HAWAII
Tuition and general student fees are waived only for regularly scheduled credit courses on a space-available basis.

IDAHO
A $5 fee per registration is charged for courses on a space-available basis.

ILLINOIS
Tuition fees are waived for regularly scheduled credit courses on a space-available basis for older students whose income is less than the current threshold for property tax relief.

KANSAS
Tuition and general student fees are waived only for auditing courses on a space-available basis.

KENTUCKY
Tuition and general student fees are waived only for regularly scheduled credit courses on a space-available basis.

LOUISIANA
Tuition and other registration fees are waived for courses on a space-available basis.

MAINE
Tuition fees are waived for undergraduate courses on a space-available basis.

MARYLAND

Tuition fees are waived for two-year college courses on a space-available basis, and up to three university or four-year college courses per term on a space-available basis for students whose income is derived from retirement benefits and who aren't employed full time.

MASSACHUSETTS

Tuition fees are waived for courses on a space-available basis.

MINNESOTA

Except for an administration fee of $6 a credit hour, collected only when a course is taken for credit, tuition and activity fees are waived to attend courses for credit, to audit any course offered for credit, or enroll in any noncredit adult vocational education courses on a space-available basis.

NEVADA

Tuition fees are waived only for regularly scheduled courses; consent of the instructor may be required.

NEW HAMPSHIRE

Tuition fees are waived for auditing Continuing Education Division courses up to a maximum of eight academic credits per semester, university and college extension courses on a space-available basis, and vocational-technical courses on a space-available basis.

NEW JERSEY

Tuition fees are waived for courses on a space-available basis; students must be formal degree candidates and

successfully complete at least six academic credits per semester.

NEW MEXICO

Tuition reduced to $5 per credit hour up to a maximum of six credit hours per semester on a space-available basis.

NEW YORK

Tuition fees are waived only for auditing courses on a space-available basis.

NORTH CAROLINA

Tuition fees are waived for auditing courses or for taking courses for credit on a space-available basis. Regular admission procedures are required.

NORTH DAKOTA

Tuition fees are waived only for auditing courses on a space-available basis.

OHIO

Tuition and matriculation fees are waived only for auditing courses on a space-available basis; approval of course instructor may be required.

OKLAHOMA

Tuition fees are waived only for auditing courses on a space-available basis.

OREGON

Tuition fees are waived for courses on a space-available basis.

RHODE ISLAND

Tuition and general student fees are waived for credit courses on a space-available basis at the discretion of the institution.

SOUTH CAROLINA

Tuition fees are waived for courses, for credit or audit, on a space-available basis; students must meet admission standards of the institution, and must not be (or have a spouse who is) employed full-time.

SOUTH DAKOTA

Tuition fees are reduced for courses to an amount equal to one-fourth of resident tuition.

TENNESSEE

Tuition fees are waived for auditing courses on a space-available basis for students 60 and older; tuition fees are waived for enrolling in credit courses on a space-available basis for residents 65 and older.

TEXAS

Tuition fees are waived for auditing courses on a space-available basis.

UTAH

Tuition fees (but not quarterly registration fees) are waived for courses on a space-available basis.

VIRGINIA

Tuition fees are waived only for auditing courses on a space-available basis. If the student has a federal taxa-

FOR RETIRED MILITARY

Forty-eight of the retirement places profiled in this book have at least one base or post where your military ID card gives you the privileges of exchange and commissary shopping.

Alamogordo, NM
Holloman Air Force Base
Albuquerque, NM
Kirtland Air Force Base
Athens, GA
Athens Naval Supply Corps School **
Austin, TX
Bergstrom Air Force Base *
Camp Mabry
Bar Harbor–Frenchman Bay, ME
Coast Guard Group Southwest Harbor
Biloxi–Gulfport–Pass Christian, MS
Gulfport Naval Construction Battalion Center
Keesler Air Force Base
Boise, ID
Gowen Field
Burlington, VT
Ethan Allen Firing Range
Camp Johnson
Camden–Penobscot Bay, ME
Coast Guard Station Rockland
Cape Cod, MA
Coast Guard Air Station Cape Cod ***
Cape May, NJ
Coast Guard Training Center Cape May ***
Charleston, SC
Charleston Air Force Base
Charleston Naval Base
Coast Guard Base Charleston ***
Charlottesville, VA
Judge Advocate General School
Colorado Springs, CO
Fort Carson
Peterson Air Force Base
U.S. Air Force Academy
El Centro–Calexico–Brawley, CA
El Centro Naval Air Facility
Fort Myers, FL
Coast Guard Station Fort Myers
Fort Walton Beach, FL
Eglin Air Force Base
Hurlburt Field
Hilton Head–Beaufort, SC
Marine Corps Air Station Beaufort
Marine Corps Recruiting Depot Parris Island
Honolulu, HI
Coast Guard Air Station Barbers Point
Coast Guard Base Honolulu
Fort Shafter
Hickam Air Force Base
Marine Corps Air Station Kaneohe Bay
Pearl Harbor Naval Base
Schofield Barracks
Key West–Key Largo–Marathon, FL
Naval Air Station Key West
Las Cruces, NM
White Sands Missile Range
Las Vegas, NV
Indian Springs Air Force Auxiliary Field
Lake Mead Annex
Nellis Air Force Base
Lexington–Fayette, KY
Bluegrass Army Depot **
Martinsburg–Charles Town, WV
Martinsburg Air National Guard Station
Melbourne–Titusville–Palm Bay, FL
Cape Canaveral Air Force Station
Patrick Air Force Base
Miami–Hialeah, FL
Coast Guard Air Station Miami ***
Coast Guard Base Miami Beach ***
Homestead Air Force Base

Myrtle Beach, SC
Myrtle Beach Air Force Base *
New Bern, NC
Marine Corps Air Station Cherry Point
Oak Harbor–Whidbey Island, WA
Naval Air Station Whidbey Island
Ocean County, NJ
Lakehurst Naval Air Engineering Center
Orlando, FL
Orlando Naval Training Center
Panama City, FL
Panama City Naval Coastal System Center ***
Tyndall Air Force Base
Pensacola, FL
Naval Air Station Pensacola
Phoenix, AZ
Gila Bend Air Force Auxiliary Field
Luke Air Force Base
Williams Air Force Base
Portsmouth–Dover–Durham, NH
Pease Air Force Base **
Portsmouth Naval Shipyard
St. Petersburg–Clearwater–Dunedin, FL
Coast Guard Air Station Clearwater ***
Coast Guard Station St. Petersburg ***
Salinas–Seaside–Monterey, CA
Fort Hunter Liggett ***
Fort Ord *
Monterey Naval Postgraduate School ***
Presidio of Monterey ***
San Antonio, TX
Brooks Air Force Base
Fort Sam Houston
Kelly Air Force Base
Lackland Air Force Base
Medina Air Force Base
Randolph Air Force Base
San Diego, CA
Camp Pendleton
Coast Guard Air Station San Diego ***
Coronado Naval Amphibious Base ***
Marine Corps Recruit Depot San Diego ***
Miramar Naval Air Station
North Island Naval Air Station
San Diego Naval Regional Medical Center ***
San Diego Naval Station
San Diego Naval Training Center
San Luis Obispo, CA
Camp San Luis Obispo
Santa Barbara, CA
Vandenberg Air Force Base
Santa Rosa–Petaluma, CA
Coast Guard Training Center Petaluma ***
Savannah, GA
Hunter Army Air Field
Travis Field
Traverse City–Grand Traverse Bay, MI
Coast Guard Air Station Traverse City ***
Tucson, AZ
Davis–Monthan Air Force Base
Virginia Beach–Norfolk, VA
Camp Elmore ***
Coast Guard Support Center Portsmouth ***
Little Creek Naval Amphibious Base
Norfolk Naval Base
Oceana Naval Air Station
Portsmouth Naval Shipyard
West Palm Beach–Boca Raton–Delray Beach, FL
Coast Guard Loran Station Jupiter ***
Yuma, AZ
Marine Corps Air Station Yuma
Yuma Proving Ground

Source: Army and Air Force Exchange Service, Coast Guard Non-Appropriated Fund Activities, Marine Corps Exchange Service, and Navy Resale System, 1990.

*Base closing proposed.
**Base will close.
***Exchange only.

ble income not exceeding $7,500, tuition fees are waived for courses taken for credit on a space-available basis. Regular admission procedures are required.

WASHINGTON

Depending on the institution, and for no more than two courses per term, tuition and general student fees are waived or reduced for courses taken for credit and waived entirely for courses taken for audit.

WISCONSIN

Tuition fees are waived for auditing courses; instructor's approval required.

DON'T PUT OFF YOUR WILL

It's human nature to avoid thinking about the need for a will. Seven out of every 10 people die without one, and eight of 10 who do have a will fail to keep it up to date. If you don't have a will when you die, the state where you live in your retirement years will write one for you according to its own statutes, and the assets you may have worked hard to accumulate will be distributed according to its laws.

Don't put off making a will because of imagined costs. A lawyer can tell you the basic fee in advance; it's usually $100 to $250 for a simple document. And it may save your heirs thousands.

Once you have a will, make a note to yourself in your calendar to review it every year. Births, marriages, deaths, hard feelings, the patching up of hard feelings, plus changes in your finances, in your health, or in federal or state laws—any of these may affect your will. Regular, periodic review helps ensure that you won't forget to make needed adjustments.

If death and taxes are inevitable—as the old saying goes—so are taxes after death. But it isn't all bad. No estate smaller than $600,000 is subject to federal tax. State tax exemptions vary greatly and often change, another reason for keeping the document up to date.

Where should you keep your will? Put it in a safe place, but don't hide it behind a painting or under a rug. If you conceal it too well, a court may rule that you don't have one! Your lawyer should have a signed copy, and the original should be in a logical place, such as a safety-deposit box or your desk. Be sure your spouse, a close relative, or a friend knows where both the copies and the original are.

Finding the Right Lawyer

When you move from one state to another, you enter a new legal environment. Even if your will is legal in your new state (and it may not be), it might not do the best possible job. So when you resettle, see a lawyer in your new area to make certain your will is one your state will recognize. Some states, for example, require that the executor of a will be a resident of the state where the deceased lived. For a legal checkup, you might have to contact a family lawyer.

The law is a competitive field. In the past, lawyers and clients usually found each other in the Rotary Club, at a church supper, or on the golf course. Since 1977, when the Supreme Court struck down laws barring the legal profession from advertising, many lawyers have gotten quite adept at promoting themselves. Just look up "Lawyers" in a telephone book's Yellow Pages, and you'll be surprised by the techniques many firms borrow from consumer goods advertising. Specialists for 24-hour divorces, personal bankruptcy, workers' compensation, and personal injury claims abound. Somewhere hidden among the listings is a professional who can advise you. How do you find him or her?

- *Satisfied clients.* If a friend or neighbor has used a lawyer's services, ask what sort of matter the lawyer handled. Some lawyers, especially in large cities, specialize in a certain branch of law and aren't interested in taking on cases outside their specialty. They aren't family lawyers.

- *Lawyers referral service.* Most state bar associations have a referral service with a toll-free telephone number. Typically, the name you are given is an attorney who practices where you live, specializes in your legal problem, and is next up in the association's data base to be referred. You can have a first interview with him or her for a stated—and very modest—fee. In that interview, you can find out whether you'll need further legal services and, if so, you can decide whether you want to continue with the lawyer to whom you were referred. You will be under no obligation to do so if you do not want to.

- *Local bar association.* If the referral service lists no lawyer in your area, try the local bar association. If you don't find it in the telephone book, inquire for the president's name at the county courthouse. You can then ask him or her for the name of a good lawyer. Be sure to make it clear that you are asking, in their capacity as president of the local association, for the name of a reliable attorney who can perform the kind of service you are seeking.

Don't talk about your legal problems to strangers. (Lawyer referral services and presidents of bar associations are professional exceptions to this rule.) People who don't know you personally aren't likely to have your best interest at heart. Be particularly wary of any recommendation that is made without your asking for it.

FINDING THE RIGHT DOCTOR

Chances are good that you'll have to choose a new physician at some point; even if you don't move after retirement, your doctor might. Finding a replacement for the person in whom you've put so much trust isn't always easy.

Give some thought to the kind of doctor you are most comfortable with. Do you want to place complete faith in your physician? Or do you have questions about your treatment? Do you like a cooperative arrangement, in which you and your doctor work as a team? It's very important to most people that they have a doctor who will listen to their complaints, worries, and concerns, rather than one who may make patients feel that they're questioning the doctor's authority.

If you're planning to move, you might ask your present doctor if he or she knows anything about the doctors in the area where you are going. Or you can get names from the nearest hospital at the new location, from friends you make, from medical societies, and from new neighbors.

When you have decided whom you want to contact, call that doctor's office, saying that you are a prospective patient, and ask to speak to the doctor briefly. You may have to agree to call back, but making a connection with a professional voice is an important step. If you can't arrange this, if the doctor is "too busy," you probably ought to go to the next name on your list. You need a physician who is readily accessible.

When you do make contact, tell the doctor enough about yourself so that he or she has a good idea of who you are and what your problems may be. If the doctor sounds "right" to you, you could ask about fees, house calls (yes, they are again being made when necessary), and emergencies. Or you may wish to save some of these questions for a personal visit. It is important to establish through the initial phone call or visit that you and the doctor will be at ease with each other.

Evaluate the doctor's attitude. If he or she doesn't want to bother with you now, you will probably get that don't-bother-me treatment sooner or later when dealing with specific problems. Make sure that

- You can openly discuss your feelings and personal concerns about sexual and emotional problems.
- The doctor isn't vague, impatient, or unwilling to answer all your questions about the causes and treatment of your physical problems.
- The doctor takes a thorough history on you and asks about past physical and emotional problems, family medical history, medication you are taking, and other matters affecting your health.
- The doctor doesn't always attribute your problems to getting older, and that he or she doesn't automatically prescribe drugs rather than deal with real causes of your medical problems.
- The doctor has an associate to whom you can turn should your doctor retire or die.

Talk with the doctor about the transfer of your medical records. Some doctors like to have them, especially if there is any specific medical problem or chronic condition. Other doctors prefer not to see them, and to develop new records.

Even if you feel fine, arrange to have a physical or at least a quick checkup. This is more for the doctor's benefit than for yours, but it will help you, too. Should an emergency occur, the doctor will have basic information about you and some knowledge of your needs, and you will avoid the stress of trying to work with a doctor who has to learn about you in an emergency.

Working

In Eagle River, Wisconsin, a World War II veteran tells how his teenage friend is mystified that the man doesn't quit his $4.25-an-hour commander's job at American Legion Post #431 and get behind the counter at McDonald's out on Highway 17. The teenager promises to pull strings with the day manager to start the older friend at $6.00. For some odd reason, says the man, he can't drum into the kid's head that the commander's job requires organizational and human relations skills, and is far more fun and interesting than fast food, even if it were done for free.

A thousand miles south, a charming woman runs the visitor's drop-in center on Central Avenue in downtown Hot Springs, Arkansas. Amid rackfuls of brochures, booklets, maps, pamphlets, and broadsides, she talks with American and foreign tourists all day long. "Ask me a question and I'll be happy to answer it. And if I don't know the answer," she adds, "I'll be happy to make one up." Her work is voluntary; so are other options at St. Joseph's hospital auxiliary, or helping high school kids with reading problems.

In a Chapel Hill haberdashery, a woman stands near the Hathaway and Pendleton shelves in the shirt alcove. The boys from Duke, UNC, and State are her customers, especially during the job-interviewing season. They haven't a clue about what goes into a good shirt nor even how to wash it. She likes this retail job much better than the one she had selling linens and bedding at a department store in a mall near Raleigh.

In Benton County, Arkansas, a man and wife, both retired from the U.S. Army Corps of Engineers, breed AKC Schipperke dogs and take in stray animals for later adoption. They advertise their Skips in *Dog World* and buyers come from all over the Mississippi and Ohio valleys. For them, it's a matter of being your own boss doing something you love rather than working a temporary job at Tyson's Foods, in nearby Springdale, when that employer is especially busy.

All are retired and each works in his own way—as a volunteer, through self-employment, or at a part-time job. Though working after retirement is by no means a concern of every older adult, it is to many. In the years immediately after retirement, nearly one in four people take a short-schedule, seasonal, or temporary job. Another one in four would do the same thing, according to surveys, but several things stand in the way.

Social Security Rules

The amount of money you can make on the job and still collect the Social Security benefits coming to you is limited. If you're under 65 and your income ex-

---

Competing for Part-Time Jobs

We can say this about college towns: for all their lively attractions, they aren't ideal grounds for older people to hunt for part-time or seasonal work. The competition is especially stiff in the following places, where the number of younger persons who look for a part-time job is more than seven times the number of sixty-ish persons searching for the same thing.

Amherst–Northampton, MA
Ann Arbor, MI
Athens, GA
Austin, TX
Blacksburg, VA
Bloomington–Brown County, IN
Burlington, VT
Chapel Hill, NC
Charlottesville, VA
Fayetteville, AR
Fort Collins–Loveland, CO
Gainesville, FL
Iowa City, IA
Madison, WI
State College, PA

Source: Woods & Poole Economics, Inc., population estimates.

---

ceeds $6,480, your benefits will be reduced by $1 for every $2 you're earning over that amount. If you're between 65 and 70 and earning more than $8,800, your benefits will be cut by $1 for every $3 you're paid over the ceiling. After age 70, these reductions no longer apply.

Keeping your earnings under the exempt amount is understandable. Not only would half or more of your excess earnings be lost through Social Security reductions, but they would be subject to income taxes as well as Social Security withholding. Explaining this to an employer unfortunately makes it seem as if you're limited in motivation.

The Market for Part-Time Jobs

Even though the number of part-time jobs has increased by 21 percent over the past decade, most of these positions are low-skill, low-paid ones with few benefits.

The big reason that there aren't more better-paying and challenging part-time jobs is the high cost to employers. Training and administrative costs, for instance, are the same for full- and part-time workers. A short work week boosts the hourly costs to employers for these expenses. In contrast, jobs that require little training—such as hamburger flipping, counter help, aisle sweeping, or cashiering—don't significantly raise the costs to employers, particularly if the job has no benefit package.

Age Discrimination

In spite of the law protecting anyone between the ages of 40 and 70 from being passed over in hiring or being involuntarily retired solely on the basis of age, this kind of discrimination still takes place in the job market.

It is also one of the most difficult job-market issues to identify. Few, if any, employers support discriminatory business practices; they are open to lawsuits if they do. Yet a large number of older workers have experienced discrimination. About the only advice career counselors can offer is that fair treatment usually comes from working for a supervisor older than yourself.

JOB FORECASTS IN RETIREMENT PLACES

Economists who follow employment trends have an old joke: If you take each local planner's forecast for job growth in his or her area and add them all together, the total number of jobs forecasted would require that every man, woman, and child hold down one day job and moonlight two others.

Fortunately, forecasters at the national level try to adopt a more balanced perspective. Although no one can predict the future with certainty, predicting where jobs will be plentiful over the next few years isn't a matter of gazing into a crystal ball. Forecasters use reliable indicators.

To start with, jobs come to where the people are. In other words, any place that has a concentration of people and is also growing is by definition a jobs mecca.

Secondly, the hot industries—retail trade, services, and finance, insurance, and real estate (known as FIRE)—will stay hot. With variation between places, this is where the real action is expected to occur in the remaining years of the 20th century. And with variation among employers, these hot industries are precisely the ones where *good* part-time jobs are found.

Unemployment Threat

If you see a good number of light-manufacturing plants with full parking lots and notice lots of hard-hat construction workers aboard growling earth-moving machines at new residential and commercial developments, you'll know that in flush times jobs are easy to find here and the pay is just great. You can also assume that, should a recession roll in, this place may be hard hit by unemployment.

One of the few things you'll find economists agreeing on is that places with large numbers of workers in manufacturing and construction are harshly affected during business slumps.

In contrast to boom-and-bust places, there are others where the pace isn't quite as fast, and where large

Job Winners, 1990–1995

RETIREMENT PLACE	New White-Collar Jobs
Phoenix–Tempe–Scottsdale, AZ	113,920
San Diego, CA	98,331
Orlando, FL	86,186
Fort Lauderdale–Hollywood–Pompano Beach, FL	81,311
West Palm Beach–Boca Raton–Delray Beach, FL	72,129
Miami–Hialeah, FL	70,051
Austin, TX	50,814
Las Vegas, NV	44,124
San Antonio, TX	43,330
St. Petersburg–Clearwater–Dunedin, FL	27,085
Virginia Beach–Norfolk, VA	26,352
Fort Myers–Cape Coral–Sanibel Island, FL	24,909
Portsmouth–Dover–Durham, NH	23,289
New Port Richey, FL	22,590
Honolulu, HI	22,353
Santa Rosa–Petaluma, CA	19,871
Tucson, AZ	19,153

Source: Woods & Poole Economics, Inc., employment forecasts.

Military Economies

At least one in every 12 workers in the following places gets paid by the Department of Defense. For this reason, military cutbacks would hit their local economies hard. Not for nothing are several of their representatives sitting on the Armed Services Committee in Congress.

Alamogordo, NM
Biloxi–Gulfport–Pass Christian, MS
Charleston, SC
Colorado Springs, CO
Fort Walton Beach, FL
Hilton Head–Beaufort, SC
Honolulu, HI
New Bern, NC
Oak Harbor–Whidbey Island, WA
Panama City, FL
Pensacola, FL
Salinas–Seaside–Monterey, CA
San Diego, CA
Virginia Beach–Norfolk, VA
Yuma, AZ

Source: Woods & Poole Economics, Inc., employment forecasts.

numbers of white-collar workers commute to downtown or suburban jobs with financial, real estate, and insurance firms. Others find their work at colleges and universities, at big medical centers in the area, or at local resorts. The employment mix in these areas is more balanced, with most of the weight going to the white-collar sector.

Finally, there are places at the opposite extreme from industrial places, not because they are thriving, but because manufacturing plays no part in their existence. These have nearly pure white-collar economies characterized by people working almost exclusively in retail trade, services, finance, insurance, and real estate.

Even though in retirement you may have little to worry about regarding being without a full-time job, local unemployment may still affect you in unforeseen ways. By boosting the competition for available work, high unemployment limits your chances of finding a part-time job should you ever want one.

Just as places can be rated for mild climates and their supply of public golf links, so also can they be rated for how vulnerable they are to joblessness during a bad business cycle. The unemployment threat is:

High
- if factory workers and construction workers hold down more than 35 percent . . .
- or if Department of Defense workers and military hold down more than 12 percent . . .
- or if together they hold down more than 40 percent

of all the jobs in the area.

Moderate
- if the number of construction workers and factory workers is between 20 and 35 percent . . .
- or the number of military and other workers for the Defense Department is between six and 12 percent . . .
- or if together they number between 25 and 40 percent

of all employment in the area.

Low
- if factory and construction workers are less than 20 percent . . .
- or Department of Defense workers and military are less than six percent . . .
- or if together they are less than 25 percent

of all the jobs in the area.

Among *Retirement Places Rated*'s 151 locations, the unemployment threat is high in 26, moderate in 73, and low in 52.

What Are the Odds?

Think of how much competition you'll meet in tracking down a good seasonal or short-schedule job. Are there crowds of voluntary part-time workers pounding the pavement everywhere, or are the odds more favorable in Phoenix and Chapel Hill than in Orlando or Albuquerque?

"Voluntary" part-timers are persons who want only part-time jobs rather than persons who resignedly take a temporary, seasonal, or short-schedule job because there's nothing else available. There are 13 million voluntary part-timers in this country. Most are older adults, 19- to 23-year-old college students, and women aged 38 to 54 easing back into the workplace.

To measure competition, *Retirement Places Rated* compares the population of these two latter groups to persons in their early 60s. In each place, the part-time job competition is:

Favorable if the number of college-age persons and women re-entering the job market is less than three times the number of persons in their early 60s.

Average if the number of college-age persons and women re-entering the job market is between three and five times the number of persons in their early 60s.

Unfavorable if the number of college-age persons and women re-entering the job market is more than five times the number of persons in their early 60s.

Among *Retirement Places Rated*'s 151 locations, the competition is favorable in 41, average in 61, and unfavorable in 49.

SCORING: Working

If you've taken early retirement from your lifelong career and want to launch a new one or simply land an interesting part-time job, are the prospects rosier in Redding, Reno, or Roswell?

To help you answer the question, *Retirement Places Rated* compares two factors in each place: the percentage rate of job growth over the next five years, and the total number of new full-time equivalent jobs forecasted in retail trade, services, and the so-called FIRE industries in each retirement place. (A full-time equivalent job is typically held by one worker; occasionally, two workers share it. Two full-time equivalent jobs roughly translate into three part-time jobs of 25 hours per week.)

The two factors—number of new jobs and rate of growth—are multiplied together to produce the score.

RANKINGS: Working

In ranking 151 retirement places for job growth, *Retirement Places Rated* uses two criteria: (1) the total number of new jobs forecast between now and 1995 in Services, Retail Trade, and the FIRE industries (Finance, Insurance, and Real Estate), and (2) the total rate of increase in these new jobs. The product of these two criteria, rounded off, is the place's score. The higher the score, the more promising the place's job outlook. Places receiving tie scores get the same rank and are listed in alphabetical order.

Retirement Places from First to Last

Rank	Score	Rank	Score	Rank	Score
1. Orlando, FL	19,468	12. Portsmouth–Dover–Durham, NH	5,320	26. St. Petersburg–Clearwater–Dunedin, FL	2,556
2. Phoenix–Tempe–Scottsdale, AZ	18,461	13. Myrtle Beach, SC	5,115	27. Salinas–Seaside–Monterey, CA	2,493
3. West Palm Beach–Boca Raton–Delray Beach, FL	17,012	14. Carson City–Minden, NV	4,300	28. Tucson, AZ	2,054
		15. San Luis Obispo, CA	4,101	29. Naples, FL	2,010
4. Fort Lauderdale–Hollywood–Pompano Beach, FL	15,041			30. Honolulu, HI	1,942
5. San Diego, CA	14,023	16. Maui, HI	4,053		
		17. Santa Rosa–Petaluma, CA	3,627	31. Key West–Key Largo–Marathon, FL	1,743
6. Austin, TX	9,857	18. Ocean County, NJ	3,500	32. Sarasota, FL	1,716
7. New Port Richey, FL	9,047	19. St. Tammany Parish, LA	3,131	33. Albuquerque, NM	1,629
8. Las Vegas, NV	7,477	20. Cape Cod, MA	2,956	34. St. George–Zion, UT	1,502
9. Miami–Hialeah, FL	7,448			35. McAllen–Edinburg–Mission, TX	1,436
10. Fort Myers–Cape Coral–Sanibel Island, FL	5,991	21. Hilton Head–Beaufort, SC	2,938		
		22. Virginia Beach–Norfolk, VA	2,892		
		23. Vero Beach, FL	2,864	36. Colorado Springs, CO	1,423
		24. Fort Walton Beach, FL	2,770	37. Gainesville, FL	1,394
11. San Antonio, TX	5,436	25. Santa Barbara, CA	2,620		

Rank	Score		Rank	Score		Rank	Score
38. Ann Arbor, MI	1,331		77. Daytona Beach, FL	547		115. New Bern, NC	224
39. Lakeland–Winter Haven, FL	1,319		78. New Paltz–Ulster County, NY	519			
40. Bradenton, FL	1,197		79. St. Augustine, FL	515		116. Petoskey–Straits of Mackinac, MI	217
41. Charleston, SC	1,196		80. Cape May, NJ	511		116. Yuma, AZ	217
42. Branson–Table Rock Lake, MO	1,194					118. Brevard, NC	216
43. Lake Havasu City–Kingman, AZ	1,188		81. Boise, ID	508		119. Grand Junction, CO	207
44. Pensacola, FL	1,060		82. Reno, NV	504		120. Canandaigua, NY	205
45. Olympia, WA	1,058		83. Eugene–Springfield, OR	501			
			83. Lexington–Fayette, KY	501		121. Columbia County, NY	198
46. Chico–Paradise, CA	1,043		85. Oak Harbor–Whidbey Island, WA	493		122. Camden–Penobscot Bay, ME	197
47. Panama City, FL	1,036					123. Hot Springs National Park, AR	194
48. Ocala, FL	1,035		86. Brunswick–Golden Isles, GA	492		124. Amador County, CA	187
49. Brownsville–Harlingen, TX	988		87. Bend, OR	483		125. Grand Lake, OK	179
50. Lancaster County, PA	929		88. Ocean City–Assateague Island, MD	480			
			89. Melbourne–Titusville–Palm Bay, FL	476		126. Clayton, GA	170
51. Madison, WI	919		90. Charlottesville, VA	469		127. Canton–Lake Tawakoni, TX	169
52. Southport, NC	899					128. Harrison, AR	160
53. Benton County, AR	892		91. Keene, NH	436		129. Houghton Lake, MI	156
54. Hanover, NH	852		92. Blacksburg, VA	412		130. Paris–Big Sandy, TN	147
55. Las Cruces, NM	840		93. Port Townsend, WA	403			
			94. Laconia–Lake Winnipesaukee, NH	398		131. Bar Harbor–Frenchman Bay, ME	146
56. Burlington, VT	839		95. State College, PA	378		131. Roswell, NM	146
57. Clear Lake, CA	835					133. Pike County, PA	145
58. North Conway–White Mountains, NH	735		96. Coeur d'Alene, ID	363		134. Fredericksburg, TX	139
59. Santa Fe, NM	733		97. Door County, WI	352		135. Red Bluff–Sacramento Valley, CA	137
60. Bloomington–Brown County, IN	718		98. Crossville, TN	351			
			99. Medford–Ashland, OR	344		136. Fayetteville, AR	132
61. Aiken, SC	703		100. Grants Pass, OR	342		137. Rockport–Aransas Pass, TX	130
62. Grass Valley–Truckee, CA	699					138. Athens, GA	122
63. South Lake Tahoe–Placerville, CA	694		101. Monticello–Liberty, NY	328		138. Hamilton–Bitterroot Valley, MT	122
64. Chapel Hill, NC	693		102. Bellingham, WA	317		140. Eagle River, WI	117
65. Traverse City–Grand Traverse Bay, MI	692		103. Athens–Cedar Creek Lake, TX	309			
			104. Biloxi–Gulfport–Pass Christian, MS	303		141. Deming, NM	116
66. Prescott, AZ	663		105. Iowa City, IA	293		141. Newport–Lincoln City, OR	116
67. Kerrville, TX	659					143. El Centro–Calexico–Brawley, CA	114
68. Fairhope–Gulf Shores, AL	651		106. Mountain Home–Bull Shoals, AR	283		144. Charlevoix–Boyne City, MI	113
69. Redding, CA	645		107. Hendersonville, NC	273		145. Lake Lanier, GA	112
70. Amherst–Northampton, MA	643		108. Martinsburg–Charles Town, WV	262			
			109. Savannah, GA	245		146. Alamogordo, NM	107
71. Twain Harte–Yosemite, CA	626		110. Asheville, NC	238		147. Carlsbad–Artesia, NM	106
72. Fort Collins–Loveland, CO	593					148. Easton–Chesapeake Bay, MD	105
73. Rehoboth Bay–Indian River Bay, DE	585		111. Wenatchee, WA	233		149. Edenton–Albemarle Sound, NC	104
74. Los Alamos, NM	571		112. Bennington, VT	232		150. Murray–Kentucky Lake, KY	103
75. New Braunfels, TX	559		113. San Juan Islands, WA	227			
			114. Kalispell, MT	226		151. Thomasville, GA	100
76. Burnet–Marble Falls–Llano, TX	549						

PLACE PROFILES: Working

The following chart shows the number of new jobs forecasted in each retirement place for Services, Retail Trade, and FIRE (Finance, Insurance, and Real Estate), the industries where the most part-time opportunities are found. The chart also characterizes the local unemployment threat—low, moderate, or high—and the competition for part-time work—favorable,

average, or unfavorable.

All figures are derived from current employment forecasts by Woods & Poole Economics, Inc., of Washington, DC, and are used here with permission.

A star (★) in front of a place's name highlights it as one of the top 20 places for part-time job opportunities between now and 1995.

	Unemployment Threat	New Jobs Forecast			Competition	Score	Rank
		Services	Retail Trade	FIRE			
Aiken, SC	high	1,939	1,659	169	average	703	61
Alamogordo, NM	high	76	111	73	unfavorable	107	146
Albuquerque, NM	moderate	10,184	4,277	1,683	unfavorable	1,629	33
Amador County, CA	moderate	464	180	31	favorable	187	124
Amherst–Northampton, MA	low	3,432	1,133	131	unfavorable	643	70
Ann Arbor, MI	low	7,691	2,053	325	unfavorable	1,331	38
Asheville, NC	moderate	1,352	1,298	−60	average	238	110
Athens, GA	low	499	472	−222	unfavorable	122	138
Athens–Cedar Creek Lake, TX	moderate	617	482	255	favorable	309	103
★ Austin, TX	moderate	15,776	17,580	17,458	unfavorable	9,857	6
Bar Harbor–Frenchman Bay, ME	moderate	459	275	63	average	146	131
Bellingham, WA	moderate	1,933	402	297	unfavorable	317	102
Bend, OR	moderate	1,914	440	548	average	483	87
Bennington, VT	moderate	551	549	219	average	232	112
Benton County, AR	high	1,030	3,528	−28	unfavorable	892	53
Biloxi–Gulfport–Pass Christian, MS	high	994	1,895	180	unfavorable	303	104
Blacksburg, VA	moderate	752	1,288	310	unfavorable	412	92
Bloomington–Brown County, IN	low	1,928	2,090	435	unfavorable	718	60
Boise, ID	moderate	2,915	1,144	1,130	unfavorable	508	81
Bradenton, FL	moderate	2,481	3,456	1,574	favorable	1,197	40
Branson–Table Rock Lake, MO	low	3,177	624	476	favorable	1,194	42
Brevard, NC	high	372	294	134	average	216	118
Brownsville–Harlingen, TX	low	3,721	2,363	586	unfavorable	988	49
Brunswick–Golden Isles, GA	moderate	1,444	1,132	328	average	492	86
Burlington, VT	moderate	3,912	1,650	495	unfavorable	839	56
Burnet–Marble Falls–Llano, TX	moderate	689	353	1,011	favorable	549	76
Camden–Penobscot Bay, ME	moderate	606	357	40	average	197	122
Canandaigua, NY	moderate	1,197	361	−30	average	205	120
Canton–Lake Tawakoni, TX	high	462	60	115	unfavorable	169	127
★ Cape Cod, MA	low	8,944	5,006	1,158	favorable	2,956	20
Cape May, NJ	low	1,186	2,093	393	favorable	511	80
Carlsbad–Artesia, NM	high	−96	−151	−5	average	106	147
★ Carson City–Minden, NV	moderate	8,143	3,190	1,166	average	4,300	14
Chapel Hill, NC	low	1,431	1,536	650	unfavorable	693	64
Charleston, SC	high	5,101	4,228	1,067	unfavorable	1,196	41
Charlevoix–Boyne City, MI	low	159	−17	91	average	113	144
Charlottesville, VA	moderate	2,248	1,485	7	unfavorable	469	90
Chico–Paradise, CA	low	4,483	1,140	964	average	1,043	46
Clayton, GA	high	−38	88	389	average	170	126
Clear Lake, CA	low	1,404	779	694	favorable	835	57
Coeur d'Alene, ID	moderate	1,542	360	132	average	363	96
Colorado Springs, CO	high	5,818	2,728	4,013	unfavorable	1,423	36
Columbia County, NY	moderate	898	201	30	average	198	121
Crossville, TN	moderate	500	257	613	average	351	98
Daytona Beach, FL	moderate	1,783	3,044	1,690	favorable	547	77
Deming, NM	low	171	31	10	favorable	116	141
Door County, WI	high	1,072	349	89	average	352	97
Eagle River, WI	moderate	205	84	6	favorable	117	140
Easton–Chesapeake Bay, MD	moderate	−4	280	−30	favorable	105	148
Edenton–Albemarle Sound, NC	high	−5	90	13	unfavorable	104	149
El Centro–Calexico–Brawley, CA	low	695	−216	−2	average	114	143
Eugene–Springfield, OR	low	3,701	2,099	−285	unfavorable	501	83
Fairhope–Gulf Shores, AL	low	779	1,597	913	average	651	68
Fayetteville, AR	low	674	32	188	unfavorable	132	136
Fort Collins–Loveland, CO	moderate	3,362	265	1,462	unfavorable	593	72
★ Fort Lauderdale–Hollywood–Pompano Beach, FL	moderate	49,832	21,705	9,774	favorable	15,041	4
★ Fort Myers–Cape Coral–Sanibel Island, FL	moderate	10,452	9,903	4,554	favorable	5,991	10
Fort Walton Beach, FL	high	4,930	3,629	2,135	unfavorable	2,770	24
Fredericksburg, TX	moderate	252	32	136	favorable	139	134
Gainesville, FL	low	5,592	2,269	754	unfavorable	1,394	37
Grand Junction, CO	low	689	328	693	unfavorable	207	119
Grand Lake, OK	moderate	283	92	226	favorable	179	125
Grants Pass, OR	low	1,068	584	255	favorable	342	100
Grass Valley–Truckee, CA	moderate	1,462	1,016	816	favorable	699	62
Hamilton–Bitterroot Valley, MT	moderate	134	128	36	favorable	122	138
Hanover, NH	moderate	3,860	897	346	unfavorable	852	54
Harrison, AR	low	233	360	42	average	160	128
Hendersonville, NC	high	346	1,136	151	unfavorable	273	107
Hilton Head–Beaufort, SC	high	3,006	5,021	1,219	average	2,938	21
Honolulu, HI	moderate	12,893	6,386	3,074	unfavorable	1,942	30
Hot Springs National Park, AR	moderate	953	124	410	favorable	194	123
Houghton Lake, MI	low	230	212	29	favorable	156	129

		New Jobs Forecast					
	Unemployment Threat	Services	Retail Trade	FIRE	Competition	Score	Rank
Iowa City, IA	low	1,114	909	213	unfavorable	293	105
Kalispell, MT	moderate	782	252	384	average	226	114
Keene, NH	high	1,601	1,169	−153	unfavorable	436	91
Kerrville, TX	low	1,106	1,012	546	favorable	659	67
Key West–Key Largo–Marathon, FL	low	3,854	2,101	1,047	favorable	1,743	31
Laconia–Lake Winnipesaukee, NH	high	1,534	657	29	average	398	94
Lake Havasu City–Kingman, AZ	moderate	1,768	1,498	1,369	favorable	1,188	43
Lake Lanier, GA	high	28	303	170	average	112	145
Lakeland–Winter Haven, FL	moderate	3,823	6,086	1,199	average	1,319	39
Lancaster County, PA	high	5,774	2,572	1,036	average	929	50
Las Cruces, NM	moderate	2,138	1,585	533	unfavorable	840	55
★ Las Vegas, NV	low	32,531	8,831	2,762	unfavorable	7,477	8
Lexington–Fayette, KY	moderate	3,705	2,418	535	average	501	83
Los Alamos, NM	low	1,357	424	159	average	571	74
Madison, WI	low	6,368	1,689	2,126	unfavorable	919	51
Martinsburg–Charles Town, WV	moderate	1,307	179	168	average	262	108
★ Maui, HI	low	6,712	4,705	1,242	average	4,053	16
McAllen–Edinburg–Mission, TX	low	4,291	3,830	945	unfavorable	1,436	35
Medford–Ashland, OR	low	1,380	1,410	192	average	344	99
Melbourne–Titusville–Palm Bay, FL	moderate	1,923	3,194	1,129	average	476	89
★ Miami–Hialeah, FL	low	45,017	14,897	10,137	average	7,448	9
Monticello–Liberty, NY	low	2,389	−73	23	average	328	101
Mountain Home–Bull Shoals, AR	high	856	292	124	unfavorable	283	106
Murray–Kentucky Lake, KY	moderate	−44	−49	−27	unfavorable	103	150
★ Myrtle Beach, SC	moderate	5,218	7,616	4,349	average	5,115	13
Naples, FL	low	4,179	3,793	1,847	favorable	2,010	29
New Bern, NC	high	435	800	154	unfavorable	224	115
New Braunfels, TX	moderate	970	682	838	average	559	75
New Paltz–Ulster County, NY	moderate	3,534	837	−223	average	519	78
★ New Port Richey, FL	moderate	10,396	8,594	3,600	favorable	9,047	7
Newport–Lincoln City, OR	low	403	30	−8	favorable	116	141
North Conway–White Mountains, NH	moderate	1,795	1,285	121	favorable	735	58
Oak Harbor–Whidbey Island, WA	high	1,020	396	539	average	493	85
Ocala, FL	moderate	2,246	2,253	1,641	favorable	1,035	48
Ocean City–Assateague Island, MD	moderate	604	1,677	393	average	480	88
★ Ocean County, NJ	moderate	13,923	3,459	1,001	favorable	3,500	18
Olympia, WA	low	3,570	1,476	906	average	1,058	45
★ Orlando, FL	moderate	48,646	23,147	14,393	unfavorable	19,468	1
Panama City, FL	moderate	2,544	3,117	320	average	1,036	47
Paris–Big Sandy, TN	high	401	74	117	unfavorable	147	130
Pensacola, FL	moderate	4,643	3,550	328	average	1,060	44
Petoskey–Straits of Mackinac, MI	moderate	692	268	52	average	217	116
★ Phoenix–Tempe–Scottsdale, AZ	moderate	59,599	21,425	32,896	average	18,461	2
Pike County, PA	moderate	321	91	74	favorable	145	133
Port Townsend, WA	moderate	718	220	316	favorable	403	93
★ Portsmouth–Dover–Durham, NH	moderate	14,699	6,206	2,384	average	5,320	12
Prescott, AZ	moderate	1,455	984	1,022	favorable	663	66
Red Bluff–Sacramento Valley, CA	low	386	72	85	favorable	137	135
Redding, CA	moderate	2,657	1,048	661	average	645	69
Rehoboth Bay–Indian River Bay, DE	high	938	1,746	1,068	average	585	73
Reno, NV	low	5,720	2,095	−1,122	unfavorable	504	82
Rockport–Aransas Pass, TX	low	53	65	225	favorable	130	137
Roswell, NM	low	376	209	178	average	146	131
St. Augustine, FL	moderate	1,071	1,151	623	average	515	79
St. George–Zion, UT	moderate	2,399	1,208	295	average	1,502	34
St. Petersburg–Clearwater–Dunedin, FL	moderate	6,793	12,269	8,023	favorable	2,556	26
★ St. Tammany Parish, LA	low	4,065	4,308	1,351	unfavorable	3,131	19
Salinas–Seaside–Monterey, CA	low	9,227	4,316	1,206	unfavorable	2,493	27
★ San Antonio, TX	moderate	21,710	14,011	7,609	unfavorable	5,436	11
★ San Diego, CA	low	61,511	20,786	16,034	unfavorable	14,023	5
San Juan Islands, WA	moderate	391	119	171	favorable	227	113
★ San Luis Obispo, CA	low	5,793	7,848	2,146	average	4,101	15
Santa Barbara, CA	low	7,491	7,953	2,295	unfavorable	2,620	25
Santa Fe, NM	low	2,254	1,779	448	average	733	59
★ Santa Rosa–Petaluma, CA	moderate	12,491	4,749	2,631	average	3,627	17
Sarasota, FL	moderate	4,184	5,200	3,460	favorable	1,716	32
Savannah, GA	moderate	2,415	648	26	unfavorable	245	109
South Lake Tahoe–Placerville, CA	low	1,880	1,674	494	average	694	63
Southport, NC	moderate	747	1,302	609	average	899	52
State College, PA	low	1,646	892	225	unfavorable	378	95
Thomasville, GA	high	−86	−2	26	average	100	151
Traverse City–Grand Traverse Bay, MI	low	1,728	2,000	161	average	692	65
Tucson, AZ	moderate	12,593	2,943	3,617	average	2,054	28

| | | New Jobs Forecast | | | | | |
	Unemployment Threat	Services	Retail Trade	FIRE	Competition	Score	Rank
Twain Harte–Yosemite, CA	low	1,389	569	588	favorable	626	71
Vero Beach, FL	moderate	4,757	2,541	1,673	favorable	2,864	23
Virginia Beach–Norfolk, VA	high	12,964	10,630	2,758	unfavorable	2,892	22
Wenatchee, WA	low	1,226	253	60	average	233	111
★ West Palm Beach–Boca Raton– Delray Beach, FL	moderate	42,067	18,980	11,082	favorable	17,012	3
Yuma, AZ	low	568	272	754	average	217	116

 ET CETERA: Working

It's dryly said that finding any job means having to listen to No, No, No, No, No . . . and No one more time before finally hearing Yes. Landing a good part-time job isn't any different, except when it means *creating* one with an employer who isn't looking, or interviewing an employer who is looking but hasn't the slightest idea what to do with an older applicant. In these situations, you may be in for a long series of Nos.

Some Unvoiced Employer Objections

While job discrimination on the basis of age is against the law, you might still be a victim of what labor economists call "statistical discrimination" when an employer assumes several things about an older person applying for a job:

- You want a job that isn't available.
- You haven't the same economic incentive to work that younger workers have.
- You don't have the stamina, skills, or flexibility.
- You want more money because you have more experience.
- Your fringe coverage—life insurance, health insurance, and pension benefits—will cost more than fringes for younger applicants.
- Your prospects for staying with a job and justifying the employer's investment in on-the-job training are less than those of a younger worker.

All of these objections somehow work themselves into the "overqualified" catch-all; it's the word most frequently used by an employer when turning down older people who've applied for a job.

Anyone who has worked 20, 30, or 40 years is overqualified by standard definition. Why not ask the employer what he or she means by being overqualified? If you'll go to work at the going rate, plus bring experience and maturity to the job, won't that mean that the cost of your productivity will be less than or equal to a younger worker's? If you're already covered by Medicare and Social Security, won't the employer avoid the cost of health insurance and a pension

plan if you're hired? If the average tenure of younger workers in certain jobs is less than the shelf life of yogurt, mightn't that make you a better bet for longevity?

PART-TIME JOB SEARCHING

The number of part-time jobs increased 21 percent over the past decade. Most of these jobs are found in retail trade, services, and in finance, insurance, and real estate. Here are some useful strategies for searching out good opportunities.

Focus on Small Businesses and Nonprofit Organizations. Large employers often have policies against part-time employment. Smaller companies are more flexible. Moreover, small businesses compete with larger employers for good workers, not by offering more money, but by offering adaptable working conditions.

Many of the most interesting opportunities are found in the nonprofit sector—libraries, museums, colleges and universities, and human service organizations. Like small businesses, they offer flexibility instead of big money.

Respond to Full-Time Job Openings. If you've identified an employer that can use your skills, button-hole the boss for a full-time job. If he or she hasn't any, suggest a part-time alternative. If the company has no experience with part-timers, suggest a trial period.

Too often, part-timers pass by advertised positions that are full-time. Many 8-hour-a-day jobs can be shared.

Don't Forget the Government. Part-time opportunities are expanding within the federal government, partly because of a 12-year-old law that requires federal agencies to introduce short-schedule positions and prorate compensation and benefits according to the number of hours worked. The good jobs, however, are reserved for persons who've previously worked for Uncle Sam for at least three years.

Almost all state governments have agencies with

part-time positions. The key is identifying the agencies and where in the state the positions are (don't assume there are no state government jobs outside of the capital city). A good place to start is the state's aging or adult services office (listed under "Relocation Resources" in the Appendix of this book).

Try Temporary Work. One major reason why agencies that supply temporary workers are hiring older persons is that the work is usually full-time for a limited period. For job-seekers with child-care needs, this isn't the most attractive situation. Agencies specializing in clerical work dominate the Yellow Pages, but firms that engage part-time engineers, accountants, and health care professionals are growing.

Volunteer. The "Me" Decade has given way to the "Decency" Decade, if you follow pop sociologists on the talk shows. Today, one of every four Americans over 14 is involved in some kind of volunteer work. The value of all their volunteered time adds up to more than $100 billion a year.

Volunteer positions frequently turn into paid positions. If anything, they provide the setting for polishing up existing job skills and acquiring new skills and experience for seeking paid employment.

Leisure Living

Leisure attractions aren't fairly distributed. Some places have more indoor and outdoor benefits going for them than others. Many of these attractions are doubly important if you want to balance fun and games with culture, and culture with the great outdoors.

COMMON DENOMINATORS

It's lucky geographic circumstances that make clam digging, hang gliding, alpine skiing, river rafting, or growing good tomatoes better in some parts of the country than in others.

But geography has little to do with more conventional activities: golfing at a public course on a weekday morning when the greens fees are cheaper; team bowling in the din at a local tenpin center; catching a movie at a showcase cinema in a shopping mall off the interstate; or dining out in a quality restaurant.

You might call these familiar activities "common denominators." They are everywhere. On a per capita basis, though, their supply varies from place to place.

Counting Stars: Good Restaurants

The most common retail establishment in this country is the one where you walk in, sit down, and order something to eat. If you enjoy an occasional dinner splurge you might as well go to a worthwhile eatery instead of a diner or a portion-controlled Casa de la Maison House where distantly prepared frozen packs of beef Wellington and veal cordon bleu are microwaved, dished out, and "menued" at 10 times what the chef paid for them.

To learn which retirement places have restaurants more than just a cut or two above average, *Retirement Places Rated* consulted the seven-volume *Mobil Travel Guide*, which since 1958 has rated restaurants across the country. The ratings are derived from two sources: customer comments and inspection reports of field representatives who dine anonymously at establishments throughout the year. Restaurants are judged by the quality of their food, service, and ambience. Ratings range from one star for a "good, better than average" restaurant to five stars for "one of the best in the country." Just 10 restaurants got this top award in 1990; one is located in each of two retirement places.

Retirement Places Rated divides the local population by the number of quality stars awarded establishments in each retirement place. Three two-star restaurants and four three-star restaurants, for example, would yield 18 quality stars. Though small places like Santa Fe, New Mexico, and Door County, Wisconsin, have fewer rated restaurants than glitzy Miami or Las

Access to Good Food

BEST RETIREMENT PLACES	Restaurants/ Quality Stars	Residents per Star
Door County, WI	20/30	944
Bennington, VT	15/35	1,059
Eagle River, WI	10/14	1,283
North Conway–White Mountains, NH	11/23	1,567
Santa Fe, NM	26/60	1,585
Easton–Chesapeake Bay, MD	6/15	1,851
Hanover, NH	21/39	1,943
Key West–Key Largo–Marathon, FL	23/41	1,961
Bar Harbor–Frenchman Bay, ME	13/23	1,970
Ocean City–Assateague Island, MD	10/19	2,086

Source: Prentice Hall Press, *Mobil Travel Guide,* 1990, and Woods & Poole Economics, Inc., population estimates.

Access to Public Golf

BEST RETIREMENT PLACES	Residents per Golf Hole
Charlevoix–Boyne City, MI	208
Myrtle Beach, SC	239
Door County, WI	242
Southport, NC	242
Hilton Head–Beaufort, SC	304
Houghton Lake, MI	318
Monticello–Liberty, NY	330
Eagle River, WI	333
North Conway–White Mountains, NH	364
Brevard, NC	371

Source: Derived from National Golf Foundation, unpublished data, and Woods & Poole Economics, Inc., population estimates.

Access to Certified Bowling

BEST RETIREMENT PLACES	Residents per Lane
Monticello–Liberty, NY	356
Rehoboth Bay–Indian River Bay, DE	599
Canandaigua, NY	645
Houghton Lake, MI	715
Wenatchee, WA	747
Traverse City–Grand Traverse Bay, MI	754
Ann Arbor, MI	781
Key West–Key Largo–Marathon, FL	821
Carlsbad–Artesia, NM	837
Charlevoix–Boyne City, MI	860

Source: American Bowling Congress, unpublished data, and Woods & Poole Economics, Inc., population estimates.

Because public regulation golf is an excellent indicator of other leisure options in a retirement place, *Retirement Places Rated* counts not the number of municipal and daily-fee courses but their total number of holes per capita. Eagle River, Wisconsin, and Carson City–Minden, Nevada, have one municipal course each, for example. But there are 36 holes at the course in the Nevada capital, and only nine at the one in the North Woods.

Counting Lanes: Tenpin Bowling

The sound of a hardwood ball striking hardwood pins was sometimes mistaken for a thunderclap in early 19th-century America. The sport has been around a long, long time indeed, and along with all its variations—skittles, fivepins, ninepins, tenpins, candlepins, duckpins, and bocce—is probably played by more people in the world than any other game.

In the United States, the dominant variation is tenpins, and nearly 71 million people take a turn at it once or twice a year. But if the 8,100 bowling centers had to depend solely on this kind of casual participation, many might quickly convert to exercise studios or oil-change shops for a steadier income. The credit for keeping the alleys in business goes to the American Bowling Congress (ABC), to which 3.2 million men belong, and the Women's International Bowling Congress (WIBC), with 3 million women members, which promote tournaments throughout the country.

Forget the idea that it's only a blue-collar, indoor sport. Doctors are prescribing it for older adults. Besides relieving the postural backache that comes from sitting too long, the physical exercise and the challenge of making the ball knock down all those pins produce better coordination of vision and mind with practically all the muscles of the body.

Another plus for newcomers is the ready-made social contacts that are part of formal bowling competition. Whether you're in Chapel Hill, Charleston, or Charlottesville, you'll find team bowling. With 1.5 million teams in 117,469 leagues around the country, what better odds can there be for meeting a group that's right for you?

Nearly every tenpin bowling center in this country

Vegas, they can still boast at least one Mobil quality star for every 2,000 people.

Counting Holes: Public Golf Courses

On a grey winter day in Benton County, Arkansas, a group of retired men and women who've challenged each other to play once a day throughout the year—rain, sleet, or shine—are duffing away in their parkas on the Belle Vista Golf Course. Everywhere, surveys show, the portion of persons of their age who play golf regularly is greater than that of any other group.

You've got three options if you're searching for golf on an idle, sunny weekend: the private course, typically part of a country club or leisure-living community open only to members and guests; a private, daily-fee operation open to all players for a fee; and a municipal course operated by a tax-supported agency such as a city, county, school, or park district.

If you can afford to join a private country club with an 18-hole course, the dues you pay buy more than valet parking and the use of the swimming pool and tennis courts. You belong to the 14 percent of golfers who don't have to kill time waiting to tee off at crowded public courses. On the other hand, if you're one of 23 million golfers in the country who regularly play a round at a daily-fee or municipal course, only six of every 10 of the nation's 13,626 courses are open to you.

Access to the Movies

BEST RETIREMENT PLACES	Residents per Screen
Ocean City–Assateague Island, MD	2,086
Burlington, VT	3,618
Brunswick–Golden Isles, GA	3,990
Athens, GA	4,132
Cape Cod, MA	4,301
Laconia–Lake Winnipesaukee, NH	4,310
Cape May, NJ	4,497
Fayetteville, AR	4,561
St. Tammany Parish, LA	5,036
Wenatchee, WA	5,232

Source: Census Bureau, *1987 Census of Selected Services*, 1990; *Motion Picture Almanac*, 1990; and Woods & Poole Economics, Inc. population estimates.

Performing Arts Calendar: 20 Outstanding Retirement Places

RETIREMENT PLACE	Dates
Phoenix–Tempe–Scottsdale, AZ	720
San Diego, CA	580
Ann Arbor, MI	434
San Antonio, TX	372
Fort Lauderdale–Hollywood–Pompano Beach, FL	344
Miami–Hialeah, FL	304
Virginia Beach–Norfolk, VA	278
St. Petersburg–Clearwater–Dunedin, FL	260
Honolulu, HI	253
Fort Myers–Cape Coral–Sanibel Island, FL	199
Albuquerque, NM	189
Orlando, FL	186
Pensacola, FL	159
Sarasota, FL	157
Santa Fe, NM	149
Austin, TX	146
Madison, WI	141
Boise, ID	139
Tucson, AZ	135
West Palm Beach–Boca Raton–Delray Beach, FL	112

Source: ABC Leisure Magazines, *Musical America: 1990 International Directory of the Performing Arts*, 1990.

is certified by the ABC for tournament competition. To rate each retirement place for bowling, *Retirement Places Rated* counts the number of certified lanes rather than the number of bowling centers to derive a per capita access score. Bellingham, Washington, for instance, and Gainesville, Florida, each have three ABC centers. There are 80 lanes in Gainesville and 60 in Bellingham. Yet Bellingham gets a higher rating than Gainesville because there are more lanes for the local population.

Counting Screens: The Movies

The number of people over 55 who regularly caught a commercial film doubled during the 1980s. This may seem odd since the studios rarely think that older adults are part of audience demographics when new picture ideas are scrutinized for whether they'll play in Peoria, Pittsburgh, and Portland. Aside from there being more people over 55 each year, another reason for increased attendance is the afternoon discount at multiplex cinemas in suburban shopping malls.

You may recall the 1940s when moviegoing was a routine family activity. Remember when John Huston won two Academy Awards—best director and best screenplay—for The Treasure of Sierra Madre? And his father, Walter, was named best supporting actor for his portrayal of the old prospector in the same film? Jane Wyman won an Oscar for her role in Johnny Belinda; Hamlet was best picture, and its star, Laurence Olivier, best actor.

The year was 1948, a time when moviegoing was the American thing to do of an evening, any evening. Popcorn was regularly swept up from the aisles between shows, the next John Wayne or Spencer Tracy film was announced on a large easel in the lobby, usherettes took you to your seat with a red-lensed flashlight, and you always got a MovieTone or Warner-Pathé newsreel with the show. There were 18,631 movie houses back then. Never again would there be so many. Most were neighborhood establishments, with a few downtown palaces for premieres and first-run screenings.

Retirement Places Rated divides the local population by the number of commercial four-wall (as opposed to drive-in) theater screens to figure access to movies. Most are in multiplex cinemas run by exhibitors like United Artists, Loews, and Cineplex Odeon at shopping malls. But the single-screen or twin Bijou or Strand kind of neighborhood theater is still alive in many retirement places.

THE PERFORMING ARTS

How do you measure the cultural goings-on in another place? If you loved your hometown's symphony, will you, after surfacing in a retirement place, have to settle for shaded seats at the annual outdoor Country Harmonica Blowoff?

Put it another way: if you exchange a big place for a smaller one, dirty air for clean, cold seasons for warm sun, the costly for the economical, do you also risk trading the lively arts for a cultural desert?

The Lively Arts Calendar

Long before a touring pianist, European boys choir, or visiting New York contemporary dance troupe comes to town for a date at the local performing arts center, it is booked by a nonprofit college or community concert association.

Does this mean you'll find the performing arts only in a big city blessed with an expensive concert hall and a nonprofit community concert association bankrolled by philanthropists, managed by paid professionals, and attended by season member-subscribers? Not necessarily.

The attendance growth at fine arts concerts is due not to turning up the volume and variety of performances in big cities but to popular interest in smaller cities and towns. And a good part of the interest comes from older fans. Among the 151 retirement places in this guide, 103 benefit from college and

Enviable Touring Artists Bookings

What will $359 get you in Iowa City? Season tickets to each of the University of Iowa's Hancher Auditorium series—all in zone 1, the best seats in the house. In New York, that money might buy two nights out at a Metropolitan Opera production, dinner, and a cab ride.

Here is the Hancher's schedule for the 1989–90 season. So much for the notion that the lively arts aren't cultivated out on the prairie.

Concert Series
10/17—Moscow Virtuosi
2/12—Warsaw Philharmonic; Zoltan Kocsis, piano
4/1—Kathleen Battle, soprano

Chamber Music Series
2/1—Lark Quartet
4/26—St. Paul Chamber Orchestra
5/1—Yo-Yo Ma, violin cello; Emanuel Ax, piano

Broadway Series
9/27–10/2—Les Misérables
1/25–27—Chess
3/2–4—Into the Woods

Innovation Afoot Series
9/22—La La La Human Steps
10/21–22—ISO & The Bobs
1/19–20—David Parsons Company

Theater Series
9/16—You Strike the Woman, You Strike the Rock
11/4—Driving Miss Daisy
1/24—"The Lunatic, the Lover, the Poet," Brian Bedford
3/6—Odyssey, National Theatre of the Deaf

Revelations Series
10/27–28—Power Failure, Rinde Eckert, tenor
4/6–7—Kronos Quartet
4/27–28—Laurie Anderson

Special Events Series
8/24—Philobus
9/24—Philip Glass, piano
10/7—Holly Near and Ronnie Gilbert, vocalists
10/30—Tendai Shomyo
11/10–12—Cats
2/26—Don Cossacks Song & Dance Ensemble
3/13—Kodo Drummers and Dancers of Sado

Young Concert Artists
11/1—Hexagon
11/8—Asako Urushihara, violin
2/7—Edwardus Halim, piano
4/18—Carl Halvorsen, tenor

Family Series
10/15—Raggedy Ann & Andy, Children's Theatre Company
2/20—American Indian Dance Theatre
2/24—Wind in the Willows, Louisville Children's Theatre

Landmark Event
12/6–8—Nutcracker, Joffrey Ballet

community arts series that regularly book touring artists.

Resident Ensembles

Besides taking in the touring attractions, people in some retirement places have the additional option of attending performances of resident ensembles.

Opera. The image of horned helmets, silvery shields, and unintelligible singing is a low-brow cliché. Fans boast that operatic stagecraft is the most demanding of the performing arts because of the unique commingling of instruments and voice with theater and dance; if you're introduced to a good production, they say, you'll be hooked for life. Thirty retirement places have live opera. Boise, Brevard, Honolulu, Madison, and Miami–Hialeah may have little else in common but they all belong to this group.

Symphony Orchestras. Orchestras are more common than opera companies. Seventy-six retirement places have at least one. Their music is heard in woodsy state parks, high-school auditoriums, philharmonic halls, impressive new civic arts centers, and small-town bandboxes and pavilions. Phoenix, San Antonio, and San Diego support "major" symphonies; that is, orchestras with budgets over $4 million.

OUTDOOR RECREATION ASSETS

For many, the great outdoors is one "destination pull" outweighing all the "origin push" factors associated with urban crime, traffic, and high costs of living. It takes in a wide range of possibilities. It might mean lying on a Gulf Coast beach, tramping the Appalachian Trail, flycasting for Rocky Mountain rainbow, daysailing on Chesapeake Bay, or just getting away from it all to a cabin on the edge of a Pacific Northwest wilderness area.

Well before the time comes for shedding job obligations, many people have already identified from past family vacations the places where, when they retire, their own ideal of the great outdoors will be right outside their door.

Resident Fishing and Hunting License Fees for Older Sportspeople

State	Eligible Age	Fishing License	Hunting/Fishing License
Alabama	65	free	—
Alaska	60	exempt	—
Arizona	70	free	—
Arkansas	65*	$10.50	—
California		$2.00	—
Colorado	64	$5.00	—
Connecticut	65	free	—
Delaware	65	exempt	—
Florida	65	exempt	—
Georgia	65	exempt	—
Hawaii	65	free	—
Idaho	70	free	$4.00
Illinois	65	exempt	—
Indiana	65	exempt	—
Iowa	65*	$8.50	$15.50
Kansas	65	exempt	—
Kentucky	65	exempt	—
Louisiana	60	exempt	—
Maine	70	free	—
Maryland	65	free	—
Massachusetts	65–69	$6.25	$9.75
	70	free	—
Michigan	65	$1.00	—
Minnesota	65	$4.00	—
Mississippi	65	exempt	—
Missouri	65	exempt	—
Montana	62	exempt	—
Nebraska	70	free	—
Nevada	65	$3.50	$5.50
New Hampshire	65	free	—
	68*	free	
New Jersey	65–69	$7.00	—
	70	free	
New Mexico	64	$1.50	—
New York	65–69	$3.00	—
	70	free	
North Carolina	70*		$10.00
North Dakota	65	$3.00	—
Ohio	66	free	—
Oklahoma	64	$6.00	$10.00
Oregon	70	free	—
Pennsylvania	65*	$10.00	—
Rhode Island	65	free	—
South Carolina	65*	free	—
South Dakota	65	$5.00	—
Tennessee	65	exempt	$6.00
Texas	65	exempt	—
Utah	65	$9.00	—
Vermont		$10.00	$18.00
Virginia	65	exempt	—
Washington	70	free	—
West Virginia	65	exempt	—
Wisconsin	65*	$15.00	—
Wyoming	65*	free	—

Source: Sport Fishing Institute, 1990 National Survey, 1990.

Exempt means no license required; free means you must carry a current license, but there is no fee; dollar figures indicate reduced fees; an asterisk (*) indicates a lifetime license; a dash (—) indicates the same eligibility rules for fishing also apply to combined hunting/fishing licenses. California reduces the fee for "eligible Senior Citizens"; Vermont offers no breaks for older sportspeople.

The Water Draw

Maryland watermen tell mainland tourists who come to Chesapeake Bay fishing villages for the oysters and soft-shell crabs that the true length of estuarine shore

Inland Water: 17 Top Retirement Places

Bar Harbor–Frenchman Bay, ME
Brownsville–Harlingen, TX
Burlington, VT
Camden–Penobscot Bay, ME
Eagle River, WI
Easton–Chesapeake Bay, MD
Edenton–Albemarle Sound, NC
Fort Myers–Cape Coral–Sanibel Island, FL
Hilton Head–Beaufort, SC
Key West–Key Largo–Marathon, FL
Melbourne–Titusville–Palm Bay, FL
Ocean County, NJ
Ocean City–Assateague Island, MD
Rockport–Aransas Pass, TX
St. Petersburg–Clearwater–Dunedin, FL
St. Tammany Parish, LA
San Juan Islands, WA

Source: Census Bureau, unpublished area measurements, 1990.

In these places, more than 15 percent of the surface area is classified as inland water, which includes ponds and lakes of surface area greater than 40 acres; streams, canals, and rivers if width is one-eight mile or more; water along irregular Great Lakes and ocean coastlines if bays, inlets, and estuaries are between one and 10 miles wide. Eight retirement places have no inland water: Alamogordo, Albuquerque, Athens (GA), Deming, Fredericksburg, Kerrville, Las Cruces, and Los Alamos.

reached by the Bay's tide would total more than 8,000 miles if all the kinks and bends were flattened out.

They say in Michigan's Roscommon County that the locals tend to live away from Houghton Lake, the state's biggest inland body of water, while the transplanted retired folks who've migrated up from Detroit or Cleveland or Chicago unerringly light on the shore like loons there for the duration.

And Oklahomans vaunt the state's collection of Corps of Engineer lakes. If you could tip the state a bit to the south, they say, the water would flow out and flood Texas for a good while.

There's not much connection between the migration of retired people on the one hand and the sight of water on the other, however. Water didn't play nearly as great a part in attracting older adults during the 1980s as did a mild climate and resort development. In fact, certain Arizona, Nevada, and New Mexico counties that were desert-dry attracted retired people at a faster rate than wet counties in other parts of the country.

For all that, you'll spot lakes, ponds, and marine bays in nine out of 10 of the 151 *Retirement Places Rated* locations. Aside from being a basic necessity for supporting life, water is regarded by most people as a scenic amenity; many regard it as a recreational amenity—as long as there is enough of it to fish in, boat on, or swim in without enduring snowmelt-cold temperatures. What's Petoskey without the Straits of Mackinac?

Or Cape Cod minus the Atlantic Ocean? Four out of five Americans today live within 100 miles of a

Federal Recreation Lands:
20 Outstanding Retirement Places

Bellingham, WA
Bend, OR
Brevard, NC
Clayton, GA
Eugene–Springfield, OR
Fort Collins–Loveland, CO
Grants Pass, OR
Hamilton–Bitterroot Valley, MT
Kalispell, MT
Key West–Key Largo–Marathon, FL
Los Alamos, NM
Miami–Hialeah, FL
Port Townsend, WA
Prescott, AZ
Redding, CA
St. George–Zion, UT
Santa Barbara, CA
South Lake Tahoe–Placerville, CA
Twain Harte–Yosemite, CA
Wenatchee, WA

More than one-third of the land area in these retirement places is set aside for national forests, parks, and wildlife refuges.

coastline; in another 10 years the Department of the Interior predicts three out of four will live within 50 miles. Not surprisingly, 47 *Retirement Places Rated* havens have an ocean or Great Lakes coastline.

Counting Acres: The Public Lands

Of all the outdoor activities that older adults take to most frequently, the leading ones—pleasure driving, walking, picnicking, sightseeing, bird-watching, nature walking, and fishing—might arguably be more fun in the country's splendid system of federal- and state-run public recreation areas.

National Forests. "Clear-Cutting Turns Off Tourists" say the bumper stickers in northwest Arkansas. So do rumbling, 18-wheel logger's trucks. Although various parts of the national forests are classified as "wilderness," "primitive," "scenic," "historic," or "recreation" areas, the main purpose of the system is silviculture: growing wood, harvesting it carefully, and preserving naturally beautiful areas from the depredations of amateur chain saws, burger palaces, miniature golf, and time-share condos.

In rainy Deschutes National Forest near Bend, Oregon, the harvest is Douglas fir. Among the widespread components of Mark Twain National Forest in the southern Missouri Ozarks, the crop is local hardwoods of blackjack oak and hickory. Within Pisgah National Forest in western North Carolina the trees are virgin oak, beech, and black walnut.

But also within the forest system are more than a

quarter of a million miles of paved roads, built not just for logging crews but for everyone. They lead to a wide variety of recreation developments: some 400 privately operated resorts, marinas, and ski lodges, plus fishing lakes and streams, campgrounds, and hiking trails.

National Parks. Where multiple use is the philosophy behind national forests, the National Park System preserves irreplaceable geographic and historic treasures for public recreation. This has been its mission every since Congress created Yellowstone National Park in adjacent western corners of the old Montana and Wyoming territories "as a public park or pleasuring ground for the benefit and enjoyment of the people" back in 1872.

The collection of national parks, preserves, monuments, memorials, battlefields, seashores, riverways, and trails makes up the oldest and largest national park system in the world. Eight million of the National Park System's 79 million acres are found in *Retirement Places Rated* areas.

National Wildlife Refuges. Wildlife refuges protect native flora and fauna from people. This purpose hasn't changed since 1903, when Theodore Roosevelt created the first refuge, Pelican Island near Vero Beach, Florida, to save the mangrove-nesting egrets from poachers scrounging for plumage to adorn women's hats.

Most of the country's 477 refuges are open for wildlife activities, particularly photography and nature observation. In certain of the refuges and at irregular times, fishing and hunting are permitted, depending on the size of the refuge's wild populations. You don't have to move to the sticks to be close to nature. One-third of the land area of Clark County, Nevada (where Las Vegas is the seat of government), is dedicated to wildlife refuges. Fort Myers–Cape Coral–Sanibel Island, Florida, has four refuges on 5,648 acres—Caloosahatchee, J. N. "Ding" Darling, Matlacha Pass, and Pine Island.

State Recreation Areas. The 10 million acres of state-run recreation areas are often equal in quality to the federal public lands, and in most states older visitors get a break on entrance fees. They range from small day-use parks in wooded areas or on beaches, offering little more than picnic tables and rest rooms, to large rugged parks and forests with developed hiking trails and campsites, and big-time destination resorts complete with golf courses, swimming pools, tennis courts, and full-time recreation staffs.

SCORING: Leisure Living

Ranking places for leisure, let's argue, can't be done with fairness. A Florida boater, hauling out his smoky

outboard motor for a tune-up, may care less for the announced dates of a local civic concert series. A

Cape Cod couple lolling on the beach may never know the joys of Wisconsin ice fishing, nor would they ever regret the loss.

There are too many differences in taste for a rating system to suit everyone. Yet it's still possible to measure the supply of specific amenities. Chamber of Commerce brochures and state tourism promotion kits do it all the time. Travelers make their own comparisons. Hearsay may hold that winter living in the northern Michigan flatwoods is as dull and lonesome today as it was for the natives who quit the area for the city generations ago, or that there's little in the way of peaceful outdoor recreation in sunbaked Orlando.

Retirement Places Rated tries a more objective approach. It neither judges the quality of music by local symphonies and opera companies nor pushes the recreation benefits of the desert over seashore or forest evirons. It simply indicates the presence of things that most persons agree enhance retirement living.

Each place starts with a base score of zero, to which points are added according to the following criteria.

Common Denominators

Places get points for how accessible four common amenities are to residents. Access is rated AA, A, B, or C (AA indicates the greatest access and C the least), and the place get points accordingly: 400 points for an AA rating, 300 points for A, 200 points for B, and 100 points for C.

1. *Good restaurants.*

A retirement place gets a rating of:	if there is one Mobil quality star for every:
AA	5,000 or fewer people
A	5,001 to 10,000 people
B	10,001 to 20,000 people
C	20,001 or more people

2. *Public golf courses.*

A retirement place gets a rating of:	if there is one public golf hole for every:
AA	750 or fewer people
A	751 to 1,500 people
B	1,501 to 2,250 people
C	2,251 or more people

3. *Bowling lanes.*

A retirement place gets a rating of:	if there is one lane for every:
AA	1,400 or fewer people
A	1,401 to 2,000 people
B	2,001 to 3,000 people
C	3,001 or more people

4. *Movie theaters.*

A retirement place gets a rating of:	if there is one screen for every:
AA	7,500 or fewer people
A	7,501 to 10,000 people
B	10,001 to 15,000 people
C	15,001 or more people

The Lively Arts Calendar

Touring Artists Bookings. In the calendar year, each date booked for touring fine arts groups to perform at local auditoriums is worth 10 points. Albuquerque's 62 bookings, for instance, are good for 620 points.

Resident Ensembles. In the calendar year, each performance date for local opera companies and symphony orchestras is worth an additional 10 points. The 41 dates for Las Vegas' two symphony orchestras and one opera company, for example, contribute 410 points to its score.

Outdoor Recreation Assets

Coastlines. Each mile of general coastline gets 10 points. The 55 miles of Pacific coastline on San Diego's western edge earn this place 550 points.

Inland Water Area. The percent of a place's surface area classified as inland water is multiplied by 50. In Clayton, Georgia, 6.7 of the 377.1 square miles of surface area is water. That works out to 1.8 percent, or 90 points.

National Forests, Parks, and Wildlife Refuges. The percent of a place's land area set aside for national forests, parks, and wildlife refuges is multiplied by 50. St. George–Zion, Utah, has 1,550,720 acres, 33.88 percent taking in the Dixie National Forest (394,503 acres) and Zion National Park (131,000 acres), giving the Desert Southwest retirement place 1,694 points.

State Recreation Areas. The percent of a place's land area set aside for state recreation areas is multiplied by 50. Vero Beach, Florida, is 313,408 acres in total area. It also has a 578-acre unit of Florida's Recreation and Parks system. This works out to .18 percent state park acreage, or 9 points.

To maintain relative parity among the three major categories—Common Denominators, Performing Arts Calendar, and Outdoor Recreation Assets—a ceiling of 2,000 points is applied to the total for each.

SCORING EXAMPLES

A rustic resort in western Montana, a southern California retirement mecca, and a small New England college area illustrate the different routes by which places arrive at their leisure-living ratings.

Kalispell, Montana (#19)

"To Hell with Heaven's Gate" read many a Kalispell bumper sticker 10 years ago. Environmentalists and more than a few cowpunchers and loggers were protesting the commotion caused by a large Hollywood production unit on location there for the filming of a story of 19th-century immigrant settlers battling powerful cattlemen. After being released and then abruptly withdrawn, the film—*Heaven's Gate*—became one of the biggest flops in moviemaking, costing United Artists nearly $40 million.

The movie's only good character, some critics said, was its ruggedly beautiful scenery. Kalispell is the access town to Flathead National Forest and the southern gateway to Glacier National Park, which straddles the Great Divide all the way up to Canada. With an inland water area of 143.2 square miles, taking in Hungry Horse Reservoir, Whitefish Lake, and Flathead Lake, and nearly 2.5 million acres of public lands, Kalispell earns the maximum 2,000 points in the Outdoor Recreation Assets category.

Kalispell and surrounding Flathead County also score well in the Common Denominators category, particularly when the hundreds of thousands of summer visitors disappear after Labor Day. The mountain resort earns three AA ratings—the highest possible—for per capita access to good restaurants, public golf courses, and bowling centers.

The Lively Arts Calendar is another story. Kalispell has one artist series, the Flathead Community Concert Association, and one resident ensemble, the Glacier Orchestra and Chorale. The combined 14 dates scheduled by these institutions are good for just 140 points.

San Diego, California (#8)

Just because one place boasts more leisure-time amenities than another doesn't always mean it's better. Myrtle Beach, South Carolina, for instance, has a greater supply of bowling lanes, movie screens, holes of public golf, and good restaurants per capita than does giant San Diego. Myrtle Beach's score for these common denominators is 1,500 points; San Diego's is 700 points. True, there are more choices in densely populated places. But there are also more people to use them. No wonder it is dryly said in Southern California that much of one's time is spent waiting in line.

San Diego's big outdoor asset is its 55 miles of Pacific shoreline from Border Field Beach at the Mexican boundary all the way up to San Clemente. That plus San Diego County's 52 square miles of lakes and reservoirs, 16 state parks and beaches, and nearly 300,000 acres of federal recreation land contribute another 1,225 points.

The lively arts calendar is where San Diego shines. The Symphony Orchestra schedules 120 performances at Symphony Hall. Operas are regularly staged at the Civic Theater and at the Old Globe Theater in Balboa Park. Suburban La Jolla is a center for chamber music. Local campus and civic auditoriums book 270 dates for touring artists. Altogether, this full lively arts calendar confers another 2,000 points to San Diego's leisure living score.

Hanover, New Hampshire (#11)

Where Kalispell's strength lies in its outdoor attractions and San Diego's in its lively arts, Hanover's advantage lies in its balance between the outdoors, the lively arts, and common denominators.

You'll search town directories in vain for tenpin bowling anywhere in Hanover and surrounding Grafton County. But the place earns three AA ratings for good restaurants, public golf courses, and commercial cinema screens. Per capita access to these amenities earns Hanover 1,200 points.

Outdoors, Grafton County's low mountain topography takes in nearly 370,000 acres of public land, including a national forest, a stretch of the Appalachian Scenic Trail, and 23 state forests and parks. Those lands, plus more than 30 square miles of natural lakes and ponds, earn the New England place 1,734 points for outdoor recreation assets.

Indoors, 64 touring artists bookings are scheduled "Under the Big Hop" at Dartmouth College's Hopkins Center. Plymouth State College east of here books another eight performances during the academic year. These dates, plus those of the New Hampshire Youth Orchestra, add 790 points to Hanover's leisure-living score.

RANKINGS: Leisure Living

Ten factors are used to derive the score for a retirement place's leisure-living assets: (1) good restaurants, (2) holes of public golf, (3) certified lanes of tenpin and candlepin bowling, (4) movie theater screens, (5) campus and civic auditorium fine arts bookings, (6) resident opera companies and symphony orchestras, (7) miles of ocean or Great Lakes coastlines, (8) inland water areas, (9) national parks, forests, and wildlife refuges, and (10) state recreation areas.

Places that receive tie scores get the same rank and are listed alphabetically.

Retirement Places from First to Last

Rank	Score	Rank	Score	Rank	Score
1. Fort Myers–Cape Coral– Sanibel Island, FL	5,197	4. St. Petersburg–Clearwater– Dunedin, FL	4,356	7. Cape Cod, MA	3,983
2. Miami–Hialeah, FL	4,700	5. Honolulu, HI	4,184	8. San Diego, CA	3,925
3. Virginia Beach–Norfolk, VA	4,425	6. Charleston, SC	4,042	9. Santa Barbara, CA	3,810
				10. Las Vegas, NV	3,791

Rank	Score	Rank	Score	Rank	Score
11. Hanover, NH	3,724	55. Amherst–Northampton, MA	2,694	102. New Paltz–Ulster County, NY	1,671
12. Santa Fe, NM	3,716			103. State College, PA	1,665
13. Sarasota, FL	3,664	56. Madison, WI	2,660	104. Gainesville, FL	1,662
14. Naples, FL	3,620	57. Redding, CA	2,649	105. Edenton–Albemarle Sound, NC	1,645
15. Orlando, FL	3,608	58. San Antonio, TX	2,641		
		59. Grand Junction, CO	2,640	106. Fayetteville, AR	1,595
16. Melbourne–Titusville–		60. Bennington, VT	2,625	107. Fort Walton Beach, FL	1,578
Palm Bay, FL	3,550			108. Lake Lanier, GA	1,565
17. Fort Collins–Loveland, CO	3,520	61. Hamilton–Bitterroot Valley,		109. Chico–Paradise, CA	1,545
18. Eugene–Springfield, OR	3,480	MT	2,606	110. Portsmouth–Dover–Durham,	
19. Kalispell, MT	3,440	62. Rockport–Aransas Pass, TX	2,600	NH	1,538
19. Key West–Key Largo–		63. Medford–Ashland, OR	2,593		
Marathon, FL	3,440	64. Door County, WI	2,576	111. Charlottesville, VA	1,528
		65. Los Alamos, NM	2,540	112. Asheville, NC	1,492
21. Burlington, VT	3,424			113. Murray–Kentucky Lake, KY	1,489
22. Phoenix–Tempe–		66. Hot Springs National Park, AR	2,524	114. Yuma, AZ	1,477
Scottsdale, AZ	3,418	67. Clayton, GA	2,505	115. Benton County, AR	1,447
23. Tucson, AZ	3,401	68. Bloomington–Brown County,			
24. Eagle River, WI	3,390	IN	2,424	116. Bradenton, FL	1,432
25. Salinas–Seaside–Monterey,		69. San Juan Islands, WA	2,400	117. Pike County, PA	1,413
CA	3,388	70. San Luis Obispo, CA	2,383	118. Lancaster County, PA	1,372
				119. Iowa City, IA	1,362
26. Ann Arbor, MI	3,364	71. Ocean County, NJ	2,372	120. Carlsbad–Artesia, NM	1,361
27. Wenatchee, WA	3,300	72. Colorado Springs, CO	2,324		
28. Pensacola, FL	3,297	73. Myrtle Beach, SC	2,312	121. Keene, NH	1,355
29. Fort Lauderdale–Hollywood–		74. Boise, ID	2,267	122. Canandaigua, NY	1,345
Pompano Beach, FL	3,293	75. Ocala, FL	2,266	123. Fairhope–Gulf Shores, AL	1,340
30. Traverse City–Grand Traverse				124. Monticello–Liberty, NY	1,319
Bay, MI	3,284	76. Cape May, NJ	2,200	125. Roswell, NM	1,265
		77. Biloxi–Gulfport–			
31. Bellingham, WA	3,250	Pass Christian, MS	2,186	126. Blacksburg, VA	1,232
32. Bend, OR	3,200	78. Reno, NV	2,176	127. Olympia, WA	1,199
33. Albuquerque, NM	3,198	79. Panama City, FL	2,151	128. El Centro–Calexico–	
34. Ocean City–Assateague		80. Branson–Table Rock Lake, MO	2,136	Brawley, CA	1,188
Island, MD	3,152			129. Southport, NC	1,146
35. West Palm Beach–		81. Brunswick–Golden Isles, GA	2,131	130. Hendersonville, NC	1,132
Boca Raton–Delray Beach,		82. Petoskey–Straits of Mackinac,			
FL	3,133	MI	2,114	131. Crossville, TN	1,124
		83. Lexington–Fayette, KY	2,055	132. Las Cruces, NM	1,068
36. Newport–Lincoln City, OR	3,125	84. Grass Valley–Truckee, CA	2,052	133. Grand Lake, OK	1,064
37. Daytona Beach, FL	3,089	85. Austin, TX	2,027	134. Columbia County, NY	1,057
38. Easton–Chesapeake Bay, MD	2,986			135. New Port Richey, FL	1,052
39. Brevard, NC	2,949	85. St. Tammany Parish, LA	2,027		
40. Grants Pass, OR	2,898	87. Alamogordo, NM	1,971	136. Harrison, AR	1,045
		88. Mountain Home–Bull Shoals,		137. Chapel Hill, NC	1,020
41. Prescott, AZ	2,894	AR	1,968	138. Deming, NM	1,001
42. Maui, HI	2,850	89. Charlevoix–Boyne City, MI	1,962	139. Clear Lake, CA	984
43. Savannah, GA	2,839	90. Red Bluff–Sacramento Valley,		140. Martinsburg–Charles Town,	
44. Laconia–Lake Winnipesaukee,		CA	1,933	WV	966
NH	2,838				
45. Hilton Head–Beaufort, SC	2,832	91. St. Augustine, FL	1,930	141. Athens, GA	960
		92. Houghton Lake, MI	1,919	142. Kerrville, TX	904
46. Camden–Penobscot Bay, ME	2,820	93. Oak Harbor–Whidbey Island,		143. Thomasville, GA	880
47. Bar Harbor–Frenchman Bay,		WA	1,903	144. Burnet–Marble Falls–	
ME	2,800	94. Lakeland–Winter Haven, FL	1,849	Llano, TX	853
47. South Lake Tahoe–		95. Santa Rosa–Petaluma, CA	1,843	145. Paris–Big Sandy, TN	812
Placerville, CA	2,800				
49. Brownsville–Harlingen, TX	2,792	96. Amador County, CA	1,839	146. New Braunfels, TX	782
50. Coeur d'Alene, ID	2,749	97. New Bern, NC	1,822	147. Athens–Cedar Creek Lake, TX	633
		98. Vero Beach, FL	1,804	148. McAllen–Edinburg–Mission,	
51. St. George–Zion, UT	2,711	99. Carson City–Minden, NV	1,774	TX	581
52. Port Townsend, WA	2,700	100. Rehoboth Bay–Indian River		149. Fredericksburg, TX	507
52. Twain Harte–Yosemite, CA	2,700	Bay, DE	1,759	150. Aiken, SC	428
54. North Conway–White					
Mountains, NH	2,698	101. Lake Havasu City–Kingman,		151. Canton–Lake Tawakoni, TX	225
		AZ	1,749		

PLACE PROFILES: Leisure Living

The following profiles are a selective catalogue of leisure-living features in each retirement place.

The profiles begin with the category **Common Denominators,** selected everyday options that ought to be available everywhere. The access rating for each item is shown in the right-hand column (AA indicates the greatest access and C the least). The Restaurants entry, besides showing the total number of local eating establishments, also tells how many of them were awarded quality stars (4 ★★ means, for example, that the place has four two-star restaurants).

The second category, **Performing Arts Calendar,** counts the annual number of dates booked at local campus and civic auditoriums for touring arts groups as reported by *Musical America*'s latest survey. The number of dates for resident opera and symphony performances is also counted.

The third category, **Outdoor Recreation Assets,** counts each place's miles of ocean or Great Lakes coastline, its square miles of inland water, and the acreage for all its state parks and national forests, national parks, and wildlife refuges. The figures for inland water include ponds and lakes if their surface areas are 40 acres or more; streams, canals, and rivers are also counted if their width is one-eighth mile or more. The water area along irregular Great Lakes and ocean coastlines is counted, too, if the bays, inlets, and estuaries are between one and 10 miles in width. Lengths of ocean and Great Lakes coastlines are estimated from state totals measured by the National Oceanic and Atmospheric Administration. A list of units of the National Park System, national forests, and national wildlife refuges is included. The following abbreviations are used in this section:

NF	National Forest	NP	National Park
NHP	National Historic Park	NRA	National Recreation Area
NHS	National Historic Site	NSR	National Scenic River
NMP	National Military Park	NS	National Seashore
NM	National Monument	NWR	National Wildlife Refuge

A retirement place's score is the sum of the points in parentheses to the right of the **Common Denominators**, **Performing Arts Calendar**, and **Outdoor Recreation Assets** headings. A star (★) preceding a place's name highlights it as one of the top 20 places for leisure living.

Information comes from these sources: ABC Leisure Magazines, *Musical America: 1990 International Directory of the Performing Arts*, 1990; American Bowling Congress, unpublished zip code data, 1990; American Symphony Orchestra League, *Orchestra and Business Directory*, 1990; Central Opera Service, *1989–1990 Directory*, 1989; National Golf Foundation, unpublished zip code data, 1990; Places Rated Partnership survey of state parks and recreation departments, 1990; Prentice Hall Press, *Mobil Travel Guide* (7 volumes), 1990; Quigley Publishing Company, *Motion Picture Almanac 1990*, 1990; U.S. Department of Agriculture, *Land Areas of the National Forest System*, 1989; U.S. Department of Commerce, Bureau of the Census, *1987 Census of Selected Retail Establishments*, 1990, *1987 Census of Selected Service Establishments*, 1990, and unpublished land and water area measurements, 1990, and National Oceanic and Atmospheric Administration, *The Coastline of the United States*, 1975; U.S. Department of the Interior, Fish and Wildlife Service, *Annual Report*, 1989, and unpublished master deed listing, 1990, and National Park Service, *Index to the National Park System and Related Areas*, 1989, and unpublished master deed listing, 1990.

Rating

Aiken, SC
Common Denominators (400 points)
Restaurants: 114
Golf courses: 4 private (81 holes); 5 daily fee (72 holes) **B**
Bowling center: 1 (14 lanes, tenpins) **C**
Movie theaters: 1 single/twin, 1 multiplex; 5 total screens **C**
Outdoor Recreation Assets (28 points)
Inland Water Area: 4.5 square miles
State Recreation Area: 1 (1,067 acres)
Score: 428 **Rank: 150**

Alamogordo, NM
Common Denominators (1,200 points)
Restaurants: 55; 1 ★, 2 ★★, 1 ★★★ **A**
Golf courses: 1 private (9 holes); 4 daily fee (45 holes); 1 municipal (9 holes) **A**
Bowling centers: 3 (44 lanes, tenpins) **AA**
Movie theater: 1 multiplex; 5 total screens **B**

Rating

Outdoor Recreation Assets (771 points)
National Parks, Forests, Wildlife Refuges:
Lincoln NF (563,686 acres)
White Sands NM (90,500 acres)
State Recreation Area: 1 (180 acres)
Score: 1,971 **Rank: 87**

Albuquerque, NM
Common Denominators (800 points)
Restaurants: 782; 3 ★, 16 ★★, 7 ★★★ **A**
Golf courses: 5 private (99 holes); 1 daily fee (27 holes); 4 municipal (63 holes) **C**
Bowling centers: 9 (264 lanes, tenpins) **A**
Movie theaters: 1 single/twin, 5 multiplex; 32 total screens **C**
The Lively Arts Calendar (1,890 points)
Touring Artists Bookings: 62 dates
Resident Ensembles:
Albuquerque Civic Light Opera (40 dates)

	Rating
Chamber Orchestra of Albuquerque (15 dates)	
New Mexico Symphony Orchestra (60 dates)	
Opera Southwest (12 dates)	

Outdoor Recreation Assets (508 points)
National Parks, Forests, Wildlife Refuges:
    Cibola NF (75,764 acres)
State Recreation Area: 1 (170 acres)
Score: 3,198   **Rank: 33**

Amador County, CA
Common Denominators (700 points)

	Rating
Restaurants: 60; 1 ★★	B
Golf course: 1 daily fee (9 holes)	C
Bowling center: 1 (24 lanes, tenpins)	AA

Outdoor Recreation Assets (1,139 points)
Inland Water Area: 15.1 square miles
National Parks, Forests, Wildlife Refuges:
    Eldorado NF (78,315 acres)
State Recreation Area: 1 (136 acres)
Score: 1,839   **Rank: 96**

Amherst–Northampton, MA
Common Denominators (600 points)

	Rating
Restaurants: 232; 1 ★, 1 ★★, 1 ★★★	C
Golf courses: 3 private (36 holes); 7 daily fee (90 holes)	B
Bowling center: 1 (32 lanes, tenpins)	C
Movie theaters: 4 single/twin, 2 multiplex; 14 total screens	B

The Lively Arts Calendar (680 points)
Touring Artists Bookings: 50 dates
Resident Ensembles:
    Five College Symphony Orchestra (10 dates)
    Project OPERA (8 dates)
Outdoor Recreation Assets (1,414 points)
Inland Water Area: 17.1 square miles
    Knightville Reservoir
    Quabbin Reservoir
State Recreation Areas: 10 (87,891 acres)
Score: 2,694   **Rank: 55**

Ann Arbor, MI
Common Denominators (1,100 points)

	Rating
Restaurants: 386; 3 ★, 4 ★★	C
Golf courses: 7 private (108 holes); 9 daily fee (144 holes); 4 municipal (81 holes)	A
Bowling centers: 13 (350 lanes, tenpins)	AA
Movie theaters: 2 single/twin, 3 multiplex; 27 total screens	A

The Lively Arts Calendar (2,000 points)
Touring Artists Bookings: 351 dates
Resident Ensembles:
    Ann Arbor Chamber Orchestra (35 dates)
    Ann Arbor Symphony Orchestra (15 dates)
    Comic Opera Guild (8 dates)
    Eastern Michigan University Symphony Orchestra
        (9 dates)
    University of Michigan Symphony Orchestra (16 dates)
Outdoor Recreation Assets (264 points)
Inland Water Area: 12.5 square miles
State Recreation Areas: 2 (16,529 acres)
Score: 3,364   **Rank: 26**

Asheville, NC
Common Denominators (700 points)

	Rating
Restaurants: 273; 1 ★, 6 ★★, 1 ★★★	B
Golf courses: 5 private (90 holes); 2 daily fee (27 holes); 2 municipal (36 holes)	C
Bowling centers: 2 (48 lanes, tenpins)	C
Movie theaters: 7 single/twin, 1 multiplex; 19 total screens	A

The Lively Arts Calendar (350 points)
Touring Artists Bookings: 20 dates
Resident Ensemble:
    Asheville Symphony Orchestra (15 dates)
Outdoor Recreation Assets (442 points)
Inland Water Area: 0.8 square miles
National Parks, Forests, Wildlife Refuges:

	Rating
Blue Ridge Parkway (5,490 acres)	
Pisgah NF (31,464 acres)	

Score: 1,492   **Rank: 112**

Athens, GA
Common Denominators (900 points)

	Rating
Restaurants: 152; 1 ★★	C
Golf courses: 1 private (27 holes); 2 daily fee (27 holes)	C
Bowling centers: 2 (56 lanes, tenpins)	A
Movie theaters: 2 single/twin, 3 multiplex; 19 total screens	AA

The Lively Arts Calendar (60 points)
Touring Artists Bookings: 6 dates
Score: 960   **Rank: 141**

Athens–Cedar Creek Lake, TX
Common Denominators (300 points)

	Rating
Restaurants: 53	
Golf courses: 2 private (27 holes)	
Bowling center: 1 (18 lanes, tenpins)	C
Movie theater: 1 multiplex; 4 total screens	B

Outdoor Recreation Assets (333 points)
Inland Water Area: 60.3 square miles
    Cedar Creek Lake
State Recreation Area: 1 (1,562 acres)
Score: 633   **Rank: 147**

Austin, TX
Common Denominators (500 points)

	Rating
Restaurants: 1,251; 2 ★, 6 ★★, 6 ★★★	C
Golf courses: 14 private (279 holes); 11 daily fee (189 holes); 4 municipal (63 holes)	C
Bowling centers: 12 (266 lanes, tenpins)	C
Movie theaters: 4 single/twin, 12 multiplex; 71 total screens	B

The Lively Arts Calendar (1,460 points)
Touring Artists Bookings: 62 dates
Resident Ensembles:
    Austin Civic Orchestra (5 dates)
    Austin Lyric Opera (9 dates)
    Austin Symphony Orchestra (63 dates)
    University of Texas Symphony Orchestra (7 dates)
Outdoor Recreation Assets (67 points)
Inland Water Area: 35.6 square miles
    Tom Miller Dam
State Recreation Area: 1 (632 acres)
Score: 2,027   **Rank: 85**

Bar Harbor–Frenchman Bay, ME
Common Denominators (1,200 points)

	Rating
Restaurants: 144; 4 ★, 8 ★★, 1 ★★★	AA
Golf courses: 2 private (18 holes); 8 daily fee (90 holes)	AA
Bowling centers: 2 (16 lanes, mixed)	C
Movie theaters: 4 single/twin, 1 multiplex; 5 total screens	A

The Lively Arts Calendar (120 points)
Touring Artists Bookings: 12 dates
Outdoor Recreation Assets (1,480 points)
Atlantic Coastline: 30 miles
Inland Water Area: 392.8 square miles
    Frenchman Bay
National Parks, Forests, Wildlife Refuges:
    Acadia NP (36,690 acres)
State Recreation Areas: 7 (2,682 acres)
Score: 2,800   **Rank: 47**

Bellingham, WA
Common Denominators (900 points)

	Rating
Restaurants: 210; 1 ★, 2 ★★	C
Golf courses: 1 private (18 holes); 5 daily fee (72 holes); 1 municipal (18 holes)	A
Bowling centers: 3 (60 lanes, tenpins)	A
Movie theaters: 2 multiplex; 9 total screens	B

The Lively Arts Calendar (350 points)
Touring Artists Bookings: 25 dates
Resident Ensemble:

Rating

Western Symphony Orchestra (10 dates)
Outdoor Recreation Assets (2,000 points)
Puget Sound Area Coastline: 30 miles
Inland Water Area: 54.1 square miles
Baker Lake
Lake Whatcom
Ross Lake
National Parks, Forests, Wildlife Refuges:
Mt. Baker NF (452,629 acres)
North Cascades NP (281,690 acres)
Ross Lake NRA (107,064 acres)
San Juan Islands NWR (3 acres)
State Recreation Areas: 2 (1,205 acres)
Score: 3,250   **Rank: 31**

Bend, OR
Common Denominators (1,200 points)
Restaurants: 138; 3 ★, 6 ★★, 1 ★★★, 1 ★★★★   **AA**
Golf courses: 1 private (18 holes); 6 daily fee (126 holes)   **AA**
Bowling centers: 3 (26 lanes, tenpins)   **B**
Movie theaters: 2 single/twin, 1 multiplex; 5 total screens   **B**
Outdoor Recreation Assets (2,000 points)
Inland Water Area: 29.3 square miles
Crane Prairie Reservoir
Wickiup Reservoir
National Parks, Forests, Wildlife Refuges:
Deschutes NF (979,533 acres)
State Recreation Areas: 9 (4,093 acres)
Score: 3,200   **Rank: 32**

Bennington, VT
Common Denominators (1,100 points)
Restaurants: 87; 1 ★, 8 ★★, 6 ★★★   **AA**
Golf courses: 3 private (45 holes); 3 daily fee (45 holes)   **A**
Bowling center: 1 (18 lanes, tenpins)   **B**
Movie theater: 2 single/twin, 1 multiplex; 3 total screens   **B**
The Lively Arts Calendar (80 points)
Touring Artists Bookings: 8 dates
Outdoor Recreation Assets (1,445 points)
Inland Water Area: 0.8 square miles
National Parks, Forests, Wildlife Refuges:
Appalachian NS Trail (375 acres)
Green Mountain NF (123,503 acres)
State Recreation Areas: 3 (931 acres)
Score: 2,625   **Rank: 60**

Benton County, AR
Common Denominators (1,000 points)
Restaurants: 130; 1 ★★, 1 ★★★   **B**
Golf courses: 1 private (18 holes); 4 daily fee
(126 holes)   **A**
Bowling centers: 3 (44 lanes, tenpins)   **B**
Movie theaters: 2 single/twin, 1 multiplex; 10 total
screens   **A**
The Lively Arts Calendar (40 points)
Touring Artists Bookings: 4 dates
Outdoor Recreation Assets (407 points)
Inland Water Area: 35.2 square miles
National Parks, Forests, Wildlife Refuges:
Ozark NF (8,197 acres)
Pea Ridge NMP (4,280 acres)
State Recreation Area: 1 (10,787 acres)
Score: 1,447   **Rank: 115**

Biloxi–Gulfport–Pass Christian, MS
Common Denominators (900 points)
Restaurants: 259; 4 ★, 2 ★★, 3 ★★★   **B**
Golf courses: 5 private (99 holes); 4 daily fee (90 holes)   **B**
Bowling centers: 5 (100 lanes, tenpins)   **B**
Movie theaters: 3 single/twin, 5 multiplex; 28 total
screens   **A**
The Lively Arts Calendar (140 points)
Touring Artists Bookings: 7 dates
Resident Ensembles:

Rating

Gulf Coast Opera Theatre (2 dates)
Gulf Coast Symphony Orchestra (5 dates)
Outdoor Recreation Assets (1,146 points)
Gulf Coastline: 45 miles
Inland Water Area: 22.7 square miles
Biloxi Bay
St. Louis Bay
National Parks, Forests, Wildlife Refuges:
DeSoto NF (61,389 acres)
Gulf Islands NS (20,000 acres)
State Recreation Areas: 2 (393 acres)
Score: 2,186   **Rank: 77**

Blacksburg, VA
Common Denominators (600 points)
Restaurants: 89; 2 ★★   **C**
Golf courses: 1 private (18 holes); 1 daily fee (18 holes)   **C**
Bowling centers: 2 (48 lanes, tenpins)   **A**
Movie theaters: 3 single/twin; 5 total screens   **C**
The Lively Arts Calendar (170 points)
Touring Artists Bookings: 11 dates
Resident Ensemble:
New River Valley Symphony (6 dates)
Outdoor Recreation Assets (462 points)
Inland Water Area: 1.5 square miles
National Parks, Forests, Wildlife Refuges:
Appalachian NS Trail (151 acres)
Jefferson NF (21,992 acres)
Score: 1,232   **Rank: 126**

Bloomington–Brown County, IN
Common Denominators (1,100 points)
Restaurants: 170; 3 ★★, 1 ★★★   **B**
Golf courses: 2 private (27 holes); 2 daily fee (36 holes);
1 municipal (18 holes)   **B**
Bowling centers: 3 (68 lanes, tenpins)   **A**
Movie theaters: 2 single/twin, 3 multiplex; 17 total
screens   **AA**
The Lively Arts Calendar (560 points)
Touring Artists Bookings: 20 dates
Resident Ensembles:
Bloomington Symphony Orchestra (6 dates)
Indiana University Philharmonic (30 dates)
Outdoor Recreation Assets (764 points)
Inland Water Area: 31.4 square miles
Lake Lemon
Monroe Lake
National Parks, Forests, Wildlife Refuges:
Hoosier NF (35,566 acres)
State Recreation Area: 1 (15,543 acres)
Score: 2,424   **Rank: 68**

Boise, ID
Common Denominators (800 points)
Restaurants: 291; 3 ★★, 1 ★★★   **C**
Golf courses: 4 private (72 holes); 4 daily fee (63 holes);
1 municipal (9 holes)   **C**
Bowling centers: 6 (138 lanes, tenpins)   **A**
Movie theaters: 5 single/twin, 3 multiplex; 21 total
screens   **A**
The Lively Arts Calendar (1,390 points)
Touring Artists Bookings: 111 dates
Resident Ensembles:
Boise Opera (11 dates)
Boise Philharmonic Association (17 dates)
Outdoor Recreation Assets (77 points)
Inland Water Area: 8.6 square miles
Lucky Peak Lake
National Parks, Forests, Wildlife Refuges:
Boise NF (4,211 acres)
State Recreation Areas: 6 (826 acres)
Score: 2,267   **Rank: 74**

Rating

Bradenton, FL
Common Denominators (900 points)
Restaurants: 243; 2 ★, 6 ★★, 1 ★★★ B
Golf courses: 4 private (72 holes); 3 daily fee (72 holes);
2 municipal (36 holes) B
Bowling center: 1 (40 lanes, tenpins) C
Movie theaters: 3 single/twin, 3 multiplex; 27 total
screens AA
Outdoor Recreation Assets (532 points)
Gulf Coastline: 20 miles
Inland Water Area: 52.2 square miles
National Parks, Forests, Wildlife Refuges:
De Soto National Memorial (27 acres)
Passage Key NWR (36 acres)
State Recreation Areas: 3 (583 acres)
Score: 1,432   **Rank: 116**

Branson–Table Rock Lake, MO
Common Denominators (1,300 points)
Restaurants: 111; 1 ★, 4 ★★, 1 ★★★ AA
Golf courses: 1 private (18 holes); 4 daily fee (54 holes) A
Bowling centers: 2 (28 lanes, tenpins) A
Movie theaters: 1 single/twin, 1 multiplex; 5 total screens A
The Lively Arts Calendar (80 points)
Touring Artists Bookings: 8 dates
Outdoor Recreation Assets (756 points)
Inland Water Area: 103.4 square miles
Bull Shoals Lake
Table Rock Lake
Lake Taneycomo
National Parks, Forests, Wildlife Refuges:
Mark Twain NF (79,944 acres)
State Recreation Areas: 2 (3,732 acres)
Score: 2,136   **Rank: 80**

Brevard, NC
Common Denominators (800 points)
Restaurants: 30
Golf courses: 1 private (18 holes); 4 daily fee (72 holes) AA
Bowling center: 1 (18 lanes, tenpins) A
Movie theater: 1 single/twin; 1 screen C
The Lively Arts Calendar (310 points)
Resident Ensembles:
Brevard Music Center Opera (6 dates)
Brevard Music Center Orchestra (25 dates)
Outdoor Recreation Assets (1,839 points)
Inland Water Area: 1.8 square miles
Lake Toxaway
National Parks, Forests, Wildlife Refuges:
Blue Ridge Parkway (1,031 acres)
Nantahala NF (4,517 acres)
Pisgah NF (82,722 acres)
Score: 2,949   **Rank: 39**

Brownsville–Harlingen, TX
Common Denominators (1,000 points)
Restaurants: 269; 3 ★, 7 ★★, 2 ★★★ B
Golf courses: 6 private (108 holes); 2 daily fee (27 holes);
1 municipal (27 holes) C
Bowling centers: 7 (146 lanes, tenpins) A
Movie theaters: 4 single/twin, 6 multiplex; 48 total
screens AA
The Lively Arts Calendar (40 points)
Touring Artists Bookings: 4 dates
Outdoor Recreation Assets (1,752 points)
Gulf Coastline: 31 miles
Inland Water Area: 262.9 square miles
Laguna Atascosa
Laguna Madre
National Parks, Forests, Wildlife Refuges:
Laguna Atascosa NWR (44,922 acres)
Lower Rio Grande Valley NWR (2,251 acres)
Palo Alto Battlefield NHS (50 acres)
State Recreation Areas: 2 (217 acres)
Score: 2,792   **Rank: 49**

Rating

Brunswick–Golden Isles, GA
Common Denominators (1,400 points)
Restaurants: 113; 3 ★, 6 ★★, 2 ★★★ AA
Golf courses: 2 private (27 holes); 3 daily fee (81 holes);
1 municipal (63 holes) AA
Bowling center: 1 (24 lanes, tenpins) B
Movie theaters: 3 multiplex; 16 total screens AA
Outdoor Recreation Assets (731 points)
Atlantic Coastline: 21 miles
Inland Water Area: 45.1 square miles
St. Simons Sound
National Parks, Forests, Wildlife Refuges:
Fort Frederica NM (211 acres)
State Recreation Area: 1 (1,268 acres)
Score: 2,131   **Rank: 81**

Burlington, VT
Common Denominators (1,400 points)
Restaurants: 219; 1 ★, 6 ★★, 3 ★★★ A
Golf courses: 1 private (18 holes); 7 daily fee
(117 holes) A
Bowling centers: 6 (118 lanes, tenpins) AA
Movie theaters: 9 multiplex; 39 total screens AA
The Lively Arts Calendar (750 points)
Touring Artists Bookings: 44 dates
Resident Ensembles:
Vermont Symphony Orchestra (22 dates)
Vermont Youth Orchestra (9 dates)
Outdoor Recreation Assets (1,274 points)
Inland Water Area: 186.9 square miles
Lake Champlain
State Recreation Areas: 5 (13,414 acres)
Score: 3,424   **Rank: 21**

Burnet–Marble Falls–Llano, TX
Common Denominators (700 points)
Restaurants: 75
Golf courses: 1 private (54 holes); 3 daily fee (36 holes) A
Bowling center: 1 (20 lanes, tenpins) A
Movie theaters: 2 single/twin; 2 total screens C
Outdoor Recreation Assets (153 points)
Inland Water Area: 53.9 square miles
Lake Buchanan
Lake Lyndon B. Johnson
State Recreation Areas: 2 (4,549 acres)
Score: 853   **Rank: 144**

Camden–Penobscot Bay, ME
Common Denominators (900 points)
Restaurants: 60; 1 ★, 4 ★★, 2 ★★★ AA
Golf courses: 1 private (9 holes); 4 daily fee (54 holes) AA
Bowling centers: 2 (16 lanes, mixed) C
The Lively Arts Calendar (260 points)
Touring Artists Bookings: 26 dates
Outdoor Recreation Assets (1,660 points)
Atlantic Coastline: 45 miles
Inland Water Area: 103.0 square miles
Penobscot Bay
National Parks, Forests, Wildlife Refuges:
Acadia NP (4,120 acres)
Franklin Island NWR (12 acres)
Seal Island NWR (65 acres)
State Recreation Areas: 6 (3,091 acres)
Score: 2,820   **Rank: 46**

Canandaigua, NY
Common Denominators (1,200 points)
Restaurants: 140; 4 ★, 5 ★★, 2 ★★★ AA
Golf courses: 3 private (36 holes); 6 daily fee (99 holes) A
Bowling centers: 5 (148 lanes, tenpins) AA
Movie theater: 1 single/twin; 1 screen C
Outdoor Recreation Assets (145 points)
Inland Water Area: 18.2 square miles
Canandaigua Lake
State Recreation Areas: 5 (841 acres)
Score: 1,345   **Rank: 122**

Rating

Canton–Lake Tawakoni, TX
Common Denominators (200 points)
Restaurants: 28
Golf course: 1 private (18 holes)
Movie theaters: 3 single/twin; 3 total screens   **B**
Outdoor Recreation Assets (25 points)
Inland Water Area: 4.6 square miles
  Lake Tawakoni
Score: 225   **Rank: 151**

★ Cape Cod, MA
Common Denominators (1,400 points)
Restaurants: 603; 12 ★, 13 ★★, 10 ★★★, 1 ★★★★   **AA**
Golf courses: 8 private (153 holes); 10 daily fee
  (144 holes); 5 municipal (99 holes)   **A**
Bowling centers: 13 (187 lanes, mixed)   **A**
Movie theaters: 5 single/twin, 6 multiplex; 45 total
  screens   **AA**
The Lively Arts Calendar (820 points)
Touring Artists Bookings: 9 dates
Resident Ensembles:
  Cape Cod Symphony Orchestra Association
    (20 dates)
  College Light Opera Company (54 dates)
Outdoor Recreation Assets (1,763 points)
Atlantic Coastline: 110 miles
Inland Water Area: 56.9 square miles
  Cape Cod Bay
  Wellfleet Harbor
National Parks, Forests, Wildlife Refuges:
  Cape Cod NS (41,932 acres)
  Monomoy NWR (2,702 acres)
State Recreation Areas: 13 (1,043 acres)
Score: 3,983   **Rank: 7**

Cape May, NJ
Common Denominators (1,100 points)
Restaurants: 450; 1 ★, 10 ★★, 2 ★★★   **AA**
Golf courses: 1 private (18 holes); 3 daily fee (45 holes);
  1 municipal (9 holes)   **B**
Bowling center: 1 (32 lanes, tenpins)   **C**
Movie theaters: 7 single/twin, 2 multiplex; 22 total
  screens   **AA**
Outdoor Recreation Assets (1,100 points)
Atlantic Coastline: 40 miles
Inland Water Area: 23.3 square miles
  Cape May Harbor
State Recreation Areas: 4 (10,809 acres)
Score: 2,200   **Rank: 76**

Carlsbad–Artesia, NM
Common Denominators (900 points)
Restaurants: 66; 1 ★, 2 ★★   **B**
Golf courses: 2 private (27 holes); 1 municipal (18 holes)   **C**
Bowling centers: 3 (64 lanes, tenpins)   **AA**
Movie theaters: 1 single/twin, 1 multiplex; 5 total
  screens   **B**
The Lively Arts Calendar (100 points)
Touring Artists Bookings: 10 dates
Outdoor Recreation Assets (361 points)
Inland Water Area: 12.6 square miles
National Parks, Forests, Wildlife Refuges:
  Carlsbad Caverns NP (46,430 acres)
  Lincoln NF (135,013 acres)
State Recreation Areas: 2 (4,107 acres)
Score: 1,361   **Rank: 120**

Carson City–Minden, NV
Common Denominators (900 points)
Restaurants: 90; 1 ★, 2 ★★   **B**
Golf courses: 3 daily fee (45 holes); 1 municipal
  (36 holes)   **A**
Bowling center: 1 (44 lanes, tenpins)   **A**
Movie theaters: 1 single/twin, 1 multiplex; 4 total screens   **C**

Rating

The Lively Arts Calendar (110 points)
Touring Artists Bookings: 5 dates
Resident Ensemble:
  Carson City Chamber Orchestra (6 dates)
Outdoor Recreation Assets (764 points)
Inland Water Area: 39.3 square miles
  Lake Tahoe
National Parks, Forests, Wildlife Refuges:
  Eldorado NF (53 acres)
  Toiyabe NF (62,115 acres)
State Recreation Area: 1 (2 acres)
Score: 1,774   **Rank: 99**

Chapel Hill, NC
Common Denominators (900 points)
Restaurants: 136; 1 ★, 4 ★★, 2 ★★★   **A**
Golf courses: 2 private (36 holes); 3 daily fee (45 holes)   **B**
Bowling center: 1 (12 lanes, tenpins)   **C**
Movie theaters: 2 single/twin, 2 multiplex, 10 total
  screens   **A**
The Lively Arts Calendar (70 points)
Touring Artists Bookings: 7 dates
Outdoor Recreation Assets (50 points)
Inland Water Area: 0.7 square miles
State Recreation Area: 1 (2,064 acres)
Score: 1,020   **Rank: 137**

★ Charleston, SC
Common Denominators (1,100 points)
Restaurants: 468; 11 ★★, 9 ★★★   **A**
Golf courses: 6 private (126 holes); 5 daily fee
  (144 holes); 1 municipal (18 holes)   **B**
Bowling centers: 7 (176 lanes, tenpins)   **A**
Movie theaters: 5 single/twin, 5 multiplex; 32 total
  screens   **A**
The Lively Arts Calendar (970 points)
Touring Artists Bookings: 19 dates
Resident Ensembles:
  Charleston Symphony Orchestra (40 dates)
  Spoleto Festival U.S.A. (38 dates)
Outdoor Recreation Assets (1,972 points)
Atlantic Coastline: 75 miles
Inland Water Area: 108.2 square miles
  Bulls Bay
  Intracoastal Waterway
National Parks, Forests, Wildlife Refuges:
  Cape Romain NWR (34,049 acres)
  Fort Sumpter NM (197 acres)
  Francis Marion NF (58,914 acres)
State Recreation Areas: 3 (1,536 acres)
Score: 4,042   **Rank: 6**

Charlevoix–Boyne City, MI
Common Denominators (1,400 points)
Restaurants: 40; 2 ★★, 1 ★★★   **AA**
Golf courses: 5 daily fee (90 holes); 1 municipal
  (9 holes)   **AA**
Bowling centers: 3 (24 lanes, tenpins)   **AA**
Movie theaters: 2 single/twin; 2 total screens   **B**
Outdoor Recreation Assets (562 points)
Lake Michigan Coastline: 10 miles
Inland Water Area: 36.8 square miles
National Parks, Forests, Wildlife Refuges:
  Michigan Islands NWR (233 acres)
State Recreation Area: 1 (3,400 acres)
Score: 1,962   **Rank: 89**

Charlottesville, VA
Common Denominators (800 points)
Restaurants: 188; 5 ★★, 2 ★★★   **A**
Golf courses: 4 private (81 holes); 1 daily fee (18 holes);
  2 municipal (18 holes)   **C**
Bowling center: 1 (40 lanes, tenpins)   **C**
Movie theaters: 5 single/twin, 2 multiplex; 15 total
  screens   **A**

Rating

The Lively Arts Calendar (520 points)
Touring Artists Bookings: 17 dates
Resident Ensembles:
Ash Lawn–Highland Opera Company (25 dates)
Charlottesville & University Symphony Orchestra (10
dates)
Outdoor Recreation Assets (208 points)
Inland Water Area: 1.1 square miles
National Parks, Forests, Wildlife Refuges:
Appalachian NS Trail (928 acres)
Shenandoah NP (29,860 acres)
Score: 1,528   **Rank: 111**

Chico–Paradise, CA
Common Denominators (500 points)
Restaurants: 243; 1 ★★   C
Golf courses: 1 private (18 holes); 2 daily fee (18 holes);
2 municipal (36 holes)   C
Bowling centers: 3 (74 lanes, tenpins)   B
Movie theaters: 2 single/twin, 2 multiplex; 9 total screens C
The Lively Arts Calendar (590 points)
Touring Artists Bookings: 48 dates
Resident Ensembles:
Chico Symphony Orchestra (6 dates)
Paradise Symphony Orchestra (5 dates)
Outdoor Recreation Assets (455 points)
Inland Water Area: 30.1 square miles
Lake Oroville
National Parks, Forests, Wildlife Refuges:
Lassen NF (49,237 acres)
State Recreation Areas: 4 (29,158 acres)
Score: 1,545   **Rank: 109**

Clayton, GA
Common Denominators (500 points)
Restaurants: 20; 1 ★   B
Golf courses: 1 private (27 holes); 1 municipal (9 holes) A
Outdoor Recreation Assets (2,000 points)
Inland Water Area: 6.7 square miles
Lake Burton
Lake Rabun
National Parks, Forests, Wildlife Refuges:
Appalachian NS Trail (190 acres)
Chattahoochee NF (148,573 acres)
State Recreation Areas: 2 (1,402 acres)
Score: 2,505   **Rank: 67**

Clear Lake, CA
Common Denominators (700 points)
Restaurants: 94
Golf courses: 6 daily fee (63 holes)   A
Bowling centers: 2 (22 lanes, tenpins)   B
Movie theaters: 2 single/twin; 4 total screens   B
Outdoor Recreation Assets (277 points)
Inland Water Area: 67.1 square miles
Clear Lake
Indian Valley Reservoir
State Recreation Areas: 3 (4,615 acres)
Score: 984   **Rank: 139**

Coeur d'Alene, ID
Common Denominators (800 points)
Restaurants: 104; 1 ★★, 1 ★★★   B
Golf courses: 1 private (18 holes); 2 daily fee (36 holes) B
Bowling centers: 2 (22 lanes, tenpins)   C
Movie theaters: 2 multiplex; 8 total screens   A
The Lively Arts Calendar (160 points)
Touring Artists Bookings: 10 dates
Resident Ensemble:
North Idaho Symphony Orchestra (6 dates)
Outdoor Recreation Assets (1,789 points)
Inland Water Area: 70.0 square miles
Coeur d'Alene Lake
Hayden Lake
Spirit Lake

Rating

National Parks, Forests, Wildlife Refuges:
Coeur d'Alene NF (242,846 acres)
State Recreation Areas: 3 (12,710 acres)
Score: 2,749   **Rank: 50**

Colorado Springs, CO
Common Denominators (1,000 points)
Restaurants: 584; 9 ★★, 3 ★★★, 1 ★★★★   B
Golf courses: 10 private (225 holes); 3 daily fee
(45 holes); 2 municipal (45 holes)   C
Bowling centers: 12 (302 lanes, tenpins)   AA
Movie theaters: 6 single/twin, 7 multiplex; 45 total
screens   A
The Lively Arts Calendar (950 points)
Touring Artists Bookings: 26 dates
Resident Ensembles:
Colorado Opera Festival (2 dates)
Colorado Springs Symphony Orchestra (65 dates)
Outdoor Recreation Assets (374 points)
Inland Water Area: 2.1 square miles
National Parks, Forests, Wildlife Refuges:
Pike NF (100,723 acres)
Score: 2,324   **Rank: 72**

Columbia County, NY
Common Denominators (900 points)
Restaurants: 82; 1 ★★, 2 ★★★, 1 ★★★★   A
Golf courses: 3 private (54 holes); 1 daily fee (9 holes) C
Bowling centers: 3 (36 lanes, tenpins)   A
Movie theaters: 2 single/twin, 1 multiplex; 5 total
screens   B
Outdoor Recreation Assets (157 points)
Inland Water Area: 9.6 square miles
Copake Lake
National Parks, Forests, Wildlife Refuges:
Martin Van Buren NHS (40 acres)
State Recreation Areas: 4 (6,808 acres)
Score: 1,057   **Rank: 134**

Crossville, TN
Common Denominators (1,000 points)
Restaurants: 35; 2 ★, 1 ★★★   A
Golf courses: 3 private (45 holes); 2 daily fee (54 holes) AA
Bowling center: 1 (16 lanes, tenpins)   B
Movie theater: 1 single/twin; 2 total screens   C
The Lively Arts Calendar (90 points)
Touring Artists Bookings: 9 dates
Outdoor Recreation Assets (34 points)
Inland Water Area: 2.1 square miles
National Parks, Forests, Wildlife Refuges:
Obed Wild and Scenic River (50 acres)
State Recreation Area: 1 (1,562 acres)
Score: 1,124   **Rank: 131**

Daytona Beach, FL
Common Denominators (1,000 points)
Restaurants: 559; 1 ★, 5 ★★, 1 ★★★   C
Golf courses: 4 private (72 holes); 9 daily fee
(180 holes); 2 municipal (54 holes)   A
Bowling centers: 8 (240 lanes, tenpins)   A
Movie theaters: 7 single/twin, 6 multiplex; 38 total
screens   A
The Lively Arts Calendar (660 points)
Touring Artists Bookings: 59 dates
Resident Ensemble:
Stetson University Orchestra (7 dates)
Outdoor Recreation Assets (1,429 points)
Atlantic Coastline: 49 miles
Inland Water Area: 151.9 square miles
Intracoastal Waterway
Lake Dexter
National Parks, Forests, Wildlife Refuges:
Canaveral NS (28,148 acres)
Lake Woodruff NWR (18,506 acres)
State Recreation Areas: 12 (8,305 acres)
Score: 3,089   **Rank: 37**

Rating

Deming, NM
Common Denominators (1,000 points)
Restaurants: 18; 1 ★   B
Golf course: 1 daily fee (9 holes)   B
Bowling center: 1 (8 lanes, tenpins)   B
Movie theater: 1 multiplex; 3 total screens   AA
Outdoor Recreation Assets (1 point)
State Recreation Areas: 2 (313 acres)
Score: 1,001   **Rank: 138**

Door County, WI
Common Denominators (1,300 points)
Restaurants: 45; 11 ★, 8 ★★, 1 ★★★   AA
Golf courses: 6 daily fee (99 holes); 1 municipal
   (18 holes)   AA
Bowling centers: 2 (18 lanes, tenpins)   A
Movie theaters: 2 single/twin; 2 total screens   B
Outdoor Recreation Assets (1,276 points)
Lake Michigan Coastline: 100 miles
Inland Water Area: 20.5 square miles
   Sturgeon Bay
National Parks, Forests, Wildlife Refuges:
   Gravel Island NWR (27 acres)
   Green Bay NWR (2 acres)
State Recreation Areas: 5 (4,959 acres)
Score: 2,576   **Rank: 64**

Eagle River, WI
Common Denominators (1,300 points)
Restaurants: 53; 6 ★, 4 ★★   AA
Golf courses: 2 private (27 holes); 4 daily fee (45 holes);
   1 municipal (9 holes)   AA
Bowling centers: 2 (18 lanes, tenpins)   AA
Movie theaters: 1 single/twin; 2 total screens   C
The Lively Arts Calendar (90 points)
Touring Artists Bookings: 9 dates
Outdoor Recreation Assets (2,000 points)
Inland Water Area: 150.5 square miles
National Parks, Forests, Wildlife Refuges:
   Chequamegon NF (6,457 acres)
   Nicolet NF (47,768 acres)
State Recreation Area: 1 (168,472 acres)
Score: 3,390   **Rank: 24**

Easton–Chesapeake Bay, MD
Common Denominators (1,500 points)
Restaurants: 57; 1★, 1 ★★, 4 ★★★   AA
Golf courses: 2 private (36 holes); 1 municipal (18 holes)   A
Bowling center: 1 (24 lanes, tenpins)   AA
Movie theaters: 2 single/twin, 2 multiplex; 5 total screens AA
The Lively Arts Calendar (50 points)
Touring Artists Bookings: 5 dates
Outdoor Recreation Assets (1,436 points)
Chesapeake Coastline: 40 miles
Inland Water Area: 67.7 square miles
   Chesapeake Bay
State Recreation Area: 1 (29 acres)
Score: 2,986   **Rank: 38**

Edenton–Albemarle Sound, NC
Common Denominators (300 points)
Restaurants: 15; 1 ★★   A
Golf course: 1 private (9 holes)
Outdoor Recreation Assets (1,345 points)
Albemarle Sound Coastline: 10 miles
Inland Water Area: 60.3 square miles
   Albemarle Sound
Score: 1,645   **Rank: 105**

El Centro–Calexico–Brawley, CA
Common Denominators (400 points)
Restaurants: 130; 1 ★   C
Golf courses: 1 private (18 holes); 2 daily fee (27 holes)   C
Bowling center: 1 (24 lanes, tenpins)   C

Rating

Movie theaters: 2 single/twin, 2 multiplex; 2 total screens C
The Lively Arts Calendar (400 points)
Touring Artists Bookings: 30 dates
Resident Ensemble:
   Imperial Valley Chamber Orchestra (10 dates)
Outdoor Recreation Assets (388 points)
Inland Water Area: 309.5 square miles
National Parks, Forests, Wildlife Refuges:
   Salton Sea NWR (9,703 acres)
State Recreation Areas: 2 (14,700 acres)
Score: 1,188   **Rank: 128**

★ Eugene–Springfield, OR
Common Denominators (900 points)
Restaurants: 438; 2 ★, 1 ★★, 4 ★★★   B
Golf courses: 3 private (45 holes); 6 daily fee (81 holes);
   1 municipal (9 holes)   C
Bowling centers: 10 (154 lanes, tenpins)   A
Movie theaters: 6 single/twin, 4 multiplex; 34 total
   screens   A
The Lively Arts Calendar (580 points)
Touring Artists Bookings: 21 dates
Resident Ensembles:
   Eugene Opera (6 dates)
   Eugene Symphony Orchestra (16 dates)
   Oregon Mozart Players (9 dates)
   University of Oregon Symphony Orchestra (6 dates)
Outdoor Recreation Assets (2,000 points)
Pacific Coastline: 30 miles
Inland Water Area: 58.2 square miles
   Fall Creek Lake
   Fern Ridge Lake
   Lookout Point Lake
National Parks, Forests, Wildlife Refuges:
   Oregon Islands NWR (12 acres)
   Siuslaw NF (243,161 acres)
   Umpqua NF (151,594 acres)
   Willamette NF (1,021,952 acres)
State Recreation Areas: 19 (4,840 acres)
Score: 3,480   **Rank: 18**

Fairhope–Gulf Shores, AL
Common Denominators (700 points)
Restaurants: 156; 3 ★, 1 ★★   C
Golf courses: 4 private (81 holes); 3 daily fee (45 holes);
   2 municipal (36 holes)   A
Bowling centers: 3 (40 lanes, tenpins)   B
Movie theaters: 1 single/twin, 1 multiplex; 4 total screens C
The Lively Arts Calendar (60 points)
Touring Artists Bookings: 6 dates
Outdoor Recreation Assets (580 points)
Gulf Coastline: 27 miles
Inland Water Area: 91.1 square miles
   Bon Secour Bay
National Parks, Forests, Wildlife Refuges:
   Bon Secour NWR (2,677 acres)
State Recreation Area: 1 (6,000 acres)
Score: 1,340   **Rank: 123**

Fayetteville, AR
Common Denominators (1,000 points)
Restaurants: 158; 1 ★, 1 ★★, 1 ★★★   B
Golf courses: 1 private (18 holes); 3 daily fee (36 holes)   C
Bowling centers: 2 (68 lanes, tenpins)   A
Movie theaters: 5 single/twin, 2 multiplex; 24 total
   screens   AA
The Lively Arts Calendar (360 points)
Touring Artists Bookings: 16 dates
Resident Ensemble:
   North Arkansas Symphony Orchestra (20 dates)
Outdoor Recreation Assets (235 points)
Inland Water Area: 5.3 square miles
National Parks, Forests, Wildlife Refuges:
   Ozark NF (23,195 acres)
State Recreation Areas: 2 (1,829 acres)
Score: 1,595   **Rank: 106**

★ Fort Collins–Loveland, CO
Common Denominators (1,000 points)
Restaurants: 280; 3 ★, 4 ★★ — **B**
Golf courses: 3 private (45 holes); 2 daily fee (36 holes);
  4 municipal (63 holes) — **B**
Bowling centers: 8 (136 lanes, tenpins) — **AA**
Movie theaters: 4 single/twin, 3 multiplex; 18 total
  screens — **B**
The Lively Arts Calendar (520 points)
Touring Artists Bookings: 31 dates
Resident Ensembles:
  Colorado State University Orchestra (6 dates)
  Fort Collins Symphony Orchestra (15 dates)
Outdoor Recreation Assets (2,000 points)
Inland Water Area: 29.0 square miles
  Horsetooth Reservoir
National Parks, Forests, Wildlife Refuges:
  Rocky Mountain NP (143,500 acres)
  Roosevelt NF (624,987 acres)
State Recreation Areas: 2 (2,616 acres)
Score: 3,520 — **Rank: 17**

Fort Lauderdale–Hollywood– Pompano Beach, FL
Common Denominators (1,000 points)
Restaurants: 1,972; 14 ★, 21 ★★, 3 ★★★, 1 ★★★★ — **B**
Golf courses: 19 private (432 holes); 20 daily fee
  (459 holes); 2 municipal (72 holes) — **B**
Bowling centers: 16 (478 lanes, tenpins) — **B**
Movie theaters: 7 single/twin, 26 multiplex; 181 total
  screens — **AA**
The Lively Arts Calendar (2,000 points)
Touring Artists Bookings: 98 dates
Resident Ensembles:
  Broward Community College Symphony (19 dates)
  Broward Symphony Orchestra (8 dates)
  Gold Coast Opera (9 dates)
  Philharmonic Orchestra of Florida (160 dates)
  South Florida Symphony Orchestra (45 dates)
  The Opera Guild (5 dates)
Outdoor Recreation Assets (293 points)
Atlantic Coastline: 25 miles
Inland Water Area: 10.2 square miles
State Recreation Areas: 2 (431 acres)
Score: 3,293 — **Rank: 29**

★ Fort Myers–Cape Coral–Sanibel Island, FL
Common Denominators (1,400 points)
Restaurants: 512; 4 ★, 16 ★★, 4 ★★★ — **A**
Golf courses: 9 private (189 holes); 15 daily fee
  (261 holes); 4 municipal (72 holes) — **A**
Bowling centers: 10 (248 lanes, tenpins) — **AA**
Movie theaters: 2 single/twin, 5 multiplex; 48 total
  screens — **AA**
The Lively Arts Calendar (1,990 points)
Touring Artists Bookings: 182 dates
Resident Ensemble:
  Southwest Florida Symphony Orchestra (17 dates)
Outdoor Recreation Assets (1,807 points)
Gulf Coastline: 38 miles
Inland Water Area: 283.0 square miles
  Caloosahatchee River Estuary
  Pine Island Sound
  San Carlos Bay
National Parks, Forests, Wildlife Refuges:
  Caloosahatchee NWR (40 acres)
  J.N. Ding Darling NWR (4,960 acres)
  Matlacha Pass NWR (244 acres)
  Pine Island NWR (404 acres)
State Recreation Areas: 7 (3,319 acres)
Score: 5,197 — **Rank: 1**

Fort Walton Beach, FL
Common Denominators (1,000 points)
Restaurants: 265; 1 ★, 5 ★★, 1 ★★★ — **B**
Golf courses: 2 private (45 holes); 6 daily fee
  (135 holes); 1 municipal (27 holes) — **A**
Bowling centers: 4 (68 lanes, tenpins) — **B**
Movie theaters: 2 single/twin, 4 multiplex; 19 total
  screens — **A**
Outdoor Recreation Assets (578 points)
Gulf Coastline: 24 miles
Inland Water Area: 59.6 square miles
  Choctawhatchee Bay
National Parks, Forests, Wildlife Refuges:
  Choctawhatchee NF (796 acres)
  Gulf Islands NS (3,500 acres)
State Recreation Areas: 2 (566 acres)
Score: 1,578 — **Rank: 107**

Fredericksburg, TX
Common Denominators (500 points)
Restaurants: 28
Golf course: 1 municipal (9 holes) — **B**
Bowling center: 1 (10 lanes, tenpins) — **A**
Outdoor Recreation Assets (7 points)
National Parks, Forests, Wildlife Refuges:
  Lyndon B. Johnson NHP (500 acres)
State Recreation Area: 1 (354 acres)
Score: 507 — **Rank: 149**

Gainesville, FL
Common Denominators (800 points)
Restaurants: 280; 1 ★★, 3 ★★★ — **B**
Golf courses: 3 private (54 holes); 2 daily fee (36 holes) — **C**
Bowling centers: 3 (80 lanes, tenpins) — **B**
Movie theaters: 2 single/twin, 4 multiplex; 22 total
  screens — **A**
The Lively Arts Calendar (270 points)
Touring Artists Bookings: 21 dates
Resident Ensemble:
  Gainesville Chamber Orchestra (6 dates)
Outdoor Recreation Assets (592 points)
Inland Water Area: 68.0 square miles
State Recreation Areas: 7 (30,043 acres)
Score: 1,662 — **Rank: 104**

Grand Junction, CO
Common Denominators (1,100 points)
Restaurants: 125; 2 ★★ — **C**
Golf courses: 1 private (18 holes); 1 daily fee (18 holes);
  2 municipal (27 holes) — **B**
Bowling centers: 2 (76 lanes, tenpins) — **AA**
Movie theaters: 4 single/twin, 2 multiplex; 16 total
  screens — **AA**
The Lively Arts Calendar (160 points)
Touring Artists Bookings: 5 dates
Resident Ensemble:
  Grand Junction Symphony Orchestra (11 dates)
Outdoor Recreation Assets (1,380 points)
Inland Water Area: 32.9 square miles
National Parks, Forests, Wildlife Refuges:
  Colorado NM (20,500 acres)
  Grand Mesa NF (252,648 acres)
  Manti-La Sal NF (4,542 acres)
  Uncompahgre NF (207,256 acres)
  White River NF (81,289 acres)
State Recreation Areas: 3 (2,456 acres)
Score: 2,640 — **Rank: 59**

Grand Lake, OK
Common Denominators (600 points)
Restaurants: 36; 1 ★★, 1 ★★★ — **A**
Golf course: 1 daily fee (9 holes) — **C**
Bowling center: 1 (12 lanes, tenpins) — **B**
Outdoor Recreation Assets (464 points)
Inland Water Area: 71.7 square miles

Rating

Grand Lake O' the Cherokees
State Recreation Areas: 5 (902 acres)
Score: 1,064   **Rank: 133**

Grants Pass, OR
Common Denominators (900 points)
Restaurants: 100; 2 ★★   **B**
Golf courses: 1 private (27 holes); 1 daily fee (9 holes)   **C**
Bowling centers: 2 (56 lanes, tenpins)   **AA**
Movie theaters: 2 single/twin, 1 multiplex; 5 total screens   **B**
The Lively Arts Calendar (60 points)
Touring Artists Bookings: 6 dates
Outdoor Recreation Assets (1,938 points)
Inland Water Area: 0.2 square miles
National Parks, Forests, Wildlife Refuges:
Oregon Caves NM (485 acres)
Rogue River NF (31,155 acres)
Siskiyou NF (374,069 acres)
State Recreation Areas: 7 (1,312 acres)
Score: 2,898   **Rank: 40**

Grass Valley–Truckee, CA
Common Denominators (500 points)
Restaurants: 108; 2 ★★, 1 ★★★   **B**
Golf courses: 2 private (36 holes); 1 daily fee (9 holes)   **C**
Bowling center: 1 (10 lanes, tenpins)   **C**
Movie theaters: 2 single/twin, 1 multiplex; 5 total screens   **C**
The Lively Arts Calendar (60 points)
Resident Ensemble:
Sierra Community Orchestra (6 dates)
Outdoor Recreation Assets (1,492 points)
Inland Water Area: 14.3 square miles
Englebright Lake
Prosser Creek Reservoir
National Parks, Forests, Wildlife Refuges:
Tahoe NF (169,050 acres)
Toiyabe NF (2,574 acres)
State Recreation Areas: 4 (5,057 acres)
Score: 2,052   **Rank: 84**

Hamilton–Bitterroot Valley, MT
Common Denominators (600 points)
Restaurants: 27
Golf courses: 1 private (9 holes); 1 municipal (18 holes)   **A**
Bowling centers: 2 (16 lanes, tenpins)   **A**
Outdoor Recreation Assets (2,000 points)
Inland Water Area: 6.5 square miles
National Parks, Forests, Wildlife Refuges:
Bitterroot NF (1,106,493 acres)
Lee Metcalf NWR (2,696 acres)
Lolo NF (8,131 acres)
State Recreation Areas: 3 (13,458 acres)
Score: 2,606   **Rank: 61**

★ Hanover, NH
Common Denominators (1,200 points)
Restaurants: 157; 6 ★, 12 ★★, 3 ★★★   **AA**
Golf courses: 1 private (9 holes); 9 daily fee (108 holes);
1 municipal (18 holes)   **AA**
Movie theaters: 2 multiplex; 10 total screens   **AA**
The Lively Arts Calendar (790 points)
Touring Artists Bookings: 72 dates
Resident Ensemble:
New Hampshire Youth Orchestra (7 dates)
Outdoor Recreation Assets (1,734 points)
Inland Water Area: 30.3 square miles
Mascoma Lake
Newfound Lake
National Parks, Forests, Wildlife Refuges:
Appalachian NS Trail (5,780 acres)
White Mountain NF (340,953 acres)
State Recreation Areas: 23 (22,618 acres)
Score: 3,724   **Rank: 11**

Rating

Harrison, AR
Common Denominators (900 points)
Restaurants: 36; 1 ★   **C**
Golf courses: 1 private (9 holes); 2 daily fee (27 holes)   **A**
Bowling center: 1 (20 lanes, tenpins)   **A**
Movie theaters: 1 single/twin; 2 total screens   **B**
Outdoor Recreation Assets (145 points)
Inland Water Area: 17.7 square miles
Bull Shoals Lake
Score: 1,045   **Rank: 136**

Hendersonville, NC
Common Denominators (700 points)
Restaurants: 97; 1 ★★   **C**
Golf courses: 1 private (18 holes); 3 daily fee (54 holes)   **A**
Bowling center: 1 (32 lanes, tenpins)   **B**
Movie theater: 1 multiplex; 4 total screens   **C**
The Lively Arts Calendar (50 points)
Resident Ensemble:
Hendersonville Symphony Orchestra (5 dates)
Outdoor Recreation Assets (382 points)
Inland Water Area: 0.5 square miles
National Parks, Forests, Wildlife Refuges:
Blue Ridge Parkway (522 acres)
Carl Sandburg Home NHS (264 acres)
Pisgah NF (17,295 acres)
Score: 1,132   **Rank: 130**

Hilton Head–Beaufort, SC
Common Denominators (1,500 points)
Restaurants: 171; 2 ★, 5 ★★, 4 ★★★   **AA**
Golf courses: 15 private (297 holes); 13 daily fee
(315 holes)   **AA**
Bowling centers: 5 (96 lanes, tenpins)   **AA**
Movie theaters: 2 single/twin, 2 multiplex; 10 total
screens   **A**
The Lively Arts Calendar (100 points)
Resident Ensemble:
Hilton Head Orchestra (10 dates)
Outdoor Recreation Assets (1,232 points)
Atlantic Coastline: 36 miles
Inland Water Area: 112.5 square miles
Port Royal Sound
State Recreation Area: 1 (5,000 acres)
Score: 2,832   **Rank: 45**

★ Honolulu, HI
Common Denominators (500 points)
Restaurants: 1,367
Golf courses: 8 private (153 holes); 9 daily fee
(162 holes); 4 municipal (63 holes)   **C**
Bowling centers: 28 (550 lanes, tenpins)   **A**
Movie theaters: 9 single/twin, 5 multiplex; 47 total
screens   **C**
The Lively Arts Calendar (2,000 points)
Touring Artists Bookings: 94 dates
Resident Ensembles:
Hawaii Opera Theatre (9 dates)
Honolulu Symphony Orchestra (150 dates)
Outdoor Recreation Assets (1,684 points)
Pacific Coastline: 135 miles
Inland Water Area: 24.2 square miles
National Parks, Forests, Wildlife Refuges:
Hawaiian Islands NWR (1,907 acres)
State Recreation Areas: 25 (9,103 acres)
Score: 4,184   **Rank: 5**

Hot Springs National Park, AR
Common Denominators (800 points)
Restaurants: 125; 1 ★, 3 ★★, 2 ★★★   **A**
Golf courses: 4 private (72 holes); 3 daily fee (72 holes)   **A**
Bowling center: 1 (24 lanes, tenpins)   **C**
Movie theaters: 1 single/twin, 2 multiplex; 3 total
screens   **C**

	Rating
Outdoor Recreation Assets (1,724 points)	
Inland Water Area: 77.5 square miles	
Lake Hamilton	
Lake Ouachita	
National Parks, Forests, Wildlife Refuges:	
Hot Springs National Park (4,835 acres)	
Ouachita NF (106,984 acres)	
State Recreation Area: 1 (370 acres)	
Score: 2,524	**Rank: 66**

Houghton Lake, MI

	Rating
Common Denominators (1,400 points)	
Restaurants: 48; 1 ★, 1 ★★	A
Golf courses: 5 daily fee (63 holes)	AA
Bowling centers: 3 (28 lanes, tenpins)	AA
Movie theaters: 2 single/twin; 2 total screens	A
The Lively Arts Calendar (50 points)	
Touring Artists Bookings: 5 dates	
Outdoor Recreation Assets (469 points)	
Inland Water Area: 52.0 square miles	
Higgins Lake	
Houghton Lake	
Lake St. Helen	
State Recreation Areas: 2 (1,390 acres)	
Score: 1,919	**Rank: 92**

Iowa City, IA

	Rating
Common Denominators (800 points)	
Restaurants: 117; 1 ★★	C
Golf courses: 1 private (9 holes); 3 daily fee (27 holes); 1 municipal (18 holes)	B
Bowling centers: 3 (60 lanes, tenpins)	A
Movie theaters: 3 single/twin, 1 multiplex; 8 total screens	B
The Lively Arts Calendar (460 points)	
Touring Artists Bookings: 40 dates	
Resident Ensemble:	
University of Iowa Symphony (6 dates)	
Outdoor Recreation Assets (102 points)	
Inland Water Area: 9.1 square miles	
Coralville Reservoir	
Lake McBride	
State Recreation Areas: 2 (2,154 acres)	
Score: 1,362	**Rank: 119**

★ Kalispell, MT

	Rating
Common Denominators (1,300 points)	
Restaurants: 131; 3 ★, 10 ★★, 1 ★★★	AA
Golf courses: 4 daily fee (81 holes)	AA
Bowling centers: 4 (46 lanes, tenpins)	AA
Movie theaters: 1 single/twin, 1 multiplex; 3 total screens	C
The Lively Arts Calendar (140 points)	
Touring Artists Bookings: 6 dates	
Resident Ensemble:	
Glacier Orchestra & Chorale (8 dates)	
Outdoor Recreation Assets (2,000 points)	
Inland Water Area: 143.2 square miles	
Flathead Lake	
Hungry Horse Reservoir	
Whitefish Lake	
National Parks, Forests, Wildlife Refuges:	
Flathead NF (1,716,287 acres)	
Glacier NP (370,200 acres)	
Kootenai NF (53,453 acres)	
Lolo NF (18,080 acres)	
State Recreation Areas: 5 (9,780 acres)	
Score: 3,440	**Rank: 19**

Keene, NH

	Rating
Common Denominators (900 points)	
Restaurants: 84; 3 ★★	B
Golf courses: 1 private (9 holes); 4 daily fee (54 holes)	A
Bowling centers: 2 (38 lanes, mixed)	B

	Rating
Movie theater: 1 multiplex; 6 total screens	B
The Lively Arts Calendar (140 points)	
Touring Artists Bookings: 14 dates	
Outdoor Recreation Assets (315 points)	
Inland Water Area: 19.0 square miles	
Spofford Lake	
Silver Lake	
State Recreation Areas: 17 (17,277 acres)	
Score: 1,355	**Rank: 121**

Kerrville, TX

	Rating
Common Denominators (900 points)	
Restaurants: 46; 3 ★★	A
Golf courses: 1 private (18 holes); 1 municipal (18 holes)	B
Bowling center: 1 (16 lanes, tenpins)	B
Movie theaters: 2 single/twin; 3 total screens	B
Outdoor Recreation Assets (4 points)	
State Recreation Area: 1 (497 acres)	
Score: 904	**Rank: 142**

★ Key West–Key Largo–Marathon, FL

	Rating
Common Denominators (1,200 points)	
Restaurants: 248; 8 ★, 12 ★★, 3 ★★★	AA
Golf courses: 3 private (72 holes); 1 daily fee (18 holes)	C
Bowling centers: 4 (98 lanes, tenpins)	AA
Movie theaters: 3 single/twin, 1 multiplex; 9 total screens	A
The Lively Arts Calendar (240 points)	
Touring Artists Bookings: 24 dates	
Outdoor Recreation Assets (2,000 points)	
Florida Straits Coastline: 160 miles	
Inland Water Area: 414.0 square miles	
National Parks, Forests, Wildlife Refuges:	
Big Cypress National Preserve (126,000 acres)	
Crocodile Lake NWR (3,998 acres)	
Everglades NP (943,630 acres)	
Fort Jefferson NM (61,500 acres)	
Great White Heron NWR (7,408 acres)	
Key West NWR (2,019 acres)	
National Key Deer NWR (7,874 acres)	
State Recreation Areas: 9 (4,876 acres)	
Score: 3,440	**Rank: 19**

Laconia–Lake Winnipesaukee, NH

	Rating
Common Denominators (1,400 points)	
Restaurants: 117; 1 ★★, 3 ★★★	AA
Golf courses: 8 daily fee (90 holes)	AA
Bowling center: 1 (24 lanes, tenpins)	B
Movie theaters: 3 single/twin, 2 multiplex; 12 total screens	AA
The Lively Arts Calendar (650 points)	
Touring Artists Bookings: 40 dates	
Resident Ensemble:	
New Hampshire Music Festival Orchestra (25 dates)	
Outdoor Recreation Assets (788 points)	
Inland Water Area: 66.9 square miles	
Lake Winnipesaukee	
State Recreation Areas: 18 (4,688 acres)	
Score: 2,838	**Rank: 44**

Lake Havasu City–Kingman, AZ

	Rating
Common Denominators (900 points)	
Restaurants: 137; 2 ★, 3 ★★, 1 ★★★	A
Golf courses: 2 daily fee (54 holes); 1 municipal (9 holes)	A
Bowling centers: 2 (36 lanes, tenpins)	B
Movie theaters: 1 single/twin, 1 multiplex; 5 total screens	C
Outdoor Recreation Assets (849 points)	
Inland Water Area: 186.0 square miles	
Lake Havasu	
Lake Mead	
National Parks, Forests, Wildlife Refuges:	
Grand Canyon NP (517,180 acres)	
Havasu NWR (11,875 acres)	
Kaibab NF (5,468 acres)	
Lake Mead NRA (795,000 acres)	

Rating

Rating

Pipe Spring NM (40 acres)
State Recreation Area: 1 (13,000 acres)
Score: 1,749   **Rank: 101**

Lake Lanier, GA
Common Denominators (900 points)
Restaurants: 132; 1 ★★, 1 ★★★   B
Golf courses: 1 daily fee (18 holes); 1 municipal
    (18 holes)   B
Bowling center: 1 (24 lanes, tenpins)   C
Movie theaters: 1 single/twin, 3 multiplex; 13 total
    screens   AA
The Lively Arts Calendar (100 points)
Touring Artists Bookings: 5 dates
Resident Ensemble:
    Lanier Symphony Orchestra (5 dates)
Outdoor Recreation Assets (565 points)
Inland Water Area: 48.5 square miles
    Lake Sidney Lanier
Score: 1,565   **Rank: 108**

Lakeland–Winter Haven, FL
Common Denominators (900 points)
Restaurants: 445; 7 ★★, 4 ★★★, 1 ★★★★   B
Golf courses: 8 private (144 holes); 9 daily fee
    (171 holes); 3 municipal (63 holes)   B
Bowling centers: 7 (240 lanes, tenpins)   A
Movie theaters: 6 single/twin, 4 multiplex; 36 total
    screens   B
The Lively Arts Calendar (430 points)
Touring Artists Bookings: 36 dates
Resident Ensemble:
    Imperial Symphony Orchestra (7 dates)
Outdoor Recreation Assets (519 points)
Inland Water Area: 187.2 square miles
    Lake Pierce
    Lake Rosalie
    Lake Weochyakapka
State Recreation Areas: 3 (13,775 acres)
Score: 1,849   **Rank: 94**

Lancaster County, PA
Common Denominators (700 points)
Restaurants: 492; 5 ★★, 5 ★★★   B
Golf courses: 5 private (81 holes); 5 daily fee (90 holes) C
Bowling centers: 10 (242 lanes, tenpins)   A
Movie theaters: 7 single/twin, 4 multiplex; 19 total
    screens   C
The Lively Arts Calendar (510 points)
Touring Artists Bookings: 26 dates
Resident Ensembles:
    Lancaster Opera Company (20 dates)
    Lancaster Symphony Orchestra (5 dates)
Outdoor Recreation Assets (162 points)
Inland Water Area: 31.5 square miles
    Muddy Run Reservoir
State Recreation Area: 1 (224 acres)
Score: 1,372   **Rank: 118**

Las Cruces, NM
Common Denominators (700 points)
Restaurants: 138; 3 ★★, 2 ★★★   B
Golf courses: 5 private (90 holes); 2 daily fee (36 holes) C
Bowling centers: 2 (42 lanes, tenpins)   C
Movie theaters: 2 single/twin, 2 multiplex; 15 total
    screens   A
The Lively Arts Calendar (260 points)
Touring Artists Bookings: 14 dates
Resident Ensemble:
    Las Cruces Symphony Orchestra (12 dates)
Outdoor Recreation Assets (108 points)
National Parks, Forests, Wildlife Refuges:
    San Andres NWR (2 acres)
    White Sands NM (52,770 acres)
State Recreation Area: 1 (40 acres)
Score: 1,068   **Rank: 132**

★Las Vegas, NV
Common Denominators (1,100 points)
Restaurants: 832; 2 ★, 11 ★★, 15 ★★★, 2 ★★★★   A
Golf courses: 3 private (54 holes); 8 daily fee
    (144 holes); 3 municipal (45 holes)   C
Bowling centers: 12 (454 lanes, tenpins)   A
Movie theaters: 8 single/twin, 12 multiplex; 88 total
    screens   AA
The Lively Arts Calendar (1,080 points)
Touring Artists Bookings: 67 dates
Resident Ensembles:
    Las Vegas Civic Symphony (5 dates)
    Las Vegas Symphony Orchestra (30 dates)
    Nevada Opera Theater (6 dates)
Outdoor Recreation Assets (1,611 points)
Inland Water Area: 209.8 square miles
    Lake Mead
National Parks, Forests, Wildlife Refuges:
    Desert NWR (828,031 acres)
    Lake Mead NRA (589,000 acres)
    Moapa Valley NWR (30 acres)
    Toiyabe NF (59,157 acres)
State Recreation Areas: 3 (58,121 acres)
Score: 3,791   **Rank: 10**

Lexington–Fayette, KY
Common Denominators (1,000 points)
Restaurants: 519; 6 ★★, 6 ★★★   B
Golf courses: 11 private (171 holes); 6 daily fee
    (99 holes); 2 municipal (36 holes)   B
Bowling centers: 6 (136 lanes, tenpins)   B
Movie theaters: 8 single/twin, 5 multiplex; 47 total
    screens   AA
The Lively Arts Calendar (1,050 points)
Touring Artists Bookings: 75 dates
Resident Ensemble:
    Lexington Philharmonic Orchestra (30 dates)
Outdoor Recreation Assets (5 points)
Inland Water Area: 0.9 square miles
State Recreation Area: 1 (10 acres)
Score: 2,055   **Rank: 83**

Los Alamos, NM
Common Denominators (500 points)
Restaurants: 29; 1 ★★   B
Golf course: 1 municipal (18 holes)   A
The Lively Arts Calendar (40 points)
Touring Artists Bookings: 4 dates
Outdoor Recreation Assets (2,000 points)
National Parks, Forests, Wildlife Refuges:
    Bandelier NM (6,483 acres)
    Santa Fe NF (30,030 acres)
Score: 2,540   **Rank: 65**

Madison, WI
Common Denominators (1,100 points)
Restaurants: 561; 2 ★, 3 ★★, 2 ★★★   C
Golf courses: 6 private (90 holes); 7 daily fee
    (117 holes); 3 municipal (63 holes)   B
Bowling centers: 24 (416 lanes, tenpins)   AA
Movie theaters: 10 single/twin, 7 multiplex; 50 total
    screens   AA
The Lively Arts Calendar (1,410 points)
Touring Artists Bookings: 90 dates
Resident Ensembles:
    Madison Opera (5 dates)
    Madison Symphony Orchestra (16 dates)
    Wisconsin Chamber Orchestra (30 dates)
Outdoor Recreation Assets (150 points)
Inland Water Area: 34.7 square miles
    Lake Mendota
    Lake Monona
State Recreation Areas: 3 (1,661 acres)
Score: 2,660   **Rank: 56**

Rating

Martinsburg–Charles Town, WV
Common Denominators (800 points)
Restaurants: 108; 1 ★★★	C
Golf courses: 1 private (18 holes); 3 daily fee (45 holes)	B
Bowling centers: 2 (52 lanes, tenpins)	A
Movie theater: 1 multiplex; 7 total screens	B

The Lively Arts Calendar (110 points)
Touring Artists Bookings: 5 dates
Resident Ensemble:
   Millbrook Chamber Orchestra (6 dates)
Outdoor Recreation Assets (56 points)
Inland Water Area: 2.6 square miles
National Parks, Forests, Wildlife Refuges:
   Appalachian NS Trail (1,100 acres)
   Harpers Ferry NHP (1,050 acres)
Score: 966   **Rank: 140**

Maui, HI
Common Denominators (600 points)
Restaurants: 215	
Golf courses: 2 private (18 holes); 7 daily fee (180 holes); 1 municipal (18 holes)	AA
Bowling centers: 2 (30 lanes, tenpins)	C
Movie theaters: 1 single/twin, 1 multiplex; 4 total screens	C

The Lively Arts Calendar (250 points)
Touring Artists Bookings: 13 dates
Resident Ensemble:
   Maui Symphony Orchestra (12 dates)
Outdoor Recreation Assets (2,000 points)
Pacific Coastline: 210 miles
Inland Water Area: 9.4 square miles
National Parks, Forests, Wildlife Refuges:
   Haleakala NP (27,500 acres)
   Kakahaia NWR (45 acres)
   Kalaupapa NHP (20 acres)
State Recreation Areas: 12 (327 acres)
Score: 2,850   **Rank: 42**

McAllen–Edinburg–Mission, TX
Common Denominators (400 points)
Restaurants: 300; 2 ★	C
Golf courses: 5 private (81 holes); 4 daily fee (45 holes); 3 municipal (54 holes)	C
Bowling centers: 3 (52 lanes, tenpins)	C
Movie theaters: 4 single/twin, 3 multiplex; 22 total screens	C

The Lively Arts Calendar (90 points)
Touring Artists Bookings: 5 dates
Resident Ensemble:
   Valley Symphony Orchestra (4 dates)
Outdoor Recreation Assets (91 points)
Inland Water Area: 12.4 square miles
National Parks, Forests, Wildlife Refuges:
   Lower Rio Grande Valley NWR (7,640 acres)
   Santa Ana NWR (2,087 acres)
State Recreation Area: 1 (587 acres)
Score: 581   **Rank: 148**

Medford–Ashland, OR
Common Denominators (1,000 points)
Restaurants: 228; 2 ★, 3 ★★, 1 ★★★	B
Golf courses: 1 private (27 holes); 1 daily fee (18 holes); 1 municipal (9 holes)	C
Bowling centers: 3 (74 lanes, tenpins)	A
Movie theaters: 4 multiplex; 20 total screens	AA

The Lively Arts Calendar (340 points)
Touring Artists Bookings: 6 dates
Resident Ensembles:
   Rogue Valley Opera Association (13 dates)
   Rogue Valley Symphony (15 dates)
Outdoor Recreation Assets (1,253 points)
Inland Water Area: 14.4 square miles
   Emigrant Reservoir
   Howard Prairie Reservoir

Rating

   Hyatt Reservoir
National Parks, Forests, Wildlife Refuges:
   Crater Lake NP (944 acres)
   Klamath NF (26,334 acres)
   Rogue River NF (411,690 acres)
State Recreation Areas: 7 (1,395 acres)
Score: 2,593   **Rank: 63**

★ Melbourne–Titusville–Palm Bay, FL
Common Denominators (700 points)
Restaurants: 550; 7 ★★, 3 ★★★	B
Golf courses: 5 private (108 holes); 3 daily fee (54 holes); 4 municipal (72 holes)	C
Bowling centers: 8 (176 lanes, tenpins)	B
Movie theaters: 3 single/twin, 4 multiplex; 35 total screens	B

The Lively Arts Calendar (850 points)
Touring Artists Bookings: 52 dates
Resident Ensembles:
   Brevard Symphony Orchestra (18 dates)
   Florida Space Coast Philharmonic (15 dates)
Outdoor Recreation Assets (2,000 points)
Atlantic Coastline: 72 miles
Inland Water Area: 299.0 square miles
   Banana Lake
   Indian River
   Lake Washington
National Parks, Forests, Wildlife Refuges:
   Canaveral NS (29,479 acres)
   St. Johns River NWR (6,254 acres)
State Recreation Area: 1 (578 acres)
Score: 3,550   **Rank: 16**

★ Miami–Hialeah, FL
Common Denominators (700 points)
Restaurants: 4,512; 5 ★, 20 ★★, 15 ★★★, 2 ★★★★	B
Golf courses: 13 private (270 holes); 7 daily fee (225 holes); 9 municipal (144 holes)	C
Bowling centers: 15 (436 lanes, tenpins)	C
Movie theaters: 10 single/twin, 28 multiplex; 196 total screens	A

The Lively Arts Calendar (2,000 points)
Touring Artists Bookings: 216 dates
Resident Ensembles:
   Greater Miami Opera Association (32 dates)
   Miami Chamber Symphony (6 dates)
   North Miami Beach Opera (4 dates)
   North Miami Beach Symphony Orchestra (6 dates)
   The New World Symphony (40 dates)
Outdoor Recreation Assets (2,000 points)
Atlantic Coastline: 50 miles
Inland Water Area: 64.2 square miles
   Biscayne Bay
National Parks, Forests, Wildlife Refuges:
   Big Cypress National Preserve (19,000 acres)
   Biscayne NP (172,000 acres)
   Everglades NP (415,700 acres)
State Recreation Areas: 5 (1,934 acres)
Score: 4,700   **Rank: 2**

Monticello–Liberty, NY
Common Denominators (1,200 points)
Restaurants: 124; 1 ★, 3 ★★, 1 ★★★	A
Golf courses: 1 private (9 holes); 10 daily fee (171 holes); 2 municipal (36 holes)	AA
Bowling centers: 9 (192 lanes, tenpins)	AA
Movie theater: 1 multiplex; 3 total screens	C

Outdoor Recreation Assets (119 points)
Inland Water Area: 20.6 square miles
   Neversink Reservoir
   Swinging Bridge Reservoir
National Parks, Forests, Wildlife Refuges:
   Upper Delaware NSR (400 acres)
State Recreation Area: 1 (1,409 acres)
Score: 1,319   **Rank: 124**

Rating

Mountain Home–Bulls Shoals, AR
Common Denominators (1,000 points)
Restaurants: 71; 1 ★, 2 ★★, 1 ★★★   A
Golf course: 1 daily fee (18 holes)   C
Bowling centers: 3 (46 lanes, tenpins)   AA
Movie theaters: 2 single/twin, 1 multiplex; 4 total
  screens   B
Outdoor Recreation Assets (968 points)
Inland Water Area: 94.1 square miles
  Bull Shoals Lake
  Norfolk Lake
National Parks, Forests, Wildlife Refuges:
  Buffalo National River (25,891 acres)
  Ozark NF (64,998 acres)
State Recreation Area: 1 (663 acres)
Score: 1,968   **Rank: 88**

Murray–Kentucky Lake, KY
Common Denominators (1,100 points)
Restaurants: 33; 2 ★★, 1 ★★★   AA
Golf courses: 2 private (36 holes); 1 daily fee (18 holes)   B
Bowling center: 1 (8 lanes, tenpins)   C
Movie theaters: 1 single/twin, 1 multiplex; 5 total screens   AA
The Lively Arts Calendar (50 points)
Touring Artists Bookings: 5 dates
Outdoor Recreation Assets (339 points)
Inland Water Area: 24.9 square miles
  Kentucky Lake
State Recreation Area: 1 (1,795 acres)
Score: 1,489   **Rank: 113**

Myrtle Beach, SC
Common Denominators (1,500 points)
Restaurants: 441; 2 ★, 7 ★★, 3 ★★★   A
Golf courses: 2 private (27 holes); 29 daily fee
  (648 holes)   AA
Bowling centers: 7 (174 lanes, tenpins)   AA
Movie theaters: 6 multiplex; 29 total screens   AA
The Lively Arts Calendar (50 points)
Touring Artists Bookings: 5 dates
Outdoor Recreation Assets (762 points)
Atlantic Coastline: 75 miles
Inland Water Area: 2.3 square miles
State Recreation Area: 1 (352 acres)
Score: 2,312   **Rank: 73**

★ Naples, FL
Common Denominators (1,400 points)
Restaurants: 241; 4 ★, 8 ★★, 9 ★★★   AA
Golf courses: 16 private (351 holes); 6 daily fee
  (108 holes)   A
Bowling centers: 3 (72 lanes, tenpins)   A
Movie theaters: 2 single/twin, 2 multiplex; 19 total
  screens   AA
The Lively Arts Calendar (220 points)
Touring Artists Bookings: 8 dates
Resident Ensemble:
  Naples Marco Philharmonic (14 dates)
Outdoor Recreation Assets (2,000 points)
Gulf Coastline: 40 miles
Inland Water Area: 112.8 square miles
  Lake Trafford
National Parks, Forests, Wildlife Refuges:
  Big Cypress National Preserve (395,000 acres)
  Everglades NP (39,262 acres)
State Recreation Areas: 4 (64,290 acres)
Score: 3,620   **Rank: 14**

New Bern, NC
Common Denominators (800 points)
Restaurants: 97; 1 ★★   C
Golf courses: 3 private (63 holes); 4 daily fee (72 holes)   A
Bowling center: 1 (16 lanes, tenpins)   C
Movie theaters: 2 multiplex; 9 total screens   A

Rating

Outdoor Recreation Assets (1,022 points)
Inland Water Area: 59.8 square miles
  Neuse River Estuary
National Parks, Forests, Wildlife Refuges:
  Croatan NF (61,125 acres)
Score: 1,822   **Rank: 97**

New Braunfels, TX
Common Denominators (600 points)
Restaurants: 72; 2 ★, 1 ★★   B
Golf courses: 1 private (18 holes); 1 municipal
  (18 holes)   C
Bowling center: 1 (24 lanes, tenpins)   B
Movie theaters: 1 single/twin; 2 total screens   C
Outdoor Recreation Assets (182 points)
Inland Water Area: 20.1 square miles
  Canyon Lake
State Recreation Area: 1 (506 acres)
Score: 782   **Rank: 146**

New Paltz–Ulster County, NY
Common Denominators (1,000 points)
Restaurants: 274; 1 ★, 4 ★★, 1 ★★★   B
Golf courses: 3 private (36 holes); 10 daily fee
  (117 holes)   A
Bowling centers: 6 (168 lanes, tenpins)   AA
Movie theaters: 4 single/twin; 4 screens   C
The Lively Arts Calendar (470 points)
Touring Artists Bookings: 41 dates
Resident Ensemble:
  Woodstock Chamber Orchestra (6 dates)
Outdoor Recreation Assets (201 points)
Inland Water Area: 30.4 square miles
  Ashokan Reservoir
State Recreation Areas: 2 (10,489 acres)
Score: 1,671   **Rank: 102**

New Port Richey, FL
Common Denominators (600 points)
Restaurants: 260; 1 ★, 2 ★★, 1 ★★★   C
Golf courses: 1 private (18 holes); 10 daily fee
  (198 holes)   A
Bowling centers: 2 (32 lanes, tenpins)   C
Movie theaters: 2 single/twin, 2 multiplex; 19 total
  screens   C
Outdoor Recreation Assets (452 points)
Gulf Coastline: 25 miles
Inland Water Area: 30.6 square miles
State Recreation Area: 1 (195 acres)
Score: 1,052   **Rank: 135**

Newport–Lincoln City, OR
Common Denominators (1,200 points)
Restaurants: 111; 1 ★, 5 ★★, 1 ★★★★   AA
Golf courses: 5 daily fee (54 holes)   AA
Bowling centers: 2 (20 lanes, tenpins)   A
Movie theaters: 2 single/twin; 2 total screens   C
Outdoor Recreation Assets (1,925 points)
Coastline: 50 miles
Inland Water Area: 11.8 square miles
  Alsea Bay
  Devils Lake
  Yaquina Bay
National Parks, Forests, Wildlife Refuges:
  Oregon Islands NWR (38 acres)
  Siuslaw NF (171,246 acres)
State Recreation Areas: 29 (2,079 acres)
Score: 3,125   **Rank: 36**

North Conway–White Mountains, NH
Common Denominators (1,200 points)
Restaurants: 144; 3 ★, 4 ★★, 4 ★★★   AA
Golf courses: 1 private (18 holes); 7 daily fee (99 holes)   AA
Movie theaters: 1 single/twin, 1 multiplex; 5 total screens   AA

	Rating
Outdoor Recreation Assets (1,498 points)	
Inland Water Area: 57.7 square miles	
Lake Winnipesaukee	
Ossipee Lake	
Silver Lake	
National Parks, Forests, Wildlife Refuges:	
White Mountain NF (145,005 acres)	
State Recreation Areas: 14 (8,133 acres)	
Score: 2,698	**Rank: 54**

Oak Harbor–Whidbey Island, WA
Common Denominators (900 points)

	Rating
Restaurants: 58; 1 ★★	C
Golf courses: 2 private (27 holes); 3 daily fee (36 holes); 1 municipal (18 holes)	A
Bowling centers: 4 (62 lanes, tenpins)	AA
Movie theaters: 2 single/twin; 3 total screens	C

Outdoor Recreation Assets (1,003 points)
Puget Sound Area Coastline: 60 miles
Inland Water Area: 11.0 square miles
Saratoga Passage
Skagit Bay
National Parks, Forests, Wildlife Refuges:
Ebey's Landing NHR (1,100 acres)
State Recreation Areas: 9 (3,379 acres)

Score: 1,903   **Rank: 93**

Ocala, FL
Common Denominators (800 points)

	Rating
Restaurants: 219; 2 ★★, 2 ★★★	B
Golf courses: 2 private (36 holes); 3 daily fee (54 holes); 2 municipal (45 holes)	B
Bowling centers: 5 (122 lanes, tenpins)	A
Movie theaters: 4 single/twin, 3 multiplex; 11 total screens	C

Outdoor Recreation Assets (1,466 points)
Inland Water Area: 52.5 square miles
Lake Bryant
Lake Kerr
Lake Weir
National Parks, Forests, Wildlife Refuges:
Ocala NF (274,773 acres)
State Recreation Areas: 2 (3,101 acres)

Score: 2,266   **Rank: 75**

Ocean City–Assateague Island, MD
Common Denominators (1,400 points)

	Rating
Restaurants: 198; 2 ★, 7 ★★, 1 ★★★	AA
Golf courses: 2 private (36 holes); 1 daily fee (27 holes); 1 municipal (9 holes)	A
Bowling centers: 2 (28 lanes, tenpins)	A
Movie theaters: 2 single/twin, 3 multiplex; 19 total screens	AA

Outdoor Recreation Assets (1,752 points)
Atlantic Coastline: 31 miles
Inland Water Area: 110.0 square miles
Chincoteague Bay
Isle of Wight Bay
Sinepuxent Bay
National Parks, Forests, Wildlife Refuges:
Assateague Island NS (23,200 acres)
Chincoteague NWR (418 acres)
State Recreation Areas: 2 (14,032 acres)

Score: 3,152   **Rank: 34**

Ocean County, NJ
Common Denominators (700 points)

	Rating
Restaurants: 565; 2 ★★	C
Golf courses: 5 private (72 holes); 3 daily fee (45 holes); 2 municipal (36 holes)	C
Bowling centers: 8 (232 lanes, tenpins)	A
Movie theaters: 6 single/twin, 5 multiplex; 33 total screens	B

The Lively Arts Calendar (130 points)
Touring Artists Bookings: 6 dates
Resident Ensemble:

Garden State Philharmonic Symphony Orchestra
(7 dates)
Outdoor Recreation Assets (1,542 points)
Atlantic Coastline: 50 miles
Inland Water Area: 113.8 square miles
Barnegat Bay
National Parks, Forests, Wildlife Refuges:
Edwin B. Forsythe NWR (10,040 acres)
State Recreation Areas: 8 (17,673 acres)

Score: 2,372   **Rank: 71**

Olympia, WA
Common Denominators (600 points)

	Rating
Restaurants: 201; 1 ★★	C
Golf courses: 1 private (18 holes); 5 daily fee (90 holes)	B
Bowling centers: 4 (64 lanes, tenpins)	B
Movie theaters: 4 single/twin, 1 multiplex; 4 total screens	C

The Lively Arts Calendar (160 points)
Touring Artists Bookings: 10 dates
Resident Ensemble:
Olympia Symphony Orchestra (6 dates)
Outdoor Recreation Assets (439 points)
Puget Sound Area Coastline: 10 miles
Inland Water Area: 47.0 square miles
Budd Inlet
Case Inlet
National Parks, Forests, Wildlife Refuges:
Nisqually NWR (1,988 acres)
Olympic NF (10 acres)
Snoqualmie NF (612 acres)
State Recreation Area: 1 (840 acres)

Score: 1,199   **Rank: 127**

★ Orlando, FL
Common Denominators (1,100 points)

	Rating
Restaurants: 1,472; 13 ★, 22 ★★, 12 ★★★, 1 ★★★★	B
Golf courses: 16 private (324 holes); 32 daily fee (549 holes); 1 municipal (18 holes)	B
Bowling centers: 21 (574 lanes, tenpins)	A
Movie theaters: 17 single/twin, 16 multiplex; 145 total screens	AA

The Lively Arts Calendar (1,860 points)
Touring Artists Bookings: 28 dates
Resident Ensembles:
Florida Symphony Orchestra (140 dates)
Orlando Opera Company (12 dates)
University of Central Florida Community Orchestra
(6 dates)
Outdoor Recreation Assets (648 points)
Inland Water Area: 297.1 square miles
Lake Apopka
Lake Kissimmee
Lake Tohopekaliga
State Recreation Areas: 4 (46,931 acres)

Score: 3,608   **Rank: 15**

Panama City, FL
Common Denominators (900 points)

	Rating
Restaurants: 262; 1 ★, 4 ★★, 1 ★★★	B
Golf courses: 2 private (36 holes); 4 daily fee (81 holes)	B
Bowling centers: 3 (56 lanes, tenpins)	B
Movie theaters: 1 single/twin, 3 multiplex; 14 total screens	A

The Lively Arts Calender (100 points)
Touring Artists Bookings: 10 dates
Outdoor Recreation Assets (1,151 points)
Gulf Coastline: 44 miles
Inland Water Area: 123.8 square miles
St. Andrew Bay
West Bay
State Recreation Area: 1 (1,268 acres)

Score: 2,151   **Rank: 79**

Rating

Paris–Big Sandy, TN
Common Denominators (300 points)
Restaurants: 54; 1 ★★ — C
Golf courses: 3 private (27 holes); 1 municipal (18 holes) — C
Bowling center: 1 (12 lanes, tenpins) — C
The Lively Arts Calendar (120 points)
Touring Artists Bookings: 12 dates
Outdoor Recreation Assets (392 points)
Inland Water Area: 77.4 square miles
  Kentucky Lake
State Recreation Areas: 2 (2,289 acres)
Score: 812 — **Rank: 145**

Pensacola, FL
Common Denominators (700 points)
Restaurants: 339; 3 ★★, 2 ★★★ — C
Golf courses: 5 private (90 holes); 2 daily fee (36 holes);
  1 municipal (18 holes) — C
Bowling centers: 8 (174 lanes, tenpins) — A
Movie theaters: 1 single/twin, 5 multiplex; 21 total
  screens — B
The Lively Arts Calendar (1,590 points)
Touring Artists Bookings: 150 dates
Resident Ensemble:
  Pensacola Symphony Orchestra (9 dates)
Outdoor Recreation Assets (1,007 points)
Gulf Coastline: 15 miles
Inland Water Area: 92.0 square miles
  Pensacola Bay
National Parks, Forests, Wildlife Refuges:
  Gulf Islands NS (22,861 acres)
State Recreation Areas: 2 (986 acres)
Score: 3,297 — **Rank: 28**

Petoskey–Straits of Mackinac, MI
Common Denominators (1,300 points)
Restaurants: 45; 5 ★★ — AA
Golf courses: 5 private (81 holes); 2 daily fee (45 holes) — AA
Bowling center: 1 (24 lanes, tenpins) — AA
Movie theater: 1 single/twin; 1 screen — C
The Lively Arts Calendar (130 points)
Touring Artists Bookings: 13 dates
Outdoor Recreation Assets (684 points)
Lake Michigan Coastline: 50 miles
Inland Water Area: 16.5 square miles
  Little Traverse Bay
  Walloon Lake
State Recreation Areas: 2 (867 acres)
Score: 2,114 — **Rank: 82**

Phoenix–Tempe–Scottsdale, AZ
Common Denominators (800 points)
Restaurants: 2,779; 18 ★, 24 ★★, 11 ★★★, 1 ★★★★ — C
Golf courses: 35 private (720 holes); 34 daily fee
  (684 holes); 9 municipal (171 holes) — B
Bowling centers: 34 (1,014 lanes, tenpins) — B
Movie theaters: 14 single/twin, 34 multiplex; 241 total
  screens — A
The Lively Arts Calendar (2,000 points)
Touring Artists Bookings: 603 dates
Resident Ensembles:
  Arizona State University Symphony (15 dates)
  Mesa Symphony Orchestra (12 dates)
  Metro Pops Orchestra (5 dates)
  Phoenix Symphony Orchestra (75 dates)
  Scottsdale Symphony Orchestra (5 dates)
  Sun Cities Symphony Orchestra (5 dates)
Outdoor Recreation Assets (618 points)
Inland Water Area: 97.9 square miles
  Apache Lake
  Bartlett Reservoir
  Canyon Lake
  Cave Creek Dam
National Parks, Forests, Wildlife Refuges:

Rating

Tonto NF (658,683 acres)
State Recreation Areas: 3 (6,260 acres)
Score: 3,418 — **Rank: 22**

Pike County, PA
Common Denominators (1,000 points)
Restaurants: 36; 2 ★★★ — AA
Golf courses: 2 private (27 holes); 2 daily fee (36 holes) — AA
Movie theater: 1 single/twin; 2 total screens — B
Outdoor Recreation Assets (413 points)
Inland Water Area: 16.0 square miles
  Lake Wallenpaupack
National Parks, Forests, Wildlife Refuges:
  Delaware NSR (550 acres)
  Delaware Water Gap NRA (16,000 acres)
  Upper Delaware NSR (260 acres)
State Recreation Area: 1 (2,971 acres)
Score: 1,413 — **Rank: 117**

Port Townsend, WA
Common Denominators (700 points)
Restaurants: 48
Golf courses: 3 daily fee (36 holes) — AA
Bowling center: 1 (12 lanes, tenpins) — A
Outdoor Recreation Assets (2,000 points)
Puget Sound Area Coastline: 15 miles
Inland Water Area: 76.7 square miles
  Port Townsend Harbor
National Parks, Forests, Wildlife Refuges:
  Olympic NF (166,992 acres)
  Olympic NP (537,335 acres)
  Protection Island NWR (313 acres)
  Quillayute Needles NWR (196 acres)
State Recreation Areas: 11 (2,482 acres)
Score: 2,700 — **Rank: 52**

Portsmouth–Dover–Durham, NH
Common Denominators (900 points)
Restaurants: 487; 2 ★, 5 ★★, 2 ★★★ — B
Golf courses: 5 private (90 holes); 10 daily fee
  (117 holes) — C
Bowling centers: 7 (146 lanes, mixed) — B
Movie theaters: 5 single/twin, 9 multiplex; 50 total
  screens — AA
The Lively Arts Calendar (130 points)
Touring Artists Bookings: 13 dates
Outdoor Recreation Assets (508 points)
Atlantic Coastline: 25 miles
Inland Water Area: 40.3 square miles
  Bow Lake
  Great Bay
  Portsmouth Harbor
State Recreation Areas: 34 (9,610 acres)
Score: 1,538 — **Rank: 110**

Prescott, AZ
Common Denominators (800 points)
Restaurants: 167; 1 ★, 7 ★★, 1 ★★★ — A
Golf courses: 2 private (36 holes); 3 daily fee
  (45 holes); 1 municipal (18 holes) — A
Bowling centers: 2 (26 lanes, tenpins) — C
Movie theaters: 4 single/twin; 4 total screens — C
The Lively Arts Calendar (200 points)
Touring Artists Bookings: 20 dates
Outdoor Recreation Assets (1,894 points)
Inland Water Area: 4.2 square miles
  Pleasant Lake
National Parks, Forests, Wildlife Refuges:
  Coconino NF (426,595 acres)
  Kaibab NF (25,119 acres)
  Montezuma Castle NM (840 acres)
  Prescott NF (1,193,974 acres)
  Tonto NF (316,917 acres)
  Tuzigoot NM (60 acres)
State Recreation Areas: 3 (720 acres)
Score: 2,894 — **Rank: 41**

	Rating

Red Bluff–Sacramento Valley, CA
Common Denominators (600 points)

	Rating
Restaurants: 64; 1 ★	C
Golf courses: 1 private (18 holes); 1 daily fee (9 holes)	C
Bowling centers: 2 (26 lanes, tenpins)	A
Movie theaters: 2 single/twin; 3 total screens	C

The Lively Arts Calendar (40 points)
Touring Artists Bookings: 4 dates
Outdoor Recreation Assets (1,293 points)
Inland Water Area: 3.1 square miles
  Black Butte Lake
National Parks, Forests, Wildlife Refuges:
  Lassen NF (188,860 acres)
  Lassen Volcanic NP (4,200 acres)
  Mendocino NF (217,104 acres)
  Trinity NF (76,947 acres)
State Recreation Areas: 2 (431 acres)
Score: 1,933   **Rank: 90**

Redding, CA
Common Denominators (600 points)

	Rating
Restaurants: 224; 2 ★★	C
Golf courses: 2 private (36 holes); 4 daily fee (45 holes)	C
Bowling centers: 3 (38 lanes, tenpins)	C
Movie theaters: 3 multiplex; 15 total screens	A

The Lively Arts Calendar (190 points)
Touring Artists Bookings: 15 dates
Resident Ensemble:
  Shasta Symphony (4 dates)
Outdoor Recreation Assets (1,859 points)
Inland Water Area: 67.8 square miles
  Shasta Lake
  Whiskeytown Lake
National Parks, Forests, Wildlife Refuges:
  Lassen NF (249,223 acres)
  Lassen Volcanic NP (66,865 acres)
  Shasta NF (468,831 acres)
  Trinity NF (30,626 acres)
  Whiskeytown–Shasta–Trinity NRA (42,450 acres)
State Recreation Areas: 4 (12,889 acres)
Score: 2,649   **Rank: 57**

Rehoboth Bay–Indian River Bay, DE
Common Denominators (900 points)

	Rating
Restaurants: 243	
Golf courses: 5 private (63 holes); 1 daily fee (18 holes)	C
Bowling centers: 7 (196 lanes, tenpins)	AA
Movie theaters: 1 single/twin, 2 multiplex; 22 total screens	AA

The Lively Arts Calendar (30 points)
Touring Artists Bookings: 3 dates
Outdoor Recreation Assets (829 points)
Atlantic Coastline: 52 miles
Inland Water Area: 37.1 square miles
  Indian River Bay
  Rehoboth Bay
National Parks, Forests, Wildlife Refuges:
  Prime Hook NWR (8,818 acres)
State Recreation Areas: 5 (6,093 acres)
Score: 1,759   **Rank: 100**

Reno, NV
Common Denominators (1,100 points)

	Rating
Restaurants: 340; 1 ★, 7 ★★, 5 ★★★, 1 ★★★★	A
Golf courses: 1 private (18 holes); 3 daily fee (54 holes); 4 municipal (63 holes)	B
Bowling centers: 7 (174 lanes, tenpins)	AA
Movie theaters: 2 single/twin, 4 multiplex; 22 total screens	B

The Lively Arts Calendar (570 points)
Touring Artists Bookings: 16 dates
Resident Ensembles:
  Nevada Opera Association (11 dates)
  Opera Festival of the Sierra (6 dates)

Reno Philharmonic (18 dates)
Sierra Community Orchestra (6 dates)
Outdoor Recreation Assets (506 points)
Inland Water Area: 232.9 square miles
  Lake Tahoe
National Parks, Forests, Wildlife Refuges:
  Anaho Island NWR (248 acres)
  Sheldon NWR (187,240 acres)
  Toiyabe NF (65,427 acres)
State Recreation Areas: 2 (19,725 acres)
Score: 2,176   **Rank: 78**

Rockport–Aransas Pass, TX
Common Denominators (600 points)

	Rating
Restaurants: 25; 1 ★★	A
Golf courses: 2 private (27 holes)	
Movie theaters: 2 single/twin; 2 total screens	A

Outdoor Recreation Assets (2,000 points)
Gulf Coastline: 23 miles
Inland Water Area: 179.1 square miles
  Aransas Bay
  Copano Bay
National Parks, Forests, Wildlife Refuges:
  Aransas NWR (52,461 acres)
State Recreation Area: 1 (575 acres)
Score: 2,600   **Rank: 62**

Roswell, NM
Common Denominators (1,000 points)

	Rating
Restaurants: 73; 3 ★★	A
Golf courses: 1 private (9 holes); 2 municipal (36 holes)	A
Bowling center: 1 (16 lanes, tenpins)	C
Movie theaters: 1 single/twin, 1 multiplex; 6 total screens	A

The Lively Arts Calendar (170 points)
Touring Artists Bookings: 4 dates
Resident Ensemble:
  Roswell Symphony Orchestra (13 dates)
Outdoor Recreation Assets (95 points)
Inland Water Area: 10.4 square miles
  Two Rivers Reservoir
National Parks, Forests, Wildlife Refuges:
  Bitter Lake NWR (24,527 acres)
  Lincoln NF (40,332 acres)
State Recreation Area: 1 (1,611 acres)
Score: 1,265   **Rank: 125**

Salinas–Seaside–Monterey, CA
Common Denominators (1,100 points)

	Rating
Restaurants: 533; 12 ★, 16 ★★, 19 ★★★	AA
Golf courses: 8 private (180 holes); 11 daily fee (207 holes); 3 municipal (45 holes)	A
Bowling centers: 6 (102 lanes, tenpins)	C
Movie theaters: 11 single/twin, 5 multiplex; 39 total screens	A

The Lively Arts Calendar (650 points)
Touring Artists Bookings: 26 dates
Resident Ensembles:
  Chamber Orchestra by the Sea (3 dates)
  Hidden Valley Opera (30 dates)
  Monterey County Symphony Orchestra (6 dates)
Outdoor Recreation Assets (1,638 points)
Pacific Coastline: 85 miles
Inland Water Area: 24.0 square miles
National Parks, Forests, Wildlife Refuges:
  Los Padres NF (304,575 acres)
  Pinnacles NM (1,283 acres)
  Salinas River NWR (364 acres)
State Recreation Areas: 15 (14,691 acres)
Score: 3,388   **Rank: 25**

San Antonio, TX
Common Denominators (600 points)

	Rating
Restaurants: 1,644; 8 ★, 12 ★★, 8 ★★★	C
Golf courses: 15 private (297 holes); 1 daily fee (18 holes); 4 municipal (72 holes)	C

Rating

Bowling centers: 19 (528 lanes, tenpins)   **B**
Movie theaters: 3 single/twin, 14 multiplex; 112 total
   screens   **B**
The Lively Arts Calendar (2,000 points)
Touring Artists Bookings: 192 dates
Resident Ensemble:
   San Antonio Symphony (180 dates)
Outdoor Recreation Assets (41 points)
Inland Water Area: 9.5 square miles
   Canyon Lake
   Colaveras Lake
National Parks, Forests, Wildlife Refuges:
   San Antonio NHP (230 acres)
State Recreation Areas: 2 (11 acres)
Score: 2,641   **Rank: 58**

★ **San Diego, CA**
Common Denominators (700 points)
Restaurants: 3,186; 8 ★, 36 ★★, 16 ★★★   **B**
Golf courses: 24 private (477 holes); 23 daily fee (441
   holes); 5 municipal (108 holes)   **C**
Bowling centers: 28 (940 lanes, tenpins)   **B**
Movie theaters: 19 single/twin, 22 multiplex; 162 total
   screens   **B**
The Lively Arts Calendar (2,000 points)
Touring Artists Bookings: 270 dates
Resident Ensembles:
   Jewish Community Center Symphony (14 dates)
   La Jolla Symphony & Chorus (14 dates)
   North Coast Symphony (8 dates)
   San Diego Chamber Orchestra (30 dates)
   San Diego Civic Light Opera (75 dates)
   San Diego Gilbert & Sullivan Company (21 dates)
   San Diego Opera (20 dates)
   San Diego State University Symphony (8 dates)
   San Diego Symphony Orchestra (120 dates)
Outdoor Recreation Assets (1,225 points)
Pacific Coastline: 55 miles
Inland Water Area: 52.5 square miles
   Cuyamaca Reservoir
   El Capitan Lake
   Lake Henshaw
   Lake Hodges
National Parks, Forests, Wildlife Refuges:
   Cabrillo NM (144 acres)
   Cleveland NF (288,240 acres)
   Tijuana Slough NWR (407 acres)
State Recreation Areas: 16 (46,971 acres)
Score: 3,925   **Rank: 8**

San Juan Islands, WA
Common Denominators (400 points)
Restaurants: 27
Golf courses: 2 daily fee (18 holes)   **AA**
Outdoor Recreation Assets (2,000 points)
Puget Sound Area Coastline: 115 miles
Inland Water Area: 89.3 square miles
National Parks, Forests, Wildlife Refuges:
   San Juan Islands NWR (379 acres)
State Recreation Areas: 14 (6,255 acres)
Score: 2,400   **Rank: 69**

San Luis Obispo, CA
Common Denominators (800 points)
Restaurants: 413; 1 ★, 5 ★★, 5 ★★★   **A**
Golf courses: 2 private (36 holes); 3 daily fee (45 holes);
   2 municipal (36 holes)   **C**
Bowling centers: 4 (84 lanes, tenpins)   **B**
Movie theaters: 5 single/twin, 1 multiplex; 16 total
   screens   **B**
The Lively Arts Calendar (470 points)
Touring Artists Bookings: 38 dates
Resident Ensemble:
   San Luis Obispo County Symphony (9 dates)
Outdoor Recreation Assets (1,113 points)

Rating

Pacific Coastline: 60 miles
Inland Water Area: 22.1 square miles
   Naciemento Reservoir
National Parks, Forests, Wildlife Refuges:
   Los Padres NF (188,908 acres)
State Recreation Areas: 12 (14,788 acres)
Score: 2,383   **Rank: 70**

★ **Santa Barbara, CA**
Common Denominators (800 points)
Restaurants: 623; 1 ★, 9 ★★, 7 ★★★   **A**
Golf courses: 9 private (153 holes); 5 daily fee (72 holes);
   1 municipal (18 holes)   **C**
Bowling centers: 6 (172 lanes, tenpins)   **B**
Movie theaters: 9 single/twin, 5 multiplex; 34 total
   screens   **B**
The Lively Arts Calendar (1,010 points)
Touring Artists Bookings: 63 dates
Resident Ensembles:
   Music Academy of the West Symphony (13 dates)
   Santa Barbara Symphony Orchestra (25 dates)
Outdoor Recreation Assets (2,000 points)
Pacific Coastline: 78 miles
Inland Water Area: 10.0 square miles
National Parks, Forests, Wildlife Refuges:
   Channel Islands NP (63,500 acres)
   Los Padres NF (628,402 acres)
State Recreation Areas: 6 (3,007 acres)
Score: 3,810   **Rank: 9**

★ **Santa Fe, NM**
Common Denominators (1,200 points)
Restaurants: 164; 1 ★, 17 ★★, 7 ★★★, 1 ★★★★   **AA**
Golf courses: 1 private (9 holes); 1 daily fee (18 holes)   **C**
Bowling centers: 3 (72 lanes, tenpins)   **AA**
Movie theaters: 4 single/twin, 1 multiplex; 12 total
   screens   **A**
The Lively Arts Calendar (1,490 points)
Touring Artists Bookings: 75 dates
Resident Ensembles:
   Orchestra of Santa Fe (29 dates)
   Santa Fe Opera (37 dates)
   Santa Fe Symphony (8 dates)
Outdoor Recreation Assets (1,026 points)
Inland Water Area: 6.9 square miles
   Cochiti Reservoir
National Parks, Forests, Wildlife Refuges:
   Bandelier NM (826 acres)
   Santa Fe NF (245,040 acres)
State Recreation Areas: 2 (355 acres)
Score: 3,716   **Rank: 12**

Santa Rosa–Petaluma, CA
Common Denominators (700 points)
Restaurants: 570; 5 ★, 8 ★★, 5 ★★★   **B**
Golf courses: 1 private (18 holes); 7 daily fee (99 holes);
   3 municipal (63 holes)   **B**
Bowling centers: 9 (180 lanes, tenpins)   **B**
Movie theaters: 1 single/twin, 5 multiplex; 24 total
   screens   **C**
The Lively Arts Calendar (610 points)
Touring Artists Bookings: 5 dates
Resident Ensembles:
   Cinnabar Opera Theater (35 dates)
   Santa Rosa Symphony Orchestra (21 dates)
Outdoor Recreation Assets (533 points)
Pacific Coastline: 35 miles
Inland Water Area: 10.2 square miles
National Parks, Forests, Wildlife Refuges:
   San Pablo Bay NWR (249 acres)
State Recreation Areas: 15 (31,363 acres)
Score: 1,843   **Rank: 95**

	Rating

★ Sarasota, FL
Common Denominators (1,100 points)
Restaurants: 459; 4 ★, 12 ★★, 7 ★★★, 1 ★★★★ — A
Golf courses: 9 private (216 holes); 15 daily fee
(333 holes); 2 municipal (63 holes) — AA
Bowling center: 1 (24 lanes, tenpins) — C
Movie theaters: 2 single/twin, 3 multiplex; 29 total
screens — A
The Lively Arts Calendar (1,570 points)
Touring Artists Bookings: 105 dates
Resident Ensembles:
Florida West Coast Symphony (24 dates)
Sarasota Opera Association (21 dates)
Sarasota–Manatee Community Orchestra (7 dates)
Outdoor Recreation Assets (994 points)
Gulf Coastline: 35 miles
Inland Water Area: 31.9 square miles
State Recreation Areas: 2 (29,338 acres)
Score: 3,664 — **Rank: 13**

Savannah, GA
Common Denominators (1,200 points)
Restaurants: 323; 1 ★, 10 ★★, 5 ★★★ — A
Golf courses: 4 private (54 holes); 3 daily fee
(117 holes); 1 municipal (27 holes) — A
Bowling centers: 5 (148 lanes, tenpins) — A
Movie theaters: 1 single/twin, 3 multiplex; 26 total
screens — A
The Lively Arts Calendar (540 points)
Touring Artists Bookings: 9 dates
Resident Ensemble:
Savannah Symphony Orchestra (45 dates)
Outdoor Recreation Assets (1,099 points)
Atlantic Coastline: 20 miles
Inland Water Area: 55.0 square miles
Ossabaw Sound
Wassaw Sound
National Parks, Forests, Wildlife Refuges:
Fort Pulaski NM (5,400 acres)
Savannah River NWR (5,527 acres)
Wassaw NWR (10,050 acres)
State Recreation Areas: 2 (1,302 acres)
Score: 2,839 — **Rank: 43**

South Lake Tahoe–Placerville, CA
Common Denominators (700 points)
Restaurants: 240; 2 ★, 2 ★★, 3 ★★★ — A
Golf courses: 2 private (36 holes); 2 daily fee (27 holes) — C
Bowling centers: 2 (28 lanes, tenpins) — C
Movie theaters: 3 single/twin, 1 multiplex; 9 total screens — B
The Lively Arts Calendar (100 points)
Touring Artists Bookings: 10 dates
Outdoor Recreation Assets (2,000 points)
Inland Water Area: 73.9 square miles
Lake Tahoe
National Parks, Forests, Wildlife Refuges:
Eldorado NF (493,667 acres)
State Recreation Areas: 8 (60,675 acres)
Score: 2,800 — **Rank: 47**

Southport, NC
Common Denominators (600 points)
Restaurants: 98; 2 ★★ — B
Golf courses: 12 daily fee (234 holes) — AA
Outdoor Recreation Assets (546 points)
Atlantic Coastline: 35 miles
Inland Water Area: 32.5 square miles
State Recreation Area: 1 (1,773 acres)
Score: 1,146 — **Rank: 129**

St. Augustine, FL
Common Denominators (700 points)
Restaurants: 151; 1 ★, 6 ★★, 1 ★★★ — A
Golf courses: 6 private (153 holes); 1 daily fee (18 holes) — C

	Rating

Bowling center: 1 (24 lanes, tenpins) — C
Movie theater: 1 multiplex; 6 total screens — B
The Lively Arts Calendar (110 points)
Touring Artists Bookings: 11 dates
Outdoor Recreation Assets (1,120 points)
Atlantic Coastline: 60 miles
Inland Water Area: 55.3 square miles
St. Johns River
National Parks, Forests, Wildlife Refuges:
Castillo NM (20 acres)
Fort Matanzas NM (228 acres)
State Recreation Areas: 4 (9,204 acres)
Score: 1,930 — **Rank: 91**

St. George–Zion, UT
Common Denominators (800 points)
Restaurants: 52; 2 ★★, 1 ★★★ — A
Golf courses: 1 private (18 holes); 2 daily fee (27 holes);
2 municipal (27 holes) — A
Bowling centers: 2 (24 lanes, tenpins) — B
The Lively Arts Calendar (180 points)
Touring Artists Bookings: 12 dates
Resident Ensemble:
Southwest Symphony Orchestra (6 dates)
Outdoor Recreation Assets (1,731 points)
Inland Water Area: 1.4 square miles
National Parks, Forests, Wildlife Refuges:
Dixie NF (394,503 acres)
Zion NP (131,000 acres)
State Recreation Areas: 4 (9,966 acres)
Score: 2,711 — **Rank: 51**

★ St. Petersburg–Clearwater–Dunedin, FL
Common Denominators (900 points)
Restaurants: 1,304; 19 ★, 22 ★★, 9 ★★★ — A
Golf courses: 9 private (234 holes); 14 daily fee
(279 holes); 1 municipal (18 holes) — C
Bowling centers: 5 (152 lanes, tenpins) — C
Movie theaters: 9 single/twin, 15 multiplex; 118 total
screens — AA
The Lively Arts Calendar (2,000 points)
Touring Artists Bookings: 224 dates
Resident Ensembles:
Florida Lyric Opera (16 dates)
Tampa Bay Opera Company (20 dates)
Outdoor Recreation Assets (1,456 points)
Gulf Coastline: 40 miles
Inland Water Area: 70.8 square miles
Lake Tarpon
Old Tampa Bay
National Parks, Forests, Wildlife Refuges:
Pinellas NWR (392 acres)
State Recreation Areas: 3 (1,642 acres)
Score: 4,356 — **Rank: 4**

St. Tammany Parish, LA
Common Denominators (700 points)
Restaurants: 170; 2 ★★★ — C
Golf courses: 5 private (99 holes); 2 daily fee (36 holes) — C
Bowling centers: 2 (56 lanes, tenpins) — C
Movie theaters: 2 single/twin, 5 multiplex; 35 total
screens — AA
The Lively Arts Calendar (50 points)
Touring Artists Bookings: 5 dates
Outdoor Recreation Assets (1,277 points)
Inland Water Area: 254.4 square miles
Lake Pontchartrain
National Parks, Forests, Wildlife Refuges:
Bogue Chitto NWR (18,188 acres)
State Recreation Areas: 2 (2,979 acres)
Score: 2,027 — **Rank: 85**

State College, PA
Common Denominators (1,000 points)
Restaurants: 173; 2 ★★, 3 ★★★ — **A**
Golf courses: 4 private (54 holes); 2 daily fee (54 holes) — **B**
Bowling centers: 4 (71 lanes, tenpins) — **A**
Movie theaters: 2 single/twin, 1 multiplex; 9 total screens — **B**
The Lively Arts Calendar (570 points)
Touring Artists Bookings: 50 dates
Resident Ensemble:
Nittany Valley Symphony (7 dates)
Outdoor Recreation Assets (95 points)
Inland Water Area: 6.1 square miles
State Recreation Areas: 6 (10,007 acres)
Score: 1,665 — **Rank: 103**

Thomasville, GA
Common Denominators (800 points)
Restaurants: 39; 1 ★★ — **B**
Golf courses: 1 private (18 holes); 1 municipal (9 holes) — **C**
Bowling center: 1 (20 lanes, tenpins) — **A**
Movie theater: 1 multiplex; 3 total screens — **B**
The Lively Arts Calendar (60 points)
Touring Artists Bookings: 6 dates
Outdoor Recreation Assets (20 points)
Inland Water Area: 2.1 square miles
State Recreation Area: 1 (1 acre)
Score: 880 — **Rank: 143**

Traverse City–Grand Traverse Bay, MI
Common Denominators (1,500 points)
Restaurants: 110; 2 ★★, 2 ★★★ — **A**
Golf courses: 1 private (18 holes); 5 daily fee (90 holes) — **AA**
Bowling centers: 3 (86 lanes, tenpins) — **AA**
Movie theaters: 3 single/twin, 1 multiplex; 10 total
screens — **AA**
The Lively Arts Calendar (750 points)
Touring Artists Bookings: 35 dates
Resident Ensembles:
Interlochen Arts Academy Orchestra (15 dates)
Traverse Symphony Orchestra (7 dates)
World Youth Symphony Orchestra (18 dates)
Outdoor Recreation Assets (1,034 points)
Lake Michigan Coastline: 75 miles
Inland Water Area: 27.8 square miles
Duck Lake
Grand Traverse Bay
Long Lake
National Parks, Forests, Wildlife Refuges:
Manistee NF (2 acres)
State Recreation Areas: 2 (232 acres)
Score: 3,284 — **Rank: 30**

Tucson, AZ
Common Denominators (1,000 points)
Restaurants: 832; 2 ★, 14 ★★, 17 ★★★, 1 ★★★★★ — **A**
Golf courses: 11 private (234 holes); 9 daily fee
(162 holes); 5 municipal (108 holes) — **B**
Bowling centers: 13 (380 lanes, tenpins) — **A**
Movie theaters: 1 single/twin, 11 multiplex; 58 total
screens — **B**
The Lively Arts Calendar (1,350 points)
Touring Artists Bookings: 50 dates
Resident Ensembles:
Arizona Opera Company (20 dates)
Civic Orchestra of Tucson (5 dates)
Philharmonic Orchestra of Tucson (9 dates)
Tucson Symphony Orchestra (51 dates)
Outdoor Recreation Assets (1,051 points)
Inland Water Area: 1.1 square miles
National Parks, Forests, Wildlife Refuges:
Buenos Aires NWR (21,281 acres)
Cabeza Prieta NWR (416,210 acres)
Coronado NF (382,027 acres)
Organ Pipe Cactus NM (329,300 acres)
Saguaro NM (81,000 acres)
State Recreation Area: 1 (5,511 acres)
Score: 3,401 — **Rank: 23**

Twain Harte–Yosemite, CA
Common Denominators (700 points)
Restaurants: 103
Golf courses: 4 daily fee (63 holes) — **AA**
Bowling center: 1 (16 lanes, tenpins) — **B**
Movie theaters: 1 single/twin; 1 total screen — **C**
Outdoor Recreation Assets (2,000 points)
Inland Water Area: 42.7 square miles
Beardley Lake
Cherry Lake
Don Pedro Reservoir
National Parks, Forests, Wildlife Refuges:
Calaveras Bigtree NF (380 acres)
Stanislaus NF (611,626 acres)
Yosemite NP (428,500 acres)
State Recreation Areas: 3 (6,288 acres)
Score: 2,700 — **Rank: 52**

Vero Beach, FL
Common Denominators (1,100 points)
Restaurants: 109; 3 ★★, 2 ★★★ — **A**
Golf courses: 5 private (126 holes); 6 daily fee
(108 holes); 1 municipal (18 holes) — **A**
Bowling centers: 3 (76 lanes, tenpins) — **AA**
Movie theater: 1 multiplex; 6 total screens — **C**
Outdoor Recreation Assets (704 points)
Atlantic Coastline: 30 miles
Inland Water Area: 42.6 square miles
Indian River
National Parks, Forests, Wildlife Refuges:
Pelican Island NWR (43 acres)
State Recreation Area: 1 (578 acres)
Score: 1,804 — **Rank: 98**

★Virginia Beach–Norfolk, VA
Common Denominators (800 points)
Restaurants: 1,267; 5 ★, 21 ★★, 7 ★★★ — **B**
Golf courses: 8 private (135 holes); 5 daily fee
(90 holes); 6 municipal (99 holes) — **C**
Bowling centers: 20 (514 lanes, tenpins) — **A**
Movie theaters: 4 single/twin, 10 multiplex; 82 total
screens — **B**
The Lively Arts Calendar (2,000 points)
Touring Artists Bookings: 90 dates
Resident Ensembles:
Old Dominion University Symphony Orchestra
(3 dates)
The Virginia Opera (24 dates)
The Virginia Symphony (103 dates)
Virginia Beach Community Orchestra (12 dates)
Virginia Beach Pops (46 dates)
Outdoor Recreation Assets (1,625 points)
Chesapeake Coastline: 55 miles
Inland Water Area: 118.7 square miles
Lynnhaven Bay
National Parks, Forests, Wildlife Refuges:
Back Bay NWR (4,589 acres)
Colonial NHP (1 acre)
Great Dismal Swamp NWR (81,862 acres)
Mackay Island NWR (874 acres)
Nansemond NWR (208 acres)
State Recreation Area: 1 (2,770 acres)
Score: 4,425 — **Rank: 3**

Wenatchee, WA
Common Denominators (1,300 points)
Restaurants: 123; 2 ★★ — **B**
Golf courses: 1 private (18 holes); 1 daily fee (18 holes);
2 municipal (36 holes) — **A**
Bowling centers: 5 (70 lanes, tenpins) — **AA**
Movie theaters: 2 multiplex; 10 total screens — **AA**
Outdoor Recreation Assets (2,000 points)
Inland Water Area: 78.1 square miles
Lake Chelan

	Rating
National Parks, Forests, Wildlife Refuges:	
Lake Chelan NRA (61,200 acres)	
North Cascades NP (66,750 acres)	
Wenatchee NF (1,302,604 acres)	
State Recreation Areas: 6 (1,285 acres)	
Score: 3,300	**Rank: 27**

West Palm Beach–
Boca Raton–Delray Beach, FL
Common Denominators (1,000 points)
Restaurants: 1,255; 7 ★, 23 ★★, 17 ★★★, 1 ★★★★, 1 ★★★★★   **A**
Golf courses: 56 private (1,557 holes); 14 daily fee
  (261 holes); 8 municipal (144 holes)   **B**
Bowling centers: 11 (376 lanes, tenpins)   **B**
Movie theaters: 3 single/twin, 11 multiplex; 89 total
  screens   **A**
The Lively Arts Calendar (1,120 points)
Touring Artists Bookings: 49 dates
Resident Ensembles:
  Florida Symphonic Pops (40 dates)
  Greater Palm Beach Symphony (16 dates)
  Palm Beach Opera (7 dates)
Outdoor Recreation Assets (1,013 points)
Atlantic Coastline: 47 miles
Inland Water Area: 235.9 square miles

	Rating
Lake Okeechobee	
Palm Beach Harbor	
National Parks, Forests, Wildlife Refuges:	
Arthur Marshall Loxahatchee NWR (2,550 acres)	
State Recreation Areas: 4 (1,074 acres)	
Score: 3,133	**Rank: 35**

Yuma, AZ
Common Denominators (800 points)
Restaurants: 100; 3 ★★   **B**
Golf courses: 1 private (18 holes); 2 daily fee (27 holes);
  1 municipal (18 holes)   **B**
Bowling centers: 3 (78 lanes, tenpins)   **A**
Movie theaters: 1 single/twin, 1 multiplex; 4 total screens   **C**
The Lively Arts Calendar (250 points)
Touring Artists Bookings: 20 dates
Resident Ensembles:
  Yuma Community Orchestra (5 dates)
Outdoor Recreation Assets (427 points)
Inland Water Area: 37.3 square miles
  Imperial Reservoir
National Parks, Forests, Wildlife Refuges:
  Kofa NWR (523,040 acres)
State Recreation Area: 1 (10 acres)
Score: 1,477   **Rank: 114**

ET CETERA: Leisure Living

RETIREMENT PLACES WITH THE BEST BASS FISHING

Black bass, the premier gamefish in North America, are found in lakes and rivers in every state but Alaska. They aren't abundant in all areas, however, and some regions do not have the large bass-holding waters that can withstand extensive public attention. *Field & Stream* recently named the 50 best fishing spots in the United States and Canada, and one or more of these bodies of water are within the following 15 retirement places.

Amherst–Northampton, Massachusetts

Located in a wilderness setting just east of Amherst, the 25,000-acre Quabbin Reservoir is the largest body of water in Massachusetts and a principal source of Boston's water supply. In addition to trout and salmon, it sports a good fishery for bass, particularly smallmouth, and is tightly managed for fishing and boating.

Branson–Table Rock Lake, Missouri

Table Rock Lake, an impoundment of the White River in southeastern Missouri, is surrounded by the Mark Twain National Forest. Its 43,100 acres are spread out in a meandering, mazelike configuration of coves and creeks that hide many bass.

Burlington, Vermont

With the Green Mountains on the east and the Adirondack Mountains on the west, 120-mile-long Lake Champlain, a natural lake on the Vermont–New York border, is nestled in the midst of some outstanding country. The premier gamefish is smallmouth bass, especially in the northern sector. Largemouth bass are abundant, too, particularly in weedy bays. In addition, walleye, trout, salmon, and perch fishing is excellent.

Hot Springs National Park, Arkansas

Lake Ouachita, a Corps of Engineers lake about 35 miles from Hot Springs, is part of the Ouachita National Forest and is known for a variety of good fishing. Largemouth and spotted (locally called "Kentucky") bass are plentiful here. Stripers, too, are abundant among the rotting timber left standing in this lake when it was flooded.

Laconia–Lake Winnipesaukee, New Hampshire

Squam Lake, location for the movie *On Golden Pond*, is noted for its smallmouth bass fishing. Its 44,000-acre neighbor, Lake Winnipesaukee, is the largest of New Hampshire's many lakes. Here, trout and landlocked salmon are the locally preferred fish, but many smallmouth and largemouth bass are caught as well.

Lake Havasu City–Kingman, Arizona

Lake Mohave, an impoundment on the Colorado River downstream from Lake Mead (see **Las Vegas, Ne-**

Another Break: Golden Age Passports

Since 1974, 4 million Golden Age Passports have been issued to U.S. citizens and permanent residents who are 62 or older. These are free entrance permits to any national park, monument, or recreation area run by the federal government and are valid for the lifetime of the holder.

With a Golden Age Passport, friends who accompany you will also be admitted free as long as everyone arrives in the same private vehicle (a car, station wagon, pickup truck, motor home, or motorcycle; busloads don't qualify). If you walk in, the passport admits you, your spouse, and children.

It isn't necessary to obtain the passport before trucking off on a combined vacation and retirement-place inspection trip. You can get one at most federally operated recreation areas where they are used and at any National Park Service regional office, national forest supervisor's office, and most ranger station offices. They aren't available by mail, however; you have to obtain one in person. All you need is proof of age—a driver's license, birth certificate, or signed affidavit attesting to your age.

There are real savings involved if you plan on frequent visits to the national parks, forests, wildlife refuges, and U.S. Army Corps of Engineers waterways. Not only are entrance fees waived (they currently range from $1 per person to $10 per vehicle), but the passport holder gets an additional 50 percent discount on federal use fees, such as parking, overnight camping, and boat launching. With camping charges well over $10 a night, and with increased parking and boat-ramp fees, 50 percent discounts can add up to a real bargain.

Most Popular National Parks in the Retirement Places

National Park Unit	Annual Visitors	Retirement Place
Acadia NP	4,502,000	Bar Harbor–Frenchman Bay, ME
		Camden–Penobscot Bay, ME
Assateague Island NS	2,418,000	Ocean City–Assateague Island, MD
Buffalo NR	1,056,000	Mountain Home–Bull Shoals, AR
Cabrillo NM	1,609,000	San Diego, CA
Canaveral NS	1,038,000	Daytona Beach, FL
		Melbourne–Titusville–Palm Bay, FL
Cape Cod NS	5,181,000	Cape Cod, MA
Delaware Water Gap NRA	2,528,000	Pike County, PA
Everglades NP	1,026,000	Naples, FL
Glacier NP	1,818,000	Kalispell, MT
Gulf Islands NS	5,198,000	Fort Walton Beach, FL Pensacola, FL
Haleakala NP	1,315,000	Maui, HI
Hot Springs NP	1,186,000	Hot Springs National Park, AR
Lake Mead NRA	8,329,000	Lake Havasu City–Kingman, AZ Las Vegas, NV
Olympic NP	2,959,000	Port Townsend, WA
Rocky Mountain NP	2,544,000	Fort Collins–Loveland, CO
Shenandoah NP	1,937,000	Charlottesville, VA
Whiskeytown–Shasta–Trinity NRA	1,352,000	Redding, CA
Yosemite NP	3,217,000	Twain Harte–Yosemite, CA
Zion NP	1,948,000	St. George–Zion, UT

Source: National Park Service, *Statistical Abstract.*

vada), is an excellent largemouth bass lake, providing good fishing on points, cliffs, brush, and other habitats that are typical of these weedless desert lakes. Cold water issuing from Hoover Dam makes the upper 15 miles more suitable for trout, but the rest of the 67-mile-long lake offers plenty of bass fishing opportunities.

Lake Lanier, Georgia

Lake Lanier is the most visited U.S. Army Corps of Engineers lake in the nation. Largemouth bass fishing among the 560 miles of shoreline, abundant coves and feeder creeks, and 38,000 acres of water supplied by the Chattahoochee and Chestatee rivers is excellent. Striped and white bass also draw anglers, but in the summer fishermen compete with weekend swimmers, water-skiers, and sailors and have to resort to weekday angling.

Lakeland–Winter Haven, Florida

The Florida Phosphate Pits, which are flooded, reclaimed phosphate-mining areas of varying size, possess an abundance of chunky largemouth bass, including plenty of trophy-size fish. There are lots of

pits in the south-central mining country, and the newest publicly accessible ones are in the Tenoroc State Reserve outside of Lakeland.

Las Vegas, Nevada

Near Las Vegas and backed by the Hoover Dam, Lake Mead has lots of good bass cover, resulting in an abundance of 1- to 3-pound largemouth bass. Stripers, too, benefit from the expanded forage base and are popular on this lake, with small fish up to 10 pounds being plentiful.

Mountain Home–Bull Shoals, Arkansas

Bull Shoals is among the best largemouth bass waters in the Ozarks, has excellent spring and fall fishing, and provides good angling throughout the year for a variety of species, including white bass and crappies. Trout and smallmouth bass are also present.

Murray–Kentucky Lake, Kentucky

Kentucky Lake and Barkley Lake are magnets for warm-water anglers throughout the Midwest. Combined, they are the second-largest man-made water system in America, and their 3,500 miles of shoreline provide

Bowling Competition in the Retirement Places

For their size, Canandaigua, New York (90 leagues, 2,614 members) and Door County, Wisconsin (52 leagues, 1,092 members) see more bowling tournaments than larger retirement places. When it comes to the number of players, however, here are the top 20 associations.

Association	Leagues	Members
Greater Phoenix (AZ)	971	24,056
San Diego (CA)	794	16,977
Madison (WI)	585	15,613
San Antonio (TX)	549	14,109
Broward County (FL)	444	12,600
Norfolk (VA)	389	11,630
Greater Orlando (FL)	375	9,133
Colorado Springs (CO)	322	9,126
Tucson (AZ)	426	8,901
Mesa (AZ)	370	8,888
Albuquerque (NM)	310	8,704
Palm Beach County (FL)	224	7,976
Greater Miami (FL)	378	7,338
St. Petersburg (FL)	294	7,176
Oahu–Honolulu (HI)	462	6,929
Lancaster (PA)	319	6,727
Austin (TX)	207	6,203
Ocean County (NJ)	198	5,083
Space Coast (FL)	204	5,300
Lexington Area (KY)	184	4,455

Source: American Bowling Congress, *Annual Report.*

countless coves, bays, finders, and hideaways for bass. Largemouth and spotted (Kentucky) bass are plentiful, and smallmouth bass have become especially prominent in recent years.

Ocala, Florida

Good largemouth fishing can be had in many areas of Florida's lengthy and renowned St. Johns River, particularly Rodman Reservoir at the northern edge of the Ocala National Forest and Lake George, upriver yet south of Rodman Reservoir.

Orlando, Florida

There are numbers of shallow, grassy lakes in Florida's Kissimmee River chain. Lake Kissimmee (the largest) and East and West Tohopekaliga are among the most prominent. West Toho is rated one of the best places for trophy bass, which is high praise in a state that has many trophy largemouth waters.

San Diego, California

San Diego's water supply lakes are small and intensively fished. Fifteen of these San Diego County Lakes are open to the public for fishing, and they have some of the best catch rates in California, including record-size Florida-strain largemouth bass.

West Palm Beach–Boca Raton–Delray Beach, Florida

Lake Okeechobee, at the western edge of this retirement place, is the most renowned of Florida's largemouth bass factories. It has over 200,000 acres of shallow, grass-filled water and is often the least affected Florida bass lake during late winter and early spring, offering fantastic fishing when the weather is stable.

GARDENING

If you are a dedicated gardener, then you're one of those hardy souls willing to deal with nature's varieties, from savage winters and sandy soils to slimy snails and slugs, in order to enjoy the splendor of June roses, vine-ripened tomatoes, and a blaze of petunias. You use the winter to read Katharine S. White's *Onward and Upward in the Garden* and the gardening catalogs, you put humus in the sandy soil, and you set out saucers of flat beer for the slugs. (No, it's not meant as a treat—they are attracted by the odor, climb in, get tipsy, and drown.)

You're also not alone if you love to garden. Of retired homeowners, 72 percent care for their lawns; 52 percent grow vegetables, with tomatoes, peppers, and cucumbers, in that order, the most popular crops. Impatiens, petunias, and marigolds are the frontrunners in annuals among the 49 percent who grow flowers; roses are far and away the most popular perennials. Forty-eight percent grow shrubs, and 86 percent of those who grow vegetables also grow berries, with strawberries, red raspberries, and blueberries the favorites. Blackberries run a poor fourth. In the Midwest, 65 percent of households grow flowers as well as vegetables; in the East, 46 percent grow both. Nearly half of western households grow both vegetables and flowers, and a surprising 45 percent of western households also grow fruits and berries.

An acre or a pot, a treat for the eye or for the palate—no matter what your aim, gardening affords the delight of seemingly inexhaustible diversity. Years of growing both flowers and food reinforce your sense of change and renewal as well as your curiosity.

But what if you decide to move after retiring? Will the roses in your new garden bloom this year? Will the tomatoes thrive in the heat or the moisture, or the lack of both? Will the beloved tulips of your northern garden do well in the warm climate of your new home? (Probably, if you refrigerate the bulbs for a few months before planting.) Will the charming flowering dogwoods of the East prosper in the wintry blasts of the North Woods? (They won't prosper, but they will survive if placed in a sheltered spot.) You'll never know if the peonies of your last home will do well in the new location unless you try to transplant some of their fleshy roots. And if you try, maybe you can disprove the doomsayers who hold that oriental poppies can never be moved once planted (their long, carrotlike root dislikes being transplanted). One old-timer claims you can't kill them.

As noted in the chapter on climate, the United

Growing Seasons and Killing Frosts

Retirement Place	Growing Season	Last Spring Frost	First Fall Frost
Albuquerque, NM	196 days	Apr. 16	Oct. 29
Asheville, NC	195	Apr. 12	Oct. 24
Bend, OR	62	June 17	Aug. 17
Boise, ID	171	Apr. 29	Oct. 16
Cape May, NJ	225	Apr. 4	Nov. 16
Kalispell, MT	135	May 12	Sept. 23
Lakeland–Winter Haven, FL	349	Jan. 10	Dec. 25
Las Vegas, NV	245	Mar. 13	Nov. 13
Lexington, KY	198	Apr. 13	Oct. 28
Medford–Ashland, OR	178	Apr. 25	Oct. 20
Miami–Hialeah, FL	365	—	—
Orlando, FL	319	Jan. 31	Dec. 17
Phoenix–Tempe– Scottsdale, AZ	317	Jan. 27	Dec. 11
Red Bluff–Sacramento Valley, CA	277	Feb. 25	Nov. 29
Reno, NV	141	May 14	Oct. 2
San Diego, CA	365	—	—
Tucson, AZ	261	Mar. 6	Nov. 23
Yuma, AZ	350	Jan. 11	Dec. 27

Source: National Oceanic and Atmospheric Administration, *Local Climatological Data,* 1986

States offers a dizzying number of variables in climate and terrain, many of which can either throw a sizable wrench into your gardening efforts or guarantee success. There are a few constraints, however, that you will find wherever you may decide to move.

Growing Seasons

The number of frost-free days ranges from a mere eight in Barrow, Alaska, to 365 in Florida's Fort Lauderdale–Hollywood–Pompano Beach, Naples, and Miami–Hialeah, and in San Diego, California. The Florida and California places would qualify as superior gardening areas from the standpoint of temperature, since killing frosts occur there less than one year in 10 and plants can be grown year-round. See the table "Growing Seasons and Killing Frosts" for figures on some representative retirement places.

Soil

All soil is made up of varying amounts of clay particles, humus, and sand. The mix you have is dependent on where you live and on what others may have done to alter the natural state of the soil. Fortunately, the majority of plants are tolerant and will grow fairly well in most soils. Some can be grown most successfully in what is known as "acid soil." Other plants like sweet, or highly alkaline, soil. The acidity or alkalinity of soil is indicated by its pH number, a figure chemists use to measure the concentration of hydrogen ions (*pH* stands for "potential of hydrogen"). The midpoint in soil chemistry is 7, or neutral, on the pH scale. Less than 7 (down to 0) means acid; more than 7 (up to 14) means alkaline.

If you send a sample of soil to a testing laboratory, you may be told that it has a pH rating of 8.5, which would explain why the clematis looks so good, why you have the best onions and lettuce you've ever grown, and why your lilies and tomatoes are in bad shape. And now you know you'll have to put some alum or sulfur in the tomato patch.

You can test your soil yourself with litmus paper purchased at the drugstore. If the blue paper turns red when placed in moist soil, the soil is acid. If the red paper turns blue or purple, the soil is sweet. If there is no change, the soil is neutral. Or, you can take a representative slice of soil from the top down to about 6 inches, mix it, and send about half a cup to your county extension agent for testing.

A word of caution: if your soil is very acid or very sweet, take time to correct it, but change the pH by no more than a point per year.

Garden Pests

Unfortunately, pests are everywhere. If you leave the beetles and gypsy moths of the East for the gardens of California, chances are good that you will have to learn to do battle with snails and slugs, pests that were never a problem to you before. The cutworm that did damage only in the early part of the growing season in New England may reproduce several times a year in warm climates. One gardener who has lived in the East, on the Pacific Coast, and in the Midwest claims to have learned three distinct gardening rules, so pronounced are the variables of good gardening from area to area. And the ants, beetles, billbugs, borers, grubs, nematodes, and webworms are always with us.

So no matter where you live, you will have to have some kind of pest control. How much pesticide and what kind depends on the local pests, how perfect you want your crop to be, and what kind of growing season you are coping with. Purists who abhor any kind of chemical spray will have to be extra diligent about the varieties of plants they buy, about keeping the gardening area free of any debris and weeds—both of which harbor insects and other pests—and about pruning assiduously.

Putting It All Together

Is there really an ideal place for retirement in America?

Various Chambers of Commerce, real estate promoters, and state tourism and economic development agencies may claim the title for their own particular locales. After all, with 25 million persons due to turn 65 during the 1990s, attracting footloose people to the Leisure Villages, Palm Shores, and Mountain Homes of this country is a highly promising growth industry.

You might even nominate your own neighborhood. The distant haven may exist somewhere for you, but living there is either unaffordable, inconvenient, or not much better than where you are now.

By this book's criteria, however, the ideal place would have the climate of Maui, Hawaii, where the Pacific Ocean keeps the air temperature from ever dropping below 65 degrees or from topping 80 degrees much of the time. It would have to be a rural place if it were to match the low crime rate of Clayton in the northeast Georgia mountains, or the inexpensive housing of Harrison in the Arkansas Ozarks. Yet the ideal spot would also have to be a big metropolitan area to duplicate San Diego's full range of health care facilities, public transportation, and continuing education opportunities. For variety in recreation, you might choose a place like Miami–Hialeah, which not only has a busy calendar of symphony orchestra performances, opera productions, and guest artist dates, but has opportunities for outdoor activities as well. For finding part-time work after retirement, the place should have Orlando's rosy prospects for job growth in the retail trade, services, and finance, insurance, and real estate industries. Finally, the ideal place should offer retired persons the low living costs of McAllen–Edinburg–Mission on the north bank of the Rio Grande in southernmost Texas.

Obviously this ideal haven is a fiction. You can explore the geography long and hard, but you will never find the single place that combines all the firsts according to this book's criteria. Moreover, because one person's haven can often be another's purgatory, and your rural retreat someone else's boondocks, one can argue that there really is no such thing as *the* ideal retirement place.

Because of better health care and increasing longevity, your active retirement years can now amount to one-quarter of your life. Choosing where to spend these years isn't easy. The first tactic is to focus on *your* preferences and needs; the section "Making the Chapters Work for You," at the front of the book, can help you identify what these preferences and needs might be.

Having said all this, one can still try to discover

If You Read this Chapter First

Readers who've skipped ahead to see how it all comes out may be surprised by the results shown in the cumulative table on pages 213–216. If you are curious about how a place receives a rank in a particular category, see the explanation of the scoring system in the appropriate chapter and bear in mind that:

- The Services, Working, and Leisure Living chapters tend to favor larger places. Smaller places have the edge in the Money Matters, Housing, and Personal Safety chapters.
- When you review the rankings in each of the chapters, note the close groupings of scores. With such close results, ranking retirement places from 1st to 151st may give the impression of greater differences among them than actually exist.
- Throughout this guide the places compared aren't towns or cities. They are counties. And though this book does not include every desirable retirement destination in America, each of the 151 places it does include are among the country's best.

America's Top Retirement Places

Retirement Place	Cumulative Score
1. Fort Myers–Cape Coral–Sanibel Island, FL	256
2. San Antonio, TX*	316
3. St. George–Zion, UT	354
4. *Pensacola, FL**	361
5. Brownsville–Harlingen, TX*	368
6. Phoenix–Tempe–Scottsdale, AZ*	387
7. Orlando, FL*	393
8. St. Petersburg–Clearwater–Dunedin, FL*	398
9. *St. Tammany Parish, LA**	399
10. Miami–Hialeah, FL*	403
11. Southport, NC*	404
12. Austin, TX	405
13. *Gainesville, FL**	410
14. *Honolulu, HI**	411
15. Mountain Home–Bull Shoals, AR	412
16. Charleston, SC*	413
17. Branson–Table Rock Lake, MO*	415
17. Sarasota, FL*	415
17. *Vero Beach, FL*	415
20. Melbourne–Titusville–Palm Bay, FL	421
21. Brevard, NC	422
22. Daytona Beach, FL	423
23. Lakeland–Winter Haven, FL	427
24. Fort Lauderdale–Hollywood–Pompano Beach, FL*	428
24. Tucson, AZ*	428
26. Virginia Beach–Norfolk, VA	430
27. Bloomington–Brown County, IN	435
27. Fort Collins–Loveland, CO*	435
29. Biloxi–Gulfport–Pass Christian, MS	437
30. Clayton, GA	438

*These places are in the bottom 25—that is, 127th or lower—in one or more of the seven factors.

Places in *italics* are newcomers to this edition.

which of the 151 places come close to the ideal.

FINDING THE BEST ALL-AROUND RETIREMENT PLACES

The method for determining America's best all-around retirement places is quite simple: The ranks of every place for each of the seven factors—money matters, housing, climate, personal safety, services, working, and leisure living—are added together for a cumulative score.

Miami–Hialeah, for example, ranks 124th in money matters, 111th in housing, 3rd in climate, 151st in personal safety, 3rd in services, 9th in working, and 2nd in leisure living. The total of these ranks (124 + 111 + 3 + 151 + 3 + 9 + 2) is 403, giving Miami–Hialeah a rank of 10th among the 151 retirement places.

Because the rating system is based on ranks, the lower the cumulative score, the better the retirement place is judged to be all around. The list that tops the following column highlights the places that rise to the top as the better spots for retirement in America.

In some respects, the list of the top 30 in this edition of *Retirement Places Rated* resembles that of the previous 1987 edition. Although their rankings have changed somewhat, 10 of the retirement places were in the top 30 before. Of the remaining places on the list, five weren't profiled at all in 1987; they are new to this edition.

By no means are these top-rated places untarnished. Seventeen rank near the bottom in one or more of *Retirement Places Rated*'s seven categories. Moreover, not one of the 151 places ranks in the upper half in all of them.

Back to the point: there isn't an ideal retirement haven in America. In spite of a blot or two, many come close through a combination of strengths. Whether their strengths are vital or unimportant or whether their blots are knockout factors or trivial is for you to decide.

RANKINGS: Putting It All Together

The following chart gives each place's rank in each of *Retirement Places Rated*'s seven chapters. On the right-hand side, the sum of these seven ranks—the cumulative score—is also shown, as is the overall rank. For example, Cape Cod's cumulative score of 577 places it 102nd overall among the 151 retirement places. As in

golf, the lower the cumulative score the better. The best possible score is 7, meaning a first-place rank in all seven chapters.

The lowest possible rank a retirement place can receive is 151, so the worst possible cumulative score would be 1,057.

Retirement Place	Money Matters	Housing	Climate	Personal Safety	Services	Working	Leisure Living	Cumulative Score	Overall Rank
Aiken, SC	55	54	49	113	145	61	150	627	129
Alamogordo, NM	16	38	68	117	143	146	87	615	122
Albuquerque, NM	106	113	93	149	28	33	33	555	93
Amador County, CA	105	133	97	37	34	124	96	626	128
Amherst–Northampton, MA	118	125	126	19	24	70	55	537	80
Ann Arbor, MI	143	126	118	134	9	38	26	594	110
Asheville, NC	59	70	84	59	31	110	112	525	70
Athens, GA	55	63	59	120	17	138	141	593	109
Athens–Cedar Creek Lake, TX	10	5	39	61	142	103	147	507	59
Austin, TX	101	51	35	119	8	6	85	405	12
Bar Harbor–Frenchman Bay, ME	99	104	134	11	44	131	47	570	98
Bellingham, WA	70	67	114	70	18	102	31	472	46
Bend, OR	100	127	133	54	62	87	32	595	112
Bennington, VT	117	123	132	44	69	112	60	657	137
Benton County, AR	58	4	83	20	130	53	115	463	37
Biloxi–Gulfport–Pass Christian, MS	15	31	27	101	82	104	77	437	29
Blacksburg, VA	47	94	91	38	16	92	126	504	56
Bloomington–Brown County, IN	52	62	103	42	48	60	68	435	27
Boise, ID	91	43	116	80	52	81	74	537	80
Bradenton, FL	86	50	14	135	60	40	116	501	55
Branson–Table Rock Lake, MO	28	22	86	10	147	42	80	415	17
Brevard, NC	25	39	70	5	126	118	39	422	21
Brownsville–Harlingen, TX	2	14	18	129	107	49	49	368	5
Brunswick–Golden Isles, GA	60	33	26	150	73	86	81	509	61
Burlington, VT	132	136	141	88	25	56	21	599	113
Burnet–Marble Falls–Llano, TX	72	2	47	31	136	76	144	508	60
Camden–Penobscot Bay, ME	75	95	134	18	53	122	46	543	84
Canandaigua, NY	119	106	128	27	83	120	122	705	145
Canton–Lake Tawakoni, TX	18	10	50	29	150	127	151	535	77
Cape Cod, MA	147	140	111	111	41	20	7	577	102

Retirement Place	Money Matters	Housing	Climate	Personal Safety	Services	Working	Leisure Living	Cumulative Score	Overall Rank
Cape May, NJ	133	130	88	115	42	80	76	664	140
Carlsbad–Artesia, NM	31	35	60	74	106	147	120	573	99
Carson City–Minden, NV	148	144	123	77	84	14	99	689	144
Chapel Hill, NC	110	120	64	77	4	64	137	576	101
Charleston, SC	66	84	40	146	30	41	6	413	16
Charlevoix–Boyne City, MI	57	70	143	24	37	144	89	564	97
Charlottesville, VA	108	118	78	62	12	90	111	579	103
Chico–Paradise, CA	82	116	62	99	21	46	109	535	77
Clayton, GA	13	25	73	12	122	126	67	438	30
Clear Lake, CA	44	79	94	129	131	57	139	673	142
Coeur d'Alene, ID	41	55	131	65	67	96	50	505	58
Colorado Springs, CO	78	48	125	111	76	36	72	546	86
Columbia County, NY	108	110	129	45	110	121	134	757	150
Crossville, TN	9	16	96	16	119	98	131	485	50
Daytona Beach, FL	60	44	17	114	74	77	37	423	22
Deming, NM	4	11	90	104	113	141	138	601	116
Door County, WI	107	96	142	7	87	97	64	600	115
Eagle River, WI	19	36	151	30	118	140	24	518	66
Easton–Chesapeake Bay, MD	135	112	89	66	46	148	38	634	130
Edenton–Albemarle Sound, NC	24	86	52	21	94	149	105	531	72
El Centro–Calexico–Brawley, CA	29	45	42	138	138	143	128	663	138
Eugene–Springfield, OR	96	115	100	93	27	83	18	532	75
Fairhope–Gulf Shores, AL	34	64	25	40	125	68	123	479	48
Fayetteville, AR	20	8	82	46	56	136	106	454	36
Fort Collins–Loveland, CO	62	30	127	84	43	72	17	435	27
Fort Lauderdale–Hollywood–Pompano Beach, FL	136	83	4	125	47	4	29	428	24
Fort Myers–Cape Coral–Sanibel Island, FL	73	24	8	48	92	10	1	256	1
Fort Walton Beach, FL	39	72	35	34	132	24	107	443	32
Fredericksburg, TX	63	9	38	8	120	134	149	521	69
Gainesville, FL	46	49	22	138	14	37	104	410	13
Grand Junction, CO	49	34	107	57	66	119	59	491	52
Grand Lake, OK	3	6	75	14	148	125	133	504	56
Grants Pass, OR	35	122	98	64	128	100	40	587	106
Grass Valley–Truckee, CA	92	124	108	47	90	62	84	607	121
Hamilton–Bitterroot Valley, MT	8	29	136	15	144	138	61	531	72
Hanover, NH	140	142	139	17	6	54	11	509	61
Harrison, AR	17	1	72	9	104	128	136	467	41
Hendersonville, NC	88	103	70	26	101	107	130	625	127
Hilton Head–Beaufort, SC	90	100	33	137	91	21	45	517	65
Honolulu, HI	146	147	2	76	5	30	5	411	14
Hot Springs National Park, AR	40	23	56	98	45	123	66	451	34

Retirement Place	Money Matters	Housing	Climate	Personal Safety	Services	Working	Leisure Living	Cumulative Score	Overall Rank
Houghton Lake, MI	12	18	149	103	49	129	92	552	89
Iowa City, IA	120	119	121	92	2	105	119	678	143
Kalispell, MT	53	57	150	75	77	114	19	545	85
Keene, NH	123	134	146	13	79	91	121	707	146
Kerrville, TX	76	3	44	52	85	67	142	469	42
Key West–Key Largo–Marathon, FL	122	141	8	147	112	31	19	580	104
Laconia–Lake Winnipesaukee, NH	121	105	147	55	71	94	44	637	132
Lake Havasu City–Kingman, AZ	14	91	67	131	140	43	101	587	106
Lake Lanier, GA	81	88	57	63	63	145	108	605	119
Lakeland–Winter Haven, FL	43	28	11	126	86	39	94	427	23
Lancaster County, PA	116	117	102	22	96	50	118	621	124
Las Cruces, NM	11	69	74	108	103	55	132	552	89
Las Vegas, NV	128	128	63	140	105	8	10	582	105
Lexington–Fayette, KY	102	82	92	91	26	83	83	559	95
Los Alamos, NM	150	143	112	2	7	74	65	553	92
Madison, WI	129	101	138	68	20	51	56	563	96
Martinsburg–Charles Town, WV	22	75	101	36	108	108	140	590	108
Maui, HI	142	148	1	107	99	16	42	555	93
McAllen–Edinburg–Mission, TX	1	37	20	96	133	35	148	470	44
Medford–Ashland, OR	98	132	104	72	37	99	63	605	119
Melbourne–Titusville–Palm Bay, FL	74	52	10	102	78	89	16	421	20
Miami–Hialeah, FL	124	111	3	151	3	9	2	403	10
Monticello–Liberty, NY	111	121	137	71	123	101	124	788	151
Mountain Home–Bull Shoals, AR	27	19	76	1	95	106	88	412	15
Murray–Kentucky Lake, KY	37	20	76	33	50	150	113	479	48
Myrtle Beach, SC	31	80	42	144	88	13	73	471	45
Naples, FL	125	89	6	85	102	29	14	450	33
New Bern, NC	38	74	48	50	64	115	97	486	51
New Braunfels, TX	65	21	37	97	23	75	146	464	38
New Paltz–Ulster County, NY	114	109	124	43	93	78	102	663	138
New Port Richey, FL	54	42	13	60	129	7	135	440	31
Newport–Lincoln City, OR	71	97	106	73	114	141	36	638	133
North Conway–White Mountains, NH	131	114	148	32	80	58	54	617	123
Oak Harbor–Whidbey Island, WA	97	99	113	6	141	85	93	634	130
Ocala, FL	23	56	19	109	135	48	75	465	40
Ocean City–Assateague Island, MD	68	59	79	136	111	88	34	575	100
Ocean County, NJ	112	46	99	49	121	18	71	516	64
Olympia, WA	84	68	110	56	40	45	127	530	71
Orlando, FL	103	61	12	142	59	1	15	393	7
Panama City, FL	41	53	31	89	124	47	79	464	38
Paris–Big Sandy, TN	6	12	80	3	137	130	145	513	63

Retirement Place	Money Matters	Housing	Climate	Personal Safety	Services	Working	Leisure Living	Cumulative Score	Overall Rank
Pensacola, FL	30	41	30	127	61	44	28	361	4
Petoskey–Straits of Mackinac, MI	95	65	143	51	70	116	82	622	125
Phoenix–Tempe–Scottsdale, AZ	104	58	53	133	15	2	22	387	6
Pike County, PA	64	102	122	28	149	133	117	715	148
Port Townsend, WA	69	92	117	41	72	93	52	536	79
Portsmouth–Dover–Durham, NH	137	139	139	35	98	12	110	670	141
Prescott, AZ	51	87	104	53	97	66	41	499	54
Red Bluff–Sacramento Valley, CA	33	66	55	105	138	135	90	622	125
Redding, CA	85	107	54	118	58	69	57	548	87
Rehoboth Bay–Indian River Bay, DE	83	108	86	87	117	73	100	654	136
Reno, NV	141	138	129	128	22	82	78	718	149
Rockport–Aransas Pass, TX	26	13	23	106	151	137	62	518	66
Roswell, NM	36	32	85	122	109	131	125	640	134
St. Augustine, FL	67	72	21	123	89	79	91	542	83
St. George–Zion, UT	7	26	81	39	116	34	51	354	3
St. Petersburg–Clearwater–Dunedin, FL	127	85	14	110	32	26	4	398	8
St. Tammany Parish, LA	44	7	28	82	134	19	85	399	9
Salinas–Seaside–Monterey, CA	145	149	68	121	68	27	25	603	117
San Antonio, TX	48	15	31	143	10	11	58	316	2
San Diego, CA	144	145	24	124	1	5	8	451	34
San Juan Islands, WA	138	131	120	23	115	113	69	709	147
San Luis Obispo, CA	139	150	51	58	51	15	70	534	76
Santa Barbara, CA	151	151	66	90	39	25	9	531	72
Santa Fe, NM	126	135	115	69	35	59	12	551	88
Santa Rosa–Petaluma, CA	149	146	65	86	36	17	95	594	110
Sarasota, FL	130	76	14	95	55	32	13	415	17
Savannah, GA	87	60	34	132	29	109	43	494	53
South Lake Tahoe–Placerville, CA	115	137	58	79	100	63	47	599	113
Southport, NC	5	27	41	4	146	52	129	404	11
State College, PA	79	98	119	25	33	95	103	552	89
Thomasville, GA	50	17	29	83	65	151	143	538	82
Traverse City–Grand Traverse Bay, MI	113	90	143	66	13	65	30	520	68
Tucson, AZ	93	81	44	141	18	28	23	428	24
Twain Harte–Yosemite, CA	89	129	94	94	75	71	52	604	118
Vero Beach, FL	80	46	6	81	81	23	98	415	17
Virginia Beach–Norfolk, VA	94	78	61	115	57	22	3	430	26
Wenatchee, WA	77	40	109	99	11	111	27	474	47
West Palm Beach–Boca Raton–Delray Beach, FL	134	93	5	145	54	3	35	469	42
Yuma, AZ	21	77	44	148	127	116	114	647	135

RETIREMENT REGIONS

If your sights are set on southwestern desert retirement, parts of five states make up that target. If you're tending toward mountain living, even more states fill the bill. Why not think of regions?

Here are 17 that look, feel, talk, and act differently from one another, yet the places within them share a number of characteristics. Few of their boundaries match the political borders you'll find in your road atlas; most of them embrace parts of more than one state and, conversely, some states are apportioned among more than one region.

On the following pages *Retirement Places Rated* describes these regions into which the 151 places seem to fall. Some have been resort country for well over a century. Some have unsophisticated, small town manners. Others are relatively new and heavily promoted. One—Florida—is nationally synonymous with retirement. Still others aren't associated with retirement by anyone but savvy residents of nearby metropolitan areas. The North Woods country of Michigan and Wisconsin is such a place for Chicagoans, Milwaukeeans, and Detroiters. So are some of the New England locations of coastal Maine and rural New Hampshire and Vermont to Bostonians and New Yorkers.

Each regional heading is accompanied by a list of places in the region, along with their overall ranks. Eleven of the regions include one or more of the 30 best all-around retirement places, and these are indicated with a star.

Whether you decide to move or end up staying right where you are, *Retirement Places Rated* hopes that your later years will rank among your best.

BIG TEN COUNTRY

Ann Arbor, MI (#110)
★ Bloomington–Brown County, IN (#27)
Iowa City, IA (#143)
Madison, WI (#96)
State College, PA (#89)

Heartland, Middle Earth, Breadbasket—the names sometimes given to the Central States evoke the change of seasons on featureless farmland, or an area mostly flown over by persons bound for either coast.

Though farming is important here, industry is more so in certain parts; though the land seems plain from the air, it is far from being homogeneous. To find Big Ten Country, take all the states that have a Lake Michigan frontage, add Minnesota, Iowa, Ohio, and Pennsylvania, and home in on the locations of their largest universities.

Four of these places (Columbus, Lansing–East Lansing, Madison, and Minneapolis–St. Paul) are also the homes of state government. Two (Ann Arbor and Evanston) are suburban parts of major metropolitan areas. Another five (Bloomington, Champaign–Urbana, Iowa City, State College, and West Lafayette) are towns where the academic calendar dominates community life.

It isn't conjecture that Big Ten Country is a retirement region. The proportion of persons 65 and over tends to be greater in college towns than it is in the nation as a whole. Big Ten universities have huge alumni organizations, and many of these alums from the 1940s and 1950s are returning for the benefits of the college town they knew years ago: past friendships, the cultural and recreational amenities, the youthful population, and the human services usually found only in large cities.

CALIFORNIA COAST

Salinas–Seaside–Monterey, CA (#117)
San Diego, CA (#34)
San Luis Obispo, CA (#76)
Santa Barbara, CA (#72)
Santa Rosa–Petaluma, CA (#110)

It certainly isn't a homogeneous area, stretching as it does from the Border Beach on the Mexican boundary all the way up to the wine country north of San Francisco. About the only natural features these five California Coast retirement places have in common is a Pacific shoreline and a mild Mediterranean climate.

All five places in this region rank high, not just for their mild climates, but also for their available services and prospects for job growth. All five rank near the bottom, however, in costs of housing and how far typical Social Security benefits will stretch.

For all that, these locations have been popular for retirement since the end of World War II. One in seven retired Navy officers lives somewhere within San Diego County, as does one in 50 retired physicians. San Luis Obispo County is now the most populous area in the country without a large central city, and much of its growth comes from attracting older persons.

Nonetheless, because of the high cost of living, a limited supply of water, and restrictions on development, population growth along the California Coast is expected to slow during the last years of this century. Indeed, some experts predict the area will lose more retired persons than it will attract. The living may be easy, but it is not cheap. Health care and housing costs along this coast are the highest in the United States.

Coastal California retirement is great for those who can afford it, but despite the many recreational and cultural amenities and the terrific weather, the costs of living in paradise can run extremely high.

DESERT SOUTHWEST

El Centro–Calexico–Brawley, CA (#138)

Lake Havasu City–Kingman, AZ (#106)

Las Vegas, NV (#105)

★ Phoenix–Tempe–Scottsdale, AZ (#6)

Prescott, AZ (#54)

★ St. George–Zion, UT (#3)

★ Tucson, AZ (#24)

Yuma, AZ (#135)

The Desert Southwest, in the southern end of the Great Basin, lies between the country's two highest mountain ranges, the Rockies to the east and the Sierra Nevadas to the west. The two mountain ranges not only add beauty, grandeur, and ruggedness to the region, they also block moist air coming from either the Pacific Ocean or the Gulf of Mexico. The entire region is high, mountainous, and dry; the valleys are dusty, with scant vegetation. The mountains and cliffsides, eroded by wind and sand, are jagged, angular, and knife-sharp.

If it's sun you're after, this is the place. Yuma is officially designated America's sunniest spot. Hot, sunny, cloudless days followed by cool, even chilly, nights are the rule here. This means you can enjoy outdoor activities in the daytime and still get a good night's rest . . . under a blanket or two.

Rapidly growing Arizona is the prototypical Sun Belt state. Tucson, a leading retirement area, has an excellent supply of health care and public transportation facilities. Metropolitan Phoenix is home to the largest retirement development in the world, Sun City.

Many parts of the Desert Southwest, however, suffer from high crime rates and high housing costs (Las Vegas ranks 140th and 128th, respectively, in these categories), and the supply of health care facilities varies greatly from location to location. Despite its rapid population growth (the eight places profiled gained more than half a million persons since 1985, for example), this is thinly settled land. There is so much space here, with such great distances even between small towns, that people who have lived in thickly populated regions like the Great Lakes or the Northeast might find it difficult to adjust to the feeling of isolation.

FLORIDA

Bradenton, FL (#55)

★ Daytona Beach, FL (#22)

★ Fort Lauderdale–Hollywood–Pompano Beach, FL (#24)

Fort Walton Beach, FL (#32)

★ Fort Myers–Cape Coral–Sanibel Island, FL (#1)

★ Gainesville, FL (#13)

Key West–Key Largo–Marathon, FL (#104)

★ Lakeland–Winter Haven, FL (#23)

★ Melbourne–Titusville–Palm Bay, FL (#20)

★ Miami–Hialeah, FL (#10)

Naples, FL (#33)

New Port Richey, FL (#31)

Ocala, FL (#40)

★ Orlando, FL (#7)

Panama City, FL (#38)

★ Pensacola, FL (#4)

St. Augustine, FL (#83)

★ St. Petersburg–Clearwater–Dunedin, FL (#8)

★ Sarasota, FL (#17)

★ Vero Beach, FL (#17)

West Palm Beach–Boca Raton–Delray Beach, FL (#42)

Perhaps because they so recently hailed from other places, few of Florida's residents are aware of the state's long and fascinating history. The land was first claimed by Spain in the 16th century, wrested away by the British, taken back by Spain, declared an independent republic by a group of ragtag Americans, and finally turned over by Spain to the United States in 1819. Very little happened in this remote, mosquito-infested outpost until the real estate boom of the 1920s. Then, dream cities sprouted up everywhere as the pitch of the real estate promoter was heard in the land. Property values increased from hour to hour, and thousands of persons bought unseen acres, many under salt water. It took three disasters—the hurricanes of 1926 and 1928 and the crash of 1929—to burst the bubble. But by then, the lure of Florida had been implanted in the American soul.

Today Florida constitutes America's tropics. The state's first tourist, Juan Ponce de Leon, didn't find his fountain of youth when he stepped ashore near St. Augustine in 1513, but modern-day retired persons, who are moving here at the rate of one thousand per week, are still trying. Whether beside a Fort Lauderdale beach, at a Fort Myers condo swimming pool, at a Miami jai alai fronton, or on a St. Petersburg park bench, they look for rejuvenation.

Florida has been elevated to its so-called "megastate" niche by a migration unique in American history. In 1950, the state had two million people; when the 1990 census figures are tallied, the total will exceed 12 million, nearly all of the increase coming from people moving in from other states. The state's population exceeded Ohio in 1984, Illinois in 1986, and Pennsylvania in 1987. It is now the fourth largest state, behind only California, New York, and Texas.

Peter Dickinson, a well-known authority on retirement, once said that if you're *determined* to find whatever it is you're searching for in retirement, you'll find it somewhere in Florida. Florida is the number one tourist destination in the world. It has nine distinct media markets, two coasts, snow, perpetual sunshine, swamps, islands, new no-down-payment homes for $45,000, and houses you can't afford if you have to ask their price. If there are two factors that account for the numbers of highly rated places here, they are climate and the near-term outlook for employment. One factor that mars their ratings, however, is unquestionably crime.

HAWAII

★ Honolulu, HI (#14)

Maui, HI (#93)

The last state to join the Union (1959), Hawaii is also the southernmost state. Just below 22 degrees of latitude, Honolulu, the capital, is as far south as middle Mexico. The state of 120 islands is 2,400 airline miles from mainland United States. Let's use the word *paradise* only once to note where it sits in the American mind. The word aptly fits; and then, again, it doesn't.

This is the only state in the tropical climate zone, officially defined as anywhere temperatures never fall below 64 degrees. Orchids grow wild here; the sun shines most of the time; the Pacific trade winds keep the islands temperate; the beaches are superb; the water is deep and blue.

The cost of living, however, is so high that this is the only state to *discourage* mainland persons from moving in for retirement. From the Commission on Aging on down to professionals selling condominiums, you're going to hear the discouraging word. Though the islands are relatively inexpensive to visit, they are unaffordable for year-round living for most retired persons.

Still, they come. Honolulu, like San Diego and San Antonio, is extremely popular with ex-military. Apropos of its size, it ranks high in services, prospects for employment growth, and leisure living. It also experiences a surprisingly modest level of crime. Maui, Kauai, and the Big Island of Hawaii are drawing older newcomers at a faster rate than Honolulu.

MID-ATLANTIC METRO BELT

Canandaigua, NY (#145)

Cape May, NJ (#140)

Charlottesville, VA (#103)

Columbia County, NY (#150)

Easton–Chesapeake Bay, MD (#130)

Lancaster County, PA (#124)

Martinsburg–Charles Town, WV (#108)

Monticello–Liberty, NY (#151)

New Paltz–Ulster County, NY (#138)

Ocean City–Assateague Island, MD (#100)

Ocean County, NJ (#64)

Pike County, PA (#148)

Rehoboth Bay–Indian River Bay, DE (#136)

★ Virginia Beach–Norfolk, VA (#26)

The area south from New York City to Washington and through the northern Virginia suburbs to Richmond is the most densely settled in America. Many cities in this region—notably Newark, Trenton, Philadelphia, Wilmington, and Baltimore—have been losing population for years.

In the midst of stagnation, however, one can easily overlook the pockets of retirement growth not visible from the Amtrak rails or Interstate Highway 95: the Atlantic beach counties, Chesapeake Bay, the Catskills, and smaller metro areas like civilized Lancaster and Charlottesville, south of Washington and northwest of Richmond.

The 130 miles of New Jersey's sandy Atlantic coastline, particularly from the tip of Cape May north to Toms River, is rebounding after years of decline. One in five residents of Ocean County is over 65, compared with the U.S. average of one in nine. The retired newcomers among them didn't have to come far; they are often New Yorkers and Philadelphians, some returning after a disappointing stint in Florida. Many planned retirement communities have been built or are being developed here, though people who want less structure can find many small seaside towns, particularly south of Atlantic City and west of the Garden State Parkway.

Farther south, you'll find retirement destinations within hailing distance of Washington and Baltimore on the Delmarva Peninsula and the shores of Chesapeake Bay. Many of the bigger summer resorts resemble Miami Beach rather than the charming, small seaside communities they once were before the opening of the Chesapeake Bay Bridge in 1952. Delaware's Rehoboth Beach, which has a winter population of 2,040 and a summer population of 50,000, calls itself the nation's summer capital because so many federal workers crowd its beaches. Ocean City, just over the border in Maryland, is also a popular resort among Washington and Baltimore residents.

MID-SOUTH

Aiken, SC (#129)

Athens, GA (#109)

Chapel Hill, NC (#101)

Crossville, TN (#50)

Lexington–Fayette, KY (#95)

Murray–Kentucky Lake, KY (#48)

Paris–Big Sandy, TN (#63)

Thomasville, GA (#82)

This region is neither north nor, with the exception of Thomasville, Georgia, too far south to be thoroughly Dixie. It's mainly in the center of the country's eastern half and includes North Carolina's and Georgia's Piedmont (but not their mountains—they are part of New Appalachia) and most of Kentucky and Tennessee.

Middle Tennessee, hemmed in by the looping Tennessee River, is gently rolling bluegrass country: fertile, well-watered, and famous for its fine livestock. The heart of the state, it is rich in tradition and history, and its rural people cling to southern folkways.

Kentucky encompasses mountains in its sandstone area, deep gorges and caves in its limestone region, and swampy flats and oxbow lagoons in the far western part of the state. This end of Kentucky is called the Purchase, after the Jackson Purchase, which bought 8,500 square miles in Kentucky and Tennessee from the Chickasaw Indians. Although Kentucky always had plenty of navigable rivers, it wasn't until the TVA projects of the 1930s and 1940s that it had a large number of lakes. These impoundments, created by dams on the Tennessee River and its tributaries, have transformed both Kentucky and Tennessee into frontrunners for fishing and water recreation.

Why is the Mid-South such an attractive retirement region? For one thing, the region lies north of more established retirement areas of the Sun Belt. Recent demographic research shows that although the

Sun Belt still remains a big drawing card for older adults, the "Retirement Belt" seems to be widening north. People are discovering the benefits of being closer to their former homes in the Midwest or Northeast, the desirability of mild, four-season climates as opposed to the monotony of the semitropical varieties, and the great advantages of low costs and low crime rates compared with many retirement areas farther south.

Furthermore, the gently rolling terrain with its pleasant scenery, the unhurried pace of life (far less manic than in many parts of Florida), and the outdoor recreational options coupled with the weather to enjoy them fully make the Mid-South a winner.

NEW APPALACHIA

Asheville, NC (#70)	★ Clayton, GA (#30)
Blacksburg, VA (#56)	Hendersonville, NC (#127)
★ Brevard, NC (#21)	Lake Lanier, GA (#119)

There's a 600-mile stretch of Appalachian Mountains from Frederick County in Virginia to Hall County, Georgia, that absorbed a good deal of antipoverty money during the 1960s and 1970s. Much of the area is still poor. Much of it, too, is as scenic as any place in the nation.

This is a land of peaks and ridges, rushing streams and thundering waterfalls. In the earliest spring days, the hillsides burst with flowering trees and shrubs: rhododendron, azalea, dogwood, and magnolia. The George Washington, Pisgah, and Chattahoochee national forests stand tall with black walnut, pine, beech, poplar, birch, and oak. The mountain vistas, especially along the Blue Ridge Parkway, show row after spectacular row of parallel mountain ridges. Distant parts of what you see from the road are so inaccessible that it's unlikely humans have regularly hiked more than 10 percent of the topography.

Because the area is bookended, so to speak, by Atlanta in the south and Washington in the north, it isn't at all unusual to encounter ex-urbanites from these major cities among the retired folks in places like Clayton in north Georgia, Asheville and Hendersonville in western North Carolina, and Blacksburg in the Virginia mountains. What is unusual are the new "Florida Clubs" formed by retired persons who settle here *after* a disappointing stint in the Sunshine State.

New Appalachia is becoming a major destination for retired persons, and many of the region's communities are virtually ideal for retirement living, offering a wide range of special services for older residents. The Appalachian counties generally combine low costs of living and housing, low crime rates, adequate health care facilities in most places, and some of the country's mildest four-season climates.

You're going to need a car to get around comforta-

bly in much of this region, though. It is a rough wilderness area abundant in natural beauty, yet it is located within reach of major eastern population centers, which eliminates the feeling of isolation so often associated with wilderness areas.

NEW ENGLAND

Amherst–Northampton, MA (#80)	Hanover, NH (#61)
Bar Harbor–Frenchman Bay, ME (#98)	Keene, NH (#146)
Bennington, VT (#137)	Laconia–Lake Winnipesaukee, NH (#132)
Burlington, VT (#113)	North Conway–White Mountains, NH (#123)
Camden–Penobscot Bay, ME (#84)	Portsmouth–Dover–Durham, NH (#141)
Cape Cod, MA (#102)	

In New England, the preferred retirement destinations aren't in heavily urbanized Connecticut, Massachusetts, or Rhode Island. One big exception is Massachusetts' Barnstable County (Cape Cod), where one in three residents over the past 15 years has been a newcomer and where one in five is now over age 65. A future exception may be in Hampshire County (Amherst–Northampton) in western Massachusetts. To find the most popular retirement spots in New England, however, look in the countryside pockets of the north, in Maine, New Hampshire, and Vermont.

In the decades since 1970, Maine's population has jumped 21 percent. By Sun Belt standards, such growth may seem paltry. For the Pine Tree State, though, it's been the fastest upsurge since the mid-19th century.

Most retired newcomers choose the rocky Atlantic coast over the hard-going farm areas and rough-cut paper- and lumber-mill towns in Maine's interior. Within the seascape counties—Hancock, Knox, Lincoln, and York—the places that draw retired people are the small lobster ports and summer resort towns off old U.S. Highway 1, places with names like Camden, Bar Harbor, Ellsworth, Wiscasset, and Rockland.

New Hampshire, too, is growing. Indeed, it is growing the most quickly of all the northeastern states—mainly at the expense of Massachusetts, its heavily taxed neighbor. You'll pay no income or sales taxes here (the only other state where this is still possible is Alaska). But you will pay handsomely for real estate along huge Lake Winnipesaukee's shoreline and around Hanover (home of Dartmouth College) and in the environs of North Conway, a resort town.

For all its attraction for disaffected New Yorkers and Pennsylvanians who come to live year round, Vermont remains the most rural state in America according to the Census Bureau. Two of every three residents here live beyond the built-up limits of cities. Much of the state unmistakably is a 19th-century Currier & Ives landscape of sugar maples, dairy farms, and steepled white Congregational churches that dominate every green town common. In early October, the brilliant fall foliage draws busloads of weekenders from Boston and New York. As a general rule, the southern counties (Bennington, for example) draw retired people, and the northern counties draw skiers.

NORTH WOODS

Charlevoix–Boyne City, MI (#97)
Door County, WI (#115)
Eagle River, WI (#66)
Houghton Lake, MI (#89)
Petoskey–Straits of Mackinac, MI (#125)
Traverse City–Grand Traverse Bay, MI (#68)

One region violating the "Law of Thermodemographics" (warm bodies eventually head south to the Sun Belt and stay there) has got to be that which includes the northern counties of Michigan's Lower Peninsula and two Wisconsin counties in Packer country near Green Bay. Winters here are long and cold. Spring, summer, and fall are lovely seasons but are all too short.

During the 1970s, this area saw a population increase unequaled since waves of Finns, Germans, Czechs, and Poles arrived 80 years previously. Growth continues, but at a slower pace. On any summer weekend, campers, RVs, and boat-trailing cars crowd the northbound lanes of I-75 out of Detroit, I-94 out of Chicago, and I-43 out of Milwaukee. The traffic offers a clue to why the formerly depressed North Woods, forested with hemlock and Norway pine, have come back.

The area's pull is strong for many vacationers from the big industrial cities of the Great Lakes. Many of these people decide to winterize their rural lakefront or flatwoods second home and retire for year-round residency.

This is recreation land with a rugged, Paul Bunyan flavor, not only in the summer months when the population doubles, but during the fall deer-hunting and winter skiing season, too. Most of Michigan's 11,000 and Wisconsin's 15,000 lakes are up here. "In some lakes," the *New York Times* reported in a profile of Eagle River and its environs, "the fishermen can see thirty feet down in waters forest green, or black, or blue, depending on the time of day or the perspective, and can retrieve dropped eyeglasses or snagged fishing lures."

In spite of high personal income and property taxes in these two North Woods states, the cost of living is still lower than in most other retirement regions. Except for small cities like Sturgeon Bay in Wisconsin and Traverse City and Petoskey in Michigan, though, you won't find much in the way of structured retirement activities or a full range of health care facilities. Nor will you find expanding job prospects. Do expect to drive a good distance for retail shopping; this is rough, beautiful, but sparsely settled, country.

OZARKS AND OUACHITAS

Benton County, AR (#37)
★ Branson–Table Rock Lake, MO (#17)
Fayetteville, AR (#36)
Grand Lake, OK (#56)
Harrison, AR (#41)
Hot Springs National Park, AR (#31)
★ Mountain Home–Bull Shoals, AR (#15)

Like New Appalachia, the Ozarks and Ouachitas of southern Missouri, northern and western Arkansas, and eastern Oklahoma are a kind of highland area with distinct folkways and geology that are undergoing rapid changes. In both areas, country craft galleries and bluegrass music festivals abound, and the mountain roads that wind through small towns also wind through some of the nation's prettiest countryside. Here, an automobile is a virtual necessity. Many Ozark and Ouachita natives can trace their family names all the way back to Carolina and Virginia mountain roots.

Nearly two million people live in these hilly plateaus (the Ozarks) and ridge-valley mountains (the Ouachitas). Mention this region and you evoke an image of small-scale subsistence farming, chickens roosting in the hickory tree out back, shoeless springs and summers, moonshining, poverty, and isolation. Applied to the rural counties, the image was accurate until the 1960s.

When the public utilities built hydroelectric dams, they produced a series of large impounded lakes in hardwood forests, which in turn produced resorts and a steady migration of retired people from Des Moines, Omaha, Tulsa, Oklahoma City, Memphis, Kansas City, St. Louis, and especially Chicago.

Some of the newcomers are what demographer Calvin Beale calls the new gentry—professional people with good incomes who can see themselves doing a bit of farming on a small section of land. Others he describes as the new peasantry, back-to-the-land types interested in raising their own food, promoting conservation, maintaining rural values, and using alternative fuel sources.

Lately, this region has been waking up to the problems that come with growth. Concerns about the loss of a special way of life are increasingly voiced; some locals say it may have already passed from the scene, never to be revived, despite local folk culture institutes and craft schools. The areas outside the biggest cities—Fayetteville and Fort Smith, Arkansas, and Springfield and Joplin, Missouri—aren't densely populated, yet some of the lakes are having pollution problems, and some of the better-known resorts are acquiring a tacky patina of liquor stores, fast-food outlets, tourist attractions, and New Age crystal shops.

PACIFIC NORTHWEST

Bellingham, WA (#46)
Bend, OR (#112)
Eugene–Springfield, OR (#75)
Grants Pass, OR (#106)
Medford–Ashland, OR (#119)
Newport–Lincoln City, OR (#133)

Oak Harbor–Whidbey Island, WA (#130)

San Juan Islands, WA (#147)

Olympia, WA (#71)

Wenatchee, WA (#47)

Port Townsend, WA (#79)

In the 1970s, no other state made so clear its desire to discourage immigration as did Oregon when its popular governor, Tom McCall, urged tourists to give the state a try. "But for heaven's sake," he quickly added, "don't come to live here." This awareness of the harm that rapid population growth can bring to beautiful, pristine land is commonly felt elsewhere in the Pacific Northwest.

Nevertheless, the near collapse of the lumber industry in Oregon and Washington in the early 1980s has caused local planners to behave like their counterparts in other states and to compete for industrial development and population growth.

Certain rural areas are being pitched as retirement havens—ironic, because older adults from the Great Lakes, the distant Northeast, and even sun-baked Southern California have been coming to this area for years to enjoy the clear air, quiet, and uncrowded space.

In the state of Washington, their destinations are most often the islands reached by bridge or ferry from downtown Seattle, and places like Olympia, Port Angeles, Port Townsend, Sequim, and Bellingham with salt water frontages. The area, with the tall Cascades and Olympic mountains in view, has a somewhat wet marine climate, low crime rates, and outstanding outdoor recreation endowments. In Oregon, retired persons settle along the Pacific Coast and in the forested cities and towns along I-5 between Portland and the California border.

Calvin Beale, a well-known demographer, observed not long ago that the popularity of the Pacific Northwest Cloud Belt just goes to show that " 'Sun Belt' is a very imperfect synonym for population growth."

During the 1970s, for example, Bend and the surrounding forested environs in Deschutes County, Oregon, made up one of the fastest-growing places west of Florida. Of more than 300 metropolitan areas in the United States, Olympia, Washington's park-like state capital, ranked in the top 10 in rate of growth over the same period, along with the Florida metro areas of Ocala and Fort Myers–Cape Coral.

RIO GRANDE COUNTRY

Alamogordo, NM (#122)

Albuquerque, NM (#93)

★ Brownsville–Harlingen, TX (#5)

Carlsbad–Artesia, NM (#99)

Deming, NM (#116)

Las Cruces, NM (#89)

Los Alamos, NM (#92)

McAllen–Edinburg–Mission, TX (#44)

Roswell, NM (#134)

Santa Fe, NM (#88)

The Rio Grande rises in the Rocky Mountains in southwestern Colorado, flows south through the center of New Mexico west of Santa Fe, through Albuquerque and Las Cruces, and serves as a 1,240-mile boundary between Texas and Mexico before emptying into the Gulf of Mexico some 60 miles downriver from Brownsville.

Like the Delta South, this area has a large ethnic population. Two of every five persons are Mexican–American, and one in 10 is American Indian. Like the Delta South, too, Rio Grande Country is distinguished by low incomes, large families, poor housing, joblessness, low levels of education, and other social problems.

Along the river's southward progress are a few pockets of phenomenal retirement growth. Not only Albuquerque but also the cities of Roswell, Deming, and Las Cruces and the settled areas around them have all seen their number of residents over age 65 jump at three or more times the average national rate. Even with the well-publicized growth that most of arid and semiarid New Mexico has experienced, there are still fewer than eight persons per square mile. The desert-mesa vastness is imposing, the distances between towns great, and the loneliness outside city limits a little scary to retired persons hailing from large cities.

The lower valley in southmost Texas isn't lonely at all. This is the number one winter tourist destination in all of Texas. Since 1980, Cameron County (Brownsville–Harlingen) and Hidalgo County (McAllen–Edinburg–Mission) have together gained 130,000 people, many of them retired midwesterners who found a climate as mild as Florida's and living costs nearly as low as Mexico's.

ROCKY MOUNTAINS

Boise, ID (#80)

Coeur d'Alene, ID (#58)

Colorado Springs, CO (#86)

★ Fort Collins–Loveland, CO (#27)

Grand Junction, CO (#52)

Hamilton–Bitterroot Valley, MT (#72)

Kalispell, MT (#85)

What does green and rugged Coeur d'Alene in Idaho's panhandle have in common with sun-baked Deming in southwestern New Mexico? Very little. Yet the Census Bureau lumps them together in a region it labels Mountain. By better reasoning, Deming, with its desert and Hispanic flavors, more properly belongs in Rio Grande Country. When it comes to certain foothill-and-mountain counties in Arizona, Colorado, Idaho, and Montana, however, the feel is definitely high-country, definitely Rocky Mountains.

In spite of the reservations many older adults have about high altitudes and cold winters, the Rockies are emerging from their vacation-only status, becoming an area where older adults are moving for year-round living.

In Colorado, one can easily distinguish between the Eastern Slope and Western Slope areas. Large cities like Colorado Springs (in a setting that reminds many of Asheville in the North Carolina mountains) and Fort Collins are Eastern Slope. Grand Junction, near the Utah border, is the population center of the Western Slope. The two slopes have different political orientations (conservative Western Slope versus Pat Schroeder liberalism) and different growth rates. In Idaho, where the population rose by more than one-third in the last 15 years, retired newcomers head for the city of Coeur d'Alene, within commuting distance of Spokane, Washington, or they settle near metropolitan Boise. In Montana, the spectacular but sparsely settled western counties—particularly Flathead, Lake, Missoula, and Ravalli—are the ones drawing older newcomers.

SOUTH ATLANTIC AND GULF COASTS

★ Biloxi–Gulfport–Pass Christian, MS (#29)

Brunswick–Golden Isles, GA (#61)

★ Charleston, SC (#16)

Edenton–Albemarle Sound, NC (#72)

Fairhope–Gulf Shores, AL (#48)

Hilton Head–Beaufort, SC (#65)

Myrtle Beach, SC (#45)

New Bern, NC (#51)

Rockport–Aransas Pass, TX (#66)

★ St. Tammany Parish, LA (#9)

Savannah, GA (#53)

★ Southport, NC (#11)

The retirement places in the South Atlantic and Gulf Coast region have a special appeal and flavor. Although the coastline is dotted with many very old cities, such as Charleston, Galveston, and Savannah, it experienced rapid growth during the 1970s.

Most of these resort-retirement areas lie in low, marshy land either on the mainland itself or on nearby barrier islands. Palmetto palms, scrub oak, dune grass, and Spanish moss swaying in the sea breezes impart a languid, relaxed mood. Fishing shanties lie scattered near the piers where shrimpers, crabbers, and trawlers moor. Stately planter-style cottages set back from the narrow street are almost hidden behind tall hedges and are surrounded by massive live oaks. Streets paved with old oyster and clam shells; small gift shops, boutiques, and shops offering seafood, gumbo, and chicory coffee; taverns and inns of all ages and sizes—these are what you'll find in every metro area, town, and village of the coastal islands.

The South Atlantic and Gulf Coast resorts are less crowded and have lower living costs than most comparable places on the Florida peninsula. Furthermore, their summer months, while sometimes uncomfortable, are less rugged than those farther south. You are likely to find newer buildings and younger people here than in some older retirement havens.

On the minus side, crime rates are high. Of the 12 retirement places in this region, only four—Edenton–Albemarle Sound, Fairhope–Gulf Shores, New Bern, and Southport—have above-average ratings for personal safety. Health care facilities can be inadequate, and while housing costs are generally low for the region, some places (such as Hilton Head–Beaufort) are expensive. Finally, these low-lying oceanside locations are subject to damage from severe tropical storms.

TAHOE BASIN AND THE OTHER CALIFORNIA

Amador County, CA (#128)

Carson City–Minden, NV (#144)

Chico–Paradise, CA (#77)

Clear Lake, CA (#142)

Grass Valley–Truckee, CA (#121)

Red Bluff–Sacramento Valley, CA (#125)

Redding, CA (#87)

Reno, NV (#149)

South Lake Tahoe–Placerville, CA (#113)

Twain Harte–Yosemite, CA (#118)

In California, three out of four residents live either in the Los Angeles basin or in metropolitan San Francisco–Oakland–San Jose. Everyone else lives in a part of the state the Beach Boys seem never to have sung about.

You might call it the Other California. Parts of it—the Mother Lode Country and the northern Sacramento Valley—are seeing a growing number of retired newcomers, most of whom are Californians.

Mother Lode Country, the mountainous interior, with alpine meadows, blizzard-filled passes, clear lakes, trout streams, and magnificent scenery, was once a mining area and now is a tourist haven. Donner Lake, a popular summer beach resort, also doubles as a winter ski area. Even in midsummer, this high mountain lake tends to be on the chilly side. Tuolumne County, roughly 100 miles to the south, contains spectacular Yosemite National Park, with all of the attendant opportunities for outstanding outdoor recreation. Although the gold rush is over, these areas continue to attract people with scenery, mountain climate, and open spaces. Places like Grass Valley, Nevada City, Truckee, and Twain Harte are seeing higher living costs, especially those associated with owning a home.

Clear Lake, on the northwest fringe of the Great Interior Valley, is California's largest natural freshwater lake and centerpiece of Lake County's resort area. In addition to excellent fishing, Clear Lake (Bass Capital of the West) offers good boating facilities.

Water recreation is also available in nearby Tehama County at Red Bluff, where Diversion Dam spans the Sacramento River. Red Bluff has some splendid Victorian homes, as does Chico downriver. Both these areas have shown substantial growth in recent years, including a sizable increase due to in-migration of retired people from densely populated Southern California.

TEXAS INTERIOR

Athens–Cedar Creek Lake, TX (#59)

★ Austin, TX (#12)

Burnet–Marble Falls–Llano, TX (#60)

Canton–Lake Tawakoni, TX (#77)

Fredericksburg, TX (#69)   New Braunfels, TX (#38)

Kerrville, TX (#42)   ★ San Antonio, TX (#2)

Of all the states, Texas perhaps occupies the most distinctive place in the American mind. To paraphrase a 60-year-old guidebook, Texas is so large that if it could be folded up and over, using its northernmost boundary as a hinge, McAllen would be plunked down in the middle of North Dakota; and if it were folded eastward, El Paso would lie just off the coast of Florida.

Out in the country, there are more internally sharp contrasts here than in any other state. Northeast Texas looks like Arkansas. East Texas is deeply southern with small farms bringing in sugar cane, cotton, and rice. Southwest Texas is mainly lonely open-range cattle country. Northwest Texas is dry and mountainous, looking like parts of New Mexico.

You'll find contrasting retirement regions, too. The lower Rio Grande valley is distinctly Hispanic and has winters as mild as Florida's. So do the Gulf Coast beaches, from South Padre Island up to just above Corpus Christi. Then there's an area in the middle of the state encompassing the lovely cedar-scented Hill Country along with Austin and San Antonio.

According to visitors, Austin, state capital and home of the University of Texas, seems to have the same terrain and natural vegetation as New England. Metropolitan Austin is growing so quickly that its population by the year 2000 is projected to be double what it was 10 years previously. In spite of negative appreciation in recent years because of the slumping Texas economy, housing costs are somewhat high. Austin is a "books and bureaucrats" city, drawing a good many retired University of Texas alumni from all over the nation along with Texas government employees.

San Antonio's appeal as a retirement destination, on the other hand, has four causes: Brooks, Kelly, Lackland, and Randolph. These are big Air Force bases. Many veterans who were posted to them during the 1940s and 1950s have returned for the mild San Antonio winters, low living costs, and pleasant Hispanic atmosphere.

West of Austin and northwest of San Antonio, the Hill Country towns (Fredericksburg and Kerrville) have spic-and-span layouts in their old sections. These are towns settled by Germans who fled their homeland in the mid-19th century. So attractive is this area that much of it is experiencing second-home development by prosperous Texans and others from outside the state.

Appendix

Relocation Resources

No single book can satisfy every reader. If you feel *Retirement Places Rated* didn't give you what you wanted or needed, here are some highly recommended recent books that might.

Dickinson, Peter, *Sunbelt Retirement*, Glenview, IL, Scott, Foresman and Company, 1987. An American Association of Retired Persons (AARP) book focusing on desirable locations in 13 southern and western states.

Dickinson, Peter, *Retirement Edens Outside the Sunbelt*, Glenview, IL, Scott, Foresman and Company, 1987. Also an AARP book, this time concentrating on places in 37 other states.

Howells, John, *Retirement Choices*, San Francisco, CA, Gateway Books, 1987. Written with humor and humanity by a journalist who prefers lifestyles over statistics. Covers the Sun Belt and Oregon.

It may be that while *Retirement Places Rated* helped you, there are still some areas where you need more information or want to do your own research. Here are some resources. A good library will have many, but you'll have to write for others.

How places present themselves. There are 596 separate Chamber of Commerce organizations promoting the benefits of living and doing business somewhere within the 151 places profiled in this book. That should give you an idea of how competitive the market is for attracting new residents, especially ones with large net worths.

Writing to Chambers of Commerce for their "newcomer's pack" produces a collection of promotional brochures, maps, business statistics, cost-of-living data, and events calendars (it may also trigger mail and telephone calls from real estate brokers). The annual *World Wide Chamber of Commerce Directory* lists the chamber name, address, and telephone number, as well as the name of the chamber's contact person, for over 4,000 locations in the United States. It is available in good libraries.

Be aware that some chambers promptly respond to your inquiry with useful materials; others do not respond at all. Frequently, you will receive more material if you identify yourself as a prospective new resident than you will if you say you're retired.

What *really* goes on in other places. If you've identified a few likely locations, a short-term subscription to their local newspapers is invaluable. After reading a month's worth, you'll have an excellent idea of consumer prices, political issues, and other matters on the mind of residents.

For the name, address, telephone number, monthly subscription cost, special features, and politics (typically independent) of each of the country's 1,635 daily newspapers, the best source is Editor & Publisher's *International Yearbook*. Note: most dailies publish Sunday editions and will fill "Sunday Only" subscriptions. Whether you want a daily or just a Sunday subscription, be sure to tell the circulation department that you want to receive the classified sections and shopping inserts. To save postage, newspapers omit these sections in mail subscriptions.

For similar information on the 6,890 semi-weekly and weekly newspapers (often the only publications covering rural areas), *Gale's Directory of Publications* is an alternative source.

General living costs. Every three months, the American Chamber of Commerce Researchers Association (ACCRA) surveys the costs of housing, food, services, transportation, and health care in 250 locations around the United States. While the ACCRA survey is modeled on what a young family of four buys, and hence isn't meant for retirement purposes, it is still enormously useful for making comparisons.

You can order a four-quarter subscription for $100, or the latest quarter's survey for $50 from:

ACCRA
1 Riverfront Plaza
Louisville, KY 40202
(502) 566-5031

Better yet, save your money. If you're thinking of

only one or two destinations, call your local Chamber of Commerce. If it belongs to ACCRA, it can readily give you cost comparisons over the telephone.

What would your house cost elsewhere? Do you know a professional appraiser? Ask him or her to do an analysis, using Marshall and Swift's *Residential Cost Handbook,* of what your home would cost in, say, Albuquerque or Austin. The handbook is a standard among appraisers and is updated every three months. Using a "Current Cost Multiplier" and a "Local Cost Multiplier," the appraiser can give you a good idea of how values differ in over 500 locations around the country.

Local "for sale" markets; a first look. Residential real estate is so competitive that many brokers now show homes on cable television, ship video tapes to newcomers who are qualified buyers, and advertise their listings in national magazines.

Remember, you are under no obligation when you request copies of these magazines. If you don't wish to be contacted by a local broker, say so to the person who takes your order.

> Homes & Land Publishing Corporation
> P.O. Box 5018
> Tallahassee, FL 32314
> (800) 874-8163

Finding and buying rural land. Pricing rural land isn't at all the same as pricing a house in the suburbs. Often there aren't enough recent sales of nearby parcels of similar size, topography, and quality to provide a basis for value. This is especially true of sloping acreage that's good for nothing but enjoying the view. For these reasons, many parcels are advertised nationally in the Strout or United Farm catalog to attract buyers who may value scenic land or agricultural acreage differently than the locals do.

Many would-be land buyers have found the prices in these catalogs are high. Nevertheless, they offer some idea of what you may be up against if your goal is a small farm or a hideaway in the mountains. Certainly the photographs and capsule descriptions will feed a daydream or two. For a free Strout catalog contact:

> Strout Realty
> P.O. Box 4528
> Springfield, MO 65808
> (800) 641-4266

The United Farm catalog is free from:

> United National Real Estate
> 4700 Belleview
> Kansas City, MO 64112
> (800) 999-1020

Buying subdivided lots. The federal government's Office of Interstate Lands Sales Registration (OILSR) maintains records of 17,000 multilot developments that are promoted in interstate commerce. If you want to do a little homework on real estate investment before making any commitment, OILSR publishes a booklet, "Buying Lots for Development," available free by writing:

> Office of Interstate Lands Sales Registration
> Room 6274
> 451 Seventh Street, S.W.
> Washington, DC 20410
> (202) 708-2716

Exchange Trial. Living in a new community before selling your house back home is a good way to evaluate the new area at your own pace before burning bridges. It's possible to swap houses with someone in the area you're interested in for a trial period. Here are three major home-exchange clubs where you can list your home in their directories for a fee of $15 to $35. You are then free to exchange letters and make appropriate arrangements. Deadlines for listings are about six months in advance of the time you might want to swap. For details, write:

> Vacation Exchange Club
> 12006 111th Ave.
> Youngtown, AZ 85363
> (602) 972-2186

> Loan-a-Home
> Two Park Lane, Apt. 6E
> Mt. Vernon, NY 10552
> (914) 664-7640

> International Home Exchange Service
> P.O. Box 190070
> San Francisco, CA 94119
> (415) 435-3497

How does your climate compare? Meteorologists at the National Climatic Data Center can take your order for comparative data that the Center publishes for any of thousands of locations in this country.

The Center's best seller is the annual *Comparative Climatic Data for the United States,* a collection of month-by-month and annual summaries for normal daily maximum and minimum temperature, average and maximum wind speed, percent of possible sunshine, rainfall, snowfall, and morning and afternoon humidity at each of 300 "first order" weather stations in this country. The cost is $3, plus $5 handling and shipping.

If the place you have in mind doesn't have a first order weather station, it may yet be one of 1,063 locations with a "cooperative" weather station. Their data are *Climatography of the United States, Series 20,* a two-page publication for each location containing freeze and precipitation probability data; tables of long-term monthly and annual mean maximum, mean minimum, and average temperature; and tables of monthly and annual total precipitation and total snowfall. The cost is $1 for each location, plus $5 handling and shipping.

All orders must be prepaid by check, MasterCard, Visa, or American Express. Call or write:

National Climatic Data Center
Federal Building
Asheville, NC 28801
(704) 259-0682

Finding crime rates in smaller places. *Retirement Places Rated* uses counties to define retirement places. One caveat: just as crime rates vary from one county to another, so do crime rates vary among towns within a *single* county. Though a retirement place may end up with a crime score that makes it look as dangerous as the rough-cut 19th-century frontier, certain towns within its county boundaries are havens of rectitude and serenity.

Two examples are Phoenix (Maricopa County), Arizona, and Daytona Beach (Volusia County), Florida. With respective rankings of 133 and 114 out of 151 retirement places, these two are among the more crime-ridden in this book. Yet despite these poor rankings, both counties contain suburban towns that contrast sharply with their more dangerous surroundings. Within metropolitan Phoenix, the towns of Avondale, Buckeye, El Mirage, and Paradise Valley are extremely safe. So are Edgewater, Lake Helen, Ponce Inlet, and Port Orange within metropolitan Daytona Beach.

How safe are Phoenix and Daytona Beach? There, as elsewhere, it all depends on where you live within the county. One source that helps you determine the relative safety of hundreds of places is the FBI's annual *Crime in the United States*. It is available in most libraries, or for $16 you can order it postpaid from:

Superintendent of Documents
U.S. Government Printing Office
Washington, DC 20402-9325
(202) 783-3238

Moving to the great outdoors. Not for nothing does this book count the acres in national parks, forests, and wildlife refuges. The 247 rural counties in the United States, where more than one-third of the land area is owned by the federal government, are retirement destinations, too, offering low-density living in the midst of spectacular scenery.

The federal agencies mentioned in this chapter have maps, listings, and descriptive brochures for recreation lands under their stewardship. For further information, send your specific requests to the following agencies. Tell them what part of the country you are interested in visiting and what kind of information you need. In some cases the agency may refer you to a district office in your area.

Department of Agriculture
National Forest Service
Publications Office
P.O. Box 96090
Washington, DC 20090-6090

Department of the Interior
Fish and Wildlife Service
Publications Unit
4401 North Fairfax Drive
Arlington, VA 22203

Department of the Interior
National Park Service
Office of Public Affairs
Public Inquiries
P.O. Box 37127
Washington, DC 20013-7127

Finding specialized hospital services. The best source is the American Hospital Association's annual *Guide to the Health Care Field*. Organized by state and by city, the guide provides a variety of information about every hospital in the United States, including address and telephone number, control (public, private, investor-owned, federal, city, state), length of stay (short term, long term), and which ones are certified for Medicare participation and accredited by the Joint Commission on Accreditation of Hospitals.

More importantly, the guide indicates which of 54 specialized facilities are available in each hospital. Cardiac intensive care, physical therapy, hemodialysis, podiatric service, psychiatric outpatient service, blood bank, home care, and health promotion, for example, are several important facilities not obtainable everywhere.

Verifying medical credentials. It is up to the states to license and regulate professions. Kentucky licenses watchmakers and auctioneers but not psychologists; Maine certifies tree surgeons and movie projectionists but not occupational therapists; Arkansas licenses insect exterminators but not opticians. Fortunately, physicians and dentists must be certified before they can practice in any state.

Check a dentist's background in the *American Dental Directory*. Check a doctor's background in the *Directory of Medical Specialists*. Both sources are updated each year, and are organized by state and by city. What to look for: medical or dental school attended, year graduated (you're not looking for a health care professional who is about to retire), specializations, and board certifications.

Quacks operate everywhere, however, because impressive-looking credentials aren't difficult to obtain. One California firm, recently shut down by the Postal Service, furnished a medical degree—complete with transcript, diploma, and letters of recommendation—to anyone for $28,000. For $5, another firm mailed out "Outstanding Service" citations. Experts testifying in a recent House of Representatives hearing estimated that one out of 50 "doctors" is doing a thriving business with fraudulent credentials, and that three out of five of their patients are over 65.

State Aging Commissions. Don't be put off by

bureaucratic-sounding titles. State aging offices are gold mines of information on government services, job openings, self-employment opportunities, volunteer activities, social programs, and taxes. They also put you in touch with other local public and private organizations for retired persons.

Alabama Commission on Aging
502 Washington Avenue, Montgomery 36130
(205)261-5743

Alaska Older Alaskans Commission
P.O. Box C, Mail Station 0209, Juneau 99811
(907)465-3250

Arizona Aging and Adult Administration
1400 West Washington St., Phoenix 85007
(602)255-4446

Arkansas Office of Aging and Adult Services
P.O. Box 1437, Little Rock 72203
(501)371-2441

California Department of Aging
1600 K St., Sacramento 95841
(916)322-5290

Colorado Aging and Adult Services Division
717 17th St., 11th Floor, Denver 80218
(303)294-5912

Connecticut Department on Aging
174 Main St., Hartford 06106
(203)566-3238

Delaware Division of Aging
1901 N. DuPont Hwy, New Castle 19720
(302)421-6791

Florida Aging and Adult Services
1321 Winewood Boulevard, Room 323, Tallahassee 32301
(904)488-2650

Georgia Office of Aging
878 Peachtree St., NE, Room 632, Atlanta 30309
(404)894-5333

Hawaii Executive Office on Aging
335 Merchant St., Room 241, Honolulu 96813
(808)548-2593

Idaho Office on Aging
Statehouse, Room 114, Boise 83720
(208)334-3833

Illinois Department on Aging
421 E. Capitol Avenue, Springfield 62701
(800)252-8966

Indiana Aging Division
P.O. Box 7083, Indianapolis 46204
(317)232-7020

Iowa Department of Elder Affairs
914 Grand Ave., Des Moines 50319
(515)281-5187

Kansas Department on Aging
610 W. 10th St., Topeka 66612
(913)296-4986

Kentucky Division for Aging Services
275 E. Main St., 6th Floor West, Frankfort 40621
(502)564-6930

Louisiana Governor's Office of Elder Affairs
P.O. Box 80374, Baton Rouge 70898
(504)925-1700

Maine Bureau of Maine's Elderly
Statehouse, Station 11, Augusta 04333
(207)289-2561

Maryland Office on Aging
301 W. Preston St., 10th floor, Baltimore 21201
(301)225-1100

Massachusetts Executive Office of Elder Affairs
38 Chauncey St., Boston 02111
(800)882-2003

Michigan Office of Services to the Aging
P.O. Box 30026, Lansing 48909
(517)373-8230

Minnesota Board on Aging
7th & Robert Streets, St. Paul 55101
(612)296-2544

Mississippi Council on Aging
301 W. Pearl St., Jackson 39201
(601)949-2013

Missouri Division on Aging
P.O. Box 1337, Jefferson City 65102
(800)392-0210

Montana Aging Service Bureau
P.O. Box 8005, Helena 59604
(406)444-5650

Nebraska Department on Aging
Statehouse Station 95044, Lincoln 68509
(402)471-2306

Nevada Division for Aging Services
505 E. King St., Carson City 89710
(702)885-4210

New Hampshire Division of Adult Services
6 Hazen Dr., Concord 03301
(603)225-0804

New Jersey Division on Aging
363 State St., CN 807, Trenton 08625
(609)292-4833

New Mexico State Agency on Aging
224 E. Palace Ave., Santa Fe 87501
(505)827-7640

New York Office for the Aging
Agency Building 2, Empire State Plaza, Albany 12223
(518)474-5731

North Carolina Division on Aging
1985 Umstead Drive, Raleigh 27603
(919)733-3983

North Dakota Aging Services
State Capitol Building, Bismarck 58505
(701)224-2310

Ohio Department of Aging
50 W. Broad St., 9th floor, Columbus 43215
(614)466-5500

Oklahoma Special Unit on Aging
P.O. Box 25352, Oklahoma City 73125
(405)521-2281

Oregon Senior Services
313 Public Service Building, Salem 97310
(503)378-4728

Pennsylvania Department of Aging
231 State St., Harrisburg 17101
(717)783-1550

Rhode Island Department of Elderly Affairs
79 Washington St., Providence 02903
(401)277-2880

South Carolina Commission on Aging
915 Main St., Columbia 29201
(803)734-3203

South Dakota Office of Adult Services
700 Governors Drive, Pierre 57501
(605)773-3656

Tennessee Commission on Aging
706 Church St., Nashville 37219
(615)741-2056

Texas Department on Aging
P.O. Box 12786, Capitol Station, Austin 78711
(512)444-2727

Utah Division on Aging
P.O. Box 45500, Salt Lake City 84115
(801)538-3910

Vermont Office on Aging
103 S. Main St., Waterbury 05676
(802)241-2400

Virginia Department for the Aging
101 N. 14th St., 18th floor, Richmond 23219
(804)225-2271

Washington Adult Services Administration
OB-44A, Olympia 98504
(206)753-2502

West Virginia Commission on Aging
State Capitol, Charleston 25305
(304)348-3317

Wisconsin Bureau on Aging
P.O. Box 7851, Madison 53707
(608)266-2536

Wyoming Commission on Aging
Hathaway Building, Room 139, Cheyenne 82002
(307)777-7986

Retirement Place Finder

The following listing, organized alphabetically by state, presents the 151 retirement places and all cities, towns, and unincorporated places with populations over 500 within their boundaries.

ALABAMA

Fairhope–Gulf Shores
(Baldwin County)
  Bay Minette, 7,770
  Daphne, 4,520
  Elberta, 610
  Fairhope, 8,720
  Foley, 5,020
  Gulf Shores, 2,830
  Lake Forest, 3,489
  Loxley, 910
  Orange Beach, 1,490
  Point Clear, 1,812
  Robertsdale, 2,450
  Silverhill, 630
  Spanish Fort, 2,364
  Summerdale, 670

ARIZONA

Lake Havasu City–Kingman
(Mohave County)
  Bullhead City, 20,160
  Colorado City, 2,560
  Kingman, 11,510
  Lake Havasu City, 19,710
Phoenix–Tempe–Scottsdale
(Maricopa County)
  Avondale, 10,660
  Buckeye, 4,030
  Carefree, 1,770
  Cashion, 3,014
  Cave Creek, 2,610
  Chandler, 81,080
  El Mirage, 4,320
  Fountain Hills, 2,771
  Gila Bend, 2,060
  Gilbert, 19,180
  Glendale, 140,170
  Goodyear, 4,830
  Guadalupe, 5,150
  Litchfield Park, 3,708
  Mesa, 280,360
  Paradise Valley, 12,490
  Peoria, 38,670
  Phoenix, 923,750
  Scottsdale, 121,740
  Sun City, 55,600
  Sun City West, 3,772
  Sun Lakes, 1,925
  Surprise, 4,960
  Tempe, 140,440
  Tolleson, 4,440
  Wickenburg, 4,240
  Youngtown, 2,320
Prescott (Yavapai County)
  Bagdad, 2,331
  Camp Verde, 6,170
  Chino Valley, 4,680
  Clarkdale, 1,970
  Cottonwood, 5,920
  Prescott, 22,480
  Prescott Valley, 5,430
Tucson (Pima County)
  Ajo, 5,189
  Catalina, 3,000

Green Valley, 8,000
  Marana, 1,780
  Oro Valley, 5,070
  Sells, 1,964
  South Tucson, 6,670
  Tucson, 385,720
Yuma (Yuma County)
  San Luis, 3,230
  Somerton, 4,810
  Wellton, 970
  Yuma, 51,000

ARKANSAS

Benton County
  Bella Vista, 6,000
  Bentonville, 10,960
  Centerton, 570
  Decatur, 1,040
  Gentry, 1,780
  Gravette, 1,310
  Little Flock, 750
  Lowell, 1,550
  Pea Ridge, 1,760
  Rogers, 22,940
  Siloam Springs, 8,730
Fayetteville (Washington
County)
  Elkins, 670
  Elm Springs, 780
  Farmington, 1,570
  Fayetteville, 40,730
  Goshen, 540
  Greenland, 750
  Johnson, 690
  Lincoln, 1,420
  Prairie Grove, 1,840
  Springdale, 26,990
  Tontitown, 570
  West Fork, 1,580
Harrison (Boone County)
  Diamond City, 740
  Harrison, 11,400
Hot Springs National Park
(Garland County)
  Hot Springs, 37,520
  Hot Springs Village, 6,000
  Lake Hamilton, 1,054
  Mountain Pine, 990
  Piney, 2,283
  Rockwell, 2,675
Mountain Home–Bull Shoals
(Baxter and Marion counties)
  Cotter, 840
  Gassville, 1,110
  Mountain Home, 8,700

CALIFORNIA

Amador County
  Ione, 4,060
  Jackson, 3,480
  Plymouth, 950
  Sutter Creek, 2,130
Chico–Paradise (Butte County)
  Biggs, 1,520

Chapmantown, 1,946
  Chico, 35,000
  Gridley, 4,310
  Oroville, 10,440
  Palermo, 2,572
  Paradise, 26,190
  Thermalito, 4,961
Clear Lake (Lake County)
  Clearlake, 10,910
  Kelseyville, 1,567
  Lakeport, 4,560
  Lucerne, 1,767
El Centro–Calexico–Brawley
(Imperial County)
  Brawley, 18,770
  Calexico, 19,400
  Calipatria, 2,940
  El Centro, 29,970
  Heber, 2,221
  Holtville, 4,980
  Imperial, 4,290
  Niland, 1,042
  Seeley, 1,058
  Westmorland, 1,940
Grass Valley–Truckee
(Nevada County)
  Alta Hill, 1,300
  Alta Sierra Estates, 2,168
  Grass Valley, 9,350
  Nevada City, 2,980
  Penn Valley, 1,032
  Truckee, 2,389
Red Bluff–Sacramento Valley
(Tehama County)
  Corning, 5,830
  Los Molinos, 1,241
  Red Bluff, 12,480
Redding (Shasta County)
  Anderson, 8,110
  Burney, 3,187
  Central Valley, 3,424
  Cottonwood, 1,553
  Johnson Park, 1,008
  Pine Grove, 1,049
  Redding, 55,400
  Summit City, 1,136
Salinas–Seaside–Monterey
(Monterey County)
  Carmel Valley, 4,013
  Carmel-by-the-Sea, 5,010
  Castroville, 4,396
  Del Rey Oaks, 1,530
  Gonzales, 3,910
  Greenfield, 6,720
  King City, 7,560
  Las Lomas, 1,740
  Marina, 29,120
  Monterey, 30,500
  Pacific Grove, 16,430
  Pajaro, 1,426
  Salinas, 101,090
  Seaside, 37,050
  Soledad, 6,720
San Diego (San Diego County)
  Alpine, 5,368

Borrego Springs, 1,405
  Carlsbad, 60,800
  Chula Vista, 126,240
  Coronado, 23,070
  Del Mar, 5,340
  El Cajon, 88,240
  Encinitas, 45,100
  Escondido, 95,390
  Fallbrook, 14,041
  Imperial Beach, 26,350
  Jamul, 1,826
  Julian, 1,320
  La Mesa, 51,840
  Lakeside, 23,921
  Lemon Grove, 23,270
  National City, 57,390
  Oceanside, 112,630
  Poway, 42,340
  Rainbow, 1,092
  Ramona, 8,173
  Rancho Santa Fe, 4,014
  San Diego, 1,070,310
  San Marcos, 25,120
  Santee, 55,500
  Solana Beach, 15,300
  Spring Valley, 52,300
  Valley Center, 1,242
  Vista, 57,220
San Luis Obispo (San Luis
Obispo County)
  Arroyo Grande, 14,090
  Atascadero, 22,120
  Cambria, 3,061
  El Paso De Robles, 16,110
  Grover City, 11,240
  Morro Bay, 9,980
  Nipomo, 5,247
  Oceano, 4,478
  Pismo Beach, 7,590
  San Luis Obispo, 38,030
Santa Barbara (Santa Barbara
County)
  Carpinteria, 12,230
  Guadalupe, 5,570
  Lompoc, 32,540
  Mission Hills, 2,797
  Santa Barbara, 79,290
  Santa Maria, 52,700
  Santa Ynez, 3,335
  Solvang, 3,870
Santa Rosa–Petaluma
(Sonoma County)
  Boyes Hot Springs, 4,177
  Cloverdale, 4,530
  Cotati, 4,930
  El Verano, 2,384
  Glen Ellen, 1,014
  Graton, 1,286
  Guerneville, 1,525
  Healdsburg, 8,910
  Monte Rio, 1,137
  Petaluma, 40,770
  Rohnert Park, 33,030
  Roseland, 8,000
  Santa Rosa, 108,220

Lacoochee, 1,800
Land O' Lakes, 4,600
New Port Richey, 14,260
Port Richey, 2,780
San Antonio, 600
St. Leo, 940
Zephyrhills, 7,350
Ocala (Marion County)
Belleview, 2,570
Dunnellon, 2,060
Ocala, 47,850
Reddick, 750
Silver Springs, 1,100
Silver Springs Shores, 4,000
Orlando (Orange, Osceola, and
Seminole counties)
Altamonte Springs, 34,550
Apopka, 10,660
Azalea Park, 7,500
Belle Isle, 4,150
Bithlo, 3,200
Campbell City, 3,000
Casselberry, 19,670
Chuluota, 2,000
Conway, 25,000
Eatonville, 2,720
Edgewood, 1,000
Fairview Shores, 6,100
Fern Park, 8,890
Forest City, 4,000
Geneva, 1,200
Goldenrod, 14,000
Holden Heights, 8,000
Kissimmee, 27,770
Lake Mary, 5,960
Lockhart, 11,000
Longwood, 13,880
Maitland, 8,980
Oakland, 680
Ocoee, 11,930
Orlando, 155,950
Orlovista, 7,000
Oviedo, 7,770
Pine Castle, 10,000
Pine Hills, 33,800
Sanford, 30,310
Sky Lake, 7,000
St. Cloud, 11,810
Union Park, 20,000
Wekiva Springs, 5,000
Windermere, 1,750
Winter Garden, 7,840
Winter Park, 23,340
Winter Springs, 22,040
Zellwood, 1,800
Panama City (Bay County)
Callaway, 11,090
Cedar Grove, 1,590
Hiland Park, 3,800
Lynn Haven, 9,320
Mexico Beach, 1,280
Panama City, 35,630
Panama City Beach, 4,370
Parker, 4,740
Southport, 2,000
Springfield, 8,320
Pensacola (Escambia County)
Century, 2,810
Ensley, 3,850
Ferry Pass Heights, 4,500
Gonzalez, 6,500
Goulding, 5,400
Molino, 1,400
Myrtle Grove, 15,000
Pensacola, 62,780
Warrington, 16,000
West Pensacola, 29,900

St. Augustine (St. Johns County)
Hastings, 620
St. Augustine, 12,710
St. Augustine Beach, 3,070
St. Augustine Shores, 2,500
St. Petersburg–Clearwater–
Dunedin (Pinellas County)
Bay Pines, 6,000
Belleair, 4,040
Belleair Beach, 1,690
Belleair Bluffs, 2,400
Clearwater, 97,520
Dunedin, 32,870
Gulfport, 11,520
Indian Rocks Beach, 4,140
Indian Shores, 1,440
Kenneth City, 4,240
Largo, 63,260
Lealman, 20,000
Madeira Beach, 5,000
North Redington Beach, 1,210
Oldsmar, 6,600
Palmer Harbor, 5,200
Pinellas Park, 40,670
Redington Beach, 1,730
Redington Shores, 2,540
Safety Harbor, 13,830
Seminole, 8,090
South Pasadena, 5,560
St. Petersburg, 239,410
St. Petersburg Beach, 9,640
Tarpon Springs, 17,310
Treasure Island, 6,800
Sarasota (Sarasota County)
Bee Ridge, 3,500
Coral Cove, 2,100
Desoto Lakes, 2,000
Englewood, 10,000
Fruitville, 3,100
Gulf Gate Estates, 10,000
Kensington Park, 3,000
Laurel, 1,500
Manasota Key, 1,200
Nokomis, 3,200
North Port, 9,520
Osprey, 1,700
Phillippi Gardens, 2,600
Pinecraft, 1,200
Sarasota, 53,280
Sarasota Springs, 14,000
Siesta Key, 7,000
Southgate, 7,500
Tri Par Estates, 1,400
Vamo, 3,000
Venice, 15,570
Venice Gardens, 7,000
Vero Beach (Indian River
County)
Fellsmere, 1,700
Florida Ridge, 5,000
Gifford, 6,300
Indian River Shores, 1,860
Roseland, 1,600
Sebastian, 7,570
Vero Beach, 18,210
Wabasso, 2,200
West Palm Beach–Boca Raton
–Delray Beach (Palm Beach
County)
Atlantis, 1,700
Belle Glade, 17,000
Boca Raton, 61,620
Boynton Beach, 45,100
Century Village, 11,000
Delray Beach, 45,160
Greenacres City, 26,190
Gulf Stream, 550

Haverhill, 1,360
Highland Beach, 3,110
Hypoluxo, 900
Juno Beach, 1,940
Jupiter, 26,480
Lake Clarke Shores, 3,300
Lake Park, 6,730
Lake Worth, 27,380
Lantana, 8,730
Mangonia Park, 1,460
North Palm Beach, 12,230
Ocean Ridge, 1,540
Pahokee, 6,510
Palm Beach, 11,160
Palm Beach Gardens, 24,280
Palm Beach Shores, 1,310
Palm Springs, 9,930
Riviera Beach, 28,090
Royal Palm Beach, 11,880
Sandalfoot Cove, 6,000
South Bay, 3,670
South Palm Beach, 1,440
Tequesta, 4,170
Wellington, 5,000
West Palm Beach, 73,050

GEORGIA
Athens (Clarke County)
Athens, 43,100
Oconee Heights, 1,200
Winterville, 870
Brunswick–Golden Isles (Glynn
County)
Brunswick, 19,470
Dock Junction, 6,500
St. Simons Island, 7,500
Clayton (Rabun County)
Clayton, 1,750
Mountain City, 800
Lake Lanier (Hall County)
Flowery Branch, 950
Gainesville, 16,860
Gainesville Mills, 1,300
Lula, 1,370
Oakwood, 1,460
Westside, 3,000
Savannah (Chatham County)
Bloomingdale, 2,440
Garden City, 9,300
Georgetown, 3,000
Pooler, 4,200
Port Wentworth, 3,640
Savannah, 146,800
Skidaway Island, 1,500
Thunderbolt, 1,880
Tybee Island, 3,280
Wilmington Island, 8,000
Thomasville (Thomas County)
Boston, 1,590
Coolidge, 930
Meigs, 1,231
Ochlocknee, 640
Pavo, 1,000
Thomasville, 18,780

HAWAII
Honolulu (Honolulu County)
Ewa, 2,637
Ewa Beach, 14,369
Haleiwa, 2,412
Hauula, 2,997
Heeia, 5,432
Honolulu, 402,400
Kahaluu, 2,925
Kailua, 40,100
Kaneohe, 33,400
Laie, 4,643

Maili, 5,026
Makaha, 8,000
Makakilo City, 8,000
Maunawili, 5,239
Mililani, 22,000
Nanakuli, 8,185
Pearl City, 35,000
Wahiawa, 16,911
Waialua, 4,051
Waianae, 5,000
Waimanalo, 3,562
Waimanalo Beach, 4,161
Waipahu, 32,300
Waipio Acres, 4,000
Whitmore Village, 2,318
Maui (Maui and Kalawao
counties)
Kahului, 15,600
Kaunakakai, 2,500
Kihei, 5,644
Lahaina, 6,500
Lanai City, 3,000
Lower Paia, 1,500
Makawao, 2,900
Napili–Honokowai, 2,500
Pukalani, 3,950
Wailuku, 11,000

IDAHO
Boise (Ada County)
Boise, 111,030
Eagle, 3,710
Garden City, 5,950
Kuna, 2,490
Meridian, 8,180
Coeur d'Alene (Kootenai County)
Coeur d'Alene, 24,690
Dalton Gardens, 2,030
Hayden, 3,530
Post Falls, 7,130
Rathdrum, 2,040
Spirit Lake, 940

INDIANA
Bloomington–Brown County
(Brown and Monroe counties)
Bloomington, 54,800
Ellettsville, 3,750
Nashville, 780

IOWA
Iowa City (Johnson County)
Coralville, 9,550
Hills, 640
Iowa City, 50,770
Lone Tree, 1,210
North Liberty, 3,150
Oxford, 620
Solon, 1,030
Swisher, 680
University Heights, 1,030

KENTUCKY
Lexington–Fayette (Bourbon,
Clark, Fayette, Jessamine,
Scott, and Woodford counties)
Georgetown, 12,910
Lexington, 225,660
Midway, 1,410
Millersburg, 1,070
Nicholasville, 15,440
North Middletown, 620
Paris, 8,230
Stamping Ground, 560
Versailles, 7,250
Wilmore, 3,530
Winchester, 17,030

Murray–Kentucky Lake
(Calloway County)
Murray, 13,760

LOUISIANA
St. Tammany Parish
Abita Springs, 1,600
Covington, 10,390
Lacombe, 5,100
Madisonville, 1,110
Mandeville, 9,900
Pearl River, 2,580
Slidell, 36,370
Sun, 600

MAINE
Bar Harbor–Frenchman Bay
(Hancock County)
Bar Harbor, 4,120
Blue Hill, 2,000
Brooklin, 700
Brooksville, 770
Bucksport, 4,490
Castine, 1,290
Dedham, 1,040
Deer Isle, 1,860
Ellsworth, 5,580
Franklin, 1,160
Gouldsboro, 1,710
Hancock, 1,590
Lamoine, 1,310
Mount Desert, 2,090
Orland, 1,900
Penobscot, 1,150
Sedgwick, 810
Southwest Harbor, 1,850
Stonington, 1,170
Sullivan, 910
Surry, 1,010
Tremont, 1,480
Trenton, 1,010
Verona, 560
Winter Harbor, 1,220
Camden–Penobscot Bay
(Knox County)
Appleton, 740
Camden, 4,440
Cushing, 1,150
Friendship, 1,040
Hope, 930
Owls Head, 1,650
Rockland, 7,940
Rockport, 3,230
South Thomaston, 1,410
St. George, 2,100
Thomaston, 3,060
Union, 1,900
Vinalhaven, 1,260
Warren, 3,020
Washington, 1,400

MARYLAND
Easton–Chesapeake Bay
(Talbot County)
Easton, 8,480
Oxford, 790
St. Michaels, 1,430
Trappe, 910
Ocean City–Assateague Island
(Worcester County)
Berlin, 3,660
Ocean City, 7,200
Pocomoke City, 3,620
Snow Hill, 2,130

MASSACHUSETTS
Amherst–Northampton
(Hampshire County)
Amherst, 32,260
Belchertown, 10,510
Chesterfield, 1,210
Cummington, 800
Easthampton, 16,330
Goshen, 760
Granby, 5,710
Hadley, 4,120
Hatfield, 3,140
Huntington, 1,930
Northampton, 28,360
Pelham, 1,480
South Hadley, 16,490
Southampton, 4,610
Ware, 9,630
Westhampton, 1,340
Williamsburg, 2,600
Worthington, 1,250
Cape Cod (Barnstable County)
Barnstable, 37,880
Bourne, 16,280
Brewster, 7,880
Chatham, 6,430
Dennis, 13,910
Eastham, 4,470
Falmouth, 26,140
Harwich, 10,210
Mashpee, 7,900
Orleans, 6,190
Provincetown, 3,500
Sandwich, 14,090
Truro, 1,380
Wellfleet, 2,550
Yarmouth, 20,020

MICHIGAN
Ann Arbor (Washtenaw County)
Ann Arbor, 107,810
Chelsea, 3,910
Dexter, 1,480
Manchester, 1,810
Milan, 4,182
Saline, 6,840
Whitmore Lake, 3,000
Ypsilanti, 23,130
Charlevoix–Boyne City
(Charlevoix County)
Boyne City, 3,780
Charlevoix, 3,370
East Jordan, 2,170
Houghton Lake (Roscommon
County)
Houghton Lake, 3,000
Roscommon, 1,170
Petoskey–Straits of Mackinac
(Emmet County)
Alanson, 560
Harbor Springs, 1,630
Pellston, 630
Petoskey, 6,160
Traverse City–Grand Traverse
Bay (Grand Traverse County)
Kingsley, 710
Traverse City, 15,810

MISSISSIPPI
Biloxi–Gulfport–Pass
Christian (Hancock and Harrison
counties)
Bay St. Louis, 10,600
Biloxi, 47,750
D'Iberville, 6,500
Diamondhead, 1,000
Gulfport, 43,410

Long Beach, 17,200
Pass Christian, 5,810
Waveland, 5,860

MISSOURI
Branson–Table Rock Lake
(Stone and Taney counties)
Branson, 4,320
Crane, 1,290
Forsyth, 1,190
Hollister, 1,880
Kimberling City, 1,680
Reeds Spring, 760

MONTANA
Hamilton–Bitterroot Valley
(Ravalli County)
Darby, 560
Hamilton, 2,880
Pinesdale, 530
Stevensville, 1,920
Kalispell (Flathead County)
Bigfork, 1,100
Columbia Falls, 3,380
Evergreen, 4,000
Kalispell, 11,960
Whitefish, 4,360

NEVADA
Carson City–Minden (Douglas
County and Carson City)
Carson City, 38,400
Minden, 1,300
Las Vegas (Clark County)
Boulder City, 11,850
Henderson, 59,310
Las Vegas, 210,620
Mesquite, 1,230
North Las Vegas, 51,450
Sun Valley, 8,822
Sunrise Manor, 63,100
Winchester, 20,000
Reno (Washoe County)
Crystal Bay, 1,200
Incline Village, 5,000
New Washoe, 3,000
Reno, 115,130
Sparks, 53,000

NEW HAMPSHIRE
Hanover (Grafton County)
Alexandria, 930
Ashland, 1,920
Bath, 870
Bethlehem, 1,770
Bridgewater, 690
Bristol, 2,430
Campton, 1,990
Canaan, 2,530
Enfield, 3,480
Franconia, 770
Grafton, 840
Hanover, 9,520
Haverhill, 3,720
Holderness, 1,740
Lebanon, 11,360
Lincoln, 1,310
Lisbon, 1,500
Littleton, 5,710
Lyme, 1,480
Monroe, 680
Orford, 1,040
Piermont, 510
Plymouth, 5,240
Rumney, 1,480
Thornton, 980
Warren, 670

Wentworth, 560
Woodstock, 960
Keene (Cheshire County)
Alstead, 1,570
Chesterfield, 2,750
Dublin, 1,500
Fitzwilliam, 2,060
Gilsum, 910
Harrisville, 1,080
Hinsdale, 3,720
Jaffrey, 5,010
Keene, 22,370
Marlborough, 1,800
Marlow, 610
Nelson, 520
Richmond, 740
Rindge, 4,140
Stoddard, 520
Sullivan, 700
Surry, 600
Swanzey, 5,720
Troy, 2,140
Walpole, 2,880
Westmoreland, 1,570
Winchester, 3,830
Laconia–Lake Winnipesaukee
(Belknap County)
Alton, 2,650
Barnstead, 2,870
Belmont, 4,750
Center Harbor, 950
Gilford, 5,190
Gilmanton, 2,590
Laconia, 16,540
Meredith, 4,740
New Hampton, 1,400
Sanbornton, 1,810
Tilton, 3,570
North Conway–White
Mountains (Caroll County)
Bartlett, 1,460
Conway, 8,250
Effingham, 730
Freedom, 810
Jackson, 670
Madison, 1,280
Moultonborough, 2,710
North Conway, 3,000
Ossipee, 2,820
Sandwich, 1,080
Tamworth, 1,660
Tuftonboro, 1,630
Wakefield, 2,550
Wolfeboro, 4,640
Portsmouth–Dover–
Durham (Rockingham and
Strafford counties)
Atkinson, 4,960
Auburn, 3,790
Barrington, 5,770
Brentwood, 2,340
Candia, 3,700
Chester, 2,350
Danville, 1,940
Deerfield, 2,360
Derry, 24,330
Dover, 23,770
Durham, 12,440
East Kingston, 1,300
Epping, 4,380
Exeter, 12,260
Farmington, 4,850
Fremont, 1,750
Greenland, 2,330
Hampstead, 5,540
Hampton, 11,760
Hampton Falls, 1,490

Kensington, 1,530
Kingston, 5,090
Lee, 2,450
Londonderry, 16,630
Madbury, 1,140
Middleton, 790
Milton, 2,660
New Castle, 870
New Durham, 1,380
Newfields, 890
Newington, 750
Newmarket, 5,840
Newton, 3,700
North Hampton, 3,740
Northwood, 2,750
Nottingham, 2,400
Plaistow, 6,130
Portsmouth, 25,970
Raymond, 7,110
Rochester, 23,370
Rollinsford, 2,450
Rye, 5,010
Salem, 25,210
Sandown, 3,310
Seabrook, 6,810
Somersworth, 10,790
South Hampton, 670
Strafford, 2,120
Stratham, 3,350
Windham, 7,490

NEW JERSEY

Cape May (Cape May County)
Avalon, 2,380
Cape May, 5,920
Cape May Court House, 4,000
Erma, 1,200
North Wildwood, 5,100
Ocean City, 15,580
Rio Grande, 2,000
Sea Isle City, 2,950
Stone Harbor, 1,330
Villas, 6,000
West Cape May, 1,260
Wildwood, 5,010
Wildwood Crest, 4,220
Woodbine, 2,710
Ocean County
Barnegat, 1,000
Barnegat Light, 650
Bay Head, 1,330
Beach Haven, 1,820
Beach Haven West, 3,000
Beachwood, 8,500
Brick Township, 65,200
Cedar Glen Lakes, 2,000
Crestwood Village, 8,000
Gilford Park, 6,000
Island Heights, 1,610
Lakehurst, 3,080
Lavallette, 2,220
Manahawkin, 2,000
Mystic Island, 5,000
New Egypt, 2,500
North Beach Haven, 3,000
Ocean Beach, 1,600
Ocean Gate, 1,500
Pine Beach, 1,790
Point Pleasant, 18,390
Point Pleasant Beach, 5,550
Seaside Heights, 2,130
Seaside Park, 1,790
Ship Bottom, 1,500
Silverton, 5,500
South Toms River, 3,950
Surf City, 1,600
Toms River, 8,000

Tuckerton, 2,670
Waretown, 1,200

NEW MEXICO

Alamogordo (Otero County)
Alamogordo, 28,520
Cloudcroft, 660
La Luz, 1,200
Tularosa, 2,680
Albuquerque (Bernalillo County)
Albuquerque, 378,480
Los Ranchos de Albuquerque, 3,370
Paradise Hills, 6,000
Carlsbad–Artesia (Eddy County)
Artesia, 11,620
Carlsbad, 27,850
Loving, 1,520
Deming (Luna County)
Columbus, 510
Deming, 11,490
Las Cruces (Dona Ana County)
Anthony, 3,300
Hatch, 1,120
Las Cruces, 56,000
Meadow Vista, 4,400
Mesilla, 2,810
Sunland Park, 6,190
University Park, 4,500
Los Alamos (Los Alamos County)
Los Alamos, 15,000
White Rock, 6,700
Roswell (Chaves County)
Dexter, 1,040
Hagerman, 860
Roswell, 44,110
Santa Fe (Santa Fe County)
Chimayo, 2,000
Santa Fe, 59,300

NEW YORK

Canandaigua (Ontario County)
Canandaigua, 12,190
Clifton Springs, 2,430
East Bloomfield, 670
Geneva, 15,520
Holcomb, 1,140
Manchester, 1,660
Naples, 1,710
Phelps, 2,180
Shortsville, 2,010
Victor, 2,360
Columbia County
Claverack, 1,000
Hudson, 8,000
Lorenz Park, 1,800
Niverville, 1,500
Stottville, 1,400
Monticello–Liberty (Sullivan County)
Jeffersonville, 540
Liberty, 4,030
Livingston Manor, 1,500
Monticello, 5,920
South Fallsburg, 2,200
Woodridge, 830
Wurtsboro, 1,300
New Paltz–Ulster County (Ulster County)
Clintondale, 1,200
Ellenville, 4,060
Glasco, 1,200
Highland, 4,000
Hurley, 5,000
Kerhonkson, 1,700
Kingston, 24,170

Lake Katrine, 2,000
Lincoln Park, 2,700
Marlboro, 2,300
Milton, 1,300
Napanoch, 1,300
New Paltz, 5,070
Port Ewen, 2,800
Rosendale, 1,200
Ruby, 1,100
Saugerties, 3,880
Tillson, 1,600
Wallkill, 2,100
Woodstock, 2,400
Zena, 1,500

NORTH CAROLINA

Asheville (Buncombe County)
Asheville, 60,290
Biltmore Forest, 1,600
Black Mountain, 4,530
Enka, 6,000
Montreat, 690
Swannanoa, 2,200
Weaverville, 2,220
Woodfin, 3,470
Brevard (Transylvania County)
Brevard, 6,090
Pisgah Forest, 2,000
Rosman, 610
Chapel Hill (Orange County)
Carrboro, 9,490
Chapel Hill, 33,540
Fairview, 1,200
Hillsborough, 3,770
Edenton–Albermarle Sound (Chowan County)
Edenton, 5,740
Hendersonville (Henderson County)
Balfour, 1,800
Barker Heights, 1,200
East Flat Rock, 4,000
Hendersonville, 8,180
Laurel Park, 1,050
Mountain Home, 1,400
Valley Hill, 2,400
New Bern (Craven County)
Bridgeton, 580
Cove City, 610
Dover, 610
Havelock, 23,560
New Bern, 19,010
River Bend, 1,640
Trent Woods, 1,270
Vanceboro, 980
Southport (Brunswick County)
Boiling Spring Lakes, 1,400
Long Beach, 3,380
Shallotte, 1,120
Southport, 3,320
Yaupon Beach, 910

OKLAHOMA

Grand Lake (Delaware County)
Colcord, 790
Grove, 4,180
Jay, 2,600
Kansas, 540
Oaks, 700
West Siloam Springs, 510

OREGON

Bend (Deschutes County)
Bend, 19,000
Redmond, 7,130
Sisters, 810
Sunriver, 1,100

Eugene–Springfield (Lane County)
Coburg, 620
Cottage Grove, 6,930
Creswell, 1,830
Dunes City, 1,130
Eugene, 105,410
Florence, 4,760
Junction City, 3,300
Lowell, 670
Oakridge, 3,460
River Road, 11,000
Santa Clara, 15,000
Springfield, 38,400
Veneta, 2,300
Grants Pass (Josephine County)
Cave Junction, 1,170
Grants Pass, 17,220
Medford–Ashland (Jackson County)
Ashland, 15,680
Central Point, 6,840
Eagle Point, 3,180
Gold Hill, 940
Jacksonville, 2,080
Medford, 43,580
Phoenix, 2,660
Rogue River, 1,590
Shady Cove, 1,230
Talent, 2,730
White City, 5,500
Newport–Lincoln City (Lincoln County)
Depoe Bay, 800
Lincoln City, 5,870
Newport, 8.050
Siletz, 1,040
Toledo, 3,350
Waldport, 1,480
Yachats, 530

PENNSYLVANIA

Lancaster County
Adamstown, 1,130
Akron, 3,760
Christiana, 1,070
Columbia, 11,230
Denver, 2,400
East Petersburg, 4,170
Elizabethtown, 9,110
Ephrata, 12,270
Lancaster, 57,200
Lititz, 8,970
Manheim, 4,900
Marietta, 2,980
Maytown, 1,500
Millersville, 7,430
Mount Joy, 6,250
Mountville, 1,690
New Holland, 4,330
Paradise, 1,100
Quarryville, 1,800
Reamstown, 1,300
Rheems, 1,300
Rothsville, 1,300
Strasburg, 2,370
Terre Hill, 1,230
Pike County
Matamoras, 2,050
Milford, 1,450
State College (Centre County)
Bellefonte, 6,260
Centre Hall, 1,120
Howard, 860
Lemont, 2,600
Milesburg, 1,440
Millheim, 830

Philipsburg, 3,430
Pine Grove Mills, 1,100
Pleasant Gap, 1,900
Port Matilda, 760
Snow Shoe, 910
South Philipsburg, 540
State College, 34,330

SOUTH CAROLINA

Aiken (Aiken County)
Aiken, 18,290
Bath, 2,300
Belvedere, 7,000
Brentwood, 2,000
Clearwater, 4,000
Gloverville, 2,700
Graniteville, 1,200
Jackson, 2,030
Langley, 1,800
Madison, 1,200
New Ellenton, 3,170
North Augusta, 16,290
Salley, 640
Wagener, 980
Warrenville, 1,100
Charleston (Charleston County)
Bucksport, 1,200
Charleston, 68,900
Folly Beach, 1,610
Forestbrook, 1,600
Hollywood, 2,910
Isle of Palms, 4,120
James Island, 25,000
Ladson, 14,000
Lincolnville, 850
Mount Pleasant, 22,070
North Charleston, 61,430
Ravenel, 2,160
Socastee, 1,100
St. Andrews, 10,000
Sullivan's Island, 1,900
Wando Woods, 5,500
Hilton Head–Beaufort
(Beaufort County)
Beaufort, 9,190
Bluffton, 790
Burton, 3,600
Hilton Head Island, 18,420
Laurel Bay, 6,000
Port Royal, 3,240
Shell Point, 2,500
Myrtle Beach (Horry County)
Aynor, 710
Conway, 13,530
Loris, 2,420
Myrtle Beach, 27,980
North Myrtle Beach, 7,280
Surfside Beach, 3,430

TENNESSEE

Crossville (Cumberland County)
Crab Orchard, 1,040
Crossville, 7,200
Paris–Big Sandy (Benton and
Henry counties)
Big Sandy, 640
Camden, 3,170
Paris, 10,470
Puryear, 690

TEXAS

Athens–Cedar Creek Lake
(Henderson County)
Athens, 11,200
Berryville, 800
Brownsboro, 830
Chandler, 1,990
Eustace, 780

Gun Barrel City, 3,100
Malakoff, 2,470
Murchison, 670
Payne Springs, 710
Seven Points, 1,090
Tool, 2,140
Trinidad, 1,480
Austin (Hays, Travis, and
Williamson counties)
Austin, 463,920
Buda, 1,470
Cedar Park, 7,020
Dripping Springs, 1,010
Florence, 990
Georgetown, 15,230
Granger, 1,240
Hays, 610
Hutto, 990
Jonestown, 1,130
Kyle, 4,000
Lago Vista, 1,400
Lakeway, 1,450
Leander, 4,110
Manor, 1,400
Pflugerville, 1,190
Rollingwood, 1,460
Round Rock, 21,900
San Marcos, 28,680
Sunset Valley, 590
Taylor, 11,640
Thrall, 640
West Lake Hills, 3,800
Woodcreek, 510
Brownsville–Harlingen
(Cameron County)
Brownsville, 102,110
Combes, 2,080
Harlingen, 54,980
La Feria, 4,470
Laguna Vista, 820
Los Fresnos, 2,780
Palm Valley, 810
Port Isabel, 4,440
Primera, 1,740
Rio Hondo, 2,110
San Benito, 21,670
Santa Rosa, 2,240
South Padre Island, 1,050
Burnet–Marble Falls–Llano
(Burnet and Llano counties)
Bertram, 1,050
Burnet, 3,990
Granite Shoals, 1,390
Kingsland, 2,300
Llano, 3,420
Marble Falls, 4,870
Sunrise Beach Village, 660
Canton–Lake Tawakoni
(Van Zandt County)
Canton, 3,170
Edgewood, 1,470
Grand Saline, 2,870
Van, 2,010
Wills Point, 3,340
Fredericksburg (Gillespie
County)
Fredericksburg, 7,660
Kerrville (Kerr County)
Ingram, 1,610
Kerrville, 19,890
McAllen–Edinburg–Mission
(Hidalgo County)
Alamo, 9,700
Alton, 4,190
Donna, 12,380
Edcouch, 3,690
Edinburg, 31,560

Elsa, 5,730
Hidalgo, 3,210
La Joya, 3,540
La Villa, 1,650
McAllen, 83,300
Mercedes, 13,910
Mission, 31,230
Palmview, 850
Pharr, 25,920
Progreso, 1,500
San Juan, 11,100
Weslaco, 24,410
New Braunfels (Comal County)
Garden Ridge, 910
New Braunfels, 27,920
Selma, 600
Rockport–Aransas Pass
(Aransas County)
Aransas Pass, 8,000
Fulton, 1,060
Rockport, 5,120
San Antonio (Bexar County)
Alamo Heights, 7,250
Balcones Heights, 3,300
Castle Hills, 5,930
China Grove, 710
Converse, 9,150
Elmendorf, 570
Helotes, 1,780
Hill Country Village, 1,540
Hollywood Park, 4,660
Kirby, 8,100
Leon Valley, 11,910
Live Oak, 9,680
Olmos Park, 2,280
San Antonio, 914,350
Selma, 528
Shavano Park, 1,890
Somerset, 1,500
St. Hedwig, 1,270
Terrell Hills, 5,540
Universal City, 12,660
Windcrest, 7,290

UTAH

St. George–Zion (Washington
County)
Enterprise, 1,010
Hildale, 1,780
Hurricane, 3,870
Ivins, 1,460
La Verkin, 2,070
Santa Clara, 1,970
St. George, 22,970
Washington, 4,660

VIRGINIA

Blacksburg (Montgomery
County)
Blacksburg, 30,380
Christiansburg, 12,480
Charlottesville (Albemarle,
Fluvanna, and Greene counties;
Charlottesville City)
Charlottesville, 41,100
Crozet, 2,600
Hessian Hills, 4,200
University Heights, 1,700
Virginia Beach–Norfolk
(Chesapeake, Norfolk,
Portsmouth, Suffolk, and Virginia
Beach cities)
Chesapeake, 147,800
Norfolk, 286,500
Portsmouth, 111,000
Suffolk, 51,300
Virginia Beach, 365,300

VERMONT

Bennington (Bennington County)
Arlington, 2,430
Bennington, 16,350
Dorset, 1,840
Manchester, 3,710
North Bennington, 1,690
Pownal, 3,640
Readsboro, 710
Rupert, 650
Shaftsbury, 3,570
Stamford, 710
Sunderland, 830
Burlington (Chittenden and
Grand Isle counties)
Alburg, 1,410
Bolton, 760
Burlington, 38,310
Charlotte, 2,760
Colchester, 14,590
Essex, 15,420
Essex Junction, 7,720
Grand Isle, 1,510
Hinesburg, 3,130
Huntington, 1,400
Jericho, 4,000
Milton, 8,190
North Hero, 530
Richmond, 3,590
Shelburne, 5,680
South Burlington, 11,420
South Hero, 1,380
St. George, 670
Underhill, 2,460
Westford, 1,600
Williston, 4,210
Winooski, 6,640

WASHINGTON

Bellingham (Whatcom County)
Bellingham, 44,960
Blaine, 2,300
Everson, 1,090
Ferndale, 4,480
Lynden, 4,420
Sumas, 730
Oak Harbor–Whidbey Island
(Island County)
Coupeville, 1,090
Langley, 720
Oak Harbor, 13,180
Olympia (Thurston County)
Bucoda, 540
Lacey, 15,630
Olympia, 29,710
Rainier, 1,020
Tanglewood, 4,000
Tenino, 1,420
Tumwater, 8,110
Union Mills, 4,700
Yelm, 1,420
Port Townsend (Jefferson
County)
Hadlock, 1,800
Port Townsend, 6,660
San Juan Islands (San Juan
County)
Friday Harbor, 1,340
Wenatchee (Chelan County)
Cashmere, 2,370
Chelan, 3,080
Entiat, 510
Leavenworth, 1,600
Sunnyslope, 1,500
Wenatchee, 18,280
West Wenatchee, 2,200

WEST VIRGINIA

Martinsburg–Charles Town
(Berkeley County)
  Bolivar, 840
  Charles Town, 3,170
  Inwood, 1,200
  Martinsburg, 13,210
  Ranson, 2,840
  Shepherdstown, 1,940

WISCONSIN

Door County
  Baileys Harbor, 830
  Brussels, 1,130
  Egg Harbor, 960
  Forestville, 980
  Gardner, 1,050
  Gibraltar, 840
  Jacksonport, 720
  Liberty Grove, 1,390
  Nasewaupee, 1,990

  Sevastopol, 2,430
  Sister Bay, 740
  Sturgeon Bay, 9,630
  Union, 860
  Washington, 650
Eagle River (Vilas County)
  Arbor Vitae, 2,340
  Boulder Junction, 960
  Cloverland, 790
  Conover, 870
  Eagle River, 1,360
  Lac du Flambeau, 2,280
  Land O'Lakes, 830
  Lincoln, 2,360
  Manitowish Waters, 660
  Phelps, 1,220
  St. Germain, 1,340
  Washington, 1,210
Madison (Dane County)
  Albion, 1,970
  Berry, 1,170

  Black Earth, 1,250
  Blooming Grove, 2,200
  Blue Mounds, 690
  Bristol, 1,870
  Burke, 3,140
  Christiana, 1,190
  Cottage Grove, 3,310
  Cross Plains, 2,380
  Dane, 990
  De Forest, 4,510
  Deerfield, 1,630
  Dunkirk, 1,900
  Dunn, 5,390
  Fitchburg, 14,270
  Madison, 175,830
  Maple Bluff, 1,370
  Marshall, 2,650
  Mazomanie, 1,380
  McFarland, 4,440
  Medina, 1,010
  Middleton, 13,410

  Monona, 8,660
  Montrose, 1,060
  Mount Horeb, 3,840
  Oregon, 4,370
  Perry, 590
  Pleasant Springs, 2,580
  Primrose, 620
  Roxbury, 1,550
  Rutland, 1,560
  Shorewood Hills, 1,830
  Springdale, 1,380
  Springfield, 2,350
  Stoughton, 8,580
  Sun Prairie, 14,250
  Vermont, 690
  Verona, 3,940
  Vienna, 1,430
  Waunakee, 4,730
  Westport, 2,910
  Windsor, 4,310
  York, 700

Source: U.S. Bureau of the Census, *Population Estimates of Governmental Units,* 1990; Rand McNally & Co., *Commercial Atlas and Marketing Guide,* 1990.

List of Tables, Maps, Sidebars & Diagrams

ABOUT THE AUTHOR

David Savageau is a member of the International Society for Retirement Planning and principal-in-charge of PreLOCATION, a personal relocation consulting firm.

He would appreciate all comments, criticisms, and suggestions for improving the next edition of *Retirement Places Rated*. Write to him at P.O. Box 1327, Gloucester, MA 01931.

Notes

Notes

Notes

Notes

Notes

Notes